Europe

## THOMAS COOK

On 5 July 1841 Thomas Cook, a 33-year-old printer from Market Harborough, in Leicestershire, England, led a party of 570 temperance enthusiasts on a railway outing from Leicester to Loughborough which he had arranged down to the last detail. This proved to be the birth of the modern tourist industry. In the course of expanding his business Thomas Cook and his son John invented many of the features of organised travel which we now take for granted. Over the next 150 years the name Thomas Cook became synonymous with world travel.

Today the Thomas Cook Group employs over 10,000 people worldwide, with more than 1600 locations in over 100 countries. Its activities include travel retailing, tour operating and financial services – Thomas Cook is a world leader in traveller's cheques and foreign money services.

Thomas Cook believed in the value of the printed word as an accompaniment to travel. His publication *The Excursionist* was the equivalent of both a holiday brochure and a travel magazine. Today Thomas Cook Publishing continues to issue one of the world's oldest travel books, the *Thomas Cook European Timetable*, which has been in existence since 1873. Updated every month, it remains the only definitive compendium of European railway schedules.

The *Thomas Cook Touring Handbook* series, to which this volume belongs, is a range of comprehensive guides for travellers touring regions of the world by train, car and ship. Other titles include:

Touring by train
*On the Rails around Europe* (Second edition January 1996)
*On the Rails around France* (Published 1995)
*On the Rails around Britain and Ireland* (Published 1995)
*On the Rails around the Alps* (Published June 1996)
Touring by car
*On the Road around California* (Second edition, publication October 1996))
*On the Road around Florida* (Published October 1995)
*On the Road around New England* (Published April 1996)
*On the Road around Normandy, Brittany and the Loire Valley* (Published April 1996)
Touring by ship
*Greek Island Hopping* (Published annually in March)

For more details of these and other Thomas Cook publications, write to Passport Books at the address on the back of the title page.

# ON THE RAILS AROUND

# Eastern Europe

## A Comprehensive Guide to Travel by Train

Edited by Anthony J.Lambert

PASSPORT BOOKS
a division of *NTC Publishing Group*

A THOMAS COOK TOURING HANDBOOK

Published by Passport Books,
a division of NTC Publishing Group
4255 West Touhy Avenue,
Lincolnwood (Chicago),
Illinois 60646-1975 USA.

Text: © 1996 The Thomas Cook Group Ltd
Maps and diagrams:
© 1996 The Thomas Cook Group Ltd

ISBN 0-8442-9992-8
Library of Congress Catalog Card
Number: 95-71565

Published by Passport Books in conjunction
with The Thomas Cook Group Ltd.

Managing Editor: Stephen York
House Editor: Kate Hopgood
Map Editor: Bernard Horton

Route diagrams drawn by ESR Ltd
Cover illustration by Michael Bennallack-
Hart

Text typeset in Bembo and Gill Sans using
  Quark XPress
Maps and diagrams created using GST
  Designworks and Macromedia Freehand

Printed in Great Britain by Silverscreen
  Print PLC, Newton Aycliffe, Co.
  Durham

*While every care has been taken in compiling this
publication, using the most up-to-date information
available at the time of going to press, all details
are liable to change and cannot be guaranteed. The
publishers cannot accept any liability whatsoever
arising from errors or omissions, however caused.
The views and opinions expressed in this book are
not necessarily those of the publishers.*

This edition written and researched by
**Kate Calvert**
**Paul Duncan**
**Robin Gauldie**
**George McDonald**
**Chris & Melanie Rice**
**Elizabeth Spencer**
**Ian Wisniewski**

Book Editor: **Anthony J. Lambert**
Series Editor: **Melissa Shales**

## ABOUT THE AUTHORS

**Anthony J. Lambert**, Book Editor for this volume, is a travel writer and photographer. He specialises in rail travel and has written 12 books as well as contributing to several national and international newspapers.

**Melissa Shales** is Series Editor, *Thomas Cook Touring Handbooks*. Former editor of *Traveller* magazine, she is the author of eight guide books.

**Kate Calvert** started travelling at the age of two and has been going ever since. Her enthusiasm for farther flung cultures was fired by a classic round-the-world trip.

**Paul Duncan** corresponds regularly for a number of British and Italian publications, and has written a number of travel books on Italy.

**Robin Gauldie** is a freelance journalist specialising in travel and tourism. He is the author of a number of guidebooks, including several covering Greece.

**George McDonald,** Scottish by birth and a journalist by inclination, lives in Belgium. Travel writing first became an obsession for him ten years ago.

**Chris and Melanie Rice** have travelled extensively in Russia and Eastern Europe and have written a number of guidebooks to the region.

**Elizabeth Spencer** is a freelance writer and journalist. A specialist on Romanian affairs, she makes regular broadcasts about topical events in the country.

**Ian Wisniewski** is a freelance travel, food and drink writer and broadcaster. His travel interests include Poland (where he travels extensively by rail) and Eastern Europe.

## ACKNOWLEDGEMENTS

The writers and publishers wish to thank all the individuals and organisations who generously gave their time and expertise in the preparation of this book, and especially the following (TB= Tourist Board; TO= Tourist Office):

Dr. A Kay; Jan Spousta, Czech Railways; Marion Telsnig, Austrian National TO, London; Lauda Air; Romantik Hotels; Radisson Hotels; Austrian Railways; Philip O'Neil; Eva Khaylova; Marian and Plamen Petkova; Plamen Starev; Vivian Anderson, Fjord Norge, Bergen; Gro Aschime, Norske Vandrerhjem, Oslo; Matti Bäckström, Oulun Matkailu Oy/Tietomaa, Oulu; Lind-Jääskeläinen, Finnish TB, London; Eeva Poukka, Helsinki City TO; Peggy Schlytter, Oslo Promotions A/S; Irmeli Torssonen, Turku City TO; Tom Ylkänen, Finnish TB, Helsinki T.O; British Rail International; Hungarian TB; Lufthansa; Austrian Airlines; Romanian Embassy Consul, London; Malév Airlines; Gheorghe Citiriga, Romanian National Railways; Mihail Dan, Romanian TB, London; Orbis, Polish National TO; LOT Polish Airlines; Polorbis Travel; Leading Hotels of the World; Millbank Public Relations; Kaldi Hannus, Annela Sepp, Estravel; Kati Kusmin, and Ene Truusa, Tallinn; Estonian TB; Tallinn TO; Helsinki City TO; Tiina Vittaniemi, Helsinki; Latvian TB; Marina Travel, Latvia; Danute Karvelyte, Egle Jakubenaite and Jelena Dudina, Lithuanian Tours; Iveta Gulbe, Riga; Soveiga Freiberga, Jurmala Information Centre; Laila Auzenberga, Latvia Tours; A Jacuka, Latgale Hotel, Rezekne; Otepää Tourist Information; Campus Travel; Estonian Railways; Latvian Railways; Lithuanian Railways; Klaus Kreher and Karin Rebbin, Deutsche Bahn, London; Agatha Suess, German National TO, London; and the staff of the *Thomas Cook European Timetable*.

### Help us update

Thomas Cook Publishing are constantly updating this and their other rail travel titles in the *Thomas Cook Touring Handbooks* series. Prices, opening hours and other details are constantly changing in these fast-developing areas of Europe. Please do send us any corrections, updates or other contributions to the next edition. All will be acknowledged; those readers whose comments are most useful will be credited in the next edition, and will receive a free copy of the new edition (or any other guide in this series) with our thanks.

If you have any other comments or suggestions to improve future editions, please use the Reader Survey form at the back of this book. All replies will be acknowledged.

5

# CONTENTS

## ROUTES AND CITIES

*In alphabetical order. For indexing purposes, routes are listed in both directions – the reverse direction to which it appears in the book is shown in italics.*

*See also the Route Map, pp. 8–9, for a diagrammatic presentation of all the routes in the book. To look up towns and other places not listed here, see the Index, p. 348.*

7

## REFERENCE SECTION

8

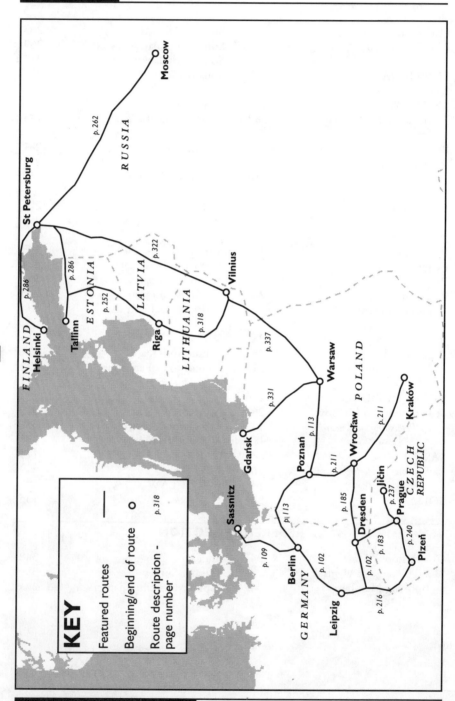

KEY

Featured routes

Beginning/end of route

Route description - page number    p.318

Moscow

RUSSIA

p.262

St Petersburg

FINLAND

Helsinki

p.286

Tallinn

ESTONIA

p.286

p.252

Riga

LATVIA

p.322

LITHUANIA

p.318

Vilnius

p.337

Gdańsk

p.331

Warsaw

POLAND

Kraków

p.211

Poznań

p.113

Wrocław

p.211

p.113

Jičín

CZECH
REPUBLIC

p.237

Sassnitz

p.185

Dresden

Prague

p.211

p.240

p.183

Plzeň

Berlin

p.109

p.102

p.102

GERMANY

Leipzig

p.216

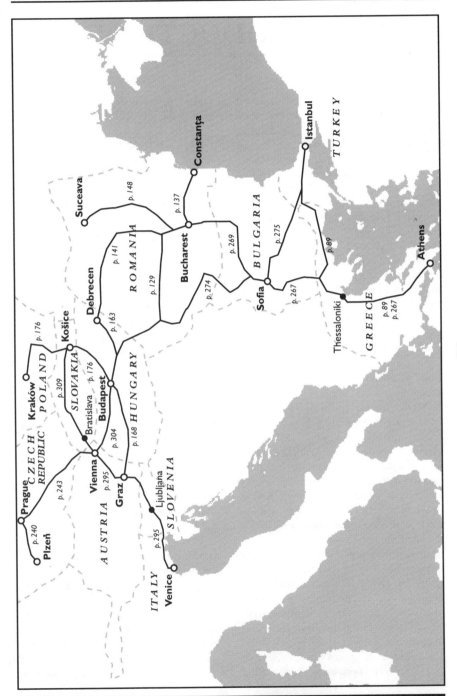

# INTRODUCTION

Train journeys are the best way to travel around Europe: even the slowest main line trains are reasonably fast; they're more comfortable than coaches – you can stretch your legs, buy refreshments or eat in a dining-car as the landscape rolls past the window; you can sleep between crisp sheets; and you're 125 times more likely to arrive safe and sound than you are travelling by road.

Safety and comfort apart, trains are also the best way to remain a part of the country you're visiting. You have a chance to meet people, from which can often come the most rewarding experiences of travel, and each station provides a fascinating vignette of local life. You can also feel you are doing your bit for the environment, since trains are the least damaging form of powered transport in terms of emissions and land use.

Many of the railways of eastern Europe are undergoing the same degree of transformation as other aspects of economies in the region. Until the break-up of the Soviet Union and its satellites, railways carried the majority of passenger and freight traffic. Now they are having to come to terms with the free market, often with dispiriting consequences for the environment – compare the pollution from road traffic in Prague or Budapest today with that of twenty years ago. However, early fears that the cold winds of deregulated competition would lead to massive railway closure programmes have proved largely groundless, though Poland in particular has lost some branch lines. The countries of eastern Europe still have good railway networks that enable visitors to reach the more rural areas as well as the principal cities and towns.

None of the railways of eastern Europe is at the cutting-edge of rail technology, so don't expect to see any high-speed trains (except between St Petersburg and Moscow). However, the character of the secondary and branch lines in eastern Europe often delights those sensitive to the qualities of a less pressured and prouder age in which station buildings, bridges and even lamps were designed to a standard rather than a price.

It is impossible to cover such a large area comprehensively in a single volume, so the routes that serve the most interesting tourist sights have been chosen. Suggestions are made in 'Useful Reading' on p. 26 for those who wish to explore countries in greater detail.

To make your journey smoother, we recommend that you also take a copy of the latest monthly *Thomas Cook European Timetable* (the 'ETT' – see p. 26) which has much more detailed timetables. Remember always to check local station timetables, because there are many more short-distance trains available than even the ETT has room to show.

Finally, eastern Europe is changing rapidly, so despite the best endeavours of the contributors, errors are bound to creep in during the life of this edition. We apologise in advance for these, and invite you to help us to keep this book up to date. Please write in with any corrections, additions or suggestions. All will be acknowledged.

**Anthony J. Lambert**

# HOW TO USE THIS BOOK

## ROUTES AND CITIES

*On the Rails around Eastern Europe* is formatted to reflect the way people actually travel by rail: not restricting themselves to one country but crossing borders (sometimes easy, sometimes a very bureaucratic process in this part of the world) and following where the international rail lines lead them.

Therefore, the book divides central and eastern Europe (including the former DDR in Germany, Greece, Turkey, and the two principal cities of European Russia) not into countries but into **recommended routes** – over thirty of them – chosen to make the most of the potential that rail offers for smooth connections between cities and nations (and often for sightseeing while travelling). For the most part each route begins and ends in a **key city**; these are major cultural and sightseeing centres or cities with important rail connections – usually they are both. Every route and every key city has its own chapter in this book. Occasionally a route ends in a town not requiring a chapter to itself, so then the town description is placed in the route chapter, e.g. Sassnitz, covered at the end of the Berlin–Sassnitz chapter.

The routes often cross borders; some of them can be travelled in a few hours, some would require at least two days to complete without stopping. But stopping is the whole point; you can break your journey for a few hours or a few days, as you wish, at towns and cities along these routes, all of which are worth visiting in their own right. Many more **smaller cities, towns, attractions and points of interest** along each route are described in the order in which you will encounter them in the direction of the route. The direction in which the routes are laid out assumes that most readers will be beginning their travel at a western 'gateway' – Athens, Berlin, Prague, Vienna, Venice – and proceeding across the continent eastwards and south to the Balkans or north to the Baltic and Russia. (If you start your tour in Athens you will find the routes leading you north towards Istanbul or Sofia.) Bear in mind that, of course, every route we have suggested can be travelled in the opposite direction to the one we have given: for instance, the Athens–Istanbul route can also be travelled in the Istanbul–Athens direction.

The order of chapters is alphabetical: chapters on key cities are usually followed by one or more chapters describing routes beginning in those cities; e.g. the chapter on Berlin is followed by routes from Berlin to Dresden, Sassnitz and Warsaw.

The routes are designed to be used as a kind of menu from which you can plan an **itinerary**, combining a number of routes which take you to the places you most want to visit. By using the **Contents List** on pp. 6–7 (which list the routes in both directions) and the planning map on pp. 8–9, you can easily plan possible tours.

## WITHIN EACH ROUTE

Each route chapter begins with a short introduction to the route, followed by a **route diagram** such as the one at the top of the next page. This summarises the route and shows the main intermediate stops, as well as intersecting routes and Side Tracks. The diagram is followed by a

Side track destinations → Halle, Merseburg, Leipzig, Erfurt

Stops on the main route

Zwickau

Intersecting route → *Leipzig – Plzen, p. 216*

section on **Trains**, giving a good idea of frequency of service and other rail travel advice; it is often divided as follows:

### FAST TRACK

This details the fastest rail service between the start and end cities, sometimes along a different line from the On Track.

### ON TRACK

This is the full route, which takes in the towns along the way. Each point-to-point service is described separately. Journey times and frequencies can only be approximate, and you should use the local timetables (at the station) to verify exact departure times, etc. You can pick and choose whether you visit all the suggested stops, or skip some of them.

### SIDE TRACK

This heading is frequently used after a description of a place, to highlight departures from there, off the recommended route, that lead to places of interest; these may be described in full or indicated in a paragraph or two. In general, Side Tracks assume a detour longer than a simple half-day trip. The extent of the Side Track (before you rejoin the main route) is shown by the grey margins and the end-sign.

### CITY DESCRIPTIONS

Whether a place is given a half-page description within a route chapter or is a key city with an entire chapter to itself, we have concentrated on practical details: local sources of **Tourist information**; **Getting around** in city centres (by public transport and on foot); **Accommodation** and **Food and drink**; post and phone **Communications**; **Entertainment** and **Shopping** opportunities; under **Sightseeing**, for reasons of space, we have often had to concentrate only on the highlights; tourist offices will provide you with plenty of extra information and ideas. The largest cities have all this detail; in smaller places some categories of information are less relevant and have been omitted or summarised. Where there is a something to say which would interrupt the flow of the main description, we have placed occasional **feature boxes**.

Although we mention good independently owned hotels in most places, we always also list the international hotel chains which have a property in the area, by means of code letters to save space, such as *IC* for Inter-Continental. Such hotels are seldom found outside large cities in in this part of Europe. The codes are explained on pp. 342–43 along with the central booking numbers for the chains

### MAPS

In addition to the diagram which accompanies each route, and the rail maps in colour at the end of the book, we provide maps of major cities (usually the central or historic area, or as far out as the main rail station where possible).

### Symbols used on city maps

| i | *Tourist Information* | 🚍 | *Bus Station* |
|---|---|---|---|
| ✉ | *Post Office* | *M* | *Metro Station* |
| † | *Church* | ✝ | *Cathedral* |

## Abbreviations

To save space the following abbreviations have often been used in the text.

### Currency Units

| | | | | | |
|---|---|---|---|---|---|
| DM | Deutsche Mark | Kč | Czech Koruna | ÖS | Austrian Schilling |
| Dr. | Greek Drachma | L. | Italian Lira | SK | Slovak Koruna |
| EEK | Estonian Kroon | Lat | Latvian Lat | TL | Turkish Lira |
| FIM | Finnish Markka | Lei | Romanian Lei | Zł | Polish Złoty |
| Ft | Hungarian Forint | Lv. | Bulgarian Leva | | |

### Addresses and Places

As well as the abbreviations, with their full versions and the English meanings, we also give the English equivalents of some unabbreviated words often found in place names and street signs. The obvious ones are not explained here (for instance, the word for 'museum' is recognisable in nearly all European languages). In this list, terms found in Germany also apply to Austria. Czech words will also be found in Slovakia.

**Altstadt** (Germany) Old Town

**Bhf** (Germany) Bahnhof; i.e. Rail Station

**blvd** (Romania) bulevardul; i.e. Boulevard

**Dom** (Germany) Cathedral

**Gara** (Romania) Station

**Hbf** (Germany) Hauptbahnhof; i.e. Main Rail Station

**-kirche** (Germany) Church

**Landstr.** (Germany) Landstrasse; i.e. Road

**pályaudvar** (Hungary) Station

**pl.** (Germany) -platz; i.e. Square

**Pza** (Italy) piazza; i.e. Square

**Rathaus** (Germany) Town Hall

**Schloss** (Germany) Castle, Palace

**stathmos** (Greece) Station

**-str.** (Germany/Austria)

**-strasse**, i.e. Street

**Str.** (Romania) Strada; i.e. Street

**tér** (Hungary) Square

**ul.** (Poland) ulica, (Czech Republic) ulice; i.e. Road

**út** (Hungary) Street

**V.** (Italy) Via; i.e. Street

**13**

## THE REST OF THE BOOK

**Travel Essentials** is an alphabetically arranged chapter of general advice for travellers in eastern and central Europe. **Travelling by Train** takes a more detailed look at how the rail system operates, what tickets or passes you will need, sleeping cars, and so on. **Country by Country** is designed to provide a basic run-down of facts and advice on each of the nations covered in this book. Information common to many destinations within a particular country is given here and not repeated in each city description. **Sample Itineraries** gives advice about planning a trip and gives some ready-made ideas for tours which you can use or adapt in your own planning.

At the end of the book, **Conversion Tables** provide a quick way of translating metric measures and Continental clothing sizes to their British and American equivalents, followed by two pages of **Hotel Central Booking Numbers and Codes**, decoding the abbreviations we use throughout the book for hotel chains, and providing information for remote booking of accommodation with them. **Through Routes** supplements our network of recommended routes with details of faster long-distance rail travel.

Finally, the **Index** is the quick way to look up any place or general subject. Use it to locate places, large and small, and topics of interest. And please help us by completing and returning the **Reader Survey** at the very end end of the book. Happy travelling!

# TRAVEL ESSENTIALS

The following is an alphabetical listing of helpful tips for those planning a holiday by rail in Central or Eastern Europe.

## ACCOMMODATION

Europe offers an excellent choice of accommodation, from five-star hotels to room only. Your main problem may lie in finding something to suit your budget. The quality of cheaper hotels in Eastern Europe may still be less than inspiring and you could do better with a private room.

City tourist offices are almost always your best starting point if you haven't pre-booked. If they don't handle bookings themselves (there's usually a small charge), they will re-direct you to someone who does. This book indicates which of the major international or national chains are represented in each city, by means of initials under the 'Accommodation' heading: e.g. 'BW, Hn, Hd' means that Best Western, Hilton and Holiday Inn have properties there. Further details can be obtained from the chain's central reservations office (for phone numbers and decoded initials see pp. 342–343) or through your travel agent. Chains that operate only in a particular country or region are noted in the 'Country by Country' section (see pp. 36–76).

### Hostelling International (HI)

For those on a tight budget, the best advice is to join **HI** (**Hostelling International**). Membership of a national association will entitle you to use over 5000 HI hostels in 60 different countries and, apart from camping, they often provide the cheapest accommodation. Membership for those over/under 18 is currently: Australia $40/12; Canada $25/12; England £9/3; Republic of Ireland £7.50/4; New Zealand $24 plus $10 joining fee; Scotland £6/2.50; South Africa R.35 (free for those under 16); USA $25/12; Wales £9/3. Buy their directory *Budget Accommodation You Can Trust* (£6.99 for the European edition). Some are open 24 hours, but most have lock-out times and reception hours are usually very limited – so check what they are and advise them if you are arriving out of hours. It is advisable to reserve accommodation – especially in summer, when many hostels fill well in advance. In winter (except around Christmas) bookings can be slow and it's worth asking if there are any special price deals available.

For information, to join, and to book accommodation in advance: **Australia**, *tel: (02) 565 1699*; **Canada**, *tel: (613) 237 7844*; **England** (and **Wales**), *tel: (0171) 836 1036*; **Republic of Ireland**, *tel: (01) 830 4555*; **New Zealand**, *tel: (03) 379 9970*; Scotland, *tel: (01786) 451181*; **South Africa**, *tel: (021) 419 1853*; **USA**, *tel: (0202) 783 6161*.

In places where **rooms in private houses** are an option, local tourist offices can usually help, by giving you a list – sometimes they will help you find space. As well as being cheaper than hotels, this form of accommodation is a good way to meet local people, but you may be expected to stay for more than one night.

### Camping

This is obviously the cheapest form of accommodation, if you are prepared to

15

carry the equipment. There are campsites in all countries covered in this book, with facilities ranging from basic (toilets and showers) to luxury sites with dining-rooms, swimming pools and complexes of permanent tents, aimed at tourists with children. The drawback is that they are often miles from the city centres. Most national tourist offices can provide a directory for their country. Either contact them before you leave home or ensure you arrive in a new town early enough to get information from the local tourist office.

## BICYCLES

In many European countries cycling is popular and the best way to explore locally. You can sometimes hire a bike at one rail station and leave it at another and this can be cheaper than going to bike-hire shops. In many countries bikes can be carried on trains (for a small fee), but advance notice may be required. If you are interested, contact the relevant national tourist office for information before you leave.

## BORDERS

Land borders between the EU (European Union) countries are virtually non-existent and it's only if you arrive/leave by air or sea that you're likely to encounter any formalities. Most former Eastern bloc countries, however, remain more bureaucratic, and you should be prepared for delays when crossing borders.

## CHILDREN

Travelling by train with children is easier than you might think – as long as you have someone to help you haul bags and pushchairs up the steps. Most children find train travel a great novelty and thoroughly enjoy themselves, but make sure

you are not short of ideas to keep them amused and have plenty of food and drink at hand.

If the children are old enough, ask them to keep a detailed travel diary. Collecting and displaying anything from tickets and postcards to dried flowers can become a whole new game. Many tourist destinations in Eastern Europe are reasonably well adapted for children and baby-sitters are not hard to find, if you ask at the local tourist office. Many hotels offer family rooms or provide a cot in a normal double. Many sights and forms of transport accept babies for free, and children under 12 for half price. For useful reading try: Maureen Wheeler, *Travel with Children*, (Lonely Planet, £5.95/US$10.95).

## CLIMATE

Most of eastern Europe has a relatively gentle climate. The summer temperature rarely exceeds 25°C (see the chart opposite), except in the far south, e.g. Athens, where it can be agonisingly hot in high summer. Winter tends to be grey and wet, with temperatures hovering around -5/+5°C, but high altitudes and areas a long way inland (e.g. Moscow) can be much colder. In the far north, midsummer is the best time to travel, to take advantage of the ultra-long days. Almost everywhere else, May and Sept are the best months.

## CLOTHING

Most of Europe is very informal these days and you will rarely need evening clothes, but make sure you have some smart casual clothes just in case. People wearing shorts or sleeveless tops may be excluded from some churches, the most traditional of which still expect women to cover their heads, so pack a long-

## Eastern European Temperatures

This chart gives an idea of the average temperatures you are likely to encounter at various times of the year in sample destinations across Eastern Europe.

|  | Berlin | Budapest | Prague | Warsaw |
|---|---|---|---|---|
| **January** | | | | |
| *Highest* | 2°C/36°F | 0°C/32°F | 2°C/36°F | 0°C/32°F |
| *Lowest* | -1°C/30°F | -5°C/23°F | -3°C/27°F | -7°C/20°F |
| **April** | | | | |
| *Highest* | 13°C/55°F | 7°C/45°F | 13°C/55°F | 13°C/55°F |
| *Lowest* | 8°C/46°F | 0°C/32°F | 5°C/41°F | 3°C/37°F |
| **July** | | | | |
| *Highest* | 23C/73°F | 21°C/70°F | 25°C/77°F | 25°C/77°F |
| *Lowest* | 17°C/63°F | 13°C/55°F | 15°C/59°F | 14°C/57°F |
| **October** | | | | |
| *Highest* | 13°C/55°F | 9°C/48°F | 13°C/55°F | 13°C/55°F |
| *Lowest* | 9°C/48°F | 4°C/39°F | 8°C/46°F | 6°C/43°F |

sleeved shirt, a shawl or large scarf. You can encounter rain or cool weather no matter where you go, so at least one sweater or jacket and some sort of rainwear are essential.

### CONSULAR SERVICES

Most embassies/consulates/high commissions will lend a helping hand if their nationals have *real* problems – and charge a small fee for any services rendered. The Australian, Canadian, UK and US consular services produce (free) leaflets outlining their services. Help should be available if: (a) your passport, or a travel document that will get you home, is stolen; (b) if there's a death or serious accident (advice on procedures, next of kin notified – probably also sympathetic help); (c) if you go to jail – don't expect sympathy, nor direct intervention, but they will explain your rights and tell you how to get a lawyer.

Should something happen to make the area dangerous (an act of God, local rebellion, etc), contact your nearest embassy or consulate to register your presence and ask for advice.

In case of real financial trouble, embassies *may* agree to make a small loan or contact next of kin with a request for help, but they do not look kindly on people who have simply overspent. Do *not* expect them to act as surrogate travel agents, banks, interpreters, etc. That is not their function. If your own country has no representation, contact one with which it has ties, e.g. Commonwealth citizens can try the British Embassy. They may help and you should at least get some advice about what to do next.

### CURRENCY

All the former Eastern bloc countries (excluding the former DDR areas of Germany) state that the amount taken out must not exceed the amount taken in, making allowance for the amount spent while there. Some such countries check the amounts on both arrival and departure, others simply query the amount taken out if they feel it is larger than they would expect. The restrictions usually refer only to banknotes/coins – if you are carrying a large amount of cash, therefore, you should declare it on arrival in order to avoid problems when you leave the country. That said, it is never advisable to carry more cash than necessary and it is sensible to take most of your money (but not all – some small-denomination local cash is essential) in the form of Eurocheques, travellers' cheques and credit cards – but don't rely too heavily on being able to use credit cards. Although technically illegal, many travellers in Bulgaria and Romania find it useful to carry a few small-denomination German notes and coins. You may still find people eager to trade on the black market in some Eastern European countries, but you could face heavy penalties if caught. You may also be ripped off by those making the exchange, or lay yourself open to muggers working with them.

Thomas Cook bureaux de change listed in this book will cash any type of Eurocheque/travellers' cheque and will replace Thomas Cook travellers' cheques if yours are lost/stolen (see also the emergency numbers in 'Country by Country' chapter). Always try to obtain a little local currency before you enter a new country. If you are unable to do so and arrive outside banking hours, the best bet (albeit an expensive option) is to ask the receptionist at a big hotel to change some for you.

In border towns and on cross-border transport, you can almost always use either of the relevant currencies (a good way to dispose of excess coins), but you generally pay less if you choose the one in which prices are marked.

## CUSTOMS

Importing narcotics and offensive weapons is banned throughout Europe – and penalties for carrying them can be very severe; so, in your own interests, do not be tempted, and do not carry things for anyone else, especially when you are crossing borders.

Professional crooks are very good at passing themselves off as harmless and in need of help and some people are languishing in jail today because they believed a hard-luck story or did someone a 'small' favour. Pornography is also banned in many countries and, since it is notoriously difficult to define, it is better to avoid carrying anything that might offend. If you have to take a prescribed drug on a regular basis, carry something (such as a doctor's letter) that will prove it is legitimate.

There are often restrictions on the import and export of plants and fresh foodstuffs (particularly meat and meat products) and you might be asked to abandon them at borders, so be careful about stocking up just before leaving a country. Before buying souvenirs, check which items are likely to be prohibited, such as those made of ivory or tortoiseshell.

### Customs Allowances in the EU
European Union member states (in this book, Austria, Finland, Germany, Greece, Italy) have set the purchase of tobacco, alcohol and perfume at the same basic allowance for each country (for the few exceptions, see the 'Country by Country' chapter), and these apply to anyone aged 17 or over.

To all intents and purposes, there are no restrictions between the EU countries for goods bought in ordinary shops and including local taxes, but you may be questioned if you have excessive amounts. Allowances are:

800 cigarettes, 200 cigars, 400 cigarillos and 1 kg tobacco

+ 90 litres wine (max. 60 litres sparkling)

+ 10 litres alcohol over 22% volume (e.g. most spirits)

+ 20 litres alcohol under 22% volume (e.g. port and sherry)

+ 110 litres beer.

The allowances for goods bought outside the EU and/or in EU duty-free shops are:

200 cigarettes or 50 cigars or 100 cigarillos or 250 g tobacco*

+ 2 litres still table wine

+ 1 litre spirits or 2 litres sparkling or fortified wine

+ 8 litres Luxembourg wine if imported via the Luxembourg frontier

+ 50 g/60 ml perfume

+ 0.5 l/250 ml toilet water.

*Some EU countries have more generous tobacco allowances for non-Europeans arriving from outside Europe, so check in the duty-free shop or with your carrier.

### Allowances for those returning home:

**Australia:** goods to the value of Aust$400 (half for those under 18) plus 250 cigarettes or 250 g tobacco and 1 litre alcohol.

**Canada:** allowances apply to anyone aged 19 or more (a year younger if you are entering AL, MN or QU). You are allowed 50 cigars and 200 cigarettes and 400 g tobacco plus 1.1 litre alcohol or 24 x 355 ml bottles/tins beer, as well as gifts not exceeding Can$60 each in value.

**New Zealand:** goods to the value of NZ$700. Anyone over 17 may also take 200 cigarettes or 250 g tobacco or 50 cigars or a combination of tobacco products

not exceeding 250 g in all plus 4.5 litres of beer or wine and 1.125 litres spirits.

**South Africa:** goods to a total value of 500 Rand. Those aged 18 or more are allowed 400 cigarettes and 50 cigars and 250 g tobacco plus 2 litres wine and 1 litre spirits plus 50 ml perfume and 250 ml toilet water.

**Republic of Ireland** and **UK:** standard EU regulations apply (see foregoing notes).

**USA:** goods to the value of US$400 as long as you have been out of the country for at least 48 hrs and only use your allowance once every 30 days. Anyone over 21 is also allowed 1 litre alcohol plus 100 (non-Cuban) cigars and 200 cigarettes and a reasonable quantity of tobacco.

## DISABLED TRAVELLERS

Europe, in theory, provides more facilities for the disabled than many other parts of the world. In practice, however, those facilities that do exist often fall short of real needs and expectations, especially in most countries of Eastern Europe and off the main routes, and there may be a shortage of helpful bystanders. Travel is feasible, but it will almost inevitably be more expensive, as it is usually only the modern trains and more up-market hotels that cater for the disabled. You will also have to throw out any thought of spontaneity and make meticulous plans, always writing and phoning ahead to make sure you have a reservation and that there is someone on hand to help you. The amount of advance warning required for trains varies.

There are two main problems to face with the trains – how to get onto them, and whether there is space for you once on board. Although modern rolling-stock tends not to have wide gaps between train and platform, in many European stations the platforms are quite low and passengers have to climb steep steps to board trains. Once aboard, only the more modern carriages provide space for a wheelchair; otherwise, space will be provided in the baggage car. Unfortunately the investment constraints on the railways of most east European countries means that there are few express trains with the kind of facilities that are becoming standard in the West. Of the countries covered by this book, Austria and Germany have the best facilities; the worst will be found in Turkey, Hungary, Greece, Bulgaria, the Czech Republic and Slovakia.

**UK information: RADAR**, *Unit 12, City Forum, 250 City Rd, London EC1V 8AF; tel: (0171) 250 3222*, publish an annual guide called *Holidays and Travel Abroad* (£5 inc. postage), which contains useful addresses and gives details of facilities for the disabled in different countries, including their trains.

**US information: SATH** (Society for the Advancement of Travel for the Handicapped), *347 5th Ave, Suite 610, New York NY 10016; tel: (212) 447 7284*.

For useful reading try: Susan Abbott and Mary Ann Tyrrell's *The World Wheelchair Traveller* (AA Publishing, £3.95); and Alison Walsh's *Nothing Ventured: A Rough Guide Special* (Penguin, £7.99).

## DISCOUNTS

In many countries reductions are available on public transport and on entrance fees for senior citizens, students and the young. Some proof of your eligibility is usually required, so always carry something that will provide evidence of your status, e.g. an official document that shows your age or a student card.

If you are a student, get an International Student Identity Card (ISIC) from your student union, as this is recognised everywhere and offers a wider range of discounts than national union cards.

Some destinations offer (for a small fee) a book of discount vouchers covering anything from museums to restaurants. Many discount passes for tourists, including some rail passes, must be purchased before you leave home as they are not available in the country itself. Contact the relevant tourist offices to ask about any such deals.

## DRIVING

If you might want to hire a motor vehicle while you are away, check requirements with the AA/RAC, or your own national motoring organisation, well before you leave, so that you have time to get any necessary documentation and additional insurance cover. Bear in mind that road accident rates tend to be higher in Eastern Europe, especially in Russia and Turkey.

To hire a vehicle (except a moped), you usually have to be over 21, with two years' driving experience. In most European countries your national licence is valid for up to six months, but you may need a translation as well and it can be easier to get an international licence. Always check that the vehicle is in good condition before you set out, with especial attention to brakes, lights and tyres (including the spare). Most road signs are standardised throughout Europe, but the quality of signposting varies widely, as do speed limits. Check for local peculiarities before you set out. In all the countries in this book traffic drives on the right.

## ELECTRICITY

With a few exceptions, European countries use 220V AC. The shape of plugs varies, though most countries have circular two-pin plugs; if you are taking any sort of electrical gadget, you should take a travel adapter. It is unlikely that you will face power cuts, but a small torch (flashlight) is a useful back-up and essential if camping.

## HEALTH

### Before you go

Europe, as a whole, is reasonably hygienic and there are no compulsory vaccination requirements. However, it is always advisable to keep your tetanus and polio protection up to date and vaccination against typhoid and hepatitis A is also a good idea. You must be able to produce a certificate against yellow fever if you have been in a yellow fever endemic zone in the six days before entering Europe. It's always a good idea to visit your dentist for a check-up before you leave home.

If you are a UK citizen, you should fill in Form E111 before you go (available from post offices). This (free) form entitles you to treatment under the reciprocal health arrangements that exist across most of Europe, but only on the same basis as citizens of the country. This means you may have to pay up-front and reclaim the cost when you return home – and/or some parts of your treatment may not be free. Procedures for each country are detailed in the booklet containing the form. It's worth visiting a pharmacy before consulting a doctor: European pharmacists tend to be well trained and may well save you medical bills by prescribing something that solves your problem.

### Risks

Although most of Europe is temperate,

there is a definite risk of sunburn in the south and in high mountain areas. Don't spend hours outdoors without using a high-factor sunblock.

Holiday romances are all very well, but don't get so carried away that you forget all about AIDS – and other unpleasant sexually-transmitted diseases. If casual sex is your scene, fine, but do take precautions – one glorious night is not worth a (short) lifetime of regret. Take your own condoms since supplies in Eastern Europe may not be dependable. Rabies exists in Continental Europe and, while the risk is very small, you should be wary of stray and wild animals. Lyme disease – caught from ticks in undergrowth – is present in Central European forests. Wear long trousers and long-sleeved shirts to avoid picking up these insects. Symptoms are similar to arthritis and if they show up within 3 months of possible exposure ask your doctor for a blood test; early treatment is nearly always effective.

### Food and water

Outside Austria and Germany, it is safer not to drink tap water. Buy canned or bottled drinks and water and do not use ice cubes. You should boil or sterilise all tap water (including the water you use to brush your teeth) if you think there may be cause for concern. Other common sources of infection in less-developed areas include unboiled unpasteurised milk, unwashed salads and fresh fruit (unless you can peel it yourself). In areas where the sea is polluted, be wary of fresh seafood. Wash your own hands before touching food.

## HITCHHIKING

If you are on a budget, you may want to try hitchhiking, rather than using public transport. This can be fun and is a good

**21**

way to meet the locals, but it can also be dangerous. To avoid trouble, don't hitch alone, or take any ride when you are outnumbered or clearly physically weaker than the people in the car. In a few countries, such as Poland, there are official schemes for getting drivers and hitchers together, so that both can feel safe. Ask at the relevant tourist offices, either before you go or once you are in the country.

## INFORMATION

Addresses of overseas **national** tourist offices are given in the 'Country by Country' chapter. We have listed **local** information offices throughout the book. Once in a new town, look for a sign displaying a lower case **i** (often black or white on a blue or green background), which is the usual symbol for information in Europe. It may indicate merely a noticeboard (or similar), but, with luck, may point you towards a tourist information office. Try to get hold of a street map in advance, so that you can find your way around if information offices are closed when you arrive.

## INSURANCE

Take out travel insurance that covers your health as well as your belongings. It should also give cancellation cover and include an emergency flight home if something goes really wrong (the hospitals in some countries are not places where you would want to linger). If you are likely to do something that might be classified as risky (e.g. ski or drive a moped), make sure your policy does not exclude that risk. (Note that if you hire a car, your travel insurance will not cover liabilities arising out of an accident; if your everyday motoring policy does not provide cover, you will have to buy a special top-up on your travel insurance.)

## LANGUAGE

Arm yourself with a copy of the *Thomas Cook European Travel Phrasebook* (£4.95/ US$7.95) if you are visiting countries where language is likely to be a problem. It contains over three hundred phrases, each translated (with phonetic spellings) into: French, German, Italian, Czech, Hungarian, Polish, Bulgarian, Romanian, Portuguese, Spanish, Greek and Turkish. Phrases cover the everyday needs of a rail traveller, from arriving in a station to booking accommodation, eating out, changing money and coping in an emergency. Your chief asset, if you have no language in common with the people you meet, will be your willingness to use sign language. If you want to know where the post office is, for example, showing someone an addressed envelope may get the message across. Smiles also go a long way towards breaking the ice and encouraging people to be helpful, but be careful that your friendliness is not misinterpreted.

Keep a pen and paper handy at all times, then you can ask people to write down such figures as times and prices. Similarly, if they don't understand your pronunciation, you can write down what you are trying to say and let them read it.

## LUGGAGE

Always travel as light as possible. The amount of space available for storing luggage on trains varies considerably. Soft-sided bags may be less secure than hard suitcases, but are lighter and easier to squeeze into cramped spaces. Backpacks are the best option if you have a lot to carry; otherwise, go for a large, zippable canvas or plastic bag, with a shoulder strap to leave your hands free.

If you're buying a backpack for the first time, shop carefully and be prepared to spend a bit more than the minimum to ensure comfort and durability (the best brands have a lifetime guarantee). Essential features are a strong internal frame, padded shoulder straps and a hip strap, to lift the bulk of the weight away from your neck. Some frames are specially adapted for women. Don't be too ambitious about how much you can carry – 50 litres for women and 60 for men is about right.

Most stations (and other transport hubs) have baggage lockers and/or manned left-luggage offices. Many stations will forward your bags to your next destination, but check that the office there will be open when you arrive.

## OPENING HOURS

A rough guide to opening hours is given in the 'Country by Country' section, but there are many variations and you should not assume that, for example, every bank will be open during all the banking hours listed – while some may stay open longer. Sunday is the usual closing day for shops and businesses (and public transport tends to be sparse).

## PASSPORTS AND VISAS

EU citizens can travel to other EU countries with a National Identity Card in lieu of a full passport, but do ensure that any identity document is valid well beyond the end of your stay. The individual requirements are given in the Country by Country section. As for non-European travellers, this book concentrates on requirements for citizens of Australia, Canada, New Zealand, South Africa and the USA. Always double-check this information, with a good travel agent or with the relevant embassies, in good time to get any necessary documents. *Anyone planning to stay more than 90 days in a* single country may need a visa and should check well before travelling.

Some countries will refuse entry to anyone who does not have an onward/return ticket and visible means of support. How this is defined can vary, but in essence it means having sufficient money to cover the cost of food, accommodation and other expenses during your stay. A credit card can be a practical way of avoiding precise cash requirements.

In many cases visa requirements have more to do with residence than with nationality, e.g. the visa requirements for an Indian living in India and an Indian living in the UK may be different. People who live abroad should check which regulations apply to them.

Where a country is not mentioned specifically, nationals of that country should assume that they need both a full passport and a visa. Even if you can theoretically obtain a visa at the border, it is probably easier and cheaper to get it in advance. Allow plenty of time, especially if you need to get several, as it can be a long process. Bear in mind that most visa departments have short, and often eccentric, opening hours. You will also need a whole stack of passport photos and will find that many countries ask you to pay in cash or by postal order and will not accept cheques or credit cards.

## PUBLIC HOLIDAYS

These have been listed under the individual headings in the 'Country by Country' section. Many are religious holidays, whose dates vary from year to year; these are given by name rather than date, in chronological order. If an official holiday falls on a weekend, the following Mon or Tues often becomes a holiday as well. Over Christmas most things close altogether; on most other public holidays a good rule of thumb is to assume that Sunday hours/schedules will apply.

There are many local festivals which are celebrated only in one town but which can disrupt everything in the area. If time is important to you, check in advance to see if your visit will coincide with any sort of holiday and, if it does, bear in mind that all transport services are liable to be severely restricted. Always double-check schedules locally.

## SALES TAX

Value Added Tax is not automatically added to most goods in Eastern European countries as it is to those in the West, but some countries impose heavy duties on items over a certain value that are being exported – as high as 300% in the Czech Republic, for example. Be sure to check the regulations regarding export if you are buying old items – nothing made before 1945 can be taken out of Poland for instance.

## SECURITY

Increasing exposure to the West, the influx of comparatively wealthy tourists, and the painful adjustment to market economies, have left many Eastern European countries with a growing crime problem. However, levels are not as high as in many other parts of the world, and the most likely risk is petty theft rather than violent crime.

The best way to avoid becoming a victim of theft is to give the impression that you are not worth robbing. Use a hidden money-belt for your valuables, travel documents and spare cash. Never carry a wallet in a back pocket or leave your handbag open and use a bag with a shoulder strap slung horizontally. In public places, take precautions with anything that is obviously worth stealing. Never

leave luggage unattended – apart from the risk of theft, many countries are very terrorist-conscious and chances are it will create a bomb scare. Use baggage lockers if you arrive at a place one morning and intend to leave the same day. When using computerised lockers, be careful that nobody sees your code.

When you're sleeping rough, in any sort of dormitory or on trains, the safest place for your small valuables is at the bottom of your sleeping-bag. In sleeping-cars, padlock your luggage to the seat and make sure the compartment door is locked at night – if necessary, ask the attendant how to lock it. There is a tendency for backpackers to trust each other, but be careful. Be particularly safety-conscious in areas around travel terminals.

Mugging is a problem in some areas, but not rife in European city centres, where pickpockets are usually the main threat. If you are attacked, let go of your bag (or anything else of obvious value) – you are more likely to be attacked physically if the thief meets with resistance. If you do run into trouble, report the incident to the local police without delay, even if it is only to get a copy of their report for your insurance company.

Carry half a dozen passport photos (useful for all sorts of purposes) and photocopy the important pages and any relevant visa stamps in your passport. Store these safely, together with a note of the numbers of your travellers' cheques, insurance policy and credit cards (keep this away from the documents themselves). If you are unfortunate enough to be robbed, you will at least have some identification – and replacing the documents will be much easier.

## SMOKING

Smoking is now banned in many public

---

> ### The Thomas Cook Worldwide Network Customer Promise
>
> Customers who purchase their travel product from any Thomas Cook Worldwide Network office are entitled to the following services at any other Worldwide Network travel location, free of all standard agency service charges:
> airline reservations;
> airline ticket reconfirmation, revalidation or re-routing;
> changes to travel arrangements;
> hotel reservations;
> car rental reservations;
> travel planning assistance;
> emergency assistance.
>
> These services are available at all Thomas Cook travel agency locations (not bureaux de change) mentioned in this book.

places in Europe, and, even where it is allowed, there may be a special area for smokers. This is likely to be less true of eastern European countries,and in any case the prohibitions are often ignored by the locals, but play safe if in doubt and ask before lighting up.

## TELEPHONES

Although phone systems are not as up to date as in the West, you should have few problems finding a phone in towns. Long-distance and international calls may be a problem and not everywhere is on direct-dial. We have commented in the text where phone calls are likely to be especially problematic. Useful telephone numbers are provided throughout the book and in the 'Country by Country' section you will find advice on how to make calls, together with emergency phone numbers.

## TIME

There are several time zones within Europe. The following list includes only the countries covered by this book.

Countries which are **GMT+1** hr in winter, **GMT+2** hrs in summer: Austria, the Czech Republic, Germany, Hungary, Italy, Poland, Slovakia and Slovenia. Countries which are **GMT+2** hrs in winter, **GMT+3** hrs in summer: Bulgaria, Estonia, Finland, Greece, Latvia, Lithuania, Romania and Turkey. Moscow and St Petersburg are **GMT+3** in winter, **GMT+4** in summer.

## TOILETS

Although not a universal concept, pictures representing a male and a female are commonly used in Europe. The term 'WC' is also quite widespread and if you see words beginning 'toilet' or 'lava' you are probably on the right track.

In some countries you may come across places where both sexes use the same facilities, even if there are separate entrances, so don't assume automatically that you are in the wrong place. The quality varies considerably. Many are modern, clean and well-equipped, others are of the hole-in-the-ground variety and not very well maintained. So be prepared for anything. This includes always carrying some paper, as you will be very lucky if you never find it missing. You can often get away with using the facilities in hotels if you look as if you might be staying there. If not,bars, cafés and restaurants are the best bet – but be prepared to buy something.

## USEFUL READING

### Thomas Cook Publications

The *Thomas Cook European Timetable (ETT)*, published monthly at £8.40, has

**25**

up-to-date details of most rail services and many shipping services throughout Europe. It is essential both for pre-planning and for making on-the-spot decisions about independent rail travel around Europe. A useful companion to it is the *Thomas Cook New Rail Map of Europe* (£5.65). Both of these publications are obtainable from some stations, any UK branch of Thomas Cook or by phoning *(01733) 268943*. In North America, contact the **Forsyth Travel Library Inc.** *1750 E. 131st St, PO Box 480800, Kansas City, MO 64148; tel: (800) 367 7984* (toll-free).

*Thomas Cook Travfsellers* (£7.99), published in the USA as *Passport's Illustrated Travel Guides* ($12.95), cover the following major European destinations: Berlin, Budapest, Greece (Mainland), Prague, Turkey, Venice and Vienna. If you plan on going as far as Athens and then seeing some of the Greek islands, you will find the Thomas Cook Touring Handbook *Greek Island Hopping* invaluable; as well as covering (literally) every island, it provides detailed, essential information on the complex ferry schedules. These guides and the *Thomas Cook European Travel Phrasebook* are available from many book shops in the UK and the USA (publisher in America: Passport Books) and from UK branches of Thomas Cook.

### Other useful books

The best series of guides are: *Lonely Planet* and *Rough Guides*, for budget travellers; the *Michelin Green Guides* for cultural sightseeing and the *AA Essential Guides* as excellent pocket guides for short stops. If you want to work for a while, buy *Work Your Way Around the World* (Vacation Work, £10.95). The *Travellers Handbook* is also extremely useful for pre-travel planning (WEXAS, £14.95).

### WHAT TO TAKE

A few really useful things are: water-bottles, Swiss Army pocket knife, torch (flashlight), sewing kit, padlock and bicycle chain (for anchoring your luggage), small first-aid kit (including insect repellent and antihistamine cream, sun-screen cream, after-sun lotion, water-sterilising tablets, something for headaches and tummy troubles, antiseptic spray or cream, medicated wet-wipes, plasters for blisters, bandages), contraceptives and tampons, they are difficult to get in Eastern Europe – try the luxury shop in the city's biggest hotel), safety matches, mug and basic cutlery, small towel, soap, toothbrush, some detergent, string (for a washing-line), travel adapter, universal plug (often missing from wash-basins), sunglasses, alarm clock, notepad and pen, pocket calculator (to convert money), a money-belt and a good book (for long journeys). For clothing, see the clothing section on p. 16. If you wear spectacles, take a spare pair and a copy of your prescription.

If you're not sure what you're doing about accommodation, take a lightweight sleeping-bag, a sheet liner, inflatable travel pillow, earplugs and eyemask (invaluable for comfort in dormitories and on some trains, even if you look a total idiot). Strong plastic containers can come in handy and pack some plastic bags of various sizes – they are useful for all sorts of things.

# TRAVELLING BY TRAIN

This chapter is packed with hints about organising an excursion around Europe by rail. Information about tickets in Western Europe has been included, as many travellers will begin their journey from a station in the West.

## INFORMATION AND BOOKING

### In the UK

Sources of international rail tickets, passes and information include: **International Rail Centre**, *Victoria Station, London SW1V 1JY; tel: (0171) 834 2345.* **Wasteels Travel**, *Victoria Station, London SW1V 1JY; tel: (0171) 834 7066.* **Campus Travel (Eurotrain)**, *52 Grosvenor Gardens, London SW1W 0AG; tel: (0171) 730 3402.* **The Rail Shop**; *tel: 0990 300 003.* **Europa Rail Ltd**, *Tavistock House North, Tavistock Square, London WC1H 0HR; tel: (0171) 387 0444.* **Ffestiniog Travel**, *Harbour Station, Portmadog, Gwynedd LL49 9NP; tel: (01766) 512340.*

### In the USA

Sources of tickets, passes and information include: **Forsyth Travel Library Inc.**, *1750 E. 131st St, PO Box 480800, Kansas City, MO 64148; tel: (913) 384 3440* (toll-free). **Rail Europe Inc**, *230 Westchester Ave, White Plains, NY 10604* and *2100 Central Ave, Suite 200, Boulder CO 80301; tel: (800) 4-EURAIL* (toll-free) or, for Eurostar, *tel: (800)-EUROSTAR* (toll-free). **DER Tours**, *tel: (800) 782 2424.* Several national rail networks have offices in the USA; infor-

mation is listed for individual countries in the Country by Country section (see pp. 36–77).

### Elsewhere

International rail information and tickets in **Australia/Canada/New Zealand** are obtainable from Thomas Cook branches (and branches of Marlin Travel in Canada). To contact **Rail Europe** in Canada, *tel: (800) 361-RAIL* (toll-free). In **South Africa** from branches of Rennies Travel (Thomas Cook network member).

## EUROPEAN RAIL PASSES

Many countries have rail passes valid only for domestic travel. Those most likely to be of interest are detailed in the Country by Country section and can usually be purchased from any branch of the national railway and its appointed agents. Your passport is required for identification, and one or two passport-size photos may be needed. Passes generally cover all the ordinary services of the national rail companies and can be used on most special services if you pay a supplement. However, if the pass has been purchased in North America there is no supplement to be paid. A few passes, such as Eurail, cover most supplements. Many passes also give free or discounted travel with privately owned rail companies (including steam and cog trains), buses and ferries. You get details of these and other extras when you buy the pass. If you are planning a long journey, consider the following international passes, which are common to most of Europe.

**27**

# Inter-Rail Passes

The **Inter-Rail Pass** has launched generations of young people into the travelling life. It can be bought by anyone who will be under 26 on the first day for which it is valid, if they have lived for at least six months in one of the European countries where the pass is valid (see list below), or are a national of that country and hold a valid passport. It can be purchased up to two months before travel begins. The current cost is £249 for a month and you can buy consecutive passes for longer journeys. You will not get free travel in the country where you buy the pass, but you may be eligible for some discount.

Inter-Rail provides unlimited second-class rail travel for a month on the national railways of: Austria, Belgium, Bulgaria, Croatia, the Czech Republic, Denmark, Finland, France, Germany, Greece, Hungary, the Republic of Ireland, Italy, Luxembourg, Morocco, the Netherlands, Norway, Poland, Portugal, Romania, Slovakia, Slovenia, Spain, Sweden, Switzerland and Turkey. There are free or discounted crossings on various ferries, so check.

### Zonal Inter-Rail Passes
These regional variations on the Inter-Rail Pass are for those under 26. The same rules about eligibility apply. For zonal passes, Europe has been divided into seven geographical zones:

1) United Kingdom and the Republic of Ireland.
2) Sweden, Norway and Finland.
3) Denmark, Switzerland, Germany and Austria.
4) Poland, the Czech Republic, Slovakia, Hungary, Bulgaria, Romania and Croatia.
5) France, Belgium, the Netherlands and Luxembourg.
6) Spain, Portugal and Morocco.
7) Italy, Slovenia, Greece, Turkey (including shipping lines between Brindisi and Patras).

Passes are available for 1 zone (15 days: £179); 2 zones (1 month: £209); and 3 zones (1 month: £229). If you have a definite route in mind, these can offer savings over the standard Europe-wide pass.

### Inter-Rail 26+ Pass
This is the same as Inter-Rail, except that it is for people over 26 and excludes Belgium, France, Italy, Morocco, Portugal, Spain and Switzerland. The current cost is £269 for a month or £209 for 15 days.

### Eurail Passes
These are available only to people living outside Europe and can be obtained from the agents listed (under 'In the USA' and 'Elsewhere') to the left.

You can get the passes once you've arrived (from French Railways in London), but at much higher prices.

Since you can buy them up to six months in advance, there is no point in waiting until the last minute.

Eurail offers unlimited travel on the national railways of: Austria, Belgium, Denmark, Finland, France, Germany, Greece, Hungary, the Republic of Ireland, Italy, Luxembourg, the

Netherlands, Norway, Portugal, Spain, Sweden and Switzerland. They also cover most private railways and a few selected ferries, such as the Hellenic Mediterranean/Adriatica di Navigazione shipping lines between Brindisi in Italy and Patras in Greece (although, as with the Inter-Rail pass, you will have to pay the port tax of approximately L.10,000 from Italy to Greece or Dr.1500 from Greece to Italy. In addition to this, Eurail pass holders must pay a high-season (June–Oct) supplement of L.15,000 from Italy to Greece or Dr.2500 from Greece to Italy). A complete list of bonuses is included on the complimentary map issued with your tickets.

The basic **Eurail Pass** has no age limit. It provides first-class travel on all services and even covers most of the supplements for travelling on express and de luxe trains. It also gives free or reduced travel on many lake steamers, ferries and buses. There are several versions, valid for 15 days, 21 days, 1 month, 2 months or 3 months. Current prices range from US$522 for 15 days to US$1468 for 3 months. The **Eurail Youth Pass** is much the same, but cheaper, as it is designed for those under 26 and is based on second-class travel. There are versions valid for 15 days (US$418), 1 month (US$598) and 2 months (US$798).

The **Eurail Flexipass** is similar to the basic Eurail pass, but allows you to travel for any 10 days (US$616) or any 15 days (US$812) within a two-month period.

The **Eurail Youth Flexipass** allows second-class travel for those under 26 within a two-month period for 10 days (US$438) and 15 days (US$588).

The **Eurail Saverpass** is designed for groups of 3–5 people travelling together at all times (between 1 Oct and 31 Mar two people travelling together is allow-

able) and offers first-class rail travel over a 15-day period for US$452, 21 days for US$578 and 1 month for US$712.

## EuroDomino Freedom Pass

This is a catch-all title for a whole series of passes allowing unlimited travel on the national railway of an individual country. They are not valid for travel in your own country. Conditions of use are the same everywhere and the options available are for any 3, 5 or 10 days within a period of one month. The passes can be purchased by non-Europeans. They cover many of the fast-train supplements.

There is no age limit, but the price depends on age. Those under 26 pay less but are restricted to second-class, while those over 26 can opt for either class. The price varies according to the size of the railway network in the country chosen. The cheapest options (of the countries covered here) are for Luxembourg: from £11 (Youth) for 3 days second-class travel to £55 for 10 days first-class travel. The most expensive passes are for France: at £99 and £359 respectively.

Passes can be purchased up to two months before travel begins. Countries currently offering them are: Austria, Belgium, Bulgaria, Croatia, the Czech Republic, Denmark, Finland, France, Germany, Greece, Hungary, the Republic of Ireland, Italy, Luxembourg, Morocco, the Netherlands, Norway, Poland, Portugal, Romania, Slovakia, Slovenia, Spain, Sweden, Switzerland and Turkey. In the UK, holders of any Euro-Domino Freedom pass can get up to 50% discount off the rail/ferry ticket from London to a Continental port. Other ferry discounts are also available.

## Europass

Available in the USA only, Europass is

valid for first-class rail travel for anything from 5 to 15 days in a 2-month period. The 5–7 day pass (US$316–400) allows you to visit three countries, 8–10 days (US$442–526) covers four countries and 11–15 days (US$568–736) covers five countries – but they must be adjacent. The basic cost covers France, Germany, Italy, Spain and Switzerland. For a supplement (from US$29 to US$90), you can add Austria, Belgium/Netherlands/Luxembourg, Greece and/or Portugal.

For those under 26 the EuroYouth Pass is available for  second-class travel; for details contact the agents listed (under 'In the USA') on p. 26. Various bonuses are available and listed on the map which accompanies the rail pass.

### Rail Europ Senior Card

This card is for those over 60. It offers a discount of 30% (sometimes more) off the cost of cross-border rail travel (excluding supplements) between the participating countries: Austria, Belgium, Croatia, the Czech Republic, Denmark, Finland, France, Germany, Greece, Hungary, the Republic of Ireland, Italy, Luxembourg, the Netherlands, Norway, Poland, Portugal, Romania, Slovakia, Slovenia, Spain, Sweden, Switzerland and the UK.

Most countries have a rail card for their senior citizens, which is needed to buy the Rail Europ Senior Card. In the UK the Senior Railcard is available to people over 60 (it costs £16 p.a.) The Rail Europ Senior Card, available from British Rail International, costs an extra £5. It becomes valid on the day of purchase and expires on the same date as the domestic card.

### TRAVEL BETWEEN WEST TO EAST

If you intend to concentrate on a few countries, a national or regional pass may make better sense, and details of these are given below. In this case, there are various offers to reduce the cost of travel between West and East. Travellers under 26 can buy a range of reduced price tickets to and from Eastern European from Campus Travel (see p. 27)

Those under 26 years of age can also receive Eurotrain or 'BIJ' discounts on one-way tickets from Eastern to Western Europe. Valid for two months and permitting stopovers, the tickets have to be obtained from a travel agency that specialises in student or youth travel: CKM Student Travel in the Czech Republic and Slovakia, Express in Hungary and Almatur in Poland, for example. Wasteels (see p. 27), which has offices throughout Europe, can also organise these tickets

An ISIC student card entitles the holder to a discount on international train tickets between the countries of Eastern Europe. It may be necessary to go a student travel office.

Single tickets, which allow unlimited stopovers within their two-month period of validity, may be better value than a pass if you want to linger where the mood takes you rather than pound the rails to get the most out of a pass.

### REGIONAL EUROPEAN RAIL PASSES

### Baltic Pass

This is available to holders of ISIC cards, full-time academic staff, and people of any nationality under the age of 26, this allows unlimited rail travel in Estonia, Latvia and Lithuania for 7 days (£13), 14 days (£18) or 21 days (£25). It can be purchased from Campus Travel (see p. 27).

Once you arrive in the Baltic states, there can be occasional hassles getting the pass validated (which must be done

30

before you board trains) and it's not as cheap as individual tickets, but still preferable unless you enjoy queuing.

## Scanrail Pass

This is available in both the UK and the USA and gives unlimited travel on the national rail networks of Denmark, Finland, Norway and Sweden. It also provides free or discounted travel on many ferries and long-distance buses – as well as good discounts at 180 Scandinavian hotels for an extra £17: ask for details of the **Bonuspass**. There is a Youth version for anyone aged 25 or less.

In the **UK** Scanrail is available from **NSB Travel Bureau**, *tel: (0171) 930 6666*, and the **International Rail Centre**, *tel: 0171 834 2345*. In the **US** these passes are available from Forsyth Travel Library (see p. 27).

Scanrail passes are obtainable inside Scandinavia, but the validity is different and the ones bought prior to arrival are far better value.

## Central Europe Pass

This is available in the USA only and provides unlimited rail travel throughout the Czech Republic, Germany, Poland and Slovakia for any 5 days within a month. The pass is available for first-class travel only and costs US$296. There are no youth reductions.

## Youth Passes

If you are under 26, there are many other discounted tickets and passes available. Some are to single destinations or for travel in single countries, others (like the examples above) to whole groups of countries. Passes come under many different names, such as Euro-Youth, Explorer Pass and BIJ (Billets International de Jeunesse).

If the Inter-Rail/Eurail passes are too general for your needs, contact an organisation that specialises in youth travel such as **Campus** or **Wasteels** (see p. 27).

### TICKETS

Always buy your ticket before travelling, unless you board at an unstaffed station, or you could face heavy penalties or even criminal prosecution. Throughout Europe tickets are easily available from many travel agents as well as at stations. Eastern Europe is a little more complicated, because rail transport systems are changing as rapidly as many other aspects of life, so finding accurate information can be difficult. On the plus side, a domestic ticket bought there is often cheaper than a ticket for exactly the same route bought outside the country.

Never buy a standard ticket without asking what discounts are available, especially if you are prepared to travel outside peak periods, such as rush hour and the weekend.

Most countries have discounts for children, but there is no set definition of what constitutes a child. They are generally classed as adults at 11/12 years, but the age at which they change from infants (who travel free) to children can range from 2 to 5 years inclusive. Quite a few countries also offer domestic rail cards which give substantial discounts to the disabled, elderly or students – although, in most cases, the international passes already mentioned are better value.

### ADVANCE RESERVATIONS

Seats on many trains cannot be booked but, when they can, it is usually worthwhile, especially in high season and around public holidays (such as Christmas and Easter), when popular routes can fill up a long way ahead and you could spend

**31**

hours standing in a crowded corridor. In some cases, you may be refused permission to board at all if there are no seats available.

For a quiet journey, with a chance to sleep, choose a seat in a compartment. For a lively journey, with conversation and panoramic views all round, choose an open carriage. In both cases, window seats are less disturbed than corridor seats. Solo travellers (particularly women) should always stick with the crowds, for security. If you are travelling during the busy summer period and have no reservation, board your train as early as possible.

Some of the major express trains – especially international trains – (usually marked in timetables by an 'R' in a box) are restricted to passengers with reservations and you can usually make a reservation about two months in advance. In all cases, booking is essential if you want sleeping accommodation. Bookings can usually be made by contacting the national railway representatives of the country through which you intend to travel. In the USA, advance reservations and sleeping-cars can be booked through **Forsyth Travel Library Inc**; *tel: (913) 384 3440* (toll-free).

## SUPPLEMENTS

Rail pass holders are often exempt from the routine surcharges applied to travel on express trains, but not always. If you opt to travel by an express service, therefore, rather than a slower alternative (there almost always is one), you should ask about supplements before committing yourself. Holders of a first-class Eurail Pass can use most of the special high-speed services in Western Europe without paying extra, but even they should check its validity if they want to use one of the new breed of luxury trains.

There's usually a fee for reserving seats but it is seldom large and is normally included in the supplementary payments for the faster trains. Sleeping accommodation (see p. 34) always attracts charges of some kind. Sort out the extras before you start your journey – and make sure you know exactly what you are paying for. You may be able to pay the supplements on the train, but it almost always costs more than doing it in advance.

## TYPES OF TRAIN

Many of the best daytime international trains are now branded EuroCity (or **EC**). To qualify, trains have to be fast and offer a certain standard of service, such as food and drink during the journey. All have names, and the EuroCity network continues to expand, now including countries such as the Czech Republic and Poland.

Many overnight trains carry names as well as numbers; some, such as the *Istanbul Express* and *Balkan Express*, having long histories. Most are just ordinary trains, but there is a new breed of high-quality night service known as EuroNight (**EN**) with air-conditioned coaches and extras such as evening drinks and breakfast, which are available even to couchette passengers.

The **IC** or InterCity label is applied by many countries to the fast long-distance trains, although there are slight variations in what they provide. The **ICE** (InterCity Express) designation also crops up in several countries, but is mostly applied to the latest high-speed trains in Germany. **IR** is the classification for inter-regional express services which make more stops than InterCity services; it is used mainly in Germany (where it stands for 'Inter-Regio') and in Italy (where it's short for 'Interregionale').

These names are all used to distinguish the faster long-distance trains from local or stopping trains. Types of train unique to a specific country are described in the Country by Country section.

Most longer-distance trains in Europe offer both first- and second-class travel, but second class is the norm for local stopping services. Where overnight trains offer seating accommodation, this is usually second class only. As a rule, in Western Europe, second class is perfectly OK for all but the most ardent comfort-seeker. A few Eastern European services still leave a lot to be desired, but tickets are very cheap and it's worth paying a little more to upgrade to first class.

### FINDING YOUR TRAIN

In small stations, you are faced with a limited choice of platforms and can usually find a friendly soul to point you in the right direction.

Most large stations have electronic departure boards or large paper timetables (often yellow for departures and white for arrivals) which list the routes, the times of departure, the relevant platforms and the arrival times at larger places. They are usually kept reasonably up to date, but watch out for nasty surprises, such as the seemingly ideal train which only runs on the third Sunday in August. In some stations, the platforms are also labelled with details of regular trains or the next departure and may even give the location of special carriages and the facilities on board.

If a platform is long it is possible that two trains will be leaving it at the same time, going in opposite directions, so double-check that you are boarding in the correct place: the trains often have destination boards on each carriage. It is necessary to be a little careful even when there is only one train, because quite a few split *en route*, with only some carriages going the full distance. If you have a reservation, all you need do is board 'your' carriage (they are all numbered, usually on cards by the entrance). If you are not booked and the destination boards are unclear, ask an official for assistance: if officials speak no English, showing your ticket should be enough for them to put you in the right portion of the train.

First-class coaches usually have a yellow stripe along the top of the windows and large number '1's on the side of the coach, on the door or on the windows. No-smoking coaches (the majority) are distinguished by signs, usually of a cigarette with a red cross, or one red band, over it. A sign near the compartment door often gives seat numbers and sometimes indicates which are reserved. In non-compartment trains, seats are usually numbered individually (on the back or on the luggage rack) and reserved seats may have labels attached to their head-rests (or the luggage racks). In many countries, however, reserved seats are not marked – so be prepared to move if someone who has booked boards the train.

Station announcements are often unintelligible, even if they are in your own language, but are sometimes important. If you hear one that you don't understand shortly before your train is due to leave, ask someone nearby whether the announcement concerned your train. The ideal is to find an official, but other travellers are often helpful. If alot of people near you start to move away hurredly, keep up, as there has probably been a change of platform.

### OVERNIGHT TRAINS

A night on the train, being rocked to sleep by the clatter of the wheels, is not to be missed. Sleeping-cars can cost about the same as a hotel but have the advantage of covering large distances as you rest and you won't waste precious holiday time in transit. You can also save quite a bit of money, if you are prepared to use couchettes or to curl up on the ordinary seats. Don't do this too often without a break, however, or you will end up totally exhausted.

The chatter of other passengers, the coming and going at stations and even the regular checks to make sure you still have all your bags can lead to a disturbed night. If you have a rail pass and the night train is due to reach your next destination too early in the morning, consider booking to a town an hour or so further along the line; you can then get some extra sleep and backtrack to the place you actually want to visit on an early train – but don't forget to check the timetables to ensure that there is a suitable early train back!

In Eastern Europe, you may be woken for Customs and Immigration checks, which can involve a search of luggage or the compartment/berth. Within Western Europe, it's unlikely you'll notice the borders, even if you're awake, and it's highly unlikely you will be disturbed. Attendants will give you an alarm call if you tell them you are leaving the train before the final destination – specify the stop rather than the time, so you can sleep longer if the train runs late. If you want to go to sleep before other passengers have arrived, switch on their berth lights and switch off the main overhead light. Sleepers and couchettes can usually be reserved up to three months in advance; early booking is recommended as space is limited. If you don't have a booking, it's still worth asking the conductor once on board. Keep some local currency handy to pay him.

## SLEEPING ACCOMMODATION

Sleeping-cars have bedroom-style compartments with limited washing facilities (usually just a wash-basin) and full bedding. WCs are located at one or both ends of the coach. An attendant travels with each car, or pair of cars, and there are sometimes facilities for drinks and/or breakfast – but be prepared to pay extra.

First-class sleeping compartments usually have one or two berths and second-class compartments have two or three berths. However, there are some special sleeping-cars (described as 'T2' in schedules) which have only one berth in first class and two in second class.

Unless your group takes up all the berths, compartments are allocated to a single sex and small unaccompanied children are placed in female compartments. In Estonia, Latvia and Lithuania berths are allocated on a first-come, first-served basis without regard to sex. You should claim your berth within 15 minutes of boarding the train or it may be reallocated. Couchettes are more basic – and much cheaper. They consist of simple bunk beds with a sheet, blanket and pillow. They are converted from the ordinary seats at night and there are usually four berths in first class and six in second class, with washing facilities and WCs at the end of each coach. Males and females are booked into the same compartment and expected to sleep in their daytime clothes.

In a few cases (notably Italy), overnight trains have airline-style reclining seats, which are allocated automatically when you make a seat reservation. These are sometimes free if you have a rail pass.

## WASHING

Showers are still rare in European trains, but a few of the luxury-class compartments include them. The Germans and Austrians are introducing 'hotel' trains with showers in some compartments. A few rail stations have low-cost showers for public use.

## EATING

Most long-distance trains in Europe have dining-cars serving full meals and/or buffet cars selling drinks and snacks. There is an increasing tendency for refreshments to be served aircraft-style from a trolley wheeled through the train. Quite a few services offer full meals only to first-class passengers, while others offer nothing but a full-scale, four-course production. Dining-cars often have set times for full meals. Buffets are usually open to both classes.

Always take emergency rations, including a full water-bottle and a packet of biscuits. Food and drink are usually expensive on trains so, if you need to save money, take a picnic.

## BAGGAGE

Lockers are invaluable if you want to look round a place without carrying heavy baggage and most stations (and other transport hubs) have them. The initial payment generally covers 24 hrs, but you are allowed to stay longer (usually up to a week, but check).

The newest lockers have display panels and are automatic: you simply pay any excess when you return. With older lockers, you have to pay the excess to station staff (at the left-luggage office, if there is one).

Baggage trolleys (where available) are usually free, but often supermarket-style: you need a coin to release them – which you get back when you return them to a stand.

35

# COUNTRY BY COUNTRY

## AUSTRIA

**Capital:** Vienna *(Wien)*.
**Language:** German; English is widely spoken in tourist areas.
**Currency:** Schilling (ÖS); 1 Schilling = 100 Groschen.

### Passports and Visas

An EU National Identity Card is sufficient. Visas are not needed by nationals of Australia, Canada, New Zealand or the USA. Others should check.

### Customs

EU nationals may import tax and duty paid items for personal use. Non-EU residents arriving from outside Europe may bring 200 cigarettes or 50 cigars or 250 g tobacco, 1 litre spirits and 2 litres wine or 3 litres beer and may bring other commodities duty free to a value of ÖS2400; ÖS1000 from the Czech or Slovak Republics or Slovenia.

### Tourist Information

There is a tourist information service of some sort in almost every small town and even village in Austria. Staff invariably speak some English. Opening times vary widely, and are restricted at weekends in out of the way places. The green 'i' is the sign to look out for, although the official name does vary – **Fremdeverkersbüro** is one of the most common.

### Useful Addresses in Australia

**Embassy,** *12 Talbot St, Forest, Canberra ACT 2603, tel: (62) 951376.*
**National Tourist Office,** *1st Floor, 36 Carrington Street, Sydney NSW 200, tel: (2) 299 3621.*

### Useful Addresses in Canada

**Embassy,** *445 Wilbrod St, Ottawa, Ontario KIN 6M7; tel: 789 1444.*
**National Tourist Office,** *2 Bloor St E./Suite 3330, Toronto, Ontario M4W 1A8, tel: (416) 9673381.*

### Useful Address in the Rep. of Ireland

**Embassy,** *15 Ailsbury Court Appts, 93 Ailsbury Rd, Dublin 4; tel: (1) 2694577.*

### Useful Addresses in South Africa

**Embassy,** *1109 Duncan St, Momentum Office Park, 0011 Brooklyn, Pretoria; tel: (12) 463361.*
**National Tourist Office,** *Private Bag X18, Parklands 2121 Jo'burg; tel: (11) 4427235.*

### Useful Addresses in the UK

**Embassy,** *18 Belgrave Mews West, London SW1X 8HU; tel: (0171) 235 3731.*
**National Tourist Office and Railways,** *30 St George St, London W1R 0AL; tel: (0171) 629 0461.*

### Useful Addresses in the USA

**Embassy,** *3524 International Court NW, Washington DC 20008; tel: (202) 895 6700.*
**National Tourist Office,** *PO Box 1142 New York NY 10108-1142; tel: (212) 944 6880 or PO Box 491938 Los Angeles, CA 90049; tel: (310) 477 3332.*

## STAYING IN AUSTRIA

### Accommodation

The **Austrian National Tourist Office** can supply information about all types of accommodation, including camping. **Hotels** are graded on the usual five-star system, but even one-star establishments are pricey. *Gasthaus/Gasthof* indicates an **inn** and *Frühstuckpension* a **bed and breakfast** place. The best value is usually a **private room** (look *zimmer frei* signs), but many require stays of several nights and some charge extra for short stays. *Jugendherberge* is the word for a **youth hostel**. In summer some universities let rooms.

Camping is popular and there are lots of sites. Standards are high, with cleanliness and efficiency the keynotes; the down-side is the high prices. Many sites open summer only. In Alpine areas there are also refuge huts – details from the local tourist office. For all accommodation it is advisable to book ahead for July, Aug, Christmas and Easter.

Several resorts, indicated by **GC** next to tourist office details, issue a guest card to visitors in higher quality accommodation. The cards entitle holders to anything from free escorted mountain hikes to discounts for ferries or museums. The cards are generally issued by *gasthofs* or hotels.

## Eating and Drinking

The Austrian pattern is: continental breakfast, lunch (1200–1400), coffee and cake in mid-afternoon, then dinner (1800–2200). Lunch is usually more expensive in cafés than in restaurants. Drinks in bars and clubs cost more than in eating places. A filling snack, sold by most butchers, is *Wurstsemmel* – slices of sausage with a bread roll. Beer is the most popular drink, but Austrian wine is good and there are multiple *schnapps* varieties. A service charge of 10–15% is included in restaurant bills. It is the custom to leave a further 5% if happy with the service.

## Opening Hours

**Banks:** in Vienna – Mon, Tue, Wed, Fri 0800–1230 and 1330–1500, Thurs 0800–1230 and 1330–1730 (some stay open through the lunch hour). Elsewhere, the norm is – Mon–Fri 0800–1230 and 1330–1500.

**Shops:** Mon–Fri 0800–1830, Sat 0800–1300 (in larger towns many stay open until 1700 on the first Sat of the month.)

**Museums:** there is no real pattern to opening times so check locally.

## Postage

Post offices can be recognised by a golden trumpet symbol and are often located close to the station or main square. They all handle poste restante (*Postlagernde Briefe*). Nationwide hours are Mon–Fri 0800–1200 and 1400–1800, but offices in major towns tend to stay open during lunch and on Sat.

The main post offices in cities frequently open 24 hrs. Stamps (*briefmarke*) can also be purchased at *Tabak/Trafik* shops.

## Public Holidays

1, 6 Jan; Easter Mon; 1 May; Ascension Day; Whit Mon; Corpus Christi; 15 Aug; 26 Oct; 1 Nov; 8, 25, 26 Dec. Many people take unofficial holidays on Good Fri, Easter Sun, Whit Sun, 2 Nov, 24 Dec and 31 Dec.

## Public Transport

The efficient Austrian **long-distance bus system** consists of orange **Bundesbahn buses**, run by ÖBB and generally based at rail stations, and yellow **Post-buses**, run by the postal system, which usually leave from beside post offices. Both serve places inaccessible to trains.

All cities have excellent **bus** and/or **tram** systems. It is possible to buy tickets on board, but cheaper to get them in advance from **Tabak/Trafik** booths. They are validated in a little machine on board, often marked with an 'E' (*Entwerter*). **Taxis** in larger cities charge by officially controlled meters. with extra charges for luggage. In smaller towns there are fixed charges and fares for longer distances are agreed beforehand.

## Telephones

It is quite easy to use ordinary pay-phones. Most boxes have instructions in English and most international operators speak it.

Even remote places have booths that take telephone cards, (*Wertkarten*), slightly cheaper than cash, available from post offices, stations and some shops or there are metered phones in post offices where payment is made afterwards.

Long distance calls are approximately 35% cheaper between 1800 and 0800 and on public holidays. To call abroad from Austria: *tel: 00*. To call Austria: *tel: 43*.

To call international enquiries and operator: *tel: 08*. Note that other dialling codes are not yet uniform. Post office phone counters can give the correct ones to use locally.

To call national enquiries and operator: *tel: 16 11*.

**Emergencies:** Police: *133*; Fire: *122*; Ambulance: *144*. Loss or theft of Thomas Cook Traveller's Cheques: *0660 6266*.

### RAIL TRAVEL WITHIN AUSTRIA

The national rail company is **Österreichische Bundesbahnen (ÖBB)**. Most lines are electrified and the railway system is fast and reliable, with *IC* trains every 1–2 hrs and regional trains timed to connect with *IC* services.

Other fast trains are: *D* (ordinary express trains often only with second-class seating); *E* (semi-fast or local trains which are usually second class); *EC*; and *EN*. Secondclass fares are higher on *EC* trains.

Most overnight trains have sleeping-cars (up to three berths) and couchettes (four or six berths). Some ordinary seating compartments are allocated exclusively for people wishing to sleep through the night.

Seat reservations cost ÖS30 (free on *EC* if made in advance). A single supplement, payable in Austria, covers first-class travel on all *EC* and *SC* trains and also (on request) the cost of seat reservations, recommended at peak times. They can be made up to three months in advance for sleeping-cars and two months in advance for couchettes.Almost every station offers left luggage facilities, and most hold an accommodation leaflet or town map.

### Fares and Passes

The main domestic passes are: **Bundesnetzkarte**, valid for first- (ÖS5400) or second-class (ÖS3600) travel for one month on all ÖBB lines, including numerous mountain railways; and the **Österreich-Puzzles** (Austrian Puzzles) Ost, West, Nord and Süd, for under-26s covering parts of the country with unlimited rail travel for any 4 days within a 10-day period (ÖS900 first class, ÖS600 second).

### BULGARIA

**Capital:** Sofia *(Sofija)*.
**Language:** Bulgarian, which is a Slavic tongue and uses the Cyrillic alphabet. English, German and French is spoken in larger hotels, restaurants and shops in main cities and resorts. Russian is more widely understood, but is unpopular.

Nodding the head up and down indicates 'no' *(ne)* and shaking it from side to side means 'yes' *(da)*.

**Currency:** Leva (Lv.); 1 Leva = 100 Stotinki. The import/export of local currency is limited to Lv.10,000 and, on leaving, you must reconvert any additional Leva into hard currency before going through passport control.

There is no restriction on the amount of foreign currency you can bring in, but amounts above $5000, or equivalent, should be declared, with exportable amounts being limited to the amount declared at import. Receipts *(bordereaux)* will be given for every exchange transaction and when you pay for accommodation. These must be retained as they will be needed when you leave.

(Travellers arriving and leaving by train should be prepared for harassment by customs officials and border police, who treat visitors as a convenient source of hard-currency additions to their salaries. Even minor infringements of the rules may be sniffed out, and the suggestion made that a suitable 'fine' – dollars and German marks are the favoured currencies – will permit the 'culprit' to stay on the train. A 'gift' of cigarettes or any western goodies may also help)

Major credit cards are accepted in larger hotels, restaurants and shops and their use is spreading.

## Passports and Visas

A full passport is required by all travellers, with six months of validity remaining. US nationals do not require a visa if travelling as a tourist and staying for no more than 30 days.

Nationals of many other countries do not require visas under certain circumstances, e.g. if travelling on organised tours pre-booked through **Balkan-tourist**. It is best to inquire. Rail travellers should have a visa before arriving, otherwise they may face border problems. All visitors should register with the police, a hotel or guesthouse within 48 hrs of their arrival.

When you arrive you will be given a *carte statistique*. Take good care of this. It has to be date-stamped every time you check into, and out of, any form of accommodation. When you leave Bulgaria, the stamps will be checked.

## Customs

The allowances are: 200 cigarettes, or 50 cigars, or 250 g tobacco products, 1 litre spirits, 2 litres wine, and 100 g perfume.

## Useful Address in Australia

**Consulate-General,** *1/4 Carlotta Rd, Double Bay, Sydney NSW 2028, tel: (02) 372 7592.*

## Useful Address in Canada

**Embassy,** *325 Stewart St, Ottawa, Ontario K1n 6K5; tel: (613) 789 3215.*

## Useful Address in South Africa

**Embassy,** *Techno Plaza E., 305 Brooks St, Melo Park, Pretoria; tel: (012) 342 3721.*

## Useful Addresses in the UK

**Republic of Bulgaria Consular Section,** *186/188 Queen's Gate, London SW7 5HL; tel: (0171) 584 9400.*
**National Tourist Office (Balkan Holidays),** *Sofia House, 18 Princes Street, London W1R 7RE; tel: (0171) 499 6988.*

## Useful Addresses in the USA

**Embassy,** *1621 22nd Street NW, Washington DC 20008-1921; tel: (202) 387 7969.*
**Balkan Holidays,** *Suite 508, 41 East*

# Bulgaria

There are some restrictions on photography and you should not use your camera at airports, railways, military installations, bridges or tunnels. Some border zones have restricted access.

Many consumer goods are hard to find, so take with you what you think you'll need in the way of films, cosmetics, toilet paper, tea-bags and medicines.

*42nd Street, New York, NY 10017; tel: (212) 573 5530.*

## STAYING IN BULGARIA

### Accommodation
In Sofia, **Balkantourist** remains a useful source, but private agencies also offer accommodation booking, information and exchange facilities. The better hotels have information desks which can be of considerable help to travellers.

### Eating and Drinking
Bulgaria produces vegetables of all kinds, which you will find in dishes such as: *bop* (lentil soup), *gjuvetch* (vegetable stew), and *kiopolou* (aubergines/eggplants). Lamb and pork are also popular.

Tea is usually green and served without milk; coffee is of the Turkish type (black, strong and with sediment), although espresso can be found in a few hotel bars. Bottled fruit juices are cheap and readily available. *Slivova* is a hangover-producing plum brandy, so take care. The aniseed-flavoured *mastika* and *raki* are also potent. The local beer is cheap, but an acquired taste. Bulgarian wine is cheap and good. The tap water is safe to drink except in the rare places where a sign indicates otherwise. Bottled water is widely available.

### Opening Hours
**Banks:** Mon–Fri 0800–1200 and 1230–1500. Private exchange bureaux remain open on Sat.
**Shops:** Mon–Fri 1000–2000, Sat 0800–1400.
**Museums:** vary widely, but the norm is 0800–1830, closing on either Mon or Tues. A 'Non-Stop' sign indicates that the establishment stays open 24 hours a day.

### Postage
Stamps *(marki)* can be bought only from post offices *(poshta)*, usually open Mon–Sat 0830–1730.

### Public Holidays
1 Jan; 3 Mar; a few days around Easter; 1, 24 May; a few days around Christmas.

### Public Transport
There are good rail and long-distance bus networks. Unusually, **buses** are slightly more expensive than trains, but both are very cheap by Western standards. At small stops, you can only buy your bus ticket once the bus is in and they can see how many spaces are available.

Local **city transport** is very cheap and runs frequently, but, as in most cities, is crowded during rush hour.

### Telephones
Coin boxes are fine for local calls, but go to the central telephone office (not necessarily in the post office) in major towns if you want to phone anywhere further afield. To call abroad from Bulgaria: *tel: 00.* To call Bulgaria: *tel: 359.* To call the international operator: *tel: 0123.* To call the local operator: *tel: 121.* Information:

*991* (international), *144* (private); *145* (state and office).

**Emergencies:** Police: *166*; Fire: *160*; Ambulance: *150*. Loss or theft of Thomas Cook Traveller's Cheques:*00 44 1733 502995* (reverse charges).

### RAIL TRAVEL WITHIN BULGARIA

The national rail company is **Bulgarian State Railways (BDZ)**. The rail system is fairly comprehensive and there are three types of train: express, fast and slow. Journeys on the electrified lines between Sofia and the other major cities are fast. Elsewhere, electrification is not complete and you should be prepared to travel slowly. Trains are very busy and seat reservations are recommended (obligatory for express trains). All medium- and long-distance trains have first- and second-class carriages and a limited buffet service. Overnight trains between Sofia and the Black Sea resorts have first- and second-class sleeping-cars and second-class couchettes.

### Stations

Station indicator boards can be confusing. One platform may serve two tracks and platforms and tracks are both numbered. Notices and signs at stations are in Cyrillic; learn what the name of your destination looks like and ask what time the train is due to arrive there, so you don't have to rely on spotting a sign. A good route map can also be helpful.

### Fares and Passes

With the exception of Sofia Central Railway Station, which has an international ticket counter, only domestic tickets are available from stations. **Rila Travel**, with offices in all cities, handle international travel. Even for local journeys, it's better to buy your ticket in advance, as there are usually long queues at stations. You can buy tickets on the trains but that costs twice as much.

### THE CZECH REPUBLIC

**Capital:** Prague (*Praha*).
**Language:** Czech is the official language of the Czech Republic. Czech and Slovak are closely related Slavic tongues, mutually intelligible by natives of both the Czech and the Slovak Republics. English, German and Russian are often also understood, although Russian is less popular.
**Currency:** Czech Korunas or Crowns (Kc); 1 Koruna = 100 Hellers. The Koruna is now fully convertible and there are no restrictions on foreign currencies. Credit cards are widely accepted in tourist areas.

### Passports and Visas

Full passports are required by everyone. Visas are not needed by EU or US nationals, but are needed by nationals of Canada, Australia and New Zealand. Others should check.

### Customs

The following allowances apply only to those who are aged 18 or over. They are: 250 cigarettes or equivalent in tobacco, 1 litre spirits, and 2 litres wine.

### Useful Addresses in the UK

**Embassy**, *28 Kensington Palace Gardens, London W8 4QY; tel: (0171) 243 1115.* **Cedok (Czech Tourist Office)**, *49 Southwark Street, London SE1 1RU; tel: (0171) 378 1526.*

### Useful Addresses in the USA

**Embassy,** *3900 Spring of Freedom St NW, Washington DC 20008-3897; tel: (202) 274 9100.*

41

**Cedok**, *10 East 40th Street, New York, NY 10016; tel: (212) 689 9720.*

## STAYING IN THE CZECH REPUBLIC

### Accommodation
You should have a choice of one–five-star hotels, private rooms and pensions, and, at a much more basic level, old-style tourist hotels, hostels and inns with a few spartan rooms. However, quality (once outside the three- to five-star range) can leave a lot to be desired. Although people are trying to upgrade as fast as possible, it can still make more sense to look at private rooms than cheap hotels. Credit cards are accepted in bigger hotels. This is the most popular of the former Eastern bloc countries and the deluge of tourists has resulted in a real shortage of beds. Always book ahead. The state tourist organisation, **Cedok**, runs booking offices across the country, as well as in London and New York (see under 'Useful Addresses').

There are plenty of campsites (usually May–Oct only), most of which cater for caravans as well. Rough camping is forbidden.

### Eating and Drinking
Lunch is around 1130–1400/1500 and dinner 1700–2200. The cuisine is rich and meat-based, but vegetarian restaurants are beginning to appear. Schnitzel and dumplings (*knedliky*) are on virtually every menu, as is *gulaš*, a spicy meat dish. Eating and drinking is cheap, especially in self-service *bufet* (where you stand while eating). *Kavárny* and *cukrárny* serve coffee (often Turkish-style) and delightful pastries. Beer halls (*pivnice*) and wine bars (*vinárna*) are good places to eat. Czech beer and Slovak wine are excellent. Budweiser originated here, but the original (*Budvar*) is better.

### Opening Hours
**Banks:** Mon–Fri 0800–1700.
**Shops:** Mon–Fri 0900–1200 and 1400–1800, Sat 0900–1200 (in Prague, shops often stay open longer). Food shops usually open earlier. Food and souvenir shops often open on Sun.
**Museums:** (usually) Tues–Sun 1000–1700. Most castles close Nov–Mar.

### Postage
There is a full postage service (including post restante), but it is slow and erratic. It is also cheap. Usual post office opening hours are 0800–1900. Stamps are also available from newsagents and tobacconists.

### Public Holidays
1 Jan; Easter Mon; 1, 8 May; 5–6 July; 28 Oct; 24–26 Dec.

### Public Transport
The rail network here is good, but there is also a comprehensive long-distance bus network, run by CSAD (although many parts are now privatised). Bus stations are well organised, with platforms, ticket offices and amazingly complicated schedule boards. Officially, you should book in advance, but you can buy tickets from the driver, although he will give priority to those with reservations.

### Telephones
To call abroad from the Czech Republic: *tel: 00*. To call the Czech Republic: *tel: 42*. Information: *121* (national) *0135* (international). **Emergencies:** Police: *158*; Fire: *150*; Ambulance: *155;* Loss or theft of Thomas Cook Traveller's Cheques: *0044 1733 502995* (reverse charges).

## RAIL TRAVEL WITHIN THE CZECH REPUBLIC

The national rail company is **Ceské Dráhy (CD)**. The rail network is cheap and extensive, but often crowded. Main lines are served by *EC* and *IC* trains (supplement payable). and express trains, *rychlík*. Other trains are *spešný* (semi-fast), which cost less, and *osobný* (slow) trains, which should be avoided.

All long-distance trains offer first- and second-class travel. Some long-distance trains have dining-cars and overnight services between cities have sleeping-cars.

Seat reservations are recommended for express. Bookings can be made at the counter marked 'R' at stations. Sleepers can be reserved at at only a few stations.

### Fares and Passes

A Czech-Slovak **Flexipass**, available in the USA only (from the Forsyth Travel Library, see p. 26), covers 5 days unlimited travel within a 15-day period throughout both the republics.

There is also an **Explorer Pass**, valid for 7 consecutive days (or multiples thereof) covering first- or second-class rail travel. It is available to anyone under 26 and to any holder of an ISIC card. It must be purchased before you go

## ESTONIA

**Capital:** Tallinn.
**Language:** Estonian (a member of the tiny Finno-Ugric language group, which also includes Finnish and Hungarian). Some Finnish could be useful and Russian is more widely understood but not popular. It can be very difficult to communicate without a dictionary or phrasebook.
**Currency:** Kroons or Crowns (EEK); 1 Kroon = 100 Sents. There are no restrictions on the import/export of any currency, but you must change some money into Kroons when you enter Estonia. Travellers' cheques can be changed at banks (and occasionally post offices) but it's easy to get caught out, so always carry some cash. Credit cards are gaining recognition, but are still only accepted in a few places.

### Passports and Visas

Full passports are required by all categories of travellers. Visas are not needed by holders of full British passports, nationals of Australia, Canada, New Zealand and the USA. Almost everyone else does, and should check. Estonian visas are also valid for Latvia and Lithuania.

### Customs

Although not a member state, Estonia applies the EU regulations (see p. 19).

43

### Useful Address in Australia

**Consulate,** *141 Campbell St, Darlinghurst, Sydney, NSW 2010; tel: (02) 212 1207.*

### Useful Address in Canada

**Consulate,** *958 Broadview Ave, Toronto, Ontario, M4K 2R6; tel: (416) 461 0764.*

### Useful Addresses in the UK

**Embassy,** *16 Hyde Park Gate, London SW7 5DG; tel: (0171) 589 3428.*

### Useful Addresses in the USA

**Embassy,** *2131 Massachussets Ave NW, Washington, DC 20008; tel: (202) 588 0101.*
**Consulate General and Tourist Office,** *630 Fifth Ave (Suite 2415), New York, NY 10111; tel: (212) 247 7634.*

## STAYING IN ESTONIA

### Accommodation

Hotels are still fairly thin on the ground. Home stays offer accommodation in farmhouses, summer cottages, homes and small boarding houses. Try to be back at your lodgings/hotel by 2200 (usual lock-out time), unless you've checked that it's all right to be later.

### Eating and Drinking

There are good cafés and restaurants in all large towns and new ones are opening all the time. Ask the waiter to recommend something if you are not sure what to have.

The pattern of eating is to have a large helping of hors d'oeuvres and modest helpings thereafter. Fish is a common ingredient. Many restaurants are open noon to midnight, with a break of a couple of hours: usually 1700–1900 (reservations are advisable, especially in the big hotels).

Tap water is not safe to drink anywhere; buy bottled water instead. Tea and coffee are widely available. The most popular drink is beer *(olu)*. Vodka and brandy are better value and some bars serve mulled wine. *Vana Toomas* is the Estonian liqueur.

### Opening Hours

**Banks:** Mon–Fri 0930–1730.
**Shops:** Mon–Fri 0900/1000–1700/1800, Sat 0900/1000–1500/1700. Shops often close for an hour or two between 1200 and 1500. In Tallinn some open Sun afternoons.
**Museums:** The days of opening vary enormously and many open for only a few days every week, so check locally. On the days they are open, this is usually 1100–1600.

### Postage

Stamps are sold by large hotels and post offices, but the service is erratic and you could arrive home before your postcards.

### Public Holidays

1 Jan; 24 Feb (Independence Day); Good Fri; Easter Mon (unofficial); 1 May; 23, 24 June; 16 Nov; 25, 26 Dec.

### Public Transport

Buses travel to more destinations than trains and can be considerably quicker. Buy tickets before boarding from the ticketing windows. Don't expect staff to speak English.

### Telephones

Some public phones are currently being replaced by cardphones, others accept sents. You can now make international calls by dialling direct. Alternatively try the post office, or for convenience the large hotels which charge a premium.

The recent modernisation of the telephone lines means calls no longer travel via Moscow and you might actually get through. It still pays to be patient, however, as the long-distance lines can be overcrowded and to book a call can take up to an hour. To call abroad from Estonia: *tel: 8, then 10.* To call Estonia: *tel: 372.* For local directory assistance: *tel: 6313 222* (from offices and establishments); *tel: 065* (from private homes). To book a call: *tel: 007* (English spoken). **Emergencies:** Police: *02*; Fire: *01*; Ambulance: *03*. Loss or theft of Thomas Cook Traveller's Cheques: *0044 1733 502995* (reverse charges)

## RAIL TRAVEL WITHIN ESTONIA

**Estonian Railways (EVR)** is the national operator. Trains fan out from Tallinn to the rest of the country (and into Latvia, Lithuania and Russia), but suburban services are the most frequent and the others tend to get very crowded. Domestic services are slow, but are very cheap.

There are two classes: 'soft' has fully upholstered seats and 'hard' has plastic/leather seats. Both convert to berths for overnight journeys. Soft is a couchette with four berths; hard may be either four-berth couchettes or an open-plan sleeping compartment. In both, there is a charge for all bedding, including mattresses. Some trains have normal two- or four-berth European sleeping-cars and some trains have only hard class, but there is no advance information about which, so ask locally.

When travelling between the Baltic States, book for soft (first) class. Through sleepers to West/Central Europe are of Western (Inter-City) type with one or two berths in first class and three berths in second class (all with full bedding included). Trains that run only by day are second class. Advance reservations are necessary (except for purely local trains) if you want to be sure of a seat.

Timetables run horizontally instead of vertically. Travel to Riga is best done overnight on one of the sleeper trains. Berths are four to a cabin and bedding is provided for a small charge. For information on trains *tel: 007*.

## Stations
Very little English is spoken at stations and buying tickets can be confusing. Stations now sell timetables for Estonian Railways.

## Fares and Passes
Two types of rail pass are available. The **Baltic Rail Explorer Pass** is for students, teachers and young people – see p.

29. The **Baltic Card**, which can be bought in Scandanavia, covers 8 or 15 days second-class travel.

### FINLAND

**Capital:** Helsinki (*Helsingfors*).
**Language:** Finnish and, in the north, Lapp/Sámi. Finnish is complicated and defies the efforts of most foreigners. Portmanteau words are common, so look for the components. Swedish, the second language, is not widely spoken, but often appears on signs after the Finnish. Knowledge of English is scattered, but there's not much problem in Helsinki. Elsewhere, you can usually find someone able to help. The Finns are friendly and it's not unusual for a passer-by to chip in if you're obviously having problems. You can also try German, which is reasonably widespread.
**Currency:** Finnmarks or Markka (FIM/Mk.); 1 Markka = 100 Pennis. **Forex** give the best exchange rates and have a branch at Helsinki station.

**45**

### Passports and Visas
National Identity Cards issued by EU countries, Iceland, Norway and Switzerland are sufficient. Visas are not needed by citizens of those countries, nor by nationals of Australia, Canada, New Zealand or the USA. South Africans do require visas.

### Customs
The usual EU regulations apply (see p. 19), but spirits may be purchased only by those aged 20 or over.

### Tourist Information
**Tourist offices (Matkailutoimistot)** can be identified by the universal 'i'. Staff speak English and there's a range of literature in English, mostly free. They pro-

vide accommodation listings and/or direct you to booking centres.

Most public buildings operate a numerical queue system, so look near the entrance for a machine dispensing numbers. The optimum time to visit (and the only time for many activities) is June–Aug. In summer mosquitoes could be a real problem, particularly in the north, so take a strong repellent. Authentic Sami articles carry a round *Duodji* token.

## Useful Addresses in Australia
**Embassy,** *10 Darwin Ave, Yarralumla, Canberra, ACT 2600; tel: (06) 273 3800.* **Finnish Railways,** *c/o Bentours International, 32–34 Bridge St, Sydney, NSW 2000; tel: (02) 247 3381.*

## Useful Addresses in Canada
**Embassy,** *Suite 850, 55 Metcalfe St, Ottawa, Ont. K1P 6L5; tel: (613) 236 2389.* **Finnish Railways,** *c/o Forestgreen Travel Inc – Scanditours, 191 Eglinton Ave E (Suite 202), Toronto, Ont. M4P 1K1; tel: (416) 483 0555.*

## Useful Address in the Rep. of Ireland
**Embassy,** *Russell House, St Stephens Green, Dublin 2; tel: (01) 478 1344.*

## Useful Address in South Africa
**Embassy,** *628 Leyds St, Muckleneuk Ext.2, Pretoria 0002; tel: (012) 343 0275.*

## Useful Addresses in the UK
**Embassy,** *38 Chesham Place, London SW1X 8HW; tel: (0171) 838 6200.* **Tourist Board,** *30–35 Pall Mall, London SW1Y 5LP; tel: (0171) 839 4048.* **Finlandia Travel Agency** (sells Finnrail), *227 Regent St, London W1R*

*8PD; tel: (0171) 409 7334/5.* **NSR Travel Bureau** (sells Scanrail), *21–24 Cockspur Street, London SW1Y 5DA; tel: (0171) 930 6666.*

## Useful Addresses in the USA
**Embassy,** *3301 Massachusetts Ave NW, Washington, DC 20008; tel: (202) 298 5800.* **Scandinavian Tourist Board,** *655 Third Avenue, New York, NY 10017; tel: (212) 949 2333.* **Finnish Railways,** *c/o Rail Europe Inc., 230 Westchester Ave, White Plains, NY 10604; tel: (800) 4-EURAIL.*

### STAYING IN FINLAND

## Accommodation
Whatever your tastes, Finland can offer accommodation to suit, from luxury **hotels** to **rough camping** (allowed anywhere *suitable*, but don't intrude on residents and leave no trace of your stay). Wherever you stay will probably have a sauna: M is for men, N for women.

Ask the Finnish tourist board for the relevant (free) brochure: *Finland Hotels* (not graded, but standards are high) or *Finland Budget Accommodation* (covers all types, including camping: 350 well-equipped and graded sites, about 70 open year-round) and get details of the **Finncheque discount hotel scheme**.

About a third of the 160 **hostels** (*Retkeilymaja*, pronounced Ret-key-loo-my-at) are open year-round: warn them if you will be arriving after 1800. Be aware however, that most of them prohibit sleeping-bags.

## Eating and Drinking
The Finns have four meals: breakfast 0700–1000; lunch 1100–1400; dinner 1600–1900; and supper 1900–midnight.

There's often a fixed-price menu which represents a considerable saving. Restaurants are expensive, but you can fill up at breakfast (included in hotel prices and consisting of a substantial help-yourself buffet). You can eat reasonably at fast-food stands (*grillit*), self-service places (*kahvila*) and bars (*baari*). *Ravintola* are more up-market restaurants, sometimes with dancing.

For self-catering, **Alepa**, **Siwa**, **Säästäri** and **Valintatalo** are among the less expensive supermarket chains.

Finnish cuisine is very cosmopolitan. Fish is a major ingredient (*lohi* indicates salmon). Try reindeer (*poro*) and *lihapullia* (meat balls); *karjalan piirakka* (rye dough filled with rice mash  topped by boiled egg); *kalakukko* (rye bread with fish and bacon) and *kiisseli* (berry mousse).

Milk, coffee, tea and hot chocolate are ubiquitous. Alcohol (including local liqueurs) is available in restaurants and bars, but only to people over 18 – and it's expensive. Beer is priced according to strength, the strongest being *olut IV*. **Alko** is the state-owned outlet for strong alcohol.

## Opening Hours

**Banks:** Mon–Fri 0915–1615, with regional variations.
**Shops:** Mon–Fri 0900–1800, Sat 0900–1400/1500. Stores and food shops: Mon–Sat 0900–1800/2000.
**Museums:** the usual closing day is Mon, but there's no norm for opening hours. Many close altogether in winter.

## Postage

Most post offices (*posti*) open at least Mon–Fri 0900–1700. The logo is a posthorn on a yellow background. Stamps can also be purchased from many shops and hotels. Postboxes are yellow.

## Public Holidays

1, 6 Jan; Good Fri; Easter Sun–Mon; May Day; Ascension Day; Whitsun; Midsummer Eve and Day (*Juhannus*); All Saints' Day; 6 Dec (Independence Day), 24, 25, 26 Dec.

## Public Transport

Timetables for trains, buses and boats dovetail conveniently. *Suomen Kulkuneovot* (published twice a year; FIM.70) covers them all in detail. It's available at bus and rail stations. Rail passes and student cards provide free or discounted travel on many buses.

Buses operate on 90% of public roads, reaching areas inaccessible by rail, particularly in the north. Bus-stops usually have a black bus on a yellow background for local services and a white bus on a blue background for longer-distance services. You can get tickets on board, but it's cheaper to buy them in advance (at bus stations or agents). Long-distance buses are comfortable, with reclining seats and ample legroom. At terminals, look for the destination, rather than the bus number.

Most towns have good public transport. If you have no pass, board vehicles at the front and pay the driver for a single journey or a multi-ride ticket. Otherwise, enter by the central door and validate your ticket in the machine (usually orange). Tickets are valid for one hour and you can change within that time. Don't expect bus drivers to speak English.

**Taxis** are free when the yellow *taksi* sign is lighted. Hailing them in the street is acceptable. They are metered, with a surcharge after 1800 and at weekends.

## Telephones

Coin boxes are being phased out, but the number of card boxes that accept credit

47

cards is increasing rapidly. If you buy a telephone card, make sure you get **Tele**, which can (at least in theory) be used nationwide – the only card that can. Tele booths have a button for English instructions. Phonecards are sold by R-kiosks (newsagents) and tourist offices, as well as Tele offices. Calls are cheapest at weekends and 2200–0800 Mon–Fri. To call abroad from Finland; *tel: 990*. To call Finland; *tel: 358* – omit the first 9 of the area code. National directory; *tel: 118*. International directory; *tel: 92 090*. International operator; *tel: 020 222*. The system is being reorganised and there's a helpline; *tel: 020 202*. Most operators speak English. **All emergencies:** *112*. Loss or theft of Thomas Cook Traveller's Cheques: *0044 1733 502995* (reverse charges)

### RAIL TRAVEL WITHIN FINLAND

The national rail company is **Valtion Rautatiet (VR)** and comfortable trains link the major towns. The logo is a stylised *VR*: often white on blue. *Pendolinos*, which can reach 220 kph, are being introduced. Reservations are compulsory for *IC* and *EP*. Sleeping-cars have one berth in first class and two or three (on top of each other) in second class. There are handbasins in each compartment and WCs at the end of each carriage. In winter, sleeping accommodation costs less Mon–Thur than at weekends. *Presidente* is a new class of sleeper coming into service; it will have a shower at the end of the carriage and two compartments with private facilities. Long-distance trains have a buffet and/or trolley service.

### Stations

Look for *Rautatieasema* or *Järnvägsstation* (or similar). There is usually a plan showing the layout of long trains, so you can locate your carriage in advance. Many stations have no trolleys, but virtually all have baggage lockers.

### Fares and Passes

The **Finnrail** pass (available at Helsinki and Turku stations) gives unlimited second-class travel on **VR** for any 3 days in a month (FIM.505), any 5 days in a month (FIM.685) or any 10 days in a month (FIM.945). There's also a first-class version: respectively FIM.760, 1030 and 1420. You can get it in the UK before you go: 3 days £81, 5 days £111, 10 days £152 (first-class: £122, £166 and £219).

### GERMANY

**Capital**: Bonn/Berlin (the functions of the capital are gradually being transferred to Berlin).

**Language**: German; English and French are widely spoken in the West, especially by young people, less so in the East. In German it is customary to roll several words into one and the polysyllabic result can be daunting. You will find it less confusing if you split the words into their component parts. *Hauptbahnhof*, for example, is an amalgam of *haupt*/chief, *bahn*/railway and *hof*/yard.

**Currency:** Deutsche Marks (DM). 1 Mark = 100 Pfennig.

### Passports and Visas

EU National Identity Cards are acceptable as are ID cards for citizens of the Czech and Slovak Republics, Hungary, Iceland, Liechtenstein, Malta, Monaco, Poland, and Switzerland.

Visas are not needed by nationals of Australia, Canada, New Zealand or the USA. Others should check.

### Customs

Standard EU regulations apply; see p. 18.

Danes must spend at least 24 hrs in Germany before taking their allowances home.

## Tourist Information

There are helpful tourist information offices in virtually every town or resort, usually within a couple of hundred metres of the station.

English is widely spoken and a wide range of English-language maps and leaflets is available. Most offices offer a room-finding service.

## Useful Addresses in the UK

**Embassy**, *23 Belgrave Square, London SW1X 8PZ; tel: (0171) 235 5033.*
**German National Tourist Office (DZT),** *Nightingale House, 65 Curzon St, London W1Y 7PE; tel: (0171) 495 3990.*
**German Rail Sales**, *The Sanctuary, 23 Oakhill Grove, Surbiton, Surrey, KT6 6DU; tel: (0181) 390 0066.*

## Useful Addresses in the USA

**Embassy**, *4645 Reservoir Rd NW, Washington DC 20007-1998; tel: (202) 298 8140.*
**Tourist Office**, *Chanin Building, 122 East 42nd St (52nd Fl), New York, NY 10168-0072; tel: (212) 308 3300.*
**German Federal Railroad (DB)**, *747 Third Ave. (33rd Floor), New York, NY 10017; tel: (212) 371 2609.*

### STAYING IN GERMANY

## Accommodation

The general standard of accommodation in the West is high, but so are prices and you will be doing well if you find a room for less than DM25 in more remote areas, or DM50 in cities. Standards in the East have improved greatly and prices have risen accordingly. All over Germany the prices vary widely according to demand.

Avoid *Messen* (trade fairs) and other special events when prices are at their highest; an events calendar is published twice yearly by the DZT. Germany is a year-round tourism and business destination, and there is no real low season for hotels. However, rates are highest between Christmas and mid-March in ski resorts and July and Aug nationwide.

**Hotels** and **boarding houses** (*Gasthof/Gasthaus*) can be booked in advance through a department of DZT: **Allgemeine Deutsche Zimmerreservierung (ADZ)**, *Corneliusstrasse 34, Frankfurt/Main; tel: (069) 74 07 67.* Advance booking is essential in high season and always advisable. **Pensionen** or **fremdenheime** are pensions and *Zimmer* means 'room' (generally in a private home). These are usually cheap but expect you to stay for at least two nights. Look for signs in the windows (*Zimmer frei* and *zu vermieten* indicate availability; *besetzt* means they are full) or book through the local tourist office. You must be prepared to pay for this type of accommodation in German cash, as credit cards and cheques are seldom accepted by small establishments.

**Jugendherberge (DJH)** are youth hostels and there are around 600 in Germany (mostly affiliated with the **HI**). In Bavaria there is an age limit of 27 elsewhere there is no limit; but preference is usually given to the young. It is necessary to book well ahead in peak season and in the East (where they are the best form of accommodation unless you can afford the top hotels). In Germany they really are youth hostels and often used by school parties, which has resulted in the introduction of a new category of accommodation, **Jugendgästehaus**, which is aimed more at young adults.

**Camping** is the cheapest form of

49

accommodation and site facilities are generally excellent, though few sites are conveniently close to stations. **Deutscher Camping-Club (DCC)**, *Mandlstr.28, Munich*, publishes an annual list of 1600 sites (price DM34.80). DZT publishes a free list and map showing more than 600 of the best sites nationwide.

There are fewer sites in the east, but you can get a list from **Camping and Caravanverband**, *Postfach 105, Berlin*. Most sites open only May–Oct and it is advisable to book a few days in advance. A few are open all year and usually have space out of season.

### Eating and Drinking

Breakfast is any time from 0630 to 1000. Lunch is around 1200–1400 (from 1130 in rural areas) and dinner 1800–2130 (earlier in rural areas).

German cuisine is fairly rich and served in large portions, with pork and potatoes the staple ingredients, but it's easy to find lighter things, such as salads. Breakfast is often substantial (and usually included in the price of a room), consisting of a variety of bread, cheese and cold meat. Germans eat their main meal at midday, with a light supper in the evening, but restaurants and pubs also offer light lunches and cooked evening meals. The cheapest way to eat is to patronise *Imbisse:* roadside stalls serving a variety of snacks, especially *Wurst* (sausage). For lunch, the best value is the daily menu (*Tageskarte*). There are simple restaurants (*Gaststätten* and *Gasthöfe*) which include regional dishes. A visit to a *Biergarten* or *Bierkeller* is a must.

### Opening Hours

These vary from place to place and are not standard even within one city. As a rule of thumb:
**Banks**: Mon–Fri 0830–1300 and 1430–1600 (until 1730 Thur). Hours have been shorter in the East, but are changing.
**Shops**: Mon–Fri 0900–1830 (until 2030 Thur) and Sat 0900–1400. Shops next to stations are permitted to sell food and drink outside these hours.
**Museums**: Tues–Sun 0900–1700 (many until 2100 Thur). Some open Mon and some close for an hour or more at lunch.

### Postage

The usual post office hours are Mon–Sat 0800–1800 and the main post office in each town has a poste restante facility. Address letters to the *postlagernde*.

All postal codes in Germany are in the process of being changed, so check that any you have are still current.

### Public Holidays

1, 6 Jan; Good Fri; Easter Sun–Mon; 1 May, Ascension Day; Whit Sun–Mon; Corpus Christi★; 15 Aug★; 3 Oct; 1 Nov★; Day of Prayer (third Wed in Nov); 24, 25 Dec; 26 Dec (afternoon). ★Catholic feasts, celebrated only in the south.

### Public Transport

All inter-city travel is by train, with buses used just for travel to remote areas. Most major bus routes are run by the railways, so you can get information about them at the rail stations.

Many big cities have a **U-Bahn** (U) underground railway and an **S-Bahn** (S) urban rail service. City travel passes cover both, as well as other public transport. International passes us-ually cover the S, but not the U. Where ferries are an integral part of the city's transport, they are often included in the city transport pass.

Local fares are expensive in the West and are fast catching up in the East. A day card (*Tagesnetzkarte*) or multi-ride ticket (*Mehrfahr-karte*) usually pays its way if you take more than three rides. If there's no machine at the stop, get your ticket from the bus driver. The usual system is to get tickets from automatic machines and then validate them in little boxes in the station or on board the vehicle.

## Telephones

In theory the Eastern and Western systems have been integrated, but the Eastern phone system still has some catching up to do. If you have important calls to make, make them in the West where the system is very efficient. Black telephone boxes have instructions in English and most operators speak it. **Kartentelefon** boxes take only cards, which you can buy at any post office, priced DM12 or DM50. To call abroad from Germany: *tel: 00*. There are a few exceptions, but the kiosks all give full information. To call Germany: *49*. To call the international operator: *0010;* national operator: *010;* directory enquiries: *001188*. **Emergencies**: Police: *110*; Fire: *112*; Ambulance: *112*. Loss or theft of Thomas Cook Traveller's Cheques: *0130 859930* (toll-free)

**RAIL TRAVEL WITHIN GERMANY**

*Deutsche Bahn (DB)* is an amalgamation of the former West German *DB (Deutsche Bundesbahn)* with the East German *DR (Deutsche Reichsbahn)*. In general, track and rolling stock in the East are older and less comfortable.There are also some privately owned railways. Tickets must be purchased before you board, unless you are prepared to pay a hefty supplement.

Long-distance trains are: *ICE* (an ultra-modern service which cruises at up to 174 mph), *IC* and *IR* plus *EC* and *EN*. The *RB* and *RSB* are modern, comfort-able regional services linking up with the long-distance network. There are also reasonably fast *Eilzug (E)* and *D* trains. Ordinary commuter trains – *City-Bahn (CB)*, *S-Bahn* and *Nahverkehrszug (N)* – are all slow services.

Most German trains offer both first and second class, but some are second class only. Overnight services often have sec-ond-class seating and sleeping accommo-dation (sleeping-cars with up to three berths and/or couchettes with four or six berths). Seat reservations are possible for most fast trains, but not local trains.

In the West most long-distance trains have dining-cars. In the East they may have either dining-cars or a buffet service.

## Stations

German stations are efficient, clean and well staffed, with facilities that include left luggage lockers (DM2) and refreshments.

The main station in each town is the **Hauptbahnhof** (Hbf) and any sizable station will be able to supply a computer print-out showing the connections along the route in which you are interested.

## Fares and Passes

The **EuroDomino Pass** (sold in North America as the **GermanRail Pass**) buys unlimited travel for any three, five or ten days in a one month period and covers all scheduled services, *S-Bahn* airport con-nections and supplements for *IC*, *EC* and *ICE* trains. Seat, couchette and sleeper reservations are extra.

German **Regional Passes** are sold only in the UK. There is no age limit and they are available for first- and second-class unlimited travel within one of 15 designated German regions for any 5 or 10 days in a 21-day period. They can be used on any *DB* trains (including *IC* and *EC*) and on the *S-Bahn*, but not on the

**51**

*ICE* unless you are prepared to pay a supplement. **Tramper-Monats** tickets (available to anyone under 23 and to students under 27) give second-class travel for a month on all *DB* trains (except the *ICE*, for which a supplement is payable) as well as on railway-run buses (*Bahnbusse*) and the *S-Bahn*.

**BahnCards** give half-price travel on all trains for a full year.

## GREECE

**Capital:** Athens *(Athinai).*
**Language:** Greek; English is very widely spoken in tourist areas and hotels and in the islands, less widely in remote mainland areas and Athens. Many people in day-to-day contact with tourists also speak some German or Italian. Station and street signs are usually in English as well as Greek characters. You may see several different versions of the same name (for example *Sindagma, Syntagma* or *Sidagma* for Athens's central square) as there is no standard transliteration.

To make things more complicated, placenames are sometimes translated directly into English, so that some maps and guides may call Plateia Syntagma 'Constitution Square'. Greek body language can also be confusing; a backward motion of the head, very like an affirmative nod, is a negative, *nai* (pronounced nay) means yes and *ochi* (pronounced very like 'okay') means no.
**Currency:** Drachmae. Coins are in denominations of 10, 20, 50 and 100; notes in 500, 1000 and 5000.

## Passports and Visas
National identity cards issued by EU countries are sufficient for entry. Nationals of the USA, Canada, Australia and New Zealand do not require visas for stays of less than three months. Others

---

### Greece

The Greek penal system is harsh and it is a crime to sell your belongings while you are there. Electrical items in particular, may be noted in your passport, when you arrive in the country.

Should you have anything of value stolen, therefore, it is essential to report the fact to the authorities immediately.

---

should check.

Turkish nationals are not permitted to enter Greece at all if their passports indicate that they have visited or intend to visit Turkish occupied Cyprus.

### Customs
Normal EU regulations apply, see p.19.

### Tourist Information
The **Greek National Tourist Office** (GNTO) provides information including hotel listings, transport schedules, archaeological sites, exhibitions, festivals and other events.

### Useful Address in Australia
**Tourist Office;** *51–7 Pitt St, Sydney NSW 200; tel: (2) 241 1663.*

### Useful Addresses in Canada
**Tourist Office;** *1300 Bay St, Main Level, Toronto, Ontario M5R 3K8; tel: (416) 968 2220.*

### Useful Addresses in the UK
**Consulate General,** *1A Holland Park, London W11 3TP; tel (0171) 221 6467.*
**Greek National Tourist Office and railway representation,** *4 Conduit Street, London W1R 0DJ; tel (0171) 734 5997.*

## Useful Addresses in the USA

**Embassy**, *2221 Massachusetts Ave NW, Washington DC 20008-2873; tel: (202) 667 3169/939 5800.*
**Tourist Office**, *Olympic Tower, 645 Fifth Ave (5th Floor), New York, NY 10022; tel: (212) 421 5777.*

### STAYING IN GREECE

## Accommodation

Greece is over-supplied with accommodation, from five-star hotels to pensions, village rooms, self-catering apartments, dormitories and youth hostels. You should have no problem finding a bed in Athens, Patras or Thessaloniki even in high summer (though the very cheapest Athens dorms and pensions are often very crowded in July and Aug).

Rooms are hardest to find over the Greek Easter period, so try to book ahead. Outside the Easter and July-Sept peaks, accommodation costs up to 30% less. You should also get a 10% discount if you stay three or more nights. Cheaper places will hang onto your passport overnight unless you pay in advance.

**Youth hostels** are not good value. **Campsites** at major sights (including Delphi, Mistra and Olympia) can be good value, with laundries, hot showers, cafés and even swimming pools. You can get a list of sites from the GNTO.

## Eating and Drinking

Greeks rarely eat breakfast (they get up at dawn and start the day with coffee and a cigarette) but many cafés in tourist areas advertise 'English breakfast'. Traditional Greek meals are unstructured, with lots of dishes brought at once or in no particular order. Lunch is any time between 1200 and 1500, after which most restaurants close until around 1930. Greeks dine late,

and you will find plenty of restaurants open until well after midnight.

The best Greek food is fresh, seasonal and simply prepared. Seafood dishes are usually the most expensive. Veal, chicken and squid are relatively cheap, and traditional salad - olives, tomatoes, onions, peppers and feta cheese drowned in oil, served with bread - is a meal in itself. Most restaurants have a bilingual Greek and English menu. In smaller places, visit the kitchen to choose what you want, or in more expensive establishments choose dishes from a display cabinet.

Coffee is easier to find than tea; iced coffee (frappé) is now more popular than the tiny, strong cups of old-fashioned Greek coffee. Tapwater is safe but heavily chlorinated. Aniseed-flavoured *ouzo* is a favourite aperitif. *Retsina* (resinated wine) is an acquired taste; many Greeks mix it with Coke. Greek brandy is on the sweet side. Draught lager is not widely available and is neither as good nor as cheap as bottled beer; Amstel, Henninger and Heineken brewed in Greece are sold in half-litre bottles.

## Opening Hours

**Banks:** (usually) Mon-Fri 0800–1400, with longer hours in busy tourist areas in peak holiday season. -
**Shops:** set their own hours; in summer most close from around midday until early evening.
**Sites and Museums:** erratic, but most should be open 0830–1500; the main Athens sites stay open until sunset in summer.

## Postage

Post offices, marked by a circular yellow sign, can be found even in quite small villages and are normally open Mon-Fri 0800–1300, Sat 0800–1200. They can change money, Eurocheques and travellers cheques.

Stamps can be bought in street kiosks and most general stores.

**Public Holidays**

1, 6 Jan; Shrove Mon; 25 Mar; Easter; May Day; Whit Mon; 15 Aug; 28 Oct; 25, 26 Dec. Everything closes for Easter (the biggest event on the Greek calendar) but bear in mind that they use the Orthodox calendar and so the dates may not coincide with the western Easter.

**Public Transport**

Most long-distance travel is by buses run by the **KTEL** consortium. All towns have well-organised bus stations with clear timetables, and buses are fast, punctual and fairly comfortable You are allocated a seat number with your ticket.

The islands are connected by a web of **ferries and hydrofoils**. The biggest gateway is Piraeus, the port of Athens, but there are also sailings from Thessaloniki, Kavala, Alexandroupolis and Volos in the north, from Nafplio and Githio in the south and from Patras for the western Ionian islands. The Greek National Tourist Office has up-to-date copies of the ever-changing schedules or buy a copy of Thomas Cook's *Greek Island Hopping*.

City transport is by **bus** or (in Athens) **trolley-bus and metro**. Services are punctual and efficient, if crowded. On most, you buy your ticket from the driver; pre-bought tickets must be validated on boarding. In towns outside Athens, **taxis** are easy to find and good value; you can use them for long inter-city journeys too, but keep your wits about you

**Telephones**

To call Greece: *tel: 30*. To call abroad

from Greece: *tel: 00*. **Emergencies**: General Emergency: *100*; Police: *100*; Fire: *199*; Ambulance *150/166*; Tourist Police (24 hr, English-speaking); *171*; Operator *100*. Loss or theft of Thomas Cook Traveller's Cheques: *0044 1733 502995* (reverse charges)

## RAIL TRAVEL WITHIN GREECE

Greek trains are run by the Greek Railway Organisation **Organismos Sidirodromon tis Ellados (OSE)** but the rail network is limited, especially north of Athens. Sleepers/couchettes are of standard European type. Reservations are essential on most express trains.

**Stations**

Facilities at Greek stations are limited. Do not expect to find left luggage and restaurant facilites or English-speaking staff.

**Fares and Passes**

Many European rail passes (see pp. 26-29) offer discounts on ferry services between Greece and Italy. There are **discount cards** for rail travel over 10, 20 or 30 days but apart from those on the main Athens-Thessaloniki route where some *IC* trains operate (advance reservation and a hefty supplement required), most services are slow and infrequent.

To make up for this, most Greek trains run through stunning scenery. If your time is limited, though, you may want to go by bus; bus fares are slightly more expensive than basic rail fares.

## HUNGARY

**Capital:** Budapest.
**Language:** Hungarian (Magyar). German is widely understood, especially near the Austrian and Romanian borders and English is spoken mainly in the tourist areas.

When asking about buses, make sure you pronounce it 'boos' as the English pronunciation is very similar to a rude word in Hungarian.

**Currency:** Forints (Ft); 1 Forint = 100 Fillers. Due to inflation, these are rarely available and pretty worthless. You can buy your currency at banks and official bureaux, but take care not to buy too much as officially you can only change back $100, which is not always readily available. Keep all your receipts. Acceptance of credit cards is becoming more widespread and most large hotels offer the facility. Eurocheques and travellers' cheques are accepted in small denominations. It is advisable to take Deutschmarks rather than dollars or sterling as prices are very often quoted in marks

### Passports and Visas

All visitors require full passports. Visas are not required by EU Nationals, Canadians or citizens of the USA.

Nationals of Australia and New Zealand must obtain visas prior to travelling. All other nationalities should check.

### Customs

The allowances are: 250 cigarettes or 50 cigars or 250g tobacco; 2 litres wine and 1 litre spirits.

### Tourist Information

**IBUSZ** is the national travel bureau, with offices all over the country, much of the literature it produces is written in English.

**Touriform** is another extremely helpful company with English-speaking staff. There is an office in central Budapest, *tel: 361 1172 200.*

### Useful Addresses in the UK

**Embassy:** *35b Eaton Place, London SW1X; tel: (0171 ) 235 2664.*

**Hungarian Tourist Office (IBUSZ):** *c/o Danube Travel, 6 Conduit St, London W1R 9TG : tel (0171 ) 493 0263.* They are very helpful and prompt in sending out information.

### Useful Addresses in the USA

**Embassy:** *3910 Shoemaker Street NW, Washington DC 20008-3811; tel: (202) 362 6730.*

**Hungarian Travel North American Division (IBUSZ):** *1 Parker plaza (Suite 1104), Fort Lee, NJ 07024; tel: (201) 592 8585.*

### STAYING IN HUNGARY

### Accommodation

There is a wide range of accommodation available of reasonable to excellent quality and some superb **hotels** of international standing in the capital. Some of the 2000 castles are being turned into hotels and here the standards vary. For the medium to lower price bracket, **private rooms** are very good value as is the small **pension**. The tourist board offer a very extensive list in all categories. Try to steer clear of the old Soviet style tourist hotels and youth hostels as they are very basic with limited facilities. **Campsites** are, on the whole, very good and can be found near the main resorts. Many have **cabins** to rent, but contact the authorities first in order to book. Camping 'rough' is not permitted and could net a hefty fine.

### Eating and Drinking

The Hungarians love their food and are very hospitable. The style of cuisine has been influenced to a large extent by Austria and Germany  as well as by Turkey. The portions are gargantuan and most restaurants offer a cheap fixed price

55

menu. Lunch is the main meal of the day, and a bowl of *goulash* laced with potatoes and spiced with paprika a must. Try smoked sausages and paprika noodles or the excellent fish. Dinner is early and you should aim to begin eating well before 2100.

In order to avoid the pitfalls of phrase book ordering, try eating in an *Önkiszolgáló* or *ételbár*. These are fairly inexpensive self-service snack bars. *Csárda* are folk restaurants usually with traditional music, but menus can be limited and slightly more expensive. Still in the moderate range are the *Vendéglő* where home cooking often features. *Étterem* are larger restaurants with a more varied menu. Check your bill carefully wherever you eat. Hungarian wines, beer and mineral water cannot be faulted, and try *pálinka*, a fire water schnapps.

## Opening Hours

There are no hard and fast rules, although only food and tourist shops are open Sun.
**Shops:** Food shops and supermarkets generally open 0600/0700–1800 Mon–Fri. Other shops open around 0900/1000–1800, Thur–2000. Shops close for lunch and half-day closing is on Sat.
**Banks:** Mon–Fri 0800/1000–1800/1900 with lunch-time closing on Sat. Some also close early on Fri.
**Museums:** usually Tues–Sun 1000–1800, whilst small museums are often only open during the summer. There's usually one day a week when the entry is free – find out from the Tourist Office or Hotel reception. All museums are closed on public holidays.

## Postage

The postal service is fairly slow but reliable; it is undergoing improvements. Postboxes are red.

## Hungary

Anyone staying in Hungary for more than a month must register at a police station within 48 hours of arrival. This is done automatically by the proprietor if you are staying at a hotel or campsite.

Crime is inreasing with westernisation, hard currency being the main target, so keep an eye on your possessions.

Now they are independent again, the Hungarians are changing their street names to get rid of the Russian influence. To avoid confusion, get an up-to-date street map on arrival in each city.

## Public Holidays

A change is expected regarding a summer bank holiday in July, but at present, holidays are as follows: 1 Jan; 15 Mar; Easter Mon; 1 May; Whit Mon; 20th Aug; 23 Oct; 25, 26th Dec.

## Public Transport

Within towns all public transport is by **bus** or **trolley-bus,** although Budapest does have an internal rail system running through the city. Long distance buses are an alternative to the rail system. Try a leisurely trip on a slow ferry along the Danube or on Lake Balaton. Taxis are good value if you bargain first and agree a price, or ensure that the meter is on.

## Telephones

Telephone service from the hotels is up to European standard but fairly costly. The use of phonecards is becoming more widespread. To call abroad from Hungary: *tel:* 00. To call Hungary: 36. **Emergencies:** Police: 07; Fire: 05; Ambulance: 04. Loss or theft of Thomas Cook Traveller's Cheques: *0044 1733 502995* (reverse charges)

## RAIL TRAVEL WITHIN HUNGARY

The rail system is first class and every town is on the **Hungarian State Railways (MÁV)** network, however most trains *(személyvonat)* are very slow. The express trains *(gyorsvonat)* and the special Blue Express *(sebesvonat)* connect Budapest with major towns and Lake Balaton.

All seats and sleepers need to be booked well in advance. Sleepers and couchettes are the standard European variety. All express trains have a snack service but this often sells out very rapidly, so it is advisable to be prepared and bring your own refreshments.

### Fares and Passes

The **Explorer Pass** gives unlimited first- or second-class rail travel in Hungary for 7 days but must be purchased before you go. **Rail cards** and other concessionary fares are available; check with the local tourist office.

All international fares must be paid in hard currency, preferably DM. Domestic fares are very cheap but prices are rising due to a small monthly rise in the rate of inflation; this means that for the next couple of years at least, first-class travel is a viable and comfortable option.

## ITALY

**Capital:** Rome *(Roma)*.
**Language:** Italian is the only official language but there are strong dialectal differences. In the cities and tourist areas many people speak some English, but it's seldom spoken at all off the beaten track.
**Currency:** Lira (L.).

### Passports and Visas

An EU National Identity Card is sufficient. Visas are not needed by Commonwealth citizens or US nationals.

---

# Italy

Women are often ·hassled in Italy. The most effective response is a look of disgust. Pickpockets are numerous in major cities, so be wary. A particularly Italian crime is for bag-snatchers to ride on motor scooters – so walk with your bag on the side away from the road.

### Customs

Standard EU regulations apply (see p. 19).

### Useful Addresses in the UK

**Consulate,** *38 Eaton Place, London SW1X 8AN;* (Visa) *tel: (0171) 259 6322.*
**Italian State Tourist Board,** *1 Princes St, London W1R 8AY; tel: (0171) 408 1254.*
**Italian Rail Travel, Wasteels,** *adjacent to Platform 2, Victoria Station, London SW1V 1JT; tel: (0171) 834 7066.*

### Useful Addresses in the USA

**Embassy,** *1601 Fuller Street NW, Washington, DC 20009; tel: (202) 328 5500.*
**Italian Government Travel Office (ENIT),** *630 Fifth Ave (Suite 1565), Rockefeller Center, New York, NY 10111; tel: (212) 245 4822 or 2324.*
**Italian Rail Travel, CIT Tours Corporation,** *594 Broadway (Suite 307), New York, NY 10012; tel: (212) 697-2100.*

## STAYING IN ITALY

### Accommodation

All **hotels** are classified according to a 5-star system and inspectors set a maximum (seasonal) rate that must be displayed in each room. It does not necessarily include showers or breakfast, but extras must be listed separately, so complain (to the tourist office if all else fails) if your bill does not agree with the rates listed. You must, by law, obtain a receipt from all hotels.

Most establishments now term themselves hotel or *albergo,* but some are still called *pension* (one-, two-, or three-star) or *locande* (one-star). There are many *private rooms,* unofficial and otherwise. You can find the unofficial ones by looking for signs saying *affitta camere,* often in shop windows. It's worth trying to bargain, but you will usually pay about the same as for a one-star hotel. *Alberghi diurni,* near stations or in the centre, are essentially **day rooms:** you can have a wash without taking a room for the night.

There is no shortage of **youth hostels,** but relatively few belong to the **HI** and the standard varies considerably. It is often just as cheap and more convenient to stay at a one-star hotel.

**Camping** is popular and there are over 2,000 sites (all tourist offices have information about their area), but they are often fairly expensive and/or difficult to reach without a car. There are few places where you can rough camp without asking permission. **Touring Club Italiano (TCI)**, *Corso Italia 10, Milano; tel: (02) 85 261 or 852 6245,* publish an annual guide. Alternatively, you can get a list from **Federcampeggio,** *Casella Postale 23, 50041 Calenzano (Firenze); tel: (055) 88 215 918,* who can also make bookings. These two organisations produce a detailed directory of campsites, *Campeggi e Villagi Turistici in Italia,* available from bookshops in Italy (L.30,000).

**Agriturismo,** *Corso V Emanuele 101, 00186 Roma; tel: (06) 852 342,* has information about staying in rural cottages and farmhouses. **Club Alpino Italiano,** *Via Fonseca Pimental 7, 20122 Milano; tel: (02) 26 141 378,* can supply details of mountain refuge huts.

## Eating and Drinking

Italians enjoy eating and there's a wide variety of food available everywhere, with pasta as just one of many options. A full meal will consist of antipasta (cold meats etc.), pasta, a main course, and fruit or cheese. Italian ice-cream (**gelato**) is among the world's best.

*Trattorie* are simple establishments which are cheaper than *ristoranti.* Most *osterie* are trendy and expensive. *Alimentari* stores often prepare excellent and interesting sandwiches. *Rosticerrie* sell good hot take aways, while *tavole calde* are cheap sit-down places. Smaller establishments seldom have menus: just ask for the dish of the day if you want something reasonably priced. Menus are displayed by the entrance.

Look for cover charges *(coperto)* and service *(servizio),* both of which will be added to your bill. Prices on *Menu Turistico* include taxes and service charges.

Coffee comes in many forms, from espresso to liqueur. There are various types of Italian beer and many fine wines. Bars are good places to get a snack, such as a roll or toasted sandwich as well as to sample the local spirit, *grappa.*

## Opening Hours

**Banks:** Mon–Fri 0830–1300 and usually for an additional hour in the afternoon (exactly when varies).

**Shops:** (usually) Mon–Sat 0830/0900–1230/1300 and 1530/1600–1900/1930. In July/Aug many close Mon morning or Sat afternoon. A few stay open all day, every day.

**Museums:** national museums and archaeological sites usually open

Tues–Sun 0930– 1300/1400 and some re-open 1600–1900, but there is no real pattern and smaller ones please themselves. Although Mon is the usual closing day, it is not uncommon for this to be Sun or Tues or for them to stay open all week. Most sites and museums refuse entry within an hour or two of closing time.

## Postage

Usual post office hours are Mon–Sat 0800–1830, but there's no Saturday opening in many small places. The postal service is slow and it's worth paying for anything urgent to be sent express. Stamps *(francobolli)* are available from post offices, tobacconists *(tabacchi)* and some gift shops in resorts. Poste restante *(Fermo posta)* is possible at most post offices, but you have to pay a small amount when you collect.

## Public Holidays

All over the country: 1, 6 Jan; Easter Mon; 1 May; 15 Aug (virtually nothing opens); 1 Nov; 8, 25, 26 Dec.

Regional saints' days: 25 Apr in Venice; 24 June in Florence, Genoa and Turin; 29 June in Rome; 15 July in Palermo; 19 Sept in Naples; 4 Oct in Bologna; 6 Dec in Bari; 7 Dec in Milan.

## Public Transport

**Buses** are often crowded, but serve many areas inaccessible by rail and tend to be punctual. Services are drastically reduced at weekends and timetables do not always reflect this fact. Tickets for long-distance and local buses are usually obtained before boarding (some local ones are bought on board). Long-distance tickets are usually available from train stations or CIT offices, while local tickets are from machines, news-stands or tobacconists.

**Taxis** are metered, but can be expensive, with a substantial flat fare to start with and extra charges for baggage, journeys out of town and travel on holidays or late at night. You can hail taxis on the street, but steer clear of unofficial ones.

## Telephones

The phone system is in a constant state of over-haul, with frequently changing numbers ranging from two to eight digits. Directories may list two numbers – try both. If they're of different lengths, the longer is likely to be the new one .

Most public phones have instructions in English and take coins, phonecards *(carte telefoniche/scheda)*, or both. Cards are available from automatic machines near the phones, tobacconists and news-stands.

You can make international calls by using a phonecard, but in some small towns you must go to an office of the state phone company, **SIP**, or (occasionally) **ASST**. They often have branches in the stations; if not, you should find one near the main post office. You may also come across the old phones that take only tokens *(gettoni)*. If so, you should be able to get the tokens from whoever owns the phone, or find an automatic dispenser nearby. *Gettoni* are often accepted as small change, so don't be surprised if you are given some instead of small denomination coins. *Scatti* phones are quite common – these are metered and you pay the operator/owner when you have finished, but they are normally in places like bars and the 'operator' may well add a service charge, so check before you commit yourself. Hotels invariably charge over the odds. To call abroad from Italy: *tel: 00.* To call Italy: *39.* For English information and assistance for intercontinental calls: *170.* For English information on calling Europe and the Mediterranean area: *176*. For local operator assistance: *15*. For local directory enquiries: *12*. **Emergencies:** Fire: *115*; Police, Ambulance and other services: *113*. Loss or theft of Thomas Cook Traveller's Cheques: *1678 72050*.

## RAIL TRAVEL WITHIN ITALY

The national rail company is **Ferrovie dello Stato (FS)**.

The **Pendolino (ETR 450)** trains reach up to 155 mph These are luxury express services between major cities. Reservations are necessary and there is the usual basic supplement to use the trains plus another (usually £10–£20) before you board (which, in first class, covers such extras as hostess service, newspapers and food). Reservations are also obligatory for *IC* and *EC* services. *IR* trains are semi-fast expresses. The *espresso* are long-distance domestic trains, with both first and second class, which stop only at main stations. The *diretto* stop frequently and are very slow, while the *locale* stop almost everywhere. The rail network is extensive and the service reasonably punctual. Some long-distance trains won't carry passengers for short distances. Sleepers have single or double berths in first class, three berths (occasionally doubles) in second class; couchettes have four berths in first class and six in second class.

Most long-distance trains have refreshment facilities. Dining-cars offer a full service at meal times and snacks the rest of the day. Buffet cars are self-service, catering coaches or bar cars. Don't drink the tap water on trains. Queues at stations are often long and it's better to buy tickets and make reservations at travel agencies (look for the **FS** symbol).

### Fares and Passes

**Biglietto Chilometrico** can be used by up to 5 people, but the allowance is divided by the number of travellers. It is valid for 3000 km, in the course of which you can have 19 different stops over a period of 2 months. The **Italian Flexicard** allows travel for any 4 days out of 9, any 8 days out of 21 or any 12 days out of 30. It should be purchased in the UK as it is available in very few other places. The **Travel-at-will** tickets allow non-Italian residents to travel on any Italian train for 8, 15, 21 or 30 days. All three domestic passes give a choice of first- or second-class travel. If you board without a ticket there is an automatic fine of up to 20% of the fare. Buy tickets for short journeys (up to 100 km) from any tobacconist.

## LATVIA

**Capital:** Riga.

**Language:** Latvian is the national language, but is spoken by only about half the population. Russian is more widely understood, but unpopular with native Latvians. Of the three Baltic countries, Latvia has the smallest indigenous population and the language, almost wiped out by Russian (as happened in Estonia and Lithuania), is on the endangered list. Latvian is an Indo-European, non-Slavic and non-Germanic language and is similar only to Lithuanian. English and German are increasingly widely spoken.

**Currency:** The new Latvian currency, the Lat, was fully introduced in Oct 1993; 1 Lat = 100 Santims. Currency exchange outfits are numerous but changing travellers' cheques isn't so easy. Credit card recognition is growing, but is far from universal.

### Passports and Visas

Full passports are required by all travellers. Visas are required universally except by nationals of Estonia, Lithuania, Hungary, UK, the Czech Republic and Slovakia. They can be obtained at the airport and the sea passenger ports (but not train border crossings) by US and most European nationals but it is advisable to get them in advance. A Latvian visa is valid for the other Baltic countries. However, the situation is liable to change so check at the nearest embassy at least three weeks before travelling.

## Customs
The following allowances are for people aged 16 or over: 200 cigarettes or 200g tobacco products, and 1 litre alcohol.

## Tourist Information
**Latvian Tourist Club,** *Skarnu 22 , Riga LV 1053; tel: 221 731.*
**The Association of Latvian Travel Agents (ALTA)** *PO Box 59, Riga, LV 1012; tel: 213 627.*

## Useful Address in Australia
**Consulate;** *PO Box 23, Kew, Victoria 3101; tel: (03) 499 6920.*

## Useful Address in Canada
**Consulate,** *230 Clemow Ave, Ottawa, Ontario K15 2B6; tel: (613) 238 6868.*

## Useful Address in the UK
**Embassy,** *45 Nottingham Place, London W1M 3FE; tel: (0171) 312 0040.*

## Useful Address in the USA
**Embassy,** *4325 17th Street NW, Washington, DC 20011; tel: (202) 726 8213/4.*

### STAYING IN LATVIA

## Accommodation
The more sophisticated accommodation

tends to cluster around Riga and the seaside resort Jurmala, once colonised by Russian holiday-makers, including Boris Yeltsin. For **bed and breakfast, farmhouse** and **self-catering** accommodation (and fishing and mushroom picking) contact **Lauku celotajs (Country Traveller)** *Republikas Sq. 2 1119, Riga, LV 1981; tel: 327 629.* Most camping facilities are in the area of Jurmala.

## Eating and Drinking
New restaurants and cafés are opening up all the time. Latvian cuisine features fish more than meat, many dishes accompanied by a richly seasoned gravy. The brown granary bread and sweet pastries are excellent. There are lots of different berries in season and they are often used in delicious ice-cream sundaes. Don't drink the tap water. Tea and coffee are both widely available. Latvian beer *(alus)* is cheap, strong and quite good – try *Aldaris* and *Piebalga. Kvass* is a mildly alcoholic rye drink which is often sold on the streets in summer. You should book a table if you want to dine in a major hotel. Many restaurants close in the late afternoon (usually 1700–1900).

## Opening Hours
**Banks:** open mainly Mon–Fri 0900–1600. Some open Sat 0900–1230.
**Shops:** Mon–Fri 0900/1000–1800/1900 and Sat 0900/1000–1500/1700 (often closed 1400–1500). Many close on Mon, as well as Sun. Food shops usually open earlier and close later.
**Museums:** days of opening vary enormously and many open on only a few days every week, most commonly from Tues or Wed to Sun, 1100–1700.

## Postage
Post offices *(pasts)* are open Mon–Fri

61

0900–1800 and Sat 0900–1300. Post boxes are yellow.

### Public Holidays

1 Jan; Good Fri; Easter Mon (unofficial); 1 May; Mothers' Day (second Sun in May); 23, 24 June (Midsummer); 18 Nov; 25, 26, 31 Dec.

### Public Transport

Public transport is still extremely cheap for Westerners and **taxis** are usually an affordable option. Try to avoid bumped-up taxi fares by negotiating a price before you get in. **Buses** and **trams** are often spilling over with passengers and can be a hotbed for pickpockets.

The **long-distance bus network** is a popular alternative to the often slow domestic train service. Buses travel to most destinations on a relatively frequent basis.

### Telephones

The old blue public phones only take tokens sold at kiosks and post offices. Look out for the new digital card phones (red, green and white). Phone cards worth 2, 5 or 10 Lats can be bought at post offices.

To call abroad from Latvia: *tel: 8 194* (from digital phones dial *00*, then the country code). For urgent connections *tel: 8 15* and pay US$1.30 per minute. To call Latvia: *tel: 371*. To call Directory enquiries: *09*.

**Emergencies:** Police: *02;* Fire: *01;* Ambulance: *03*. Loss or theft of Thomas Cook Traveller's Cheques: *0044 1733 502995* (reverse charges)

### RAIL TRAVEL WITHIN LATVIA

The national rail company is **Latvian Railways (LVD)**. Domestic services can be unbearably slow although the network appears to be improving. Toilets on board are often without running water and are sometimes even closed. Timetables run horizontally rather than vertically.

There are two classes: 'soft' (first) and 'hard' (second), the same as in Estonia – see p. 45. Prices are relatively low, so it is worth booking soft class for extra comfort. Through sleepers to West/Central Europe have one or two berths in first class and three berths in second class. All include full bedding. All day trains are hard class. Reservations are necessary except for purely local journeys.

### Fares and Passes

For details of passes, see Estonia, p. 45. Kiosks line the streets and station forecourts. From here buy either individual or, more sensibly, several tickets which are validated on board the buses or trams; alternatively buy from the driver. The same tickets apply for both. For longer stays a monthly transport ticket can prove convenient and, if you have student ID, an even cheaper solution.

On the spot fines are charged for unauthorised travel.

### LITHUANIA

**Capital:** Vilnius.
**Language:** Lithuanian. Lithuanian and Latvian belong to the same language group and are Indo-European in origin. Russian is still common on signs around the traditional lines of communication, the railways and the telephones. However while Russian may be helpful, this reminder of the years of Soviet occupation would be unpopular and a phrasebook is indispensible. **Currency:** Lithuanian Litai; 1 Litas = 100 Cents. There are no restrictions on the import/export of foreign currencies.

# Lithuania

I t isn't worth bringing cigarettes with you, as they are not taxed in Lithuania, which makes them very cheap. Western brands are widely available.

Travellers' cheques can be cashed at some banks and at major tourist hotels: US$ or DM are best. Recognition for credit cards is limited, but growing.

## Passports and Visas

All visitors require full passports. Visas are required for those who are not nationals of the UK, the US, Australia, Iceland, Denmark, Poland, the Czech Republic or Slovakia. Visas are no longer issued at borders or airports. For most Westerners, Lithuanian visas are also valid in Latvia and Estonia, but check first.

## Customs

Allowances are constantly changing, so you will need to check just before travelling. The present allowance is: 200 cigarettes or 50 cigars or 250 g tobacco and 1 litre spirits, or 2 litres wine.

## Useful Address in Australia

Consulate, 26 Jalanga Crescent, Aranda, ACT 2614; tel: (062) 53 2062.

## Useful Address in Canada

Consulate, 235 Yorkland Blvd, Suite 502, Willowdale, Ontario M2J 4Y8; tel: (416) 494 8313.

## Useful Address in the UK

Embassy, 17 Essex Villas, London W8 7BP; tel: (0171) 938 2481 or 937 1588.

## Useful Address in the USA

Lithuanian Consulate-General and National Tourist Office, 420 Fifth Avenue, New York, NY 10018; tel: (212) 354 7840.

## STAYING IN LITHUANIA

## Accommodation

Builders are moving fast to meet the demand, but hotel accommodation – especially at the more comfortable end of the market – can still be very hard to come by. Booking in advance is strongly recommended. Prices are often listed in DM or US$, suggestive of the fact that they bear little relation to local costs. An alternative to hotels is to go to the agencies who arrange accommodation with local families. If looking away from the capital, book ahead or at least have some names, addresses and phone numbers. Check out any accommodation before you part with your money.

## Eating and Drinking

Local specialities include: cepelinai (the national dish – meat balls in potato), blynai (mini-pancakes) and kotletas (pork cutlets). Fish and dairy products are common ingredients of all dishes.Lithuanians eat their evening meal early and you should aim to order by 2000, even in places which are theoretically open much later. Service is leisurely so relax and make an evening of it. Leave no more than 1 Litas as a tip.

Do not drink tap water, opt for bottled water instead. Tea and coffee are widely available. Vodka (the best is Kvietine) and very sweet liqueurs are the main spirits. Lithuanian beer is becoming increasingly hard to find (the best is Utenos alus) as the drinking-places prefer to sell Western brands. The beer bars in Vilnius are worth a visit if you want to see 'the other side' of Lithuania. They are usually large

63

rooms where snacks and watered-down beer are sold to sometimes belligerent hard drinkers.

## Opening Hours

**Banks:** opening hours vary, but you can be reasonably sure banks will be open Mon–Fri 0930–1230. Some open earlier and/or close later; some also open on Sat.

**Shops:** (large shops) Mon–Fri 1000/1100–1900; many also open Sat until 1600. Some close for lunch (1400–1500) and also on Sun and Mon. The local shops have their own systems and there is no pattern to this at all.

**Food shops** have longer hours: Mon–Sat 0900-1400 and 1500–2000, Sun 0800–1400.

**Museums:** these open on different days and at different times. Most are closed Mon and open at least Wed and Fri (entrance to many is free on Wed). Most are open at least 1100–1700, but a few open only in the morning or the afternoon, so you must check locally.

## Postage

All towns have a post office with an international telephone service.

## Public Holidays

1 Jan; 16 Feb; 11 Mar; Easter Sun and Mon; the first Sun in May; 6 July; 1 Nov; 25, 26 Dec.

## Telephones

To call Lithuania: *tel: 370.* To call abroad from Lithuania: *tel: 8 10 + country code.* To call the international operator: *tel: 8 194* (English spoken). Directory enquiries: *09.* **Emergencies:** Police: *02;* Fire: *01;* Ambulance: *03.* Loss or theft of Thomas Cook Traveller's Cheques: *0044 1733 502995* (reverse charges)

### RAIL TRAVEL WITHIN LITHUANIA

The Lithuanian railway company is **LG**. There is a reasonable rail network linking Vilnius with the other Lithuanian towns. Domestic services are both very slow and very cheap. The different classes of rail travel and details of fares and passes are the same as in Estonia, see p. 45.

## POLAND

**Capital**: Warsaw *(Warszawa).*

**Language**: Polish; many older Poles speak German or French, while younger Poles (particularly students) are more likely to speak English in tourist areas. Russian is widely understood, but not popular.

**Currency**: Złoty (Zł.). You will be asked to fill in a currency declaration form on arrival. Any Polish money you have left can be re-converted when you leave. The most useful foreign currencies are British pounds, American dollars or German marks. You are unlikely to be able to change travellers' cheques or Eurocheques other than at large banks or certain **Kantor** exchange offices. Kantor sometimes give better rates than banks and their opening hours are longer. A branch of **Thomas Cook** will also be able to change your travellers' cheques, free of charge in the case of Thomas Cook travellers' cheques, at: *Orbis Travel, ul. Marszalkowska 142, Warsaw.*

Credit cards are widely accepted in large establishments and their use is increasing elsewhere, but they are still far from universal.

## Passports and Visas

All visitors require full passports. British passport holders do not require visas (but your passport must be valid for at least six months after your planned departure date from Poland), nor do nationals of the

USA or the Republic of Ireland. Nationals of Australia, Canada, New Zealand and South Africa do need visas. Others should check.

## Customs

The following allowances are for people aged 17 or over: 250 cigarettes or 50 cigars or 250g tobacco, 1 litre wine, and 1 litre any other alcoholic beverage.

## Tourist Information

**IT** tourist information centres operate within most major towns and cities, offering national as well as local information, and can usually help with accommodation. In the absence of an IT office, there will often be an **Orbis** office which can provide tourist information, arrange excursions and help with accommodation.

## Useful Address in Australia

**Embassy,** *7 Turrana St, Yarralumla ACT, 2600 Canberra; tel: (06) 273 12 08/11.*

## Useful Address in Canada

**Embassy,** *443 Daly Ave., Ontario K1N 6H3, Ottawa 2; tel: (613) 789 0468.*

## Useful Address in the Rep. of Ireland

**Embassy,** *5 Ailesbury Rd, Dublin 4; tel: (1) 283 08 55.*

## Useful Address in New Zealand

**Commercial Counselor,** *17 Upland Road, Kelburn, Wellington; tel: (4) 471 24 56.*

## Useful Address in South Africa

**Embassy,** *14 Amos St, Colbyn, Pretoria 0083; tel: (12) 43 26 31.*

## Useful Addresses in the UK

**Embassy,** *47 Portland Place, London*

*W1N 3AG; tel: (0171) 580 4324.* **Polish National Tourist Office (Orbis),** *Remo House, 310-312 Regent Street, W1R 5AJ; tel: (0171) 580 8811.*
**Polish State Railways** *c/o* Orbis; *tel: (0171) 580 8811.*

## Useful Addresses in the USA

**Embassy,** *2640 16th Street NW, Washington, DC 20009; tel: (202) 234 3800.* **Polish National Tourist Office (Orbis),** *275 Madison Avenue, Suite 1711, New York, NY 10016; tel: (212) 338 9412.*

### STAYING IN POLAND

## Accommodation

Orbis runs a chain of international and tourist standard **hotels** across the country, and some less expensive **motels**. Otherwise, your best bet will probably be a **pension** or **private room**.

In popular holiday areas, you may be able to hire a **holiday cottage** for a longer stay. In high summer **youth hostels** and **university rooms** are also available. With a rapidly developing economy, a wide range of accommodation is becoming easier to find outside the major centres, and you can usually rely on tourist offices to help. But equally, find a good, up-to-date hotel listing and be prepared to make your own arrangements.

## Eating and Drinking

Simple meals and snacks can easily be obtained at cafés and fast food outlets, while *zajazdy*, reasonably priced roadside inns and cafés, serve typical Polish food and pastries. Many restaurants close around 2100 but those in hotels stay open later, often serving until around 2300. Classic national dishes include potato

65

pancakes, stuffed cabbage leaves, cabbage and sausage stew, *pierogi* (a large-scale ravioli), baked cheesecake and doughnuts.

There's a heavy emphasis on soups, which can be sweet as well as savoury. Typical ingredients include fish, pork, game and soured cream. A vast range of Polish mineral waters are drunk in preference to tap water, which is best avoided.

Tea is served black and in glasses, usually with lemon, but you can specify that you would like tea with milk. Virtually all wine is imported and expensive, while Polish beer, generally lager, has a distinctive fresh taste. The vast range of clear and flavoured vodka is excellent and inexpensive.

## Opening Hours
**Banks:** Mon–Fri 0800–1500/1800.
**Shops**: Mon–Fri 0800/1100–1900, Sat 0900–1300.
**Food shops:** Mon–Fri 0600–1900, Sat 0600–1300.
**Museums:** these vary greatly, but are usually open Tues–Sun 1000–1600. They seldom open on public holidays and are often closed the following day as well.

## Postage
Post offices *(Poczta)* open Mon–Sat 0700/0800–1800/2000 (main offices). Note that the word *Przerwa* on the glass windows means break and the booth is closed between the times shown. In each city, the post offices are numbered (the main office is always 1) and the number should be included in the post restante address. Post boxes are green (local mail), blue (air-mail), or red (long-distance mail).

## Public Holidays
1 Jan; Easter Sun–Mon; 1, 3 May; Corpus Christi; 15 Aug; 1, 11 Nov; 24, 25, 26 Dec.

## Public Transport
**PKS buses** are cheap and more practical than trains for short trips or off-beat destinations. Tickets include seat reservations (the seat number is on the back) and can be purchased in advance from the bus station. In rural areas, bus drivers will often halt away from official stops if you wave them down.

## Telephones
Until recently public telephones were operated exclusively by telephone tokens on sale at post offices and Ruch kiosks. Newer telephones operate on telephone cards and if you can find one, these are much more efficient.

To call Poland: *tel: 48*. To call abroad from Poland: *tel: 901*. To call an English speaking operator: *tel: 903*. **Emergencies:** Police: *997*; Fire: *998*; Ambulance: *999*. Loss or theft of Thomas Cook Traveller's Cheques: *0044 1733 502995* (reverse charges)

The Polish national rail service is operated by **Polskie Koleje Panstwowe (PKP),** with some minor lines run by **Lubusz Koleje Regionalna (LKR).** The rail network is extensive, cheap and punctual, but make sure you know what type of train you're taking, as ordinary services can be very slow. Express trains link all major cities, though travelling in Eastern Poland is far less streamlined and usually involves circuitous routes.

At stations, departures *(odjazdy)* are on yellow paper and arrivals *(przyjazdy)* on white. The express trains *(ekspres – prefixed 'EX')* and direct trains *(pospieszny)* that are almost as fast are printed in red. The black *osobowy* trains are the slowest.

Trains usually have first- and second-class accommodation and Westerners generally feel first class is worth the extra cost (about 50% more, but still cheap by Western standards).

Overnight trains usually have first- and second-class sleepers, as well as second-class couchettes.

Reservations are needed on all express and some direct services. Most long-distance trains have buffet services and the WARS (buffet) carriages can be good for a snack and a drink.

## Stations
Virtually all major stations provide left-luggage and refreshment facilities. Don't expect ticket clerks to speak English.

## Fares and Passes
There is a **Polrail Pass,** which allows an unlimited number of rail trips on some routes for 8, 15 or 21 days, but normal fares are very cheap and it's usually more economical to buy ordinary single and return tickets.

## ROMANIA

**Capital:** Bucharest *(Bucures, ti).*
**Language:** Romanian. It is a Latin-based language with a strong affinity to French, the country's second language. German is widely spoken, especially in Transylvania where Hungarian is spoken also. English is spoken in most major cities.
**Currency:** Lei. The import/export of currency is forbidden, it is advisable to bring dollars or DM into the country as currency rather than travellers cheques. Only change your currency at official exchange offices or banks.

Do not change money on the black market, although the rate is higher, so is the chance of having it instantly stolen.

### *Romania*

Gypsies are a problem in Romania and (with some justification) are blamed for most thefts, so be especially wary when they are around.

Many things which are readily available in the West are hard (if not impossible) to get in Romania and you should take your own supply of routine medication and toiletries. Don't expect to find paper, soap and towels in public facilities.

Street names are being widely changed in many cities. Be prepared for discrepancies between signs and maps.

Protection against hepatitis A is to be recommended.

The number of outlets accepting credit cards is increasing in the larger cities.

## Passports and Visas
All visitors require full passports and visas, obtainable from the Romanian Embassy or the airport in Bucharest, at a slightly higher charge.

## Customs
The allowances for adults are: 200 cigarettes or 300g tobacco. 2 litres spirits and 4 litres wine or beer.

## Useful Addresses in the UK
**Embassy:** *Arundel House, 4 Palace Green, London W8 4QD; tel: (0171) 937 9667.*
**Romanian National Tourist Office:** *83a Marylebone High Street. London W! 3DE; tel: (0171) 224 3629*

## Useful Addresses in the USA
**Embassy :** *1607 23rd Street NW Washington DC 20008-2809; tel: (202) 232 4747.*
**Romanian National Tourist Board:**

*347 Madison Ave, Suite 210 New York NY 10177; tel: (212) 697 6971.*

## STAYING IN ROMANIA

### Accommodation

**Hotels** vary a great deal in quality, even within the same category and prices tend to be high. Rooms may be booked in advance for both hotels and **private apartments** at the local tourist offices but beware as commission charges are usually quite steep. At most Romanian stations, touts may be found hawking their rooms. These may be quite cheap but often very nasty and far out in the suburbs, so check them out before you agree to anything.

It is advisable to book well in advance in the mountains and at the **Black Sea** coastal resorts especially in the summer as hotels become very full with Romanian holiday makers. Avoid **campsites** if at all possible as they can be really quite grim.

### Eating and Drinking

There are many restaurants in the main cities, offering a variey of foods. Meat is usually chicken, pork or beef. Up in the mountains there is a possibility that you may be offered bear, but it is very expensive. Unsmoked frankfurters *(Pariser)* equal the ones in the West, and *Creme Wurst,* is a light liver sausage. Vegetables are limited and very expensive, as is fresh fruit, although it can be easy to buy at markets.

Fish, especially the fresh Danube carp *(krap)* and cakes *(prejitura)* are delicious.

Spirits and wine are very cheap, a bottle of local Vodka can cost as little as £0.80. Try the *tuica* (pronounced 'tswica') or *palinka* – two local plum brandies. Drink is easily obtainable with a vast selection, including the usual western fizzy drinks and their own fruit drinks, such as Kiwi crush. Tap water is perfectly safe to drink but highly chlorinated.

Coffee is usually *Turcesca* or *Nes*. Turcesca is ground coffee, Turkish style, and usually sweetened, unless you specify *fahar zacher* (no sugar). Nes is more like a sweetened chicory coffee. Milk is not easily obtainable, and seldom offered.

### Opening Hours

**Shops:** there is no rule of thumb; many markets open at the weekend as well as during the week, though shops don't often open Sun. Stalls selling cakes and soft drinks, and a host of other items are available almost all day. In Bucharest there are many 24 hr outlets. Larger shops usually open 0830/0900–1300 and again at 1500–1800/2000. Small food shops can open at 0600 and don't close till late. **Banks:** hours here are fairly strict, Mon-Fri 0900–1200/1300. There are many to choose from.

**Museums:** times vary, so try to check first. Many don't open Mon, but open Sun for family visits.

### Postage

Post is slow and letter boxes are rare to find especially in the country, they are yellow and marked *Posta*. Few postcards can be found to purchase.

### Public Transport

In Bucharest there is the metro, and there are bus services in all towns. Trains are the best option for long-distance travel, and there are passenger ferries along the Danube. Local transport is cheap and convenient, though often crowded. Taxis can be a lottery – always make sure that the driver starts the meter when you begin your journey.

## Telephones

Telephone cards costing about 10/12000 Lei are readily available from many city outlets. Local calls are fairly easy to make but it is almost impossible to call out of the country unless you happen to find someone (or a hotel) who has a foreign line. There are offices where you can send international faxes in major cities. To call Romania, *tel: 40.* To call from Romania, *tel: 00.* **Emergencies:** Police: *955;* Fire: *981;* Ambulance: *961.* Loss or theft of Thomas Cook Traveller's Cheques: *0044 1733 502995* (reverse charges)

### RAIL TRAVEL WITHIN ROMANIA

The rail system in Romania is mainly electrified and links all major cities. The stations are often without raised platforms which makes boarding and alighting difficult for the elderly and the handicapped. The Rail Company is **Caîle Ferate Romane (CFR)** and the signs to look out for are **CFR** or **SNCFR**. Tickets may be bought in advance from agencies, or from the station, one hour before departure. It is essential to book in advance.

rAvoid the *Persoane*, as they are very slow. *Accelerat* and *Rapide* are the express trains and the *IC* are the fastest, but most expensive. However, costs for the western traveller for first-class travel on the *IC* are reasonable. Food is only available on inter-city trains and for long distance travel.

On long distance journeys, sleepers (*Wagons de dormit*) or couchettes *(cos, eta)* are advisable. The toilets are not particularly savoury on most trains, so avoid using them if at all possible. Students' international travel tickets purchased from Campus Travel (p. 26) should be accepted although there is no official rul-ing as yet according the Director of Railways.

## Fares and Passes

Tickets may be purchased for individual fares at about 400 Lei a trip. Day passes cost in the region of 1000 Lei. Both weekly and monthly passes are available and are good value because they can be used as often as wished. The monthly ticket costs about 18000 Lei, but prices vary from town to town and are in the process of rising, so ask whePFn you get there. Passes may be usually be purchased from tobacconist shops.

### SLOVAKIA

**Capital:** Bratislava.
**Language:** Slovak is a Slavic tongue closely related to Czech. Some Russian and German, and a little English, are also understood. Shops where the staff are linguists tend to have signs saying so.
**Currency:** Slovak Korunas or Crowns (SK.); 1 Koruna = 100 Hellers. Import and export of Crowns is not allowed, but there are no restrictions on foreign currencies. Credit cards are becoming more widely accepted in Bratislava and some tourist areas.

## Passports and Visas

Full passports are required. Visas are not needed by nationals of the EU or the USA. Nationals of Canada, Australia and New Zealand need visas and passports valid for at least six months. Others should check.

## Customs

The following allowances apply to people who are aged 18 or over. They are: 200 cigarettes, or 50 cigars, or equivalent in tobacco, 1 litre spirits, and 2 litres wine.

## Tourist Information

**Bratislava Information Service (BIS)**, *tel: 333715* or *334370*, has information about the city and also Slovakia in general. Staff can speak English and can arrange accommodation. **Satur** can help with accommodation as well as booking tours and train journeys.

## Useful Addresses in the UK

**Embassy,** *25 Kensington Palace Gardens, London W8 4QY; tel: (0171) 243 0803.* **Satur (Slovak Tourist Office),** *49 Southwark Street, London SE1 1RU; tel: (0171) 378 6009.*

## Useful Addresses in the USA

**Embassy,** *Suite 380,2201 Wisconsin Ave, Washington DC 20007; tel: (202) 965 5160.* **Slovakia Travel Service,** *Suite 3601, 10 East 40th Street, New York 10016; tel: (212) 213 3865.*

## STAYING IN SLOVAKIA

### Accommodation

You should have a choice of one- to five-star **hotels, private rooms** and **pensions**, old-style tourist hotels, **hostels** and **inns** with a few spartan rooms. However, quality (once outside the three- five-star range), although it has improved greatly in recent years, can leave a lot to be desired. It may make more sense to look at private rooms than cheap hotels. Some places insist on payment in hard currency.

Private rooms, **youth hostel** beds and hotel rooms can be booked through a variety of agencies. Local tourist information offices can also help with the search for accommodation. Local individuals also offer rooms to arriving travellers: if the price is indicated in advance and the rooms seem acceptable on viewing, this can be the ideal solution for budget travellers.

### Eating and Drinking

Lunch is around 1130–1400/1500 and dinner 1800–2130/2200. The cuisine tends to be rich and meat-based, but vegetarian restaurants can also be found.

*Brynzopé haluš*, a dumpling with grated cheese, is typical of Slovak cuisine. Slovak food is very similar to Hungarian; Schnitzel and dumplings (*knedliky*) are on virtually every menu, so is *gulaš*, a spicy meat dish with wine. Eating and drinking is cheap, especially in a self-service *bufet* (where you stand while eating). *Kavárny* and *cukrárny* serve coffee (often Turkish-style) and delightful pastries.

Beer halls (*pivnice*) and wine bars (*vináma*) are good places to eat. Slovak beer is almost as good as Czech, and Slovak wine is excellent.

### Opening Hours

**Banks:** Mon–Fri 0800–1700.
**Shops:** Mon–Fri 0900–1800, Sat 0900–1200. Food shops usually open earlier and often open on Sun.
**Museums:** (usually) Tues–Sun 1000–1700. Most castles close on national holidays and from Nov to Mar.

### Postage

There is a full postal service (including post restante) which, although cheap, is slow and erratic. Usual post office opening hours are 0800–1900. Stamps are also available from newsagents and tobacconists.

### Public Holidays

1, 6 Jan; Good Fri; Easter Mon; 1 May; 5 July; 29 Aug; 1, 15 Sep; 1 Nov; 24–26 Dec.

## Public Transport
The rail network is good, but there is also a comprehensive long-distance bus network. Bus stations are fairly well-organised.

Officially, you should book in advance, but you can buy tickets from the driver, although he will give priority to those with reservations.

## Telephones
To call Slovakia: *tel: 42*. To call abroad from Slovakia: *tel: 00*. Information: *120* (national); *0149* (international). **Emergencies:** Police: *158;* Fire: *150;* Ambulance: *155*. Loss or theft of Thomas Cook Traveller's Cheques: *0044 1733 502995* (reverse charges)

### RAIL TRAVEL WITHIN SLOVAKIA
The national rail company is **Zeleznice Slovenskej Republiky** (**ZSR**). The rail network is cheap and extensive, but the trains are often crowded. The fastest trains are *expresný*, but *rychlík* cost as much as the express. The few *spešný* (semi-fast) trains cost less. *Osobný* (slow) should be avoided.

All trains offer both first- and second-class travel. Most long-distance trains have dining cars and overnight services between cities have sleeping-cars. Sleepers/couchettes are of standard European type.

Seat reservations are recommended for travel by express train, bookings can be made at the station counters marked 'R'.

To reserve sleepers, you must go to an office of the official tourist board. It is now possible to make couchette reservations at the main Bratislava station.

## Fares and Passes
A **Czech-Slovak Flexipass** covers 5 days unlimited travel within a 15-day period throughout both the Republics. There is an **Explorer Pass** for 7 consecutive days (or multiples thereof) which covers first- or second-class rail travel. It is available to anyone under 26 and to any holder of an ISIC card, but must be purchased (from Campus Travel – see p. 26) before you go.

### SLOVENIA
**Capital:** Ljubljana.
**Language:** Slovene. Although a Slavic language, it is written with Roman characters. English and German are often spoken by those involved with tourism, and Italian is spoken along the coast (the part of Istria in Slovenia was once part of Italy).
**Currency:** Tolar (1 tolar, 2 tolarja, 3 tolarji, and so on).

## Passports and Visas
Visitors from the European Union, Scandinavian countries, Australia, Canada Israel, Japan , New Zealand or the USA do not require a visa. All other nationals should consult the Slovenian Consul or Embassy before departure about visa requirements.

## Customs
Goods purchased in Slovenia exceeding 9000 tolars are eligible for tax refunds. Most border crossings have duty free shops.

## Tourist Information
Apart from a good Tourist Information Centre in Ljubljana, the country's travel agencies have a reputation for being very helpful to independent travellers. Look for signs that read 'Turist Biro'. The Slovenian travel agency Kompas has offices abroad (see below)

71

## Useful Address in Australia

Kompas, *Suite 401, 115 Pitt St, Sydney, NSW 2000; tel: (02) 233 4197.*

## Useful Address in Canada

**Kompas**, *Suite 535, 4060 Ste-Catherine W, Montreal, PQ H3Z 2Z3; tel: (0514) 938 4041.*

## Useful Addresses in the UK

**Embassy**, *Suite 1, Cavendish Court, 11–15 Wigmore Street, London W1H 9LA; tel: 0171 495 7775.*
**Slovenian Tourist Board**, *2 Canfield Place, London NW6 3BT; tel: (0171) 372 3767.*

## Useful Address in the USA

**Embassy**, *1525 New Hampshire Ave NW, Washington, DC, 20036; tel: (202) 667 5363.*
**Kompas**, *2826 E Commercial Blvd, Fort Lauderdale, FL 33308; tel: (0305) 771 9200.*
**Kompas**, *10662 El Adelante Ave, Fountain Valley, CA 92708; tel: (0714) 378 0510.*
**Slovenian Tourist Office**, *122 East 42nd Street, Suite 3006, New York, NY 10168 0072; tel: (212) 682 58 96.*

## Accommodation

**Hotels** are divided into four categories: L (deluxe), A (first class), B (superior) and C (for those on lower budgets – though bedrooms have hot and cold water, an en suite bathroom is unusual in this category). However, the rating system gives any hotel whose rooms have en suite facilities a higher rank than one of better quality that doesn't. A hotel price list published each year is available from Slovene tourist agencies. Outside Ljubljana, prices are highest in July and August, with smaller seasonal increases in June and September. Accommodation is only in short supply only, as a rule, in July and August.

The Protocol Service, *Brdo Castle, Predoslje; tel: (064) 221 133*, runs a variety of luxurious castle hotels that are well worth investigating.

Tourist offices also have lists of **private rooms** for rent. These are categorised by I and II grades, the former having private shower and toilet, the latter hot and cold water in the room but shared bathroom and toilet. A 30 per cent surcharge is sometimes made for stays of less than two or three nights, especially on the coast.

Over 120 working farms also provide accommodation, sometimes offering horse riding or other sports; information and bookings from *Zadruzna Turisticna Agencija VAS, Miklosiceva 4, 61000 Ljubljana; tel: (386 61) 12 56 172.*

It is possible to stay in **colleges and hostels**. Contact the Holiday Association of Slovenia (PZS), *Parmova ulica 33, Ljubljana; tel: (061) 312 156.* It is not necessary to have a Hostelling International card, although of you do you may well qualify for discounts.

There are numerous, mostly small but well-equipped, **campgrounds**, many of which have related sports facilities and children's playground. It is illegal to camp rough.

## Eating and Drinking

Places to eat go by many different names in Slovenia. A restaurant where you are served by a waiter is a *restavracija*, while a *gostilna* is an inn which generally serves, in a rustic setting, national dishes. Both sometimes have a set menu (*dnevno kosilo*) at lunch – this is usually the most inexpensive option. There are also self-service places (*samopostrezna restavracija*) where you can eat standing up. People eat fast food in an *okrepcevalnica*, and they snack in a *bife* or a *krcma*.

Slovenia's position at a crossroads of Pannonian, Alpine and Mediterranean cultures is reflected in its cuisine: you may encounter sausages and sauerkraut, strudel or the Balkan *burek* pie of layered meat and cheese.

Soup is regarded as an almost indispensable part of lunch. Elaborate breads stuffed with sweet fillings, meat or vegetables are often produced for holidays and festivals.

The north-eastern part of Slovenia is renowned for its white wines, which have been produced since the occupation of the region by the Celts, before the arrival of the Romans who improved viticulture. Some are produced using the champagne method.

On the coast and in the karst region, red wine grapes are mostly grown. Cellars in Dobrova, Vipava, Sezena and Koper may be visited. Wines labelled 'uvoz' (imported) should be avoided, but metal and plastic stoppers are accepted substitutes for cork.

## Opening Hours

**Banks** are normally open from 0800–1800 on weekdays, 0800–1200 on Saturdays.

**Shops** are normally open on weekdays from 0730–1900 without closing for lunch, from 0730–1300 on Sat. Only on-duty pharmacies and the occasional private shop are likely to be open on Sun.

Most stores accept the principal credit cards.

## Postage

Post offices are normally open from 0800–1800 on weekdays, 0800–1200 on Saturdays. A poste restante service is available at central post offices. Larger offices also offer fax services, money exchange (cash and travellers' cheques)

## Public Holidays

1 and 2 Jan; 8 Feb; Easter Sunday and Monday; 27 Apr; 1 and 2 May; 25 Jun; 15 Aug; 31 Oct; 1 Nov; 25 and 26 Dec.

## Public Transport

Some tourist destinations can be reached directly only by bus, such as Bohinj and Istria. Services are frequent and inexpensive. You can usually buy your ticket as you board a bus, whether local or long-distance. However, the busiest time is Friday afternoon when buses leaving Ljubljana are usually full, so a reservation is advisable.

Regrettably Ljubljana dispensed with its environmentally friendly trams decades ago, and now relies on diesel buses. They have a fare box beside the driver, or you can buy bus tokens at news-stands. A day pass can be bought at two red kiosks marked 'LPP' at Slovenska cesta 55.

Taxis are available in most towns. City taxis have meters; in smaller towns agree a price in advance. Tipping is optional – simply round up the fare.

## Telephones

The best place to make a telephone call, if you are not staying in a hotel, is the post office or telephone centre (Ljubljana's, at *Prazakova ulrica 3*, is open 24 hours a day).

Public telephones operate on tokens or magnetic cards. The cards can be bought only at post offices, but the tokens are also be purchased at newsagents. However, they are useable only in the area of purchase, rather than nationally,

**73**

so do not buy more than you need locally.

**Emergencies:** Police: *92*; Fire: *93*; Ambulance/rescue: *94*. Loss or theft of Thomas Cook Traveller's Cheques: *0044 1733 502995* (reverse charges)

To make an outgoing international call; *tel 00*. To call Slovenia; *tel 386*. For international operator, *tel 901*; for international directory, *tel 989*; for directory assistance for Slovenia, *tel 988*.

## RAIL TRAVEL WITHIN SLOVENIA

The Slovenian Railways (Slovenske zeleznice – SZ) network comprises 1198 km of routes, 496 of them electrified. Most of the principal tourist destinations can be reached by comfortable intercity trains at very reasonable fares. Amongst the scenic routes are Ljubljana–Zagreb, Ljubljana–Pivka (covered by Ljubljana–Venice trains) and Jesenice–Nova Gorica.

*Prihodi* means arrivals, *odhodi* departures. Tickets should be bought before travel, but can be purchased from train conductors at a small supplement. Steam trains are operated over various routes during the summer.

For information contact: **Slovenija Turist**, *Slovenska 58, 61000 Ljubljana; tel: (386 61) 131 50 55.*

## TURKEY

**Capital:** Ankara.

**Language:** Turkish; French, English and German are also spoken to some extent in Istanbul and coast resorts.

**Currency:** Turkish Lira (TL.). On departure you can reconvert Lira into hard currencies only up to the value of US$100, so don't change more than necessary and keep exchange receipts.

## Passports and Visas

All travellers require a passport. Nationals

---

## Turkey

Protection against hepatitis A, polio and typhoid is recommended and also against malaria if you plan to visit Asian Turkey. Be wary of drinking tap water and milk.

Drug laws are so stringent that you can get into trouble for just being in the company of a user – and Turkish jails are not pleasant – so steer well clear.

Turkey is an Islamic country (albeit liberal) and you must be careful not to offend. Use your right hand (or both hands) to pass and receive things – never the left hand alone.

Women should always dress modestly take take special care when visiting mosques. Also remember to remove your shoes.

Never forget mosques are places of worship and it is priviledge for non-muslims to enter at all; few Islamic states permit such visits.

Bargaining is the norm, and to be enjoyed. You are likely to be offered tea during the course of the haggling – this is a courtesy and payment is not expected, not does accepting it put you under obligaiton to buy.

---

of Ireland, Italy, the UK, USA, Austria, Spain, Portugal and Israel must buy visas on arrival. They are not needed by nationals of the other EU countries, Australia, Canada or New Zealand. Others should check.

## Customs

Turkey joined the European Customs Union in Jan 1996, so regulations are likely to change; check with your Turkish Tourist Office.

In addition to the usual prohibitions,

there are restrictions on goods like photographic film, so get full details from the Turkish tourist office before you go.

If buying expensive or antique carpets, be prepared to pay duty for them on your return. Customs officials are seldom fooled by receipts that undervalue carpets, so don't waste your time getting them.

**Tourist Information**
Most coastal resorts and some larger towns have small municipal tourist offices, which offer a limited range of sightseeing information but little else. Limited English is usually spoken.

**Useful Addresses in the UK**
**Consulate-General**, *Rutland Lodge, Rutland Gardens, London SW7 1BW; tel: (0171) 589 0360.*
**Turkish Tourist Office**, *170/173 Piccadilly (1st Flr), London W1V 9DD; tel: (0171) 734 8681/2.*

**Useful Addresses in the USA**
**Embassy**, *1606 23rd St NW, Washington, DC 20008; tel: (202) 387 3200.*
**Turkish Tourist Office**, *821 UN Plaza, New York, NY 10017; tel: (212) 687 2194/6.*

**STAYING IN TURKEY**

**Accommodation**
There are plenty of **hotels** in main towns and cities and at coastal resort areas, though much of Turkey's Aegean coast and most of the Black Sea coast remains quite untouched by tourism.

Prices and types range from the luxurious and ultra-expensive to dirt-cheap and cockroach-ridden, although the quality doesn't always match the price.

The cheapest city hotels are often shabby and unappealing, with a clientele to match, but above rock bottom they are usually clean and comfortable. Always check out the room and the plumbing before you agree to take it.

In high summer, look for somewhere with air-conditioning or a fan, and always take your own plug (they are rarely provided). Eager touts often hang around bus and train stations.

**Eating and Drinking**
Both eating and drinking are very cheap in Turkey, if you stick to local food – and there's really no reason not to, as the Turkish cuisine is excellent.

Food tends to be fairly plain and based on whatever vegetables and fruit are in season, with fresh seafood, lamb and chicken (other meats are found, but less often). *Pide,* a pizza-like, meal-sized snack of unleavened bread topped with a choice of minced lamb, cheese, eggs, vegetables and herbs, is perfect if you're on a budget. Puddings are usually very sweet, many featuring semolina, honey and nuts.

Coffee (black and very strong) is an expensive rarity but tea (black, sweet, often vanilla-flavoured and very cheap) is easily available. You will have to specify if you want your drink unsweetened. You may be given milk with your tea at breakfast, but seldom at any other time. There is a wide choice of local wines, some of them very good. *Raki* (anisseed-flavoured spirit drunk with water) is popular.

The local beers are palatable. Most spirits are imported. Be wary of drinking tap water and milk.

In cities, eating-places are open most of the day. In smaller places the normal eating hours are 1200–1500 and

75

1900–2200. In most restaurants there is a counter where you can see what's on offer, and it's customary to have a good look.

If you don't speak Turkish, just point at whatever appeals to you.

## Opening Hours

**Banks**: Mon–Fri 0830–1200 and 1330–1700.

**Shops**: Mon–Sat 0930–1300 and 1400–1900. Shops in tourist areas often open until 2100 and also on Sun. The covered bazaar in Istanbul is open Mon–Sat 0800–1900.

**Museums**: (generally) Tues–Sun 0900/0930–1630/1700. Palaces keep much the same hours, but tend to close Tues or Thur rather than Mon.

## Postage

Post offices have yellow **PTT** signs. The main offices in Istanbul and Ankara open 24 hrs daily, smaller offices across the country open Mon–Fri 0830–1230 and 1330–1730.

## Public Holidays

1 Jan; 23 Apr; 19 May; 30 Aug; 29 Oct. There are also two three-day Muslim festivals (at the end of Ramadan and Kurban Bayrami), but the dates for these depend on the lunar calendar and vary considerably from year to year.

## Public Transport

The rail network covers only the major cities and goes nowhere near many of the most popular tourist areas. Outside the major cities, look to the **buses,** of which there are many, with services to absolutely everywhere. There are also luxury **long-distance coaches,** which come with lace at the windows and videos upfront.

Reserve in advance to choose a good seat (well worth it, given the quality of some of the roads and driving).

For local transport, the best option is to use the *dolmus* (shared minibuses or taxis) which run on standard routes and leave as soon as they have a full load. *Dolmus* means 'stuffed' and the Turkish notion of a full load means people hanging out of the window and sitting on your lap.

## Telephones

To call Turkey: *tel: 90.* To call abroad: *tel: 99.* Operator: 155, directory enquiries: 153.

**Emergencies**: Police: *055;* Fire: *000;* Medical and general emergencies: *077.* Loss or theft of Thomas Cook Traveller's Cheques: *00 800 44 914895* (toll-free).

## RAIL TRAVEL WITHIN TURKEY

The national rail company is **Turkiye Cumhuryeti Devlet Demiryollan (*TCDD*)**. Rail services in Turkey are slow and the system is limited to a handful of routes linking the major cities.

The fastest express trains are the *mototren, ekspres* and *mavi tren.* Overnight services usually have sleeping-cars and couchettes, both of which should be booked in advance. You should reserve seats on the better trains. The food in dining-cars is both good and cheap.

## Stations

Services at railway stations are basic. English is not usually spoken, though staff – like most people in Turkey – often go out of their way to try to help.

## Fares and Passes

European rail passes (see p. 27) are valid in European Turkey (i.e. between Edirne and Istanbul).

# THOMAS COOK TRAVELLERS

This series of 192-page compact (192mm x 130mm) guides, each fully illustrated in colour with completely new research and mapping, has been created for the holidaymaker of the 1990s by Thomas Cook Publishing and leading guidebook publishers AA Publishing.

## Features include

* Facts at your fingertips
* Background information on history, politics and culture
* Descriptions of major sights and lesser-known places
* A 'get-away-from-it-all' section
* A shopping and entertainment guide
* An A–Z help list packed with practical information
* Tips on 'finding your feet'
* Up to 10 city walks or excursions with full-colour maps

**Titles in the series include: Athens, Berlin, Budapest, Istanbul, Moscow & St Petersburg, Prague, Venice and Vienna**

Available in the UK from Thomas Cook shops and book shops, UK price £7.99, or by mail order from Thomas Cook Publishing, Dept (TPO/EER), P.O. Box 227, Peterborough PE3 8BQ, UK. Tel: (01733) 268943. These guides are published in the USA as Passport's Illustrated Guides from Thomas Cook, and are available from bookstores.

# SAMPLE ITINERARIES

Here are eight themed tours using many of the recommended routes, with a few digressions and short cuts added. You can adapt them to your own interests and timescale or just use the general ideas to plan your own itinerary.

The routes start in a variety of principal cities. Reaching them by air is straightforward, but holders of European-wide passes may prefer the pleasure of train travel.

Naturally you can choose to 'start' the tours at any of the en-route cities they include. The suggested overnight stops are always in **bold** type.

## 1. CLASSIC EAST EUROPEAN CITIES

**19 days**

*For those who want to 'do' the most important cities of Eastern Europe in one trip, this takes in as many of the cities with major cultural attractions as possible.*

Days 1, 2: **Berlin** (p. 93). Day 3: Berlin–**Dresden** (p. 102 and p. 180). Day 4: **Dresden**. Day 5: Dresden–**Prague** (p. 183 and p. 228). Days 6, 7: **Prague**. Day 8: Prague–**Vienna** (p. 243 and p. 297). Days 9, 10: **Vienna**. Day 11: Vienna–**Budapest** (p. 304 and p. 154). Days 12, 13: **Budapest**. Day 14: Budapest–**Kraków** (p.176 and p.200). Day 15: **Kraków**. Day 16: Kraków–**Warsaw** . Day 17: **Warsaw** (p. 325). Day 18:

Warsaw–**Poznań** (p. 113). Day 19: Poznań–Berlin.

## 2. A CASTLE TOUR

**11 days**

*Despite the ravages of various wars, Eastern Europe has numerous castles, varying from remnants of stone-built fortresses to wonderfully preserved palatial piles that are castles in name only. Perhaps the greatest concentration is the 70-odd castles and palaces that lie between Prague and Mannheim; to see them all would take over a month, so this is a shorter tour of some of the finest examples in a concentrated area of east Germany and Czech.*

Day 1: **Dresden** (p. 180) for the Zwinger Palace and a 50-minute journey by train to Moritzburg, where the moated castle was used by Augustus the Strong as a shooting lodge to entertain up to a hundred guests. Day 2: **Dresden**. Day 3: Dresden–**Zwickau** (p. 217), stopping off at Rochsburg (p.108) for Schloss Rochsburg, a 12th-century castle rebuilt in 1470, which contains a fine museum. Rochsburg is reached by changing from a Dresden–Zwickau train at Glauchau. Day 4: **Zwickau**, taking the train to Weida for Schloss Osterburg (p. 216), parts of which date from almost every century between the 12th and 18th. Day 5: Zwickau–**Leipzig** (p. 216), stopping off at Altenburg to see the commanding castle that has elements dating back to 800, though most was put up in the 18th century. Day 6: **Leipzig** (p. 213) for a day visit to the famous World War II prison of Colditz Castle, dating from the 11th century. Day 7: Leipzig–**Prague** (p. 216 and p. 240), stopping off at Cheb for the 12th-century castle. Day 8: **Prague** (p. 228). Day 9: Prague–**Dresden** (p. 183), stopping off at Königstein for the impressive castle above the Elbe. Day 10: **Dresden**, for day visit to Weesenstein on the branch to Altenberg that leaves the main Dresden–Prague line (p. 183) at Heidenau. In a dramatic position overlooking the River Muglitz, the castle dates from 1300. Day 11: **Dresden**, for day visit to Bautzen on the Dresden–Wroclaw line (p. 185) for Schloss Ortenburg.

## 3. AROUND ROMANIA
**20 days**

*Although Romania still bears the scars of the oppressive Ceausescu dictatorship, and some hotels may not come up to western standards, many of the country's towns are rich in character. Fortified churches and painted churches, internally and externally, are just two of the building types characteristic of parts of Romania.*

Day 1: **Bucharest** (p. 124). Day 2: **Bucharest**. Day 3: Bucharest–**Constanţa**, the port and resort on the Black Sea. Apart from the Roman sites in the area and the beaches along the coast, there is the option of a 2–3-day trip north to Tulcea for the Danube Delta nature reserve, one of Europe's finest bird sanctuaries. Day 4: **Constanţa**. Day 5: Constanta–**Galąti** (p. 137), situated on the Danube. Day 6: Galąti–**Suceava** (p. 149), the old capital of Moldavia. This area is renowned for its painted churches, so allow more time here if you are interested in these remarkable survivals from the 16th century. Many can be reached by local train or bus. Day 7: **Suceava**.

Day 8: Suceava–**Iaşi** (p. 148), a later capital of Moldavia with several fine churches and monasteries. Day 9: **Iaşi** (150–151). Day 10: Iaşi–**Braşov** (p. 133–134), a medieval town in attractive setting. A change of train will almost certainly be necessary at Ploiesti. Day 11: Braşov–**Oradea** (p. 141). This journey can be made either by travelling to Satu Mare and changing or, for a shorter journey, changing at Jibou. Oradea has a remarkable for the legacy of *fin de siècle* buildings from the city's days as part of the Austro-Hungarian empire. Day 12: Oradea–**Cluj-Napoca** (p. 141), which has several museums about Transylvania and a good botanical garden. Day 13: Cluj-Napoca–**Alba-Iulia** (p. 141), which has a magnificent fortress built in 1714–41. Day 14: Alba-Iulia–**Sighişoara** (p. 141), one of Romania's best preserved medieval towns and birthplace of Vlad the Impaler. Day 15: **Sighişoara**. Day 16: Sighişoara–**Sibiu** (p. 141). This journey can be done by returning towards Alba-Iulia and changing at the junction of Copsa Mica (for a mercifully short look at one of Romania's most polluted eyesores) for Sibiu. Once the seat of Austrian governors of Transylvania, the town has plenty of interest and is close to lovely walking in the Fagaras Mountains. Day 17: **Sibiu**. Day 18: Sibiu–**Arad** (p. 141). Another town with lots of c.1900 Austro-Hungarian buildings. Day 19: Arad–**Timisoara** (p. 129). Day 20: Timisoara–Bucharest (p.129).

## 4. BALTIC AND RUSSIAN CAPITALS
**18 days**

*St Petersburg and Moscow have long been major tourist destinations, but the Baltic capitals are still relatively undiscovered. Their*

79

*character and buildings are quite different from the country that once ruled them, though evidence of Russian influence remains.*

Day 1: **Helsinki** (p. 188). Day 2: Helsinki–**Tallinn** by boat or train (p. 286 and p. 281). Day 3: **Tallinn**. Day 4: Tallinn–**Riga** (p. 252 and p. 247). Day 5: **Riga**. Day 6: Riga–**Vilnius** via Radviliskis (p. 313, p.318 and p. 320). Day 7: **Vilnius**. Day 8: **Vilnius**, for excursion by train to the beautiful castle at Trakai (p. 317). Day 9: Vilnius–**Pskov** (p. 324). Though reduced to ruins in World War II, much of the old city has been restored, and there are fine examples of church architecture. Day 10: **Pskov**. Day 11: Pskov–**St Petersburg** (p. 322). Days 12, 13, 14: **St Petersburg**. Day 15: St Petersburg–**Moscow** (p. 262 and p. 221). Days 16, 17: **Moscow**. Day 18: Moscow–Helsinki via St Petersburg (p. 262 and p. 286).

**5. A TOUR OF POLAND**
18 days

*Despite the tragic destruction wrought by wars, Poland still has some of Europe's finest towns and cities – the meticulous restoration of the main square in Warsaw took decades and is regarded as a landmark in such work. This tour takes in some of the best centres.*

Day 1: **Warsaw** (p. 325). Day 2: **Warsaw**. Day 3: Warsaw–**Gdańsk** (p. 331). Given the proximity of neighbouring Gdynia and Sopot, it is probably best to base yourself in Gdańsk and use local trains to visit other sites in the area. Days 4, 5: **Gdańsk**. Day 6: Gdańsk–**Torun** (p. 113), which is second only to Kraków in terms of architectural heritage. You change trains at Ilawa. Day 7: **Torun** (p.120). Day 8: **Torun**, for excursion by

train to Bydgoszcz (p. 113 and p. 119). Day 9: Torun–**Poznań** (p. 113), which was the 10th-century capital of Poland. Because Poznań is the venue for many international trade fairs, it is unwise not to book accommodation in advance. Day 10: **Poznań**. Day 11: Poznań–**Szczecin** (p. 113). Day 12: **Szczecin** (p. 114), taking the train to nearby Stargard Szczecin, which has fine Gothic, Renaissance and baroque buildings. Day 12: Szczecin–**Kraków** (p. 113, p. 211 and p. 200). Days 13, 14, 15: **Kraków**. On one of the days take a side trip to Zakopane (p. 205). Day 16: Kraków–**Przemysł** (p. 209). Day 17: **Przemysł**, taking a train back towards Kraków to visit nearby Rzeszów (p. 207). Day 18: Przemysł–Warsaw. There are direct trains to Warsaw, without returning via Kraków.

**6. THE NEW EUROPE**
11–16 days

*Visit the merging nations of eastern Europe in this variable-length trip.*

**CENTRAL EUROPE ONLY**

Day 1: Berlin–**Prague** (p. 183 and p. 228). There are many direct trains between the cities. Day 2: **Prague**. Day 3: Prague–**Budapest** (again there are trains which obviate the need to go via Vienna, as described on p. 243 and 304). Day 4, 5: **Budapest**. Day 6: Budapest–**Vienna** (p. 304 and p. 297). Day 7: **Vienna** (p. 297). Day 8: Vienna–**Warsaw** (p. 309, p. 200 and p. 325). Day 9: **Warsaw**. Day 10: Warsaw–**Berlin** (p. 113). Day 11: **Berlin**.

**BALKAN EXTENSION**

As far as Prague, then:

# Planning an Itinerary

Practicable trips are easy and fun to plan if you remember a few golden rules:

1. Work out train times with an up-to-date copy of the *Thomas Cook European Timetable*, and always read the footnotes to the tables, which give exceptions or further information. When travelling, recheck the timings at the station – not only because train schedules can change, but also because there may be convenient local trains which the Thomas Cook timetable doesn't have space to include. A copy of the *Thomas Cook New Rail Map of Europe* isn't essential but increases your planning potential. (For details of both publications see p. 26.)

2. Don't plan quick change-overs – leave plenty of time between train. It's better to spend an unexpected wait of hour or two viewing the town than miss your connection through unforeseen delays.

3. Unless you have accommodation pre-booked, plan to arrive in your overnight stop with enough time to find the accommodation you want. Make the tourist information office your first call on arrival.

4. Build in plenty of time towards the end of your trip to return to your home base – try not to plan on a 24-hr dash back across Europe to reach your plane or ferry on time.

5. Build in as many routes as possible that use frequent train services.

6. Don't plan in great detail – fill in the detail as you travel. This gives you more flexibility (to stay another day in an unexpected gem of a town, or take an interesting detour on the spur of the moment) and helps you cope with the unexpected, such as alterations to rail schedules. It is also more fun – after all, if you wanted a totally planned trip you wouldn't be travelling this way.

81

Day 3: Prague–**Bratislava** (p. 243, though there are direct trains which avoid Vienna, and p. 122). Day 4: **Bratislava**. Day 5: Bratislava–**Budapest** by direct train (p. 154). Day 6: **Budapest**. Day 7: Budapest–**Bucharest** (p. 129 and p. 124). Day 8: **Bucharest**. Day 9: Bucharest–**Sofia** (p. 269 and p. 264). Day 9: **Sofia**. Day 10: Sofia–Budapest–**Vienna** (p. 274, p. 304 and p. 297). Day 11: **Vienna**. Day 12: Vienna–**Kraków** (p. 309 and p. 200). Day 13: **Kraków**. Day 14: Kraków–**Warsaw** (p. 200 and p. 325). Day 15: **Warsaw**. Day 16: Warsaw–**Berlin** (p. 113 and p. 93).

## 7. MOUNTAINS, LAKES AND RIVERS
**15 days**

*A tour for those who prefer walking beside water or amongst hills to cultural pursuits.*

Day 1: **Vienna** (p. 297) for walks beside the Danube. Day 2: **Vienna**, for excursion to the nearby Neusiederslee. Day 3: Vienna–**Budapest** (p. 304 and p. 154). This journey can also be done by boat down the Danube. Day 4: **Budapest**. Day 5: Budapest–**Lake Balaton** (p. 169–170 There are numerous resorts around Lake Balaton from which to choose. Day 6: **Lake Balaton**. Day 7: Lake Balaton–Budapest–**Sofia** (p. 129, p. 274 and p. 264). By using local trains, especially to the east along the scenic railway to Tulovo, or south into the Rila Mountains, you can reach some spectacular country for walking. Days 8, 9: **Sofia**. Day 10: Sofia–**Bucharest** (p. 269 and p. 124). There is a series of interconnected lakes to the north of Bucharest, close to the Village Museum. Day 11: Bucharest–**Constanţa** (p.138).

If sitting on a beach is not your thing, this part of the itinerary could be omitted, or you could take the train to Tulcea for a tour of the Danube Delta and its outstanding birdlife. Day 12: **Constanţa**. Day 13: Constanţa–**Sibiu** (p. 137 and p. 141). Once the seat of Austrian governors of Transylvania, the town has plenty of interest and is close to lovely walking in

the Făgăras Mountains (p. 134). Day 14: **Sibiu**. Day 15: Sibiu–Budapest–Vienna (p. 129, p. 134, p. 304 and p. 297).

## 8. ANCIENT EUROPE
**16 days**

*A greater understanding of the great civilisations of the eastern Mediterranean can be developed by visits to the museum and ancient sites that border the Aegean Sea.*

Days 1, 2, 3: **Istanbul** (p. 193). Day 4: Istanbul–**Plovdiv** (p. 275) for the remains of Trimontium and the Achaeological Museum. Day 5: **Plovdiv**. Day 6: Plovdiv–**Sofia** (p. 275 and p. 264) for the National Archaeological Museum. Day 7: **Sofia**, for side trip by bus to Rila Monastery. Day 8: Sofia–**Thessaloniki** (p. 267) for its Archaeological Museum and sites that date back to the 4th century. Day 9: **Thessaloniki**, taking train to Lithoro for walk or taxi up Mount Olympus (the full walk takes about two days). Day 10: Thessaloniki–Larissa–**Volos** (p. 267) for its Archaeological Museum. Day 11: Volos–Larissa–**Athens** (p. 267, p. 89 and p. 83). Days 12, 13, 14: **Athens**. If you want to explore the sites of the Peloponnese, which has a railway line that permits a circular tour (as well as one of the world's great railway journeys, from Diakopto–Kalavrita), you will need to add at least three more days. Day 15: Athens–**Xànthi** (p. 89), for its old quarter. Day 16: Xànthi–Istanbul (p. 89).

82

# ATHENS

Modern Athens is a noisy, bustling city of more than 4 million people. The city has doubled in size in less than a generation. Many Athenians manage somehow to live a laid-back, village-style life amid the concrete apartment blocks which stretch to the horizon from the prominent landmark of the Acropolis, and hardly a corner is without a tiny café or tavern.

Most visitors, though, come to see the ancient city where the seeds of modern democracy, philosophy, medicine and art were planted. Worth seeing, too, are the many Orthodox churches dating from the Byzantine era.

## TOURIST INFORMATION

The **Greek National Tourist Organization (EOT)** maintains two information offices just off *Platia Syntagma*: one in the **National Bank of Greece**, *Karageorgi Servias 2*; *tel: 322 2545* or *323 4130*, (Mon–Fri 0800–1400 and 1530–2000; Sat 0900–1400); the other in the **General Bank**, *Ermou 1*; *tel: 325 2267* or *325 2268*, (Mon–Fri 0800–1800; Sat 0900–1300). Both offices offer sightseeing information leaflets, more practical individual fact sheets, local and regional transport schedules and up-to-date opening times of sights. There are also EOT offices (not dependably open) in the **East Terminal** of the airport, *tel: 961 2722* and in **Piraeus Zea Marina**, *tel: 413 5730*. The **tourist police** in Athens (*tel: 171*) can help with lists of licensed accommodation. Their head office is *Singrou 7; tel: 923 9224*.

## ARRIVING AND DEPARTING

### Airports

**Athens International Airport** is 10 km south of *Platia Syntagma* in central Athens. Olympic Airways flights, both domestic and international, use the West Terminal; *tel: 926 9111*. Bus no. 90 runs to *Syntagma*, also at 30 mins intervals.

All other airlines use the East Terminal; *tel: 96 991*. Bus no. 91 runs between the terminal and *Syntagma* every 30 mins during the day and every hour during the night.

### Stations

Trains from Thessaloniki, Northern Greece, Bulgaria and Europe use **Larissa Station** (**Stathmos Larisis**), *Theodorou Diligiani; tel: 524 0646* or *524 0601*. Trains from Patras and the Peloponnese use the **Peloponnese Station** (**Stathmos Peloponisou**); *tel: 513 1601*. The stations are small and unimpressive; in fact, if you are looking for a prominent station worthy of a capital city you may even miss them.

The two stations are only 200 yards apart, Peloponnese being behind Larissis over the metal footbridge. They are about 2 km north-west of *Syntagma* (tram no. 1). The nearest metro stop is currently *Victoria*, about 500 m to the east.

International rail tickets can be bought at Larissis station or at the **OSE offices** in Athens: *Karolou 1; tel: 522 2491, 6 Sina St; tel: 362 4402*; and *Filellinon 17 ; tel: 522 4302*. For domestic railway timetable information, *tel: 145*; for international services, *tel: 147*.

**83**

## Ferries

The **Piraeus Port Authority** handles services to the Greek islands, *tel: 451 1311* or *453 7107*. The port itself, 8 km southwest of Athens, is served by train and metro. The tourist office will give you an all-island ferry timetable, which changes monthly.

If you are planning an island-hopping interlude, Thomas Cook's guidebook *Greek Island Hopping*, in the same series as this one, combines a guide to every Greek island with authoritative ferry timetable information.)

### GETTING AROUND

The free map of Athens available from the tourist office is excellent. It indicates trolley-bus routes and metro stations and gives details of bus services. Central Athens, from *Omonia* to *Syntagma* through the *Plaka* to the Acropolis, is increasingly walkable thanks to a ban on traffic in several core blocks. Don't think about walking any further than this in July and August, when the heat and smog are unbearable.

## Metro (Subway)

There is currently only one metro line in Athens, which runs from Piraeus north to the centre of town, where there are stations at *Monastiraki* (for the Acropolis and the Plaka), *Omonia* (for the Archaeological Museum) and *Victoria* (for the main-line stations), then on to *Kifissia*.

Tickets are available from station kiosks or self-service machines; validate them in the machines at station entrances.

A cross-town metro line, with stations at *Syntagma* and *Larissis* mainline stations, is being built. The building work is quite disruptive, although it has thrown up interesting archaeological finds, such as two Roman wells at *Syntagma*.

## Trolley-buses and Buses

Buy tickets from blue booths near bus stops or from kiosks throughout Athens. Validate tickets on board. The network is far more comprehensive than the metro; the tourist office map gives clear details. Most routes pass through either *Syntagma* or *Omonia*.

## Taxis

Taxis in Athens are hard to find, especially during the rush hour, around lunch-time and early afternoon. Sharing a taxi is normal – all passengers pay full fare. Some airport taxi drivers will overcharge unwary visitors; agree a fare before getting in.

### STAYING IN ATHENS

## Accommodation

The **Hellenic Chamber of Hotels** provides a booking service for hotels in Athens. They can be contacted before arrival at *Stadiou 24, Athens; tel: 323 6962*, or after arrival in Athens at *Karageorgi Servias 2*, off *Syntagma*; *tel: 323 7193*, next door to the tourist office in the National Bank.

Hotel groups represented in Athens include *Ch, Hn, IC, Ma* and *Nv*. The tourist office itself has a standard list of class A–C hotels. Ask for details of class D and E hotels if you are looking for cheaper options. Athens has many private hostels catering to budget travellers. Some tout for business at stations and on the trains arriving in Athens from Patras. Standards vary widely.

Hostels cluster in the *Plaka* area, which is noisy but ideally located for the main sights, or in the area between *Victoria* and the stations (where the tackiest accommodation is found). Some of the cheapest 'hostel' accommodation near the station is extremely overcrowded in high season,

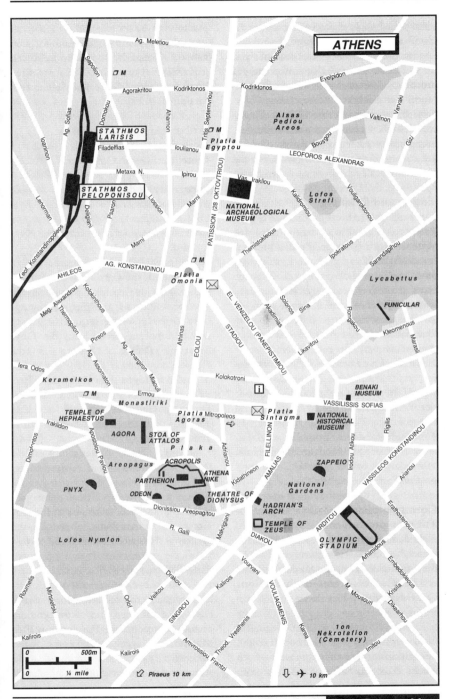

**ATHENS**

Ag. Meletiou
Kipselis
Evelpidon

M
Agorakritou
Kodriktonos
Kodriktonos
Kodriktonos
Varvaki
Valtinon
Gizi

Sapolion
Domokou
Aharnon
Tritis Septemvriou

**STATHMOS LARISIS**
Filadelfias
Ioulianou

**Aisas
Pediou
Areos**
Bousgou

**LEOFOROS ALEXANDRAS**

Ag. Sofias
Ioannon

Metaxa N.
Ipirou
Marni
M
**Platia
Egyptou**

Vas. Irakliou
Kaldromou
**Lofos
Strefi**
Voulgaroktonou

Lenorman
Ag. Konstandinopoleos
**STATHMOS PELOPONISOU**
Deligiani
Psaron
Liosion

PATISSION (28 OKTOVTRIOU)

**NATIONAL
ARCHAEOLOGICAL
MUSEUM**

Ipokratous
Sarandapihou
**Lycabettus**

Marni
Themistokleous
Solonos
Sina

**AHILEOS**
**AG. KONSTANDINOU**
M
**Platia
Omonia**
Akadimias

**FUNICULAR**
Rongakou
Kleomenous

Meg. Alexandrou
Thermopilon
Kolokinthous
Pireos
Ag. Anargiron
Miaouli
Athinas
EOLOU
STADIOU
EL. VENZELOU (PANEPISTIMIOU)
Likavitou
Marasli

Iera Odos
Assomaton

**Kerameikos**
Kolokotroni
i

M
Ermou
**Monastiriki**

**BENAKI
MUSEUM**
**VASSILISSIS SOFIAS**
Riglis

**TEMPLE OF
HEPHAESTUS**
Iraklidon
**Platia
Agoras**
Mitropoleos
Adrianou
**Platia
Sintagma**
**NATIONAL
HISTORICAL
MUSEUM**

Dimofontos
Apostolou Pavlou
**AGORA**
**STOA OF
ATTALOS**
**P l a k a**
FILELLINON
AMALIAS
Inodou Atikou
**VASSILEOS KONSTANDINOU**

**Areopagus**
**ACROPOLIS**
Kidathineon
**ZAPPEIO**
Arianou

**PNYX**
**PARTHENON**
**ATHENA
NIKE**
Erathostenous

**ODEON**
**THEATRE OF
DIONYSUS**
**National
Gardens**

Dionissiou Areopagitou
Makrigiani
**HADRIAN'S
ARCH**
ARDITOU
Amimidous

R. Galli
**TEMPLE OF
ZEUS**
DIAKOU
**OLYMPIC
STADIUM**
Embedokleous

**Lofos Nymfon**
Vourvani
Krisila
Dikearhou
Imitou

Roumelis
Mintsefaki
Drakou
Veikou
Kaliroiis
Vresthenis
VOULIAGMENIS
M. Mousouri
Karea

Oriol
SINGROU

Kalirois
Kalirois
Amvrossiou Frantzi
Theod. Vresthenis
**1 on
Nekrotafion
(Cemetery)**

0        500m
0    ¼ mile
Piraeus 10 km
10 km

with tight-budget travellers sleeping on the floor and in the corridors. However, except during the height of summer you should have plenty of options. The **HI hostel**, *57 Kypselis St; tel: 822 5860*, 2 km north of *Syntagma Square* (trolley nos. 2/4/9), is further out than most of the private hostels. **Camping** is not a good idea; campsites are up to an hour from the centre by bus, dirty and poorly serviced, and not dramatically cheaper than hostels.

### Eating and Drinking

On a tight budget, eat on the move: *giros*, slices of veal kebab with onions, tomatoes, yoghurt and fries wrapped in flat bread, is a meal in itself and there are lots of other street snacks to choose from. *Plaka* restaurants tend to be touristy, but those at *Plateia Filiki Eterias*, off *Kidathineon* on the edge of the *Plaka*, are a little less so. Try **Bakalarakia**, a basement fish restaurant at *Kidathineon 41*, for cod Athenian style; **Eden**, at *Flessa 3; tel: 3248 858* serves vegetarian food; **Apotsos**, at *Venizelou 10*, for superb lunchtime snacks and old-style decor; or **Baktairakis**, by the corner of *Mitropoleos* and *Monastiraki*, for filling traditional dishes and wine from the barrel. For even cheaper eats, head for the Pankrati suburb, north of the *National Gardens* and *Stadiou*.

### Communications

The main **post office** is at *Eolou 100; tel: 321 6063*, Mon–Sat 0730–2030. One branch is in *Syntagma; tel: 323 7573*, Mon–Sat 0730–2030 and Sun 0730–1330.

The **Greek Telecommunications Organisation (OTE)** has an office open 24 hrs at *Patisson 85*. The office at *Stadiou 15; tel: 322 1002*, is open Mon–Fri 0700–2400 and Sat–Sun 0800–2400. International calls can be made at both offices. You can make local calls from public coin boxes and international calls from those which bear the orange 'international' legend. You can also make calls from metered phones at 'periptero' street booths all over the city. The dialling code for Athens is *301*.

### Embassies and Consulates

**Australia:** *Mesoghion 15; tel: 644 7303.*
**Canada:** *Ioannou Gennadiou 4; tel: 723 9511.*
**New Zealand:** *Semitelou 9, Athens; tel:7239 510/9.*
**UK:** *Ploutarchou 1; tel: 723 6211.*
**USA:** *Vassilissis Sofias 91; tel: 721 2951.*

### ENTERTAINMENT

Most cinemas show the latest English language movies with original soundtrack and Greek subtitles; see the English-language daily *Athens News* for listings. See traditional music and dance with the **Dora Stratou Dance Theatre** in the *Philopappous Theatre; tel 324 4395*. The **Sound and Light** show on *Pnyx Hill; tel: 322 1459*, is not to be missed. **Absolut Dancing Club**, *Fillelinon 23; tel: 3237 197*, is still Athens's most popular dance venue.

During the **Athens Festival** (June–Sept) events staged in the **Odeon of Herodes Atticus**, an open-air Roman theatre, include ancient Greek drama plus classical music and ballet, performed by Greek and international companies and orchestras. For information, *tel: 322 1459*.

### SHOPPING

For gold and silver jewellery, ceramics, leather goods and fashion with a Greek slant – lots of linen and cotton knits in bright colours – try the **Pandrossou Flea Market**, between *Monastiraki* and *Mitropoleos Square*. For antiques, junk, army surplus, antique clothing and camp-

86

ing gear, the original **Flea Market** on *Ifestou*, on the opposite side of *Monastiraki*, is a better bet.

## SIGHTSEEING

### The Acropolis

To many, the **Acropolis** symbolises Greece. The 'high city' served as Athens' stronghold until it was converted into a religious shrine in the 13th century BC.

Pericles built the **Parthenon** (Home of the Virgin), between 447 and 432 BC. Designed by Iktinus and Phidias, it is the finest example of Doric architecture still in existence. Close examination of the temple reveals irregularities: columns are closer together at the corners, where light can shine between them; columns are of differing widths and bulge one third of the way up; the roof line is curved. The combined effect is one of the finest optical illusions ever devised, giving the impression from afar of perfect symmetry. Today, the temple maintains its grandeur, despite the intrusions of scaffolding and cranes as part of a long-term EU-funded restoration project. Most of the dramatic friezes that adorned the Parthenon's exterior, the controversial Elgin Marbles, are in the British Museum, London, although the Acropolis Museum has some fragments.

The **Erechtheum**, to the north-west of the Parthenon, is most notable for its six *caryatids* – graceful sculptures of women. Due to the detrimental effects of air pollution, the originals have been removed and replaced by the replicas on display today. Four of the originals are on display in the Acropolis Museum.

The delicate **Temple of Athena Nike** (Victory), with its eight small columns, stands perched on the south-west corner of the Acropolis. Built around 420 BC, during a pause in the Peloponnesian War,

the temple was once the only place from where you could look out to the sea over the defensive walls; it is considered one of the finest Ionic buildings left in Greece.

The bulky **Propylaea**, the great gateway to the Acropolis, takes up most of the western end of the hill and today welcomes thousands of visitors. Arrive early if you want any peace or uninterrupted photo opportunities.

The **Acropolis Museum**, to the east of the Parthenon, contains some interesting material.

### Beyond the Acropolis

From the Acropolis you obtain extensive panoramic views of Athens and beyond. Most of the city suburbs are anonymous concrete swathes, distinguished only by dark green awnings, but in areas close to the Acropolis you can pick out many other ancient ruins. Just below the Acropolis hill, on the south side, are two ancient theatres. The **Theatre of Dionysus**, built in the 4th century BC, was the oldest in Greece and thus can lay claim to being the first in the Western world. Only bare ruins remain, although the plan of the theatre can be identified easily, especially from above. The Roman **Odeon of Herodes Atticus** has been reconstructed and is, once again, in use as a theatre. The remains of the **Temple of Olympian Zeus** are also clearly visible, east of the Acropolis. There are only a few surviving columns but it is still possible to absorb the grandeur of what was the largest temple in Greece. Next to it is **Hadrian's Arch**, constructed by the enthusiastic Roman builder-emperor to mark where the ancient Greek city ended and his new city began.

Across *Vassilissis Olgas*, to the north, are the **National Gardens**, which stretch up to Syntagma Square and offer a break from

**87**

Athens' infamous traffic. The **Olympic Stadium**, across *Vassileos Konstandinou* from the National Gardens, stands on the site of an ancient Athenian version and was host to the first modern Olympics in 1896.

To the north-west of the Acropolis lie the extensive ruins of the **Agora**, the central focus for much of ancient Athens' commercial and intellectual life. In the Agora is one of the best-preserved ancient Greek buildings, the immaculate **Temple of Hephaestus** or **Thesseion**, built in 440 BC and decorated with elaborate friezes. The **Stoa of Attalos**, built by King Attalos II in the 2nd century BC, has now been restored as a museum displaying objects found during excavations of the Agora. There are entrances from *Adrianou, Thissio,* just off *Monastiraki,* and the path on the north side of the Acropolis. The **Areopagus**, below the entrance of the Acropolis, was the open-air meeting place for the city-state's supreme court.

Across the rail lines from the Agora is **Kerameikos Cemetery**, the burial place for influential Athenians of ancient times. The **Kerameikos Museum**, *148 Ermou St*, contains discoveries from the cemetery. Round to the west of the Acropolis is **Pnyx Hill**. Here the *Ecclesia tou Demou*, or public assembly, of the Athenian State met.

### The Plaka

Huddled below the Acropolis on its north and east sides is the most appealing part of the city. The old-fashioned streets of the Plaka – reprieved and the last minute from demolition and redevelopment in the 1980s – are lined with tall stucco-fronted mansions dating from the 19th century. Many old buidings are being renovated. There are few cars and plenty of shops, cafés and leafy squares.

### Museums and Churches

For an incomparable collection of relics from Athens and many other Greek sites, head to the **National Archaeological Museum**, *44 Patission; tel: 821 7717*. The line-up of exhibits is both exhaustive and exhausting: allow yourself a full day. Exhibits range through Minoan frescoes, Mycenaean gold, a selection from a phenomenal collection of over 300,000 coins, sculptures, *kouroi* and much more.

There are plenty of other museums offering their own insights into Greek life, both modern and ancient. The **Museum of Cycladic and Ancient Greek Art**, *4 Neofitou Douka St*, concentrates on the simple yet powerful sculptures from Greece's most ancient civilisation, in the Cyclades Islands. The **National Gallery and Alexander Soutzos Museum**, *Vassileos Konstantinou*, has a general but uninspired collection of mainly 19th-century Greek painting. The diverse, entertaining collection in the **Benaki Museum**, *Koumpari St* and *Vassilissis Sofias Ave*, includes everything from ancient Greek relics through to mementoes from the War of Independence. The **Byzantine Museum**, *Vassilissis Sofia 22*, houses icons from this later glory of Greek culture.

Several churches survive in Athens from the 10th–13th century. These include **Agia Kaphikareas**, *Ermou*; **Agios Eleftherios** (or **Panagia Gorgoepikoos**), near *Mitopoleos Square*; and **Agia Apostoli**, near the Agora. The **Byzantine Museum**, *Vassilissis Sofias 22*, shows elements of the Byzantine influence from the 4th century onwards.

From **Lycabettus Hill**, the highest in Athens at 278m, the view surpasses even that from the Acropolis. Take the funicular railway up and the path down for the best round-trip.

# ATHENS–ISTANBUL

This route links Greece and Turkey. As well as connecting Greece's two major cities, it passes through some dramatic scenery. Between Athens and Thessaloniki it bypasses the ancient site of Delphi, skirting the Mt Parnassos massif and passing through rugged mountain country betwen Amfiklia and Lamia. North of Larissa it runs through the lovely Vale of Tembi to emerge on the north Aegean coast in the shadows of Mt Olympus. East of Thessaloniki the line runs briefly north towards the Bulgarian border, then parallels the Aegean shore, through the gentle, pastoral scenery of rural Thrace, before crossing the Evros river into Turkey.

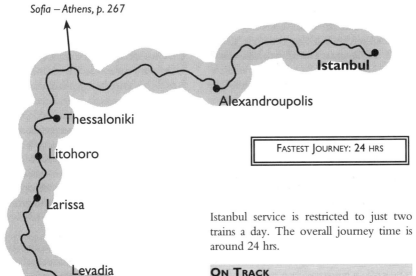

Sofia – Athens, p. 267

**89**

FASTEST JOURNEY: 24 HRS

Istanbul service is restricted to just two trains a day. The overall journey time is around 24 hrs.

## ON TRACK

### Athens–Thebes–Levadia
Ten trains a day taking 1 hr 30 mins from Athens to Thebes and 50 mins from Thebes to Levadia.

### Levadia–Larissa
Up to 11 trains a day with journey times of between 2 hrs 30 mins and 4 hrs 30 mins. The faster trains have refreshment cars, but also require a supplement.

## TRAINS

ETT Tables: 970, 974

### FAST TRACK
A change of train at Thessaloniki is required and the Thessaloniki to

## Larissa–Litohoro–Thessaloniki

A frequent service links Larissa with Thessaloniki, but most trains do not call at Litohoro and many of those that do, stop only on request. Larissa to Litohoro takes just over 1 hr and Litohoro to Thessaloniki takes nearly 2 hrs.

## Thessaloniki–Alexandroupolis

Five trains a day link these towns with journey times ranging from 5 hrs 30 mins for the two expressess, to 7 hr 30 mins for the other trains.

## Alexandropoulis–Istanbul

Two trains a day make the 10 hr journey (one overnight).

## THEBES (THIVAI)

**Station**: tel: (0262) 27 531, 1 km north of the centre. Modern Thebes is a dull little town with no outstanding points of interest. A small Archaeological Museum and remnants of a 13th-century castle, both in the town centre, help to pass the time between trains.

## LEVADIA

**Station**: tel: (0261) 28 046, 3 km from the centre, but taxis are available.
**Tourist Police**: tel: (0261) 28 551.
Levadia is a common stopping point for travellers en route to Delphi, 56 km west. The town fulfilled a similar role in ancient times. Those heading to the **Oracle at Delphi** could stop at Levadia's **Oracle of Zeus Trofonios** on top of Profiris Ilias, one of the two hills overlooking the town. The remains of a 14th-century castle that was built over the site of the Oracle can still be seen.

## LARISSA

**Station**: tel: (041) 236 250, 1 km from the centre.

**Tourist Office**: EOT, 18 Koumoundourou St; tel: (041) 250 919. **Tourist Police**: 86 Papanastasiou St; tel: (041) 227 900 or 222 152.

Larissa, capital of Thessaly, is one of the few rail junction towns in Greece and has the distinction of having recorded the hottest summer temperatures in Europe. The **Archaeological Museum** houses some ancient relics of the city.

### ⇄ SIDE TRACKS
### FROM LARISSA

**Volos** was an important town in the Mycenean age and is now the main base from which to explore the beautiful, mountainous **Pelion** peninsula to the east. The city itself, from where Jason set sail in the Argo in search of the Golden Fleece, has little to offer except a reasonable **Archaeological Museum**. There are fairly ˌfrequent trains from Larissa, taking about 1 hr. **Station**: Odos Papadiamandis; tel: (0421) 23 712 or 25 759. **EOT Office**: Platia Riga Fereou; (0421) tel: 36 233. **Tourist Police**: 217 Odos Alexandras; tel: (0421) 27 094.

The major tourist attraction in northern Greece, **Meteora**, is reached by bus from **Kalambaka**, to which there are five trains a day from Larissa, with a change in Paleofarsalos. The full journey takes about 2 hrs 30 mins. Paleofarsalos is 'On Track' between Athens and Thessaloniki, if you want to visit Meteora without going to Larissa.

Kalambaka has an early 14th-century **Cathedral**, which contains some 13th–14th-century paintings and a lovely marble pulpit. **Roman remains** are still visible around the cathedral. **Tourist Police**: 10 Odos Hatzipetrou; tel: (0432) 22 813.

The town is one gateway to the valley of the Meteora, 24 perpendicular rocks which soar to 600m. In the 11th century Byzantine monks began to build monasteries on the summits. Exactly how they managed this is still something of a mystery; St Barlaam, the first abbot, is said to have flown to the top mounted on an eagle. Later occupants used precarious pulley-lifts. By the 14th century there were 24 monasteries perched on the top, but the number of inhabitants decreased and only 5 are still occupied. Nowadays their function has as much to do with showing visitors round as with religion. As in all Greek monasteries, there is a strict dress code - not shorts or bare shoulders for men or women; skirts must cover the knee 🔄

## LITOHORO

**Station**: *tel: (0352) 81 990*, near the coast, 5 km east of town. Buses run between the station and the town.

**Tourist Office**: *Odos Ag Nicolaou 15; tel: (0352) 81 250* (in the Town Hall). Mon–Sat 0900–1400 and 1700–2100, and Sun 0900–1400. The **HI**; *2 Enipeos St; tel: (0352) 81 311* or *82 176*, has information on the various climbs. More reliable information is available from the **Greek Alpine Club (EOS)** office, *Kentriki Platia, 60200 Litohoro; tel: (0532) 81944*.

Litohoro is the jumping-off point for the 2917m-high **Mt Olympus**, the home of the ancient gods. You don't need any special equipment (other than suitable footwear) for the full ascent, but it does demand real fitness and takes two days. Book a bunk in one of the mountain refuge dormitories (hot meals and drinks available) through the EOS office. Getting to the top involves taking a taxi or hitching a lift to the car park 6 km from Litohoro, at the 1000 m level; then hiking

through wooded ravines to the refuge at around 2000 m. It is best to spend the night here before making the final, demanding trek to the tops; the final 100 m traverse to **Mitikas**, the highest peak, requires strong nerves.

> 🔄 **SIDE TRACK**
> **FROM LITOHORO**
> **Dion** is one of the finest and least-visited archaeological sites in Greece. There are several buses daily from Litohoro village and station to Dion village, 8 km north of Litohoro and 2 km west of the site. Highlights are the marble and mosaic floors, the Sanctuary of Isis, and a length of the paved road which led to Olympus. The **museum**, in the centre of the village, has a fine collection of finds from the site. 🔄

## THESSALONIKI

**Station**: *tel: (031) 517 517*, about 1 km west of the town centre. Bus no. 3 runs from the station to the centre, passing **Platia Aristotelous**.

**Tourist Information**: EOT Office, *8 Platia Aristotelous; tel: 271 888* or *222 935*. Mon–Fri 0800–2000 and Sat 0830–1400. There is an information desk at the station which can help direct you there. **Tourist Police**: *Odos Dodekanissou*, near *Platia Dimokratias; tel: 544 162*.

### GETTING AROUND

Thessaloniki is a large city, but many of the interesting sights are within 10–15 mins walk of the tourist office. Buses cover the city comprehensively. Buy tickets from the conductor, who sits at the rear.

### ACCOMMODATION

As befits a major city, Thessaloniki has a full range of accommodation – ask the tourist office for a list. The cheaper hotels mostly cluster along *Egnatia St* – the continuation of *Monastiriou St*, east of the station. There's a fairly central **youth hostel**: *44 Al. Svolou St; tel: (031) 225 945.*

## COMMUNICATIONS

The main **post office** is at *45 Tsimiski St; tel: 264 208* and the main **telephone office** is at *27 Karolou St (Ermou St).*

## CONSULATES

**UK**: *8 Venizelou St; tel: (031) 278 006.*
**USA**: *59 Nikis St; tel (031) 266 121.*

## SIGHTSEEING

Thessaloniki, the second largest city in Greece, was founded in 315 BC by Kassandros and named after his wife, the sister of Alexander the Great. The name means 'Victory in Thessaly'. The city became strategically vital to the Romans, straddling the Via Egnatia, their highway between Constantinople and the Adriatic, and later to the Byzantines and their Turkish conquerors. It was one of the greatest cities of the Ottoman Empire, rejoining Greece only in 1913. The old town was destroyed by fire in 1917 and Thessaloniki today is a modern, busy city, laid out along a crescent bay.

A **Museum of Byzantine Art and History** is housed in the **White Tower**, the most prominent surviving bastion of the Byzantine-Turkish city walls. The superb **Archaeological Museum**, opposite, contains the contents of Macedonian Royal Tombs discovered at Vergina in 1977. The exceptional gold-trimmed armour, weapons and gold-leaf headdresses are eclipsed by the charred bones of the buried king, believed to be Philip II of Macedonia, father of Alexander the Great. There's also a **Folklore Museum**, *Vassilissis Olgas 68*, with a fine series of exhibits on the vanished folkways of

northern Greece. Thessaloniki's Roman heritage includes remains of the **Forum**, *Odos Filipou*, the **Palace of Galerius**, *Platia Navarinou*, the **Baths**, next to Agios Dimitrios church, and the distinctive **Arch of Galerius**, beside **Odos Egnatia**, near *Platia Sintrivaniou.*

The city also has a fine collection of **Byzantine churches**, the most notable of which are **Agios Georgios** and the restored 4th-century **Agios Dimitrios** rotunda. Many of these are being restored and are closed with no opening date set.

## ALEXANDROUPOLIS

**Station**: *tel: 26 395* or *26 212*, by the port. At the eastern extremity of northern Greece, this dusty, sleepy little port and railway town is little more than a stopping place for travellers heading to or from Turkey.

> **SIDE TRACK FROM ALEXANDROUPOLIS**
>
> **Samothraki**, about 20 km south of Alexandroupolis, is dominated by the tree-covered slopes and bare summit of **Mt Fengari**, the highest mountain in the Aegean archipelago. The island's main attraction is the striking **Sanctuary of the Great Gods**, the site where the Winged Victory of Samothrace, now in the Louvre, was discovered. There are remnants of a theatre, Temple of Hera, and other buildings and an interesting small museum.
>
> A daily ferry between Alexandroupolis and **Kamariotissa**, the island port, takes two hours; in high season, hydrofoils do the trip in one hour. There are plenty of places to stay in Kamariotissa; the Sanctuary is just outisde the hamlet of **Paleopolis**, 10 km from the village. ◤

# BERLIN

Once famous for being divided, Berlin is now just as famous for being reunited. The events of 9 November 1989, when people from East and West Berlin tore down the barriers which had kept them apart since 1961, are by no means ancient history. The only remaining trace of the infamous Wall is a ribbon of wasteland lining the western part of the city, but melding the two halves will take time. East Berliners, used to a society which guaranteed them jobs and a certain (admittedly low) standard of living, are still coming to terms with the insecurity that goes with their new-found freedoms. West Berliners, from the ostentatiously wealthy Mercedes set to the thriving avant-garde arts and revolution scene, were taken aback to find their 'island city' no longer an enclave but just another big German city. Not that Berlin will ever be anything but exciting: its delight in dabbling with whatever is new and experimental ensures that, and as the hub of the new Germany it is in the middle of its biggest adventure yet.

The main **VTB** (tourist information office) in the **Europa Centre**, *Budapester Str. 10787; tel: (030) 262 60 31*, opens Mon–Sat 0800–2230, Sun 0900–2100. There are also offices at **Tegel Airport** and the two of the three main railway stations: **Zoo Bahnhof**, *tel: (030) 313 90 63*, open Mon–Sat 0800-2300 and **Hauptbahnhof**, *tel: (030) 279 52 09*, open Mon–Sun 0800–2000. For written enquiries contact the central administration at *Martin-Luther-Str.105, 10825 Berlin.* **Thomas Cook bureaux de change**: *Friedrichstr. 56*; **Schönefeld Airport**.

**Airports**
Most flights from the West are to **Berlin-Tegel Otto Lilienthal Airport**, *tel: (030) 60 91 21 39*, 8 km from the centre of town. Bus nos. 109 and 128 connect with the U-bahn; the first to *Jakob-Kaiser-Platz* and the second to *Kurt-Schumacher-Platz*. Allow about an hour. Taxis are not much more expensive.

**Schönefeld Airport** (19 km south-west) served the East in the days of the Berlin Wall and since reunification the destinations haven't changed much. For enquiries *tel: (030) 60 91 21 39*. The S-bahn runs to Hbf (29 mins) and **Zoo** (48 mins), main-line trains to Lichtenberg (19 mins).

**National buses**
These are run by **ZOB** (Zentraler Omnibusbahnhof), *tel: (030) 301 80 28*. The main station is at Kaiserdamm. Buses run daily to all major cities and smaller towns.

**Stations**
Berlin's two major stations for long-distance main-line trains are **Berlin Zoologischer Garten** (shortened to

93

Zoo), *Hardenbergplatz 11* in the western part of the city and **Berlin Hauptbahnhof** (Hbf), *Am Hauptbahnhof*, in the east. Some main-line trains also stop at **Berlin Friedrichstr.**, *Georgenstr. 14-18*, midway between the two larger stations; and at **Berlin Lichtenburg**, *Weitlingerstr. 22*, 4 km. east of Hbf.

For all rail information ask at the **Bundesbahn Information Office**, *Hardenbergstr. 20; tel: 19419.* Open Mon–Fri, 0830–1830.

### GETTING AROUND

Berlin's efficient public transport network combines buses, trams, underground and surface trains. Free photocopied street maps can be picked up from the tourist offices. A more comprehensive version costs DM5–DM10 from newsagents. Train maps are easy to find but for bus maps you must go to the **BVG information centre**, outside Zoo Bahnhof, *tel: (030) 256 2462.* Open Mon–Fri 0800–1800, Sat 0700–1400 and Sun 0900–1600. Here you can get the *Region Berlin Linienplan* (DM3) and free smaller transport maps. Taxis are plentiful, especially in the west, and relatively inexpensive; they can be flagged down on the street or from ranks at stations, airport and other key points.

### Public Transport

The 20 lines of the U–bahn (underground) and S-bahn (suburban surface trains) offer quick transport to most spots within the 40 km diameter of Berlin. The stations are easily recognised by the white U on a blue square or white S on a green circle and lines are colour-coded and numbered. Direction is indicated by the name of the final destination. Bus-stops are indicated by a green H on a yellow background. Buses are also convenient and a good way

to see the city. Take the no. 100 from Zoo Bhf to *Alexanderplatz* for a tour of west and east including the **Tiergarten avenues**, the **Reichstag**, the **Brandeburg Gate** and **Unter den Linden**, ending conveniently close to **Museum Island**. No. 12, which runs along an east–west axis through the city, is another good sightseeing route.

### Tickets

Tickets can be bought from automatic machines on station platforms, bus drivers or ticket offices and are validated by punching the ticket once on board or on the platform. A single allows travel on any bus, train or tram for a period of 2 hours. A *Sammelkarte* (the equivalent of four singles) is a cheaper option and a *24-Stunden-Karte* (24-hour ticket) can be even more economical if you are planning several journeys. The *Berlin WelcomeCard* costs DM 29 and allows you unlimited free use of public transport throughout the city and its suburbs; you also get reductions on city tours, museums, theatres and tourist attractions in Berlin and Potsdam. Buy *WelcomeCards* at stations, bus ticket offices, hotels, or the tourist information offices at Hauptbahnhof, Tegel airport, or the Brandenburg Gate. Weekly (Mon–Sat) tickets are also available.

### Boats

For daily boat trips along the **River Spree**, go to the restaurant terrace at the **Kongress Halle**, *Greenwich-Promenade* in Tegel, **Tiergarten pier** or **Wannsee pier**. For information *tel: (030) 394 49 54* or *(030) 810 0040.*

### Bicycles

You can rent bikes for the day, the evening or the weekend from **Christoph Beck**, *Zoo/Ernst Reuter Platz, tel (030) 312*

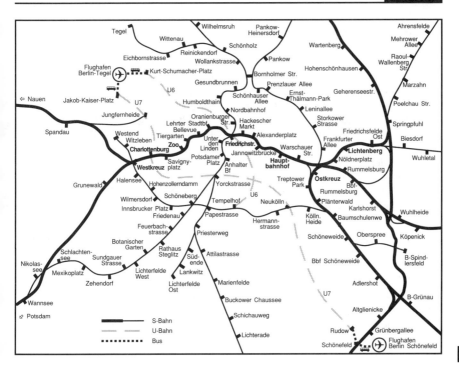

*19 25.*

## Guided Walks

From Apr–Oct walks with English-speaking guides start at 1030 daily from the McDonalds on *Hardenbergplatz*, opposite the main entrance to Zoo Bhf (look for the guide wearing a 'Berlin Walks' badge). An introductory city walk lasting 2½–3 hrs takes in the **Brandeburg Gate** and the **Reichstag**, **Unter Den Linden**, **Museum Island**, what remains of the Wall, and **Checkpoint Charlie**. Three themed walks cover the buildings of the Third Reich, Jewish Berlin, and the now-vanished **Berlin Wall**.

## STAYING IN BERLIN

## Accommodation

Most up-market tourist accommodation is in the west, especially in the environs of **Zoo**, **Ku'damm** and **Charlottenburg**. Since unification, rooms in the east have been slightly cheaper and of lower standard, a situation which is rapidly changing. The tourist information offices will make reservations for a small fee and give advice, addresses and telephone numbers. **Thomas Cook network member** *Reisebüro Helios, Uhlandstr. 73; tel: (030) 860 0050* also makes hotel reservations. There is a wide range of top quality, international hotels, including *BW, Ch, Ex, Fm, GT, Hn, Ib, IC, Ke, Mp, Nv, Pe, RC, Rd, Rn*. For a list of cheap hotels and hostels (including prices) ask for the *Accommodation for Young Visitors* booklet at the Tourist Office. Prices start at about DM35 for hostels, and cheap hotel rooms (pensions) start at about DM70 for a single and DM90 for a double. Near the Zoo station, **Arco Pension**; *Kurfurstendamm 30, Ecke Uhland-str, 1000 Berlin 15* is a recommended cheap hotel option with rooms from around DM 70. Other places around DM 90 include: **Apart Hotel Hanse**; *Jenaer-str. 2, 10717 Berlin; tel: 211 90 53*; **BCA Lichtenberg**, *Rhin-str. 159, 10315 Berlin; tel: 540 01 12*; **BCA Wilhelmsberg**, *Landsberger Allee 203, 13055 Berlin; tel: 49 77 40*; **Hotel Berliner Ho**, *Taentzien-str. 8, 10789 Berlin; tel: 25 49 50*; **Hotel Kurfürstendamm am Adenauerplatz**, *Kurfurstendamm 68, 10707 Berlin; tel: 88 46 30*; **Hotel Suden**, *Neukollner-str. 217, 12357 Berlin; tel: 66 00 80*; **Hotel-Pension Wittelsbach**, *Wittelsbacherstr. 22, 10707 Berlin; tel: 87 63 45.*

**Apartment Sharing Centres** (*Mitwohnzentralen*) arrange vacant room and apartment rental for a fee based on the cost of the accommodation. There are several such centres, the one at *Kurfurstendamm 227/228; tel: (030) 88 30 51* is near Zoo. Most Berlin **campsites** are out of town; for a list ask at the tourist office. A few minutes walk from Tegel U-bahn, an **international youth-camp** offers places for DM9 a night.

### Communications
There is a **24-hour post office** at Zoo Bahnhof where you can also collect **Post Restante** mail. Post offices are usually open Mon–Fri 0900–1800; Sat 0900–1200. To phone Berlin from abroad, *tel: 49* (Germany) + *30* (Berlin) + *number,* to phone Berlin from elsewhere in Germany, *tel: 030 + number.*

### Eating and Drinking
Berlin has a huge array of restaurants, cafés, bars and street stalls, from typically German establishments to kebab houses and pizzerias. In the centre, there are con-centrations around Zoo station and **Ku'damm**; the bland Europe Centre shopping mall, opposite the station, has a reasonable choice of fast-food snackeries and a popular Irish pub which serves Guinness. In the east of the city, head for the **Nikolai quarter** or **Gendarmenmarkt**. For a treat, try the cakes at coffee shops, while for cheap food and a happy evening's drinking, head for the pubs (*kneipe*) around *Savigny Platz*, *Kreuzberg* and *Prenzlauer Berg*. **Café Kranzler**, at the *Charlottenberg* end of the Ku'damm; *Kurfurstendamm 18-19: tel 885 77 20*; is a three-storey gem of wedding-cake architecture, with Berlin's finest coffee and cakes; for a real Berlin meal of beer, pickles, pork hocks or meat rissoles try **Wilhelm Hoeck**; *Wilmersdorfer-str. 149*; *tel: 341 81 74*. For the best pizza in town head for **Gorgonzola Club**, *Kreuzberg, Dresdner-str. 121; tel: 615 64 73*. Other recommended eating places include; **Zur letzten Instanz**, *Waisenstr 14-16*, founded in 1621, claims to be the oldest bar in Berlin; **Rockendorfs Restaurant**, *Waidmannslust, Dusterhauptstr 1*, is at the opposite end of the gourmet scale with two Michelin stars – owner-chef Siegfried Rockendorf is Berlin's gourmet king. **Henne**, *Leuschnerdamm 25*, is a Kreuzberg brasserie specialising in grilled chicken; **Jolesch**, *Muskauer Str 1*, serves Viennese style cooking; **Osteria No 1**, also in Kreuzberg, is a lively Mediterranean establishment. **Berlin's Hard Rock Café** is in *Wilmersdorf, at Meinekestr 21*, with the usual Hard Rock burger-oriented menu. A good bet if you are with a crowd is **Meinecke X**, *Meineckestr. 10*, just off the Ku'damm, a typical Berlin *kneipe* where huge lumps of *eisbein* (pork knuckles) and glasses of wheat beer are the order of the day. **Grossbeerenkeller**, *Grossbeerenstr 90*, is a Kreuzberg joint for night-owls,

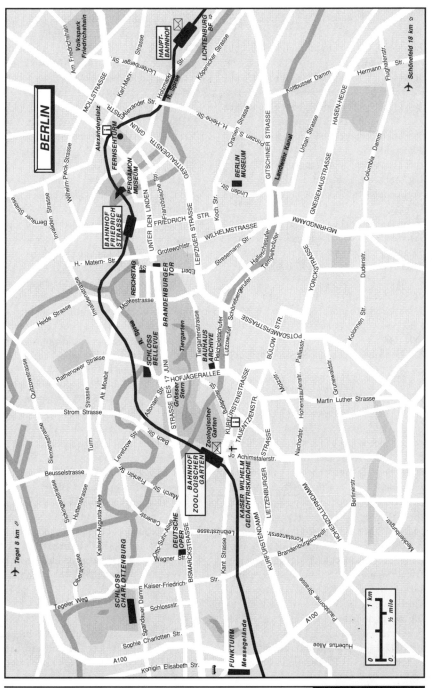

open until 0300 (0400 Fri, Sat and Sun). **Herta**, *Schluterstr. 75*, is another early-hours bar and restaurant, popular with students and close to *Savignyplatz*. **Jodelkeller**, *Adalbertstr 81*, is an old hippie-biker hangout in Kreuzberg. Guinness fans head for **James Joyce Tavern**, *Joachim-Friedrich-Str 30*, and Irish bar with porter, whiskey, darts and Irish music. **Kumpelnest 3000**, *Lutzowstr. 23*, near the Tiergarten, is another good late-night bet, open until 0500 and attracting a very wide mix of drinkers.

### Embassies and Consulates
**Australia**: *Kempinski Plaza, Uhlandstr.181–3; tel: (030) 88 00 880.*
**Canada**: *IHZ Building, Friedrichstr.95; tel: (030) 261 1161.*
**New Zealand**: *Bundeskanzlerplatz 2–10, Bonn; tel: (030) 228 070.*
**UK**: *Unter den Linden 32–34; tel: (030) 201 840.*
**USA**: *Neustadtische Kirchstr; tel: (030) 238 5174.*

### ENTERTAINMENT
Berlin has a well-deserved reputation for diverse and non-stop entertainment, from opera, theatre and film to club-land and rock. There are several listings magazines: *Zitty and Tip*, available from newsagents for about DM4. For listings in English, try the Tourist Office monthly *Check Point* or the quarterly overview magazine *Berlin berlin*, DM3.50. *Oranienstr.*, in the Kreuzberg district, is the heart of a busy club and music bar scene; current favourites include **Schnabel-Bar, Alibi, J-Bar, Lola** and the **Cosmopolitan Club**, with a 600 sq. m. dancefloor. **A-Trane Jazzclub**, *Bleibtreustr 1*, is an elegant jazz club; live music starts around 2200. **Bar jeder Vernunft**, *Scaperstr 24*, is a dance club with Art Nouveau decor;

**Knaack Club**, *Greifswalderstr 224*, has two discos, a concert hall and five giant pool tables and plays dance music all night, every night. **Quasimodo**, *Kantstr.12*, is a live jazz, funk and blues venue which attracts the occasional celebrity jam.

### SHOPPING
Berlin is not one of Europe's great shopping bargains. West Berlin's Cold War-era taste for total ostentation has been reinforced by the even more status-conscious attitudes of newly-rich easterners. Those not equipped with D-marks, Swiss francs or Japanese yen will find prices startlingly high.

The West still has greater variety and hosts Berlin's chief shopping boulevard **Kurfürstendamm**, 3 km of boutiques and cafés. *Fasanenstr.* has designer shops, while Kreuzberg, the centre of alternative Berlin, revels in cheap ethnic and trendy clothing and jewellery. The main street for records, second-hand clothes and cafés here is *Oranien-str.*

At the other end of the shopping spectrum, the giant **KaDeWe** department store on Wittenberg-platz is the ultimate temple of Berlin's consumer society. Away from the centre, each of Berlin's 23 districts has its own shopping areas, such as *Schonhauser Allee*, in *Prenzlauer Berg*; and *Wilmersdorfer Str.* in *Charlottenburg*.

For flea market (*Flohmarkt*) shopping, try the **Trodelmarkts** at *Str. des 17. Juni* (Sat and Sun; S-bahn: *Tiergarten*), and *Charlottenburg*, **Ku'-damm-Karree**, (daily, except Tues). **Winterfeld-platz** is the central food market (Wed and Sat, 0800–1400; U-Bahn: *Zoo*).

### SIGHTSEEING
Zoo Bahnhof is central for sightseeing in the west. From here the **Charlottenburg Schloss** (U-Bahn: *Sophie Charlotte Platz*)

lies two S-bahn stops south-west in the district of the same name.

## Charlottenburg

**Schloss Charlottenburg**, *Schlossgarten* (entrance opposite corner of *Schloss-str* and *Spandauer Damm*) was built between 1695 and 1699 by Frederick I (immortalised in the statue in the Court of Honour) as a summer retreat for Princess Sophie Charlotte, later his queen. The palace, a fine example of the baroque style, has beautiful, geometrically-landscaped gardens and museums with impressive Egyptian and antique collections.

## Ku'damm

Running roughly westward from the Zoo intersection, 3 km-long **Kurfursten-damm** is lined with bland shops, restaurants, cafés and cinemas at its eastern end but after a few blocks turns into a dull and soulless traffic artery. With the fall of the wall, the *Ku'damm* – as Berliners call it – is gradually losing some of its importance as the western city's most prestigious street. Opposite Zoo Bhf is the **Gedachtnis-kirche** (Kaiser Wilhelm Memorial Church), its maimed and gaping tower left unrepaired in memory of World War II.

Next to this is the neon-covered **Europa Centre**, a bland shopping mall. *Budapester Str.* leads past the observation tower in the Europa Centre to the **Zoologischer Garten** (zoo) and **Tiergarten**. This was the former hunting ground of the kings of Prussia and one of the oldest parts of Berlin. In the middle of the wooded parkland stands the **Siegessaule**, a 67 m column built to celebrate 19th-century Prussian victories over Denmark (1864), Austria (1866) and France (1870–71). Worth climbing for the view.

To the west is **Schloss Bellevue**, residence of the Federal President, and to the east the 1960s Kongresshalle.

## The Great Divide

All that remains of **Checkpoint Charlie**, the **Berlin Wall** crossing point featured in a hundred spy stories, is a swathe of rubble-strewn waste land and the nearby **Checkpoint Charlie Museum**, which tells the story of the many ingenious, desperate and only sometimes successful attempts to flee the GDR into West Berlin. In all, 75 would-be escapees were shot trying to cross the 3 m-high wall and its perimeter of traps, wires, searchlights and alarms.

The towering **Brandenburg Gate**, *Pariser Platz*, which stands between *Str. den 17 juni* (the date in 1953 when 200–400 anti-Soviet protestors were shot) and **Unter den Linden**, was built in 1788-91 as a triumphal arch for Prussia's victorious armies. The current gate is a post-war copy of architect Carl Gotthard von Langhans' building, which was itself an interpretation of the Propylaia of the Acropolis in Athens. Closed by the building of the Wall, it became a symbol of the divided Germany and was reopened in Dec 1989. An even more powerful symbol stands just to the north: the **Reichstag**. Built in 1871 to house the imperial parliament, it is still pocked with the bullets of the Red Army's final push on Berlin. It was the scene of the ushering-in of a new era when the new German parliament met for the first time in 1990, and will again become the seat of parliament for a reunited Germany in 2000.

## Unter den Linden

The spine of pre-war Berlin, this is still an impressive broad boulevard flanked by monumental public buildings, almost all of which needed restoration after World War

**99**

II. During the Cold War, it became the focal point of the Eastern sector but at the same time a cul-de-sac ending in the Brandenburg Gate and the Wall. With reunification, it is rapidly becoming once again Berlin's most important street, flanked by smart shops, government buildings, and the offices of international corporations. Behind the **Deutsche Staatsoper** (opera house) stands the Catholic Cathedral of **St. Hedwig** (founded in 1809). Further along, **Humboldt University** numbers Einstein, Marx and Engels amongst its more famous alumni.

The **Baroque Zeughaus** (Arsenal), one of the most visually impressive buildings on the street, now houses the Museum of German History. Since reunification, the museum's Marxist and pro-Soviet outlook has been revised yet again to reflect the new capitalist orthodoxy. Also look out for the **Deutsche Staatsbibliothek** (library) and the **Kronprinzen Palais**.

### Nikolaiviertel (Nikolai quarter)

The oldest streets in the city cluster by the riverside around the restored 13th-century twin-towered **Nikolaikirche**, *Nikolaikirchplatz*, Berlin's oldest building, which now houses the **Brandeburg March Museum**. The tiny district's sense of age is a cunning illusion, as the entire quarter was reconstructed from scratch in the mid-1980s, one of the last positive achievements of the socialist East. The **Knoblauchhaus**, *Postr.*, houses a wine bar and a small museum of 19th-century life. The quarter is packed with bars and cafés.

### Museuminsel

'Museum Island', on the River Spree, houses several excellent museums, which together have (but do not display) some

1.2 million works of art. The most famous is the **Pergamon Museum**, one of Europe's best collections of antiquities, including Egyptian and Byzantine art. The museum's proudest possession is the 2175 year old Pergamon altar; other treasures include the bust of Nefertiti and the astonishing Processional Way from Babylon. The **Bode Museum**, *Monbijoubrucke*, in the north-west corner, houses early Christian art, Egyptian works and 15th–18th century paintings. The **Nationalgalerie** is strong on 20th-century art and particularly the Expressionists, including work from the Brucke and Blaue Reiter schools. There is also a 19th-century collection.

From here take the **Rathausbrucke**, past the **Berliner Dom** and the **Palast der Republik** to *Rathausstr.* The Rotes Rathaus (Red Town Hall, so called on account of its bricks), leads to the base of the Fernsehturm. This 365 m spike, piercing a globe-shaped revolving restaurant and viewing gallery at 200 m, can be seen from all over the city. Built under the communist regime, it was nicknamed the 'Pope's Revenge' – sunlight reflecting from the silvered globe forms a giant cross, anathema in the atheist DDR.

### Berliner Grunewald

West of the city centre, the Berliner Grunewald (S-Bahn: *Grunewald*) is a vast expanse of parkland with the Havel forming a wide lake on its western edge. The Teufelsberg, its highest point, is 120 m-high landmark. In the 17th and 18th centuries it was a royal hunting preserve. The Jagdschloss (hunting lodge) beside the Grunewaldsee (close to the junction of Koenigsallee and Huttenweg) is a relic of those times, begun in 1542 for the Elector Joachim II of Brandeburg and frequently altered by his successors in the following centuries. Gothic in style, its Renaissance grand hall has a lovely panelled ceiling and some fine paintings are on display.

## Wannsee

The Wannsee, a large lake formed by the River Havel, is a popular weekend getaway for Berliners especially in summer. It is a pleasant place for a picnic, and Schloss Pfaueninsel, *Pfaueninselchaussee*, in landscaped grounds on an island in the lake, is well worth visiting. More a folly than a real castle, is a quaint building designed in imitation of a romantic Italian ruin and built as a summer residence for King Friedrich Wilhelm II between 1794 and 1797. (S-bahn: *Wannsee*, then bus nos. 216 or 316).

## Kopenick

**Schloss Kopenick**, Schlossinsel (Castle Island), Berlin-Kopenick, is a striking baroque building dating from 1677 and built on the site of earlier 16th- and 9th-century hunting lodges. It has an attractive stucco interior and houses the **Museum of Arts and Crafts**.

### SIDE TRACKS FROM BERLIN

### BABELSBERG

Germany's answer to Hollywood lies on the southern outskirts of the city. The Babelsberg film studios, *Grossbeerenstr.* (S-bahn: *Babelsberg*, bus nos. 690 or 691, or Regionalbahn to Drewitz Bhf) made their first film in 1912 and quickly became Europe's largest studio complex. Many of the famous actors and directors who later ended up in 1930–40s Hollywood – Marlene Dietrich, Billy Wilder, Erich von Stroheim and Fritz Lang among them – began their careers here. Home of the Defa production company, which made 1300 films – 700 of them under the DDR regime – Babelsberg is enjoying a new lease of life, attracting Hollywood names like Gerard Depardieu and Nick Nolte. Do not be put off by the unprepossessing exterior, inside are film sets imitating medieval markets, pirate caves, and paradise islands, together with the largest collection of film props in the world. You can visit the editing and props rooms and even have yourself made up with the shocking cosmetics of your choice.

### POTSDAM

**Tourist Office**: *Touristenzentrale, Freidrich-Elbert-Str.5; tel: (0331) 21 100,* open Mon–Fri 1000–1800, Sat–Sun 1100–1500.

Potsdam is a purpose-built fantasy of landscaped gardens and palaces, 30 km south-west of Berlin (easily reached by S-bahn or rail from Zoo, Hbf or *Friedrichstr.*, journey time about 20 mins). Founded in 993, the town came into its own from the late 17th century, when it became the seat of the Hohenzollern kings, who welcomed exiled Protestants of talent from all over Europe. Its architectural treasures – most of them dating from the 18th century - have earned it World Heritage Site status. The best feature is the 12-roomed Rococo **Sanssouci Palace** (1745–47) set in the huge Park Sanssouci. A leisurely walk through the park reveals the Chinese Tea House (1754–7), the pagoda-like Drachenhaus, Schloss Charlottenhof, and the Romische Bader (Roman Baths) (both early 19th century). There are more delightful 17th century buildings in the town itself and on the other side of the Havel River, in Babelsberg Park. ⟰

101

# BERLIN–DRESDEN

The route loops through the most historically and architecturally interesting towns and cities of eastern Germany, ending up at Dresden, the most beautiful city in Saxony. For much of the way the scenery is unexciting, but there are a number of interesting Side Tracks, including a foray into the Harz Mountains.

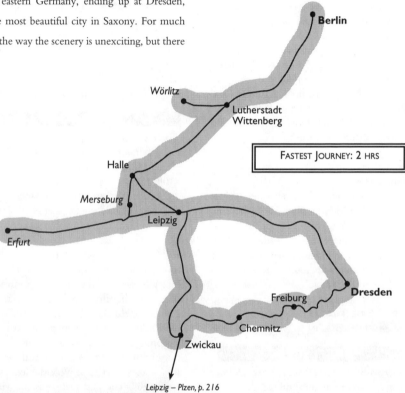

Berlin

Wörlitz

Lutherstadt
Wittenberg

FASTEST JOURNEY: 2 HRS

Halle

Merseburg

Leipzig

Erfurt

Freiburg    Dresden

Chemnitz

Zwickau

Leipzig – Plzen, p. 216

## TRAINS

### FAST TRACK

➡️ Most trains for Dresden and points on this route leave from Berlin-Lichtenberg Hbf. A train every 2 hrs with catering services and a supplement payable takes the direct route, 2 hrs. This service is expected to be increased to hourly during the winter of 1996/7.

## ON TRACK

### Berlin–Lutherstadt Wittenberg–Halle

Trains run every 2 hrs and take 75 mins between Berlin and Lutherstadt and 50 mins between Lutherstadt and Halle.

### Halle–Leipzig

A very frequent service, journey 30 mins.

## Leipzig–Dresden

An hourly service taking 1 hr 30 mins. InterCity trains have dining cars but require supplements.

## Leipzig–Chemnitz

A train every hours taking 1 hr 25 mins.

## Chemnitz–Freiberg–Dresden

An hourly service with all trains calling at Freiberg. Chemnitz to Freiberg takes 70 mins, Freiberg to Dresden 35 mins.

## LUTHERSTADT WITTENBERG

**Station: Hbf**; *tel: (03491) 2406.*
**Tourist Office**: *Collegienstr. 29; tel: (03491) 2239 or 2537* open Mon–Fri 0900–1800 (1700 Nov–Mar), Sat–Sun 1000–1400.

### ACCOMMODATION AND FOOD

**HI** is in the **Residenzschloss**, *Schloss Str.; tel: (03491) 3255.* Private rooms can be booked through the tourist office; *tel: (03491) 414848.* Bed and breakfast accommodation includes **Frühstück-pension An der Stadkirche**, *Mittelstr. 7; tel: (03491) 410871;* mid-priced accommodation on the edge of town includes the **Hohe Muhle**, a century-old inn, *Wittenbergerstr. 10, Reinsdorf b. Wittenberg; tel: (03491) 50066;* **Waldhotel Vogel**, *Tonmark 10; tel: (03491) 51137.*

The century-old **Rattschanke**, *Markt 14,* is a traditional cellar restaurant with a fine reputation for fish dishes. By Wittenberg's river harbour, **Zum Schiffchen**, *An der Elbe 6,* has a pleasant terrace (summer only).

### SIGHTSEEING

Wittenberg's place in history was assured when in 1517 the theologian and church reformer Martin Luther, who held the chair at its university, began his intellectual assault on the corrupt values of the Catholic Church by nailing his 95 theses to the door of the castle church. Luther enjoyed the protection of the Elector Frederick the Wise of Saxony. The DDR government dubbed the city Lutherstadt Wittenberg when seeking a better relationship with the Lutheran Church in the 1970s and 80s.

Start your tour of the city on the main street, *Collegienstr.* The **Lutherhalle**, *Collegienstr. 54,* was first an Augustinian monastery, then Luther's residence. Its history is explained in a small exhibition, and there is also an exhibit on Lucas Cranach the Elder, Frederick the Wise's court painter, who was also a prominent political figure in Reformation-era Wittenberg and a friend of Luther's. The building is now part of the Augusteum, part of the original 16th-century **University**.

The **Luthereiche** (Luther Oak) at the east end of *Collegienstr.* marks the spot where Luther set the Reformation irrevocably in motion by burning the papal bull demanding that he recant or face excommunication. The **Melancthonhaus**, *Collegienstr. 60,* home of Luther's fellow-reformer Philipp Schwarzerd (known by the classical Greek form of his name, Melancthon), contains a historical collection. Melancthon's apartments have been artfully restored.

Statues of Luther and Melancthon stand in front of the **Rathaus** (Town Hall), *Marktpl..* The motto on one side of Luther's plinth reads 'Believe in the gospel' while on the other is inscribed the first verse of his most famous hymn 'Ein feste Burg ist unser Gott' ('A mighty fortress is our God'). The Rathaus, begun in 1522 and completed more than half a century later (its Renaissance main door is dated 1573) is a combination of Renaissance and Gothic styles and is surmounted by a statue representing Justice. Also on the *Marktpl.* are a handful of Renaissance townhouses, one of which was the birthplace in 1515 of the painter Lucas Cranach the Younger; a plaque marks it. The **Marienkirche** (St Mary's), *Kirchpl.*, stands next to the *Marktpl.*, which is overlooked by its two eight-sided towers. The church was completed in 1470. The altarpiece and reredos painted by Lucas Cranach the Elder portray Luther, Melancthon, and scenes from the Gospels. More paintings on religious themes by both Cranach and his son adorn the interior of the church.

Wittenberg's other sights include the **Residenzschloss** and the **Schlosskirche** (castle church), both on *Schloss Str.* The massive bronze portals of the Schlosskirche are engraved with Luther's 95 theses. The original church and its wooden doors were destroyed by the French in 1760 during the Seven Years War, and the present building with its round tower and crown-like spire dates from the late 19th century. Climb the 289 steps for a fine view of the Elbe valley. The Residenzschloss was built for Luther's patron Frederick the Wise (whose bronze mausoleum, topped by a sword-wielding bronze, is in the Schlosskirche), and now houses Wittenberg's small natural history museum.

### OUT OF TOWN

**Worlitz**, 19 km west of Wittenburg (buses from Wittenberg Hbf) is an outstandingly pretty village built around a series of lakes. Its most delightful feature is the **Schlosspark**, with a perfectly-preserved white castle, a decorative Gothic palace, and an enormous landscaped garden. **Tourist Office**: *Neuer Wall 103; tel: (034905) 20216*, Apr–Oct Mon–Fri 0900–1800, Sat–Sun 0900–1200, (Nov–Mar: Mon–Wed and Fri only).

### HALLE

**Station**: Hbf; *tel: (0345) 2027765.*
**Tourist Office**: In the *Roter Turm, Markpl. 1; tel: (0345) 2023340*, Mon, Tues, Thur and Fri 0900–1800, Wed 1000–1800, Sat 0900–1300, Sun (Apr–Sept only) 1000–1400. To get to the tourist office, turn left out of the station forecourt and walk through pedestrian tunnels and the pedestrianised *Leipzigerstr.* for 900 metres to the *Alter Markt*, centre of the old town. The wide range of free publications includes a German-language entertainment and listings magazine, *Halle Blitz.* Bus, tram and S-Bahn network maps are available from the tourist office. Historic sights are concentrated around the Markt, within 1 km of Hbf.

### ACCOMMODATION AND FOOD

Chains include *Ma.* **HI** is at *August Bebel Str. 48A; tel: 03451 24716.* Tourist office reservations; *tel: (0345) 2028371, fax (0345) 502738.* Mid-priced accommodation in and near the centre includes **Pension Am Alten Markt**, *Schmeerstr. 3; tel: (0345) 2025636*, the most centrally located beds in town; **Pension Am Krahenberg**, *Am Krahenberg; tel: (0345) 2026714*; **Pension Ammendorf**, *Georgi Dimitroffstr. 7-8; tel: (0345) 77995*; **Pension Giebichenstein**, *Burgstr. 11; tel: (0345) 2029103*; **Pension Hause**, *Burgstr. 70; tel: (0345) 2021004.* Private rooms can be booked through the tourist office accommodation service; *tel: (0345) 2028371.* A list of cheaper accommodation is also available from the DB information desk in the Hbf. **HI**: *August Bebel Str. 48a; tel: (0345) 2024716.* Church hostel accommodation also at **Villa Juhling**, *Evangelische Kugendbildungsstatte, Semmelweisstr. 6; tel: (0345) 5511699.*

**Gildenhaus St Nikolaus**, *Grosse Nikolaistr. 9-11*, is a traditional Halle restaurant in an historic building; **Dompfaff**, *Dompl. 5*, has a huge open-air terrace with a long wine list and regional specialities; **Alter Zollkeller**, *Ankerstr. 2*, is a cavernous cellar-restaurant.

## SIGHTSEEING

Halle is the largest city in the state of Saxony-Anhalt, with an inner core of attractive restored buildings. To reach the inner city turn left out of Hbf and follow pedestrianised *Leipzig Str.* to the *Marktpl.*. Dominated on one side by the stark modern **Ratshof**, this historic square is worth the walk, with a colourful weekday market selling all sorts of produce. A statue of the composer George Frederick Handel (1685-1759), erected on the centenary of his death, stands in the square, close to the **Roter Turm** (Red Tower), a Gothic church tower which now houses the tourist office. Around the square stand the **Hausmannsturme** and the **Blaue Turme**, relics of two 13th-century churches demolished in 1529 to make way for the **Marktkirche Unser Lieben Frauen**, the church which now connects them. The **Marktschlosschen**, *Marktpl. 13*, is a miniature palace containing a collection of musical instruments and a small art gallery.

Music lovers should head for the **Handel-Haus**, *Grosse Nikolai Str.* The composer's birthplace houses a collection relating to his life and work as well as recordings of his best known compositions, which are also performed at the annual **Handel Music Festival** each June. The **Dom** (cathedral), *Dompl.*, is a blend of architectural styles; in the first half of the 16th century the original Dominican monastery was converted into a cathedral, and following the Reformation, the building was again remodelled in baroque style. The **Moritzburg**, north of the Dom, was a 15th-century bishop's palace and now houses the **Staatliche Galerie**, with a good collection of Expressionist paintings.

**Burg Giebichstein** (tram no. 8 from *Marktpl.*) is a complex of castle ruins overlooking the Saale River, north of the city centre. The **Unterburg**, sacked during the Thirty Years War, was rebuilt in the late 17th century in baroque style and now houses an art college, while above it the earlier Oberburg is a picturesque ruin in the best Romantic tradition.

**SIDE TRACKS FROM HALLE**

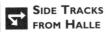

**HARZ MOUNTAIN RAILWAY**

The **Harzer Schmalspur Bahnen**, a network of narrow-gauge steam railways, connects the small towns of the Harz Mountains. Steam trains hauled by powerful 2-10-2 tank engines have served the Harzquerbahn route between **Nordhausen Nord** (about 1 hr from Leipzig or Halle Hbfs) and **Wernigerode** (about 90 mins from Berlin Zoo Hbf) since 1897 and scheduled steam services still operate all year round. The 60 km trip takes about three hours and the wooded mountain scenery of the Harz makes a welcome change from the flat farmland of much of Saxony. You can also connect at **Eisfelder Talmuhle**, about an hour from Nordhausen, with the Selketalbahn narrow-gauge steam line to **Gernrode** and at **Drei Annen Hohe**, 2 hrs out of Nordhausen, with the Brockenbahn, where steam engines take 50 mins to chug to the highest narrow-gauge station in Germany, at 1125 metres above sea level. There is a splendid view of the **Hochharz**

National **Park** from the **Brocken** summit, which until 1992 was a sealed military area.

Harzquerbahn trains leave from their own station opposite Nordhausen Nord Bf; *tel: (03631) 628151.* There are three departures daily for Wernigerode and four additional trains terminating at Drei Annen Hohe.

**Harzer Schmalspuren GmbH,** *Forkestr. 17, 38855 Wernigerode; tel: (03943) 588143, fax: (03943) 32107.*

## MERSEBURG

Virtually a suburb of Halle (14 km from the city centre), Merseburg has its own station and can also be reached by tram no. 5 from Halle *Marktplatz.* It is prettily sited on the Saale river and its cathedral and castle, **Schloss Merseburg,** are worth a short detour from the direct route between Halle and Leipzig. The **Dom** (cathedral), *Dompl.,* holds traces of an 11th-century Romanesque predecssor and was rebuilt in the 13th and 16th centuries in elegant Gothic. Within is a noteworthy collection of tombs of several local counts and bishops and a Romanesque chapel. The Schloss, next to the cathedral, was built and added to between 1483 and 1665. It embodies Renaissance, Gothic and baroque elements. Also worth seeing are the 15th–16th century Renaissance **Rathaus,** *Marktplatz,* and the neighbouring churches of **St Maxim** and **St Thomas.**

## ERFURT

**Station: Hbf,** *Bahnhofstr.; tel: (0361) 19419,* is at the south-eastern corner of the centre. Erfurt is about 90 mins from Halle or Leipzig Hbf.

**Tourist Office:** *Bahnhofstr. 37; tel:*

*(0361) 26267.* Open Mon–Fri 0900–1800 and Sat 1000–1500. *Krämerbrücke 3; tel: (0361) 23436.* Open Mon–Fri 0900–1230 and 1330–1700, and Sat–Sun 0900–1100.

### ACCOMMODATION

The few hotels are usually booked well in advance, but private rooms are often available. **Zimmervermittlung Brigitte Scheel,** *Paulinzeller Weg 23; tel: (0361) 41 38 38,* offer a 24-hour telephone booking service. **HI:** *Hochheimerstr. 12; tel: (0361) 26705,* south of the centre (tram nos 5/51). Reasonably priced hotels, when available, include **Landhotel Burgenblick,** *Am Zwetschgenberg 1; tel: (036202) 81111* and **Hotel Gasthaus zu Melchendorf,** *Haarbergstr. 2; tel: (0361) 41 62 03.*

### SIGHTSEEING

The stylish Thuringian capital dates from the 8th century and much of it survived the Allied bombs. **Peterskirche,** once a magnificent Romanesque structure, dominates **Petersberg,** the larger of two hills to the west of the Altstadt, but the main attraction now is the view of the city. The smaller hill, **Domhügel,** is reached by monumental steps from *Dompl..* The **Dom** (cathedral) was founded in the 8th century, but took several centuries to complete. Parts are Romanesque, but most of it is Gothic. It is noted for Gloriosa, one of the world's largest bells, High Gothic choir stalls, 15th-century stained glass and an enormous hall. The distinctive triple-towered **Severikirche,** alongside, has a five-aisled nave, creating a false impression of size. The treasures include the fine pink sandstone sarcophagus of St Severus, an alabaster relief of St Michael and a

15th-century font. The *Altstadt* is a rewarding place to stroll, almost every street being lined with superb buildings. **Fischmarkt** contrasts the Renaissance **Zum Breiten Herd** with the classically balanced **Zum Roten Ochsen** and the 19th-century **Rathaus**, noted for its interior Romantic frescos with Thuringian themes.

Just south, **Prederigerkirche** has a plain façade that belies the gloriously intact Gothic interior. A magnificent Annunciation adorns the rood screen and the stained glass has floral motifs. On the other side of Fischmarkt is **Krämerbrücke**, a medieval bridge lined with 33 half-timbered shops that looks more like a medieval alley than a bridge: it's best appreciated from the waterside. Just east of the *Altstadt* is **Volkskunde**, a folklore museum.

In the 15th century, Erfurt was noted for its retables and a superb example can be seen in **Reglerkirche**, *Bahnhofstr.* To the north, in a Baroque palace, is **Angermuseum**, covering the decorative arts through the centuries.

**Cyriaksburg**, a castle south-west of the centre (bus no. 2), houses a museum tracing the history of gardening and is set in large grounds that host a permanent garden show, **Internationale Gartenbauaustellung** (Iga).

## WEIMAR

**Station:** Hbf; *tel: (03643) 19419*, is 10 mins walk north of the centre (bus no. 4). Leipzig is about 1 hr away.

**Tourist Office:** *Marktstr. 4; tel: (03643) 2173*. Open Mon 1000–1800, Tue–Fri 0900–1800, Sat 0900–1300.

The area of interest is concentrated in Altstadt and easily walkable.

Hotel rooms are in short supply, but the tourist office can arrange private rooms, as can **Werse & Reiseshop**, *Kleine Kirchgasse 3; tel: (03643) 3642*. **HI:** *Carl-August-Allee 13; tel: (03643) 2076*, 2 mins from Hbf; and *Zum Wilden Graben 12; tel: (03643) 3471*.

### SIGHTSEEING

Although it's of no great size, Weimar represents all that is best and worst in Germany. The entire *Altstadt* has been listed as a historical monument, steeped in the greatest of German culture, while, outside the town, the Buchenwald concentration camp represents the true horrors of the Nazi regime.

The largely neo-classical **Schloss**, *Burgpl. 4*, houses a vast collection, including Dürer's *Hans and Elspeth Tucher* and outstanding 16th-century Cranach paintings. The Gothic **Stadtkirche St Peter und Paul**, *Herderpl.*, contains a large triptych: either Lucas Cranach's last work or executed by Lucas Cranach junior (one of three painter sons) as a memorial to his father. Opposite the neo-Gothic **Rathaus** (Town Hall) in *Marktpl.* is the eye-catching gabled **Cranachhaus**, where Cranach the Elder spent his last years, while **Bachstube** was where Bach lived during his stint as leader of the court orchestra.

Germany's two greatest writers both lived in Weimar. Schiller spent the last three years of his life at **Schillerhaus**, *Schillerstr.*, and his rooms are much as they were then, with drafts and early editions of his works. The nearby *Theaterpl.* features a monument to Schiller and Goethe, both of whose works were first performed in the Deutsches Nationaltheater. **Goethehaus**, *Frauenplan 1*, is in two parts, one a museum devoted to the author, the

107

other an evocative baroque mansion where he lived for some 50 years. **Goethepark**, to the east of the centre, contains the simple **Gartenhaus**, which was Goethe's first home in Weimar and later became his retreat. It contains a selection of his possessions and drawings. At the western edge of the park, the **Liszthaus** is the beautifully maintained residence of the Austro-Hungarian composer, who moved to Weimar in 1848 to direct the local orchestra for 11 years. He later returned, to spend the last 17 summers of his life at the house. His piano and some scores are among the exhibits.

The grim site of **Buchenwald** is a few km north of Weimar town centre and is marked by a huge tower commemorating the 65,000 who died here under the Nazis. Tours to the site are organised by the Tourist Office. 🔼

## LEIPZIG

See p. 213.

## ROCHSBURG

**Station:** *tel: (030) 19419.*

**Schloss Rochsburg**, *09322 Rochburg; tel: (037383) 703,* open year-round, Tues–Sun, 0900–1530. There is an **HI** hostel within the castle.

The late 12th-century fortress was rebuilt in 1470 by Arnold of Westphalia.Standing above the River Mulde, it contains and a museum filled with fine 18th- and 19th-century works of art and furniture. The elaborate late Gothic tracery vaulting of the chapel was the work of Kaspar Kraft and the sandstone Renaissance altar was added by Andreas Lorenz in 1576.

## CHEMNITZ

**Station: Hbf**, *tel: (0371) 471 0600.*

**Tourist Office:** *Strasse der Nationen 3; tel: (0371) 62051.*

Chemnitz is a stolid industrial town. Partly levelled during World War II, it was rebuilt in the worst style of DDR urban architecture. The sole surviving traditional buildings are around the *Markt*, where you will find the white-painted Renaissance **Altes Rathaus** and its century-old successor, the **Neues Rathaus**. Next to it stands the **Jakobikirche**, with an elegant Jugendstil facade added at the turn of the century. A reminder of Chemnitz's days as Karl-Marx-Stadt – it was renamed in honour of the author of the Communist manifesto in 1953 and reverted to its older name in 1990 – is the massive bronze bust of Marx at the corner of *Brückenstrasse* and *Strasse der Nationen*.

## FREIBERG

**Station: Hbf**, *Bahnhofstr; tel: (03731) 23602,* 2 km from Altstadt centre.
**Tourist Office:** *Burgstr. 1; tel: (03731) 23602.* Midway between Chemnitz and Dresden, Freiberg was founded as a silver-mining centre and its historic centre – for once unscathed by war damage – was extensively restored during the 1970s and 80s. Walk along *Burgstrasse*, with several splendid Renaissance mansions, to the centre of the old town, the **Obermarkt**. On its east side is a Gothic **Rathaus**. Opposite stands a contemporary church, the **Petrikirche**. However, Freiberg's greatest jewel is the cathedral, **Dom** or **Marienkirche**. Unimpressive on the outside, it conceals a gorgeous interior, of which the most striking features are the 13th-century Goldene Pforte (Golden Portal) and the Tulpenkanzel (Tulip Pulpit) with its allegorical figures. Within the church is the sepulchre of the Electors of Wettin, dominated by the sarcophagus of the Elector Moritz.

# BERLIN–SASSNITZ

This route runs north from Berlin to the Baltic, passing through attractive rural scenery which is more varied than much of Germany's farmland. On either side are the rivers and lakelands of Mecklenburg-Pomerania and stops include several pretty towns. At the end of the line is Germany's largest island.

FASTEST JOURNEY: **4** HRS **30** MINS

## TRAINS

**ETT Tables: 669, 676**

### FAST TRACK

→ Three through trains a day but a service every two hours is available by changing trains in Stralsund. The journey takes 4 hrs 30 mins.

### ON TRACK

**Berlin–Neustrelitz**
A regular service operates between Berlin and Neustrelitz, a 75- min journey, with most trains calling at Oranienburg and Fürstenburg.

**Neustrelitz–Neubrandenburg**
A train every two hours taking 30 mins.

**Neubrandenburg–Stralsund**
Approximately every two hours with journey times of 1 hr 30 mins.

**Stralsund–Sassnitz**
Frequent service taking 1 hr.

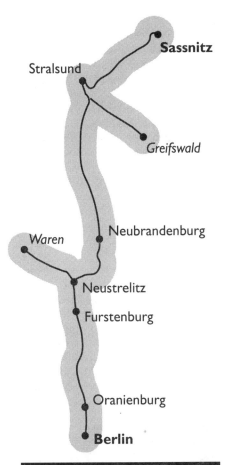

**109**

## NEUSTRELITZ

**Station**: Hbf; tel: *(03981) 580.*
**Tourist Office**, *Markt 1; tel: (03981) 253119*, May–Sept Mon–Fri 0900–12200 and 1300–1700, Sat 100–1300; Oct–Apr Mon–Fri 0900–1200, 1300–1630.
  Private rooms can be found through the tourist office and: **Joachim Ahnsehl**, *Fürstenbergerstr 55, Strelitz-Alt; tel: (03981) 7348;* **Hans-Jochen Brentfuhrer**,

## Sachsenhausen and Ravensbruck

The sites of these two concentration camps lie along this route. Sachsenhausen is signposted from the station at Oranienburg (30 mins S-Bahn from Berlin), and Ravensbruck from the station at Fürstenburg 15 ,mins on by rail from Oranienburg. The walls, barbed wire, prison barracks and torture chambers of Sachsenhausen are preserved as a horrible reminder of what humanity is capable of. Ravensbruck's Wall of Nations lists the countries from which its victims were brought to be murdered.

*Schulstr 2, Strelitz Alt; tel: (03981) 44 34 25*; **Norbert Heller**, *Wesenbergerstr 38, Strelitz-Alt; tel: (039810 20 41 64*; **Gabriele Koch**, *Fürstenberger Str 5, Strelitz Alt; tel: (03981) 7717*; **Erhart Weber**, *Furstenseer Landstr 4, Strelitz Alt; tel: (03981) 2986*. There are several pleasant cafés and beer gardens in the town.

Neustrelitz's main attraction is the **Schlossgarten**, an 18th-century landscaped park laid out on the shore of the **Zierke See**, with a collection of rather kitsch baroque statuary and fountains.

### ⮌ SIDE TRACK FROM NEUSTRELITZ

### WAREN

Waren (approx 45 km/1 hr by rail), founded in the 13th century, is an attractive little town with many surviving or restored half-timbered buildings, standing on the shore of the 116 sq km **Muritzsee**, eastern Germany's largest lake. The Muritzsee is ringed by a 450,000 hectare forest, part of which, the Damerow **nature reserve**, shelters

a herd of rare European bison and a number of endangered bird species. **Weisse Flotte** (White Fleet) cruisers sail on the lake and surrounding rivers and **canoes** and **sailing dinghies** can be hired. **Tourist office**: *Kiezstr 13a; tel: (03991) 16 80 14.* ⮌

### NEUBRANDENBURG

**Station**: Hbf; is just outside the city walls. **Tourist Office**, *2 Ringstr, Wiekhaus no 21; tel: (0395) 44 23 18*, Mon–Fri 0800–1600, is 250 m from Hbf, signposted on the right just before the 14th-century **Johanniskirche**; and *Turmstr 11; tel: (0395) 582 22 67*, Apr–Sept Mon–Fri 0900–1800, (Oct–Mar 1000–1700) Sat 0900–1200.

Private rooms bookable through tourist office. **HI**, *Ihlenfelderstr 73; tel: (0395) 4225801*, 1 km from Hbf, bus no. 7. Mid–range: **Hotel Weinert Garni**, *23 Ziegelbergstr; tel: (0395) 581230*, just outside the old town (550 m from **Neues Tor**); **Harmonika Herberge**, *Katharinenstr 10; tel: (0395) 581670*. More expensive, just outside the Neues Tor, **Hotel CTK**, *Grosse Krauthoferstr 1; tel: (0395) 5560*. For refeshment, try **Torcafe** in Friedlander Tor,. **Cafe im Reuterhaus**, *Stargarderstr 35* in the 19th-century home of poet Fritz Reuter, or **Ums Eck**, *Turmstr 28*.

Ringed by painstakingly restored medieval walls, Neubrandenburg's old inner city is known, accurately enough, as the 'City of the Four Gates'. The best way to see these is to walk the 2.3 km circuit of the walls anticlockwise from the **Johanniskirche**, stopping at the tourist office en route. The first of the four gates is the **Treptower Tor**, now housing the city museum. Next is the **Stargarder Tor**, close to which is the massive 13th-century **Marienkirche**. The **Neues Tor**, at the opposite end of *Pfaffenstr* from the church, is the least impressive of the town gates, but the **Friedlander Tor**, your last stop before returning to Hbf, has a complex of fortifications. For a breath of fresh air, duck through the Treptower Tor, cross the ring road and follow *Promenade am Oberbach*, the canalside walk and cycle path, past a series of bright-painted boathouses to the **Tollensesee**, a huge lake surrounded by woodland with marked hiking trails.

## STRALSUND

**Station: Hbf;** *tel: (030) 19419*, approximately 1 km from the Innenstadt.
**Tourist Office: Ostee-Tours Zentrale Zimmerborse**; at Hbf, Mon–Fri 0900–1800, Sat 0900–1200, and at *Ossenreyerstr 23; tel: (0381) 29 38 94*, handles hotel, guesthouse and bed and breakfast bookings in Stralsund and on Rugen and offers an information service.

### ACCOMMODATION AND FOOD

Beds in the Innenstadt are more expensive and hard to find in summer and at weekends; book in advance through Zentrale Zimmerborse. There are two **HI: Jugendherberge Stralsund**, centrally located at *Am Kutertor 1; tel: (03831) 29 21 60* and less centrally at **Jugendherberge Stralsund-Devin**, *Strandstr 21; tel: (03831) 27 03 58*. Cheap rooms within 10 mins walk of the centre are available through the Zimmerborse.

If you can afford it, stay on board the luxury ship-hotel, the **Good-Morning-Hotel Astoria**, anchored in the harbour with a fine view of the waterfront at *An der Fahrbrucke Kai 1; tel: (03831) 28 01 10-17*. Other expensive hotels include **Hotel Schweriner Hof**, *Neuer Markt 1; tel: (03831) 26 82 0*, a prettily-restored neo-classical building in the heart of the old town, and the modern **Parkhotel**

**Stralsund**, *Lindenallee 61; tel: (03831) 47 40*. Moderate pensions and guesthouses include **Pension Quast**, *Greifswalder Chaussee 54; tel: (03831) 27 05 32*; **Pension Ziegler**, *Tribseerstr 15; tel: (03831) 29 74 11*; **Pension Kemari**, *Frau-Neumannstr 3; tel: (03831) 27 05 33*. Places to eat and drink in the Innenstadt include the arty **Bistro Duett**, *Alter Markt 9*; **Cafe Lutt**, *Alter Markt 12*; and seafood restaurants: **Nurfisch** at *Hewilgeiststr 92* and **Gastmahl des meeres**, *Ossenreyerstr 49*.

### SIGHTSEEING

Blocks of low-rise apartments conceal an impressive collection of medieval buildings in the old quarter, **Innenstadt**, which is built around the harbour which made the city one of the wealthiest in the Baltic in the Middle Ages. Built around three lakes – the Moorteich, Knieperteich and Frankenteich – Stralsund was founded in 1209 by Prince Jaromir of Rugen. Some its finest buildings are on and around the *Alter Markt* – the heart of the old city – including the **Rathaus**, date from this 13th-century era of prosperity. The most striking feature, its soaring brick façade, is pierced by six enormous star-decorated windows and topped by seven pointed turrets, symbolic of the cities of the Hanseatic League. Next to the Rathaus stands the equally magnificent **Nikolaikirche** (St Nicholas church), completed in the mid-14th century. The town's other churches include the vast Gothic **Marienkirche** (St Mary's), overlooking the *Neuer Markt*. Built between 1384 and 1473, its western tower equals that of the Nikolaikirche. Also worth seeing is the **Katarinenkloster**, originally a monastery, which now houses the **Stralsund Maritime Museum**. Head for *Fischmarkt* for a view of the harbour, where a handful of working fishing boats share space with a larger fleet of small yachts. The waterfront is lined with gracious stucco-fronted merchants' houses and a jumble of ramshackle red brick waterhouses. Stralsund also has its own **Weisse Flotte** (White Fleet), *Fahrstrasse 16; tel: (03831) 26 81 16*, with pleasure cruisers which sail around the city lakes and across the Sound to Rugen.

The **Kultour tourist pass**, available from the Stralsund city information office and the HI, costs DM16 and offers free entry and discounts on museums and sights in Stralsund and Greifswald

> **SIDE TRACK**
> **FROM STRALSUND**
> **Greifswald** (45 km/1 hr by rail east of Stralsund); **tourist office**, *Schuhhagen 22; tel: (03834) 3460*, is a Hanseatic town with a small treasury of Gothic, baroque and Renaissance buildings. Highlights include a Gothic cathedral, the **St Nikolaidom**, dating from the 13th century, and a 13th–14th century **Marienkirche**. Also worth seeing are the imitation-Renaissance **Rathaus**, rebuilt in 1736 after the Gothic town hall burned down, and the University, housed in baroque 18th-century buildings.

## RUGEN

Stralsund is the gateway to Rugen, Germany's largest island, which is separated from the mainland by the 1 km wide **Strelasund**, from which the medieval city got its name. The road and railway are carried across the sound by a causeway. The island and its Baltic seaside villages were a haven for members of the Communist elite during the days of the GDR and still enjoy a reputation as a summer resort which rather over-sells the reality. Accommodation can be booked in

advance through Sassnitz or Stralsund tourist offices or through **Tourist-Incoming Putbus**, *Bahnhofstr. 2; tel: (038301) 60513*.

## SIGHTSEEING

Manmade attractions in **Putbus** (train or bus from Sassnitz) include the elegant **English garden**, laid out for the Swedish royal family in 1808, when Rugen was in Swedish hands. **Jagdschloss Granitz**, *Lancken Granitz* (8 km northeast of Putbus town centre) is an attractive neo-Gothic building overlooking the sea, built in 1836 as a hunting lodge for Prince Wilhelm Malte I of Putbus. Four wings surround a tall central observation tower, added in 1844, which you can climb by a giddying cast-iron spiral staircase. Within the lodge is a fine marble dining hall and a hunting museum. **Jasmund National Park** is a vast area of coast and beech forest north of Sassnitz, with an excellent network of hiking trails. Off Rugen's west coast, the car-free island of **Hiddensee**, with several small beaches, also offers long walks on kilometres of beach and sand dunes. Ferries sail two or three times daily from Stralsund.

## SASSNITZ

Sassnitz, a small town of drab apartment blocks, sits overlooking a large harbour from which ferries cross the Baltic to Sweden and the Danish island of **Bornholm**. The small **tourist office**, 500 m from Hbf at *Hauptstr 1* (behind the large Kurhotel Sassnitz); *tel: (038392) 32037* Mon–Fri 0800–1900, is not outstandingly helpful. Some Stralsund–Sassnitz rail services involve a bus transfer from Lietzow, 12 km away. For those in a hurry, there is a taxi rank at the Hbf. The mid-range **Hotel Garni Zum Hafen**, *Hafenstrasse 3; tel: (038392) 2 23 06*, is handily located for both Hbf and ferry harbour.

# BERLIN-WARSAW

This journey crosses the vast Central European Plain to link two cities that suffered greatly during World War II, but which are now reviving dynamically. The scenery is pleasant and the route, following the Piast Trail, links some of Poland's most historic cities.At Poznań you can transfer to the Kraków–Poznań route to reach southern Poland and from there the Czech Republic and Hungary.

Krakow – Poznan, p. 211

Krakow – Poznan, p. 211

113

FASTEST JOURNEY: 6 HRS 30 MINS

## TRAINS

**ETT Tables:** 56 ,675, 851, 850

### FAST TRACK

Three trains a day link Berlin and Warszawa. Two day expresses from Berlin Hbf and 1 overnight from Lichtenberg. The day expresses are to EuroCity standards and take 6 hr 30 mins. The overnight train has sleeping cars and couchettes and takes 9 hr.

### ON TRACK

**Berlin–Szczecin**
The two through trains a day from Berlin Lichtenberg take around 2 hr 30 mins. A few other services are available by changiung trains at Angermünde.

**Szczecin–Stargard Szczenski**
Frequent local service taking 45 mins.

**Stargard Szczenski–Poznań**
Frequent but irregular service, journey 2–2½ hr.

**Poznań–Warsaw**
Eleven trains a day provide a good service but there are some gaps in it. The journey takes around 3 hr 30 mins.

## SZCZECIN

**Station:** **Szczecin Główny**, *ul. Kolomba; tel: (091) 41 00 11,* or *935* (train times). Facilities include restaurant, currency exchange and left-luggage. **Tourist Office:** *ul. Ks. Kard. Wyszyńskiego 26, 70-203 Szczecin; tel: (091) 34 04 40, 33 84 20,* open Mon–Fri 0900–1700 (week-end opening may be introduced for summer seasons in 1996). Offers plenty of information on Szczecin and the surrounding regions, together with advice on accommodation and a reservation service.

### ACCOMMODATION AND FOOD

**Hotel Neptun** is a typically reliable Orbis hotel at *ul. Matejki 18; tel: (091) 88 38 83,* and like its neighbour the executive-style **Radisson**, *pl. Radła; tel: (091) 59 55 95,* is centrally located.

**Youth hostels** operate in the summer season at *ul. Monte Cassino 19; tel: (091) 22 47 61* and *ul. Grodzka 22; tel: (091) 33 29 24.* **Camping** is at *ul. Przestrzenna 23; tel: (091) 61 32 64.* The **Pomerania Accommodation Bureau** (within the Pomorski Hotel) is at *pl. Brama Portowa 4; tel: (091) 360 51.*

For typical Polish (and German) food try **Admiral**, *ul. Monte Cassino 37; tel: (091) 34 28 15;* and **U Klemensa**, *ul. Szarotki 3; tel: (091) 22 67 50.* with **Café Brama**, *pl. Hołdu Pruskiego*, an atmospheric café within the original Royal Gate.

### GETTING AROUND

Most sights are within walking distance. Trams cover the city well, with a no. 3 departing from the railway station and passing Brama Portowa, a good central location at which to begin sightseeing. Tram tickets for single, daily or weekly travel are available from Ruch kiosks.

### ENTERTAINMENT

As a cultural centre Szczecin provides options such as the **Szczecin Philharmonic Orchestra**, *pl. Armii Krajowej 1; tel: (091) 22 12 52.* **Pleciuga Puppet Theatre**, *ul. Kasztuba 9; tel: (091) 370 05,* and the **Opera House**, *ul. Korsarzy 1; tel: (091) 325 81.* Nightclubs include **Tango**, *pl. Batorego 2*; and **Paradise**, *ul. Rydla 92.*

### SIGHTSEEING

City and regional sightseeing can be booked through **PTA Travel Agency**, *ul. Mazurska 29; tel: (091) 88 32 63, 34 18 93* or **Orbis**, *ul. 3 Maja 1; tel: (091) 426 18.* Boat trips around Szczecin and to the nearby port of **Świnoujście** can be booked through **Żegluga Sczecińska**, *ul. Jana z Kolna 7; tel: (091) 33 28 18.*

The city of Szczecin was founded in 1243, having been an important trading post since the 11th century. As capital of the Duchy of Pomerania the city grew in importance both as a military stronghold and a trading centre after gaining maritime trading rights from King Władysław Jagiellon in the 14th century. After the Thirty Years War, in 1648, Pomerania was divided between Sweden and Brandenburg, with Szczecin in Swedish hands.

In the 18th century Pomerania was under Prussian rule, with the Berlin–Szczecin railway opening in 1843. Szczecin became part of Poland again after World War II. Much of the city's 19th-century design remains, in the form of wide avenues and squares, with about a quarter of the city's area accounted for by water. Szczecin is a major centre of shipbuilding, trade and culture.

Start sightseeing at the baroque **Brama Portowa** (Harbour Gate), built in 1725, on *al. Niepodległości*, and continue along *ul. Wyszynskiego* to the **Cathedral of St James the Apostle**, at no. 19, which was a parish church in 1187, and has been continuously rebuilt until restored to its original Gothic character since its destruction during World War II. It became a cathedral in 1983. Opposite is the **Ratusz** (Town Hall) in the *Old Market Square*, dating from 1450 though its present baroque form is late 18th-century. It is now also used for exhibition space by the **National Museum** in Szczecin and houses the **U Wyszaka** restaurant.

Continuing along *ul. Farna* is **pl. Orła Białego** (White Eagle Square) with its baroque well-cum-fountain, statue of the Goddess Flora, and the baroque **Pod Globusem Palace**, where Zofia of Anhalt-Zerbst, better known as Empress Catherine II of Russia, was born, and now a medical college. At the top of *ul. Farna* is the **Castle of Pomeranian Dukes**, one of the city's most important monuments, originally constructed in 1346 and rebuilt in 1575 It houses a cultural centre, opera and concert hall. You can climb the tower for spectacular city views, and if you're there at noon you'll also hear a bugle call. Vaults in the eastern wing contain sarcophagi of Pomeranian dukes.

## Museums

**Muzeum Narodowe** (National Museum), *ul. Staromłyńska 27; tel: (091) 33 60 70,* open Tues, Thur 1000–1700, Wed, Fri 0900–1530, Sat–Sun 1000–1600, containing Polish art and antique table silver. Other branches of the National Museum (same opening hours) are at *Wały Chrobrego 3,* with marine and African art, coin collections and metalwork, and at *ul. Staromłyńska 1,* with contemporary Polish art. **Muzeum**

**Historyczne Miasta Szczecina** (Museum of the City of Szczecin) in the **Ratusz** (Town Hall), *pl. Rzepichy 1; tel: (091) 34 72 49,* open Tues, Thur 1000–1700, Wed, Fri 0900–1530, Sat–Sun 1000–1600, covering the 10th–17th centuries.

## STARGARD SZCZECIŃSKI

**Station**: **Stargard Szczeciński**, *ul. Dworcowa;* tel: *(092) 77 36 00.* with facilities including left-luggage and café.

**Tourist Office**: There is no 'it' office, though city information and advice on accommodation can be obtained from **PTTK**, *ul. Łokietka 3a;* tel: *(092) 77 66 36,* open Mon–Fri 0900–1400.

### GETTING AROUND

A short walk from the station leads to the Old Town, with all the sights in close proximity.

### ACCOMMODATION AND FOOD

Hotels include **Staromiejski**, *ul. Spichrzowa 2;* tel: *(092) 77 22 28,* with hostel style accommodation at **Hotel PTTK**, *ul. Kuśnierzy 5;* tel: *(092) 77 31 91,* which are both close to the Old Town. Notable among the restaurants is the traditional **Ratuszowa**, *ul. Kramarska 1;* tel: *(092) 77 62 14 ,* by the Town Hall.

### SIGHTSEEING

This is one of the oldest Pomeranian towns, dating from 1243, and an important trading centre after a port was built on the river Inie in 1283. This led to fierce trading rivalry with Szczecin, but Stargard Szczeciński eventually came second. Although almost half the town was destroyed during World War II, careful renovation means there are superb Gothic, Renaissance and baroque buildings.

Starting in the Old Town, proceed along *ul. B Chrobrego* passing the 15th-century Gothic **Kościół sw. Jana Chciciela** (church of St John the Baptist). Turn left in to *ul. Kazimierza Wielkiego*, then left again into *Bolesława Krzywoustego*, past **Kościół Najswiętszej M Panny** (Church of the Blessed Virgin), classified as one of the country's finest Gothic churches, dating from the 13th century.

Turn into *ul. Mariacka*, passing **Baszta Jenców**, a 13th-century tower, and the **Ratusz** (Town Hall) which is 13th-century Gothic with 17th-century baroque additions. *Ul Mieszka 1* leads to the **Park Piastowski**, with the 15th-century fortified **Basteja** building (now a museum). Continue along *Sukiennicza* past the **Brama Pyrzycka**, the town's oldest gateway, dating from the 13th century. In the adjoining **Bolesława Chrobrego** park is **Baszta Morze Czerwone**, a 15th-century tower, and the 19th-century neo-Gothic **sw. Piotra i Pawła** (St. Peter and Paul) **Russian Orthodox Church**. During the summer the park also has an amphitheatre.

## Museums

The **City Museum** is at *Rynek Staromiejski 2/3; tel: (092) 77 25 56*. **Basteja**, *Park Piastowski 1; tel: (092) 77 18 85* is a military museum.

## POZNAŃ

**Station**: the main station, **Poznań Główny**, *ul. Dworcowa 1; tel: (061) 52 72 21*, is a short bus ride from the town centre. It has a 24-hr rail information office; *tel: (061) 66 12 12*, tourist information, currency exchange, left-luggage, cafés and kiosks.

Most international trains stop here, although some arrive and depart from

**Starołęka Station**, 5 km to the south-east.

**Tourist Office:** With its Old Town Market Square location, the Tourist Office at *Stary Rynek 59, 61-772 Poznań; tel: (061) 52 61 56*, is very good for city, regional and national information, as well as advice on accommodation. There is also an office at *ul. Gramarska 32; tel: (061) 52 98 05*, open Mon–Fri 0900–1700, Sat 1000–1400, with an office at the station; *tel: (061) 66 06 67*, open Mon–Fri 0800–1600. Look out for *Poznań Magazine* which contains useful listings and practical information.

### GETTING AROUND

While the centre is easily walkable, tram and bus lines also operate, with tickets for single journeys, daily or weekly travel available from Ruch kiosks. Radio Taxi's can be called on: *919*.

### ACCOMMODATION AND FOOD

Poznań has several Orbis hotels, including **Hotel Polonez**, *al. Niepodleglosci 36; tel: (061 69 91 41*, mostly designed for trade fair delegates on expense accounts (reserve ahead as finding hotel rooms during trade fairs, which are held throughout the year, is difficult. Prices are usually higher during trade fairs.

Less expensive options include **Dom Turysty** (in what was originally the Mielzyński Palace) with rooms and dormitory accommodation, ideally placed in the Old Town Market Square, *Stary Rynek 91; tel: (061) 52 88 93*. There is a **Youth Hostel** at *ul. Berwinskiego 2; tel (061) 66 36 80*. Rooms in private accommodation can be booked through **Orbis**, *pl. Gen. W. Andersa 1; tel: (061) 33 02 21*. **Campsites** are **Poznań Strzeszynek**, *ul. Koszalinska 15; tel (061) 48 31 29*, open May–October, while

**Malta,** *ul. Krańcowa 98; tel: (061) 76 61 55,* is open all year round and closer to the centre.

It's easy to find food at all prices in Poznań with plenty of cafés and fast food outlets, particularly around the Old Town. For traditional Polish food in the Old Town Market Square try **Stara Ratuszowa** at *no. 55; tel: (061) 51 53 18,* and **U Dylla** at no. *37/39; tel: (061) 52 17 76.*

There are plenty of **exchange** offices (*Kantor*); for Western Union Money transfer contact Bank Zachodni, Stary Rynek 73/74.

There is a **US consulate,** *ul. Chopina 4; tel: (061) 55 10 88.*

ENTERTAINMENT

Poznań's cultural options include the **Stanisław Moniuszko State Opera,** *ul. Fredry 7; tel: (061) 52 82 91,* **Poznań State Philharmonic,** *ul. Sw Marćina 81; tel: (061) 52 47 08,* and the **Polish Theatre of Dance, Poznań Ballet Co,** *ul. Kozia 4; tel: (061) 52 42 41.*

**SIGHTSEEING**

Poznań is the provincial capital of **Wielkopolska** and was the 10th-century capital of Poland, with the first bishopric also founded over 1000 years ago. The 17th and 18th centuries saw Swedish invasions, after which the city was under Prussian rule for 125 years, being finally freed at the end of the 18th century, and then falling to the Nazis in World War II.

Poznań has always been an important trading centre, lying at a geographical crossroads, which has resulted in a rich architectural heritage. Trading elements continue, as Poznań hosts Central and Eastern Europe's largest international trade fairs.

Poznań's focal point is **Stary Rynek** (the Old Market Square) with ornamental, gabled burghers' houses. At no. 1 is the 16th-century **Ratusz** (Town Hall), one of Europe's finest Renaissance buildings, which is best visited at midday when two mechanical goats emerge from above the clock to lock horns. The Town Hall also houses the **Muzeum Historii Miasta Poznańia** (Historical Museum of the City of Poznań; *tel: (061) 52 80 11,* open Mon, Tues, Fri 1000–1600, Wed 1200–1800, Sun 1000–1500, featuring Gothic vaults and the **Chamber of the Renaissance,** which has a beautifully painted, coffered ceiling (1555). In front of the Town Hall is a rococo fountain, and a copy of the pillory used for 16th-century floggings.

Also in the square at *no. 45* is the **Muzeum Instrumentów Muzycznych** (Museum of Musical Instruments); *tel: (061) 52 08 57,* open Tues, Sat, 1100–1700, Wed, Fri 1000–1600, Sun 1000–1500, which is considered one of the finest collections of its kind, totalling about 2000 instruments and including a room dedicated to Chopin. The city also hosts the **Henryk Wieniawski International Violin Competition** (Nov). At no. 3 in the Market Square is **Wielkopolskie Muzeum Historyczne** (Historical Museum of the Wielkopolski Region); *tel: (061) 52 94 64,* open Mon–Sat 1000–1800, Sun 1000–1500, it includes exhibits on the victims of the Katyn massacre. At no. 41 (but with the entrance in *ul. Klasztorna*) is the **Muzeum Farmacji** (Pharmacy Museum); *tel: (061) 51 66 15,* open Tues–Wed 1200–1700, Fri 1000–1500. At no. 84 is the **Muzeum Literackie Henryka Sienkiewicza** (The Literary Museum of Henryk Sienkiewicz); *tel: (061) 52 24 96,* open Mon–Fri 1000–1700, tracing one of Poland's greatest writers, who won the Nobel Prize for literature in 1905 with *Quo Vadis*. **Muzeum Archeologiczne** (the Archeological Museum), located in the 16th-century Renaissance **Górków Palace**, *ul. Wodna 27; tel: (061) 52 82 51*, open Tues–Fri 1000–1600, Sat 1000–1800, Sun 1000–1500, has a range of exhibits from 15,000 BC–7000 BC.

In the partially reconstructed **Przemysław Castle**, *Góra Przemysława; tel: (061) 52 20 35*, the **Arts and Crafts Museum** has artefacts dating from the 12th century. **Muzeum Narodowe** (The National Museum), at *al. Marcinkowskiego 9; tel: (061) 52 80 11*, has a fine art and scultpure collection from the 12th–20th centuries, together with Dutch, Spanish and Italian masters. **Muzeum Etnograficzne** (Ethnographic Museum), *ul. Grobla 25; tel: (061) 52 30 06*, is open Tues, Wed, Fri, Sat 1000–1600, Sun 1000–1500.

Numerous churches form an outer ring around the *Old Town Market Square*. One of the finest is the archetypally baroque **Kościół Farny** (Poznań's parish church), dedicated to St. Mary Magdalene. Its neighbour, the **Jesuit Monastery**, was once Napoleon's residence and is now the venue for Chopin concerts.

The island of **Ostrów Tumski** in the middle of the **River Warta** contains the oldest part of Poznań. Here stands the **Cathedral**, first built in the 9th century, greatly extended in the 14th century, and heavily restored after World War II. Within the 19th-century **Golden Chapel** lie the tombs of Mieszko I and Bolesław the Brave, Poland's first two kings.

Poznań's greenery is well above average, with two zoos and a vast palm house (part of Poland's largest botanical garden).

For picnics, **Park Chopina** is only 250 m from the *Old Market Square* and there are more parks and lakes within 1 km. On the edge of the city is the 100 sq km **Wielkopolski Park Narodowy** (Great Poland National Park), easily accessible by train.

## GNIEZNO

**Station**: Gniezno, *ul. Dworcowa; tel: (066) 21 11*. Facilities include left-luggage and café, and is within walking distance of the town centre, next to the bus station.

**Tourist Office**: Gniezno lacks an 'it' office, although tourist information and advice on accommodation can be obtained from **Orbis**, *ul. Rynek 7, 62 200 Gniezno; tel: (066) 26 37 01*, with some information also available from **Dom Kultury**, *ul. Łubieńskiego 11; tel: (066) 26 35 23*. The bookshop next door to Orbis sells town maps and guide books to the cathedral, which is easily found (head west from the market square).

### ACCOMMODATION

The options are limited, with only a few hotels, such as **Hotel Lech** (also a sports centre with sports hall and swimming pools), *ul. Jolenty 5; tel: (066) 26 23 85*, and the **Hotel Pracowniczy**, *ul. Armii Poznań; tel: (066) 26 47 29*. There is also a **youth hostel** at *ul. Pocztowa 11; tel: (0661) 13 23*.

### SIGHTSEEING

Gniezno (which means 'bird's nest') is small but historically important, having been briefly the capital of Poland in the 11th century. Excavations have revealed settlements dating from the early stone Age. The main attraction is the Gothic **Cathedral** (originally dating from the 10th century), which has 14 chapels and

Romanesque bronze doors (1170) depicting the life of St Adalbertus (one of the patron saints of Poland), while his red marble tomb and silver shrine are found within the cathedral, together with a **Museum of Religious Art**. The **Museum of the Origins of the Polish State**, *ul. Kostrzewskiego 1; tel: (066) 26 46 41*, traces early Polish history.

> **SIDE TRACK**
> **FROM GNIEZO**

## BYDGOSZCZ

**Station: Bydgoszcz Główny**, *ul. Zygmunta Augusta 7; tel: (052) 22 06 61/2*. Facilities include currency exchange, restaurant, shops and arcades with barbers, washing facilities and left-luggage.

**Tourist Office**: *ul. Zygmunta Augusta 10, 85-082 Bydgoszcz; tel: (052) 22 84 32*, open Mon–Thur 0730–1530, Fri 0730–1500. Located opposite the main entrance to the railway station, there is plenty of city and country information, together with advice on accommodation and a reservation service.

### ACCOMMODATION AND FOOD

Accommodation for all budgets is easily found. The premier address is the centrally located **Pod Orłem**, *ul. Gdańska 14; tel: (052) 22 18 61*, built in 1896 in the Secessionist (Art Nouveau) style and recently restored. The **Youth Hostel** is at *ul. Sowińskiego 5; tel: (052) 22 75 70*, on the edge of town. The **Accommodation Bureau** is at *ul. Długa 37; tel: (052) 22 88 61*.

A wide range of cafés and restaurants can easily be found, with one of the best restaurants serving local cuisine being **Karczma Słupska**, *al. 1 Maja 28; tel: (052) 22 15 22*.

### GETTING AROUND

Buses operate throughout the city, with no. 77 going from the railway station to the Old Town and city centre, though this is equally walkable. Tickets for single journeys, daily or weekly travel can be bought from Ruch kiosks. For radio taxis call *919*.

### SIGHTSEEING

Sightseeing and excursions can be organised through **Orbis**, *ul. Gdańska 25; tel: (052) 22 16 27*. Boat trips lasting an hour leave from *Rybi Rynek* (a market square in the Old Town) during the summer season.

Established as a city in 1346, Bydgoszcz became a stronghold of Polish resistance against the Teutonic Knights in the 15th century. During this period it developed into a major trading port (being on the junction of the Vistula and Brda rivers), and many of the city's 16th-century buildings were established with its new found wealth. The Swedish invasion in 1655 partially destroyed the city, with Saxon and Prussian invasions following. Bydgoszcz was under Prussian rule following the 1772 partition of Poland, returning to Poland in 1920.

Reaching the *Old Town* by crossing the river on *ul. Mostowa*, you pass 18th- and 19th-century granaries, beyond which is the *Rybi Rynek*. Continuing along *ul. Mostowa* to the **Stary Rynek** (Old Market Square) with its historic buildings, its cafés and various shops, turn left down *ul. Farna*, passing the **Urząd Miejski** (Town Hall), and continue onto the the 15th-century Gothic **Farny church,** with

**119**

several baroque altars. Turn left into *Przy Rzece* by the canal (known as Bydgoszcz's Venice) with distant views of granaries and a buckwheat mill.

Turn right into *ul. Długa*, and take the first left down *ul. Jezuicka* with the 17th-century **Kolegium Jezuickie** (Jesuit College), then continue along *ul. Długa*, turn left into *Podwale* and continue until you reach the **Hala Targowa** (Covered Market), adjacent to which is an open air market with bric-a-brac, flowers, fruit and vegetables.

Turning left into *ul. Magdzińskiego* gets you back to the Old Market Square, right by the 18th-century public library, which combines baroque and neo-classical. **Muzeum Okręgowe im. Leona Wyczółkowskiego** (Regional Museum), *ul. Gdanska 4; tel: (052) 22 16 08*, open Tues–Wed 1000–1800, Thur–Sat 1000–1600, Sat–Sun 1000–1400, is rich in paintings, including contemporary. Another branch (same opening hours) at *ul. Mennica 1; tel: (052) 27 03 93*, is housed in a former granary. **Muzeum Tradycji POW** (Museum of the Polish Army) is at *ul. Czerkaska 2; tel: (052) 28 20 27*, open Mon, Tues, Thur, Fri 1000–1400, Wed 1200–1800, Sat–Sun 1000–1400.

## TORUŃ

**Station**: the main station is **Toruń Główny**, *ul. Kujawska 1; tel: (056) 272 22*, with left-luggage facilities and a restaurant. Five other stations feature the name Toruń; nearest to the old town is **Toruń Miasto**. From the main station, bus nos. 22 and 24 will take you to the old town centre.

Tickets are available from Ruch kiosks.

**Tourist Office**: Located on the ground floor of the **Ratusz** (Town Hall), *Rynek Staromiejski1, 87–100 Toruń; tel: (056) 109 31*, open Tues–Fri 0900–1800, Mon and Sat 0900–1800 (Sun 0900–1300 in summer season).

### ACCOMMODATION AND FOOD:

**Orbis** hotels include **Helios**, *ul. Kraszewskiego 1/3; tel: (056) 250 33*, overlooking a central park and only a few minutes walk from the Old Town.

Among the hostels are Dom Wycieczkowy PTTK, *ul. Legionów 24; tel: (056) 238-55*, and in the summer season only a youth hostel at *Szkoła Podstawowa 17, ul. Rudacka 15; tel: (056) 272-42*. The **campsite** is *Tramp, ul. Kujawska 14; tel: (056) 241 87*.

Eating at all budget levels is easily found, with some highlights in the *Rynek Nowomiejski* (New Market Square) being the baroque café **Pod Modrym Fartuchem** at no 8; *tel: (056) 214 88*, and **Piwnica Pod Aniołem** at no 1; *tel: (056) 270-38 extn. 50*, being an atmospheric cellar beneath the Ratusz (Town Hall).

### SIGHTSEEING

Guides can be booked through **Centrum Usług Turystycznych** (Center for Tourist Services), *ul. Fosa Staromiejska 6; tel: (056)104-22*, while sightseeing and various excursions can be arranged through **Orbis**, *ul. Mostowa 7; tel: (056) 217-14*. **Boat trips** along the Wisła (Vistula river) depart from the landing stage on *Bulward Filadelfijski*.

Toruń (the capital of Pomerania) is second only to Cracow in terms of architectural heritage. The city was founded by the Order of Teutonic Knights (1233), and became part of the Hanseatic League, benefiting greatly as a trading town from its location by the Wisła (Vistula) River. Prospering between the 13th–15th centuries, Toruń fell first to the Swedes and then to the Prussians, only becoming part of Poland again in 1919.

The city's main claims to fame have been the production of gingerbread, made in various guises and elaborately decorated with icing sugar, and its most famous citizen, astronomer Nicolaus Copernicus, who first established that the earth moved around the sun.

A good starting point for sightseeing is the *Rynek Staromiejski* (Old Market Square) featuring the 14th-century **Old Town Hall** which is now home to the **Regional Museum;** *tel: (056) 270 38,* open Tues–Sun 1000–1600, with a wealth of 17th–19th century Polish paintings. Nearby is a monument to Copernicus, erected in 1853. The burgher's house at *no. 35,* called **Pod Gwiazdą** (literally 'under the star') was originally 15th century with ornate baroque additions and a 17th-century hanging staircase. The building also houses the **Muzeum Sztuki Dalekiego Wschodu** (Museum of Far Eastern Art); *tel: (056) 211 33,* open Tues–Sun 1000–1600. Near the market square is **Dom Kopernika** (Nicholas Copern-

icus' House), at *ul. Kopernika 15/17; tel: (056) 267 48,* open Tues–Sun 1000–1600 (in the house which was his family home), with various Copernicus memorabilia.

Heading south-east leads to the **Ruiny Zamku Krzyżackiego** (ruins of the Teutonic Castle); the castle was destroyed in 1454, but its still offers the best preserved remnants of the medieval city walls, and a good impression of how the castle would have looked.

Toruń also has several fine churches, including the Gothic **Franciscan Hall Church of St Mary's**, on the old market square. The 14th-century **St James's Church**, by the *Rynek Nowomiejski*, has Gothic flying buttresses and frescoes. Technically the oldest church is the Gothic **Św. Jana** (St. John's), *ul. Zeglarska,* most of which is mid 15th-century, although the Presbytery is 300 years earlier.

The **Muzeum Etnograficzne** (Ethnographic Museum), *Wały Sikorskiego 19; tel: (056) 280 91,* open Mon, Wed, Fri 0900–1600, and additionally in the summer season on Tues, Thur, Sat, Sun 1000–1800, has Poland's finest collection of folk art and crafts arranged within a living Skansen museum that includes a reconstructed village setting. The **Planetarium,** *ul. Franciszkańska 15/21; tel: (056) 260 66,* open Wed–Sat 1000–1700, Tues, Sun 1000–1600, has commentaries in English

**121**

# BRATISLAVA

The capital of Slovakia usually suffers by comparison with its three better advertised near-neighbours, Budapest, Prague and Vienna. There is some justice in this, but Bratislava has much more going for it than it is usually given credit for. In particular, the old city centre, much of which is undergoing a needed process of restoration, is tranquil and atmospheric.

## TOURIST INFORMATION

**Bratislava Information Service (BIS),** *Panská 18; tel: 333715, 334370,* open Mon–Fri 0800–1800, Sat, Sun 0800–1300). Staff speak English and can arrange accommodation, *tel: 334325.* Maps of the town are available, as are brochures about the city and Slovakia in general. **Satur** *Jesenského 5; tel: 367624,* open Mon–Sat 0900–1700, can arrange accommodation, as well as tours and bus and train journeys. **CKM,** *Hviezdoslavova námestie 16; tel: 334114,* open Mon, Wed 1000–1730, Tue, Thur, Fri 0900–1600, is the place for cut-price accommodation and travel information and bookings.

## ARRIVING AND DEPARTING

Most trains serve the main station, **Hlavná Stanica,** *tel: 20444 84* or *498275,* 1.5 km north of old town centre. There are exchange and catering facilities. At the international ticket counter there will usually be an English speaker. Go downstairs to reach the trams (no. 1 to old town). **Nové Město** station (*tel: 60702*) is about 3 km north-east of the centre (accessible by tram).

**Hydrofoils** run between Bratislava

and Vienna, and back, twice daily, leaving from the **River Terminal** on *Fajnorovo nábr 2;* in which is located **Blue Danube Travel,** *tel: 362266.* The journey takes about an hour.

## GETTING AROUND

As the old town is compact and not over-burdened with traffic, walking is pleasant there; elsewhere public transport is a must. An efficient tram system links the old town with the suburbs. The route network is displayed inside trams and at major stops. Buses are frequent, although often crowded. Tickets available include one- and seven-day passes. **Taxis** are less expensive and with more honest drivers than those of Prague, but it is still best to agree a price before starting out.

## STAYING IN BRATISLAVA

### Accommodation

Hotels are relatively expensive because there are few of them. There are no booking agencies in the station but locals offer private rooms to arriving travellers at prices often far lower than those of hotels. **BIS** book private rooms and hotels. **CKM** has a wide variety of accommodation, including university dorms in the summer and a student hotel open all year round. Try also **Satur.** Hotel chains in Bratislava include *Fm, IC* and *IH.* **HI:** *Bernolákova 3; tel: 497725.*

### Eating and Drinking

The regional speciality is *bryndzove halusky* (potato pasta with ewe's cheese and diced fried bacon), but Austrian and Hungarian dishes are also popular.

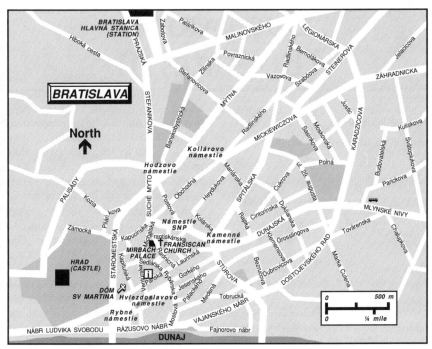

## Communications

The main **post office** is on *Predstaničné nám*, open Mon–Fri 0800–1800. For outgoing international calls, first dial *00*.

## Consulates

**Canada:** *Kolárska 4; tel: 361277.*
**UK:** *Grösslingová 35; tel: 364420.*
**USA:** *4 Hviezdoslavovo nám; tel: 330861, 335083 or 333 338.*
**Citizens of Australia, New Zealand** and **South Africa** can contact the British Embassy in case of emergency.

## SHOPPING

Shops are open Mon–Sat 0900–1800/1900. Pottery, porcelain, wood-carvings and and hand-embroidered clothes make for excellent souvenirs.

## SIGHTSEEING

Bratislava is really two cities: the elegant and intimate old town centre, **Staré Město,** with its many cobbled courtyards; and a forest of high-rise apartment blocks on the outskirts. The **Castle** is the most distinctive sight in town. Fortifications date back to at least the 9th century, but the main castle was burnt down in 1811 during the Napoleonic wars. The present structure is 1960s vintage and displays some of the exhibits from the **Slovak National Museum's** collection. There's a good view of the unusual design of the **SNP bridge** across the Danube. During Bratislava's period as Hungarian capital, 11 kings were crowned in **St Martin's Cathedral,** across *Starometska* from the castle. The old town conservation area, largely pedestrianised, also contains the **Mirbach Palace,** Radicna St, and the **Franciscan Church,** one of Bratislava's oldest surviving structures, dating back to 1290.

# BUCHAREST
# (BUCUREȘTI)

This cosmopolitan city of 1½ million people, founded by the legendary shepherd Bucur, became Romania's capital in the mid 19th century. Decades of misrule and megalomaniac building projects, to say nothing of the fighting in 1989, have left their mark on what was once one of the most elegant cities of eastern Europe, but as it faces up to a painfully changing future Bucharest remains a fascinating metropolis.

## TOURIST INFORMATION

All major hotels carry tourist information, as does the **ONT-Carpati Information Office** 7 *Blvd Magheru; tel: Str. 312 25 98 or 614 51 60* (metro: *Piața Romana*). There are branches at Otopeni Airport and at the Gara de Nord. ONT-Carpati will arrange tours, hotel bookings and will offer maps.

## ARRIVING AND DEPARTING

### Airport
**Otopeni**, *tel: Str. 633 66 02 or 212 16 02*, is 16 km from the centre. There is a good bus service (no: 783) to the city centre, costing 500 lei (around £0.20). Taxis only accept US dollars (or occasionally DM), and charge anything from $15 upwards. Negotiate before you travel.

### Stations
Virtually all trains stop at **Gara de Nord**, *Calea Griviței; tel: 952* for general information. There are occasional services from other Bucharest stations but these are very slow trains. All tickets and reservations must be purchased in advance and can be obtained at **CFR** offices no sooner than ten days in advance of travelling or later than the day prior of the journey. Tickets are obtainable on the day itself from the station up to and no later than two hours before departure. CFR agencies in Bucharest are located at: *44 bis Blvd Brătianu; tel: Str. 613 40 08; 139 Calea Griviței; tel: Str. 650 72 47/650 36 45; 10–14 Str. Domnița Anastasia; tel: Str. 613 26 42/43/44, 615 56 86, 613 90 21 and 614 98 19.* Ask about the special rates for senior citizens and minors. A word of warning for the not so nimble: as elsewhere in Romania, there are virtually no platforms and the step onto the train is therefore exceptionally high. Pickpocketting and theft is carried out on a major scale, so be ultra-careful with all possessions.

## GETTING AROUND

A good street map is essential as many of the streets have changed and still are changing, their names. Bucharest is built on Parisian lines, with wide tree-lined boulevards radiating out from the Arc de Triomphe.

### Metro, Buses and Trolley-buses
The metro is frequent and fast, covering most of central Bucharest and the Gara de Nord. There are three main lines and most city maps carry a metro plan. Change may be obtained at the turnstiles, but there may a be a long queue, as coins are in very short supply.

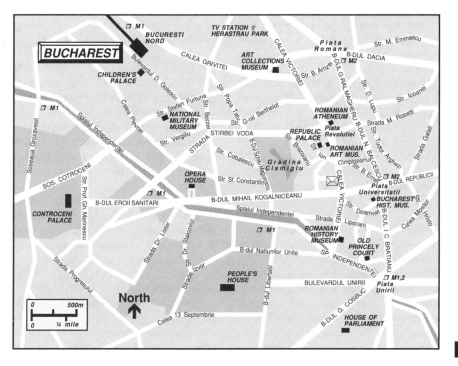

BUCHAREST

♩ M1
BUCURESTI
NORD

TV STATION ⇧
HERASTRAU PARK

Piata
Romana

Str. M. Eminescu

B-DUL DACIA
♩ M2

CALEA GRIVITEI

ART
COLLECTIONS
MUSEUM ■

CALEA VICTORIEI

Str. B. Amzei

DUL G-RAL MAGHERU

CHILDREN'S
PALACE

Bulevardul D. Golescu

Str. D. Lupu

Str. Icoanei

♩ M1

Calea Plevnei

Splaiul Independentei

Soseaua Grozavesti

Str. Stefan Furtuna

Str. NATIONAL
MILITARY
MUSEUM

Str. Vergiliu

Str. Popa Tatu

Str. Berzei

STRADA

STIRBEI VODA

Str. G-ral Berthelot

Str. B-dul Schitu Magureanu

Str. Cobalcescu

ROMANIAN
ATHENEUM
●

B-DUL N. BALCESCU

Strada M. Rosetti

Str. Tudor Arghezi

Strada Galati

REPUBLIC
PALACE

Piata
Revolutiei
■

ROMANIAN
ART MUS.
■

Str. Ion Brezoianu

Cimpineanu

B-DUL REPUBLICII
♩ M2

SOS. COTROCENI

Str. Prof. Gh. Marinescu

B-DUL EROII SANITARI

Gradina
Cismiglu

B-DUL Ernest

Str. D.

Str. Icoanei

CONTROCENI
PALACE

OPERA
HOUSE
■

♩ M1

Str. Sf. Constantin

B-DUL MIHAIL KOGALNICEANU

Piata
Universitatii

CALEA VICTORIEI

Str. Doamnei

♦ BUCHAREST ⇧
HIST. MUS.

Calea Mosilor

Strada Dr. Lister

Strada Dr. Dr. Staicovici

Splaiul Independentei

Strada Lipscani

B-DUL I C BRATIANU

Calea Hristo

♩ M1

ROMANIAN
HISTORY
MUSEUM ■

OLD
PRINCELY
COURT
■

Strada Progresului

Strada Izvor

Strada Sf. Dr. Staicovici

B-dul Natiunilor Unite

SF. INDEPENDENTEI

PEOPLE'S
HOUSE
▪

B-dul Libertatii

BULEVARDUL UNIRII

Piata
Uniril

♩ M1,2

North
⬆

Calea 13 Septembrie

B-DUL G. COSBUC

HOUSE OF
PARLIAMENT
■

0 ├─────┤ 500m
0 ¼ mile

125

Buses and trolley-buses run throughout inner and outer Bucharest. They are dirty, very full and very cheap. Tickets must be obtained before boarding, from orange kiosks marked RATB. Fines for boarding without a ticket are very hefty. Check your route at major stops or obtain a route map from the kiosks.

## Taxis

Taxis are relatively inexpensive by Western standards and are fairly easy to hail, but it is a hit-and-miss affair whether you find a state-run cab or a privately owned one. Check that the drivers switch on the meter before you start the journey. The cars may be very old and often in a poor state of repair, and, as there is so much unemployment in Romania, anyone with a car will take to the streets. It is wisest to phone **Titan** (*tel: 953*) or

**Criscars** (*tel: 946*) to order a cab in advance; waiting time is usually 5–10 mins, and the price around 600 Lei per km. Your name, address and phone number will be logged, as will the driver's number. Consider planning your route from a street map and give a copy of this to the driver, in case of any dispute.

## STAYING IN BUCHAREST

### Accommodation

**ONT** (see Tourist Information) can arrange both hotel and private rooms. There is a service charge of around 30%. Private rooms usually come with breakfast, but check first. Expect to pay US$20–30 (in dollars) a night for this. Some landlords will include an evening meal in this price, or will offer one at around US$5. This is expensive, even though food is very costly for the Romanian. Hotel prices vary dramatically and one- and two- star hotel prices are in the same price-range or a little above the cost of private rooms, so this is worth considering. Avoid the unofficial touts at the station; although their rooms will be cheaper than the standard rate, they will often be in outlying suburbs and of a very rough standard. In some areas, water is switched off during the night and at times during the day. Hot water may only be available twice or three times a week, so be warned.

Accommodation in Bucharest is not cheap. Western-style hotels include the **Inter-Continental**, Str. Balcescu; the **Bucureşti**, 63-81 Ave Victoriei; the **Dorobanţi**, Calea Dorobanţilor; and the new **Sofitel**, 2 Blvd. Expozitiei. Although a little out of the centre, the Sofitel is incorporated in the World Trade Centre business and conference complex does have a shuttle service to and from the town and the airport. Close to the station, at Blvd. Dinicu Golescu; tel: Str. 638 26 90, is the recently refurbished two-star **Hotel Astoria**, owned by the railway company. There are suites, single and double rooms at reasonable prices, and a comprehensive restaurant.

**Student hostels** are inexpensive. Ask ONT for details. These are generally open to young people in the summer months. Have your student ID handy.

### Eating and Drinking

Food is basic, with few fresh vegetables on offer. Meat is generally pork or lamb and is usually fried and called *friptura*. *Sarmale* are stuffed cabbage leaves and *mititei* are small, tasty grilled or fried meatballs. Chicken and locally caught fish are usually excellent, especially the carp (*krap*). *Mamaliga* is a dish as varied as the regions of Romania made from golden maize, and

may be eaten alone or as an accompanying dish to most main meals.

Milk is virtually unobtainable and coffee is thick, black and sweet. *Nes* is unlike our own Nescafé, and is a sweetened chicory coffee, usually drunk without milk. The wines are superb, especially from the Murfatlar region. Soft drinks are interesting and varied and the bottled water is of the sparkling variety. The tap water is perfectly safe to drink, but highly chlorinated.

The Romanians love cakes and pastries and these are generally excellent. A plethora of cafés and stalls selling colas and snacks are mushrooming everywhere, and the occasional pizza bar may be found. 24-hour fast food cafés are open in many places.

The hotels mentioned above are safe bets for dining out. There is also a superb and authentic Chinese restaurant, **Nan Jing**, at the Minerva Hotel, 2–4 Str. Gheorghe Manu; tel: Str. 650 6010 – booking advisable. Near the Gara de Nord is a new restaurant and snack bar, **<&>**, 68 Calea Griviţei; tel: Str. 659 7923. The snack bar serves a creditable thin-crust pizza; and the restaurant menu includes other Balkan cuisines besides Romanian, and even Italian and Lebanese dishes. **Mc Moni's** is mini-chain with a good reputation; it has restaurants at 28 Blvd Mărăşti; tel: Str. 311 2342 and 42 Str. Occidentului; tel: 659 2984, a pizzeria at 37 Str. Berthelot; tel: 613172, and a coffee shop at 3 Piaţa Rossetti; tel: 615 5998.

For budget eating, in addition to the many pizzerias and burger bars, there is reasonable choice of picnic items in food shops, street markets and delicatessens throughout the city.

### Communications

The main **post office**, 10 Str. Matei Millo;

*tel: Str. 614 40 54*, is round the corner from the main **telephone office**, *37 Calea Victoriei*. There are few letter boxes to be found.

Unless an establishment has an international phone line, it is difficult to phone out of the country or even to numbers outside Bucharest. International calls can be booked via the international operator on 971, but they can take anything from 5 minutes to 5 days to connect. Most hotels graded two-star and above have international phones and faxes. Out-of-town calls may be booked with the local operator on 991.

A new phone book has just been issued and there is a directory enquiry service but the full name and address is needed to obtain the number. Since May 1995, the numbers and exchange codes in Bucharest have been changing, causing utter confusion, as there is no service which can re-direct callers. Romania plans to have a direct-dial service in 1996/7, but its introduction may be delayed.

The area code for Bucharest if phoning from outside the city is (01).

## Money

Always change your money at official banks or exchange offices and keep your receipts, as you may be expected to show them at the hotel when paying the bill in Lei.

## Embassies

**Canada:** *36 Str. Nicolae Iorga; tel Str. 650 63 30.*

**UK:** *4, Str. Jules Michelet; tel: Str. 611 16 34.*

**USA:** *7–9 Str. Tudor Arghezi; tel: Str. 210 40 42.*

Citizens of Australia, New Zealand, South Africa and the Republic of Ireland should contact the UK Embassy.

## ENTERTAINMENT

Bucharest has many nightclubs, discos and casinos, as well as bars and pubs of varying quality. The **casino** at the Inter-Continental (see 'Acommodation') is said to be the best in Eastern Europe. The restaurant/nightclub **Odobeşti**, *207 Calea Moşilor; tel: 610 4745*, is one of several that features a 'Folies-Bergere'-type revue.

Cinema-going is very popular, and many places show undubbed English-language films: try the **Bucureşti**, *4–6 Blvd Mihail Kogălniceanu* or the **Mioriţa**, *127 Calea Moşilor*.

## SHOPPING

*Calea Victoriei* is the most prestigious street for boutique-style shopping. There are three department stores: **Unirea**, *1 Piaţa Unirii*; **Eva**, *9 Blvd Gen. Magheru*; and **Tineretului**, *37 Blvd Unirii*.

**Street markets** abound, one of the best being in *Piaţa Amzei*, where you can buy everything, including Russian caviar, for a bargain price if you are prepared to haggle. Watch out for short weight goods. There is a Sunday book market in the side streets around the Inter-Continental, off *Blvd Nicolae Bălcescu*, which often has some English-language bargains.

## SIGHTSEEING

Bucharest was once named 'The Little Paris of Eastern Europe'. The **Arc de Triomphe**, built 1918–19, dominates its wide piazza, and was built with tree-lined boulevards radiating from it, just as in Paris, but built 5 metres wider and longer than their Parisian originals. In spite of the military atmosphere conveyed by the machine-gun-toting guards fronting museums and other places of interest, there is evidence of a great deal of the elegant splendour of the past, much of which has been retained, even though sizeable

**127**

chunks of the old city were demolished during the Industrialisation period in the mid 1970s. This was to make way for the growing need for budget housing and, in later years, for the building of the **Casa Poporului** (People's House) (metro: *Izvor*), the second-largest building in Europe. The roads to the Palace are wide and triumphal. Hand-laid fountains lie in sunken beds in the middle of *Blvd Unirii*. The maginificent façade of the flats belies their true nature, as they are minute and less serviceable than their monolithic counterparts in the suburbs. After the execution of Ceauşescu, in 1989, all building work stopped.

Due to the large number of flower-filled parks, many with lakes, Bucharest has also been nicknamed 'The Garden City'. **Herăstrău Park**, built by Nicu Ceauşescu, younger son of the former president, has many water sports and tennis courts to offer. Here too is the **Village Museum**, *28–30 Şos Kiseleff*, close to the Arc de Triomphe. This offers a fascinating taste of the architecture and styles of homes, mills and other buildings from around the country. Close, too, is the **Ilie Nastase Sports Centre**. The **Grădina Cişmigu** (Cishmigu Park) on *Blvd Kogălniceanu*, opposite the imposing **Town Hall** and **Ministry of Justice**, is large and sprawling, filled with tree-lined paths and vast flower beds.

*Calea Victoriei*, with its many museums and boutiques and the splendid **Bucureşti Hotel**, is the Regent Street or 5th Avenue of Bucharest. There you will find the **History Museum of Romania** at no. 12, the **Arts Collection Museum** at no 11, the **National Art Museum** at 49-53 and the **Gheorghe Enescu** museum at no 141. Another museum worth visiting is the **History Museum of Bucharest**, *2 Blvd Brătianu*, which forges some links

with the legend of Dracula. The Presidential **Cotroceni Palace** houses the **National Museum**, *1 Blvd Geniului*.

The air of optimism that filled the streets early in 1990 after the coup against Ceauşescu is vanishing along with the memorials of that period. *Piaţa Universităţii* (metro: *Universităţii*) still bears the daubings on the walls and all around the city, especially at the **TV Station** in *Calea Dorobanţilor* (metro: *Aviatorilor*), where bullet holes are still visible. Much of the fighting took place around the **Ministry of Defence**.

Nearby is the **National Theatre**, *2 Nicolae Bălcescu*. One of the few **Jewish Theatres** left in the world can be seen at *15 Str. Julin Barasch*. The **Opera**, *70-72 Blvd Mihail Kogălniceanu*, rebuilt after the major earthquake that devasted Bucharest in the 1970s, is splendid.

Look out for the many magnificent churches and monasteries dotted around the city. Their architecture is of varying styles, such as Gothic, and date back as far as the 13th century. The ancient **Synagogue** is at *Str. Sfincta Vineri*, hidden behind *Blvd Unirii*.

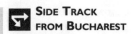

### SIDE TRACK FROM BUCHAREST

## SNAGOV

**Station: Snagov Plaja** is the station to alight at, not Snagov Sat. There are two trains a day between Bucharest and Snagov in each direction.

Only 40 km north of the capital, Snagov, the playground of Bucharest, boasts a beautiful lake surrounded by magnificent villas. On the island in the lake, the 15th-century **Monastery** (accessible by motor boat service) houses the tomb of Vlad Tepeş (Vlad the Impaler – see p. 131).

# BUCHAREST–BUDAPEST

From Bucharest to Arad the train speeds through picture-postcard villages and tiny stations (don't be surprised to see the stationmaster/mistress run out to see you safely through!). The journey continues through the Prahova valley, past churches which vary in style as the region changes, until in Transylvania they resemble miniature Kremlins. Don't miss the opportunity to stop awhile at historic Braşov and Timişoara.

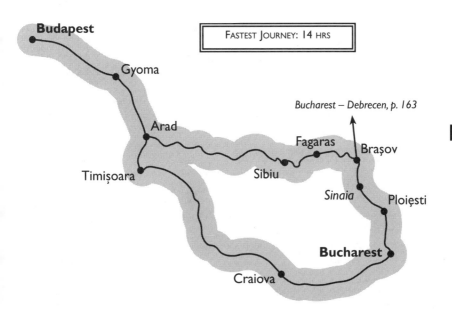

FASTEST JOURNEY: 14 HRS

Bucharest – Debrecen, p. 163

129

---

## TRAINS

**ETT Tables:** 950, 954

### FAST TRACK

➡ Six trains a day make the 14-hr journey. Advance reservations are required on all services.

## ON TRACK

**⮡ Bucharest–Ploieşti**
Frequent service taking 45 mins.

**Ploieşti–Braşov**
Frequent service taking 2 hrs.

TRAINS

### Braşov–Făgăraş–Sibiu–Arad

Six trains a day. Braşov to Făgăraş takes 1 hr 15 mins, Făgăraş to Sibiu takes 2 hrs and Sibiu to Arad takes around 5 hrs.

### Arad–Gyoma

5 trains a day with journey times of around 3 hrs.

### Gyoma–Budapest

Nine trains a day taking 2 hrs 30 mins.

### Bucharest–Craiova

A good service throughout the day lasting 3 hr.

### Craiova–Timişoara

Eight trains a day. 5 hour journey.

### Timişoara–Budapest

One direst service at inconvenient times. Other services available by changing trains at Arad. Journey time at least 6 hr.

## CRAIOVA

**Station**: **CFR** railway information, *Complex Unirea, Piaţa Unirii; tel:(051) 11 16 34.*

### ACCOMMODATION

A gigantic inlaid roundabout fronts the semi-circular **Hotel Jiul**, *1–3 Calea Bucureşti; tel :(051) 11 56 55* . One of the official bureaux de change is situated in the hotel, as is a swimming pool. They offer live entertainment, hairdressing and much more. Smaller are the **Parc**, *16 Str. Bibescu; tel: (051) 11 72 57*, and the one-star Minerva, *1-3 Str. Mihail Kogălniceanu; tel: (051) 13 33 00.*

### SIGHTSEEING

Craiova lies in the south-west of Romania, close to the former Yugoslavian border. It is a large city with well over a quarter of a million inhabitants. As a settle ment it dates back to the Neolithic Age. Towards the end of the 19th century, Craiova had become an economic centre and the first Workers' Party was founded in the city in 1891. In 1944, Craiova played an important role in the national insurrection, destroying the resistance of Hitler's occupying army. Today industrialised Craiova boasts a large University with ten faculties , and a National Theatre.

The oldest building in the town is the **Casa Băniei**, The Money House, *14 Str. Matei Basarab*. It was built during the reign of Constantin Brincoveanu replacing the house of the ruling Craioveşti family. It is very elegant, with stone pillars and has exhibits of old traditional carpets, glass and wooden icons, local national costumes and old household utensils.

The **Art Museum**, *15 Calea Unirii*, is in what was the Jean Mihail Palace. It is divided into three sections: the Romanian Gallery, the Brâncuşi Chamber (devoted to the works of the leading Romanian sculptor), and the Universal Gallery, with many works from the Dutch, French, Flemish and Italian schools. The **National Theatre**, *11 Str. Alexandru Ioan Cuza*, is an institution in the traditional style from the mid 1850s.

The **Parcul Poporului** (People's Park), *Calea Dunării*, at 95 hectares is the largest in the country. The **Botanical Gardens**, *Str. Iancu Iianu*, date from 1955 and contain several delightful gardens with international themes, such as the Chinese and Italian gardens, as well as an area devoted to the local flora of Oltenia.

## TIMIŞOARA

**Station**: Timişoara has two **CFR** information and ticket offices: *2 Blvd Republicii*, and *40 Blvd Gheorghe Lazăr, tel: (056) 19 18 89.*

**Tourist Office:** There are two: **Banatul**, *2 Str. 1 Mai; tel: (056) 19 19 07, 19 19 09 or 19 19 10*, and **Biroul de Turism şi Tranzactii**, *26 Blvd Revoluţiei din 1989; tel: (056) 13 31 48.*

## ACCOMMODATION

The best-rated hotel is the **International**, *44 Blvd C.D.Loga; tel: (056) 19 93 39.* Although very small, this four-star establishment boasts a complex for swimming and entertainment, conferences, shops and a bureau de change, as well as a terrace restaurant. The three-star **Continental**, *3 Blvd Revoluţiei; tel: (056) 19 41 44*, offers much the same but is a vast tower block. Next to the tourist office is **Hotel Banatul**, *3–5 Str. 1 Mai; tel: (056) 19 19 03.*

## SIGHTSEEING

Timişoara is an old university town in the Banat region of Romania. It is close to the border with the Serbian part of former Yugoslavia, and during the recent conflicts, huge convoys of petrol and munitions could be spotted trundling across, breaking the UN-imposed embargo. Romania has long held an alliance with Serbs and renewed this in 1993.

The broad and rambling River Timiă runs behind the city and the Bega Canal runs through. It was the Royal Hungarian seat of residence between 1307 and 1342, during the reign of King Carol Robert d'Anjou. A great citadel was built in the city in 1441. Its industrial development began as early on as the 18th century and has led the country's technological research

**Huniades Castle**, *1 piaţa Huniade*, is a sight that alone justifies a stop in Timişoara. Built during 1307–1342, enlarged by Iancu Hunedoara in 144, it underwent grand restorations in 1856.

Inside there are the added attractions of the natural history and local history museums. There is an amazing collection of some 21,000 precious and semi-precious stones and an exceptional exhibit of ornithology.

The **Ethnographical Museum**, *4 Str. Popa Şapcă*, is an open-air exhibition of the local way of life, its pavilions centred in the **Pădure Verde** (Green Park) There are many examples of the local costume, textiles, architecture encrusted wood and painted glass, for example. The **Art Museum**, *1 Piaţa Unirii*, houses a collection of decorative Oriental art, German graphics, paintings from Austrian, the Dutch, French, Flemish and Italian schools, as well as modern Romanian art.

The 18th-century **Old Town Hall**, *1 Piaţa Libertăţii*, is a pretty baroque building. Nearby at no. 12 is the **Roman Catholic Cathedral**, built 1736-73. There is also a **Serbian church**, *12 Str. Em. Ungureanu*, with a series of fine paintings.

Running along the bank of the canal there is a necklace of parks. In the **Parcul Catedralei**, *Blvd 30 Decembrie*, stands the Eastern Orthodox cathedral). Here too is the replica of the Romulus and Remus statue, a gift to Timişoara from the people of Rome. Crossing the canal there is the delightful iron **Hannibal's bridge**, held up by elephants at the spans, recalling a tradition that the Carthaginian general passed through here with his elephants..

## PLOIEŞTI

**Station:** *17 Blvd Republicii; tel: 14 20 80.*
**Tourist Office: Prahova SA**, *12 Blvd Republicii Bloc 33 B; tel: (044) 14 13 51*, and **Concordia**, *Str. Gen Lazar; tel: (044) 12 59 41.*

## ACCOMMODATION

There are three hotels worth considering.

The two-star **Hotel Central**, *1 Blvd Republicii; tel: (044) 12 66 41*, is as centrally located as its name implies. Also two-star is **Hotel Prahova**, *11 Str. Dobrogeanu Gherea; tel: (044) 12 68 50*. **Hotel Turist**, *6 Str. Tache Ionescu; tel: (044) 12 61 01*, boasts only one star but has sports facilities. All three hotels have lifts, restaurants and snack bars.

### SIGHTSEEING

The town dates back to 1545, when it was first mentioned in Romanian historical documents and housed one of the main residences of Mihail Bravura (King Michael the Brave). In 1599 the King elevated the town's status to that of city and it grew rapidly in importance up to the 17th century, to the detriment of the earlier established cities nearby. Slowly but surely, Ploieşti became the artisan and commercial centre of the region. In the second half of the 19th century Ploieşi became the hub of the oil industry in Romania, a position it still enjoys today.

Due to its economic importance and early industrialisation, Ploieşti can claim several 'firsts': in 1871 the first 'Socialist Circle' was born in the city, and in 1890 Romania's first strike took place there, which eventually led to the Peasants' Revolt of 1907. The culmination of the industrial action born in Ploieşti was Romania's national strike in 1920.

Ploieşti played an important anti-Hitler rôle during the war whilst Romania was allied with Germany, by sabotaging the war machine in the Prahova valley. Gaining control of the oilfields was vital to Germany in both World Wars; in 1944 the city was heavily bombed by the Allies as a result.

Ploieşti has its share of museums. Opening times vary and there is usually one day a week day when they are closed.

It is advisable to check with the tourist office first. The fact that Ploieşti is one of Romania's principal oil centres is not forgotten and a museum dedicated to its importance is the **Petroleum Museum**, *10 Str. Dr. Bagdasar*, showing the evolution of the machinery used to extract oil and the development of its uses.. There is a fascinating **Clock Museum**, *1 Str. 6 Martie*, containing over 2000 timepieces dating from the 18th century onwards.

The **History Museum**, *10 Str. Teatrului*, can be found in the ancient building of the School of Commerce, a designated architectural monument in itself, designed in 1865 by the architect Al. Orăscu . There is a rich collection of Palaeolithic tools, ancient coins and documents mapping the history of the city from its earliest days.

The **Art Museum** (at was what was called *1 Blvd Gh Gheorghiu Dej* – possible name change) holds a large collection of paintings from some of Romania's leading artists, such as Nicolae Grigorescu and Corneliu Baba, as well as signed sculptures by Ion Vlasiu, Ion Jalea and others. There is also an exhibition of appliqué and decorative art.

The **Natural History Museum** is found within the Palace of Culture (*1 Str. N. Krupskaia* – possible name change). Ion Luca Caragiale is to Romania what Shakespeare is to England, and his house, *1 Str. C T Grigorescu*, is a museum where there are photographs of his family, articles, letters and personal effects. The building itself dates back to the 18th century.

One of the strangest sights is the **Shoe Monument** in *Piaţa Gării de Sud*.It was realised by the sculptor Vasilescu, to commemorate the heroism of the soldiers who fought for independence between 1877–78. Another statue, found behind the Cultural Palace, is the **Statue of**

**Liberty**. It was sculpted in Paris in the 19th century and is dedicated to the 'citizens of Ploieşti, – defenders of public liberty'. There are many churches, but the most interesting is the **Church of the Princes**, *63 Str. Matei Basarab*, which was built in 1639 by Matei Basarab, reconstructed in 1742 and renovated several times since.

### SIDE TRACK
### FROM PLOIEŞTI

## SINAIA

Sinaia, 'the Pearl of the of the. Carpathians', is a popular summer and winter mountain resort, with many hotels, mostly along *Blvd Carol 1*. There are many walks, ski tracks, ski lifts and cable cars. Whilst still a village, it became the playground of royalty, due to its sheer beauty, at the foot of the snowy Bucegi mountains. In 1880 the village was elevated to town and health spa status.

The 112-year-old **Peleş Palace** was built in German Renaissance style during the reign of King Carol (1866–1914). It took ten years to build due to the War of Independence (1877–78). Later additions include a hunting cottage now called **Foişor** and the 70 room **Pelişorul** (Little Peles) Palace in 1903, where King Carol's heir, Ferdinand (1916-27) lived during the summer. King Carol's wife, Elisabeta of Wied, wrote books under the pen name of Carmen Sylva in Sinaia.

The Germanic influence is very dominant yet there is a pleasing mixture of Hispanic, Italian and English renaissance styles within the decor of the 160 rooms and innumerable bathrooms. One of the most interesting

rooms is the carved oak library where there is a secret door, behind which was the imperial suite complete with theatre, where in 1906 the first film in the country was projected.

One of the many sights of the Bucegi mountains is the skull-like rock formation known as 'The Sphinx'. ◭

## BRAŞOV

**Station:** *53 Str. Republicii; tel: (068) 14 29 12*. One of the most attractive in Romania the station lies about 2 km north of the old town. Bus no 4 runs from the station to *Piaţa Sfatului* and *Piaţa Unirii* in the old town.

**Tourist Office: Biroul de Turism şi Tranzacţii SA**, *45 Str. Republicii; tel: (068) 14 46 96*, in the old quarter is generally open Mon–Fri 0800–1600. **Cristianul SA**, *1 Str. Toamneei; tel: (068) 18 71 10; 18 71 32; 18 83 46*. Maps of the area are available.

### GETTING AROUND

Many of the streets have changed their names recently, although remnants of Blvd Lenin or Karl Marx may still be seen around. Certainly the local people remember the old names better than the new ones at present. Whilst in the area, car hire is easily arranged for touring the area, but public transport and taxis are inexpensive and there are occasionally organised tours to Dracula sites.

### ACCOMMODATION

The choice of hotels in Braşov is extensive from the large four-star **Aro-Palace**, *27 Blvd Eroilor; tel: 068 14 28 40*, to the **Timpa**, *68 Str. Matei Basarab; tel: 068 11 51 80*, a one star hotel which does have rooms with bath or shower, whilst many of the other smaller hotels have shared facilities. There are several quite good

**133**

hotels in the *Blvd Eroilor* and *Str.Republicii* area but at Western prices. Private rooms are on offer – and the standard is usually a better than in Bucharest – by asking the locals usually found outside the stationor at the tourist offices. A little higher, up in **Poina Braşov**, the hotels offer a wide range of activities, especially the **Alpin**, *Poina Braşov; tel: 068 26 23 43*, offering hunting, riding and tennis as well as ski activities.

**SIGHTSEEING**

Once the more industrial area of Ploieşti has been left behind, the train travels through some extremely pretty countryside with open fields and winding rivers flowing near the railway line for much of the journey up to Sibiu, through some spectacular mountain scenery in the Predeal Valley.

The twin towns of Braşov and Poina Braşov rank among the prettiest summer/winter resorts in Europe. The winter sports facilities are excellent for downhill and cross country skiing and the area is close to central cities such as Bucharest as well as the Transylvanian cities of Sibiu and Timişoara. Poina Braşov is 13 km away by train.

One of the three local single-track railways can be found in Braşov and the cable car to the top of **Mt Timpa** offers spectacular views. The aerial view of the **Town Hall** (nicknamed the Trumpet Tower ) in *Piaţa Sfatului* is stunning. It was from there that the trumpeter sounded the warning of impending danger during the 15th-century. Nowadays the sounds of rock and pop concerts can be heard echoing through the rafters. Romania's history is on display in the **Regional History Museum** at the town hall. This includes the oldest existing document in the Romanian language.

Another first for Braşov was the first language school to be built in Romania. Now it is the **Museum of Romanian Culture**, *2 Piaţa Unirii*. The complex, in the old city quarter, includes a 15th-century wooden church.

The 14th-century Gothic **Black Church** in *Str. Curtea Bisericaii Negre* is one of the finest churches in Romania, exhibiting old prints of Braşov and the region. Another fine church is the **Bartolemeu**, *251 Str. lungă,* built in 1260.

**SIDE TRACKS FROM BRAŞOV**

The elegant winter resort of **Predeal** is close by, and 26 km away is **Bran Castle**, marketed as the home of Count Dracula. There are regular tours to the castle.

**FAGĂRĂŞ**

**Tourist Office:** None. For tourist information ask at the Braşov office.

The small town of Făgăraş lies almost halfway between Braşov and Sibiu and is an important centre for Romania's busy chemical and industrial equipment industry. Făgăraş is noted for its distinctive local costume and its ancient **fortress**, situated in the Olt Valley and built in 1310 on the site of an original 10th-century palisade. During 1599–60 the fortress belonged to King Michael the Brave.

The **Church of St Nicholas**, *116 Str. Tudor Vladimirescu,* was built in 1697 and has been kept intact, richly ornate with original paintings. At **Simbăta de Jos** 13 km away is a baroque chateau built by Iosif Brukenthal in 1770. The Brukenthal name is synonymous with art collections in this part of the world (see Sibiu).

**SIBIU**

**Station:** *6 Str. Nicolae Bălcescu; tel: (069)*

*21 20 85,* large and central with taxis readily available outside.

**Tourist Office: Biroul de Turism şi Tranzacţii,** *4 Str. Komhauser; tel: (069) 42 61 15,* and **Continental,** *2–4 Calea Dumbrăii; tel: (069) 41 09 10.*

## ACCOMMODATION

The leading hotel is the **Impăatul Romanilor** (Roman Emperor), *4 Str. Nicolae Bălcescu; tel: (069) 41 64 90,* close to the centre of town and the station. It is very imposing and has many amenities including family apartments. Most of the hotels in the city, such as the **Bulevard,** *10 Piaţa Unirii; tel: (069) 41 34 44,* and the **Silva,** *1 Aleea Mihail Eminescu; tel: (069) 44 21 41,* offer a variety of entertainment and facilities.

## SIGHTSEEING

The university city of Sibiu lies in the heart of mountainous Transylvania. The name is a derivation of the River Cibin which runs through the town. Sibiu's history dates back to the Paleolithic age. In Middle Ages Sibiu was rebuilt as a fortified town after the original was burnt down by the Tatars, who ransacked and pillaged the area in 1241. The old fortifications still surround the city.

In 1375 Sibiu became the economical centre of Transylvania and remains so today. It is well known as a centre for wine and beer, textile manufacture and the production of the classic Romanian salami, *Salame de Sibiu.*

Transylvania was for generations under German influence, and both modern German and the ancient Sax are still widely spoken; Sibiu is also known by its German name of *Hermansstadt.* Between 1703–1790 and again from 1849–67 Sibiu was the residence of the Prince of Transylvania. Since then it has been the home of the Governor (now called Mayor) of the surrounding county. Its most famous Governor in recent times was Nicu Ceauşescu, younger son of the former President.

Sibiu is also the home of the 'King of the Gypsies', currently the larger than life figure of Ion Cioba, who lives in a large mansion on the outskirts of the town.

The university and its student apartments are close to the Town Hall, but the old city square and the cobbled streets and arches around have not lost their ancient charm, with colourful flower stalls and market booths, yet both the old town and the new co-habit successfully.

Sibiu has one of the most famed art galleries in Romania with a collection of European art. Mrs Popescu, the curator of the **Brukenthal Museum,** *4 Piaţa Republicii,* is very knowledgable and can arrange tours. This has the distinction of being the oldest museum in Romania, and become a State museum in 1948. The baroque **Brukenthal House,** *8 Str. Avram Iancu,* was the home of Count Michael Brukenthal.

The old **Town Hall,** *2 Blvd 1 Mai,* is architecturally very interesting, and its Exhibition of the History of Sibiu presents the evolution of the ancient defence systems of the city. The **Casa Haller** (Haller House), *10 Piaţa Republicii,* built in Gothic style in 1470, combines the old architecture with transformations which took place during the renaissance.

There is a **Pharmaceutical Museum** at *26 Piaţa 6 Martie* which shows the advance of the pharmaceutical industry over more than 150 years, and a **Natural History Museum** at *1 Str. Cetăţii.* This street has many of the old towers and fortifications open to view. Sibiu has also several beautiful churches, including the **Reform Church,** *Piaţa Griviţei,* the

**Chapel of the Cross**, *Piaţa Gării*, and the **Orthodox Church**, *17 Str. Reconstrucţiei*.

In the summer, there is an open-air **village museum** combining actual examples of regional architectural styles from across the country with demonstrations of village life and crafts. For the summer programme, ask at the Tourist Bureau.

## ARAD

**Station:** for train information contact the ticket office, *1 Str. Unirii; tel: (057) 12 177.*

**Tourist Office: Biroul de Turism şi Tranzacţii**, *14–16 Piaţa Avram Iancu; tel: (057) 21 37 56*, and **Zarandul**, in the Hotel Parc; *tel: (057) 21 26 15*. Both supply local maps.

### ACCOMMODATION

The two main hotels are enormous. **Hotel Parc**, *25 Blvd General Dragalina; tel: (057 21 28 59*, close to the right bank of the River Mureş, has an unusually high number of single rooms. The three-star **Hotel Astoria**, *79–81 Blvd Revoluţiei; tel: (057) 21 66 50*, can be found on the main street of the city. Both are owned by the State. The private hotels such as **Hotel Aradealul**, *98 Blvd Revoluţiei; tel: (057) 21 18 40* (see below for its history), are quite small, but for groups willing to share, or families, a few rooms for 3 or 4 people are available.

### SIGHTSEEING

The city is large and sprawls along the river. The Arad area is agriculturally one of the most fertile in Romania and its history dates back to the Dacians. Arad was occupied by the Turks between 1552 and 1686. The first Romanian pedagogic school was founded in Arad in 1812 and on 22 March 1848 the city united at a grand assembly to abolish slavery, feudal privileges for the minorities and to allow freedom of the press. During World War I Arad forged close links with the Hungarian government in order to resolve the boundary problems in Transylvania.

The **Hotel Aradealul** was re-built in 1841 on the site of an ancient travellers' inn and is a fine example of the local neo-classic style. Once it was the most important hotel in Arad: regular concerts offered in its vast salon featured Franz Liszt (1846), Johann Strauss the younger (1847), Brahms (1879) and more recently Pablo Casals (1912).

The **Old Theatre**, *1–3 Str. Gheorge Lazăr*, opened in 1817 and is the oldest theatre in Transylvania. It notched up another first in 1907, as it changed its identity and became the first permanent cinema in Romania. The **Theatre** at *103 Blvd Revoluţii*, built in 1874, contains a museum relating to the history of the theatre in Arad.

The Philharmonic orchestra has its chambers in the **Palatul Culturel** (Cultural Palace), *1 Piaţa Enescu*, which is also the home of the main **museum** in Arad. There are archeological, ethnographical and historical exhibits to be seen in separate sections.

For those interested in medieval religious artefacts, a visit to the **Monstir de Simeon de Stylite**, *172 Str. Dunării*, built between 1760 and 1762 and reconstructed in 1955, should prove interesting.

On the left bank of the River Mureş there is an **obelisk** and a visitable ancient **fortress**. The obelisk was erected to honour the soldiers of Arad who defended the city. Another monument, this time in remembrance of those who fell in 1944 liberating Transylvania, can be seen at *Piaţa Avram Iancu*.

# BUCHAREST–CONSTANȚA

Romania is a country of contrasts. The bustling port of Constanța (Constanza) on the Black Sea (Pontus Euxinus, the 'Sea of Hospitality', to the Romans) is the turntable of the coastline, the Mecca of regular trains from all areas. The journey from Bucharest takes just 3 hours.

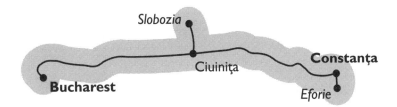

FASTEST JOURNEY: 3 HRS

Slobozia

Ciuinița

Constanța

Bucharest

Eforie

137

## TRAINS

**ETT Table:** 958

**FAST TRACK**

 **Bucharest–Constanța**
Eleven trains a day, journey time 3 hrs

**ON TRACK**

 **Bucharest–Ciuinița–Constanța**
The same eleven daily trains serve the full route. Journey time to Ciunita from either direction is about 1½ hrs.

### CIUINIȚA
Ciuniţa is of no great interest in itself, but is the jumping-off point for a diversion to Slobozia.

 **SIDE TRACK FROM CIUINIȚA**

### SLOBOZIA
**Station:** There is a railway and ticket office: **CFR**, *1 Blvd Unirii; tel: 043) 14 919.*
**Tourist Information:** Slobozia does not have its own tourist office yet, but any information needed can be

obtained from the **Ialomița Council,** Slobozia, *29 Str. Matei Basarab; tel: (043) 21 132 74.*

Slobozia was developed in 1604 on the site of a more ancient village called Vaideei, at the time of King Michael the Brave (Mihai Bravura). It is a pretty little town, with its share of churches and monuments, but its chief claim to fame is a bizarre new tourist attraction. Still not completed but already functional, **Southfork** is a replica of the American ranch made popular in the TV series *Dallas*. The programme is immensely popular in Romania and so is the new tourist sight. Returning to reality, *Str. Matei Basarab* is the main street and most of the sights are there, such as the **Monastir Slobozia de Ianache** (Monastery), founded in 1633 by Marshal Ianache Caragea and built by Matei Basarab. The street is complemented by two parks and the sports stadium. Worth a visit, at no. 30, is the **Museul Județean** (Departmental Museum), which highlights the folk traditions of the region, including the beautiful embroidery and woven carpets. 🖄

## CONSTANȚA

**Station**: 2 km west of the town, to which it is connected by a trolley-bus service. For train bookings and information, contact **CFR**, *4 Str. V Canarache; tel: (041)61 49 60)*, or **Oficiul PTTR Mamaia**, *tel: (041)61 79 30/61 82 12.* **Tourist Office:** There are two tourist offices, **Litoral SA**, *8741 Mamaia, Hotel București; tel: (041) 53 11 52/83 13 34,* and **Danubius,** *22 Blvd Republicii; tel: (041) 61 58 36/61 94 51.*

### ACCOMMODATION

There are a great many hotels to choose

from, mainly in Mamaia, which is one of the most popular resorts among the Romanians themselves. Advance booking is advisable, especially during the hot summer months. **Hotel Rex** in Mamaia, *Stațiunea Mamaia; tel: (041) 83 15 95)* is a very popular beachfront hotel with its own pastry shop and programme of entertainment. The **București**, *Stațiunea Mamaia; tel:(041) 83 13 60,* is made up of mainly family apartments with several double rooms. The three-star **Riviera**, *Stațiunea Mamaia; tel: 041) 83 10 19,* is a massive tower block with over 200 rooms. At the other end of the spectrum there are innumerable simple, small hotels, such as the **Pescăriuș**, *tel:(041) 83 16 73,* or the **Sulina**, *tel: (041) 83 15 96,* with single rooms as well as family apartments and double rooms.

The hotels in Constanța itself are generally very small, such as the **Intim**, *9 Str. Nicolae Titulescu: tel: (041) 61 78 14).* The largest is the **Palls**, *5–7 Str. Remiss Operand; tel:(041) 61 46 96,* which offers, amongst its limited facilities, entertainment of sorts.

Constanța is well provided with restaurants, as befits a resort of its size, and not just in the hotels. The choice includes Chinese, Italian and other cuisines, in what is one of the most comopolitan corners of Romania.

### SIGHTSEEING

Constanța's origins date back to the 5th century BC, when it was founded by the Greeks. In 61 BC the city, then known as **Tomis**, was occupied by the Romans. Ovid, the Roman poet, was exiled and died here. During the second half of the third century AD the population increased rapidly as Tomis became the centre for migrant families and the capital of the region. Fortifications, still visible today, were built to protect the area from invasion, especially from the Bulgars. Its name was changed to Constantia in honour of the Emperor Constantine during the early medieval period, when it was the chief port of the Byzantine Empire's fleet. After the 1877–78 War of Independence the region joined Romania. Such was Constanţa's importance that in 1905 the Russian battleship *Potemkin* anchored in the port after its famous mutiny, whereupon the crew proceeded to jump ship and make their escape. In 1944 the citizens fought hard to prevent the Nazis from destroying Constanţa, its naval installations and shipyards.

Today the old and the new cities mingle in harmony. The largest coastal resort of **Mamaia** is an extension of Constanţa, lying just north of the city.

The **Museum of the Sea** (Natelul Palace *15 Str. Remus Opreanu)* is opposite the site of the ancient port of Tomis. Here the visitor can see a collection of ancient flora and fauna found in the Black Sea and the Ocean. **The Aquarium** (*1 Blvd 16 Februarie)* has on exhibit some of the largest sturgeon ever caught as well as some 130 species of Black Sea fish. Other sites with a natural history slant are the **Natural Science Complex** and the **Delfinarium**, in the popular park at **Lake Tăbăcăriei.** By contrast, there are several attractions devoted the heavens: a **Planetarium,** an **Astronomic Observatory** and the **Solar Station** which presents films and documentaries on astronomy, biology and the cosmos. (For the new street names and latest programmes, please ask at the tourist offices). **The Muzeul Marinei Român** (Romanian Marine Museum), *53 Str. Traian,* charts the naval history of the region from Greek triremes onwards. All around Constanţa there are remains of Roman

---

### Ovid

Publius Ovidius Naso, 43 BC–AD 17, known to Latin scholars as Ovid, is Constanţa's most illustrious ex-citizen. A respectable married Roman, he neverthless made his reputation with frank and amusing poetry on sexual themes, including the classic *Art of Love.* The 'immorality' of this work was the pretext for his exile from Rome, at the age of 50, by the Emperor Augustus, to Tomis at the outermost reaches of the Roman Empire. Ovid hated Tomis, its harsh climate and ignorant citizens, and complained about it incessantly in his later poetry, coupled with fruitless appeals for his release from exile. He continued to write poetry for 10 years until his death, but the only work inspired by Tomis itself was a treatise in verse on Black Sea fish, which he gave up half-way through.

**139**

thermal baths, fortifications and statues. The 14th-century Genoese ship, *Str. Romulus Opreanu,* is worth a look, as is the **Archaeological Museum,** *12 Piaţa Ovidiu,* in the same square as Ovid's statue, which was sculpted by the Italian Gitore Ferrari in 1887.

### SIDE TRACKS FROM CONSTANŢA

The coastal region of the Black Sea, the **Littoral,** boasts some 245 km of seaside. Constanţa is the springboard for the exotically named resorts, each catering for different needs, with soft, white sandy beaches. The next stops along the railway line going south, are **Eforie Nord,** 14 km away by train and **Eforie Sud,** 17 km away. These are spa resorts, whose black sapropelic mud and brackish waters of **Lake**

**Tekirghiol** draw hundreds of thousands annually from all over the world, for the rheumatic cures, amongst others, on offer. Costineşti, 14 mins away by train from Eforie Sud, is a youth resort purpose-built in the 1980s. The side-track can be continued past modern purpose-built resorts to the ancient town of Mangalia, 43 km from Constanţa.

### EFORIE

**Stations:** Each resort has its own **CFR** train information and ticket office. Nord: *11 Blvd Republicii; tel: (041) 61 79 30/61 82 12.* Sud: *1 Str. Oituz; tel: (041) 61 82 12.*

**Tourist Offices:** The tourist office for both resorts is at Eforie Nord, in the **Hotel Steau del Mare**, *tel: (041) 74 28 84.*

Many of the hotels are built along the sea wall and there are solariums, restaurants and funfairs to entice the holidaymaker. **Hotel Steau Del Mare**, *39–43 Str. Tudor Vladimirescu; tel: (041)74 28 80.* There are a host of hotels of chose from mainly along the *Aleea Perla Mări* or *Str. Tudor Vladimirescu.* The **Bran**, *7 Str. Tudor Vladimirescu; tel: (041) 74 14 21* is a smallish hotel with many amenities. The **Europa**, *19 Str. Republicii; tel: (041) 74 29 90,* and the **Hefaistos**, *tel: (041) 74 17 55,* are extremely large and fairly impersonal. The hotels are all rather smaller in Eforie Sud, with most in *Str. Faleză*, such as the **Riviera**, *8 Str. Faleză; tel: (041) 74 15 33,* or the **Ancora**, *10 Str. Faleză; tel: (041) 74 29 38.* The **Excelsior**, *4 Str. Faleză; tel: (041) 74 16 54,* is one of the largest in the resort.

As both the resorts were built in the 20th century there are few specific sights, only the enjoyment of the sea, the hot and cold pools, the lush vegetation and the well-kept parks.

### COSTINEŞTI

**Tourist Office:** For rail and other tourist enquiries contact, the **youth tourist bureau**, *tel: 041 61 82 12.*

This resort was developed by Nicu Ceauşescu whilst Youth Secretary, in the 1980s and was therefore exempt from the curfew orders found elsewhere. Here the students were able to dance the night away in discos and bars. It is still a resort catering students on an international level. The accommodation is basic and the atmosphere is lively. There are campfires to be found at the beach and beach games galore. There are a few hotels, such as the 341-bed **Amiral**, *1 Staţiunea Costineşti; tel: (041) 74 16 34.*

### MANGALIA

**Tourist Office:** There is no local tourist office, but there is a local **CFR** for railway information, *16 Str. Stefan Cel Mare; tel: (041) 75 28 18.*

Mangalia, ancient Callatis, has a 3000-year history. The remains of the old Grecian walls can still be seen. The **Archaeological Museum of Callatis** has a large collection of artefacts from the Greek and Roman times, such as sculpture and statuettes, vases and sarcophagi. Another interesting site is the **Mosque de Sultan Esmahan**, *Str. Mircea cel Batrin,* built in 1590, and the Muslim cemetery it encircles.

There are many hotels to choose from, such as the **Mangalia**, *35 Str. Rozelor; tel: (041) 75 20 52,* and several more on *Str. Teilor,* but advance booking in the summer months is essential.

# BUCHAREST–DEBRECEN

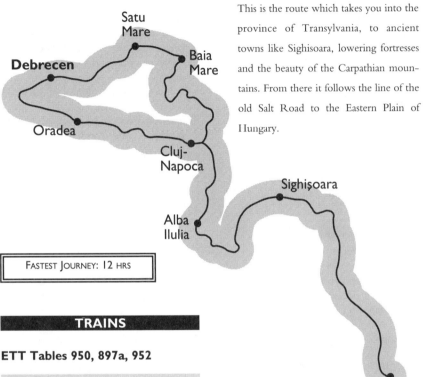

This is the route which takes you into the province of Transylvania, to ancient towns like Sighisoara, lowering fortresses and the beauty of the Carpathian mountains. From there it follows the line of the old Salt Road to the Eastern Plain of Hungary.

FASTEST JOURNEY: 12 HRS

141

## TRAINS

ETT Tables 950, 897a, 952

### FAST TRACK
No through trains. One through service a day possible by changing trains at Carei. Journey time around 12 hrs. Advance seat reservations are required for all these services.

### ON TRACK

**Bucharest–Sighişoara**
Seven fast trains a day taking nearly 5 hrs.

**Sighişoara–Alba Iulia**
Three train daily taking around 2 hrs.

**Alba Iulia–Cluj Napoca**
Seven trains a day make the journey in between 2 and 3 hrs.

**Cluj Napoca–Oradea**
Four express trains and one local are available on this route. Journeys vary from 2 hrs 30 mins to 4 hrs.

**Oradea–Debrecen**
Change trains at Püspökladány. Journey 4 hrs.

**Bucharest–Baia Mare**

Just 2 trains each day, one of which is overnight, taking some 12 hr.

**Baia Mare–Satu Mare**

11 trains a day taking between 50 and 80 minutes.

**Satu Mare–Debrecen**

One through train takes 4 hrs.

## SIGHIŞOARA

**Station:** tel: (065)77 18 86. About 1 km north of the centre. **CFR Agency** 2 Str. Decembrie 1; tel: 065) 77 18 20 for reservations.

**Tourist Office:** Information is available at the CFR Agency and at the Hotel Steaua.

### ACCOMMODATION

The only hotel is the **Steaua**, 12 Str. Decembrie 1; tel: (065) 771930. Although it has a monopoly, it manages to remain friendly and reasonably priced. There is also a **campsite**, **Dealul Gării**, tel: (065) 71046, 4 km out of town in the direction of Medias.

### SIGHTSEEING

Sighişoara is a delightful Transylvanian town set in medieval fortifications, as are most in the area. Said to be the most picturesque town in Romania, it is situated in the Tinaveni Valley on the Tirnava Mare river.

The remains of the 3rd-century **fortifications** may still be seen around the main square. There are some fine churches; one in particular, the **Coteau church**, 7 Str. Scolli, built in the Flamboyant Gothic style between 1345 and 1516, has some remarkable frescos. The 15th-century **Monastery**, 8 Piata Muzeului, is famous for its bronze baptismal fonts dating back to 1440. **Vlad Tepeş** (see box opposite) lived in Sighişoara before he became Prince of Wallachia, and his birthplace is near the monastery. The town is still strongly dominated by its Austrian/Saxon background, and the ancient Sax language (an archaic dialect of German) can still be heard spoken here and around the region. Transylvania was settled in the early Middle Ages with colonies of 'Saxons', i.e. German tradesmen and craftsmen, deliberately attracted by the local rulers in an attempt to improve the economy.

## ALBA IULIA

**Station:** 2 km south of the town. For railway information, contact the **CFR** at 1 Str. Moţilor; tel: (058) 81 36 89.

**Tourist Office: Biroul de Turism şi Tranzacţii**, 2 Str. Parcului; tel: (058) 81 21 40 is close to the Cultural Union.

### ACCOMMODATION AND FOOD

**Hotel Parc**, 4 Str. Primăverii; tel: (058) 81 17 23, is a smallish, modern-style hotel with pleasant overhanging balconies and surrounded by hedges and greenery. There are many restaurants to choose from, such as the **Hanuc cu Berze**, 17a Str. Republicii; tel: (058) 83 01 28, or the more sophisticated restaurant/bar **Mosquito**, 33 Str. Aurel Vlaicu; tel:(058) 83 00 25. This establishment has a games room and a swimming pool on the terrace which is open during the summer season.

### SIGHTSEEING

Alba Iulia is the capital town of the county of Alba and is situated in western Transylvania, where Hungarian influence has been traditionally dominant. The eastern side of the town is dominated by the border of the Plateau of Secaşe, whilst

## Vlad the Impaler

Vlad Tepeş – Vlad the Impaler – is both a prominent character in Romanian history and a figure of legend, a legend complicated by the publication of Bram Stoker's Gothic tale *Dracula* in 1897. The very name Transylvania is known to many Western visitors only through the novel (which was denounced as anti-Romanian throughout the Ceauşescu era). The real story of this late-medieval Romanian ruler is, if anything, even more blood-curdling than that of his fictional reincarnation as the vampire Count Dracula. Add to this the separate traditions of vampirism in Transylvania, which inspired Stoker's novel, and the fact that Vlad's father was called Vlad Dracul, and the confusion is multiplied.

The historical Vlad was born in Sighişoara in the 1430s, son of Vlad Dracul ('the Dragon' – so-named from his being made a knight of the Order of that name by the King of Hungary). Wallachia, Transylvania and other provinces of what is now Romania were then a battleground in the struggle between Hungary and the Ottoman Empire for domination of the Balkans. Minor rulers played off one side against the other in order to carve out their own domains. Vlad Tepeş spent part of his youth as a hostage at the Sultan's court, and was installed as Prince of Wallachia after the murder of his father. His appearance was said to be terrifying; certainly his cruelty is well documented. He executed personal and political enemies, criminals and prisoners of war in thousands, usually by the excruciating process of impalement alive on wooden stakes; on one occasion a Turkish army is said to have turned back after finding 20,000 of their comrades, taken captive in previous battles, impaled on stakes lining the road to Vlad's fortress. Betrayed by his brother and the Transylvanian nobility, as well as the Saxon townspeople of the region, Vlad was finally assassinated and beheaded in 1476. Despite his atrocities, he was regarded by many Romanians as a folk-hero of their fight against the Turks, and the pre-1989 regime virtually canonised him.

His reappearance as Dracula was invented by the late-Victorian tour de force of Bram Stoker, who never visited Romania but came across Vlad's blood-stained history while researching vampirism in the British Museum Library for his novel. There is no evidence that Vlad was regarded as a vampire in his own time, but the belief in 'undead' corpses was, and to some extent still is, widespread in Hungary and all the Balkan countries which came under Ottoman influence (the word 'vampire' is derived from the Turkish for a witch). Outbreaks of supposed vampire activity were common in all periods in the eastern half of the Austro-Hungarian Empire, and interest in the phenomenon among western Europeans was well established before Stoker wrote *Dracula,* which joined a long existing tradition of vampire stories. Much of the paraphernalia familiar from the novel and its cinematic spin-offs, such as the belief in garlic as a prophylactic and the lack of a shadow or reflection among vampires, derives from authentic Romanian folk traditions.

Associations with the real Vlad abound in Transylvania; his birthplace is in Sighişoara and his tomb in Snagov, but there is no proven association with Bran Castle, billed for tourists as Dracula's castle, although it looks the part.

**143**

on the west, there are the mountains of Trascău and Metalliferes. It nestles at the confluence of the rivers Mureş and Ampoiu. Alba Iulia lies in a wine-growing area and the hills all around are filled with vineyards, with vast vegetable fields close to the rivers. Developed since the Neolithic age, the town has in recent years been the subject of several interesting and important archaeological finds, including in 1959 the vestiges of a large, fortified, wooden Iron Age citadel and in 1969, some 10 km from Alba Iulia on the heights of Piatra Craivii, the remains a Dacian village.

Alba Iulia has kept its ancient Roman name; it was at one time the seat of the Governor-General of the Roman province of Dacia, which covered most of what is now Romania. During the Middle Ages Alba Iulia became a centre of Catholicism; it was attacked by the Tatars in 1241, 1658 and 1661, and was established as the autonomous capital of Transylvania during the second half of the 16th century.

The medieval **Fortress** was constructed over the original defences; consisting of seven bastions; a central fort; and six gates. it is richly ornamented in baroque style and is the largest in Transylvania. The leaders of the Popular Revolution of 1784 were imprisoned in its dungeons. The 14–15th century **Prince's Palace**, Str. Mihail Viteazu, was transformed into barracks in the 18th century. The twin **Palaces** of **Apor** and **Bethlem Mikloş**, Str. Unirii, are situated on the perimeter of the fortress; built in Renaissance style, they date from the 17th century. The old **library** in the fortress complex contains some ancient and very rare manuscripts dating back to 1665, as well as a fragment of the Codex Aureus written on parchment during the 8th century AD.

The Roman Catholic Cathedral of **Sf Mihai** (St Michael's) is considered by many to be the most outstanding medieval building in Transylvania. Built in stages between the 13th and 17th cen-

turies, it was constructed on the site of an 11th-century place of worship destroyed by the Tatars in 1241. The basilica and the transept were built between 1247 and 1291 in Romanesque style, whilst the Gothic design of the choir dates from the 14th century.

## CLUJ-NAPOCA

**Station:** 20 mins walk from the centre. There are two **CFR** offices for railway enquiries and tickets: **Cluj-Napoca International**, 9 Piaţ Unirii; tel: (064) 11 24 75), conveniently near to the tourist office, and **Cluj-Napoca**, 20 Piaţa Mihail Viteazu; tel: (064) 11 22 12, for local information. Try contacting International first.

**Tourist Office:** There are two tourist information offices: **Continental**, 1 Str. Napoca; tel: (064) 11 14 41, and **Turism Transilvania**, 10 Piaţa Unirii; tel: (064) 19 11 14/10 04 58.

### ACCOMMODATION AND FOOD

The selection of hotels in all price ranges is very large. The **Transilvania**, 1–3 Str. Călăraşi; tel: (064) 13 44 60, is very large and offers one of the most extensive list of amenities in Romania, including cabaret, dancing and a bureau de change. **Hotel Univers T**, 53–55 Str. Tineretului; tel: (064) 15 46 86, has a fitness room, tennis courts, billiards and a large restaurant. It is situated on the lake. There is a wide choice of restaurants, bars, fast food restaurants all around the town.

### SIGHTSEEING

Cluj-Napoca is one of the largest cities in Romania. It is divided into industrial and residential zones and is criss-crossed by rivers; the Little Someş (Someşul Mic); the Morii Canal and Piriul Nadaş.

There is a great deal of Hungarian

influence in the area: in the 1848 Diet of Cluj, a union between Transylvania and Hungary was forged by representatives of Hungary, the Saxons and the Sekels. However, in 1894 the people of Cluj founded the movement to liberate Transylvania from the 'oppression of the Austro–Hungarian Empire ruled by Emperor Franz Joseph'. After 1900 the city replaced the old Empire's authority and government with Romanian leadership. Today there is still ethnic tension between the Romanians and the Hungarian-speaking population. The current Romanian mayor is trying to eradicate the Hungarian language and remove ethnic Hungarians from their homes. On the other side of the coin, there is a Hungarian television station and theatre, and the ethnic minority want to have their own University.

Cluj-Napoca, like the rest of Transylvania, is steeped in history, dating back to the Roman era. It developed as the economic centre of the region, and remains so today, second only to Bucharest in size. From the 16th century increased trade brought a great deal of culture to the city and the establishment of the faculties of jurisprudence, theology and philology, and later of natural science, law and medicine. Cluj also became one of Romania's leading Jewish centres.

Cluj is a very green city, with many parks all around the city. The **Botanical Gardens**, *42 Str. Republicii*, has areas devoted to many different sections of the floral world, including exotic and ornamental plants. Within the gardens there is also a Botanical Museum. The **Open Air Museum** in the Hoia Woods has assembled 130 houses and rustic buildings of the region. The **Ethnographical Museum**, *21 Str. 30 Decembrie*, was built in the Empire style at the end of the 18th century, and furnished by Redoute. It depicts the costumes and customs of Transylvania with some 40,000 exhibits.

Cluj has a fine **Opera House**; ask for details of the programme at one of the Tourist Offices or your hotel.

The house where Matei Corvin (King Mattyas Corvinus of Hungary, 1458–90) was born, *6 Str. Matei Corvin*, is the oldest in the city.

There are several interesting churches scattered around the city, as well as a citadel and monastery including the Gothic-style Cathedral of **Sf Mihai** (St Michael), *Piaţa Libertăţii*, the oldest religious building in Cluj. It contains some very valuable paintings from the 16th century. The **Art Museum**, *30 Piaţa Libertăţii*, is housed in the baroque **Bánffy Palace**. The **Tailor's Bastion** is a 15th-century fortification which was reconstructed by the Prince of Transylvania, Gabriel Bethlen in 1624–29 and restored in 1959.

**145**

## ORADEA

**Station**: North of the town, with trams to the centre. The **CFR** office for rail enquiries and tickets is at *2 Blvd Republicii; tel: (059) 13 05 78*.

**Tourist Office: Crişul**, *2 Str. Teatrului; tel: (059) 13 07 37/13 05 08*, is conveniently close to the Hotel Astoria. The other is **Lucun**, *1 Str. Gen Traian Moşolu; tel: (059) 13 66 13*.

### ACCOMMDATION

The three star **Hotel Dacia**, *1 Aleea Stradului; tel: ( 059) 11 86 56*, is large and rather uninteresting to look at but it lies on the river bank. There are two quite nice hotels in the *Str. Teatrului*: **Astoria** at no. 1, *tel: (059) 13 07 45)*, and **Transylvania** at no. 2, *tel:( 059) 13 05 08/13 07 45*.

### SIGHTSEEING

Oradea is a very busy border post between Romania and Hungary and the principal city of Bihor County. Built on the terraces along the left bank of the River Criş Repede it lies at the foothills of the Piemintaine hills which precede the Carpathians. After the founding of the Eastern Orthodox Church it became a flourishing religious centre.

Due to its geographical position at the apex of Transylvania, Hungary and the Banat region, Oradea soon became a commercial area, too. Between 1880 and 1906 the first regular magazine in Romania, *Familia*, was published in Oradea, which contributed to the extension of Romanian culture and became a vehicle for the leading writers and poets of the country.

The **Muzeul Ţării Crişurilor** (Museum of the Criş Rivers Land), *2 Str. Stadionului*, is very diversified; its chief curiosity is a collection of 13,000 painted eggs, representing a craft tradition of the region. The museum is housed in the grounds of the 18th-century **Episcopal Palace**, modelled on Vienna's Belvedere Palace. The grounds also contain giant sequoias, as well as the baroque **Roman Catholic cathedral**, Romania's largest.

Another fine church is the **Biserica cu Lun** (Moon Church, so called from the unusual lunar clock on its façade), *Piaţa Victoriei*.

### BAIA MARE

Station: The **CFR** railway office is at *57 Str. Victoriei; tel: (062) 42 16 13*, close to the river bank.
**Tourist Office: Biroul de Turismşi Tranzacţii**, *29 Str. Gh Şincai; tel: (062) 41 21 62/41 21 63/41 32 49*, one of two tourist offices, is close to the Hotel Maramureş. The other office, **Mara SA**, *1*

*Str. Culturil; tel: (062) 41 41 77/ 41 10 43*, lies on the street which crosses the river.

### ACCOMMODATION

The privately run **Hotel Carpaţi**, *16 Str. Minerva; tel: (062) 41 48 16*, has a western-style lobby with shops, but is fairly small as modern hotels go. It is situated on the banks of the river right in the town centre. **Hotel Maramureş**, *37a Str. Gh. Şincai; tel:(062) 41 65 55*, has two restaurants, bars, hairdressing salons and other facilities.

### SIGHTSEEING

This small town is close to the Hungarian and Ukrainian borders, in the Săsar valley at the foot of Mount Gutii. It lies at an altitude of 245 m; the climate is one of the most temperate in the region.

Documents pinpoint Baia Mare's history to at least 1329; it acquired its present name, meaning 'Great Mine', in 1564. Precious metals were mined in the area and Baia developed rapidly after giving its riches to the royal treasury. The mining of non-ferrous metals is still a significant industry, but the town has also developed a tourist infrastructure.

An impressive **Monument to Romanian Soldiers** stands at the point where the old and the modern parts of town meet, at the entrance to the **Town Park**. Also in the park is the **Ethnographical and Popular Art Museum**. Perhaps one of the world's more unusual art museums, the **Plastique Art Museum**, *8 Str. 1 Mai*, exhibits modern sculptures. graphical designs and other more recent art forms . Nearby is the **Departmental Museum**, its natural science exhibits including examples of local mineralogy. Within walking distance is the **Bastionul Monetăriei** (Money Bastion), *1–2 Str. Bicazului*, a vestige of the ancient fortifications.

In the square is the **House of Iancu de Hunedoara**, also known as Elizabeth's House – Iancu was the father of Mátyas Corvinus, one of Hungary's greatest monarchs and builder of the Matthias Church in Budapest (see p. 160). Within the massive walls, which date back to the 15th century, is an exhibition of the 'Flowers of the Mines'.

Two more towers, **Stephen's Tower**, in *Str. Crişan*, and the **Munitions Tower** were built in the mid 1400s. Within the surrounds of Stephen's Tower are the remains of the Cathedral of **Sf Stefan** (St Stephen), built in 1347 but demolished a century later.

The ancient **Jesuit residence** was built close to the tower in 1696. Originally the old High School was founded in the residence, today the building continues as a local school. The Jesuit Church itself, **St Trinity**, was built in baroque style.

There is a **Teatrul de Păpusi** (puppet theatre) in town, amongst the more usual theatres, and the **Complexul Astronomic Popular** (astronomy complex), which offers a planetarium, sun chamber, and an observatory.

## SATU MARE

**Station**: The **CFR** office is at 9 Piaţa 25 Octombrie; tel: (061) 71 12 02.

**Tourist Information**: **Biroul de Turism şi Tranzactii**, 7 *Str. Traian; tel: (061) 73 79 18.*

### ACCOMMODATION

The two main hotels in Satu Mare are the imposing **Dacia**, 8 *Piaţa Libertăţii; tel: (061)71 42 76,*with fountains playing in front of the grand façade, and the **Aurora**, 11 *Piaţa Libetrăţii; tel: (061) 71 49 46,* which is smaller but offers far more amenities; both are of these old and well-established hotels are classified as two-star.

### SIGHTSEEING

This large, sprawling town is situated on the north of the East Plain on the two banks of the River Someş. The name is derived from the Latin *fossatum* (village surrounded by a ditch) which the villagers transformed into 'Sătmar' ('large village'). Satu Mare was a fortress town in early days, then by the Middle Ages, became a flourishing city. Nowadays Satu Mare is a metropolis with ethnic Hungarians, Austrian and Germans living alongside the Romanian population.

The *Piaţa Libertăţii* is the main area of tourist interest. The square's impressive façade in the Viennese Secession style, built in 1909, has been Satu Mare's town emblem for generations.

The **Reform Church** and the **Roman Catholic Church**, both built in the 1780s, are in the square. The Reform Church, destroyed in 1944 and later restored, is in baroque style, but the neo-Classical Catholic church is the more impressive of the two.

There is only one museum of importance in the town, the **Departmental Museum**, 21 *Piaţa Libertăţii*, with its sections on archaeology, antique and modern Romanian paintings and ceramics in the Art gallery, some fine very valuable bronzes from the Roman-Dacian age and a local history department. There is a large sports and fitness centre on the banks of the River Someş, with thermal baths, a swimming pool and sports facilities.

The area around Satu Mare is best appreciated for its scenery and the fruit orchards of the pretty nearby villages; The countryside of **Maramureş** still echoes the notes of the ancient and harmonious wooden 'Pan pipes'. The region is also famed for its peasant tradition of exotic and delicate 'lace carvings' in wood, often adorning the gateways to homes.

**147**

# BUCHAREST–SUCEAVA

Between Bucharest and Suceava the train passes through the beautiful Prahova valley. The aeas round Suceava, in Moldoviţa, is renowned for its beauty and pleasant climate. The town itself is one of Romania's most important cultural centres.

**Suceava**

**Paşcani**   *Iaşi*

FASTEST JOURNEY: **6** HRS

**148**

*Galaţi*

**Buzau**   *Braila*

**Bucharest**

## TRAINS

**ETT Table:** 955

### FAST TRACK

Seven trains a day with journeys of around 6 hrs. Most trains offer refreshments onboard.

### ON TRACK

**Bucharest–Buzău**
Frequent service taking 1 hr 45 mins.

**Buzău–Pascani–Suceava**
Seven trains a day with journey times of 3 hr 30 mins for Buzău to Pascani and just over 1 hr for Pascani to Suceava.

## BUZĂU

**Station: CFR** railway information and official ticket office, *18b str. Unirii; tel:*

*(038) 11 135,* is conveniently close to the the tourist office.

**Tourist Office: Biroul de Turism și Tranzactii,** *Block 1 Str. Unirii; tel: (038) 41 38 50.*

There are quite a few hotels to choose from. Although small, the **Tineretului,** *1 Str. Mesteacănul; tel:(038) 41 35 41,* has ten pin bowling for its guests, but there is no lift. Another worth considering is the larger **Hotel Pietroasa,** *1 Piața Dacia; tel: (038) 41 19 42 or 41 20 33.*

Buzău, capital of Buzău county, is large and sprawling, nestling between several forests on the right bank of the **River Buzău.** For years it has been considered as the gateway into Transylvania and Moldova. Some 1600 years old, Buzău has always been a military centre and has thus been destroyed on numerous occasions, rising like the phoenix from its ashes in 1600, 1659, 1768-74 and lastly in 1807. At the end of the 19th and during the early 20th century it was redeveloped and modernised, and many public buildings were added. Buzău has become one of the industrial centres of Romania.

Wandering through the streets the tourist will find many pleasing statues and architectural sights, such as the delightful Town Hall and the **Ethnographical Museum,** *8 Str. Războieni.* This is inside the **Vergu-Mănăilă house** and is a monument to the architecture of the 18th century. There are some very interesting exhibits of local folk costume, decorative textiles, ceramics and some very ancient utensils from the surrounding area. In the **Dumbrava Cemetery** there are some old and, unusual busts, monuments and headstones. The **Departmental Museum,** *50 Str. Bălcescu,* contains ancient coins, Neolithic ceramics, pieces from the Bronze Age and ancient historical documents as well as a room devoted

to the history of art.

Should the restaurant in the **Parcul Crîng** (Cring Park) be open, this is very pleasant as the park is in a wooded layout. Another fine park is the **Parcul Judeţului** (Youth Park). In the park is a statue to Gheorghe Enescu, one of the most famous Romanian composers of international status, whose best-known work in the West is the *Romanian Rhapsody.* The nearby forests are worth visiting. **Frasin** is a nature reserve with some very unusual and rare plants. **Spătaru** is very similar, and only about 10 km away there is a seasonal thermal spa.

**SIDE TRACK FROM BUZĂU**

**GALAŢI**

**Station:** rail information at the **CFR** office and ticket bureau, *Block BR2, Str. Brăilei; tel: (036) 35 121.*

**Tourist Office: Galtour SRL,** *15 Str. Domnească; tel: (036) 41 40 46/46 07 04* and **Dunărea SA,** *1 Str. Nicolae Bălcescu; tel: (036) 41 22 27/41 80 41.*

For accommodation, try the **Hotel Galaţi,** *12 Str. Domnească; tel: (036) 46 00 40,* or the **Constant International,** *1 Str. Sidergiştilor; tel: (036) 46 11 32.*

Galaţi is a city of around a quarter of a million inhabitants, situated on the banks of the Danube between the river branches Siret and Prut. Built in terraces, it has been occupied since at least the 1st century AD; there is evidence of a fortress dating from that era. Galaţi played an important role in the development of Moldovia, one of the first regions of Romania. In 1484 it lost its status as a port, but 400 years later this was reinstated after the

**149**

Treaty of Adrianapol (1829) and many ships were constructed there. Locally, Galaţi is famous as one of the leading centres of strike action between 1888 and 1920. In 1944 the town was partially destroyed and the railway sabotaged by the Germans after Romania broke its alliance with them and joined the rest of Europe against Hitler.

There is a **Museum of Contemporary Art**, *141 Str. Domnească,* which has a large collection of mainly postwar paintings, sculpture, graphic art and appliqué. The **Librarie V. A. Urechia**, *44 Str. Primaverii,* holds over 500,000 books and 3000 manuscripts and letters, dating from around 1500. The **Muzeul Istorie** (History Museum), *80 Str. Alexandru Ioan Cuza,* has sections devoted to archaeology, ancient and medieval history and a selection of bronzes and ceramics. The **Modern History Museum**, *46 Str. Mihail Bravu,* shows the history of Galaţi and personal objects relatingto several important Romanians throughout more recent history. There are several interesting churches and parks throughout the town and pleasant walks along the Danube bank.

## PAŞCANI

This is the stop at which to change trains for Iaşi.

### ↴ SIDE TRACK
### FROM PAŞCANI

## IAŞI

**Station:** There is a very large **CFR** office near the Hotel Unirea for rail tickets and enquiries, *9-11 Piaţa Unirii; tel: (032) 14 76 73 / 14 52 69.*
**Tourist Office: Moldova SA**

**Turism**, *29 Str. Anastasie Panu; tel: (032) 14 64 00* and **Tourism Agency of Moldova**, *4 Blvd Ştefan cel Mare şi Sfânt; tel:(032) 11 22 89.*

As one would expect. there are a host of hotels to choose from, like the **Hotel UOTB Nicolina**, *12 Str. Trotuş; tel: (032) 12 43 74.* In the same block with the same phone number but with different facilities is the **Basarabia**, *12 Str. Trotuş; tel: (032) 12 43 74.* The **Unirea**, *5 Piaţa Unirii; tel: (032) 14 21 10,* is a huge place, as is the **Moldova**, *31 Str. Anastasie Panu; tel: (032) 14 22 25,* where one of the official money exchange offices is to be found.

**Iaşi** , capital of Iaşi county and once of Moldavia, is only 21 km away from the Russian border. It is a large, important city lying in the Moldavian plain on the terraces of the Bahlui hills, and between the arms of the River Bahlui and the rivulet Nicolina. **Iaşi** has been inhabited since the Palaeolithic era, according to archaeological finds. Those of the 7th-14th centuries prove that this was a densely populated city, beginning as the residential capital of the nobility then turning into an economic centre for the region, after the construction of the royal residence in the 15th century. The Turks, Tartars, Poles and the Cossacks in turn burnt and pillaged Iaşi, the last attack as recently as 1821. Great fires over the years 1776–1882 also destroyed much of the old city. From the 17th century, Iaşi was known as one of the leading cultural centres of Romania and during the second half of the 19th century, the most prestigious names in Romanian literature such as Ion Creangă and Mihai Eminescu formed a literary group, 'Junimea', which was based here. Iaşi is divided into sections, **Dealul Copoului** is the University city, the oldest in the country and second in size and importance to Bucharest.

Throughout Romanian towns and cities there are streets named after Mihail Kogălniceanu. In Iaşi one can visit the museum that was once the house of the famous writer, journalist, politician and academician, *15 Str. Mihail Kogălniceanu*. There are many exhibits that concern his multilateral activities.

The tourist to Iăsi cannot fail to notice the many statues, busts and monuments throughout the parks and squares. They commemorate the lives of the many famous citizens of this town, especially from the arts. The **Literature Museum** *(4 Str. I.C.Frimu)* contains a richesse of documentation relating to modern Romanian literature. **The Palace of Culture** *(1 Str. Palatului)* is an edifice built in neo-Gothic style at the turn of the 20th century. There is an imposing tower with a clock which chimes the hour. Inside there is a series of museum chambers, including the **Museum of Moldavian History**, charting the area's development since paleothic times, and the **Art Museum**, with a collection of Dutch, Italian, French and Flemish works, as well as the local Moldavian folk designs, including carpets and embroideries. The **Biserica Sf Nicolae** (Royal Church of St Nicholas), *65 Str. A Panu,* was founded in 1491–92 and restored by French architects in 1888–1904. It is very close to the 17th-century **Casa Dosoftei**, the 'House of the Arcades', *69 Str. A*

*Panu,* which houses a literature museum, but mainly of interest for its architectural style. The **National Theatre Museum**, *5 Str. Vasile Alecsandri,* illustrates the Romanian's love of the theatre and culture since the Middle Ages up to the present day. ⚱

## SUCEAVA

**Station:** There are two passenger stations, Gara Suceava and Suceava Nord. Both are connected to the town centre by trolley-bus.For rail enquiries and tickets: **CFR**, *8 Str. Nicolae Bălcescu; tel:(030) 21 43 35.*

**Tourist Office:** at the Hotel Tineret.

### ACCOMMODATION

Every main street has a hotel to chose from, most with either a one- or two-star classification. The one-star **Hotel Tineret**, *5 Str. Mitropoliei; tel: (030) 21 58 56*, remains popular. The slightly smaller, two-star, **Hotel Balada**, *8 Str. Mitropoliei; tel: (030) 22 31 98*, has a restaurant. Perhaps the best hotels are the **Arcaşul**, *4–6 Str. Mihai Viteazu; tel: (030) 27 10 94*, where there is often live entertainment available, and the **Bucovina**, *5 Str. Ana Ipitescu; tel: (030) 21 70 48*, where there is a foreign exchange desk in reception.

### SIGHTSEEING

The chief town of the area of Moldavia known as Bucovina, Suceava is in the uppermost corner of the country, close to the borders with the Ukraine and Moldova (not to be confused with the Romanian province of Moldavia). Archeological discoveries have dated its existence to before the Neolithic Age and after the Dacian era, Suceavans co-existed with a migrant Slav population.

The history of the area is one of suc-

151

cessive annexation. Between 1457 and 1504, there was a period of particular brilliance under the reign of Stephen the Great. Decline set in when the royal seat moved to Iaşi. In 1600 Moldavia joined with Transylvania and Wallachia and Michael the Brave's army to form a united Romania, with Suceava as the capital of Moldavia. During 1775, however, Bucovina was annexed by the Austrians. Nevertheless, the citizens of Suceava felt strong Romanian ties throughout, and thousands enrolled as volunteers into the Romanian army during 1887–88, as well as forming an active underground movement of terrorists in order to break these unnatural alliances. Bucovina was returned to Romania after World War I. Suceava was once the seat of a large Jewish community, thousands of whom perished in the Holocaust.

In Suceava itself the old **Cetăţea Sucevei (Suceava Fortress)** is one of the predominant sights. *(Str. Citătii).* Built 1374-91, it forms a quadrangle surrounded by towers and arc-like bastions. It was partially demolished originally, by order of the Turks, then over the centuries, fell to ruins. The restoration of a greater part of the fortress was undertaken during 1961-70. **The Fortress de Şcheia,** *(by Str. Ilie Pintilie)* was built in the north of the town during the 14th century. The 17th-century **Hanul Domnesc** (Prince's Inn), *5 Ciprian Porumbescu,* is now a museum. This too was restored in the 1960s, and contains exhibits of north Romanian pottery, Moldavian national dress, carved wood pieces and part of the interior of a peasant cottage. For those interested in archaeology, this may be found in the History section of the **Departmental Museum,** *33 Str. Ştefan cel Mare,* where there are documents and photographs which illus-

trate the history of the region, as well. The **Natural Science Museum** *(23 Str. Ştefan cel Mare)* has a collection of rare species of flora and fauna of the region. Folklore is represented at the home of the local folklore expert, **Simeon Florea Marian,** (1847-1907) *(4 Allea S. F. Marian).*

The local churches of Suceava are wonderful, especially the **Biserica Mirăuţi,** *(19 Str. Mirăuţi)* built at the end of the 14th century. After 1401 it became the Moldavian Cathedral where the official Princely ceremonies were performed. The **Biserica Sf Gheorghe,** nicknamed the **New Cathedral** *(1514-22)* has some fascinating old paintings inside while fragments of the exterior frescos remain. In 1606 the Armenian **Monastery-Fortress de Zamca** *(Str. Zamcii)* was built and fortified 1690-1. It contains certain elements of Gothic and oriental design.

## OUT OF TOWN

The tour of the **five historical churches** in Bucovina is a must . They are feudal monuments to the reign of **Ştefan cel Mare,** Prince Stephen the Great, who reigned for around half a century (1475–1504). Pope Sixtus IV conferred the title 'Christ's Athlete' on the Prince after his valiant and successful attempts with the region's armies, to vanquish the Turks during the Ottoman conquests.

It is possible to reach them by train, but so slowly that each monastery entails travelling the best part of a day. The tourist agencies in Suceava organise tours by road, and these are more convenient.

Art historians have yet to unravel the secret which has kept the paintwork of the Bucovinian churches in such excellent condition. UNESCO has catalogued the five houses of God as 'values of universal art' (*sic*).

**Veroneţ Monastery** was built in 1488, in the village of the same name. It has been called the 'Sistine Chapel of the East', with its fairy-tale frescoes. It took a little under four months to complete, and has lasted more than five centuries, despite pollution and the ravages of the weather. Veroneţ is Byzantine art at its best, with a multitude of panels painted on a background of blue. The panels have been compare to those of the Renaissance painters Giotto or Ciambue and the mosaics to those in the Kahrie mosque in Istanbul.

**Humor** is close by and is known by the name of 'Miniatures on the Lawn'. It can be found 6 km from the tiny village of **Gura Humorului** and has the appearance of a page from an ornate ancient manuscript. Built in 1583, the vault has a similarity to the one at Moldoviţa, giving a floating appearance. Along the southern wall there is a composition of paintings and embroideries representing a poem depicting 24 scenes of the Virgin Mary saving the city in 626 after the Persian attack. Other scenes along the walls depict the devil in the guise of a greedy woman, in a jocular fashion, which gave the monastery its name; a *hora* danced by a group of five, inviting guests at a feast to join in, and images of the Prodigal Son. In the 15th century there were workshops close to the church, where miniature painters worked.

**Moldoviţa Monastery**, only a few km away, like Veroneţ, is presented predominantly in blue, and has been nicknamed 'A Parchment in Blue' for this reason. It is larger than the Monasteries of Veroneţ and Humor. It was built in 1532 and the paintings were undertaken during 1537. Again, the exterior walls are totally

covered in fine frescoes with hundreds of portraits and scenes including the 'Jesse Tree', similar to the one to be seen at Veroneţ. One of the largest and most valuable compositions is the tribute to the siege of Constantinople, the only one of its kind in the world.

**Sucevitia**, called a 'Poem in Green and Light', lies under gentle green hills in the fields, and is encased behind four walls with towers at each corner, rather like a citadel. There are many legends within this 16th-century monastery; one of them depicts the head in black stone of a woman who allegedly carried her own ox cart for thirty years. The fresco of the 'Tree of Jesus' depicts our Judgement Day' and is painted on the outside wall. It is remarkably modern, with saints tumbling from the skies being carried by angels and martyrs. There is a gallery of over a hundred faces representing Pythagoras, Plato, Sophocles and other worthies. The building of this great church was under the auspices of the Movillă family, who were great churchmen and politicians in the area. The family originated from the Ukraine, and it was Petru Movillă who founded the Eastern Orthodox Church, breaking away from Catholiscism.

**Arbore**, known as the 'Strange Vision' is the smallest of the churches and dimly lit. To counteract the darkness, the windows overlooking the nave are large. This is a church whose hues are predominantly green. In fact, there are five shades of green intertwined, giving a very feminine appearance, complementing the figures of the female saints. Outside the church are the two great stone slabs with their fifteen deep indentations where the original paints were mixed by the Moldavian artists who decorated the church.

153

# BUDAPEST

One of the most beautiful cities in the world just has to be Budapest. Nestling between the Buda Hills and the river Danube ( in Hungary, the Duna), the city blends its Roman roots through centuries of architectural splendour with the modern energetic life it enjoys. Historically Budapest is not one, or even two, cities but three – the old Roman city of Óbuda, the later replacement Buda established on Várhegy and the thriving commercial centre of Pest, which only formally joined the other two in 1872. Today Budapest, visually exciting and historically significant, exotic enough to thrill without threatening, is rightfully enjoying a renaissance as one of the most interesting and welcoming cities in Europe.

## TOURIST INFORMATION

All main hotels carry a very extensive selection of tourist information, as do the tourist bureau offices located in all towns. **Tourinform,**2, *Süto út; tel: 117 9800* (metro: *Deáktér*) are very helpful and have multilingual staff. Open daily 0800–2000.

**Ibusz**, the Hungarian tourist organisation, mainly operate to book accommodation and organise tours but are usually in the position to offer good advice. They have offices throughout Budapest opening hours usually at 0800–1800/2000.

The branch at *6 Vigadó út; tel: 118 6466 is* open Mon–Fri 0900–1700. The most useful office in central Budapest is at *3 Petőfi tér; tel: 118 5707* or *118 4842* (metro: *Deák* or *Ferenciek tére*), open 24

hours. In addition there are branches at **Ferihegy Airport** (open 0700–2100), the **International Pier** (0700–2100) and at the three stations (0800–1800/2000). **Nyugati** *(tel: 112 3615);* **Keleti** *(tel: 122 5429)* and **Déli** *(tel: 155 2133).*

Ibusz have a desk in reception at most major hotels Mon–Sat 0800–2000 and Sun 0800–1200, though this may vary.

## ARRIVING AND DEPARTING

### Airport

**Ferihegy** airport lies about 15 km southeast of Budapest. There are two terminals. Most of the airlines use Terminal 1 *(tel: 157 2122),* whilst **Malév** (Hungarian Airlines) and its partner **Alitalia** plus a couple of others use Terminal 2. *(tel: 157 7831).* This number is also used for general enquiries. At Ferihegy the staff are most helpful to the disabled traveller, even to the extent of sending a special bus with a low step to the aeroplane for those with difficulties in boarding.

To get to the city centre, there is an extortionate taxi service and an extremely inexpensive no. 93 bus, which can be picked up outside the terminal building and takes you in to Köbánya-Kispest on the outskirts of Budapest; from there metro line 3 takes you into the centre of Budapest. Some large hotels have their own collection service.

There is a moderately priced shuttle service which will take you directly to your hotel by minibus. Book it at one of the desks inside the terminal, but be prepared for a long and chaotic wait until your name is called.

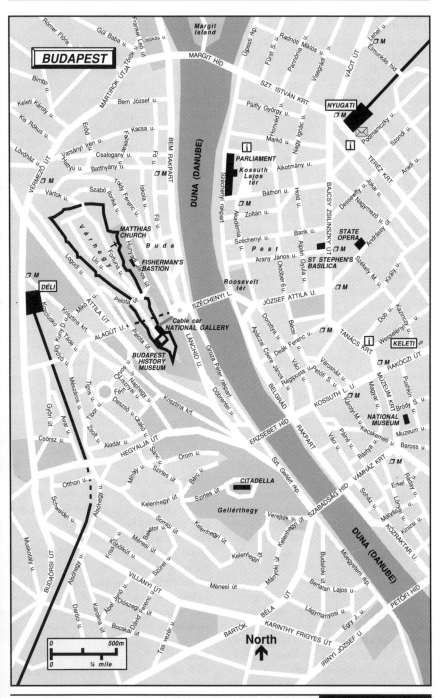

## Stations

Budapest has long been an important rail crossroads of Europe: the first trains ran here in 1850. There are three major stations in Budapest. These are: **Nyugati Pályaudvar** (West Station), *Nyugati tér; tel: 149 0115;* **Keleti Pályaudvar** (East Station), *Baross tér; tel: 113 6835;* and **Déli Pályaudvar** (South Station); *Magyar Jakobinusok tér; tel: 175 6293.* Always check from which station your train leaves, as there are no hard and fast rules. Trains from Romania may arrive at Keleti or Nyugati, for example. All three stations are fairly central and close to hotels. They are on the metro, Keleti and Déli on line 2, Nyugati on line 3.

For **rail information**, contact **MÁV**, *73–75 Andrássy út; tel: 1 220 660.*

Budapest is an easy city to get around if you have a street and transport guide. These are obtainable from the metro ticket kiosks.

The Danube runs north to south, with the Buda hills to the west and Pest to the east. There are 22 districts, indicated by Roman numerals, which appear in addresses and on maps. Buda has six districts, Pest has fifteen and there is one on the more commercial island of **Csepel** in the south. The fashionable and expensive **Várhegy** (Castle Hill) is classified as district I, district V the **Belváros** in Pest, the 'Left Bank' of Budapest, opposite Castle Hill.

Budapest is a city well worth covering on foot, as lurking behind each corner is another architectural delight even though tourist sights are fairly far apart. The public transport system is first-class and very speedy, especially since the recent refurbishment of the metro tunnels.

## Metro (Subway)

The metro service is fast and inexpensive. Stations are denoted by signs displaying a large letter M. As there are only three lines, it is relatively easy to use. All lines intersect at *Deák tér.* Line M1 is the second oldest in Europe, built shortly after London's Metropolitan line. It runs just below *Andrássy út.* Tickets are available from kiosks in stations or machines, where the exact change is needed. All tickets must be stamped, on line M1 this is done on board, but on lines M2 and M3 they must be stamped in the machines at the station entrance. Tickets are non transferable, which means that if you change line you need a new ticket. One- and three-day travel passes are available. Also available are ten-day packs of tickets for the price of nine. For visitors staying longer, the weekly/monthly passes, (photo required) are worth considering.

### Buses, Trams and Suburban Trains

For areas not on the speedy metro and for those who wish to soak in the delights of bustling Budapest, the bus and tram system is very useful, as it covers the city extensively. A similar method for ticket stamping exists, with a machine on board the bus. Eastern European countries are energetic in punishing those without a valid ticket: pleading ignorance does not carry any weight. The suburban network of **HÉV** trains travel several kilometres out of the city boundary as well as embracing the ruins of Aquincum and the old town of Óbuda. The maps available at the metro stations cover all suburban routes. The trains run parallel with the roads for much of the time.

### Taxis

Well-kept taxis are in abundance, so it is

not too difficult to find one even at the height of the season or in the pouring rain. Remember to check that the meter is running. Have the address of where you are going written down and give the driver a copy. This ensures that there is no argument about having misunderstood your destination.

## STAYING IN BUDAPEST

### Accommodation

New hotels are springing up like mushrooms in order to cope with the city's deservedly growing popularity. The five-star **Aquincum**, *1036 Budapest III, Árpád fejedelem utja 94; tel: 250 3360*, opposite the Danube in Óbuda, has superb facilities, including an enormous pool and fitness area where treatments are given under medical supervision for a large number of ailments. At its sister establishment the **Thermal Hotel Helia**, *1133 Budapest XIII, Kárpat út 62–64; tel: 270 377*, in Pest, just across the river, the rooms are more basic but still extremely comfortable. On Buda Hill one of the more interesting hotels can be found on the second floor inside the Palace itself. The first staircase into the building is truly regal, then the shock sets in. The lift is miniscule and more like a goods lift. The entrance into the hotel itself is through a dark brown door sporting a cardboard sign reading **Hotel Kulturinov**. This hotel, *1014 Budapest I, Szentháromstág tér 6; tel: 155 0122*, is more like a hostel; the rooms are very basic and the facilities are limited. However, even though it is in Budapest's finest district, in a building that formerly housed royalty and latterly a (Russian-style) cultural centre, it is reasonably inexpensive and ideal for the undemanding tourist on a tight budget. Opposite the Kulturinov is the **Budapest Hilton**, *1014*

*Budapest I, Hess András tér 1–3; tel: 175 1000*, which is built into the beautiful Matthias Church.

Even if you cannot stay there, try to visit the world-famous **Gellért**, *1111 Budapest XI, Szent Gellért tér 1; tel: 185 2200*, which sports the most amazing Turkish baths and swimming pool. Other hotels in Budapest include the superb *Ke*, and the *Hy, Ib, Ma* and *Rd*.

**Private rooms** are less expensive than the hotels and the joy of having a local host usually adds to the pleasures of absorbing the atmosphere of the city. There are few rooms available in the centre of town: they are usually found a few stops away from the centre. These as well as the hotel and pension accommodation are bookable at the **Ibusz** offices, or at any of the other tourist agencies. Outside the main ones, and especially at the Ibusz office at *3 Petöfi tér*, you may well find people offering private accommodation. It is advisable to check out private accommodation before booking, although you will usually find it to be safe and clean, and the Hungarians have a tradition of excellent hospitality.

**Youth hostel and student accommodation** is on the increase. Hostel organisations advertise widely at the stations and often offer free transport to the hostels. **More Than Ways**, *152 Dózsa György út; tel: 129 8644*, is the organisation to contact for accommodation in university dormitories. There are 19 hostels in Budapest affiliated to *HI*: for a list, contact your national *HI* or the **Hungarian Youth Hostel Federation,** *21 Konkoly Thege; tel: 156 2857,*. The youth travel service is **Express** at *16 Szabadság tér.*

**Camping** is available in a few sites, mainly found in the Buda hills, accessible by bus. Accommodation is crowded and failities are very basic. They are listed in

157

tourist information leaflets. A brochure is available from **Tourinform**, *Sütö utca; tel: 117 9800*, and your national office of the Hungarian Tourist Board may be able to provide a copy before you travel. Camping at unregistered sites is forbidden.

## Eating and Drinking

The city abounds with restaurants at all price levels serving traditional food such as goulash, paprika schnitzel and chicken. Typical of such places is **Kalocsai Paprika Csárda**, *Budapest VIII, Bláthy Ottó út 14–15; tel: 133 5972*.

Recently voted eastern Europe's No. 1 restaurant (and deservedly so) is the 101-year old **Gundel**, *1395 Budapest XIV, Állatkerti út P 2; tel: 122 1002*, now part-owned by Ronald Lauder (son of Austrian-born cosmetics queen Estée Lauder). In the evenings traditional Hungarian violinists serenade the guests.

There is also a good selection of other national cuisines – French, Chinese, Italian, and so on. Vegetarians are generally not well catered for, but **Vegetárium**, *3 Cukor utca*, is an exception. Try one of the many **coffee houses** for pizza, coffee and ices; a good one is **Bravo**, *Budapest XI, Fehérvári út 23*. At the other end of the scale, there are several **McDonalds** in the city. The supermarkets are well stocked with cold meats and other foods, which makes picnic lunches inexpensive.

## Communications

The main **telephone office** is at *17–19 Petöfi út; tel: 117 5500*. The main **post office** is conveniently next door. There are 24-hour post offices near Nyugati and Keleti stations, at *51 Teréz körút* and *11 Baross tér* respectively. The dialling code for Budapest is *1*.

## Embassies

**Australia:** *30 Délibáb út; tel: 153 4233*
**Canada:** *32 Budakeszi út; tel: 176 7711*
**New Zealand:** There are no diplomatic representation, in emergencies contact the British Embassy.
**South Africa:** *1–3 Rákóczi út; tel: 266 2148*
**UK:** *6 Harmincad út; tel: 118 2888*
**USA:** *12 Szabadság tér; tel: 112 6450*

## Money

Only change currency in official places; there are plenty of them. **Ibusz** at *6 Vigadó utca* (the **Thomas Cook network member**, offers foreign exchange and travellers' cheque refunds. **American Express** is at *Deák Ferenc utca 10; tel: 266 8671*.

There is always plenty for all tastes in Budapest. Check with the monthly listings guides available from hotel reception areas. The English *Budapest Sun* newspaper also has listings.

Music has always featured highly in Hungarian priorities, and the stunningly beautiful **Opera House**, *22 Andrássy út; tel 153 0170*, now 110 years old, was the first modern theatre in the world. There are guided tours at 1500 and 1600 hours every afternoon. **Operetta**, too, has its place, and the less ornate **Vigado Concert Hall** at *Vigado utca 2; tel: 117 0869* is usually packed for its very patriotic programme of light music. Seats are not reservable, so be early to get a good spot. **Organ recitals** are often given at the **Matthias Church**, *Várhegy*, and at **St Stephen's Basilica**. The **Franz Liszt Academy of Music**, aptly found at *8 Liszt Ferenc tér; tel: 142 0179* and the **Philharmonia**, *Vörösmarty tér; tel: 117 6222*, frequently host classical concerts.

Folk music is still popular in Hungary; for information on venues, etc., contact **Folklör Centrum**, *47 Fehérvári út; tel: 145 2160.*

There is a wide choice of **cinemas**, many showing English-language films (the key word to look out for in listings is *Angolul).*

Other possibilities for nightlife are the many pubs to be found all over the city; the **nightclubs** in the red light area in district VII are only for the extremely broad-minded.

As well as the Hotel Gellért's **thermal swimming pool**, there are other examples of this Budapest speciality at varying prices – either public or at the Thermal hotels such as the Aquincum or Helia (contact the **Danubia Hotels** office *Margitsziget; tel: 112 1000* for information and prices). Other spas include **Dandárutcai**, *5–7 Dandár út; tel: 113 7084,* and **Király**, *Fö út; tel: 115 3000.*

**SIGHTSEEING**

**Buda**
The hills of Buda offer a marvellous view of the city and the Danube. The area is on the UNESCO list of protected cultural centres. On the west of the hills are woods and paths for rambling. Railway enthusiasts will love the cogwheel railway from *Szilágyi Erzsébet fasor* which circumnavigates the woods. There is also a chair-lift and **Gyermekvasút**, a narrow-gauge Children's Railway.

On **Gellérthegy (Gellért Hill)**, looking down on the city and the Royal Palace, is the gigantic **Liberation Monument**, which commemorates the Soviet liberation of Budapest, offering one of the best views in the city. Here too is the **statue of St Gellért**, raised at the place from which this luckless Italian missionary was thrown to his death inside a wooden barrel.

**Várhegy** (Castle Hill) was first built on in the 13th century and is perhaps the most historic and important feature in Budapest; the streets there have retained their medieval form. Walk up the hill from *Déli* or *Moskva* metro stations or ride up on the **Sikló**, the world's second-oldest funicular, from *Clark Adám tér* at the end of the Chain Bridge. There is also a shuttle bus service from *Moskva tér.* To enjoy the area at its best, take a horse-drawn fiacre ride from *Szentháromság*; the price should be about 600 Ft. Don't miss *Fortuna út* (Fortune St), which takes its name from the old Fortuna Inn, now the **Museum of Catering and Commerce**, at no. 4, worth a visit for its replicas of an entire pastry kitchen and food shops of past times.

The **Palace** was originally built as part of the fortifications of the city during the Middle Ages. It was redesigned during the Renaissance and reconstructed during the Hapsburg era. The Nazis occupied it during World War II and then it was almost totally destroyed by the Soviets. Once again it has been rebuilt, but only the foundations and the ramparts remain.

There are three museums in the Palace: the **Budapest History Museum,** the **Museum of Contemporary History** and the **Hungarian National Gallery**.

The **Halászbástya** or **Fisherman's Bastion** presents a well-known icon of Budapest; this beautiful building, with a magnificent roof, was erected at the turn of the century. It was here, legend has it, that the fishermen defended their city during the Middle Ages. Other stories say that they sold their catch in the square. Whatever the truth, the view is magnificent. The square is always filled with tourists, especially during public holidays,

## History and Influences

Contrary to popular belief, Budapest is not made up of two cities but three. The old Roman city of Óbuda, on the west bank of the Danube, close to the frontier and spa town of Aquincum, was defeated by the barbarian invasions. The site was taken over by a tribe of the Magyar people who were to become the dominant ethnic group of Hungary. A short distance away, overlooking the Danube, the town of Buda was later established on Várhegy (Castle Hill), gradually replacing Óbuda and better able to resist invasion, especially that of the Tartars in 1241. It was after the devastation of that invasion that King Béla IV built the first fortress on Buda Hill. King Louis the Great brought his court to Buda and successive kings enlarged the palace, culminating in the artistic and architectural splendours of the reign of King Mátyás Corvinus. Buda was the capital of an independent Hungary until the Turkish invasion in 1541 and rule of the Ottoman Empire. Just over a hundred years later, in 1686, the Austrians liberated and revitalised the almost derelict towns of Buda and Pest. Thus began over three centuries of Austrian rule and cultural influence.

Buda continued as an important city until Hungary's autonomy under the *Ausgleich* (Compromise) of 1867, which established the Dual Monarchy of the Austro-Hungarian Empire. Pest by that time had become a thriving business city on the eastern banks of the Danube. Frequently cut off from the opposite shore because of flooding and ice, the two (Buda and Óbuda had already been considered as one town) were only joined in 1872. This was largely due to the building of a more substantial bridge, the Margaret Bridge, than the Széchenyi Chain Bridge built in the 1840s. By the turn of the century Pest greatly exceeded Buda in size.

when the area is awash with street entertainers and market stalls of all sorts.

The **statue of St Stephen** (Szent István), legendary King of Hungary, is overlooked by the **Mátyas Church.** Here lies the tomb of King Béla III. The church was originally built in the 13th century and extended during the 19th. During the Ottoman domination it was used as a mosque. Next to the church are the remains of a **Dominican Abbey** which are incorporated within the modern Hilton Hotel. The streets around are cobbled and the houses are fine examples of baroque and Gothic stonework.

Still in Buda, visit the picturesque **Margit-sziget** (Margaret's Island). Cars are only allowed to go as far as the hotels; the miles of walks along the river are beautiful. Known as the Isle of Rabbits during the 11th century, the island is 2.5 km in length. It was renamed after Princess Margaret, daughter of King Béla IV, who lived on the island, as had the Roman nobility before her. On the island you will find two swimming pools, an open-air theatre, churches and Turkish remains. In the **Japanese Garden** near the 1911 **Water Tower** is the so-called **Musical Fountain**, which produces neither water nor music.

To the north of Castle Hill is the exclusive suburb of **Roszadomb** (Rose Hill), an area of smart *fin-de-siècle* villas .

### Óbuda

Further to the north is **Óbuda** (Old Buda), connected to Margit-sziget by the **Árpád Hid** (bridge). Only a street or two remains to show where the original settlement stood. One quaint feature is the silver statues of ladies holding up umbrellas, dotted around the square. The Hotel Aquincum stands close to the ruins of the remains of **Aquincum**, a Roman spa town during the 2nd and 3rd centuries. (HÉV stations *Aquincum* and *Romai-Furdo.)* Next door, in *Lajos út*, Hungarian Radio occupies what was once the **Óbuda Synagogue**. The history of Budapest is charted in the **Kiscelli Museum**, *Bécsi út*, housed in a building that was a monastery in the 18th century, and later a barracks.

## Pest

This is the busy commercial part of the city, built in two semi-circular avenues with broad tree-lined boulevards radiating from it. Here is the elegant shopping street **Vád út**, and the street cafés of **Vörösmarty tér,** the artists' hang-out. The imposing **Parliament** building (built 1885–1905 by Imre Steinl), with its 700 rooms and innumerable courtyards, can be visited by a pre-arranged guided tour (from the tourist office). The **National Museum**, *14–16 Múzeum körút*, contains what are believed to be the coronation regalia of St Stephen, presented by the Pope Sylvester when the King converted to Christianity, amongst other remains of Hungary's chequered history. The regalia were smuggled to America for safety at the end of World War II, and returned to Hungary by President Carter in 1978. The 19th-century **St Stephen's Basilica** is another memorial to Budapest's patron saint. It is the largest church in the city, and contains the mummified head of the saint. Both the Basilica and the **Central Synagogue** are being restored at present. The synagogue, *2-8 Dohány út,* is one of Europe's largest, holding 3000 people. Special features are Imre Varga's metal weeping willow memorial to the victims of the Budapest ghetto and the museum, built on the site of the birthplace of

Theodor Herzl, founder of Zionism. Special heritage tours can be arranged through **Chosen Tours**, *tel: 166 5165*, or the **Jewish Federation**, *12 Síp út; tel: 142 1333.* The area contain sevral very old synagogues.

A thousand years of Magyar existence is commemorated by the cold-looking **Millenary Monument** in *Hösök tére* (Heroes' Square). The whole area, including the frescoes on the surrounding buildings, is currently being renovated. Nearby is the leafy **Városliget** (City Woodland Park) area, with its permanent circus and zoo. (It was in the amusement arcades of this park that Ferenc Molnár, Hungary's internationally best-known writer, set his story of *Liliom*; Rodgers and Hammerstein later adapted it to an American, and musical, setting, as *Carousel*.) The Park contains the fairytale **Vajahunyad vára** castle, modelled on the Hunyadoara Castle in Romania, birthplace of one of Hungary's greatest kings, Mátyás Corvinus.

Also in the City Woodland Park region is the **Közlekedési Múzeum**, Budapest's transport museum, *11 Városligieti út; tel: 114 20565*, open 1000–1600/1800, including weekends (free entrance on Weds). Permanent and temporary exhibitions include the History of the Railway. It has two branches elsewhere: the **Kossuth Ship Museum** (next to the Chain Bridge) and the **Underground Railway Museum** in *Deák tér* metro station.

One cannot leave Budapest without wandering down **Andrássy út,** Budapest's most famous avenue, where the **Opera House** can be found. Just around the corner is the **Liszt Museum**, *35 Vörösmarty út,* where the composer lived.

Budapest also has museums to two other famous Hungarian composers: **Béla**

## Bridges along the Danube

A cruise along Budapest's river is highly recommended. **Legenda**, *Trencsényi utca 16* (no phone), include a video film commentary as part of the trip. The **Elizabeth Bridge** was rebuilt 1961–64 after the original's destruction in World War II, as was the **Liberty Bridge**, originally the Franz Josef Bridge when built in 1894–96.

The next one, **Petöfi Bridge**, has been modernised three times, latterly in 1980. Originally called the Miklos Horthy Bridge on its construction in 1933, it was renamed in 1950 after Hungary's leading poet, Sandor Petöfi.

The oldest and most distinctive structure is the **Széchenyi Chain Bridge**, built by Scottish engineer Adam Clark to a design by (the unrelated) William Tierney Clark and rebuilt in 1948 – parts of the original are still visible nearby. W T Clark had already perfected the design in a smaller version with the suspension bridge at Marlow, Buckinghamshire, in England, and this inspired István Széchenyi, the nobleman who was the driving force of the project to bridge the Danube. The **Margaret Bridge** was the second to be built over the Danube, in 1872, taking its French engineers four years to construct. The present bridge was rebuilt in 1946 after wartime destruction (it was blown up by the occupying Nazis while being used by hundreds of commuters during the rush hour, with heavy loss of life).

The final and busiest of the Danube bridges is the **Árpád Bridge**, begun in 1939. The remains of an ancient Roman bridge have been discovered near it – the first bridge in Budapest, and the last, until the great era of bridge-building began in the 19th century.

**Bartók** is commemorated at his former villa at *29 Csalán út; tel: 176 2100* (open Tues–Sun) and the **Zoltán Kodály Memorial Museum** is at *1 Kodály Körönd*, halfway down *Andrássy út* from the City Woodland Park.

### ⤴ SIDE TRACKS FROM BUDAPEST

Take the regular HEV suburban service from *Batthyány tér* to picturesque town of **Szentendre** on the Danube Bend. You can connect with the Vienna–Budapest route (p. 305) by continuing on to **Esztergom**.

### SZENTENDRE

Szentendre (St Andrew) lies on the entrance to the Danube Bend and is only 20 km north of Budapest.

This is an artists' colony, with quaint, narrow streets. Horse drawn buggies and carts meander through leafy lanes. There are many churches, such as the **Belgrade Cathedral** (1764) with a tall red tower pointing out of a walled courtyard; it contains the **Serbian Ecclesiastical Museum**, a collection of sacred icons and pictures.

The river flows alongside the cobbled street where the restaurants are in close proximity to each other; however the best are to be found around the square. In *Sas utca* there is a **Dolls Museum** open Wed–Sat..

**Magyar Szabadtéri Néprajzi Múzeum** (Outdoor Ethnographical Museum) is 3 km out of town *(Sztaravodai út PF; tel:(26) 310 183)*. The museum comprises a Nature Conservation Area and a collection of architecture and exhibits depicting the Hungarian way of life. ⬛

# BUDAPEST–DEBRECEN

This route crosses the Great Hungarian Plain, the Nagyalföld, the massive prairie which is the traditional home of cattle herds and the *ciklós* or Hungarian cowboy, until it reaches historic Debrecen, the seat of Hungarian independence. En route you can take one or two detours to the less-visited and unspoilt towns in the south.

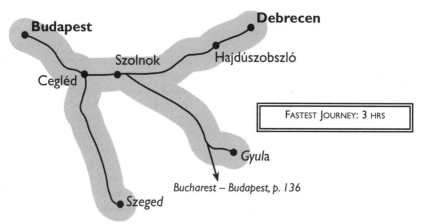

Budapest

Debrecen

Szolnok  Hajdúszobszló

Cegléd

FASTEST JOURNEY: 3 HRS

Gyula

*Bucharest – Budapest, p. 136*

Szeged

163

---

## TRAINS

**ETT Table: 898**

### FAST TRACK
A roughly hourly service taking 3 hrs.

### ON TRACK

**Budapest–Cegléd–Szolnok–Hajdúszobszló–Debrecen**
The frequent trains between Budapest and Debrecen all call at Szolnok and most call at Cegléd and Hajdúszobszló. Budapest to Cegléd takes nearly 1 hr, Cegléd to Szolnok 25 mins, Szolnok to Hajdúszobszló 1 hr 20 mins and Hajdúszobszló **to** Debrecen 15 mins.

## CEGLÉD
From Cegléd you can make a worthwhile detour to the town of Szeged.

### SIDE TRACK FROM CEGLÉD

## SZEGED
**Station:** This is situated in a drab modern area of the town; there are buses from it to the centre.
**Tourist Office: IBUSZ**, *2 Klauzál tér; tel: (62) 417 177,* and the **Hungarian Tourist Service**, *1 Victor Hugo utca; tel: (62) 311 711,* are well equipped to offer all manner of help. **Szeged Tourist**, *7 Klauzál tér; tel: (62) 321 800,* has a register of accommodation available.

## ACCOMMODATION AND FOOD

There is a **campsite** in the **Napfény Hotel and Nyaralótelep** complex, *4 Dorozsmai út; tel: (62) 325 8000/325 450.* The hotel itself is not really recommendable, unless you are not too fussy. None of the hotels in Szeged is impressive: either the location is noisy or the rooms expensive or shoddy, or both. **Szeged Tourist** (see above) can find rooms in private accommodation, which are probably a better option.

The situation is rather better when it comes to eating out. Szeged is noted for specialities such as the deliciously appetizing *szegediner* goulash, made with the local paprika, and Pick Salami. Another speciality is *szegedi halászlé*, fish from the Tisza cooked as a soup.

Watching salami being manufactured is quite fun and tours at the **Pick factory**, *10 Felső Tisza,* take place on Tues and Thur during the afternoon.

## SIGHTSEEING

Szeged is a form of the word for 'island'. The town lies in the southern section of the Hungarian *puszta* or Great Plain, at the junction of the rivers Maros and Tisza. It was almost completely destroyed by floods in 1879. The Tisza was named after the city engineer, Lajos Tisza, who rebuilt the city in an intricate pattern of squares circular streets, all named after major European cities which contributed towards the reconstruction. Recently *Odessa* has been renamed *Temesvári körút,* after Timişoara, to mark Hungary's involvement with its Transylvanian neighbour during the events of 1989.

Szeged is a university town, as well as the cultural and economic capital of the region; it is noted for its late-summer **Open-Air Theatre Festival**, held in the precincts of the **Votive Church** or Cathedral, built in fulfilment of vows made after the great flood of 1879, when only 250–300 houses remained standing.

This church is set in one of the most beautiful squares in Hungary, *Dóm tér* (Cathedral Square). Its twin towers, 91 metres high, dwarf the 54-metre high dome built in Byzantine style. Inside the cathedral there is a most unusual Madonna, the **Szeged Madonna in Szür** (Szeged Madonna in a cloak.) The statue wears a long, embroidered shepherd's cloak, and is also adorned with slippers and butterflies. The organ, one of Europe's largest, has some 10,000 pipes.

The **Serbian Orthodox Church**, behind the Votive Church, is sadly not often open to visitors. It contains a tree-like structure fashioned in gold with sixty icons dripping from it like leaves.

The **Musical Fountain** in *Dugonics tér* really does play, unlike that in Budapest, but only three or so times a day during May to October (a timetable is published). It was erected in 1979 to commemorate the great flood of a hundred years before.

The **Old Synagogue**, *12 Hajnóczy utca*, built in 1843, has markings on the wall to show how high the flood waters rose. The **Great Synagogue**, between *Hajnóczy utca* and *Gutenberg*, was built in 1903 and is reputed to be the most beautiful in Hungary. It is amply decorated with a huge dome and twenty-four massive pillars representing the hours of the day. A star of David is perched like a crown at the top of the dome with rays of light encircling it.

There is a **flea market** on *Vam tér* (at the beginning of *Szabadkai út*) and two fruit and vegetable markets at *Mars tér* (which was the site of the infamous Star prison for political prisoners during the 1950s) and *Szent István tér*.

## SZOLNOK

Change trains at here to reach Gyula and the Bucharest–Budapest route (page 136).

### SIDE TRACK
### FROM SZOLNOK

## GYULA

**Station:** North-west of the centre.
**Tourist Office: Ibusz**, *3 Hét vezér utca;tel:(66) 463 028*, is open 0800–1600.

### ACCOMMODATION AND FOOD

Gyula has both a thermal and an ordinary **campsite**: **Thermal Camping and Motel**, *16 Szélsö út; tel:(66) 463 551*, and **Márk Camping**, *5 Vár út; tel: (66) 361 473*. Although very small the latter site has a beautiful view of the castle. The best hotel in town is the **Aranykereszt**, *2 Eszperantó tér; tel: (66) 463 163*,overlooking the canal. The **Höforrás**, *2 Rábai utca; tel: (66) 361 544*, has an inlaid roof and decorative chimneys. The **Agro**, *5 Part utca; tel:(66)463 522*, has well-laid-out gardens at the rear of the building and is situated in a leafy, quiet road. The **Park**, *15 Part utca; tel; (66) 463 711*, has its own swimming pool and sauna. The **Üdülö Egyesülés**, *34 Tibork; tel: (66) 362 555 / 363 560*, looks like a mushroom, with its bright red roof. This tiny and attractive hotel

has a restaurant and is only 200 m from the Castle baths.

The local speciality is the spicy *Gyula kolbász*, a thin tasty sausage. There is a plethora of restaurants, from the ultra-smart one at the Arankereszt Hotel to the pizzeria and cafés selling delicious cakes and pastries.

### SIGHTSEEING

This pretty little town lies 4 km away from the Romanian border on the Great Plain. It is a restful spa town on the banks of the river Körös. The ancient brick Gyula castle is the only one in the area and it took about a hundred years to complete during the 13th and 14th centuries. Restoration work was undertaken in the 1950s. The town was divided into ghettos between 1703–11 after it had been liberated from the Turks. The quarters are still named after their former inhabitants: Magyarváros (Hungarian Town); Németváros (German Town) and Nagy Románváros and Kis Románváros (Large and Small Romanian Town). An ethnic minority group of Romanians still lives in Gyula and its environs.

Gyula's chief historic building is the 14th-century **Castle**. The **Castle Museum** (open Tues–Sun) exhibits documents on its history. Every summer the **Gyula Castle Theatre** puts on performances in the amphitheatre inside the red castle walls near the pond. Also in the Castle park is a famous **spa**, with 12 pools.

The little house at *1 Erkel tér* doubles as a café and a museum, with quaint old utensils and 1840 Biedermeier furniture and furnishings.

The **Ferenc Erkel House**, *6 Apor Vilmos tér*, is where the composer of

165

the Hungarian National Anthem was born (1810-93). He was also the founder of the Hungarian National Opera. Open Tues–Sun 1000–1700. On the other side of the road is the house devoted to honouring the elder and younger Albrecht Dürer, better known for their association with Nuremberg, who lived here for some time (Albrecht the younger may have been born here). Albrecht senior was a goldsmith; his more famous son was one of the greatest German artists.

The **György Kohán Museum**, *35 Béke Sugárút*, holds more than 3000 of this local painter's works, left to the town on his death in 1966. ⬛

## HAJDÚSKOBOSZLÓ

**Tourist Office: Hajdútourist**, *2 József Attila utca; tel: (52) 362 966*. **Hungarian Tourist Service**, *Szilfákalja út; tel: (52) 362 448*. **Ibusz**, *4–6 Hősök tere; tel: (52) 362 041*. All can offer maps, advice and information.

There are dozens of hotels and pensions, to choose from. Noteworthy is the **Hotel Délibáb**, *4 József Attila út; tel: (52) 362 366*, was the result of an oil exploration that sprang up spa water instead of liquid gold. The hotel is large and popular with a night-bar restaurants and patisserie. **Campsite: Káplár Camping**, *Hajdúböszörmény; tel: (52) 371 388*, just off the motorway.

This small spa town is great on recreation and is to Hungary what Brighton is to London or Coney Island to New York. Only 20 km away from Debrecen, it makes an ideal outing, especially if you are travelling with kids who may be bored with churches and museums. Nearly all the activities centre around one street, split into four sections, *Debreceni út; Szilfákalja út; Hősök tére* and *Dózsa utca*.

Apart from enjoying the air, the holiday atmosphere and the thermal amenities, there is little else except an exhibition of the local 'black pottery on Mondays.

The word *Hajdú* means cattle-drover, and many of the towns and villages around Debrecen begin with that prefix, as this was the main occupation of the villagers. The title was granted to them after they staunchly fought against the Habsburgs with Prince István Bocskai of Transylvania.

## DEBRECEN

**Station:** Located on *Piac utca*, about 20 mins walk (or a tram-ride) away from the centre.

**Tourist Office: Hungarian Tourist Service**, *Piac utca 20; tel: (52) 312 250*, and **Ibusz**, *11–13 Piac utca; tel: (52) 315 555*.

### ACCOMMODATION AND FOOD

The three-star **Aranybika Hotel**, *11–15 Piac utca; tel: (52) 416 777*, is supposedly the best in Debrecen, offering a casino, night-club, bars, restaurants and patisserie. **Termál Hotel**, *9-11 Nagyerdei körút; tel: (52) 411 888*, has two-star classification but boasts amenities beyonds its class, including, as its name suggests, pools and thermal cures. **Civis**, *Kálvin tér; tel: (52) 418 522*, is a newer and brasher three-star hotel. There is a **campsite** at **Termál Camping**, *102 Nagyerdei körut; tel: (52) 412 456*, connected with the hotel of the same name, and another one at **Dorcas Centre Camping**, *Erdöspuszta ; tel: (52) 368 900*. Prices vary and are usually displayed in DM.

Dining out at all price ranges is not difficult in this univeristy town. The restaurant of the Civis Hotel has around thirty or more vegetarian dishes on its menu, including the stuffed cabbage for which the town is famed. Students eat at the **Mátyás Pince**, *1 Ajtó utca*: it is cheap, there is a bar and the atmosphere in the ancient cellar is fun.

## SIGHTSEEING

Debrecen is the third-largest town in Hungary, dating back to 1361 and famed for its religious heritage (see box opposite) and its **International Flower Carnival**, unique in Eastern Europe. St Stephen's Day, 20 Aug, is celebrated withn a parade to rival Rio: over a million flowers made up into astonishing compositions adorn floats, people and houses. The parade wends its way through the city to the **Nagyerdei Stadion** (Great Forest Stadium) where a 2½-hrr programme of events follows.

Every visitor makes a beeline for the **Református Nagytemplom** (Great Reformed Church), built in 1823 after the fire of 1802, on a site where churches have stood since the 12th century. It has become the symbol of Debrecen; it was here that the declaration of independence from Austria was read out. There is a superb organ behind the pulpit. The bell was recast from that of the previous church in 1873 but is rarely rung. Twin towers 61 m tall are topped with giant cupolas and have a clock in each tower.

A **monument to Lajos Kossuth**, leader of the 1848 uprising against the Habsburgs, was erected in 1914 at the front of the building, whilst behind is a **Garden of Remembrance** for those whom the Habsburgs sent into slavery for their Calvinist beliefs. This is depicted in the **Column of the Galley-Slaves**.

The **Református Kollégium** (Reformed College) lies to the north on *Kálvin tér*. It was built in 1675 but there had been a college on the site since 1568. Some 530,000 books are kept in the

## The Calvinist Rome

Debrecen was so nicknamed from its role as the centre of the Calvinist Reformation in Hungary in the 16th century. The Turks conquered the area in 1535, yet Calvinism continued to flourish and the citizens were allowed to build the Reformed College in 1538. During the 17th century it was the turn of the Habsburgs to enter and liberate the town from the Turks but as Catholics, they attempted to repress Calvinism. Intolerance worked both ways; the Calvinists had long banned other religions from the area, and well into the 18th century they led notorious persecutions of 'witches'.

Debrecen has played a leading role in Hungarian national aspirations. In 1848, Lajos Kossuth led a revolt to gain Hungary's independence from the Habsburgs and he announced this from the Great Reformed Church. In 1944, while Budapest was in turmoil and under siege, Debrecen became the seat of Parliament until the time was right for its return to the capital in March 1945.

library, including a comprehensive collection of old Bibles and other valuable manuscripts. Nearby to the west is the **Déri Museum**, *Déri tér*. It holds a unique collection of art treasures, Egyptian mummies and sarcophagi, and examples of Eastern Asian art.

Debrecen is a very pleasant town to wander through, with its **Nagyerdei Park** and boating on the lake and its thermal spa complex. Try visiting the Flea Market, *Vágó híd utca*, next to the Sports Stadium, or the covered market at *Csapó utca*, the ideal place to buy fruit and salad vegetables for a picnic.

# BUDAPEST–GRAZ

This route leads from the Hungarian capital to Graz, the chief city of the Austrian province of Styria. There is no quick way of making the journey: it deliberately uses a number of train services to take you through the attractive towns and countryside of western Hungary. There is a long detour around the shores of central Europe's largest lake. which is well worth pursuing, for the seaside-like resorts of Balaton.

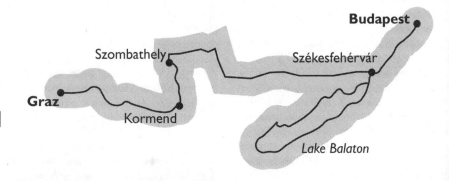

## TRAINS

**ETT Tables:** 891, 829

There is no fast or direct route.

### ON TRACK

**Budapest–Székesfehérvár**
Frequent service taking around 1 hr.

**Székesfehérvár–Szombathely**
Thirteen trains a day, journey 2 hrs 40 mins.

**Szombathely–Körmend**
Around 9 trains a day.

**Körmend–Graz**
Change trains at Szentgotthard.

### SZÉKESFEHÉRVÁR

**Station:** To reach the town centre, walk up *Prohaszka utca.*
**Tourist Office: Ibusz,** *2 Andy Endr utca; tel: (22) 311 510,* is in the old town.
   Hotels are pretty grim in general; the best is the 100-year-old **Magyar Király**, *10 Fő utca ; tel: (22) 311 262.* The **Alba**

**Regia**, *1 Rákóczi utca; tel:(22) 313 484*, is a very modern hotel with but expensive, not far from the Garden of Ruins.

This town was the first Royal Hungarian capital, its name Székesfehérvár ('white castle seat', German *Stuhlweissenburg*), a reminder of Árpád, the 'white king' and founding father of Hungary, who settled in the town. It remained the royal capital for centuries and is the oldest Magyar town in the country. St Stephen built a basilica in which Hungary's kings would be crowned and buried. for more than 500 years. Throughout the centuries the town increased in importance until 1688 when the Ottoman and Habsburg Empires were dividing up the country. Parliament was removed to Bratislava and Székesfehérvár was no longer a major city. In the 19th century the marshes were drained and the city began to expand outwards, but it was not until after World War II that it developed into an industrial area.

The present **St Stephen's Cathedral** was built in the 13th century; outlines of a previous church are visible. There is a lovely crucifix in the north wall which has been dedicated to the victims of the 1956 Revolution against communism. Concerts are held in St Stephen's Cathedral and **Bory Castle**.

> **SIDE TRACK: LAKE BALATON LOOP**
>
> From Székesfehérvár it is possible to take a circular tour of **Lake Balaton**, stopping at whatever resorts take your fancy along the way. The suggested route goes anti-clockwise, following the north shore first and then doubling back along the southern coast up to the starting point. The entire lake, the largest in Europe out-

side Scandinavia, is encircled by the railway. Allow yourself at least two or three days, and study the timetables to estimate where you will want to spend a night: this inland sea is a magnet for Hungarian holidaymakers, and accommodation can be very difficult to find if you do not book ahead. It is impossible to mention here every resort: they vary from fair-sized towns to small villages, but we have tried to select the most interesting.

**Lake Balaton** (from the Slav *blatno*, 'marsh') covers 598 sq km. The Romans knew it as *Pelso*, and they built a fort at Fenékpuszta (Valcum). The Magyars found the lake an excellent line of defence as well as a resource for good fresh fish and water and they settled, developing the area with churches and villages. During the 18th century, Germans, Slovaks and Croats settled into the surrounding hills giving the area a truly cosmopolitan flavour and many new towns. It was not until late into the 19th century when disease killed off the flourishing wine-growing industry, that Balaton became a playground for the wealthy. The Communist government commandeered their holiday homes for their own usage after World War II, building villas for the workers' and increasing the accommodation available. Since 1989 many have been turned into hotels and pensions.

The first resort of any consequence is **Balatonakarratya**. It was built around a 400-year-old elm tree a few metres away from the railway station. Legend has it that Prince Rákoczi tied his horse to the tree before proclaiming Hungary's freedom from the Habsburgs. Camping at **FKK Piroska**, *15 Aligai út; tel: (88) 381*

169

*084.* (FKK stands for *Frei Körper Kultur*, i.e. naturism, which is popular around Balaton.) Next is **Balatonkenese.** Eat at the **Zsindely Csárda**, *25 Táncsics utca*, walk along the raised **Partfö** (180 m above sea level) for excellent views and examine the caves along the Partfö wall where the villagers were said to have hidden from the Turks.

**Balatonalmádi** is the third largest resort on the north bank of the lake and has been popular since 1877. Most of the lake's houses are built from the distinctive red sandstone found at Balatonalmádi. The town is a port and the railway station is at the very centre of town. Beautiful beaches lie in the south of the town while to the north is **Oreg-hegy** (Mount Oreg). The view from the top is worth the long climb up to the Wesseléni Tower. Accommodation includes the **Aurora**, *14 Bajcsy Zsilinsky*, a 12-storey hotel with a private beach, and **Inter-Európa Club Hotel**, *15 Neptun utca; tel: (88) 339 150*,cottage-style. There are also three campsites.

Covered in vines at the foot of Somióhegy is the tiny, peaceful village of **Alsóörs**. **Felsőörs** is 2 km inland and totally unspoiled.

## BALATONFÜRED

**Station:** *Dobó István.* The **Pier** for lake steamers is on *Vitorlás tér.*
**Tourist Office: Ibusz**, *4a Petőfi Sándor; tel: (86) 342 327*, is open 0830–1600 or even later during the peak season, including Sat.

There are many hotels to choose from. **Fúred Hotel**, *20 Széchenyi utca; tel: (86) 343 033*, is a gigantic hotel on the water's edge with almost every kind of amenity imaginable. The

country hotel **Park**, *24 Jókai ut; tel: (86) 343 203*, is considered the resort's top hotel. Hotels **Annabella**, *25 Deák utca; tel: (87) 342 222*, **Marina**, *26 Széchenyi utca; tel: (87) 343 644*, and **Margaréta**, *29 Széchenyi utca; tel: (87) 343 824*, are all spa hotels offering treatment. **Füred Camping**, *24 Széchenyi utca; tel: (86) 343 823*, has bungalows available and live entertainment on site. plus many sporting activities.

Balatonfüred is the oldest resort and perhaps the most popular on the north side of Lake Balaton. It is a renowned spa resort where the carbonated waters have been recognised as perfect for healing those with heart and circulation problems. The Bath houses were built in 1743. In 1831 the first Hungarian-language theatre was founded, and in 1846 the first steamship cruised from the harbour through the Lake. While in the area, a visit to the **wineries** is recommended, the Riesling is especially good. There is a good **market** (*Arácsi utca*) specialising in bakery products. If you are in the area on 25 July, St Anne's Day, take a stroll in *Gyógy tér*, and watch the locals turn out at the Sanatorium in their beautiful costumes for the annual, resplendent **Anna Ball**.

Moving on along the lake, another popular resort is **Tihany**, perched on the Tihany peninsula, which was once an island. This juts out 5 km into the lake, and is a nature reserve which almost joins the two shores. The tiny village has a beautiful Baroque Abbey (1740–45) in splendid yellow, with twin towers each with its own clock face. Take a walk round the Open Air Museum, once an old fishing village, where there are some beautiful old peasant cottages to be seen, with thatched roofs.

**Örvényes**, **Balatonudvari**, **Balatonakali** and **Balatonszepezd** are four pretty little villages running along the north shore of the lake. The remains of Roman settlements have been discovered. At Örvényes there is an old water mill, now a museum , which was in use during the 19th century. Balatonudvari has a cemetery which is the subject of a preservation order, as it contains some beautiful heart-shaped memorials again from the 19th century. Balatonakali and Balatonszepezd are best known for their fine wines, especially the muscatel. These can be sampled at the local inns. Camping is available at several sites.

A few km inland lies the market town of **Nagyvázsony**, with its 1100 inhabitants. This region is one of the prettiest in Central Transdanubia. Kinizsi Castle just south of the town centre was built in the 15th century. It was a gift from King Mátyás Corvinus to Pál Kinizsi after his army had defeated the Turks. The castle was originally the home of the Vezsenyi family, now it is a museum. The Village Museum, *21 Bercsényi utca*, is a tiny peasant's house where once the local coppersmith had his workshop.

**Révfülöp**'s natural heart-shaped banks make it the ideal harbour for ships which regularly ply to Boglärille. Near the harbour are the remains of a 13th-century church. There are a couple of pensions and a campsite in the town.

Like Tihany, the **Szigliget** peninsula was once an island. The thatched cottages in the village are so picturesque, that they have been desig-

nated listed buildings. Szigliget is still unspoiled by tourists and partly due to its solitude and calm, the village has become the Hungarian writers' centre where accommodation is offered whilst they work in what was the Eszterházy Palace. (Fö tér), The building is most impressive.

## KESZETHELY

**Tourist Office: Ibusz**, *1–3 Széchenyi utca; tel: (83) 314 320*, open 0830–1600. There are no less than four campsites, and the choice of hotels is fairly extensive. There are also many restaurants and fast food places to choose from.

The largest town on the lake, Keszethely lies just as the lake bends towards the south bank in the Zala region. There are sandy beaches and many holiday activities. In 1745 Kristóf Festetics had a small (34-room) **Palace** built here. In 1883 it was enlarged greatly and the palace now possesses more than a hundred fine rooms. The garden designs were the work of an English landscape gardener, E. H. Miller. Inside the Festetics Palace there is much to see; the southern wing contains one of the most impressive exhibitions, the Helikon Library. This has close to 100,000 books, as well as a large collection of objets d'art, portraits, furniture and bric-a-brac.

There are two beaches at Keszthely, the Helikon, south of the pier and the Városi close to it. For the railway enthusiasts a vintage steam railway runs between Keszthely and Badacsonytomaj, Jul–Aug.

**Héviz** is situated on Europe's largest thermal lake, Gyógy-tó. Lying 7 km away from Kezsthely, in the

171

Parkerdő (Park Forest), it was developed by Count György Festetics in 1795 when he had the first wooden bath house built, but only reached popularity at the turn of the 19th century. All activities centre on the the lake, whose waters reach 34°C in summer and 26°C in winter. Eighteen million gallons a day rise through a spring and are radioactive and sulphuric. There are several piers, a quaint covered bridge and a pavilion to enjoy, as well as the Carbona Sports Centre, *Zrínyi utca*, where there is bowling, a swimming pool and a large number of tennis courts for hire.

**Balatonberény** is the first village as the loop of the lake is rounded onto the south bank. The scenery on this side of the lake is not generally as picturesque as the north side yet the towns, villages and resorts link up with each other to form an almost continuous chain long the 70 km of lakeside.

**Balatonmáriafürdö** is close to the railway but peaceful.

**Balatonszemes** is a small town at the mid-point of the south shore of the lake. Above the railway, on a gentle slope is the main residential area, while the fairly recently built holiday complex, with its pools and sports, lies on the shore of the lake. What used to be the old post office is now the Postal Museum, *36 Bajcsy Zsalinsky út.* **Köröshegy** boasts a 15th-century Franciscan one-aisled church which is still in use, noted for its organ recitals. Whilst in the town, sample the wines from the towns wine caves.

The *Jenő Kvassay promenade*, 2 km long, is a firm favourite with the holidaymakers of **Balatonföldvár**. At an altidude of 108 metres there are some lovely views and the largest marina on the lake. Within the harbour is sunny little **Galambsziget** (Doves island). Near the station there is a fountain of carbonated water, a reminder of the rich mineral splendour of the region.Camping for 600 is available at **Magyar Tenger Camping**, *6 Kemping utca; tel: (84) 340 240*, and for another 300 at **Naro Camping**, *4–8 Kismartoni utca ; tel: (84) 340 966.*

## SIÓFOK

**Tourist Office: Ibusz** head office is at *174 Fő tér; tel: (84) 311 066.* **Hungarian Tourist Service**, *41 Fő utca; tel: (84) 310 117.* Opening hours 0800–1600 (later during high season).

### ACCOMMODATION

There are several **campsites** at and around the resort, such as the large **Aranypart Nyaralótelep**, *183–5 Szent László utca; tel: (84) 352 801.* For **hostels**, contact the **Trade School Holiday Homes**, *46 Erkel Ferenc utca; tel: (84) 310 131.* Private rooms can be found through the tourist agencies or looking for the *Zimmer Frei* signs. This kind of accommodation is rare, however. There is a glut of hotels, yet space is at a premium. The **Aranypart Hotel**, *82 Beszédes Jósef; tel: (84) 312 722*, is one of the priciest but has a lot on offer, as does the larger **Azúr**, *11 Vitoriás utca; tel: (84) 312 419*, but perhaps the best hotel is the **Aranyhíd**, *69–71 Jószef sétany; tel: (84) 311 633*, with its own pier and a 500-metre stretch of private beach.

### SIGHTSEEING

The last town on the anti-clockwise route, Siófok lies on the mouth of the tiny River Sió. It is the largest town on the south bank of the lake and is very popular because of its excellent amenities. The advent of the railway, as elsewhere along the lake, meant that Siófok was even more accessible and the tourist trade began to develop with the introduction of the Budapest–Fiume line in 1861. The value of this natural gateway to the Danube was soon discovered and the Sió Canal was built in 1863. There was already a fleet of ships on Lake Balaton, but now they could join the Danube which from that point increased their importance and value in trading. In 1866 the park had been added and with the advent of the promenade, shops and restaurants, a new playground was born.

As Siófok is a relatively new resort, the sights are mainly modern. The lock (Krúdy sétany) near the ferry pier always has a fascination when it is being operated, and the Balaton navy headquarters is nearby (Hungary being one of the few landlocked nations to have a navy). Perhaps the oldest sights are in the József Beszédes Museum, 2 Sió utca, alongside the canal. There is a collection of old photographs and hydro engineering which explain the history of the lake and how it was drained. The Meteorological Research Centre is housed inside the green tower opposite the ferry pier.

Close to the centre of town there is the Nagy Strand, the large public beach. The best known beach is the Aranypart (Golden Beach), where the hotels have their own sections of private beach. The Ezüstpart (Silver Beach) is west of the harbour and is not quite so luxurious. 🛈

## SZOMBATHELY

Station: This busy station is on Éhen Gyula tér, and a no 7 bus leads straight into town.

Tourist Office: Ibusz, 3–5 Kálmán út; tel: (94) 314 141, is open 0800 – 1600 on weekdays and to 1200 on Sat.

### ACCOMMODATION

There is really only one decent hotel in the town itself, the Savaria, 4 Mártírok tere; tel: (94) 311 440). Across the lake is the Claudius, 39 Bartók Béla körut; tel:(94) 313 760. Expensive. Campsite: Tópart Camping, Kondics utca; tel: (94) 314 766, by the lakes, is small, with a few bungalows to rent out. The accommodation is very basic but the location is beautiful.

### SIGHTSEEING

Szombathely was one of the prosperous towns on the Bernstein (Amber) trade route founded by the Roman Emperor Claudius. In 107 it was the capital of the Roman province of Pannonia Superior. Almost totally destroyed by earthquake in 455 the town of Savaria as it was then known disappeared for generations. Szombethely resurfaced in the reign of Charlemagne. In the 18th century the Austrian Empress Maria Theresia created a new interest in the town and it became the seat of a bishopric. During World War II, the town was decimated once again and almost all the ancient buildings were lost.

Szombathely Cathedral (built in 1797) was almost totally destroyed during the last few days of the war. The red and white marble pulpit escaped, as did a couple of the Maulbertsch original frescoes. The Bishop's Palace, 3 Berzsenyi tér, was more fortunate in that all the Maulbertsch frescoes survived. Due to

173

their rarity, viewing is by special arrangement only; frescoes by István Dorfmeister, however, and other items are open to the public. Opposite the Cathedral is the **Eölbey House**, built in 1796, which houses the **Revolution Museum**. **Járdányi Paulovits István Romkert**, the Garden of Ruins, is behind the cathedral, displaying discoveries made in 1938. Part of the old Roman road has been excavated and the mosaics are very interesting. The **Szombethely Gallery**, *12 Rákótczi utca*, has a fine collection of 20th-century Hungarian art. On the other side of the street, the Moorish-style **music school and Bartók Concert Hall** was in fact originally a Synagogue designed in 1881. Only a memorial plaque indicates the spot where '4228 of our Jewish brothers and sisters were deported to Auschwitz on 4th June 1944'. The **Vas County Village Museum**, *Árpád utca*, contains some 12 houses imported from all over the region and set out in a semi-circle.

## KÖRMEND

**Station:** Just north of the town centre. **Tourist Office: Savaria Tourist**, *11 Rákóczi utca; tel: Körmend 161*. The town is not yet on the main telephone line so all calls must be connected by an operator.

The place is so small that even the Hungarian Tourist Service do not include any accommodation in their official lists, but in fact there are a couple of hotels. The **Rába**, *24 Becsényi utca; tel: Körmend 89*, has 20 rooms and is conveniently close to the railway and bus stations. The **Halászcsárda** pension, *24 Becsényi utca; tel Körmend 69*, has 9 double rooms. Savaria can organise cheap dormitory accommodation in the summer.

The **Rába Historical Collection**,

the 18th-century riding school and **City Theatre** are in the **Batthyány-Strattman Palace**. This is one of the finest of the Transdanubian mansions, built on the walls of a 12-14th-century castle. There is an exhibition which highlights the past events and town history.Every summer there are the **Körmend open air concerts** in the 13th-century park.

## GRAZ

**Station:** *tel: (0316) 1717*. Rents bikes. **Tourist Office:** *Hbf; tel: (0316) 916837* Mon–Fri, 0900–1300, 1400–1800, Sat 0900–1200, 1300–1700, Suns and holidays 1000–1500. An office at *Herreng. 16; tel: (0316) 8352410*; trams nos 3 or 6 from the station to the *Hauptpl.* or approx 15 mins walk, opens Mon–Fri 0900–1900, Sat 0900–1800, Sun 1000–1500 (May–Oct), Mon–Fri 0900–1800, Sat 1000–1500 Sun and holidays 1000–1500 (Nov–Apr). It offers give-away city map with a more detailed one for sale (ÖS25) plus regional information.

### GETTING AROUND

A 24-hour bus and tram ticket costs ÖS40, or for 10 trips ÖS140. There is a shuttle bus from the airport to hotels four times a day depending on flight times. The *Graz Total* booklet lists eating places and all cultural events.

### ACCOMMODATION AND FOOD

The tourist office can book accommodation (fee is ÖS30 per hotel). At the top end is **Grand Hotel Wiesler**, *Grieskai 4–8; tel: (0316) 90660* (very expensive) in a quayside property, or the **Hotel Erzherzog Johann**, *Sackstr. 3–5; tel: (0316) 811616* (expensive), with rooms on 19th-century scale. Alternatives are the two-star **Hotel Strasser**, *Eggenberger*

174

*Gurtel 11; tel: (0316) 913977* (moderate) near the station. **HI: Jugendgasthaus Graz**, *Idlhofg. 74; tel: (0316) 914876*, is 20 mins walk from the station or bus no. 50. **Camping Central** is at *Martinhofstr. 3; tel: (0316) 281831*, south of the city close to the local *Strassgang* station. Chains with property here include *BW* and *Rk*.

Cheap eating places cater to Graz's many students, while the area beside the *Hauptpl.*, centring on *Mehlpl.*, is alive with numerous cafés, notably **M1**, *Mehlpl. 1*, with great views. Most popular for food is probably **Gastwirtschaft**, *Harlbarthg. 4*. More expensive is the **Landeshaus-Keller**, *Schmiedg. 9*, in the *Landeshaus* itself. Or check out the *Bauernmärkte*, Mon–Sat 0700–1230, *Kaiser-Josefpl. and Lendpl.*; Mon–Sat 0500–2000, *Hauptpl.*; Mon–Fri 0700–1800, Sat 0700–1230 at *Jakominipl.*

### ENTERTAINMENT

Music schools are big here, resulting in high quality **street performance**. The **Opera House** is the venue for major cultural events. July–Sept sees candlelit concerts at the **Eggenbergerschloss** and **open-air concerts** Jul–mid-Aug in the **Generalihof** with jazz Thurs. **Styriarte**, Jun and Jul, is a classical music festival with a different theme each year. The **Steirischer Herbst** (Styrian autumn) international contemporary arts festival (Sept–Oct) includes anything from mime to jazz. There is also a **street art festival** Aug.

### SHOPPING

**Kastner & Öhler**, a high tech department store in the heart of old *Altstadt* buildings, is one of the smartest places to shop. For local cheeses try **Delikatessen F. Nussbaumer**, *Paradeisg. 1*, There is a stylish local craftshop under **Café M1**.

**Steirisches Heimatwerk**, *Herreng.* offers genuine *Trachten* (traditional costumes).

### SIGHTSEEING

The Tourist Office organises 2-hr tours daily Apr–Oct, Sat Nov–Mar, for ÖS75. The **medieval centre** with small streets packed with shops and cafés, hinges round the **Hauptplatz**, with nearby the delightful 16th-century Italian-influenced **Landeshaus**. On the hill above are the remains of the town's former castle – a **bell tower** of 1556, expensively ransomed from the French. But the most intriguing spot is the **Landeszeughaus**, *Herreng. 16; tel: (0316) 8017 4810* – in effect a supermarket for arms where local lords would equip their men. Built in the 17th century, it is still the world's largest historical armoury, with 30,000 muskets, rifles, suits of armour and shields,

The **Mausoleum**, erected next to the cathedral 1614–1638, was designed as Emperor Ferdinand II's tomb, impressive for its unabashed mannerist/baroque style. The **Dom** (cathedral) itself is decorated outside with the well-worn **Scourges of God mural**, a reminder of the Black Death, Turkish invasion and plagues of locusts.

The **Neue Galerie**, *Sackstr. 16; tel: (0316) 829155* shows 19th- and 20th-century Austrian painting in the fine **Palais Herberstein**. The **Alte Galerie**, *Neutorg. 45; tel: (0316) 80174770*, has medieval through to baroque works. The **Kunstgewerbe**, *Neutorg. 45; tel: (0316) 80174780*, combines modern artists' works and ethnic and social history exhibits. Slightly out of town (bus no. 1 from *Hauptpl.*) is the **Eggenberger-schloss**, *Eggenbergeralle 90; tel: (0316) 583264*, built in 1625 with, including false ones, a window for each day of the year.

**175**

# BUDAPEST–KRAKÓW

From Hungary into Poland, this route passes through the Büuk Hills, named from their beechwood forests, with autumn colour to match New England's. If you are lucky you will catch sight of some of the Lipizaner horses, famous as the mounts of Vienna's Spanish Riding School, which are bred in these hills. There is also a side-track to Hungary's best-known wine region.

**Kraków**

*Vienna – Kosice, p. 309*
←

**Kosice**

*Eger*

**Miskolc**

**FASTEST JOURNEY: 12HRS**

**Fuzesabony**

**Budapest**

## ON TRACK

**Budapest–Füzesabony–Miskolc**
Nine or ten trains a day run between Budapest and Miskolc, stopping at Fuzesabony en route. Budapest to Fuzesabony takes 1 hr 45 mins, Fuzesabony to Miskolc takes 45 mins.

## TRAINS

**ETT Tables: 95b, 899**

### FAST TRACK
→ One through overnight service with sleeping cars and couchettes taking 12 hrs. A day service is available by changing train at Hatvan.

**Miskolc–Kosice**
Four of the Budapest trains continue on to Kosice in Slovakia. Moskolc to Kosice takes 1 hr 40 mins.

**Kosice–Kraków**
Two expresses link Kosice with Kraków, taking 7 hrs for the journey.

## FÜZESABONY

This is the jumping-off point for Eger. There are also three direct trains daily from Budapest.

### ⤴ SIDE TRACK FROM FÜZESABONY

## EGER

**Station:** There are two stations, the main station by *Deák Ferenc utca* and Egervár station, a few min away from the castle, for local destinations north of Eger.
**Tourist Office: Hungarian Tourist Service**, *2 Dobó tér; tel: (36) 312 807*, are very knowledgeable about Eger and the surrounding area. **Ibusz** is at *Bajcsy-Zsilinsky utca; tel: (36) 312 526.*

### ACCOMMODATION

There is a good choice of hotels. The tiny **Romantik Hotel**, *26 Csiky S. utca; tel: (36) 310 456*, has its own beach, bureau de change and shops. **Flora Hotel**, *5 Fürdő; tel:(36) 320 211*, is large and includes a sauna, solarium and massage amongst its vast number of facilities. The **Minaret**, *3 Harangöntő; tel: (36) 410 473*, is a quaint gable-roofed hotel with a very extensive range of facilities to tempt the guest. There is also a **campsite** for 2000 with bungalows available, at **Autós Caravan Camping**, *79 Rákóczi út; tel: (36) 310 558.*

### SIGHTSEEING

In 1241 the Mongols destroyed the town Saint Stephen had built up as his diocese. The Turks tried to invade twice. First in 1552 its 80,000 strong army was defeated by the local 2000 force made up of men and women, but the second attempt in 1596 suc-

ceeded and the Turks ruled for a hundred years. After their departure Eger once more became the see of a bishop and flourished, industry developed and the town became an educational centre.

At the southern foot of the Bükk Mountains, Eger is one of the most beautiful towns in the country and one of Hungary's best known wine regions, famed for its *Egri Bikavér*, 'Bull's Blood'. Try the wines at the **Bormúzeum** (Wine Museum), *1 Városfal utca*, or at **Szépasszony-völgy** (Valley of the Beautiful Women). Bull's Blood itself may be sampled in the many cellars going down the hill into the valley. Walk there; drink the wines at a few forints per glass; listen to the gypsy bands but take a taxi back; you'll need to, as you most probably will have a *macskajaj* ('cat's wail', a Hungarian hangover.)

Among the more sobering sights is the 13th-century **castle** on Castle Hill. Steeped in ancient history and like most others in the region, it was blown up by the Habsburgs. Bishop Károly Esterházy used the stones to construct his own buildings. Much has been rebuilt since the 1950s.

The ancient foundations of the 12th-century **St John's Cathedral** have been excavated. **István Dobó Museum** in the Bishop's Palace section of the castle exhibits models of what the castle looked like, as well as some of the original furnishings and ceramics. The Art Gallery contains mainly portraits of leading Hungarians. Guided tours are available from the ticket office.

On the way down to town stands **Főzékesgyhaz** (Classic Cathedral). It is an enormous structure with huge

**177**

statues on the roof of Faith, Hope and Charity. Inside there is a wealth of beautiful art in the form of paintings and sculpture.

On the opposite side of the road (*Szabadság*) is the old **Lyceum**, which is now a teachers' training college. The ceiling fresco (1778-79) in the library is stunning, with over a hundred figures representing the delegates at the Council Of Trent (1545-63), and there are tens of thousands of ancient books and manuscripts inside the oak cupboards. On the third floor there is an observatory with 18th-century astronomical equipment.

**Érseki palota**, the Bishop's Palace, *1–3 Széchenyi utca,* built in 1764–66 in the form of a horseshoe, leads to the main shopping area of Eger, with many beautiful 18th-century buildings such as the **Carlone House** (no. 13) home of an Italian painter, and the **Apothecary Museum** at no. 14. At no. 15 is the **Cistercian Church** and further down at no. 59 is the **Rác Church**, the Serbian Orthodox church founded in 1799. Inside there is a beautiful iconostasis in gold leaf.

One of the most beautiful baroque churches in Hungary is the **Minorite Church**, *Dobó tér.* During medieval times this was the site of the market square, the hub of the village as it was then. On the opposite side of the square towers a tall **minaret** topped with a cross. There are 100 spiral steps winding their narrow way to the top, which offers a spectacular vista. The **park** a little way south from the centre has a very large open-air and a covered pool, open 0830–1900 and genuine Turkish thermal baths open 1200–1800 (alternate days for men and women.)

## MISKOLC

**Station:** in the east of town, on *Zója tér.* A 15-min ride by tram will bring you into the centre.

**Tourist Office: Isbuz**, 3–9 Széchenyi út; tel: (46) 324 411, have a register of private rooms available to rent, and all the hotels and other details. They also operate a bureau de change. Open 0800–1630 weekdays, 0800–1200 Sat. **Hungarian Tourist Service** operate from *1 Mindszent tér; tel: (46) 348 921.*

### ACCOMMODATION AND FOOD

Miskolc has some fine hotels, such as the **Juno**, *2–4 Csabai utca; tel: (46) 364 411.* **Pannonia**, *2 Kossuth Lajos; tel: (46) 329 425,* is a well-run member of a large chain of Western-style hotels in the eastern European area.

In the suburb if Miskolc-Tapolca, 7 km, bus no. 2 or no. 102 from the centre of town, the **Kikelet Panzió**, *6 Győri utca; tel: (46 366 811,* is a nice little pension.

Go to Avas Hill for the best selection of restaurants and cafés, where there are also many hotels and the local wine cellars plunging to a depth of 10 to 100m.

### SIGHTSEEING

Miscolc is Hungary's second- or third-largest city, depending on whose statistics you believe. Large and industrialised, with the usual accompanying social problems, it is nevertheless steeped in history and has sights worth stopping for.

The view from the top of the 243-metre **Avas Hill** is beautiful. Just below the mountain on the northern slopes called **Kis Avas** (Little Avas) is the **Calvinist Reformed Church**. It was built in Gothic style in 1414, but destroyed by fire and rebuilt 1560–69. It is thought that the wooden pews came from Diósgyör Castle. In 1557 the free-standing bell tower was added.

**Diósgyör Castle** is in the now indus-trial Diósgyör district of town. This four-towered fortress, now in ruins, was first destroyed in 1241, and there was a history of rebuilding and destruction until 1678, when the Habsburg army finally demol-ished it. At present it is undergoing reconstruction yet again and some of the towers are now standing, as are parts of the east wing and the foundations of the Knight's Hall. There was originally a double gate tower and a five cornered bastion. During the summer there are events staged in the grounds. Next to the castle are the **Castle Baths**, which stay open until 1800 during the summer.

The **National Theatre**, *Széchenyi utca*, is a very fine-looking building, and beyond that is *Városház tér,* where many more imposing official buildings are stretched along both sides of this narrow red paved pedestrian-only street.

There is a superb Black Madonna of Kazan, a gift from Catherine the Great of Russia, at the **Görögkeleti templom** (Greek Orthodox Church and Museum), 7 *Deák tér*. The iconostasis surrounding the statue holds 100 beautiful icons. Another beautiful object is the **Mt Athos Cross**, brought to Miskolc by Greek set-tlers in the 18th century It is richly encrusted with jewels. The church, built in 1785-88, is open Tue–Sun 1000–1800. *Szabadság tér* is a delightful square where the **Ottó Herman Museum** can be found in a baroque house on the cor-ner. Herman discovered the prehistoric remains of the area and the museum houses archaeological and folk exhibits as well as an extensive collections of Neolithic pieces.

## OUT OF TOWN

Considered a suburb of Miskolc, 10 km out of town, is the health resort of **Lillafüred**, 320 metres above sea level. There are many ways to travel there from Miskolc itself, such as by taking the no. 101 bus from Miskolk to Majális Park and then changing onto a no. 5 or 15. Another way is by no. 68 bus from *Andrássy tér* direct. Then there is the nar-row-gauge train which goes from Miskolc via Lillafüred to Garadna. This is a must for railway enthusiasts, with one of the most attractive rides in Hungary, but there are only about fifteen trips a year, so check with one of the tourist offices. The line branches off at Papígyár for a 23 km ride up to the paper factory which causes so much pollution to the Szinva stream. Its redeeming feature is that the scenery it travels through is breathtaking. A ride is well worth the dreadful smell the factory emits!

You can stay at the **Hotel Palota**, *1 Erzsébet Sétany; tel:( 46 331 411,* on the Garadna River where it meets the River Szinva. It looks like the castle in Disneyland with towers and cupolas ris-ing up in front of a backdrop of tree cov-ered mountains. Apart from its spa, Lillafüred is famed for its limestone caves. There are around six hundred caves in the Bükk mountains, three which are open to the public with a guided tour. They are close to the Hotel Palota. The **Petőfi** or **Anne's cave** has evidence of now long-extinct flora in its walls; **István cave** on the Eger road is a stalactite cave, the long points hanging downwards a fantastic sight and the temperature an even 10°C throughout. **Szeleta cave** has evidence of the hunting tools used during the Ice Age.

# DRESDEN

Dresden is best known for its idealised china figurines – the inspiration for millions of kitsch imitations – and for the tragic Allied air raid of 1945. Restoration in the half century since World War II has been extensive and is still going on, to make Dresden once again eastern Germany's most attractive big city.

## TOURIST INFORMATION

**Tourist offices**: *Prager Str. 10; tel: (0351) 495 5025* (near Hbf), open Apr–Oct, Mon–Sat 0900–2000 (–1200 Sun); Nov–Mar, Mon–Fri 0900–1800 (–1400 Sat, –1300 Sun). **Neustadter Markt** (*Fussgangertunnel*); *tel: (0351) 53539*, Mon–Fri 0900–1800, (–1600 Sat), Sun 1000–1600. **Saxony state tourist office**: *Friedrichstr.24; tel: (0351) 496 9703*, Mon–Fri 0900–1800, (–1600 Sat), Sun 1000–1600. **Thomas Cook network member: Thomas Cook Reisebüro** *Scharfenburger Str.66 tel: (0351) 851 2100.*

## ARRIVING AND DEPARTING

**Stations: Hbf**; *tel: (0351) 471 0600*; **Neustadt**; *tel: (0351) 51185*; **Dresden–Klotzsche Airport**; *tel: (0351) 5890 30 80* is 9k m north of the city, with flights to major German cities and a few international flights, *tel: (0351)5890 35961*

## GETTING AROUND

Dresden has trams, buses and a suburban railway system (S-Bahn). There are 15 tram lines covering the entire city. Main transfer points in the city centre are Hbf, Neustadt Bhf, and the SV-Bahnhof Mitte. A 24-hour ticket, valid on buses, trams and SV-Bahn, costs DM5.

## STAYING IN DRESDEN

### Accommodation

Hotel groups in Dresden include *Hn, BW, Hd, Ib, IC, Ke, Mc, SL* and *Tp*. More expensive hotels include **Hotel Am Terrassenufer**, *Am Terrassenufer 12; tel: (0351) 4409500, fax 440 9600*; **Hotel Residenz Alt Dresden**, *Mobschatzerstr.29; tel: (0351) 432 1830, fax (0351) 432 1839*; **Hotel Coventry Cottage**, *Hulsestrasse 1; tel: (0351) 274 3014, fax (0351) 274 3014*. Moderate accommodation includes three hotel ships moored on the Elbe right in the city centre, **Hotelschiff Elbresidenz**; *tel: (0351) 459 5003, fax (0351) 495 5137*, **Hotelschiff Florentina** and **Hotelschiff St Caspar**; *tel: (0351) 459 0169, fax (0359) 459 5036*. Budget accommodation in private rooms can be found through the tourist office.

### Eating and Drinking

There are two good restaurants in the **Semperoper**, the **Steakhaus** and the **Opernplatz**, both *Theatrepl. 2*. **Altmarktkeller**, *Haus Altmarkt, Wilsdrufferstr. 19-21*, is a cavernous cellar restaurant in the old town; **Luisenhof**, *Berganhnstr.8*, has fine vioews and is known as the 'balcony of Dresden'; **Bierhaus Dampschiff**, at the **Dresden Hilton**, *An der Frauenkirche 5*, has a large open-air beer garden; **Café Sphinx**, *Altmarkt 16/17*, has a big open-air terrace in the heart of the old city.

### Money

**Deutsche Verkehrsbank AG**, *Hbf*, Mon–Fri 0700–1930, Sat 0800–1600

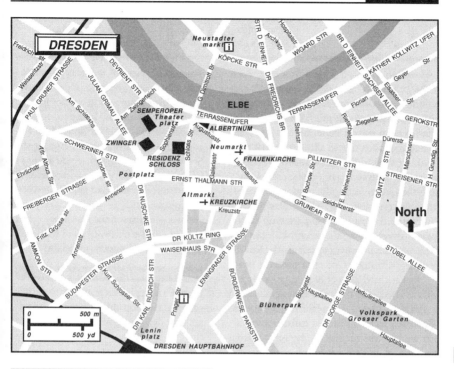

## ENTERTAINMENT

Dresden is the venue each summer (usually in May or June) of one of Europe's most important festivals of classical music and opera, the **Dresdner Musikfestspiele**.

## SIGHTSEEING

Dresden existed as a city by the early 13th century and grew in importance with the building of the first bridge across the Elbe in 1275. In the last quarter of the 13th century Heinrich, Margrave of Meissen, fortified the city. His successors later became dukes, then kings of Saxony. Many of the city's finest baroque buildings date from the reign of its most illustrious ruler, Augustus the Strong, who ruled from 1694–1733. There are city tours by tram, including a guided tour of the Zwinger palace, daily from *Postplatz* at 1000 and a range of guided walking tours,

infromation from the Tourist Office.

From Hbf, *Prager Str.* leads to the Altmarkt, past the Church of the Holy Cross, on to the **Newmarkt** and the **Frauenkirche** (Church of Our Lady), destroyed in the 1945 bombing and now being restored. The **Residenzschloss**, *Residenzplatz*, was also destroyed in 1945 (not for the first time – it burned down in 1701 and was rebuilt by Augustus the Strong) and is also being rebuilt. Another victim of the raid was the **Semperoper** (**Opera House**), *Theaterpl. 2*, built in 1831 and fully restored in the mid 1980s. Dresden's gem, however, is the **Zwinger Palace**, *Sophienstr.* Designed by the court architect Matthaus Poppelmann in 1704 as the centrepiece of Augustus the Strong's new city and a venue for all the entertainments of the royal court. Above its main courtyard rises the **Kronentor** (Crown

Gate), a triumphal arch built to celebrate Augustus's ascent to the throne of Poland in 1697. Within the palace are a gallery of old masters, zoological and historical museums, and a collection of fine porcelain.

On the south bank of the Elbe, the **Albertinum**, *Bruhlsche Terrasse*, is a grandiose museum built in 1884/87 on the foundations of the old city arsenal and housing a collection of works by modern painters, sculpture and coin collections, and the Green Vault, the treasure-room of the Dukes of Saxony. The **Bruhlsche Terrasse** is a former rampart with casemates overlooking the river, laid out in 1739/48 as a pleasure garden for the Saxon Prime Minister, Count Bruhl; it was known as the 'Balcony of Europe' because of the fine views over the Elbe.

East of the *Altstadt*, the **Grosser Garten** park, originally a formal baroque garden, was as one of the 'English' gardens so beloved of 19th-century German landscape architects. Dresden's biggest and prettiest park, it has its own narrow-gauge railway, the **Dresdner Parkeisenbahn**, whose trains make the 5.6 km trip around the park in 30 mins. Operated by schoolchildren, it runs between Apr and Oct.

The southern suburb of **Pillnitz** was the summer residence of the Saxon court. Its two most important buildings, the **Wasserpalais** (Riverside Palace) and the **Bergapalais** (Hill Palace) were built between 1720 and 1722 and now house an **arts and crafts museum**.

⟲ **SIDE TRACKS FROM DRESDEN**

## MEISSEN

38 mins from Dresden Hbf, Meissen is the home of the famous china more widely and less accurately known as Dresden, with an exhibition hall, demonstration workshop and gift shop; *Talstr. 9*. *Moritzburg* (a 50-min trip from Dresden Hbf, changing at *Radebeul Ost* onto a steam train) boasts an immaculate moated hunting lodge, the **Jagdschloss**, one of the most imposing in Europe. built by Duke Moritz of Saxony between 1542 and 1546 and added to by his successors. August the Strong, Elector of Saxony and King of Poland, transformed the earlier building into a splendid baroque palace between 1723 and 26. Nearby stands the **Fasanenschlosschen**, a simple but elegant royal residence built (1769–82) for Friedrich August III of Saxony.

## ELBE CRUISES

Dresden is the home port of the world's oldest fleet of paddle steamers, which sail through the Saxon Switzerland of the Elbe Valley south of the city between Apr and Oct. Other steam vessels sailing on the Elbe include the *Krippen*, built in 1882 and recently restored to its original glory and the *Sachsenwald*, a steam tugboat – the last of its kind still afloat. **Sachsichsche Dampschiffahrtsgesellschaft**, *Georgenstr. 6; tel: (0351) 5023877*. **Sachsenwald**, *am Hausberg 12, Pirna; tel: (03501) 2624*. **Krippen**, *Siebenicher Str. 29a; tel: (03521) 452600*.

## WINDBERGBAHN

Germany's first mountain railway, the Windbergbahn, was built in 1856 and winds steeply upward from the Plauenschergrund valley to the Obergittersee plateau. There are superb views of Dresden and its surroundings. The 11.4 km journey from *Dresden Hbf* to *Gittersee Bhf* takes 40 mins each way and scheduled trains operate between May–Oct from Dresden Hbf. ⬛

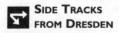

# DRESDEN-PRAGUE

From Dresden, this route runs southeast along the Elbe valley through the beautiful mountain region known as the 'Saxon Switzerland'. In the mid-18th century it was romaticised in oils by Bernardo Bellotto, nephew of Canaletto, who was commissioned by Augustis II of Saxony to paint views of Dresden and its surroundings. Until the fall of the Berlin Wall and the raising of the Iron Curtain, this part of Germany was off-limits to foreign visitors.

**Dresden**

**Königstein (Bad Schandau)**

**Pirna**

183

**Prague**

FASTEST JOURNEY: 3 HRS

## ON TRACK

## TRAINS

**ETT Tables:** 60.

## FAST TRACK

Service every two hours. The journey takes three hrs.

**Dresden–Pirna**
Frequent local S-Bahn service taking 25 mins.

**Pirna–Prague**
Eight services a day changing trains at Bad Schandau.

### PIRNA

**Station: Hbf;** *tel: 030 19 4 19.*
This small town has a cluster of well-preserved historic buildings including the **Rathaus**, *Marktplatz*, a 17th-century building with a baroque tower added in 1718; the adjoining 15th-century **Marienkirche** has a Gothic belfry and a high altar added in 1615. The town is dominated by the Sonnenstein fortress, dating from as early as the 15th century.

**SIDE TRACK
FROM PIRNA**

### SCHLOSS WEESENSTEIN

Five km west of Pirna, the castle clings to a crag overlooking the river Muglitz. The oldest part of the building, the inner round tower, was built in 1300, with a ring of outer battlements added in 1575 and a chapel, built much later in 1738–41. Fine stucco ceilings, marble fireplaces and leather wall hangings grace the interior.

### KÖNIGSTEIN

**Station: Hbf,** Bad Schandau/Königstein. **Festung Königstein** crowns a flat-topped hill above the Elbe and dates from the 12th century, when it belonged to the King of Bohemia (Wenzel I, celebrated in the carol as Good King Wenceslas). Passing into the hands of the Saxon Electors, it became a strong border fortress and prison. Its most striking features are the massive main gate, built in 1590, the arsenal, built in 1594, and the Friedrichsburg, an octagonal summer villa built in 1589 and rebuilt in 1721.

# DRESDEN-WROCŁAW

The journey through Lower Silesia passes through forests and agricultural land (predominantly wheat and sugar beet), into historic Polish territories lost under the 1772 partitions of Poland, and only regained from Germany after World War II.

FASTEST JOURNEY: 4 HRS

Bautzen

Wrocław

Dresden

185

## TRAINS

**ETT Table:** 55

### FAST TRACK

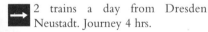 2 trains a day from Dresden Neustadt. Journey 4 hrs.

### ON TRACK

**Dresden–Bautzen**
A train every 2 hrs makes the hour-long journey.

**Bautzen–Wrocław**
The two through trains between Dresden and Wrocław call at Bautzen, journey time Bautzen to Wrocław 3 hrs.

## BAUTZEN

This very attractive small town, close to Germany's border with Poland, was repeatedly the scene of ferocious battles because of its strategic position commanding a crossing of the River Spree. It was destroyed during the Thirty Years War (1618-48) and almost levelled in fierce fighting between Napoleon's retreating troops and a Russian and Prussian army in 1813. Like several other cities of the region, including Dresden, the town was founded by the Slavic Sorabians who originally populated this corner of what is now Germany; the German Bautzen is a version of the earlier Sorabian name Budysin.

Commanding the city is the **Ortenburg**, a 15th-century fortified palace overlooking the Spree, which now houses a history museum. Also worth seeing are the **Rathaus**, *Hauptmarkt*, built in 1732 and the **Ratskeller**, with a fine vaulted interior and 19th century baroque facade. The **Petridom** (St Peter's Cathedral), *Fleischmarkt*, is a Gothic style church built in the 13th–15th centuries. Like some other churches in Germany, this has been shared by Protestant and Roman Catholic congregations since the Reformation. Originally a grille separated them; the cathedral still has a separate altar for each group of worshippers.

## WROCŁAW

**Station: Wrocław Główny**, *ul. Piłsudskiego 104; tel: (071) 68 54 64*, and *933/4/5* (for train timetable). The station is a superb late 19th century neo-Gothic building, with its 200-metre long main hall making it one of Germany's largest stations when built (Wrocław, known as Breslau, was then under Prussian rule). Facilities include left-luggage, restaurants, cafés, currency exchange, shops and kiosks.

**Tourist Office:** Located in the main market square at *Rynek 14, 50-101 Wrocław; tel: (071) 44 31 11*, open Mon–Fri 0900–1900, Sat 1000–1600 (summer season); Mon–Fri 0900–1700, Sat 1000–1400 (winter season). Free information is limited though there's plenty to buy, with accommodation advice too. Look out for the free magazine *Welcome to Wrocław and Lower Silesia* with listings and practical information.

### GETTING AROUND

Trams link the city, with tickets for single journeys, daily or weekly travel available

from Ruch kiosks. Tram nos. 9 and 11 will take you from the railway station to *pl. Dominikanski*, a few minutes from the Market Square. Radio taxis can be called on *919*.

### ACCOMMODATION

There are plenty of hotels at various price points. Period grandeur is expensive at **Dwór Wazów**, *ul. Kiełbaśnicza 2; tel: (071) 72 34 15*, adjacent to the main market square. Far less expensive is the **Hotel Monopol**, *ul. H Modrzejewskiej 2; tel: (071) 370 41*, which is renowned for its Art Nouveau style but needs restoration. Tourist grade Orbis hotels offer inexpensive options. The **Accommodation Bureau** for private lodgings is **Odra-Tourist**, *ul. Piłsudskiego 98; tel: (071) 368 11*. The **Youth Hostel** is at *ul. Kołłztaja 20; tel: (071) 388 56*, and within walking distance of the centre. **Campsites** include *ul. Na Grobli 16/18; tel: (071) 344 42*, on the banks of the Oder river at the edge of town.

### EATING AND DRINKING

Wrocław offers everything from international fast food to traditional Polish, particularly around the Market Square, where the many vaulted cellar bars include **Spiż** under the **Ratusz** (Town Hall), *Rynek-Ratusz 2; tel: (071) 44 52 67*, with its own working micro-brewery visible behind the counter, and inexpensive bar food.

### ENTERTAINMENT

The **Opera House** is at *ul. Świdnicka 35; tel: (071) 386 41*. A charming Art Nouveau theatre-café is **Pod Kalamburem**, *Kużnicza 29a; tel: (071) 44 57 28*. Nightclubs include the sophisticated **Dwór Polski**, *Rynek 5; tel: (071) 72 48 98*, and the more bustling **Pałacyk**, in a converted palace, at *ul. Kościuszki 34,* every night from 2100–0500. Annual festivals include **Polish Contemporary Music** (Feb), **Jazz Music** (Mar), and **Modern Polish Plays** (Jun).

## SIGHTSEEING

Renowned for Gothic and baroque architecture, Wrocław is Poland's fourth biggest city and 'capital' of Silesia, which became part of Poland in the 10th century. From the 14th century Silesia was ruled by Bohemia, by Austria in the 16th century and Prussia in the 18th century, returning to Poland again after World War II, having been two thirds destroyed.

Starting in the Market Square, the **Ratusz** (Town Hall), a superb example of Silesian Gothic, dates from the 12th century with a 16th century astrological clock, and houses the **Muzeum Historyczne** (Historical Museum), *Rynek-Ratusz, tel: (071) 44 13 34,* open Tues–Fri 1000–1600, Sat 1100–1700, Sun 1000–1800. Heading north is the 1860 **Dom Miejski**, the main civic building within the architectural cluster in the centre of the Market Square. Nos 2–11 are outstanding examples from the 13th century. In the north west corner of the Market Square is the 14th-century Gothic church **Św. Elżbiety** (St. Elizabeth's) with an 86 m tower making it the city's tallest. By the Market Square is *pl. Solny* with market stalls, Renaissance buildings, and the **Nowa Giełda** (New Stock Exchange), an early 19th-century neo-Classical building.

South of the Market Square is **ul. Świdnicka**, laid out in 1242 and the city's busiest street with department stores, cafés, street traders, the **Opera House** (built 1837-1841) and the 16th-century **Corpus Christi church**.

Heading north from the Market Square along *ul. Sw. Katarzyny* and *ul. Piastowa* passes the old tram depot, now a covered market, and leads to **Ostrów Tumski**. Ostrów means 'island' in old Polish, and this most historic part of town, with traces of 9th-century fortifications, is now a complex of Gothic religious architecture, including: **St John the Baptist's Church, St Bartholomew's Church** and **St Egidus' Church,** all 13th century, and the 14th-century **Church of Our Lady on the Sand**.

From Ostrów Tumski take ul. Grodzka to the **University,** an 18th-century baroque building overlooking the Oder river, with a baroque **Aula Leopoldina** (Assembly Hall) *pl. Uniwersytecki 1; tel: (071) 40 22 71,* open Mon, Tues, Thur–Sun 1000–1530.

## Museums

**Muzeum Narodowe** (National Museum), *ul. Powstańców Warszawy 5; tel: (071) 388 30,* open Tues–Wed, Fri–Sun 1000–1600, Thur 0900–1700, Sat 1100–1700, with 14th-19th century Silesian and Polish art.

**Muzeum Panoramy Racławickiej,** *ul. Purkiniego 11; tel: (071) 44 23 44,* open Tues–Sun 0900–1800. The *Panorama of the Battle of Racławice* is a 19th-century painting, 120 by 15 metres, housed in a specially built rotunda, commemorating Tadeusz Kościuszko's defeat of Russian troops in 1794.

City sightseeing and excursions can be booked through **Orbis,** *Rynek 9-11; tel: (071) 382 91/2.* Book boat trips along the Oder river at *ul. Wróblewskiego 1; tel: (071) 22 36 18.* A **tram café** dating from 1929, called Baba Jaga, makes sightseeing tours on Sat–Sun, book at *pl. Teatralny; tel: (071) 57 72 32.*

187

# HELSINKI

Notwithstanding a population of half a million, Helsinki still retains something of the atmosphere of an overgrown fishing port. The de facto capital of Finland since 1917 also bears the imprint of previous occupations. Swedish is still the second language here, while Russian influence is nowadays confined to the sphere of architecture. Helsinki is a singularly compact city, and welcomes tourists, although prices are steep.

## TOURIST INFORMATION

**Helsinki City Tourist Office**, *Pohjoisesplanadi 19; tel: 169 37 57 or 174 088,* opens May 2–Sept 30, Mon–Fri 0830–1800 and Sat–Sun 1000–1500; Oct 1- Apr 30, Mon–Fri 0830–1600. This is a comprehensive resource centre for visitors – brochures, reservations for sight-seeing, guides, accommodation listings and separate regional service desks. An alternative is the **Finnish Tourist Board**, *Eteläesplanadi 4; tel: 4030 13 00,* open Mon–Fri 0830–1700, Sat 1000–1400.

The **Thomas Cook Network** licensee is **Finland Travel Bureau**, *Kaivokatu 10a; tel: 182 63 51.* They provide a variety of services to visitors, including assistance under the Thomas Cook Worldwide Customer Promise.

## ARRIVING AND DEPARTING

### Airport
**Vantaa Airport**, information and timetable enquiries, *tel: 9600 81 00.* Helsinki's international airport is 20 km north of the .city. Finnair buses depart from the terminal at 20-min intervals between the hours of 0500 and 2400. The 30-min trip to the central railway station costs 24FIM. A cheaper alternative is the local bus, no. 615.

### Stations
**Rautatieasema** station is at *Rautatientori; tel: 1010 115 or 0100 121* (timetable enquiries 24 hrs). Services include currency exchanges and numerous shops, fast food outlets and cafés, both upstairs and in the subway. The left luggage office is open daily from 0635 to 2200 only. There are daily services to Moscow and St Petersburg and to most destinations within Finland. The Art Deco station is one of Helsinki's most celebrated public buildings, completed in 1916.

### Ferries and Buses
There are regular daily **ferry** sailings to Tallinn and Stockholm. The **Viking Line**, *Mannerheimintie 2; tel: 123 577,* open daily 0700–2130 and **Silja Line**, also *Mannerheimintie 2; tel: 9800 74552,* open daily 0800–2000. Both depart from the main harbour. Ferries to Tallinn depart from the **West Terminal** (Länsisatama), *Hietasaarenkuja.* Bus no. 15. **Tallink Travel Shop**, *Erottajankatu 19; tel: 2282 1277,* open Mon–Sat 0830–1900. The **long-distance bus** station is just across *Mannerheimintie* from the railway station. For timetable information, *tel: 9600 4000*

## GETTING AROUND

### Public Transport
Helsinki is well served with buses and

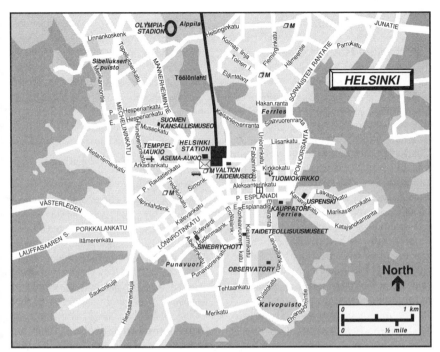

trams and there is also a single metro line, running from Kamppi to Mellunmäki via Rautatientori (Central Station). For bus and tram information, *tel: 0100 111*

### Tickets

Tickets are valid on buses, metro and trams. Passengers can either buy a single ticket, cost 9FIM or a 10-trip ticket, cost 75FIM. Better value may be to buy a Tourist Ticket, for one (25FIM) three (50FIM) or five (75FIM) days. The **Helsinki Card** entitles the user to free entry to more than 50 museums, boat trips to the Zoo and Suomenlinna Fortress and other concessions. Single tickets are sold on board buses and trams, single and 10–trip tickets can be bought from machines on metro stations, other tickets can be bought from Rautatientori Metro Station, from R-kiosks and shops displaying the double arrow symbol.

### Taxis

Official cabs (marked *Taksi*) have a yellow roof light to indicate if the vehicle is for hire. There are a number of taxi ranks in the city centre; or you can ring **Helsinki Taxi Center**, *tel: 700 700*. Bear in mind, however, that taxis are entitled to run meters from the moment your call is picked up.

## STAYING IN HELSINKI

### Accommodation

Helsinki has accommodation of every category, much of it centrally located. For help with accommodation, contact the **Hotel Booking Centre** at the railway station; *tel: 171 133*. Hotel chains in Helsinki include *Rd, IC, BW* and *Rm*. Many hotels offer saunas inclusive in the price. Two good-value medium-price hotels are **Helka**, *P. Rautatiekatu 23; tel:*

440 581, and **Cumulus Kaisaniemi**, *Kaisaniemenkatu 7; tel: 172 881*. The Finnish **Youth Hostel Association** is at *Yrjönkatu 38 B15; tel: 6940 377*. The central hostel is **Stadionin Retkeily-maja**, *P. Stadionintie 3B; tel: 496 071*, where bikes can also be hired. There are several other hostels in the city, some open only in the summer. Another budget option is the **YMCA Interpoint**, *Vuorikatu 17; tel: 173 44 257*. Beds cost from 50FIM a night and it's only a few blocks north of the railway station. There are campsites at **Rastila**, *Vuosaari; tel: 316 551*, and at **Espoo Camping Oittaa**, *Espoo; tel: 862 585*.

## Eating and Drinking

Helsinki caters for every taste in food and ambience but prices can be off-putting. Drinks are highly expensive, especially wines – fortunately water is usually served with meals. **Fazer's** restaurant and pastry shop, *Kluuvikatu 3; tel: 666 597*, offers local dishes at reasonable prices – help yourself to bread and delicious cream cheeses. **Kluuvi**, *Kluuvikatu 5; tel: 659 014*, is a large but relaxed establishment, specialising in pizza and pasta. **Café Strindberg**, *Pohjoisesplanadi 33; tel: 652 262*, overlooks the Esplanade and serves good coffee. There are dozens of pubs and bars. You can drink by candlelight in **Vastarannan Kiiski**, *Salomonkatu 15; tel: 694 1383*, or join the crowd at the Irish bar, **Molly Malones**, *Kaisaniemenkatu 1; tel: 171 272*. For combining drinking and sightseeing you can't do better than the **Koff Pub-Tram**, which leaves from the Pohjoisesplanadi between 1000 and 1500; 30FIM includes the price of a beer or soft drink. There's a toilet on board!

## Communications

The main **post office** is on *Manner-heimintie 11*, open Mon–Fri 0900–1700. The Poste restante (general delivery) at the same address is open Mon–Fri 0800–2100, Sat 0900–1800, Sun 11.00–2100.

To phone Helsinki from abroad: *tel: international code +3580 + number*; to phone Helsinki from elsewhere in Finland: *tel: 90 + number*.

## Money

Banking hours in Finland are Mon–Fri 0915-1615. There are money changing facilities all over Helsinki, for example **Helsinki Oy**, *Pohjoisesplanadi 21*, open Mon–Sat 0800–2200 and Sun 0900–1800. If you cash six cheques at once, the bank charge is the equivalent of cashing a single cheque (30 FIM). Major credit cards are accepted in most hotels, restaurants and department stores.

## Embasssies and consulates

**Australia:** no embassy, contact Australian Government Information Office, *Museokatu 25a; tel: 447 233*
**Canada:** *Pohjoisesplanadi 25b; tel: 171 141*
**New Zealand:** no embassy, contact British embassy.
**Republic of Ireland:** *Erottajankatu 7a; tel: 646 006*
**South Africa:** *Rahapajankatu 1A5; tel: 658 288*.
**UK:** *Itäinen Puistotie 17; tel: 661 293*.
**USA:** *Itäinen Puistotie 14a; tel: 171 931*.

## ENTERTAINMENT

Helsinki has a lively night life during the summer months. For listings see the free, English-language magazines *Helsinki this Week* and *Helsinki Guide*. The best place to head is the area around *Aleksanterinkatu* and the streets off *Mannerheimintie*. Pubs are popular meeting places for planning a night on the town. There are a number of night restaurants with cabaret, discothèques (many of them in hotels), rock cafés, jazz clubs (**Hot Tomato** and **Storyville** are very popular) and casinos. Most clubs close at between 0300 and 0400.

The main venue for symphony and other concerts is **Finlandia Hall**; concerts are also held in churches. **Finnish National Opera** is another important musical venue. There are several theatres, notably the **National**. Helsinki's 30 cinemas all show films in the original language. There are several major summer festivals, including the **Arts Festival** (Jun–Jul) and the **Helsinki Festival** (Aug–Sept); see the listings magazines for events. Helsinki's main sporting venue is the **Olympic Stadium**. In August look out for the international athletics meeting between Sweden and Finland.

## SHOPPING

Shopping hours are 0900–1700/1800 weekdays and 0900–1400/1500 Sat. For after-hours shopping (to 2200 nightly) try the precinct under the railway station. The main shopping streets are *Mannerheimintie* and *Aleksanterinkatu* – Helsinki's premier department store, **Stockmann's**, is at no. 52. The Esplanade is lined with upmarket showrooms and boutiques advertising Finnish designer names. *Kauppatori* (Market Square) is the best place to look for hand-crafted souvenirs:: hand-knitted hats, hessian puppets, clay ducks, painted earrings in wood and metal, woven baskets and much else besides.

## SIGHTSEEING

A useful introduction to Helsinki is to take **tram 3T** from *Kauppatori*. The figure-eight route takes in most of the major sights and there is sometimes a commentary in English. The city is best enjoyed on foot. The **Helsinki Tourist Assoc-**

**iation** organises city walks with English-speaking guides in summer. Contact HTA at *Lönnrotinkatu 7B; tel: 601 966*. There are any number of **boat tours** exploring Helsinki's fascinating coastline. The starting point is *Kauppatori*.

## Waterfront

Take the pulse of the city by strolling through the colourful harbour district. *Kauppatori* is the focus of Helsinki's markets – stalls selling freshly caught fish, fruit and vegetables make way for an enticing array of local crafts. In the winter months head for the 19th-century indoor market or **Kauppahalli** on *Eteläranta (Open Mon–Fri 0800–1700; Sat 0800–1400)*. Overlooking the market is the charming **Havis Amanda** fountain – the seductive sea nymph was considered risqué when first unveiled in 1908. The neo-classical **Town Hall** just behind the square was conceived as a hotel by C. L. Engel in 1833. Nearby, at the corner of *Mariankatu*, is the **President's Palace**, built as a private home in 1814 and later remodelled by Engel. The gilded cupolas of the red-brick **Uspensky Cathedral** are an interesting counterpoint to Helsinki's neo-classical architecture. The Cathedral, overlooking the harbour, was built for the city's Russian Orthodox community in 1868 and now serves the Finnish Orthodox Church (open Apr–Sept, Mon, Wed–Fri 0930–1600 Tues 0930–1800; Sat 1000–1600; Sun 1200–1500). South of *Kauppatori* is *Ehrenströmintie,* which skirts the old health resort of **Kaivopuisto** (Spa Park). The little neighbourhood of quaint Russian dachas (country cottages) is now occupied by several major embassies. A row of striking Art Nouveau buildings forms the backdrop to the yachting marina at picturesque **Merisatama Harbour.**

## Senate Square

In 1812 Helsinki became the capital of the Russian Grand Duchy of Finland. To reflect its enhanced status, the German architect C. L. Engel was commissioned to build a new architectural centrepiece around the **Senate House** (now Government Palace) which occupies the eastern side of the square. The entire ensemble is in the Empire style fashionable in the early 19th century and echoes the contemporary architecture of St Petersburg.

The jewel in the crown is undoubtedly the green-domed **Lutheran Cathedral**. The interior is impressive for its restraint. There is an attractive altarpiece and a handsome pulpit with ornate baldacchino. Statues of the great religious reformers including Mikael Agricola, who brought the Reformation to Finland, complete the decoration (open Mon–Sat 0900–1700/1900 May-Sep; Sun 1200–1800). In the centre of the square is a statue of Tsar Alexander II, who did much to advance Finnish autonomy in the 19th century. Opposite the Senate House is the **University** and to the south is the former governor-general's residence, now the Town Hall.

## Mannerheimintie

Helsinki's main thoroughfare stretches from the leafy **Esplanade** in the south to way beyond the **Olympic Stadium** – the 72-metre tower is a good vantage point over the city. The street honours the great statesman Marshal Carl Gustaf Mannerheim, hero of the independence movement and of the campaigns of World War II. (If you want to know more there is a house museum on *Kalliolinnantie 14*, open Fri–Sun 1100–1600) Just off *Kaivokatu* is the station and the complex of art museums which includes **The Finnish National Gallery** (open Tues and Fri 0900–1700; Wed and Thurs 0900–2100; Sat and Sun 1100–1700). Beyond the station are a number of important buildings: the severe granite **Parliament** building; the **Helsinki City Museum**, located in an elegant neo-classical mansion (open Wed–Sun 1100–1700); the **National Museum** (open Tues–Sun 1100–1600) and the sleek, white marble **Finlandia Hall**, designed in the 1970s by award-winning architect, Alvar Aalto. Also worth seeing is the modern **Temppeliaukion Kirkko** (Rock Church) on *Temppelikatu* (open Mon–Fri 1000–2000; Sat 1000–1800; Sun 1200–2000) and, off *Sibeliuksenkatu*, **Sibelius Park**, which has a monument to the famous composer by Eila Hiltunen.

## The Islands

One of Helsinki's most attractive features is the neighbouring islands, four of which are easily reached by ferry departing from *Kauppatori*. **Korkeasaari** boasts the world's northernmost zoo, with more than 1000 animals. There are small beaches and landscaped picnic areas, open daily, 1000–2000 May–Sept (to 1600 Oct-Apr). **Suomenlinna** (Sveaborg) is an island fortress built by the Swedes in the 18th century to fend off Russian encroachment. The entire network of defences is open to the public and there's a café and two small beaches (open all day). **Pihlajasaari** has the best beaches for swimming (including bathing huts); there is also a café and woodland paths to explore (open Jun–Aug, daily 0900–2100). The open-air museum at **Seurasaari** comprises 80 buildings from Finland's past, including a wooden church, medieval peasant huts and some examples of traditional Lapp architecture (open Jun–Aug, daily 1100–1700).

# ISTANBUL

Istanbul is unique; the gateway to Europe or to Asia, depending on which way you are travelling. To the ancient Greeks it was Byzantium. The Emperor Constantine christened it Constantinople, relocating his capital here from Rome in AD 330. Constantinople it remained until renamed by Kemal Atatürk, father of modern Turkey, in 1923. When the Roman Empire in the west collapsed in the fifth century AD, Constantinople turned eastward to rule a thousand-year empire. In 1453 it fell to Sultan Mehmet II. As the Ottoman Empire grew in strength, the city became the glittering, cosmopolitan capital of an even greater empire stretching from the Danube to the Red Sea – the city was as much Greek, Armenian, and Balkan as Turkish. This complex heritage, and its own vibrant street life, make it one of the world's most fascinating cities.

## TOURIST INFORMATION

**Main Office**: *57 Mesrutiyet Cad., Beyoglu; tel: 245 6875* or *243 3472*. **Branches**: Atatürk Airport; *tel: 573 7399* or *573 4136*; Karakoy Maritime Station; *tel: 249 5776*; Hilton Hotel, *Cumhuriyet Cad., Harbiye; tel: 233 0592*; and Sultanahmet Meydani; *tel: 518 1802*. Open Mon–Fri 0830–1230 and 1330–1730, they distribute free maps and guides (in English) and have details on local transport. If you have any problems, look for the special tourist police, *tel: 527 4503* or *528 5369,* who can be recognised by their beige uniforms and maroon berets.

## ARRIVING AND DEPARTING

### Airport
**Atatürk Airport** (*tel: 573 7617* or *573 3530*) is in Yeşilköy, 15 km west of Istanbul. Buses run every half-hour between Atatürk and the THY (Turkish Airlines) terminal at Şişhane.

### Stations
**Sirkeçi Station** (*tel: 527 0050* or *520 6575*), near the waterfront at Eminönü (express tram or 10 mins walk beside tram line to *Sultanahmet*) serves trains to Europe via Greece or Bulgaria. The bureau de change in the station will exchange only cash, but there are others immediately outside and automatic cash dispensers in the forecourt. Rail services to Asian Turkey and beyond use **Haydarpaşa Station** (*tel: 336 0475*), across the Bosphorus (by ferry).

## GETTING AROUND
The city is split in two by the Bosphorus straits. The Asian side is more properly called *Uskudar*. The European side is itself split by the Golden Horn (*Halic*), an inlet of the Bosphorus. Most of the historic tourist sights are in *Sultanahmet*, south of the Golden Horn, but much of the more interesting streetlife is to be found in the *Galatasaray/Beyoglu* districts to the north, between the Golden Horn and *Taksim Square*.

There is one **express tram** line, running from Sirkeçi station west along *Divan Yolu* and *Millet Cad.*, out to the old city walls. Buy tickets from kiosks by the stops: place them in metal containers at the entrance to the platforms. Istanbul's oldest trams and tramline, dating from the turn of the century, have been reprieved and refurbished and run down the 1.2 km length of *Istiklal Cad.*, the Beyoglu district's fashionable pedestrianised shopping street. They connect with the **Tunel**, a short, steep, underground railway built in 1875 to connect the hilltop avenue – then the main thoroughfare of the smart European quarter called Pera – with the warehouses and docks of the Golden Horn.

Large fleets of **buses** cover most of Istanbul, but routes can be confusing and there is no bus map, so ask for details at major stops or tourist offices. The major departure points are *Taksim Square, Eminönü* (near the Galata Bridge) and *Beyazit*. Tickets can be bought at kiosks or from street vendors and are put into machines on board. Depending on the route, one or two tickets may be required.

The yellow **taxis** in Istanbul offer a simpler alternative to the buses. Fares are cheap, but ensure that the driver starts the meter when you get in. Fares double between midnight and 0600. The unique **dolmus** (communal taxis) run on set routes and cram remarkable numbers of passengers into huge, decrepit American cars or Japanese minibuses.

**Ferries** run regularly across the Bosphorus, between *Karaköy* on the European side and *Haydarpasa* and *Kadiköy*; and between *Eminönü* on the European side and *Üsküdar*. Schedules can be confusing and piers chaotic, so ask at the tourist office, or consult Thomas Cook's guidebook *Greek Island Hopping*.

## STAYING IN ISTANBUL

### Accommodation

Chains include *Hd, Hn, Hy, Ke, Pe, Pu, Rd, Sh* and *Sw*. Most budget accommodation lies in the **Sultanahmet** district, in the back streets between *Sultanahmet Square* and the water and especially in *Yerebatan Cad*. **HI:** *6 Caferiye Sok; tel: 513 6150*. There is also a collection of similarly priced private hostels. Although basic and often crowded, these are cheap and marvellously placed for Istanbul's main sights, only 2 mins walk to the Blue Mosque. There are often a few people hawking rooms to arriving rail passengers, but they are usually touting for establishments far from the centre. Make sure you know where they are and how to get there before accepting.

Most of Istanbul's top-range hotels congregate north of the Golden Horn around *Taksim* and *Harbiye*, rather characterless areas a considerable distance from the main sights. There are, however, plenty of hotels south of the Golden Horn, so it is possible to stay in this more atmospheric part of the city without having to slum it, with a particular concentration of hotels of all categories in *Beyazit, Laleli* and *Aksaray*. The tourist offices have a comprehensive list. Arguably the nicest hotel in Istanbul is the **Ayasofya Pansiyonlari**, a refurbished row of traditional wooden homes, prettily painted and furnished in Ottoman style, immediately behind the Aya Sofya church. (*Sogukcesme, 34400 Sultanahmet–Istanbul, tel: 513 36 60, Fax: 513 36 69*). Rooms cost around US$75 double. The Ayasofya has spawned a host of cheaper imitators in traditional wooden mansions; there are several in the streets just east of Aya Sofya and Topkapi. A cheaper option on the other side of Sultanahmet is **Hotel Antique** (*K. Ayasofya Cad., Ogul Sok No. 17, tel: 516 49 36/516 09 97; fax: 517 63 70*) where rooms are around US$35 double. On **Büyük Ada**, an island in the Sea of Marmara some 40 mins away by fast catamaran, the magnificently ramshackle

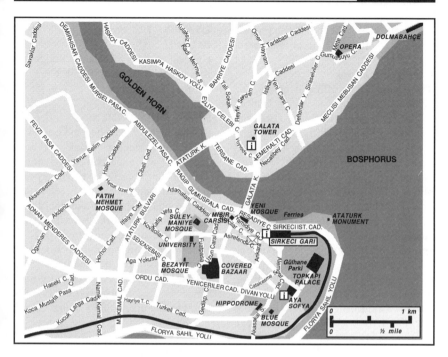

**Splendid Otel**, in a domed 19th-century wooden building, costs $82 double.

There are four **campsites** around Istanbul, all a long way from the centre and offering no advantages to campers without vehicles.

## Eating and Drinking

Istanbul's eating options are as varied and colourful as the city itself. Surprisingly, **Sultanahmet** is a restaurant desert, with very few places to eat or drink. In the daytime, head for the **Grand Bazaar**, where there are lots of indoor and outdoor cafés, or the **Laleli** district around the university.

Istanbul, located near two seas, is naturally a great place for seafood, though it is relatively expensive. It's also a great place for vegetarians, with plenty of meat-free dishes and wonderful fresh fruit. The best place to eat is in *Çiçek Paşaji* (Flower Passage), off pedestrianised *Istiklal Cad.*,

where a covered arcade and the alleys around it are packed with restaurant tables. The cheapest places are in the lane behind the arcade.

**Bakirköy**, further along the railway line towards the airport, is another good area. Further afield, the settlements on either side of the Bosphorus are renowned for their seafood restaurants, which often afford dramatic views across the straits. These include **Ortaköy**, by the European end of the Bosphorus bridge, where, along with much eating, there is live music and dancing. Further north, the towns of **Humeli Kavagi** (European side), and **Anadolu Kavagi** (Asian side), are popular destinations amongst day-trippers on Bosphorus excursions. Both places seem to revolve around their copious fish restaurants. Another good expedition is the ferry or fast catamaran trip to **Büyük Ada**, the biggest of three small islands in the Sea of

Marmara. The car-free island has a harbour lined with fish and meat restaurants.

## Communications

The **main PTT office** is at *25 Yeni Postane Cad.*, near Sirkeçi Station. However, there are many branches throughout Istanbul which generally have shorter queues, both for postal services and for making telephone calls. You can make international calls at all the major PTT offices. **Pay phones** require *jetons* (tokens), which come in small, medium and large sizes and can be bought from kiosks. Few pay phones seem to function. A small *jeton* should suffice for a local call; long-distance attempts require many large ones. Some new card phones are being introduced (cards available from PTT offices). The dialling code for Istanbul is *212* (north of the Bosphorus), or *216* (south of the Bosphorus).

## Money

There are plenty of bureaux de change around Istanbul, especially in *Sultanahmet* and in the covered market. Commissions and rates vary considerably, so it is worth checking several offices. Due to extremely high inflation, exchange rates date rapidly, although prices stay reasonably constant in terms of Western currencies. Automatic cash dispensers are becoming more common and are convenient; it is often cheaper to get a cash advance on a credit card and pay the handling charge than to pay commission at a bank or bureau.

## Consulates

**Australia:** *58 Tepecik Yolu, Etiler; tel: 257 7050.*
**Canada:** *107 Buyukdere Cad., Gayrettepe; tel: 272 5174.*
**UK:** *34 Mesrutiyet Cad., Beyoglu; tel: 244 7540.*

**USA:** *104–108 Mesrutiyet, Tepebas¯ i; tel: 251 3602.*
Citizens of **New Zealand** and **South Africa** can contact the British Consulate in cases of emergency.

## ENTERTAINMENT

Istanbul nightlife is limited and centres on eating and drinking. There are some expensive and unpleasant discos around Taksim, but the sleazy and potentially dangerous red-light scene in the streets around the top of *Istiklal Cad.* makes the district unappealing after dark. Several international hotels and restaurants offer folklore floorshows featuring music, song and belly-dancers. The **International Arts Festival** is in June and July. Its main venues are the Cemal Resit Rey Hall, Harbiye, and the Atatürk Cultural Center, Taksim.

## SHOPPING

Shopping and street life provide the best of the city's entertainment. The most famous of the markets is the **Kapali Çarşi** (Covered Bazaar), *Beyazit*: go along *Divan Yolu* from *Sultanahmet*. Not just a shopping street, but an entire district, with around 5 km of lanes, streets and alleys, the bazaar never disappoints. The pressure to buy something is strong; if you are just sightseeing, keep moving, because the bite goes on if you so much as pause to browse. There are thousands of shops and stalls here, roughly grouped according to merchandise, with whole alleys selling gold, silver, brass or leather. If you are going to buy anything, haggle hard; the bargaining process is a sport in itself and accompanied by a succession of glasses of tea brought from the nearest café (the shopkeeper pays). Around the bazaar is a good selection of carpet shops; here too, haggling is the order of the day. There are some bargains to be had (though bear in mind that you will have to pay customs duty on your return home) but as with any work of art it takes considerable knowledge and expertise to tell the difference between first-rate and second-rate products.

The **Misir Çarşisi**, the spice bazaar near the Yeni Mosque, is equally interesting, with mounds of herbs and spices and confectioners selling dozens of different kinds of sticky Turkish delight and other colourful sweets. At weekends, the pet and pot-plant market in the square outside sells everything from geraniums to goldfish and jars of wriggling leeches. There's also a thriving street market along the waterfront by the new Galata Bridge. It mainly sells clothes, including convincing imitations of leading-brand denims; you'll also find lots of shops selling suspiciously cheap brand-name jeans on the streets leading up to Beyoglu from the Galata Bridge.

## SIGHTSEEING

Its 2000-year history has left Istanbul full of monumental buildings that fight for prominence, creating a memorable skyline of domes and minarets, best seen from the Bosphorus at dawn, or the top of the **Galata Tower**, north of the Golden Horn. Built in 1348 by the Genoese, this now serves as a club and bar. Unlike so many other historic cities, Istanbul has been untouched by war since the Turkish conquest, so its history is more or less intact. On the other hand, the runaway development of the 1980s swept away whole districts of picturesque – if insanitary – older buildings in favour of modern suburbs.

## Topkapi

If you see nothing else in Istanbul, see the magnificent **Topkapi Palace**, seat of the Ottoman Sultans from the 15th to the 19th centuries. The complex, at the tip of the old city peninsula, has now been converted into an encyclopaedic collection of the Imperial treasures, stretching through three courtyards. Allow at least a half day to take in the cream of the exhibits, which include Islamic armour, imperial robes, jewellery and precious objects, porcelain and miniatures.

The third of the palace courtyards holds the **Halls of Audience**, the **Library of Ahmet III** and, more strikingly, the glittering wealth of the **Imperial Treasury**, a staggering display of ostentation. Over-bejewelled daggers and great balls of emeralds jostle for position with gold and silver caskets and costumes stiff with silver thread and cloth of gold. Look out for the ingenious mechanical toys sent to the Sultans by European rulers eager to curry favour, and for the ruby-studded cranium of St John the Divine, seized from the monastery of Patmos.

In the centre of this inner sanctum the **Pavilion of the Holy Mantle** houses religious artifacts, including sacred relics of the Prophet Mohammed, brought to Istanbul when the Ottoman sultans assumed the leadership of the entire Islamic world. One of the most fascinating parts of the Topkapi is the extensive **Harem** area, which housed the concubines and children of the sultans, with their attendant eunuchs. The harem can only be seen on tours, so you should go there as soon as you get to Topkapi to book for the next scheduled.

There are great views over the Bosphorus from the Palace terrace (where there is a café-restaurant), and within the Topkapi complex are several first-rate museums. Signposted off the first courtyard are the **Archaeological Museums**, consisting of the **Archaeological Museum** itself, guardian of the Alexander

Sarcophagus, the **Museum of the Ancient Orient** and **Cinili Kiosk**, the tiled pavilion, built by Mehmet the Conqueror. The 18th-century **Ahmet III Fountain** stands at the entrance to the Topkapi. The **Church of St Irene**, the first built in Constantinople, predating even Aya Sofya, is now also a museum.

## Aya Sofya

Work on **Aya Sofya**, formerly the Basilica of Aghia Sophia (Holy Wisdom), was started by Constantine in AD 347, but its present form is mainly due to substantial reconstruction by the Emperor Justinian in the 6th century. Aghia Sophia served as the cathedral of Constantinople until the Turkish occupation of 1453, when it was converted into a mosque. In 1935 Atatürk turned it into a museum; a convenient non-secular label, as Aya Sofya has no conventional exhibits to offer, just the building itself. Its massive bulk can seem drab and clumsy compared to the more graceful and beautifully-proportioned mosques nearby. Inside, massive marble pillars support a vaulted dome 31 m in diameter and 55 m high. Aya Sofya was the the largest domed structure in the world until St Peter's in Rome was built, and its interior impresses more with its size than its decoration. Although there are some splendid mosaics around the gallery (head up the sloped flagstone walkway), the interior is an uneasy mixture; the Christian frescoes which adorned the dome in Byzantine times were covered by abstract patterns while Aya Sofya was a mosque; the decor that remains is an odd compromise.

### The Mosques and Museums

Undoubtedly the most beautiful of Istanbul's many mosques is the **Suleiman-iye**, built between 1550 and 1557 for Sultan Suleyman the Magnificent by his court architect Mimar Sinan. Seen from the banks of the Golden Horn, the complex of domes and spires is the most striking sight in the old city.

Opposite Aya Sofya, the **Blue Mosque** or **Sultanahmet Mosque** was built in 1609–16 for Sultan Ahmet I in a clear attempt to outdo Justinian's Aya Sofya. Together, the two buildings form one of Istanbul's most dramatic cityscapes. The flamboyant Ahmet equipped his mosque with six minarets, a move which caused ructions with the religious authorities as it equalled the number at Mecca. Ahmet defused the situation by paying for a seventh to be built at Mecca. The exterior of the Sultanahmet is more appealing than Aya Sofya's, almost mesmeric with its sequence of nested half-domes. Thousands of turquoise *Iznik* tiles – from which the mosque gets its epithet – pick up the gentle washed light that filters in through the windows. It is certainly worth braving the touts and hustlers outside in order to view the interior. Entry is permitted outside prayer times. Be polite but firm with those who will try to convince you that it is necessary to pay ridiculously large sums for a tour, or to be let in, or to have your shoes looked after. Locals simply walk in carrying their footwear. On summer evenings a rather brash sound and light show redeems itself with some captivating floodlighting.

The **Hippodrome**, focus of Byzantine life in Istanbul, was sited in what is now the broad open space of *Sultanahmet* west of the Blue Mosque. Three columns dating from the early centuries of the Byzantine era mark the site: the 4th-century **Column of Constantine**, the 6th-century **Obelisk of Theodosius**, and the bronze **Serpentine Column**. A few fragments of the Hippodrome wall can be seen nearby. Across from the Hippodrome, the **Ibrahim Paşa Palace** houses the **Museum of Turkish and Islamic Art**, including some priceless ancient Persian carpets. On the other side of the Blue Mosque are the **Mosaic Museum**, with some Byzantine mosaics, and the quaintly named **Turkish Carpets Museum**. This latter represents the more staid end of the carpet industry in Istanbul.

The **Yeni Mosque** (meaning 'new', although built between 1597 and 1633) is unmissable to those arriving at *Eminönü* or crossing the Galata Bridge. There are a miserly two minarets here. Work started on the **Fatih Mosque** only ten years after the Turkish conquest. The mosque is named after Istanbul's conqueror, Fatih Sultan Mehmet, who is buried there. Istanbul's oldest mosque, however, is the **Beyazit**, next to the covered market.

The **Yerebatan Saray**, a giant cistern beneath *Sultanahmet*, is one of many which provided water for the city from the fourth century on. The huge cavern, its domed and vaulted roof supported by more than 300 stone pillars, was fed by water led in by aqueducts from sources outside the city. You enter the cistern from *Yerebatan Cad.* and explore it by pathways just above the surface of the water.

Some distance west of *Sultanahmet*, the old **City Walls**, now partially restored, stretch across the landward end of the peninsula from the Sea of Marmara to the Golden Horn. Built at the command of the 5th-century Emperor Theodosius, they protected all the land approaches to the ancient city.

## OUT OF TOWN

The **Bosphorus strait**, leading north from the Sea of Marmara to the Black Sea, is sprinkled with impressive imperial palaces and pavilions built by a succession of sultans. The best way to see them is by boat; popular excursion trips run up to *Rumeli Kavagi* and *Anadolu Kavagi* from *Eminönü*, pier 3. Three boats run each way Mon–Sat; on Sun and bank holidays there are five each way and prices are halved.

The most prominent palace en route – and the one not to miss – is the **Dolmabahce**, which has a 600-metre water frontage. Built by Sultan Abdulmecit in the 19th century, this served as the final seat of the Ottoman sultans. It is an astonishing compromise between what the sultans thought of as modern European style and their age-old love of lavish adornment. In the enormous reception room, the weight of a four and a half ton chandelier is supported by 56 columns and glitters with 750 bulbs. Atatürk died here in 1938. On a hill set back from the Bosphorus is the **Yildiz Palace** complex, built by Sultan Abdulhamit II at the end of the 19th century, as the absolute power of the sultans was crumbling. The palace is set in an elaborate park planted with flowering shrubs and trees from all over the world and has beautiful panoramic views of the Bosphorus. The **Sale Pavilion** (the only part currently open) reveals the dream-like luxury in which the sultans lived: small wonder that they took little notice of the world outside.

The Asian bank also has its fair share of imperial residences. Just north of the **Bosphorus Bridge**, the first to join continents, is the **Beylerbeyi Palace**, another 19th-century construction, this time the work of Sultan Abdul-aziz. The 19th-century sultans took turns to adorn the Bosphorus with extra palaces. Further north the **Goksu** or **Kucusku Palace** served as the summer residence of Abdulmecit. The second bridge across the Bosphorus, the **Fatih Sultan Mehmet Bridge**, is to the north.

199

# KRAKÓW

Kraków became the capital of Poland in 1040, moved from Gniezno by King Casimir the Restorer. Rebuilt after the 1241 Tartar invasion, the city entered a golden age in the 14th century, though Warsaw became the capital in 1596. When Poland was partitioned at the end of the 18th century, Kraków became part of the Austro-Hungarian Empire. Under the Nazi occupation, it was headquarters for the General Gouvernement, being liberated by Soviet forces in 1945, when a sudden advance saw the Nazis retreat, without implementing a planned programme of complete destruction. Thus Kraków was one of a few Polish cities to survive the War, and its cultural significance, not to mention beauty, is immense. Poles regard it as the spiritual heart of the country; UNESCO lists it as one of the world's 12 most precious cultural sites, with a wealth of Gothic, Renaissance and baroque architecture.

## TOURIST INFORMATION

The **Tourist Information Office**, *ul. Pawia 8, 31-154 Kraków; tel: (010) 22 60 91, 22 04 71*, (by Kraków Główny), is open Mon–Fri 0900–2100, Sat 0900–1500 in the summer season, otherwise Mon–Fri 0800–1600. Free information is limited though there is plenty to buy, and some accommodation, particularly hostels, can be booked there. Similar information and services are available from **Tourist Offices** at *ul. Florianska 37,*

*31-019 Kraków; tel: (012) 21 77 64*, open Mon–Fri 0900–1800, Sat–Sun 0900–1500, and *Sukiennice 1/3, Rynek Główny, 31-042 Kraków; tel: (012) 21 77 06*, open Mon–Fri 0900–1800, Sat 0900–1300. **Orbis** has a central office at *Rynek Główny 41; tel: (012) 22 40 35*, open Mon–Fri 0800–1900, Sat 0800–1400 and also at the **Cracovia Hotel**. The monthly magazines *Welcome to Kraków*, and *What, Where, When Kraków*, have practical information and listings, available from hotel lobbies.

## ARRIVING AND DEPARTING

### Airport

**Kraków Balice Airport**: *32-083 Balice; tel: (012) 11 67 00*, is 15 km from Kraków, with **LOT Polish Airlines** offering direct flights to London, Paris, Vienna, Zurich, Frankfurt, Cologne and Rome. For tickets and flight information the LOT office in Kraków is at *ul. Basztowa 15; tel: (012) 22 50 76*. From the airport take a taxi, or bus B leaving every 30 mins, which reaches the centre in about 20 mins, terminating by the Old Town.

### By Train

**Station: Kraków Główny** (main station), *pl. Kolejowy; tel: (012) 933* and *22 41 82* (domestic information), or *22 22 48* (international), has currency exchange, a PKO bank, left-luggage facilities, restaurant and kiosks. The station is only a few mins walk from the Old Town. **Płaszów Station,** for trains to **Oświęcim** (Auschwitz), **Wieliczka** salt mines and some night services, is about 30 mins from the centre by Tram no. 13, or take a train from Kraków Główny. Train tickets can also be bought at the Orbis office.

### GETTING AROUND

The **Stare Miasto** (Old Town), encircled by the **Planty**, a park-like belt of greenery where the city walls once stood, is pedestrian only. Beyond this is a network of buses and trams, with tickets sold at Ruch kiosks for single journeys, one day or weekly travel. Punch one end of the ticket on board (spot checks are carried out). When taking night buses and trams, tickets can be bought from the driver. *Kraków Plan Miasta*, the city map with a distinctive red and yellow cover, is marked with bus and tram routes, and sold at Ruch kiosks and bookshops (don't be surprised if street names have changed, as Communist references are being phased out).

Taxis are relatively cheap with radio taxis the cheapest. Find them at the station, taxi ranks throughout the Old Town, or by phoning *919*.

### STAYING IN KRAKÓW

#### Accommodation

For those on a limited budget finding a bed can be difficult between July and August, although pension style accommodation under private ownership is increasingly becoming available. **Waweltour** operates a *Biuro Zakwaterowań* (Accommodation Bureau) at *ul. Pawia 8; tel: (012) 22 19 21, 22 16 40*, which can also book rooms in hostels.

It is also quite common to be approached by accommodation touts at the station, but remember to check the location and price before agreeing. In addition to modern Orbis hotels such as

**Hotel Cracovia**, *ul. Marszałka Focha 1; tel: (012) 22 86 66*, there are period townhouse hotels within the Old Town, such as the (expensive) 1912 Secessionist style **Hotel Francuski**, *ul. Pijarska 13; tel: (012) 22 51 22*, and the moderately priced **Hotel Polski Pod Białym Orłem**, *ul. Pijarska 17; tel: (012) 22 15 29*. Chain hotels include: *Fm* and *Hd* **Hostels** are at *ul. Kościuszki 88; tel: (012) 22 19 51*, and *ul. Oleandry 4; tel: (012) 33 88 22*, both about 15 mins walk from the town centre, while **Dom Turysty** at *ul. Westerplatte 15; tel: (012) 22 95 66*, is at the edge of the Old Town. There are three **campsites**; **Krak**, *ul. Radzikowskiego 99; tel: (012) 37 21 22*, has the highest ranking as well as a café and restaurant.

#### Eating and Drinking

**Rynek Główny** and the surrounding streets are full of expensive and inexpensive restaurants and cafés. For traditional Polish food at the top end of the market try **Staropolska**, *ul. Sienna 4; tel: (012) 22 58 21*, and **Wierzynek**, *Rynek Główny 15; tel: (012) 22 10 35*, which has a 600-year history and comes complete with suits of armour, 18th-century tiled stoves and classical frescos. Jewish food (with music) can be enjoyed at **Ariel**, *ul. Szeroka 17; tel: (012) 21 38 70*. The art nouveau café **Jama Michalika**, *ul. Floriańska 45; tel: (012) 22 15 61*, is renowed for pastries, ice-cream and cabaret. Among the numerous Old Town cellar bars is **Piwnica pod Baranami**, *Rynek Główny 26*, while **Bar Wegetarianski**, *ul. Sw. Gertrudy 7*; is open all day for vegetarian food. For picnics, go to the delicatessen-style grocers (east side of square), with benches along the Planty park providing an ideal picnic base. All night delis include **Delicje**, *ul. Basztowa 12*.

## Communications

The main post office (with Poste Restante), *ul.Westerplatte 1; tel (012) 22 48 11*, is open Mon–Fri 0730–2030, Sat 0800–1400 and Sun 0900–1600. The telephone section is open 24 hours (be prepared to queue). Telephone cards, needed for international calls, and the increasingly out-moded telephone coins are also on sale.

## Consulates

USA: *ul. Stolarska 9; tel: (012) 22 12 94, 22 13 68.*

## Money

Central Kraków is full of **Kantors** (currency exchanges) which usually offer a higher rate than banks and hotels. Change travellers cheques at **Pekao bank** (there is a branch in. *Rynek Główny*), open Mon–Fri 0730–1900, Sat 0730–1730. When changing money try to have undamaged notes without any writing on them, as these can be refused. For Western Union money transfer contact **Prosper Bank**, *ul. Miodowa 11; tel: (012) 22 42 02*. Credit cards are rapidly gaining sway and are accepted in many hotels, restaurants and shops.

### ENTERTAINMENT

Evening activities are becoming far more varied, with regular concerts, cabaret and nightclubs that stay open late. Concert halls include the **Karol Szymanowski National Philharmonic**, *ul. Zwierzyniecka 1; tel: (012) 22 43 64*, and **Juliusz Słowacki Theatre and Opera Stage**, *pl. Sw. Ducha 3; tel: (012) 22 45 75*. For jazz try U **Muniaka** on *ul. Florianska; tel: (012) 22 15 61*, and **Ogródek Muzyczny**, *ul. Jagiellonska 6; tel: (012) 21 60 29*, which also serves Polish and Breton cuisine. Cabaret venues

include **Cafe Cabaret**, *ul. Św. Jana 2; tel: (012) 21 96 37*, and **Jama Michalika**, *ul. Florianska 45; tel: (012) 22 15 61*. Films are usually undubbed and the 18 cinemas are a popular source of entertainment. Annual events include the **Days of Organ Music** (Apr) held in Kraków's churches, the **International Festival of Short Feature Films** (May), the **International Festival of Street Theatre** (July), **'Krakówiak' International Meeting of Youth Folk Ensembles** (Aug), the **Folkart and Crafts Market** (Sept) and the exhibition of **Christ Child's cribs** (Dec).

### SIGHTSEEING

The Old Town is frequently referred to as a vast museum, though the city actually has around 30 museums with over 2 million works of art. A walking tour, which can be booked through Orbis, is an ideal way to begin sightseeing. Horse-drawn carriages can be found opposite Hawełka restaurant at no. 34, golf buggies at **St Wojciech's Church**, and rickshaws at **Adam Mickiewicz's** monument. Kraków sightseeing and various options including Wieliczka salt mine are also offered by companies like **Point Travel Agency**, *ul. Armii Krajowej 11; tel: (012) 23 78 94* and **Inter-Crac**, *Rynek Główny 14; tel: (012) 22 58 40*.

### Rynek Główny

With each side measuring 200 m, this is one of the largest and most beautiful medieval market places in Europe. The size of the **Sukiennice** (Cloth Hall) that stands centre-stage, and the surrounding burgher's houses and churches create a unique atmosphere.

The Cloth Hall was originally a Gothic roof over trading stalls, being enlarged in the reign of Casimir the Great. Following

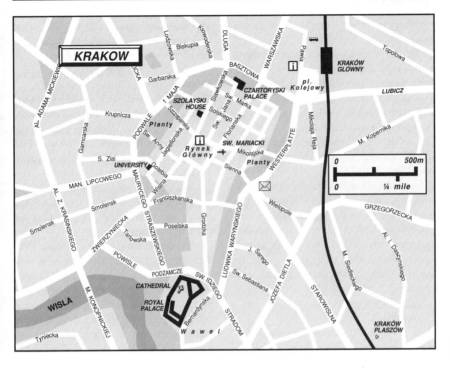

a fire in 1555 it was reconstructed in the Renaissance style, and is still a thriving commercial concern, filled with stalls selling amber, silver, folk-art and superior souvenirs. A branch of the **National Museum,** on the first floor of the **Sukiennice**; *tel: (012) 22 11 66,* is open Wed 1000–1530, Thur 1200–1730, Fri–Sun 1000–1530, housing 18th- and 19th-century historical Polish paintings and sculptures.

The **Ratusz** (City Hall Tower) *Rynek Główny 1; tel: (012) 22 09 62,* is open Wed 0900–1500, Thur 1100–1800, Fri–Sun 0900–1500, (closed second weekend each month), is all that remains of the Gothic Town Hall, destroyed in the 1820s as part of a civic rebuilding programme. In addition to historical exhibits, there is a great view from the top, and an atmospheric bar in the basement,

**Stanczyk w Ratuszu** (open 1000–0100). In the opposite corner of the square is the Romanesque **St. Adalbert's Church,** which is the oldest and possibly the smallest church in Kraków, while further north the Gothic **Mariacki** (St Mary's Church) was built on the ruins of a Romanesque church destroyed by Tartars. Legend has it that a watchman was shot down from the church tower by Tartar invaders as he played the *hejnał* to raise the alarm. The *hejnał* is still repeated on the hour, with a short pause after a few bars, signifying the time it took for a replacement to take over from the original watchman. The Mariacki's wooden Gothic altar is 13 m high and adorned by 200 figures, created over 12 years by Wit Stwosz, the 15th-century master carver from Nuremberg. **Kraków University** is the second oldest in Central Europe, receiving its royal charter in 1364. It was renamed the Jagiellonian University, under the patronage of the eponymous Polish royal family in the early 15th century. Famous alumni include the Polish astronomer Nicolaus Copernicus and Pope John Paul II, while the current student population is about 60,000. The oldest college is **Collegium Maius**, *ul. Jagiellonska 15; tel: (012) 22 05 49,* open Mon–Fri 1100–1430, Sat 1100–1330. A magnificent example of Gothic and now a museum, numerous artefacts include 35 globes, with one dating from 1510 and featuring the earliest illustration of America, marked 'a newly discovered land.' Tours also take in the lecture rooms, dining room, assembly hall and professors' apartments.

## Museums

With so many museums in Kraków, it's as well to get a detailed guide book from the tourist office. Admission is free in many museums on Sundays. The 18th-century **Czartoryski Palace,** *ul. Św. Jana 19; tel: (012) 22 55 66* is open Tues–Thur, Sat 1000–1730, Fri 1200–1730, Sun 1000–1500, with exhibits including a large collection of ancient art, and old masters like Rembrandt and Leonardo da Vinci. Two other branches of the **Muzeum Narodowe** (National Museum) are **Kamienica Szollayskich** (Szollayski House), *pl. Szczepanski 9; tel: (012) 22 70 21,* open Tues 1000–1800, Wed–Sun 1000–1530, which has 14th–18th-century art and sculpture, while **Galleria Sztuk XX w.** (Gallery of 20th Century Art), *al. 3 Maja; tel: (012) 34 33 77,* open Tues–Sun 1000–1800, has Polish paintings and sculpture. The **Jan Matejko Museum**, *ul. Florianska 41; tel: (012) 22 59 26,* open Tues–Wed, Fri–Sun 1000–1530, Thur 1200–1800, details the

life of Poland's greatest historical painter, within the house where he spent much of his life and also features his studio.

## Wawel

The **Cathedral** and fortified **Royal Castle** (both built by King Casimir the Great) are the most important museums in Kraków, standing high on **Wawel Hill** and bordered by the Wisła (Vistula) river. Open Tues–Sat 0930–1430, Sun 1000–1500 on Wawel Hill, *Wzgorze Wawelskie 5; tel: (012) 22 51 55* for the castle and *(012) 22 26 43* for the Cathedral Museum.

The Cathedral's present Gothic form dates from 1320–1364, with the first church constructed here in the 11th century. Relics of the earlier building are displayed in the castle's west wing. The most famous of the 19 side chapels, built in Renaissance and baroque styles, is the golden-domed Renaissance **Zygmunt-owska** (Sigismund's Chapel), built 1519–31. As the site of coronations and funerals, 41 of Poland's 45 kings are buried in the Cathedral, along with national heroes and poets. Climb the cathedral tower for a good view and see the 2.5 m diameter **Zygmunt Bell**, rung to celebrate church or national holidays.

Some of the Royal Castle's Gothic fragments, such as the **Danish Tower** and **Kurza Stopa** (Hen's Foot) still exist, but the majority of the Castle was rebuilt in the Renaissance style after a fire in 1502–36. The vast courtyard with three-storey arcades is considered one of Europe's finest examples of Renaissance architecture. Displayed in the **Komnaty Królewskie** (Royal Chambers) are 142 exquisite Arras tapestries depicting biblical scenes, commissioned in the mid 16th century. The Treasury houses European and Oriental weapons, some of which were captured by King Jan III Sobieski when he defeated the Turks at Vienna in 1683. There is also a collection of royal jewels and coronation regalia.

## Kazimierz

Now part of Kraków, **Kazimierz** was originally a separate city, founded in 1335 when Poland was the only European country to welcome Jews. Among the numerous Renaissance buildings is **Synagoga Stara** (Old Synagogue) on *ul. Szeroka 24; tel: (012) 22 09 62,* open Wed–Thur, Sat–Sun 0900–1530, Fri 1100–1800 (closed the first weekend of each month) with Gothic and Renaissance architecture dating from the late 15th century, this is the oldest synagogue in the country, and now a museum depicting Jewish history and culture in Poland. The Renaissance **Remuh synagogue** still serves its religious purpose, and has a graveyard which is one of the oldest Jewish burial grounds in Europe with Rennaissance and baroque tombstones, and a wailing wall built of old tombstones.

 **SIDE TRACKS FROM KRACÓW**

### OŚWIĘCIM

Trains (1 hr 45 mins) leave from Kraków, mostly from Płaszów station. **Station: Auschwitz**, the German name for Oświęcim, is synonomous with the atrocities of the Holocaust. In this, the largest concentration camp, between 1.5 and 2 million people from across Europe, mainly Jewish, met brutality and death at the hands of the SS. Men, women and children were transported here in cattle trucks, often surviving for up to 10 days. Cyanide gas pouring from the shower heads poi-

soned up to 2000 at a time, while others met hard physical labour and passed daily through gates bearing the inscription *Arbeit Macht Frei* (Freedom through Work). The camp was liberated by Soviet forces in May 1945, and regular screenings of their films are shown in several languages.

Nearby **Birkenau** was an even more efficient Nazi death factory. **National Museum of Auschwitz-Birkenau**, *ul. Wiezniow Oswiecimia 20; tel: (012) 240 21.*

## WIELICZKA (MAGNUM SAL)

Trains leave from Kraków Płaszów.

### TOURIST INFORMATION

Contact the **Tourist Office** at *ul. Daniłowicza 10, 32-020 Wieliczka; tel: (012) 78 73 02* or *78 73 66.*

**Wieliczka** salt mine, *Park Kingi 1,* features along with Kraków on UNESCO's heritage list. Mined for 700 years, it has 350 miles of tunnelling with 2040 chambers, from 64–135 m underground. Still in use, it used to provide 40% of the area's wealth. The mine is a dazzling feat, with 40 chapels carved entirely from salt, while larger than life size salt statues of, amongst others, Copernicus and St. Anthony, can be seen in the tunnels. Most magnificent of all is the main chapel with salt chandeliers and even salt relief pictures on the walls. Guided tours in English. Open daily 0800–1800 from Apr 16– Oct 15, and 0800-1600 out of season.

## ZAKOPANE

Once south of Kraków, lush undulating meadows lead to the wooded foothills of the Tatra Mountains and its

**205**

'capital' Zakopane which provide stunning views, while the valleys are dotted with chalet-style wooden houses. **Station**: **Zakopane Dworzec**, Główny, ul. Chramcówki 35; tel: (0165) 145 04, has left-luggage facilities (between 0500–2300) and currency exchange. **Tourist Information**: There is no 'it' office, but information is available from **Trip**, ul. Kościuszki 23, 34-500 Zakopane; tel: (0165) 159 47, 145 77, open Mon–Fri 0900–1600, Sat 0900–1300, which has limited town and regional information and advises on accommodation.

### GETTING AROUND

Zakopane is easily covered on foot and the station is central, though there is also a bus service with tickets available from Ruch kiosks for single, daily or weekly travel. Taxis are fairly cheap, call **Radio Taxis**; tel: 120 87.

### ACCOMMODATION AND FOOD

There is a wide range of accommodation from well-equipped hotels to simple hostels, though as Zakopane is now an all-year-round holiday destination it is best to book well in advance. **Hotel Kasprowy Wierch** is a wooden building in the local style at ul. Krupówki 50B; tel: (0165) 127 38, while an efficient modern option is **Hotel Helios**, ul. Słoneczna 2a; tel: (0165) 154 00. Both these hotels are very central. The **Accommodatoon Bureau** is at ul. Kościuszki 19; tel: (0165) 127 63. One of several **hostels** is **DWP Kolejarz**, ul. Kościuszki 23; tel: (0165) 154 68, located in the centre of town. The best **campsite** is Pod Krokwią, ul. Zeromskiego, tel (0165) 122

56. Local cuisine in Highland surroundings includes **Obrochtówka**, ul. Kraszewskiego 10a; tel: (0165) 639 87, while folk music is also provided every Thurs at **Chata Zbójnicka**, ul. Jagiellońska; tel: (0165) 142 17.

### ENTERTAINMENT

Clubs include **Morskie Oko**, ul. Krupówki 30 for jazz, with **David**, ul. Kasprusie 7, being a popular disco.

**Tatran Autumn Festival** (Sept) includes the International Festival of Highland Folklore.

### SIGHTSEEING

Town and regional tours can be organised through **Trip**, and **Orbis**, ul. Krupówki 22; tel: (0165) 141 51. Book guides for mountain hikes at **Centrum Przewodnictwa Tatrzańskiego**, Rondo Kuźnickie; tel: (0165) 637 99.

The earliest references to Zakopane date from the 16th century, with the indigenous residents being the Górale (Highlanders), traditionally shepherds and farmers, though tourism is now the main earner.

Although Zakopane is at the centre of a vast national park comprising mountains, lakes and forests, it is also a centre of Highland folk arts and crafts, with the local architecture (known as Zakopane style) featuring ornate wooden houses and churches, many of which are over 100 years old. The main road, ul. Krupówki, is full of interesting examples. Zakopane has applied to host the 2006 Winter Olympics.

**Muzeum Stylu Zakopiańskiego, im. Stanisława Witkiewicza** (Museum of Zakopane Style, dedicated to Stanisław Witkiewicz), Willa Koliba, ul. Kościeliska 18; tel: (0165) 136 02, is open Tues–Sun 1000–1400. One of the earliest villas built in the Zakopane style, in 1892–4, for the eponymous painter, features Highland interiors and folk art. **Karol Szymanowski Museum,** *ul. Kasprusie 19; tel: (0165) 631 50,* open Tues–Sun 1000–1600, is dedicated to this Polish composer. **Jan Kasprowicz Museum,** *Harenda 1; tel: (0165) 634 26,* open Tues–Sun 1015–1515. The eponymous poet lived here between 1923–6, and the house celebrates his work which often drew on Highland folk culture. **Museum Tatrzanskie** (Tatra Museum), *ul. Krupówki 10; tel: (0165) 152 05,* open Tues–Sun 0900–1600, has many ethnographic exhibits.

## RZESZÓW

**Tourist Board:** There is no 'it' office, though tourist information and advice on accommodation, as well as Western Union money transfer can be obtained from **Orbis,** *ul. Rynek 7, 35-073 Rzeszów; tel: (017) 34 366, 371 29,* open Mon–Fri 0900–1700, Sat 0900–1200.
**Station: Rzeszów Dworzec Główny,** *pl. Dworcowy 1; tel: (017) 338 33, 344 12.* Facilities include left-luggage, washing, café and shops.

### ACCOMMODATION AND FOOD

**Hotel Rzeszów,** *al. Cieplińskiego 2; tel: (017) 374 41,* is a short walk from the centre and Old Town. **Cafe Murzynek,** *Kościuszko 7, tel: (017) 365 10,* is the most engaging in the Old Town and has an adjacent currency exchange.

### ENTERTAINMENT

Festivals include the **World Festival of Polish Folklore Groups** every three years (1996, 1999).

### SIGHTSEEING

Founded in 1354 by King Kazimierz Wielki (Casimir the Great) Rzeszów has had a tradition of handicrafts including weaving and shoemaking, though it is also an educational centre with a branch of the Marie Curie-Skłodowska University, a college of Civil Aviation and a Theological Seminary. In the 17th century it was privately-owned by the Lubomirski family, until the 1772 partitions of Poland which brought Rzeszów under Austro-Hungarian rule. Sightseeing and excursions can be arranged through Orbis.

Starting in the **Rynek** (Market Square) is the ornate **Ratusz** (Town Hall), dating from the 18th century, together with various period buildings (currently being restored). Head south along *ul. T Kościuszki* to the **Kosciół Farny** (Farny church), originally 15th century Gothic, rebuilt in the 17th century and extended with side naves and a rococo altar. The presbytery contains Renaissance graves of local dignitaries, while a separate 17th-century **dzwonica** (bell tower) is decorated with an Archangel's silhouette. Turning into *ul. 3 Maja,* you pass the **Liceum Ogólnokształcące,** originally established as a Collegium in 1650 and now a lycée. Former pupils include General Sikorski who played such an important role during World War II. Continuing along *ul. 3 Maja* takes you past the **Kosciół Sw. Krzyża** (Church of the Holy Cross), a superb baroque example built in 1645, the highly eclectic Polish bank PKO at *no. 23* built in 1908 with a mix of baroque, neo-classical and Neo-Gothic elements, **Zorza,** *no. 28,* is a neo-classical cinema complete with marbled interiors, reaching the Lubomirski family's baroque **Summer Palace** just before turning left into *al. pod Kasztanami* (literally avenue 'under the chestnut trees') with its eclectic, late 19th-century and early 20th-century villas, including the neo-baroque *no 6*, *no. 8* was built in the Swedish style as was *no. 10*, known as **Pod Sową** (Under the Owl) which has an ornamental sundial, while *no. 18* is an art nouveau mansion block. On the other side of this street is the moated **Zamek** (Castle) originally the Lubomirski family's home and now the Courthouse. Dating from the 15th century, the Castle was rebuilt in the 18th century.

**Muzeum Okregowe** (Regional Museum), *ul. 3 Maja 19; tel: (017) 360 83*, open Mon, Fri 1000–1700, Tue–Thur 1000–1500, Sun 0900–1400, has city and regional history, including Polish porcelain from the 17th-20th century. The museum is housed in a 17th-century monastery with interiors that include ornate vaulted ceilings. **Muzeum Etnograficzne** (Ethnographic Museum), *Rynek 6; tel: (017) 620 217*, is open Tues, Fri 0900–1400, Fri 0900–1700, Sunday 0900–1400, featuring folk art and crafts.

## ŁAŃCUT

**Tourist Board**: Although there is no 'it' office tourist information and advice on accommodation is available from **PTTK**, *ul. Dominikańska 1, 37-100 Łańcut; tel: (017) 20 52, 31 84*, open Mon–Fri 0700–1500, and from **Trans Euro-Tours**, *ul. Kościuszki 2, 337-100 Łańcut; tel: (017) 25 49 99*, open Mon–Fri 0900–1700, Sat 0900–1300.

**Station**: Łańcut, *ul. Kolejowa, tel: (017)*

25 23 17. Facilities include left-luggage and kiosks.

## GETTING AROUND

Bus nos 9 and 12 go from the station to the **Rynek** (Market Square) which is in the centre, and only a few minutes walk from **Łańcut Palace**. Alternatively, a 30 mins walk to the Palace passes by great examples of local architecture. Leaving the railway station by the main entrance walk straight ahead, turning left into *ul. Żeromskiego*, then right into *ul. Grunwaldzka*, with its traditional wooden villas, and at the top of this long road is the Palace entrance.

## ACCOMMODATION AND FOOD

The most atmospheric (and moderately priced) hotel is **Zamkowy**, actually within Łańcut Palace, *ul. Zamkowa 1; tel: (017) 25 26 71/2*. The adjoining restaurant is open daily 0900–2100. A hostel right by the market square is **Dom Wycieczkowy PTTK**, *ul. Dominikańska 1; tel: (017) 25 45 12*.

## SIGHTSEEING

Łańcut was founded in the 14th century by King Kazimierz Wielki (Casimir the Great) and subsequently the town was privately-owned by aristocratic families including the Lubomirskis and Potockis. Under Austro-Hungarian rule after the 1772 partitions, Łańcut became part of Poland again in 1919. The Palace was 'nationalised' in 1945, the last owner, Count Alfred Potocki, having fled the Nazis in 1939.

The Market Square is at the centre of the Old Town, containing classical buildings as early as the 14th century, and adjacent to it are the former

**Dominican Monastery complex,** *ul. Dominikańska 1*, and the **Kościół Farny** (Farny Church), *ul. B. Prusa,* built in the late 15th century and rebuilt at the end of the 19th century. Łańcut Palace, *ul. Zamkowa 1; tel: (017) 25 20 08,* open Mon–Sat 0900–1430, Sun 0900–1600. The Palace was built in 1629-1642, initially as a fortified building, which resisted a Swedish siege of 1657. Subsequent rebuilding turned it into a residential palace with baroque, rococo, neo-classical and *belle epoque* elements. The interiors are magnificent with a vast collection of paintings, sculpture, furniture, tapestries, porcelain and *objet d'art.* Set amidst Italianate gardens within a romantic park, complete with an orangery housing a winter garden, and coach houses.

**Muzeum Judaików** (Museum of Judaism), *pl. J Sobieskiego;* is only open during the summer season (call Łańcut Palace for opening times), featuring exhibitions of Jewish culture within a synagogue built in the 18th-century, when Łańcut became a major centre for the Hassidim sect. **Muzeum Branżowe Fabryki Wódek 'Polmos'** (Museum of Vodka Production) is at *ul. Grunwaldzka 79.*

An annual **music festival** is held at Łańcut Palace (May).

## PRZEMYŚL

**Station: Przemyśl Główny,** *pl. Legionów; tel: (010) 78 68 59,* (tickets), *935* (train information). Originally built in 1860 when the Kraków-Lvov railway line was constructed, the station was rebuilt in 1895 in a neo-baroque style with magnificent interiors complete with chandeliers, frescos and a wooden canopy over the adjacent platform. Facilities include left-luggage, café, restaurant and various kiosks. Just as you pull into the station admire the stone viaduct over the railway line, constructed in 1869.

**Tourist Board:** *ul. Ratuszowa 8, 37-700 Przemyśl; tel: (010) 78 73 09,* open Mon–Fri 0800–1800, Sat 0800–1400, provides city and regional information, together with advice on accommodation. Look out for the magazine *Welcome to Przemyśl,* which has listings and practical information.

### GETTING AROUND

The main sights are within walking distance of the railway station, though there is also a network of buses. Tickets can be bought from Ruch kiosks.

### ACCOMMODATION AND FOOD

The **Hotel Marko,** *ul. Lwowska 36a; tel: (010) 78 92 72,* has the highest ranking (three stars) and is located some distance from the railway station (bus nos 2, 9, 10 and 11 provide a fast connection to the Old Town).

Less expensive options include the pension **Pod Białym Orłem,** *ul. Sanoca 13; tel: (010) 78 61 07,* ideally located at the edge of the **Zamkowy Park,** close to the market square, with a nearby campsite, **Zamek Camping** at *ul. Wyb. Piłsudskiego 8a; tel: (010) 78 56 42.*

There is a wide range of eating options at various prices, with fast food and cafés abundant in the Old Town, such as the **Pizzeria Margherita,** *ul. Rynek 4; tel: (010) 47 347,* and **Cafe Śródmiejksa,** *ul. Francziszkańska 33; tel: (010) 59 33.*

### ENTERTAINMENT

See what's showing at the **Fredreum**

**Theatre in the Castle**, box office at *Rynek 15; tel: (010) 78 25 43.*

### SIGHTSEEING

Located 12 km from the border with the Ukraine, and always prosperous as a commercial cross-roads, Przemyśl was fought over and ruled briefly by the Ukraine and Hungary in the 13th century before being taken back into Polish hands by King Casimir the Great and flourishing in the 15th century. Under Austro-Hungarian rule after the 1772 partition of Poland, Przemyśl became a military stronghold. The network of forts, which faced a Russian onslaught during World War I, are now tourist attractions.

The town is once again an important link between the Ukraine, CIS and Western Europe, and its architectural heritage is being carefully restored now that Przemyśl is prospering again.

City tours and regional excursions, including the nearby **Bieszczady Mountains**, can be booked through **Orbis**, *pl. Legionów 1; tel: (010) 78 52 65* (by the railway station).

Setting off from the railway station, turn right into *ul. Mickiewicza* passing the 17th century church and cloister of the Reformati on the junction with *ul. Jagiellońska*. Crossing over to continue along *ul. Franciszkańska* there are remains of the 16th-century **Town Walls**, the 18th-century baroque **Clock Tower**, and **Franciscan Cloister**, dating from 1235, with the 18th-century church having Gothic, neo-classical and baroque elements. Skirting the **Rynek** (Market Square) with its 16th- and 17th-century buildings, leads to *ul. Grodzka* with, on the left side, the 18th-century Roman Catholic **Bishop's Palace**, the 15th-

century **Capitular School**, and the 15th-century **Roman Catholic Cathedral** which combines original Gothic, neo-Gothic and baroque elements. Just beyond these buildings, along *ul. Zamkowa*, is the 17th-century **Theological College** and, set within its own park, is the **King's Castle** built in a Gothic style in 1340 by King Casimir the Great, though only the entrance gateway remains from that time, with the remainder rebuilt in a Renaissance style in the 16th century.

Turning left from *ul. Grodzka* along *ul. Waygarta* are two former **Dominican Cloisters** of the 16th and 18th centuries, now used as administrative centres by the town council. Turning right into *Wyb. Marszałka Piłsudskiego* and then right again into *ul. Kościuszki*, passes by the former **Cloister of the Order of St. John,** originally a hospital and now an English Language college, the former **Palace of the Pawlikowski Family** from Medyka (who were important patrons of the arts) built in the 17th century and used as the **Ratusz** (Town Hall) since 1855.

**Muzeum Narodowe Ziemi Przemyskiej** (National Museum of the Przemyśl Region), *pl. Czackiego 3; tel: (010) 78 33 25,* open Tues, Wed, Fri 1000–1800, Thur, Sat, Sun 1000–1400, with a collection of archeological, ethnographic icons and Medieval Byzantine artefacts housed in a late 18th-century Greco-Catholic Bishop's Palace.

**World War I Museum,** *Fortress Gate, ul. Sanocka; tel (010) 78 97 35,* open in summer season only. **Archdiocesan Museum**, *pl. Czackiego 2; tel: (010) 78 27 92,* open by appointment. ◪

# KRAKÓW–POZNAŃ

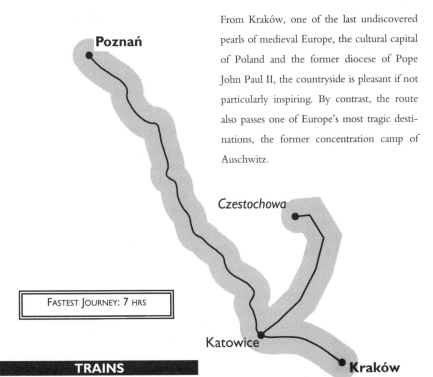

Poznań

Czestochowa

Katowice

Kraków

FASTEST JOURNEY: 7 HRS

From Kraków, one of the last undiscovered pearls of medieval Europe, the cultural capital of Poland and the former diocese of Pope John Paul II, the countryside is pleasant if not particularly inspiring. By contrast, the route also passes one of Europe's most tragic destinations, the former concentration camp of Auschwitz.

**211**

## TRAINS

ETT Table: 861.

### FAST TRACK

➡ Six trains a day operate on this route although not all of them are at convenient times of the day. The journey takes around 7 hrs.

### ON TRACK

**Kraków–Katowice**
A frequent service taking 1 hr 30 mins.

**Katowice–Poznań**
Four trains a day taking 5 hrs.

## KATOWICE

**Station: Katowice Główny,** *pl. Dworcowy; tel: (03) 53 75 36,* has left-luggage facilities and information on accommodation.

**Tourist Office:** Located on the first street on the right as you leave the station at *11 ul. Młynska; 42-200 Katowice; tel: (03) 53 97 87.* Open Mon–Fri 0900–1700, Sat 0900–1300 has city information and can give helpful advice on accommodation.

### GETTING AROUND

The Museums and Main Market Square are within walking distance of the station, though buses and trams also operate. Single journey- , daily- and weekly-tickets are available from Ruch kiosks. Radio taxis can be ordered by dialling *919*.

### ACCOMMODATION AND FOOD

Orbis hotels include **Hotel Silesia**, *ul. Piotra Skargi 2; tel: (03) 59 62 11)*, and **Hotel Warszawa**, *ul. W Rożdieńskiego 16; tel: (03) 59 60 11*. For regional cuisine try **Karczma Slupska**, *ul. Mariacka 1.*

### SIGHTSEEING

As the largest city in Poland's industrial heartland (principally coal and steel), Katowice also has some points historic of interest. City tours and excursions can be organised through **Orbis** at *al. Korfantego 2; tel: (03) 58 86 66*. The **Muzeum Sląskie (Silesian Museum)**, *al. Korfantego 3; tel: (03) 58 56 61*, offers Polish paintings and sculpture, while the **Diocesan Museum**, *ul. Jordana 39; tel: (03) 51 21 60*, has a collection of religious art.

The **Historical Museum of Katowice**, *ul. Ks. Szafranka 9; tel: (03) 51 50 69*, traces the city's evolution. The **Wojewódzki Park** has a planetarium, observatory, cable car and big wheel. Within easy reach is the **Upper Silesian Ethnographic Park**, *ul. Parkowa 1, Chorzów; tel: (03) 41 07 18*, with many historic examples of traditional wooden architecture.

### SIDE TRACK FROM KATOWICE

## CZĘSTOCHOWA

**Station:** Częstochowa Dworzec Główny, *ul. Piłsudskiego 38, tel: (034)*

*24 26 51*, has left-luggage facilities and information on accommodation. There is also a tourist information point at the station open Mon–Sat 0800–2000, June– September.

**Tourist Board:** *al. Najswiętszej Marii Panny 65, 42-200 Częstochowa; tel: (034) 24 13 60*. Open Mon-Fri 0900–1800, Sat–Sun 0100–1600 with city information and advice on accommodation.

### GETTING AROUND

The city centre and **Klasztor OO. Paulinów na Jasney Górze** (The Jasna Góra Monastery), *ul. Kordeckiego 2; tel: (034) 65 66 88*, open 0530–2100 daily, is about 20 mins walk from the station, or take bus no. 18. The monastery is Poland's most important shrine, dedicated to the Virgin Mary, whom the country has always revered. Originally 13th century, it was rebuilt and heavily fortified in the 17th century, and resisting a Swedish siege further promoted the cult of the Virgin Mary. The painting of the so-called Black Madonna is 15th century and has been attributed with miraculous powers.

The monastery's museum, arsenal, tower and treasury are open daily 0600–1200, 1530–1700. The **Muzeum Okręgowe** (Regional Museum) in the **Ratusz** (Town Hall), *pl. Biegańskiego 45; tel: (034) 24 44 24*, is open Wed 1200-1800, Thur–Sat 0900–1500, Sun 1000–1500.

Trains for Częstochowa, which is also an industrial centre, leave from Katowice Dworzec Główny, taking about two hours. Pilgrims from all over the world arrive throughout the year, though Aug 15 and 26 are the most important days. ⬛

# LEIPZIG

Leipzig is, after Berlin, eastern Germany's most important city and is capital of the state of Saxony. At first glance it can appear rather grim, and clearly shows its 19th-century industrial roots; however, it contains buildings surviving from as early as the 12th century.

The city is rich in cultural history: Goethe set his play *Faust* here, Mendelssohn was conductor of its symphony orchestra between 1835 and 1847, and Bach lived and worked in Leipzig for most of his life. It is one of Europe's opera capitals, and its Gewandhaus orchestra is perhaps the world's most distinguished.

## TOURIST INFORMATION

There is no tourist office at Hbf. Cross *Willi-Brandt-Pl.* by the underpass to *Sachsenpl. 1*, 400 m from Hbf, tel: *(0341) 71040*, open Mon–Fri 0900–1900, weekends 0930–1400. There is also a branch at **Leipzig-Halle Airport**, tel: *(0341) 2241847*, Mon–Fri 0700–2100, Sat 0840–1430, Sun 0900–1800.

Tourist office sells city guides and excursion guides and offers free accommodation list and an accommodation booking service. **Thomas Cook Network member: Thomas Cook Urlaubreisen**, *Geitheimerstr. 60; tel: 341 657 0100.*

## ARRIVING AND DEPARTING

**Airport**: **Leipzig-Halle Airport**, tel: *(0341) 22 40*, is 18 km from the city centre. Shuttle buses operate from Hbf.

**Station**: **Hbf**; tel: *(0341) 19419*. With 26 platforms and a vast, echoing hall, Leipzif Hbf is the largest termini in Europe, a monument to the great railway era of the 19th century. It was badly bomb-damaged during World War II and has been extensively restored, but is no less impressive for that. **Bayerischer Bahnhof**, a few minutes south of the Ring, is used only for local services. Built in the 1840s, it was destroyed during World War II and its neo-classical façade was restored after the war.

## GETTING AROUND

Leipzig's public transport system, **RVL**, is a combination of trams, buses, and an S-bahn network. Multiple-trip tickets can be used on the entire system. A network map is available free from the RVL office just outisde the east entrance to Hbf at *Willy-Brandt-Pl. 1; tel: (0341) 9600406*. Most of the main sights are within easy walking distance of Hbf, within the inner circle formed by *Willy-Brandt-Pl., Goergring, Rosspl., Martin Luther Ring, Dittrichring, Goerdellerring* and *Trondinring*. **Taxis:** tel: *(0341) 74 11; (0341) 401 4103;* or *(0341) 982222.*

## STAYING IN LEIPZIG

### Accommodation

Chain hotels include *IC, Do, Me, Ma* and *Hd*. **HI:** *Am Auensee, Gustav Esche Str. 4; tel and fax: (0341) 57189.* **Camping Am Auensee** is next door at *Gustav Esche Str. 5; tel: (0341) 4611977; fax: (0341) 4611997* (tram nos 10, 11 or 28).

Cheaper **guesthouse** accommodation is bookable through the tourist office in

213

## Musicians in Leipzig

From 1723–50 Johann Sebastian Bach was musical director of the church of **St Thomas** (a late-Romanesque building which began its existence as a chapel monastery). It is worth visiting, whether or not you're interested in music, for its diverse archtectural styles which include a Gothic choir and 16th-century octagonal tower. Amongst the many tributes to Bach in St Thomas are: a modern bronze tomb designed by Nierade and Tieman in 1950; the 1909 statue designed by Carl Seffner in the graveyard; the centre of Bach studies in the church square with a permanent exhibition on his life and work; an unusual tribute can be found in the Festaal in the form of ceiling- and wall-paintings by Oeser. There is another Bach archive in the baroque and rococo **Gohliser Schlösschen**, *Menckestr*, to the northwest of the railway station

Mendlessohn's connections with Leipzig are also strong. He founded the first music conservatoire in Germany here, with Robert Schumann as one of the professors. He was also responsible for the rise in prominence of the Gewandhaus orchestra during the mid-19th century.

Richard Wagner was born in Leipzig in 1813 and studied musical composition at the city's University. His *Symphony in C Major* was performed at the Leipzig Gewandhaus in 1833, 12 years before he earned public acclaim for *Rienzi*. His *Ring* cycle was performed at the Leipzig opera house in 1878.

**214**

city centre or airport. Mid-range pensions in the centre include **Am Zoo**, *Pfaffendorferstr. 23; tel: (0341) 9602432.* Cheaper pensions and hotels garni in the suburbs (3–6 km from the centre) include **Herberge zur Alten Bäckerei**, *An der Muhle 12; tel: (0341) 4792066*; **Pension Lindenau**, *Georg-Schwarz-Str. 35; tel: (0341)27454*; **Pension Petit**, *Am Eichwinkel 8b; tel: (0341) 33 60 70*; **Pension Zahn**, *Schmiedebergestr. 18; tel: (0341) 42 61 40.*

### Eating and Drinking

There are plenty of places to eat and drink in the city centre. The most expensive restaurants are to be found in the international chain hotels which have appeared since unification. Leipzig is also well provided with cheaper cafés and bistros.

**Mövenpick**, *Naschmarkt 13*, is a value-for-money chain restaurant with choice of self-service or table service, open-air terrace; **Paulaner-Palais**, *Klostergasse 3–5*, is a beer and wine tavern with terrace; **Zwiebelchen**, *Peterstr. 113*, offers affordable vegetarian specialities (the name means 'little onion'). **Auerbachs Keller**, *Madlerpassage, Grimmaische Str. 2–4*, opposite the old town hall, is a historic restaurant dating from 1530 with Faustian connections. Leipzig's **Ratskeller**, in the Neues Rathaus, is vast. **Zill's Tunnel**, *Barfussgässchen 9*, offers Saxon cooking in one of the oldest restaurants in town. Other inexpensive choices include **Café am Bruhl**, *Richard-Wagner-Pl. 1*, **Café Corso**, *Grimmaische Str. 12–14*, **Café de Saxe**, *Am Markt 11/15* **Café Schloss Wilhelmshohe**, *Hainstr. 10*, and **Concerto**, *Thomaskirchhof 13*. **Zum Coffe Baum** (The Coffee Tree), *Kleine Fleischergasse 4*, is a monument in its own right. Leipzig's oldest coffeehouse, it dates back to at least 1694 and Liszt, Wagner, and Goethe were among its patrons.

**Money**

There is an exchange office at Hbf, the **Deutsche Verkehrsbank AG**, open Mon–Fri 0700–1930, Sat 0800–1600.

## SIGHTSEEING

From Hbf, cross *Willy-Brandt-Pl.* and walk through *Sachsenpl.* to enter the Altstadt, which is mainly pedestrianised and contained within a peripheral road, the Ring. The best place to start exploring is the *Marktplatz*, the centre of the old town, around which stand some of the city's most striking historic buildings. On *Naschmarkt* stands the **Old Bourse**, begun in 1687, now a theatre and concert hall. A statue of Goethe, dating from 1903, stands outside. The splendid red and yellow **Altes Rathaus** (Old Town Hall), *Marktpl.*, is all the more remarkable for the speed with which it was built – it was begun in 1556 and completed within nine months, a remarkable feat at a time when large public buildings usually took years or even decades to complete. It was restored in 1672 and its tower was redesigned in 1744 in baroque style to complement the towers of the churches of St Nikolai and St Thomas. The **Neues Rathaus** (New Town Hall), *Burgpl.*, built at the beginning of this century, is a clumsy building erected on the site of the Pleissenburg, Leipzig's earliest fortress. Its 111-metre central tower is being refurbished and when reopened will give a fine view of the old town.

Johann Sebastian Bach served as cantor in the Gothic **Thomaskirche** (St Thomas' church), *Klostergasse*, for the last 27 years of his life. He is commemorated

by a monument outside the church, commissioned by Mendelssohn, while the **Bachmuseum** opposite has a large collection of memorabilia. On the wide *Augustuspl.* one of Europe's newest and most elegant concert halls, the **Neue Gewandhaus**, faces the 18th-century **Opera House**; it is the home of the Gewandhausorchester, the oldest and largest orchestra in the world. The **Grassi-Museum** complex, *Johannisspl.*, is worth visiting for its **musical instruments museum**, with more than 3,500 intruments, some still in use, and the **Museum für Volkerkunde**, featuring ethnological displays from all over the world. The 12th-century **Nikolaikirche** (St Nicholas' church), *Nikolaistr.*, is more interesting inside than its grimy, much-restored exterior suggests.

For a breath of fresh air, turn right as you leave Hbf and walk along *Trondlinring*, turning right again onto *Pfaffendorfer Str.* to the **Rosental**, an enormous landscaped park, and the **Zoo**.

215

> **SIDE TRACK**
> **FROM LEIPZIG**
> **Schloss Colditz**, an 11th century castle notoriously used as a prison for Allied captives during World War II, stands on a crag above the pleasant small town of Colditz on the River Mulde, reached by DB trains from Leipzig Hbf to **Grossbothen**, then by a 12 km scenic railway. There is a tour of the castle, which is being turned into a museum, and the **Städtisches Museum** in Colditz itself has a collection of ingenious devices made by prisoners to aid their escape attempts; despite supposedly watertight security, a surprising number of inmates got out of the castle, though most were recaptured. ▣

# LEIPZIG–PLZEŇ

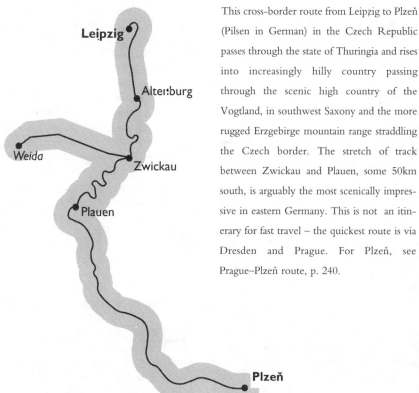

This cross-border route from Leipzig to Plzeň (Pilsen in German) in the Czech Republic passes through the state of Thuringia and rises into increasingly hilly country passing through the scenic high country of the Vogtland, in southwest Saxony and the more rugged Erzgebirge mountain range straddling the Czech border. The stretch of track between Zwickau and Plauen, some 50km south, is arguably the most scenically impressive in eastern Germany. This is not an itinerary for fast travel – the quickest route is via Dresden and Prague. For Plzeň, see Prague–Plzeň route, p. 240.

216

## TRAINS

**ETT Tables:** 674, 875, 870, 777

### ON TRACK

#### Leipzig–Altenburg–Zwickau
An hourly service links these towns. Leipzig to Altenburg takes 40 mins, Altenburg to Zwickau 45 mins. Some trains depart from Leipzig Bayerischer station rather than the usual Hbf.

#### Zwickau–Plauen
A frequent service with a journey time of around 1 hr.

#### Plauen–Plzeň
No through trains operate, indeed only one train a day takes the direct route across the border into the Czech Republic. Using this train a change of train is required at Cheb.

## ALTENBURG

**Station: Hbf,** *Bahnhofpl.,* 10 mins from north of the centre.

**Schloss Altenburg,** overlooking the town, is Altenburg's main attraction. Strategically located commanding a pass through the hills, the castle is one of the region's oldest, with remnants of a Slavic circular rampart built as early as 800 AD. Two centuries later, the Holy Roman Emperor Otto I built a larger castle, of which a single tower known as the Flasche survives, and in the 12th and 13th centuries it was converted into a fortified royal palace. In 1826 the town became the capital of the Duchy of Saxony-Altenburg. The present palace dates from the 18th century. In the town centre, the **Rathaus,** Weibermarkt, is an attractive Renaissance building. Also worth looking at is the Seckendorff'sche Palais, Alter Markt.

## ZWICKAU

**Station: Hbf,** *Bahnhofstr., tel (0375) 592712.*
**Tourist Office:** *Haupstr 6, tel (0375) 293713,* open Mon–Fri, and Sat a.m. Private rooms are bookable through tourist office. Mid-range hotels include **Hotel Stadt Zwickau,** *Bahnhofstr 67, tel: (0375) 8030* and **Hotel Merkur,** *tel: (0375) 294280.*

Though very much an industrial city – the tiny, plastic-bodied Trabant cars were built here – Zwickau's old town centre is attractive enough, with a collection of historic buildings around its hub, the *Hauptmarkt.* The **Rathaus** has a florid baroque front, an addition to an earlier medieval hall. It is outdone by the even more elaborate front and five-stepped gable of the **Gewandhaus,** the Renaissance hall of the drapers' guild, now a theatre. The **Dom,** also on *Hauptmarkt,* is a late Gothic building with a fine, highly

decorated interior and a baroque tower which gives a fine view of the inner city. **Robert Schumann Haus,** *Hauptmarkt,* is dedicated to the life and music of the composer. Also in the old town are the **Schiffchenhaus** (Little Ship House), at the corner of *Domhof and Munzstr.,* a 15th-century building shaped like a ship's bow. The **Pulverturm** (Gunpowder Tower), *Nikolaistr.,* is the sole surviving remnant of the medieval ramparts.

Take a train from Zwickau Hbf to **Schloss Osterburg,** *07570 Weida, tel (036603) 2775,* open Apr-Nov, Wed-Sun 0900-1730. **HI** within castle. Built by the rulers of Weida in the 12th century, the fortified complex has been known as Osterburg since the 17th century.

## PLAUEN

**Station: Oberer Bhf,** *Bahnhofstr.,* on the Leipzig–Nuremberg line and **Unterer Bhf,** *Elsterstr,* for the line through the Vogtland to the Czech border.
**Tourist Office:** corner of *Bahnhofstr.* and *Radelstr.; tel (03741) 224 945.*

Rooms and pensions are bookable through tourist office. Plauen is not outstandingly interesting in its own right but is the best base for those planning to explore the hilly scenery of the Vogtland plateau. The *Alter Markt* is dominated by the looming bulk of the modern town hall, but the **Altes Rathaus,** *Alter Markt,* is more attractive, and houses the **Plauen Lace Museum,** devoted to the town's best-known product. On *Syrastr.* the **Roter Turm** (Red Tower), surrounded by ruined ramparts, is all that remains of the castle of the Vogts, the feudal rulers of the region in the early centuries of the Holy Roman Empire. You can find out more about them in the **Vogtland Museum,** *Nobelstr.,* located in three handsome 18th century mansions.

**217**

# LJUBLJANA

Slovenia's capital, dominated by a castle-topped hill, preserves a lovely old centre filled with interesting buildings and other sights. It is the focus of Slovenian culture – its museums highlight it – and, as largest city in Slovenia, takes pride of place as political and economic centre as well. Most parts of the country are accessible from Ljubljana. Taking the train, or the bus, you can reach the Alps, or the sea.

## TOURIST INFORMATION

The **Tourist Information Centre** at *Slovenska cesta 35; tel: 061 215 412,* is open Mon-Fri 0800–1900, and on Sat and Sun 0800–1200 and 1600–1900. Ask for up-to-date maps for walking tours of the city (they have multi-lingual ones too). The **Cultural Information Centre**, hard by *trg Francoske Revolucije 7; tel: 061 214 025,* and open Mon-Fri 1000–1300 and 1700–2000 (Sat 1000–1300, will provide information about what's on, listings, festivals and other entertainments. Ask for the free booklet listing all the city's museums and galleries. Since this is the capital of a country noted for its Alpine peaks, its skiing and walking, visit the **Alpine Association** at *Dvorzakova ulica 9; tel: 061 312 553,* and get their maps and guides. The office is open 0800–1500, Mon-Fri only.

## ARRIVING AND DEPARTING

### Airports
**Brnik Airport**, 28 km north-west of Ljubljana; tel: *064 222 700,* is the only airport in Slovenia to receive regular international flights. There are car rental firms, a hotel booking centre, a tourist information office, a post office and a duty-free shop.

**Adria Airways**; *tel: 064 221 441,* the national airlines, runs buses between the city centre (*Trg Osvobodilne Fronte,* in front of the post office) and the airport for all incoming and departing flights. City buses also make the round trip – depart from platform 28 in the main bus station. The airport is open 0600–2200.

### Stations
The main railway station is also at *Trg Osvobodilne Fronte; tel: 131 5167.* All local, national and foreign trains arrive and depart from here. You can change money here and there is a 24-hour left-luggage depot.

## GETTING AROUND

Much of Ljubljana can be seen on foot – the city centre is compact. The old suburbs and the outlying areas can be visited by bus or taxi.

### Buses
The main **bus station** is at *Trg Osvobodilne Fronte* – to the north of the centre. Buses are run by **LPP** and passes can be purchased from their head office at *Celovska ulica 160; tel: 159 4114,* open 0645–1900 Mon-Fri and 0645–1300 Sat, and from the kiosks marked 'LPP' at *Slovenska cesta 55.* The city bus service is comprehensive and regular and are definitely the best way to get around. The service starts at around 0500 and lasts until midnight. Pay as you climb on.

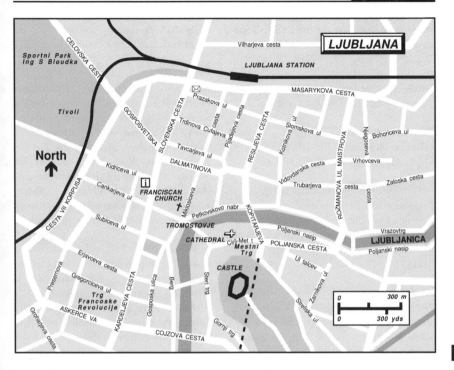

## Taxis

Taxis can be hailed in the street or found at a rank. They can also be called, *tel: 9700/9706.*

## STAYING IN LJUBLJANA

### Accommodation

There is an enormous range of accommodation available in the city, but not much variety. The luxury hotels are what you would expect from any European city – best are the **Slon** and the Art Nouveau **Grand Hotel Union**. Middle and inexpensive are neglected categories but there are pensions/guesthouses and good private rooms available to rent. The best place to find out about these is the Tourist Information Centre. They have a list. Bear in mind that many of these are not in the centre but out in the suburbs –

savings on room price have to be weighed against extra transport fares.

There is a variety of hostels. Again, make enquiries at the tourist office. They tend to be premises vacated by student during their summer breaks and are generally clean, cheap and friendly places to stay. There are just two **campsites** worth investigating. Only the **Jezica**, *tel: 372 901*, on the Sava River at *Dunajaska cesta 270a*, is convenient for the town centre (take buses nos 6 or 8 for about 7 km). The other, the **Smlednik**; *tel: 061 627 002*, is at Dragocajna, just under 20 km from Ljubljana. It is open May–Oct.

### Communications

The main **post office** is at *Slovenska cetsa 32*, open Mon–Fri 0700–2000 (1800 Sat). There is a poste restante (general delivery) service. Telephone calls can be made from here, but the main **telephone centre** – best for international calls – is at *Prazakova ulica 3*, open weekdays 0700–2000 (Sat 0700–1800, Sun 0800–1200). It also serves as a post office. The area code for Ljubljana is 061.

### Embassies
**UK:** *Trg Republike 3/IV; tel: 125 7191.*
**USA:** *Prazakova ulica 4; tel: 301 427.*

## ENTERTAINMENT

Entertainment in Ljubljana offers a rich variety of alternatives. The best time to come though is during the summer when the city's excellent cultural festivals are held.

### Nightlife
From gambling at Ljubljana's **Casino**, to a variety of clubs, pubs, bars and the gay **Klub K4**, there is something for everyone here.

### Cinemas, theatres and concerts
First-run films are screened at the **Kino Komuna** at Cankarjeva cesta 1, while classics can be seen at the **Kinoteka** at *Miklosiceva cesta 28.* There are seven theatres here, and the city is home to the **National Drama Theatre** at *Erjavceva cesta 1,* and the **National Youth Theatre**, *Vilharjeva ulica 11* (the Festival Hall). The **Glej Theatre**, *Gregorciceva ulica 3*, is the home of experimental theatre groups. The Slovenian Philharmonic Orchestra and the RTV Slovenija Symphony Orchestra are based in the **Cankarjev Dom** on *Trg Republike.*

### Festivals
Summer festivals include **Festival of the Arts** (July-August), **Summer in Old Ljubljana** (an outdoor chamber music festival), the **International Wine Fair** (August-September) and the **International Jazz Festival** (June-July).

## SHOPPING

Ask at the tourist office for their brochure entitled *Where to Shop.* Slovenia is famous for its folklore; folk items are a good buy. Go to the **Samec** shop at *Stari trg 15*, or to the **Dom** shop, *Mestni trg 24*. There is an **antiques and flea market** on Sunday mornings on *Pogarcarjev trg* and *Adamic-Lundrovo nabrezje.* **Sidro**, *Kongresni trg 3*, sells herbal teas and natural remedies, another Slovenian speciality.

## SIGHTSEEING

The most important sights in Ljubljana include the baroque **Cathedral of St Nicholas**, the nearby Renaissance **Bishop's Palace** and the 18th-century **Seminary** (all in *Pogarcarjev trg*). The **Franciscan Church**, *Presernov trg*, has a baroque altar by Francesco Robba.

The old city is dominated by **Ljubljana Castle**, situated on Castle Hill, which is worth visiting for its archaeological collections, the 15th-century **Chapel of St George**, and its magnificent views out over the city. In the old city itself stands the 18th-century **Robba Fountain**, which emulates Bernini's in Rome's Piazza Navona, and a variety of interesting civic buildings, palaces and churches – including the 17th-century **St Florian** on *Gornji trg.*

Ljubljana's museums highlight Slovenian culture. The **National Museum**, *Muzejska ulica*, contains local archaeological finds, while the **National Gallery**, *Cankarjeva ulica 20*, houses collections including paintings by the Slovene Impressionists. The **Museum of Modern Art**, *Cankarjeva cesta 15*, houses the permanent collection of 20th-century Slovenian art.

# MOSCOW (MOSKVA)

There's no city in the world quite like Moscow and if you've not been here, you can't really say you've seen Russia. It's a tough uncompromising place, not given to turning on the charm for visitors, but keep your sense of humour and you'll get along fine. Spend at least two or three days seeing the sights and soaking up the atmosphere.

## TOURIST INFORMATION

There is as yet no city information office in Moscow. The **Intourist** or service desk in any major hotel will help with tours, restaurant bookings, theatre tickets and travel, but only to a limited extent with accommodation. Its headquarters at *Mokhavaya ulitsa 13; tel: 292 2365,* is really only able to deal with tours.

The large hotels also sell up-to-date maps and provide some of the English-language listings publications free of charge. These include *Moscow Times* (daily), *Time Out in Moscow* (weekly), *Where in Moscow* (a directory with maps and telephone listings), *Moscow from A to Z* (guide, mostly listings) and *Traveller's Yellow Pages and Handbook for Moscow.*

## ARRIVING AND DEPARTING

### Airport

**Sheremetevo:** for flight information *tel: 578 7518.* Moscow's international airport is located 30km north-west of the city. There are two terminals: Sheremetevo 1, handling domestic flights, and Sheremetevo 2 for all international arrivals and departures.

Facilities (rather run-down) include currency exchange, car rental, 24-hour duty-free shops, bar and restaurant. As the entry and departure formalities are still heavily bureaucratic, allow plenty of time for delays. If at all possible pre-book your transfer from the airport to the hotel. The alternative is a two-stage bus and metro journey starting from outside the terminal. One bus leaves for *Rechnoi Vokzal* metro station (every 30 mins – last bus 2030), the other for the Central Airport Station, near *Dinamo* metro station (every 90 mins – last bus 2200). You'll be pestered with offers for taxi rides from the moment you leave Arrivals. The cost is exorbitant, so at least negotiate a price first.

### By Train

**Leningradsky Vokzal** (alternative name **Oktyabrskaya**), *Komsomolskaya ploshchad 3; tel: 262 9524.* For trains to St Petersburg and Helsinki. Nearest metro *Komsomolskaya.* The oldest of Moscow's eight terminals, dating from 1851. **Rizhsky Vokzal**, *Rizhskaya ploshchad; tel: 266 1372.* For trains to most Baltic destinations. Nearest metro *Rizhskaya.* **Belorussky Vokzal**, *Tverskaya Zastava ploshchad 1; tel: 973 8191.* For trains to Berlin, Warsaw, Kaliningrad, Minsk and Vilnius. Nearest metro *Belorusskaya.* This attractive building dates from 1870s.

The facilities in all these terminals are primitive and the toilets are appalling! There is no information in English apart from the **Intourist** office at Leningradsky Vokzal. Keep an eye on your bags at all times. All mainline/international tickets must be paid for in hard currency. Apply

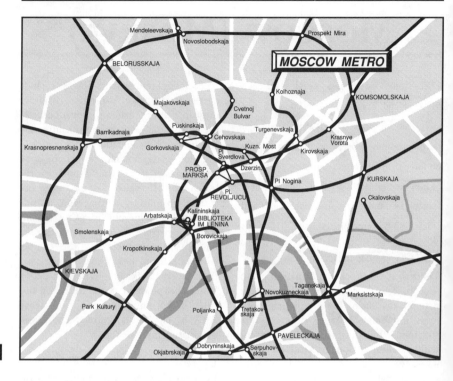

**MOSCOW METRO**

to your hotel or the **Intourtrans** office, *Ulitsa Petrovka 15/13; tel: 927 1181,* metro *Turgenevskaya.*

## GETTING AROUND

Moscow is a vast city which, the Kremlin, Red Square and one or two other sights apart, cannot be negotiated on foot. Fortunately Moscow's public transport system, especially the metro, is second to none. All transport runs from 0530 to 0100. There is no authorised transport map, but most city maps include bus and tram routes and a metro plan.

## Tickets

Tickets for all forms of local transport are sold at metro stations and kiosks. Buy *yedinye bilyeti* and you'll be able to ride on any form of transport for a month. All tickets are either punched on board the vehicle or in the booking hall of the station. To travel on the metro you can also buy tokens (*talony*), which should be dropped into the turnstiles at the top of the escalator.

## Metro

Built as a showpiece of Socialism in the 1930s and 40s, the Moscow metro is comprehensive, cheap, extremely reliable and a work of art in its own right. Lavishly decorated with marble, mosaics, gold and glass, each of the station interiors is intended to highlight a revolutionary or proletarian theme. The most impressive station interiors include Ploshchad Revolyutsii, Komsomolskaya, Mayakovskaya, Kievskaya and Park Kultury. A basic knowledge of the

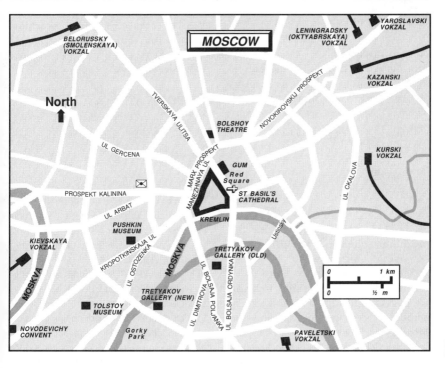

North ↑

YAROSLAVSKI VOKZAL

LENINGRADSKY (OKTYABRSKAYA) VOKZAL

BELORUSSKY (SMOLENSKAYA) VOKZAL

**MOSCOW**

KAZANSKI VOKZAL

TVERSKAYA ULITSA

NOVOKIROVSKIJ PROSPEKT

BOLSHOY THEATRE

UL GERCENA

KURSKI VOKZAL

MARX PROSPEKT

MANEZHNAYA UL

GUM
Red Square

UL CKALOVA

PROSPEKT KALININA

ST BASIL'S CATHEDRAL

UL ARBAT

KREMLIN

KIEVSKAYA VOKZAL

PUSHKIN MUSEUM

KROPOTKINSKAJA UL

UL OSTOZENKA

MOSKVA

TRETYAKOV GALLERY (OLD)

Ustinskij

UL BOLSAJA ORDYNKA

MOSKVA

TRETYAKOV GALLERY (NEW)

UL DIMITROVA

UL BOLSAJA POLJANKA

0                1 km
0                ½ m

TOLSTOY MUSEUM

NOVODEVICHY CONVENT

Gorky Park

PAVELETSKI VOKZAL

223

Cyrillic alphabet is all but essential for negotiating the metro. Remember that each station has its own name, even two stations on the same site but on different lines. Stations are indicated by a large red letter M. Indicator boards in the station give exit and transfer information. Check you're on the right line and heading in the right direction by studying the route map on the tunnel wall. If you're changing lines, look for a sign with the word *perekhod* and the name of the station you want. To get back to street level, follow the signs *vykhod*. Lost property, *tel: 222 2085*

### Other Public Transport

There are relatively few **trams** in Moscow. Look for the signs (T) hanging on wires above the street and adjacent to the stop. For **bus**es the sign is (A) and for **trolley-buses** (m). All these vehicles are extremely crowded and there is a considerable amount of re-routing, often with no notice. Expect to be pushed and shoved throughout any journey; if you can't move near enough to the exit, shout *pazhalsta*! Lost property, *tel: 923 8753*

### Taxis

There is no shortage of cabs in Moscow, but not all vehicles are authorised or roadworthy. To avoid being overcharged order a cab in advance from the hotel (allow at least 1 hr). If you hail a taxi on the street, look for the official cabs – yellow with a chequered band on the door. Never take a private taxi without being clear about the price in advance and never get into a cab where there is already another passenger. To call for a taxi, *tel: 927 0000.*

## Accommodation

Moscow is fast making up the historic shortfall of accommodation for foreigners, but there is still some way to go. There is a heavy bias towards the luxury end of the market Hotel chains in Moscow include *IC, Ke, Nv, Pe, Pu* and *Rd*. There are several famous luxury hotels, dating back to the pre-revolutionary period, such as the **National**, *Okhotny ryad 14/1; tel: 203 6539*, the equally splendid **Metropol**, *Teatralny proezd 1/4; tel: 927 6000*, and the **Mezhdunarodnaya I and II**, *Krasnopresnenskaya naberezhnaya; tel: 253 2382*.

Several medium-priced hotels have central locations. The **Ukraina**, *Kutuzovsky prospekt 2/1; tel: 243 3030* is a wedding-cake skyscraper overlooking the Moskva river. The rooms are clean and comfortable but don't bother with breakfast! The **Intourist Hotel**, *Tverskaya ulitsa 3/5; tel: 203 4008* is a soulless tower block within striking distance of Red Square and the Kremlin. Although Moscow has a number of lower-priced hotels they can't be recommended simply because the facilities don't come up to western standards. You might try the **Belgrad** Hotel, *Smolenskaya ploshchad 5; tel: 248 1643*, which at least is clean and safe.

In the budget category there are the following: **Prakash Guest House**, *Profsoyuznaya 83; tel: 334 2598*, **Sputnik**, *Leninsky prospekt 38; tel: 938 7057*. The **Traveller's Guest House**, *Bolshaya pereyaslavskaya 50; tel: 971 4059*, is on the 10th floor of an anonymous office block. It's American-run, clean and welcoming and will help you with travel arrangements and other problems.

It's now possible to stay with a Russian family – **Host Families Association**, *Tavricheskaya ulitsa 5 kv.25, St Petersburg; tel: 275 1992* will find rooms in Moscow.

## Eating and Drinking

Eating out in Moscow is expensive; however the proliferation of private restaurants in the last decade means that at least you won't have a problem with choice. If you're out sightseeing and feel the need for a bite to eat, head for *Tverskaya ulitsa*, the **Arbat** or any major hotel or shopping mall. European and American cuisines as well as Russian are now widely available and there's a wide range of ethnic restaurants – the best are those of the former Soviet republics, Georgia for example. Russian caterers have yet to acknowledge the existence of vegetarians.

The major **fast-food** chains are now well established. Moscow also has a number of western-style delicatessens. GUM is a good source, so is the **Sadko Arcade**, *Krasnogvardeysky proezd 1*. On no account buy food from street vendors.

**Razgulyai**, *Spartakovskaya ulitsa 11; tel: 267 7613* offers Russian cuisine and gypsy music and is patronised by locals. More sedate and serving Russian nouvelle cuisine is the **Atrium**, *Leninsky prospekt 44; tel: 137 3008*. **La Cantina**, *Tverskaya ulitsa 5; tel: 926 3684* is located near the Kremlin and serves Tex-Mex in convivial surroundings. **Art Café Cappuccino**, *Suvorovsky bulvar 12; tel: 290 1498* serves excellent pizzas.

## Communications

**Central Post Office: Glavny Pochtant**, *Myasnitskaya ulitsa 26/2; tel: 928 6311*; open Mon–Fri 0800–2000, Sat 0800–1900, Sun 0900–1900. The most convenient post restante (general delivery) is the Central Telegraph Office,

**Tsentralny telegraf**, *Tverskaya ulitsa 7; tel: 924 9004.* **Telephones:** the local area code is 095. For local calls you'll need to buy *zhetony* (tokens) at the metro. Making an international call is much easier than it was, as most large hotels now have direct dial phone booths.

### Consulates

**Australia:** *Kropotkinsky pereulok 13; tel: 956 6070,* metro: *Park Kultury.*
**Canada:** *Starokonyushenny pereulok 23; tel: 956 6666,* metro: *Kropotkinskaya.*
**New Zealand:** *Povarskaya ulitsa 44; tel: 290 1277,* metro: *Barrikadnaya.*
**Republic of Ireland:** *Grokholsky pereulok 5; tel: 288 4101,* metro: *Prospekt Mira.*
**South Africa:** *Bolshoy Strochenovsky pereulok 22/5; tel: 230 7854,* metro: *Serpukhovskaya.*
**UK:** *Sofiyskaya naberezhnaya 14; tel: 230 6333,* metro: *Biblioteka imeni Lenina.*
**USA:** *Novinsky bulvar 19/23; tel: 252 2451,* metro: *Barrikadnaya.*

### ENTERTAINMENT AND EVENTS

For tickets to all major events and venues enquire at the service or Intourist desk at your hotel; alternatively **IPS Theatre Box Office** in the Hotel Metropol. You'll pay western rates and in hard currency but there's really no alternative.

Russia is famous for its high culture. The **Bolshoy** opera and ballet companies perform at the theatre of the same name, *Teatralnaya ploshchad 1; tel: 292 3119,* or sometimes at the **Palace of Congresses** in the Kremlin, *tel: 929 7901.* The main venues for concerts are the **Tchaikovsky Concert Hall**, *Triumfalnaya ploshchad 4/31; tel: 299 0378* and the **Moscow Conservatory**, *Bolshaya Nikitskaya ulitsa 13; tel: 229 3687.*

There are two venues of the **Moscow State Circus**: *Tsvetnoy bulvar 13; tel: 200 6889* and *Prospekt Vernadskovo 7; tel: 930 2815.* For foreign films see the listings in the *Moscow Times* or contact: **Americom House of Cinema**, *Radisson Slavyanskaya Hotel, Berezhkovskaya naberezhnaya 2; tel: 941 8386.* The **Moscow International Film Festival** takes place in May every odd-numbered year.

For a uniquely Russian experience, visit the famous 19th-century **Sandunovskaya banya** (baths), *Neglinnaya ulitsa 14; tel: 925 4631.* (For opening times etc., ask at your hotel.) Ice hockey is played at the **Ice Palace of TsKA**, *Leningradsky prospect 39; tel: 213 6590.* See listings magazines for details of games, and of soccer matches (Mar–Oct).

The most impressive celebrations in Russia take place during the **Christmas** and **New Year** period. Musical concerts and various folk events also take place during the **Russian Winter Festival** (25 Dec–5 Jan). The traditional Soviet **anniversaries** (1 May and 7 November) are still marked by small-scale demonstrations, while **Victory Day** (9 May) is commemorated by veteran marches. **Russian Independence Day** (12 Jun) – head for Red Square or the main parks to see what's going on.

### SHOPPING

Moscow's main shopping street is *Tverskaya ulitsa.* Of several malls, the most famous is **GUM**, *Krasnaya ploshchad 3,* now stocked mainly with western goods. Typically Russian souvenirs include the painted Palekh lacquer boxes, matryoshka nest dolls, blue and white Gzhel pottery, carved wooden toys, balalaikas and miniature samovars, colourfully embroidered shawls and of course the traditional Russian fur hat. Apart from the malls, the best place for souvenirs is the **Izmailovsky Park street market** at weekends.

**225**

Coach tours and excursions are organised by **Intourist VAO**, *Mokhovaya ulitsa 13; tel: 292 2037* (payment in hard currency only) and other travel companies. In summer, about the best and cheapest way of seeing Moscow is to take a boat trip on the Moskva river. Numerous embarkation points include the Ustinsky Bolshoy bridge, near the Rossiya Hotel, and the pier behind the Kiev railway station.

## The Kremlin

Metro *Ploshchad Revolyutsii* Open Fri–Wed 1000–1700, but closed on other occasions at short notice, so check before setting out. The main entrance is through the **Kutafaya Tower** on *Manezhnaya ulitsa,* where tickets are sold to all sights open to the public. Moscow's first kremlin (*kreml* means 'fortress') was founded in 1156 but the present complex dates from the late 15th century, when Tsar Ivan III imported Italian architects for the latest in Renaissance engineering.

The **Cathedrals** are among the greatest artistic monuments in Russia and were the scene of all the great ceremonies of state until the demise of the monarchy in 1917. **Uspensky Sobor**, the Cathedral of the Assumption, is the work of a Bolognese architect, Aristotele Fioravanti. The interior walls and pillars are covered with 17th-century paintings of breathtaking beauty – some of the panels of the iconostasis are much are older. See also the exquisitely carved throne of Ivan the Terrible. Russian architects from Pskov built **Blagoveshchensky Sobor**, the Cathedral of the Annunciation, in just five years (1484–89). Used as a private chapel by the Tsar and his family, it is decorated with frescos by the medieval master Theodosius. The exuberantly decorated exterior of **Arkhangelsky Sobor**, the Cathedral of the Archangel, is a clue to the Venetian origins of the architect, Aleviz Novy. It is the burial place of Russia's earliest rulers, Ivan the Terrible among them.

The **Patriach's Palace**, including the **Church of the Twelve Apostles**, is now the **Museum of 17th-Century Life and Applied Arts**. The exhibitions here include two rooms furnished in the style of a wealthy boyar's residence. Some of the displays are borrowed from the **Oruzheynaya Palata** (Kremlin Armoury). This vast and stunning collection comprises priceless objects made for the Tsar and his court and also gifts presented by foreign dignitaries over the centuries: armour, gold and silverware, robes and regalia, jewellery, including some of the famous Fabergé eggs, and royal coaches.

A number of the buildings and palaces, including the massive white and gold **Nicholas Palace** and the almost hidden **Terem Palace**, aren't open to the public. From the famous 'Red' (or ceremonial) Staircase outside the **Granovitaya Dvorets** (Palace of Facets), Tsars processed to their coronation – the stairs were destroyed by Stalin, but rebuilt in 1994. Also in the Kremlin are the 81-metre **Ivan the Great Bell Tower**, the **Tsar's Bell and Cannon**, the **Arsenal, the** former **Senate** (where the President of Russia still has an office) and the modern **Palace of Congresses**.

### Red Square

Running parallel to the eastern side of the Kremlin wall is **Red Square** (Krasnaya Ploshchad): metro *Ploshchad Revolyutsii*. The most familiar sight here is **St Basil's Cathedral**, built by Ivan the Terrible to commemorate a victory over the Tatars at Kazan in 1552. Now a museum (open Wed–Mon, 1000–1700 summer; 1100–

1600 winter; closed first Mon every month), the interior is a dark, mysterious maze of corridors, vestibules, twisting staircases and partly restored chapels. ·

In front of the Kremlin wall where many Communist worthies, including Stalin, are buried, is the **Lenin Mausoleum**, where the Soviet leader has been interred since his death in 1924. There are persistent rumours that this monument will close when the Soviet leader's body is reburied in St Petersburg (open Tues–Thurs, Sat 1000–1300; Sun 1000–1400).

Opposite the mausoleum is the elaborate shopping arcade known as **GUM** (State Universal Store), a reminder that Red Square was originally a market place. The late 19th-century interior, with its enormous glass roof galleries, stuccoed archways and iron bridges, now contains a mere fraction of the original thousand stalls. Two monuments demolished in the Stalin era have recently been restored. The **Kazan Cathedral** originally dates from 1636 and is now a functioning church. The **Iberian Gate** near the red-brick **Historical Museum** (currently closed) takes its name from a tiny chapel dedicated to the Iberian Virgin which stood over the two arches.

## Other Sights

Presiding over *Teatralnaya ploshchad* (Theatre Square) is the stunning neo-classical façade of the **Bolshoy**, home to the world-famous opera and ballet companies. Tchaikovsky's *Swan Lake* was premiered in this building in 1877.

The most outstanding of all Moscow's fortified monasteries is the **Novodevichy Convent**, *Novodevichy proezd,* metro: *Sportivnaya* (open Wed–Mon 1000–1800 summer; 1000–1700 winter; closed last day of each month). Founded specifically for the daughters of noblewomen by Tsar

Basil III in 1524, this majestic architectural ensemble contains the 17th-century **Church of the Assumption**, where some of the best choral singing in Russia takes place on Sundays. Much of old Moscow was destroyed by Stalin's planners in the 1920s and 30s. One fragment to survive is the **Arbat** (metro: *Arbatskaya*), a charming 19th-century residential quarter now the haunt of buskers and street artists and the focal point of Moscow's embryonic café culture.

Moscow should be better known in the West for its magnificent parks – **Gorky Park** has views across the Moskva River as well as amusements, a theatre and ice skating rink (metro: *Park Kulutry*, trolley-buses: 4, 7, 62). **Izmailovsky Park** contains the hunting lodge where Peter the Great grew up; it's also famous for its weekend art and souvenir markets (metro: *Izmailovsky Park*).

## Museums

The recently re-opened **Tretyakov Gallery** houses the largest collection of Russian art in the world, some 50,000 paintings in all. Original building: *Lavrushinsky pereulok 10,* metro: *Tretyakovskaya*. New building: *Krymsky Val ulitsa 10,* metro: *Park Kultury* (open Tues–Sun 1000–1900). The **Pushkin Fine Arts Museum** has a fine collection of old masters and French Impressionist and post-Impressionist art. *Ulitsa Volkhonka 12,* metro: *Kropotkinskaya* (open Tues–Sun 1000–1900). The evocative **Lev Tolstoy Estate-Museum** is where the author spent the winters of 1882–1901. All 16 rooms have been meticulously preserved, offering a fascinating eye view on upper-class life of the period. *Ulitsa Lva Tolstova 21,* metro: *Kropotkinskaya* (open Tues–Sun, 1000–1700; closed last day of month).

**227**

# PRAGUE (PRAHA)

Prague has been transformed since the 1989 'Velvet Revolution' to become one of Europe's most popular tourist destinations. It is a beautiful city, with a well-preserved historic centre, and it is justly famed for its superb 17th-century baroque architecture. It has acquired a laid-back, 'anything goes' reputation that sits side-by-side with a newly elegant, fashionable lifestyle and the creative energy of a city that knows it is going places.

Prague has a fascinating history, a lively music scene, a vast number of museums and churches, friendly bars, good restaurants, and a wealth of open green spaces. Allow yourself several days at least to do it justice.

## TOURIST INFORMATION

The main office of the **Pražská informační služba** (Prague Information Service, known as PIS) is at *Na príkopĕ 20,* near *Václavské námĕstí* (Wenceslas Square); *tel: (02) 54 44 44.* Open Mon–Fri 0800–1900, weekends 0800–1530 (later in summer). There are also PIS offices at *Staromĕstské námĕstí 22, tel: (02) 24 21 28 44* in the heart of the old town, and at the **Central Railway Station** *(Hlavní Nádraží).* PIS also distributes useful free publications.

## ARRIVING AND DEPARTING

### Airport
**Ruzynĕ Airport** is 16 km west of the city (flight enquiries, *tel: (02) 36 78 14/36 77 60),* with a 24-hour currency exchange booth, an accommodation bureau, post and telephone facilities at the airport, and a restaurant open from 1000 to 2000. The no. 119 bus runs from the airport to Dejvická metro station, from where other public transport connections are available. **Czech Airlines** (ČSA) run a bus service every 30 mins, 0530–1900, to their terminal in Staré Mĕsto, *Revoluční 25;* travel time is 30 mins. **Czech Airhandling**'s excellent mini-bus service runs door-to-door, but costs more.

### Stations
**Praha Hlavní Nádraží** (Central Railway Station), *Wilsonova, tel: (02) 26 49 30,* is the city's main station. It is a big, modern station with a tourist information office, train information and seat reservation desk, bureaux de change (open 0800–1800), hotel and private room reservation desks, left luggage, post, telephone, showers, and restaurant, kiosk and other catering services. Some long-distance and international services also operate into **Nádraží Praha-Holešovice**, *tel: (02) 80 75 05,* in the 7th district (a little way out), which also has train information and local accommodation offices. Both stations are on Metro Line C, which connects to the city centre. **Praha-Masarykovo nádraží** (Metro Line B), *Námĕstí Republiky,* does not operate international services but internal services often stop here and it is a good starting point for trips to the countryside. For both local and international service enquiries, call the central railway information service, *tel: (02) 24 22 42 00/24 61 40 30.* Some local services begin and end at **Praha-Smíchov** (Metro Line B).

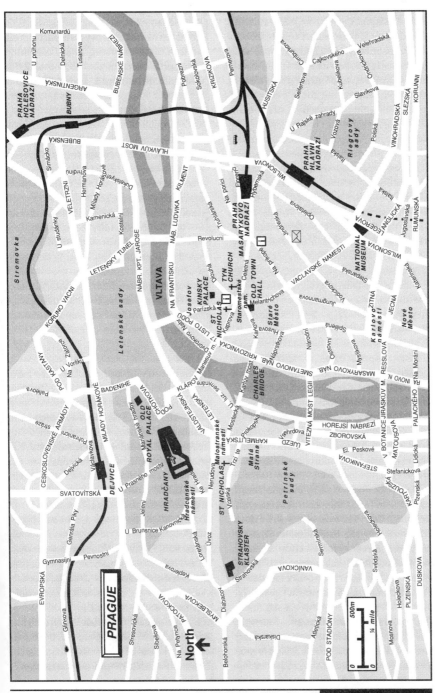

## GETTING AROUND

Visiting the main attractions is easy, as they are mostly confined to small areas, particularly in the city centre and on the **Hradčany** (Castle Hill). Nevertheless, you will need to use some public transport. PIS offices issue free street plans. The most reliable and up-to-date map, by Kartografie Praha (1:20,000), includes public transport routes .

**Wenceslas Square** *(Václavské náměstí)* is very lively by day, with all manner of shops, hotels, and fast-food places. However, parts of it also double as the red light district at night (extending into the surrounding streets).

### Tickets

Single tickets *(jízdenky)* allow you 1 hr on the metro, or 1 leg of a bus or tram journey. A better buy is the inexpensive 5-day **tourist ticket** *(denní jízdenka)*, which is valid on all forms of public transport. Tickets are on sale at *tabák* (tobacconists/newsagents) or from metro station ticket desks and (with exact change) slot machines. Punch your ticket when boarding and punch a new ticket when changing vehicles (the fine for riding without a valid ticket is almost 40 times the regular fare). Children aged up to 10 travel free; those aged 10–16 for half price. Alternatively, a **Prague card**, available from, Čedok, (travel agency) *Na příkopě 18,* or American Express, *Václavské náměstí 56,* combines a 3-day transport ticket with free entry to major sights. Beware of pickpockets while travelling on public transport, especially if crowded and on the main tourist routes.

### Metro, Trams and Buses

A wonderfully efficient and modern **metro** (3 lines: A, B and C) covers most areas you are likely to visit, except

Hradčany (Castle Hill). There is also a good network of **trams** running on main arteries and across the river. All public transport runs from about 0500 to 2400. The infrequent **night trams** all stop at *Lazarská,* just off *Václavské náměstí* (Wenceslas Square).

You will rarely need to use **buses** unless you are staying out in the suburbs. The **Central Bus Station** is at *Křižíkova 4, tel: (02) 24 21 10 60* – it is often impossible to get through and it may make sense to queue at the information desk – (metro: *Florenc).* All forms of public transport are subject to route and timetable changes, as the system is renovated and responds to changing demands, so it is a good idea to get up-to-date information from the tourist office. Buses are usually more frequent and faster than trains for getting to locations just outside Prague.

### Taxis

Avoid taxis, if at all possible – bare-faced over-charging of foreigners by ridiculous amounts is endemic and there have been cases of violence against passengers who refuse to stump up. Always agree a fare before getting in or make sure that the meter is switched on and begins with the normal minimum fare. If a taxi ride is unavoidable, get one called rather than hailing one in the street. *Tel: (02) 35 03 20/34 24 10/24 91 15 59/33 99.*

## STAYING IN PRAGUE

### Accommodation

Although Prague is gradually expanding the range and quality of its hotels, many are over-priced for what they offer. If you prefer to stick to a well-known chain, the following have hotels in Prague: *Fm, IC, IH* and *Pe.* The 5-star

Savoy Hotel, *Keplerova 6; tel: (02) 24 30 24 30*, is an ideal place to stay, if one can afford it, otherwise there is always the Sunday jazz brunch in its Hradčany Restaurant. The **Grand Hotel Evropa**, *Václavské nám. 25; tel: (02) 24 22 81 17*, is one of the city's landmarks, an art nouveau extravaganza in an ideal location on Wenceslas Square. Perhaps the best-known pension is **Pension Unitas**, *Barolomějská 9; tel: (02) 24 32 77 00*, which is owned by the Sisters of Mercy, although they are worldly enough to accept credit cards. It was formerly a prison operated by the secret police and its most famous former inmate was the current President Václav Havel himself.

**Botels**, boat hotels on the Vltava River, are an interesting, mid-price option. Try **Admirál**, *Hořejší nábřeží; tel: (02) 24 51 16 97*; **Albatros**, *nábřežíL. Svobody; tel: (02) 24 81 05 47*; or **Racék**, *na Dvorecké louce; tel: (02) 24 4 60 51*.

**Accommodation Bureaux: AVE**, *Hlavní nádraží; tel: (02) 24 22 32 26/35 21*, is one of the best-known, and although not the cheapest offers good value for money. It has offices at the airport (open 24 hrs) and at the Central and Holešovice railway stations. AVE can provide accommodation for individuals or groups in hotels ranging from 1 to 5 stars, and also in boarding houses, youth hostels and private apartments. Open daily 0600–2300. **Čedok**, *Na příkopě 18, tel: (02) 24 19 71 11* (open Mon–Fri 0900–1800, weekends 0830–1630), can make a computer check on hotels with vacant rooms.

For **youth-orientated information**, try **RHIA**, *Skolská 1; tel: (02) 24 91 45 14*, which specialises in low-cost rooms and can also book youth hostel accommodation; or **CKM**, *Jindřišská 28 ; tel: (02) 26 05 32/26 85 07*, (open daily 0900–1800), or the **Junior Hotel (Youth Hostel) reservation office**, *Žitná 12; tel: (02) 29 29 84*, (open 24 hrs daily). In July, Aug and Sept, CKM also lets cheap rooms in student hostels and a similar service is provided by **Uniset**, *Spálená 5, tel: (02) 24 91 01 13*. You can also call the **Student Hostel Booking Office**, *tel: (02) 53 99 51/59*. Some hostels worth trying are **Hostel Sokol**, *Hellichova 1; tel: (02) 24 51 06 07*, located in the Malá Strana district and with a roof terrace looking out on the Petřín Hill; and **Libra-Q**, *Senovážné nám. 21; tel: (02) 24 10 25 36*, centrally located, with both dormitories and rooms.

There are several **campsites** within the city boundary: **Triocamp Praha**, *Dolní Chabry, tel: (02) 66 41 11 80*; **Intercamp Kotva Braník**, *tel: (02) 46 13 97*; **Caravan Camping Císařská Louka**, *tel (02) 54 01 29*. For central information, contact **UAMK**, Mánesova 20, *tel: (02) 24 22 16 35*. Closed at weekends.

Accommodation **hawkers** wait for visitors arriving by train. You can try them if you want to stay in a private apartment and have the chance to meet ordinary Czechs. Agree a price in advance. The arrangements are generally safe, but the quality of the accommodations can only be judged on arrival. Or use one of the many private agencies, such as **Unitour**, *tel: (02) 24 14 29 36*.

## Communications

The **Central Post Office** and **Poste Restante** (General Delivery) are at *Jindřišská 14*, off *Václavské náměstí*, *tel: (02) 24 22 88 56/90 51* (24-hr service for letters, parcels, telegrams and telephones). Otherwise, post office opening hours are Mon–Fri 0800–1800. There are conveniently located post offices at the airport,

231

at Praha Hlavní Nádraží (Central Railway Station), on *Wilsonova*, and inside Hradčany Castle. Stamps and phonecards can be purchased at post offices or from *tabák*.

The telephone system is erratic, but improving, and the older, coin-operated telephones are seldom reliable. The modern phone booths accept phone cards. Local calls (coins only) are made on the yellow and black telephones; long-distance calls on the grey ones. All card phones have instructions in English. For an English-speaking operator, *tel: (02) 0135;* to make collect calls, *tel: (02) 0132.* The Prague area code is *02.*

## Eating and Drinking

The restaurant scene in Prague has expanded enormously in recent years, and quality has gone up dramatically, but the city still lags behind comparably sized cities in western Europe. Nevertheless, a wide variety of international cuisines is now on offer, and the quality and presentation of the Czechs' own cuisine has improved. The latter, however, can often be stodgy and unimaginative. *Knedliky* (dumplings) are on almost every menu.

There are three main categories of eating house: *restaurace* (restaurant), *vinárna* (wine-bar/restaurant) and *pivnice* (beer cellar). Prices range from expensive in fashionable inner-city locations to great value in hiss'n'spit dives serving locally brewed beer. A mid-price level of restaurants mostly frequented by the young and chic, has emerged. These pay finer attention to quality and are often housed in characterful old premises. As happens in tourist zones all over the world, a few restaurants may take advantage of the transient nature of their clientele to overcharge. Waiters are good at making 'mistakes' with the prices and the change, so

check both carefully against your bill.

Although touristy, the classic **U Flekú** beer garden and cellar, *Křemencova 11; tel: (02) 2491 5119,* is worth a visit for its black ale. Several Prague breweries have their own 'pubs', while others serve the legendary Pilsner Urquell, Gambrinus or Budweiser beers. Other establishments which can be recommended include **Verlyba**, *Ostrovní 23, tel: (02) 24 91 23 91;* **Pizzeria Kmotra**, *V Jirchářích 12, tel: (02) 24 91 58 09;* **Caférestaurant Gany's**, *Národní 20, tel: (02) 29 76 65.* Do not miss the chance to visit a typical Czech pub, of which there are dozens in Malá Strana and the Old Town.

Should you get fed up with typically stodgy Czech dumplings, pork and heavy fillings, vegetarian food is available at **Bufet Adonis**, *Jungmannova 21, tel: (02) 26 89 08;* **Green Bar Jonáš**, *Na Poříčí 10, tel: (02) 23 21 64 37;* **Konírna** salad bar, *Anenská 11;* **Jo's Bar**, *Malostranské máměstí 7.*

If you want to chat in English over one of the many excellent Czech pilsener beers (the city's favourites are Staropramen and Velckepopoviký Kozel), try **Jáma**, *V jámě 28;* **Hogo-Fogo**, *Salvátorská 4, tel: (02) 23 17 023;* **Ethno-bar**, *Husova 18, tel: (02) 26 67 04;* **Andy's Café** (very American), *V kolkovně;* or **Chapeau Rouge** at the corner of *Štupartská and Jakubská.*

**McDonalds** and other burger and pizza restaurants and take-aways are easy to find in the centre.

## Embassies and consulates

**Australia:** *Čínska 4, Praha 6; tel: (02) 24 31 00 71.*

**Canada:** *Mickiewiczova 6, Hradčany, Praha 6; tel: (02) 24 31 11 08.*

**UK:** *Thunovská 10, Malá Strana; tel: (02) 24 51 04 39.* (The UK embassy acts for

232

citizens of the Republic of Ireland and New Zealand; in emergencies, South African citizens can enquire here also.) **USA:** *Tržiště 15, Malá Strana; tel: (02) 24 51 08 47.*

## Money

Banking hours are usually Mon–Fri 0900–1700 (but the Komerční Bank at *Na příkopě 42* is open from 0900–1900 and on Saturday from 0900–1300). Street bureaux de change mostly charge very high commissions and should be avoided if possible. For fair dealing, go to **Thomas Cook**, *Národni 28; tel: 21 10 52 77*, or the **Živnostenská Banka**, *Na příkopě 20*. There are plenty of automatic cash-dispensers, accessible by cards of the established international brands. Travellers cheques and Eurocheques are widely accepted, and so increasingly areh credit cards, especially in upmarket establishments.

## ENTERTAINMENT

Consult the English-language newspaper *The Prague Post* for weekly listings of events. The Czech publications, *Program* (weekly), and *Přehled* (monthly) and *Kultura v Praze* (monthly, issued also in English) also give details of what's on.

Prague offers an excellent choice of classical music (look for posters and advertisements or pick up a handout from a street distributor – it is hard to avoid them). The **Smetana Hall**, *Náměstí Republiky 5; tel: (02) 22 32 58 58*, with its distinctive art nouveau façade from 1906, is the home of the Czech Philharmonic Orchestra.

There is also a strong theatre scene (mostly in Czech, but with occasional English performances). The grandest of all the theatres is the **National Theatre** (Národní divadlo), *Národní třída 24, tel:*

*(02) 24 91 34 37*, a neo-Renaissance-style building dating from 1883, in which theatre, opera and ballet are performed. There are also many delightful and easily understood puppet and mime shows, such as those at **Black Theatre**, *Pařížská, tel: (02) 23 29 191*; **Studio Gag Borise Hybnera**, *Národní 25, tel: (02) 24 22 90 95*; **Ta Fantastika**, *Karlova 8, tel: (02) 24 22 90 78*; and the famed **Laterna Magika**, *Národní 4, tel: (02) 24 21 26 91*.

The rock and disco scene exploded into life with the end of Communist rule and has been booming ever since, with cult discos like **Bunkr**, *Lodecká 2, Staré Město, tel: (02) 24 81 04 75* – originally a bomb shelter for Party bigwigs. There are also **Rock Café**, *Národní 20, tel: (02) 24 91 44 16*; **Roxy**, *Dlouhá 33, tel: (02) 231 63 31*. If this is your scene, make sure you visit **Radost FX**, *Bělehradská 120*; and **Subway-rock Club**, *Na Příkopě 22*.

For good jazz, Czech or international, traditional or modern, try places like **Agartha Jazz Centrum**, *Krakovská 5, tel: (02) 24 21 29 14* (while there, you can visit the CD shop with numerous Czech jazz discs); or **Reduta**, *Národní 20, tel: (02) 24 91 22 46;* or **Metropolitan Jazz Club**, *Jungmannova 14, tel: (02) 24 21 60 25;* or the **Press Jazz Club**, *Parízska 9; tel: (02) 24 32 62 82*.

## SHOPPING

Bohemian crystal glass, which is of excellent quality, is far cheaper here than the same product sold in western Europe or the USA. There is a big selection at **Bohemia Crystal Shop-Jafa**, *Maiselova 15; tel: (02) 24 81 00 09*. **Bohemia-Moser**, *Na příkopě 12; tel: (02) 24 21 12 93*, offers a mailing service. **Karlovarský Porcelán**, *Parízska ul.; tel: (02) 231 77 34*, is another shop with good choice and

233

quality. In the picturesque narrow streets of *Malá Strana* and *Staré Město* are plenty of small souvenir shops, selling glass, ceramics, wooden toys and puppets. The selection of goods in the city is now incomparably wider than pre-1989. The streets off *Václavské náměstí* boast numerous luxurious shops and boutiques. For cheaper goods, food and other essentials try one of the main department stores: **Prior Kotva**, *Náměstí republiky;* **Bílá labut'**, *Na Poříčí;* **Prior Máj**, *Národní 26;* **Krone**, *Václavské náměstí;* and **K-Mart**, *Spálená*. Look out for the daily **fruit and vegetable market** at the intersection of *Havelská* and *Melantrichova* in the Old Town.

Shop opening times vary, but only a few now maintain the restricted schedule of former times. Most are open Mon–Sat from 0800 to 1900 or 2000, and sometimes even later, and often also on Sunday.

## SIGHTSEEING

Old Prague is divided into *Staré Město* and *Nové Město* to the east, and *Malá Strana* and *Hradčany* to the west of the River *Vltava*. At the heart of *Staré Město* is the picturesque *Staroměstské náměstí* (Old Town Square), (metro/tram nos 17 and 18: *Staroměstská*), a time-capsule ringed by medieval and baroque structures. Find time to visit the **Staroměstská radnice** (Old Town Hall), with its astrological clock, the baroque **Kostel Sv. Mikuláše** (St Nicholas Church), built by the great Prague architects, Christoph and Kilian Ignác Dientzenhofer, the baroque **Kinsky Palace**, the somewhat forbidding but very ancient **Kostel panny Marie před Ty'nem** (Tyn Church), and the Gothic **U Kamenného zvonu** (House of the Stone Bell). The 1915 **Monument to Jan Hus** in the middle of

the square is a traditional rallying point for Czechs – Hus was a 15th-century religious reformer who fought against a corrupt Catholic church and foreign domination of Bohemia.

*Nové Město* is a less compact area with fewer sights, but all visitors to Prague should spend some time in the famous, lively *Václavské náměstí* (Wenceslas Square) (metro: *Můstek or Muzeum*), which witnessed the climax of the 'Velvet Revolution' in 1989. At the top end is the **National Museum** (see under Museums) in front of which stand an equestrian statue of **St Wenceslas** and a shrine to **Jan Palach**, who burned himself to death on 16 January 1969 in protest at the Warsaw Pact invasion of Czechoslovakia.

### West Bank

*Malá Strana* is a picturesque district of narrow cobbled streets and diminutive squares squeezed between the river and the wedge-shaped plateau of *Hradčany*. Here, *Malostranské náměstí* (Lesser Quarter Square) is particularly worth visiting (metro/tram nos 12 and 22: *Malostranská*), dominated by the Dientzenhofer's other **Kostel Sv. Mikuláše** (Church of St Nicholas), and ringed with baroque palaces. Not far away are the even more delightful *Velkopřevorské náměstí* (Grand Prior's Square) and the adjoining *Maltézské náměstí* (Square of the Knights of Malta), which contain some interesting churches and palaces, together with the celebrated **John Lennon Wall**, a pop-art folly (tram nos 12 and 22: *Hellichova*).

### Hradčany

This huge hilltop castle is the focal point of Prague (tram no. 22: *Malostranské náměstí/Pražsky' hrad*). Dominating the whole complex is the magnificent **Katedrála Svatého Víta** (St Vitus Cathedral), the core of which was built by Matthew of Arras and Peter Parler between 1344 and 1385. Highlights include the Wenceslas Chapel, with walls studded with precious stones, the late-Gothic Royal Oratory, the fabulous baroque Tomb of St John Nepomuk by Fischer von Erlach and the oak panel reliefs in the ambulatory.

Nearby, much of the **Stary´ Královsky´ Palác** (Old Royal Palace) was built by Benedikt Ried for King Vladislav Jagiello in the 15th century. Don't miss the magnificent late-Gothic **Vladislav Hall**, the so-called Riders' Stairway (which was used by mounted knights who jousted in the hall) and the **Bohemian Chancellery**, where the most famous of Prague's four defenestrations occurred, when Protestant nobles threw Frederick II's ambassadors from the window in 1618.

To the north-east are the **Klášter Sv. Jiří** (Convent of St George) and the Romanesque **Bazilika Sv. Jiří** (Basilica of St George). Near this is the **Lobkowicz Palace**, which contains a museum of Bohemian history. At the north of the castle plateau, *Zlatá Ulička* (Golden Lane) is lined by diminutive Renaissance houses. **Franz Kafka** lived at no. 22, between 1916 and 1917 (it is now a bookshop owned by the Kafka Society).

While the many splendid buildings of the Hradčany are of course the main attraction, there are also some splendid ornamental gardens which make for pleasant walks in the sunshine and scented air.

Beyond the *Hradčany* itself is an attractive area beginning with *Hradčanské náměstí* (Hradčany Square). Take tram nos

12 or 22 to *Malostranské náměstí* and walk up *Nerudova*. Note the graffitoed **Schwarzenberg Palace** on the south side (housing the War Museum), the **Tuscany Palace** to the west and the noble **Archbishop's Palace** to the north. If you walk up *Loretánská*, you come to the imposing **Černín Palace**, from whose window Foreign Minister Jan Masaryk plunged (or was pushed) to his death in 1948. Nearby is the **Loreta** shrine, an imitation of the famous Loreto near Ancona that claims to possess the house of the Virgin Mary. The baroque **bell-tower** has a much-admired carillon and the **cloisters, the Santa Casa** and the **Treasury** are all worth a visit. Beyond the Loreta is the **Strahovsky´ Klášter**, (Strahov Monastery), take tram no. 22: *Památník písemnictví,* whose star attraction is the **Philosophical Hall** with marvellous frescos by Franz Anton Maulpertsch. **Petřínsky sady** (Petřín Hill) is a green and scenic area adjacent to Hradčany, reachable by a funicular from *Újezd,* and crowned by a range of notably stange architectural features, such as a downsizd Eiffel Tower, a mirror maze, a mock-Gothic castle, and, less eccentrically, an Observatory.

### Charles Bridge

This beautiful, medieval sandstone bridge, commissioned by Charles VI in 1357, remained the city's only permanent river crossing until 1836. At each end are high towers, and the parapet is lined by baroque statues (mainly 1683–1714, with a few copies and later works). Note especially Jan Brockoff's **St John Nepomuk** (1683), a vivid depiction of Wenceslas IV's Vicar-General who, according to legend, was flung from the bridge for refusing to reveal the secrets of the Queen's confession to the King.

**235**

## Galleries and Museums

The rich **National Gallery** collection is scattered round four venues: the **Šternbersky' Palác** (Sternberg Palace), *Hradčany náměstí 15* (tram no. 22: *Pražsky' hrad*), with major works by European masters, including Breughel, El Greco, Dürer, Rembrandt, Klimt, Cézanne, Manet, Dégas and Picasso. The **Klášter sv. Jiří na Pražském hradě** (St George's Convent), *Jiřské naměstí 33,* houses old Bohemian art. The **Anežský Klášter** (St Agnes Convent), *U milosrdny'ch 17* (tram nos 5, 14 or 26: *Revoluční)* is devoted to 19th-century artists of the Czech national revival and the **Zámek Zbraslav** (Zbraslav Castle), *Zbraslav nad Vltavou* (metro: *Smíchovské nádraží,* then bus nos 129 or 241) has a remarkable display of 19th- and 20th-century Czech sculpture.

The **Národní Museum** (National Museum), *Václavské náměstí 68* (metro: *Muzeum*), is chiefly interesting for its architecture and pantheon. More stimulating is the **Museum hlavního města Prahy** (Museum of the City of Prague), *Na Poříčí 52,* (metro/tram nos 3/8/24: *Florenc*), which has Antonín Langweil's model of the city (1826) featuring 2228 buildings. Of the many other museums, give priority to the fine collection of furniture and glass at the **Uměleckoprůmyslové Museum** (Museum of Decorative Arts), *Ulice 17, listopadu 2;* the **Franz Kafka Permanent Exhibition**, *U Radnice 5* (Metro or tram nos 17 or 18: *Staroměstská,* for both of these); and **Bertramka, Mozartova 169**, (tram nos 4, 6, 7 or 9: *Bertramka*), a 17th-century villa which houses an exhibition of Mozart's life and work.

For contemporary Czech art, visit: **České Muzeum Výtvarných Umění,** *Husova 19–21;* **Valdštejnská Jízdárna,** *Valdštejnské náměstí 3* (Metro *Malostranská*); **Dům U Kamenného zvonu,** *Staroměstké náměstí;* and **Gallerie Rudolfinum,** *Alšovo nábřeží 12.* For photography, there is the **Prague House of Photography,** *Husova 23.*

## Other sights

Prague has a superb array of church architecture, from Romanesque rotundas to Josip Plečnik's stunning, 1933 **Kostel nejsvětějšího srdce páně** (Church of the Sacred Heart), *Náměstí Jiřího z Poděbrad* (metro: same name). Also find time to visit the fine **baroque Kostel Svatého Jakuba** (St James), *Malá Štupartská* (metro: *Náměstí Republiky*) and the remarkable **Kostel nanebevzetí panny Marie a Karla velikého** (Church of the Assumption of Our Lady and Charlemagne), *Ke Karlovu,* (metro: *IP Pavlova*), with lovely Gothic star vaulting. The old Jewish ghetto of **Josefov** (metro/tram no. 17: *Staroměstská*) was swept away in 1893, leaving behind the only preserved and functioning medieval synagogue in Central Europe and a haunting **Old Jewish Cemetery**. The surrounding buildings (which include the **Old–New Synagogue**, the rococo **Town Hall** with a Hebraic **clock** and the **Pinkas Synagogue** with a holocaust memorial) constitute a **National Jewish Museum** (one ticket for access to all sights).

At *Vyšehrad* (metro: *Vyšehrad*), south of *Nové Město,* the ancient citadel where the Slavic tribes first settled, sights include the Slavín Pantheon of leading Czechs in the **cemetery** next to the **Church of St Peter and St Paul** and breathtaking views over the **Vltava** from the bastions.

236

# PRAGUE–JICIN

The main reason for making this trip is to visit the Český Ráj (the Czech – but more usually translated as Bohemian – Paradise National Park). It is beautiful indeed, and makes a welcome break from too many museums and petrol fumes in Prague. The route is best done as a round trip, with the segment from Jičín to Turnov either being done on the local train, or even better, on foot through the most scenic sections of the Český Ráj. The suggested routing, Prague–Turnov–Jičín, could equally be done in reverse as Prague–Jičín–Turnov.

> FASTEST JOURNEY: 3 HRS 30 MINS

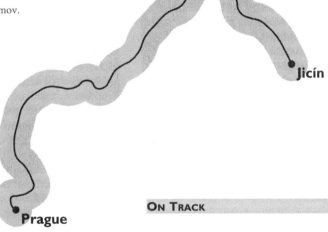

**237**

## TRAINS

**ETT Tables:** 876.

### FAST TRACK

➡ Changing trains at Turnov is the only route.

## ON TRACK

▮▮▶ **Prague–Turnov**
Three express trains and six slower trains run from Prague's **Praha Hlavní Nádraží**, (Central railway station) every hour or so to Turnov, and although at 2 hrs 30 mins the train takes an hour longer than the bus from Prague, the extra time is worth it as the train follows a more scenic route.

## Turnov–Jičín

There are small local trains every two hrs in summer between Turnov and Jičín, 23 km apart as the crow flies, but almost double this on the winding railway line, following a splendidly scenic route through the **Český Ráj** and stopping at tiny country stations on the way.

For travellers who are short of time, this is the best way to see the area. Those with extra time and energy on their hands would do better to hike for at least part of the way, following one of the colour-coded routes marked on Klub Českych Turistu's 1:50,000-scale *Hiking Map 19* of the Český Ráj. This could involve just a one-day walk, or perhaps three for the full route, camping or staying at local accommodation on the way.

### TURNOV

**Station**: The railway station lies to the west of the Jizera river, about 1 km from the town centre's main square, *Nám. Českého Ráje* on the east side. For the town centre, take *Nádrazní*, go under the railway bridge, and cross over the *Jizera* on *Palackého*.

**Tourist Office**: The **Čedok** office is in the town centre, at *Nám. Českého Ráje 26,* and can help with accommodation. A better bet for rail travellers is **Čechotour**, beside the station at *Nádrazní*, which has information about the Český Ráj and will also help with finding accommodation.

### ACCOMMODATION AND FOOD

The limited hotel, pension, bed and breakfast and student housing (July–Sept only) in the town can be booked by one of the offices listed above.

The **Hotel Karel IV** at *Žižkova 501; tel (0436) 238 55* and the **Sport** at *Koškova 1766; tel: (0436) 228 22* are good hotels with restaurants and should

be pre-booked in the main tourist season and at weekends.

There are often some private rooms to rent on the road towards the château, which could be your best bet.

### SIGHTSEEING

There is not very much to see in Turnov, as its main function is to act as a gateway to the Český Ráj. However, the **Český Ráj Museum** at *Skálova 71* (0900–1600, closed Mon), though small, contains some interesting archaeological, historical and mineralogical exhibits from the nearby national park zone as well as ethnographical displays from the area.

### ČESKÝ RÁJ

**Stations**: The two main stations giving access are at Turnov to the north-west and Jičín to the south-east, but there are also numerous small stations and wayside halts. Of these the two most useful are at **Hrubá Skála**, for access to the heart of the Český Ráj; and at **Libuň**, for the Prachovské Skály, a fairy-tale landscape of tall volcanic towers. From both of these stations the nearby scenic areas can easily be reached on foot.

**Tourist Information**: The Čedok and Čechotour offices in Turnov and Jičín are the best places, but some of the bigger hotels, such as the **Hotel Zámek** at *Hrubá Skála* have information offices, where maps and brochures are available.

### ACCOMMODATION

This area gets very busy in the summer and although it is still big enough to find plenty of peace and quiet, accommodation is not so easy to come by.

The **Hotel Zámek**, *tel: (0436) 91 61 12,* and **Hotel Štekl**, *tel: (0436) 91 62 84,* both at *Hrubá Skála*, are excellent hotels at a reasonable price, but need to be pre-booked, especially at peak times. The same applies to the excellent **Hotel Skální Město**, *tel: (0433) 35 13* and the less costly **Turistická Chata**, *tel: (0433) 35 41*, in the *Prachovské Skály*. There are **campsites** at *Sedmihorky, Komárovský Rybník* and *Prachov.*

In addition, very many of the country cottages round about have rooms for hire, with bed and breakfast (they are mostly advertised in German: *Zimmer frei*).

Campers can, of course, stay at one of the official campsites, but there is no problem with setting up a tent in any likely space (but not on farming land without permission).

### SIGHTSEEING

This area is not called the Bohemian Paradise for nothing and has been a popular place for weekend breaks for over a century.

But while there are individual points of interest – such as **Trosky Castle** (0800–1700, closed Mon), the ruins of a 14th-century fortress atop the twin peaks of a basalt outcrop and with a kiosk for welcome refreshments in the grounds – it is the Český Ráj as a whole that attracts. This highly scenic area combines a protected landscape of weathered towers of volcanic rock, with rugged woods and hills, and some rolling agricultural scenery dotted with flower-bedecked cottages.

The **Prachovské Skály** merits a day to itself, for exploring this wonderland of tall and slim volcanic stacks that attracted poets and artists from Prague in the 19th century. The area is rich in rare minerals and semi-precious stones, and local artisans sell jewellery made from them.

From Apr–Oct, certified rock-climbers can climb the sandstone pinnacles and sign their name in the 'visitor's book' at the top.

## JIČÍN

**Station**: The railway station is about 1 km south-east of the town centre, along *Fugnerova.*

**Tourist Information**: Čedok and the Jičín tourist information office are at *Husova 64.*

### ACCOMMODATION

The choice of accommodation is fairly limited. The **Hotel Start**; *Revoluční 836; tel: (0433) 233 63* and the **Pension Bohemia**, *Markova 303; tel: (0433) 244 31* represent the top end of the spectrum. There are several better value pensions, which along with campsites and bed and breakfasts add up to plenty of budget options. Try **Sportcentrum**, *Valdštejnovo náměstí 2; tel: (0433) 219 77*, for information on accommodation.

### SIGHTSEEING

Jičín is an ideal place to stop whilst exploring this region, not only is it situated amongst the most impressive scenery of the Český Ráj, but it is also a good base for hiking tours.

Jičín's would-be benefactor was the 17th-century Habsburg Baron Valdštejn, who claimed Jičín in the Thirty Years' War and made it the capital of his personal empire. He was in the throes of embellishing the town when he was assassinated in 1634. The main square, *Valdštejnovo náměstí*, which he rebuilt in stone in the 1620s, is named after him.

The **Valdštejn Château** and the renaissance-baroque **Kostel sv Jakuba** (St James's Church) are both on the square, while the **Kostel sv Ignáce** (St Ignatius's Church) is just to the west of the square. The **Okresní Museum** (Regional Museum) occupies part of the château and is open 0900–1700, closed Mon.

239

# PRAGUE–PLZEŇ

Plzeň has virtually become synonymous with beer (Pils or Pilsner), disguising the fact that the city of Plzeň is an important administrative and industrial centre. It also has some points of intrinsic interest and is the gateway to two of the Czech Republic's – and indeed Europe's – most handsome towns: the historic spas of Mariánské Lázně (Marienbad) and Karlovy Vary (Karlsbad).

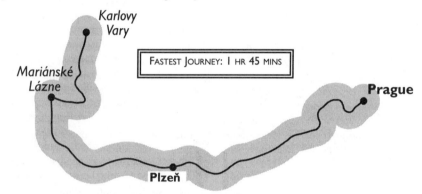

**Karlovy Vary**

**Mariánské Lázne**

FASTEST JOURNEY: 1 HR 45 MINS

**Prague**

**Plzeň**

## TRAINS

**ETT Table:** 870.

### FAST TRACK

→ **Prague–Plzeň**
About 12 trains a day run from Prague's **Praha Hlavní Nádraží** (Central railway station) to Plzeň in summer, some of them express trains which do the journey in 1 hr 45 mins and the remainder slow trains which take 30 mins longer. The bus from Prague is, however, more frequent, faster than the slow train and may be more convenient.

## PLZEŇ

**Station:** The railway station lies about 1 km south-east of the town centre, across the Radbuza river. To get from there to the town centre, turn right from the exit and after the tunnel turn left onto *Americká*, cross the river, and turn right on either *Frantiskánská* or *Smetany*, which lead to the main square, *Náměstí Republiky*.

**Tourist Office:** The **Čedok** office is in the town centre, at *Sedláčkova 12; tel: (019) 22 37 03*, and provides local information and can also arrange accommodation. **CKM** at *Dominikánská 1* can also book private accommodation.

### ACCOMMODATION

Plzeň has some pretty dreary suburbs and it would be best to steer clear of them. *IH* has the only chain hotel. Other good places are the **Central**, *Náměstí Republiky 33; tel: (019) 22 67 57* and the **Panorama**, *V. Lomech 11; tel: (019) 52 43 23*. For travellers on a restricted budget, the **Western Bohemia University**, *Bolevecká 30; tel: (019) 22 30 49* has student hostel rooms available during the summer months. Likewise with the **Ostende** campsite at Velký Bolevecký lake north of town (take the no. 20 bus from the station). Otherwise, the private and pension accommodation available from Čedok and CKM is fairly abundant.

### EATING AND DRINKING

The main hotels have fine but expensive restaurants, while in the area around *Náměstí Republiky* are restaurants and cafeterias to suit most tastes and prices. A specially Plzeň-style treat is the **Prazdroj Brewery restaurant**, beside the brewery gate, where beer is the favoured tipple.

### SIGHTSEEING

Touring the breweries is probably the main reason for stopping at Plzeň, and the **Pilsner-Urquell Prazdroj Brewery**, *U Prazdroje*, some of whose equipment dates from 1842, has paid-for guided tours lasting one hour that leave from Mon–Fri at 1230 (the commentary is usually in German). For slightly less commercially-oriented information, there is the **Pivovarské Muzeum** (Beer Museum), *Veleslavinova 6*, located inside a 15th-century malt house (open Tues–Sun, 1000–1800). The busy main square, *Náměstí Republiky*, has a series of interesting points, including the 16th-century **Radnice** (Town Hall), the Gothic **Kostel sv Bartoloměje** (St Bartholemew's Church), and a column dating from 1681 to the memory of plague victims.

### SIDE TRACKS FROM PLZEŇ

### MARIÁNSKÉ LÁZNĚ

Trains leave every hour or so from Plzeň to Mariánské Lázně, taking 1 hr 10 mins for the trip.

**Station:** *tel: (0165) 53 23.* The train and bus stations stand side by side on *Nádražní nám,* about 1 km from the town centre. To get there, take either the no. 5 trolleybus from in front of the station, or if you prefer to walk, turn right outside the station on *Nádražní* then left on *Hlavní třída* and keep going along this main boulevard.

**Tourist Information:** The **Info-centrum** in Dům Chopin, *Hlavní třída 47; tel: (0165) 2474* or *2482,* dispenses heaps of maps, leaflets and brochures, as well as having lists of accommodation (open Mon–Sat 0900–1800 in summer). **Čedok**, *Třebízského 2/101; tel: (0165) 22 54* also has information and can arrange accommodation. The **Lázenská Informační Služba**, *Mírové Nám. 104/06; tel: (0165) 21 70* is the spa information service and has details about the various cures on offer and can also book rooms and courses of treatment at sanatoria in the town.

### ACCOMMODATION AND FOOD

There are plenty of expensive hotels in Mariánské Lázně, many of them with spa options. *Ex* and *IH* each have a hotel here. There are also several **campsites** around the town, the closest being the **Start Motel** (also with bungalows) just south of the railway station. There are several junior **hostels** in town, the most interesting being the **Juniorhotel Krakonos**, *Okres Cheb; tel: (0165) 26 24,* in a down-at-heel mansion in the hills just east of the Kolonáda. Bed and breakfast is also available in private homes. Information from Čedok or one of the other information services listed above.

There are numerous restaurants along and just behind the western side of *Hlavní Třída,* covering everything

241

from fast-food to typical Czech food and other international cuisine. The **New York** restaurant at *Hlavní Třída 233* has live jazz on weekend evenings in summer from 2000–2300.

### SIGHTSEEING

Mariánské Lázně is a beautiful small town, scenically situated. The elegance of its mineral spas, public buildings, hotels and other facilities recalls the bygone age when taking the waters was *de rigueur* for Europe's well-heeled leisure classes. The town hosts a **Chopin Festival** every Aug.

Many of the finest sights are grouped in the northern complex around the magnificent Lázenská Kolonáda, a carefully restored neo-baroque colonnade. At its northern end is the neo-classical **Křížový Pramen** (Cross Spring), the first spa in Mariánské Lázně. Outside, at the southern end of the colonnade is the **Zpívající Fontána** (Singing Fountain), certainly the most popular tourist spot in town. The fountain jets play in time to classical music recordings. Among the notable churches is the **Kostel sv Vladimíra** (St Vladimir) and the **Anglikánský Kostelík**, both on *Ruská*, and the octagonal, neo-Byzantine **Kostel Nanebevzetí Panny Marie** on *Goethevo nám*. The **Městské Muzeum**, *Goethevo nám 11; tel: (0165) 27 40*, (open Tues–Sun 0900–1600) has information and displays on Mariánské Lázně and on some of the famous people who have visited it, including Goethe.

If time permits, get out of Mariánské Lázně, onto one of the hiking trails around the town, all offer fine views. The spas themselves are a major attraction, of course, but only a few are open to non-guests. These include the

magnificent **Nové Lázně**, *Reitenbergerova 53; tel: (0165) 30 01*.

### KARLOVY VARY

Karlovy Vary is equally famous a spa town as Mariánské Lázně, but is bigger and more industrial. Nevertheless in its old spa zone it has some of the most notable architecture in the country. The 1 hr 30 mins train journey from Mariánské Lázně is very scenic.

**Station: Dolní Nádrazí**; *tel: (017) 233 77* is where trains from Mariánské Lázně arrive (direct trains from Prague and Plzeň arrive at the **Hlavní Nádrazí** (Main station) across the Ohř river. The inter-city bus station is just outside Dolní Nádrazí. **Tourist Information**: **Čedok** is at *Moskevská 2; tel: (017) 222 92* and can arrange private rooms.

### ACCOMMODATION

Karlovy Vary is very popular in the summer and gets very crowded. Čedok is the essential stop for anyone without accommodation: they can get hotel rooms and rooms in private houses. Some smaller hotels only accept payment in German marks. *IH* has a hotel here.

### SIGHTSEEING

The main sights are more or less lined up on the pedestrian promenades along the banks of the Teplá stream, going as far as the **Mlýnská Kolonáda** (Market Colonnade) on *Lázeňská*, and beyond. Here a fantastic procession of buildings rings the changes on architectural style. The twin towers and giant dome of the 18th-century **Kostel sv Maří Magdaleny** (Church of St Mary Magdalene) in *Nám. Svobody* dominates the ensemble. ◪

**242**

# PRAGUE–VIENNA

This route connects two of Europe's great cultural cities – one of them a long-time popular target for tourists and the other a more recent favourite – via Brno, the historic capital of Moravia. The scenery is rugged in some places and rolling in others. In particular it affords a glimpse of the Czech countryside, much of which retains a feel of bygone days in Europe.

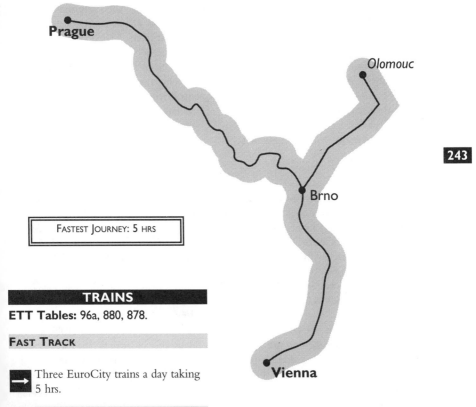

Prague

Olomouc

243

Brno

FASTEST JOURNEY: 5 HRS

Vienna

## TRAINS

**ETT Tables:** 96a, 880, 878.

### FAST TRACK

Three EuroCity trains a day taking 5 hrs.

### ON TRACK

**Prague–Brno**
An almost hourly service of Inter City trains taking just over 3 hrs.

**Brno–Vienna**
Three trains a day to Wien Sudbahnhof. Journey is around 2 hrs.

## BRNO

**Station**: The main station, **Hlavní Nádraží**, is on *Nádražní ul; tel: (05) 422 148 03* or *422 275 62*. For town centre cross this street and head up *Masarykova* towards *Náměstí Svobody*.

**Tourist Office: Taxatour** in the Central Station, 24 hours daily, and **Brno Informační služba**, Old Town Hall, *Radnická 4–10; tel: (05) 422 110 90*; open Mon–Fri 0800–1800, Sat–Sun 0900–1700 (closed Sun, Oct–Apr). Both can help with accommodation of all categories, as can **Čedok**, *Masarykova 37; tel: (05) 422 109 42*, open Mon–Fri 0900–1800 (1700 winter), Sat 0900–1200. There is another Čedok office at the **Exhibition Centre**, *Vystaviste 1; tel: (05) 411 511 11*, but this naturally caters mostly for exhibition visitors. Free maps are available from the tourist offices, but a better map for getting around is Géodezie Brno's 1:12,000 city map.

### GETTING AROUND

Public transport in the city is very good, with buses and trams running from early morning to midnight, followed by a minimal night service of buses. Most of the sights in the city are within walking distance. Use the same tickets for buses and trolley buses, they can be bought from PNS newsagents, yellow ticket machines and hotel receptions.

Taxi drivers are not nearly so rapacious as those of Prague, but they do not like to lag too far behind: always agree a price before getting in or at least ensure that the meter is running.

The bus station on *Benšova ul.* can be reached via a walkway from the train station and is the place for out-of-town services. Both stations have lockers and you can find a 24-hour left-luggage service at the train station.

### MONEY

The **Komerční Bank** at *Náměti Svobody 21* offers good exchange rates and commission of just 1 per cent, as do other banks in the town. Private bureaux de change charge at least 5 per cent, and some even more.

### ACCOMMODATION

The Taxatours office at the station is a good bet for low-cost hotels, pensions and private rooms, as is the Čedok office on *Masarykova*. In the summer months, **CKM**, *Česká 11*, can arrange accommodation in student hostels. Hawkers may approach you at the station, although not so many as in Prague, but the same rules apply: check the location on a map before going there and get an indication of the price and facilities if possible.

An option in the moderate price range and near to the station is the **Hotel Metropole**, *Dornych 5, 60200; tel: 337114-5*. Budget accommodation can be found at the **Hotel Avion**, *Ceskà 20; tel: 4221 5016/4232 1303*, designed in the 1920s by Bohuslav Fuchs. If you can afford to splash out, try the expensive **Grand Hotel**, *Třída 1. Màje 18–20, 65783; tel: 23526*, also near the station and the departure point for Čedok tours.

Hotels in Brno include *BW, Hd, IH*.

### EATING AND DRINKING

Similar general points apply of the kind of food on offer in Brno as for Prague, except that the style tends more towards the Hungarian as opposed to the Austrian, with paprika more in evidence.

In addition, Brno, being a less tourist-oriented city, has fewer restaurants, and a thinner choice of international cuisine styles.

The area around the railway station is good for cheap buffets, while around

*Náměti Svobody* are better quality snack bars and small restaurants. **Černý Medvěd**, *Jakubské Náměstí 1; tel: (05) 422 145 48*, gives good international quality at reasonable prices. For a drink along with some live rock or jazz music, try **Pohadká**, *Ve Smečkách 3; tel (05) 236 227 69*.

### SIGHTSEEING

Once capital of the Austrian crown land of Moravia, Brno, a city of some 400,000 inhabitants, has many historic buildings, but marks of the 19th-century industrial boom remain. Founded in the 10th century, it stands at the confluence of the Svratka and the Svitava rivers, and became part of Bohemia in 1229 before being declared a free city in 1243. Armaments have always been an important industry in Brno (the famous Bren gun used extensively by the British Army in World War II was developed here).

The city has some lovely old streets and squares and a colourful outdoor cabbage market.

Chief sights (most of which close Mon) are within 1 km of the station. Nearby, **Dóm Na Petrově**, the Cathedral of Sts Peter and Paul), crowns Petrov Hill; the Swedes got this far in 1645, laid siege to Brno, and in the process destroyed the then Gothic cathedral, which was subsequently rebuilt in baroque style. The 13th-century **Špilberk Castle**, the citadel atop **Špilberk Hill**, was rebuilt in the 19th century after suffering extensive damage in the Napoleonic wars.

A little way south-west of the castle, in *Mendlovo Náměstí*, is the Augustinian Abbey, now a museum, where in the 19th century the monk Gregor Mendel worked out the fundamentals of genetics by studying the breeding of pea plants in the abbey garden. Garden and pea plants are still

there, and a statue of Mendel faces the church.

The **Old City Hall**, *Radnická ul.*, has Gothic-, Renaissance- and baroque-style elements. Its early parts are the oldest extant construction in Brno. The Gothic portal is by the renowned Brno artist, Anton Pilgram. In the entrance is a wheel made in 1636 as part of a bet to fell a tree, make a wheel and roll it 50 km to Brno in one day. In the crypt of the **Kapucínské Klášter** (the Capuchin Monastery) are over 100 mummified bodies, air-dried in 1650, amongst which is that of the now headless Baron Trenck (1711–49), commander of the pandour troops.

The **Brno International Festival of Music** takes place in Sept and Oct and there are many international trade fairs at the **Brno Exhibition Centre**.

### SIDE TRACKS FROM BRNO

The **Moravský Kras** is a dramatic area in the middle of a forest north-east of Brno, with limestone rocks that form a series of jagged canyons and giant caves filled with stalagmites and stalactites, often with undeground rivers flowing through them. Important traces of prehistoric settlements have been found in some caves. There are four slow trains and two buses a day to nearby **Blansko** (journey time: 1 hr), which contains a museum of the Moravský Kras.

The baroque château of **Slavkov u Brna**, 20 km east by bus, dates from 1752, although it was restored in the 1950s after being heavily damaged in World War II. It has an English-style country garden. The nearby town of Slavkov u Brna has a 16th-century Renaissance Town Hall. The locality is best known as the site of the Battle of Austerlitz in 1805. In what became known as the 'Battle of the Three Emperors', Napoleon brilliantly and decisively defeated a combined Austro-Russian army, having first dangled before them the prospect of their doing the same to his own. The 26 m Austerlitz Memorial stands atop the Pratzen Heights and nearby there is a museum and snack bar.

## OLOMOUC

A beautifully situated old town on the banks of the Morava, can be reached by frequent bus (every hour or so) or by infrequent and slow train from Brno. It is one of those scenic gems that often get overlooked by tourists intent on better publicised destinations. A university town, it was capital of Moravia from the 12th century until the mid-17th century, and it retains much of the historic interest one would expect from

an old capital. Since the departure of the Soviet soldiers who had been stationed nearby for 20 years, Olomouc has become one of the more lively cities of Moravia, partly due to its growing student population. Among the sights to look for are the 14th-century **Town Hall** (Radnice) in *Horní Náměstí*, and the adjacent, splendidly baroque **Trinity Column** (Sousosí Nejsvě#08tějsí trojice). In addition, the main square has two beautiful baroque fountains. In *Václavské Náměstí* stands the **St Wenceslas Cathedral** (Dóm Svatého Václava), which has been rebuilt and restored several times since its founding in the 11th century. Its main aspect is now Gothic and neo-Gothic. Mozart was laid up for six weeks with smallpox in its deanery in 1767. Every July the national garden festival Flora Olomouc is held here. 🔼

# RIGA

The capital of Latvia, Riga is an old Hanseatic port with a turbulent history and plenty of reminders of its long-established German, Swedish and Russian connections. It's also the closest thing in the Baltic States to a real metropolis with a thriving commercial centre, wide-ranging culture and a burgeoning night-life. An extra plus is the proximity of the Kurzeme coastline, with its infinite expanse of white dunes and beaches.

## TOURIST INFORMATION

In the absence of a city information office, try the following: **Latvian Tourist Club**, Skarnu iela 22; tel: 221 731, for brochures, maps and leaflets; **Latvia Tours**, Grecinieku Str. 22/24; tel: 221 896, and **Marina Travel Ltd**, Smilshu iela 14; tel: 213 082, for help with accommodation. A quicker alternative may be to get hold of the listings magazine, Riga in Your Pocket, available from bookshops and newsstands.

## ARRIVING AND DEPARTING

### Airport

**Lidosta Riga**; tel: 207 009. Riga airport is located 8 km south west of the city centre. Facilities in the single terminal include currency exchange, baggage room, post office, news-stand and small duty-free shop. Bus no. 22, departing every half-hour, will take you straight into town.

### Station

**Centrala Stacija** (Central Station),

Stacijas laukums; tel: 233095. The station, a large modern building, is just a few mins walk from the centre of town. For information (Russian and Latvian only), go to the window to the right of the main booking hall. There's a currency exchange office opposite (open 0830–2130. For tickets to local destinations (including the seaside) go to the small hall with a separate entrance to the right of the station. The baggage room is in the basement and there are lockers next to platform 6. For shops, bars and cafés, even a hairdresser's, go to the lower hall adjacent to the platforms. Take special note that the advance booking office is in another building entirely, on Turgeneva 14; tel: 234396. English is spoken here and the staff are helpful. International trains depart for Tallinn, Warsaw, Berlin, Moscow and St Petersburg.

### Buses

**Autoosta** (bus station) Pragas iela; tel: 213 611. Open 0500–2400. International destinations include Berlin, Tallinn, Vilnius, Klaipeda and Warsaw.

## GETTING AROUND

Most of the major sights are in the Old Town and are easily managed on foot.

### Public Transport

Riga has a comprehensive local transport network of trams, trolley-buses and buses, operating 0530–0030. Some central routes have an hourly night service.

Tickets for all public transport are sold at news-stands, kiosks, post offices and sometimes on the vehicle. There is a sin-

247

gle flat fare for most destinations. All tickets must be punched on board.

**Taxis**

State-owned taxis, *tel: 334 041.* Taxis abound in Riga but you're advised to stick to the official cabs (orange and black markings) wherever possible. Make sure the meter is switched on and agree on a price beforehand – don't expect to pay more than 3 Lats for any daytime journey across the city.

**Accommodation**

There's a wide range of accomodation, much of it reasonably priced and fairly central.

Hotel chains in Riga include *Mp, Rd.* If money is no object you'll probably want to stay in luxurious surroundings in the German-run **Hotel de Rome**, *Kalku 28; tel: 222 841.*

A number of medium-priced hotels are being upgraded and offer value for money. A good case in point is the **Viktorija**, *A. Čaka iela 55; tel: 272 305.* A clean and spacious alternative, though a little further out, is the **Brigita**, *Saulkalnes iela 11; tel: 623 000.*

There's a fair spread of budget accomodation but most places have only a few rooms so you'll have to book in advance. **Radi un Draugi**, *Marstalu 1; tel: 220 372,* is a new modern pension in the heart of the Old Town. For bed and breakfast try **Patricia**, *Elizabetes iela 22/4a; tel: 284 868,* or the small guest house belonging to the **Tourist Club of Latvia**, *Skarnu 22; tel: 221 731.*

**Youth hostels** are thin on the ground. For the latest information contact Head Office, *Minsterijas 8/10; tel: 225 307* or try the hostel **Imantu**,

*Zolitudes 30; tel: 413 847* (take the local train to Jurmala and alight at Imanta).

**Eating and Drinking**

Old Riga in particular abounds with eating places of every category, from the gourmet restaurant to the humble snack bar. A pavement café culture, too, is well-established in the squares, especially *Doma Laukums.*

Riga may be a port, but it's not a particularly cosmopolitan city – there are relatively few ethnic restaurants and the first authentic fish restaurant has only recently opened. **Zivju**, *R. Vagnera iela 4; tel: 216 713,* is relatively expensive but the English-speaking staff will help you negotiate the menu. For Italian cuisine, head for **1739**, *Skarnu 6; tel: 211 398.*

The Art Deco ambience of **Andaluzijas Suns**, *Elizabetes iela 81/3; tel: 288 304,* makes it popular with locals, so book in advance. For a genuine Latvian flavour try **Sena Riga**, *Aspazijas blvd; tel: 216 869.* **Fredis Café**, *Audeju iela 5; tel: 213 731,* has excellent, tasty snacks and a buzzing atmosphere. A close rival in both respects is **Pie Kristapa**, *Jauniela 25/9; tel: 227 530.* Fast food chains (e.g. McDonalds) have arrived in Riga, but the best pizzeria is **Lulu Pica**, *Gertrudes 27; tel: 296 818.*

If you're buying food for picnics, look no further than the famous Zeppelin hangars, the location of the **Central Market**, *Pragas 1,* open 0700–1800 (Sun and Mon 0700–1600).

Latvia is well-known for its beers, such as *Aldaris,* and you'll find them on sale virtually everywhere. The bar in the courtyard of St John's Church, off *Jana iela,* has a nice atmosphere but like other cafés in the old town closes around 1700. For late-night drinking try the new, welcoming **Dublin Irish Bar**, *R. Vagnera*

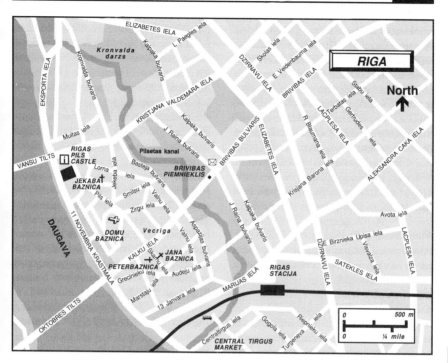

*iela 16*; or the raucous **Piebalga**, *Laipu iela 7*.

## Communications

**Central Post Office**, *Brivibas iela 21; tel: 224 155*. Open 24 hrs. The local telephone area code is 2 (8 for digital phones). Look out for the new card or coin-operated pay phones – the old blue phone booths only take tokens. If you're calling abroad, the **International Telephone Centre**, *Brivibas iela 33*, is open Mon–Sat 0900–2000, Sun 0900–1900

## Consulates

**Canada:** *Doma Laukums 4; tel: 783 0141.*

**UK:** *Alunana 5; tel: 733 8126.*

**USA:** *Raina Blvd 7; tel: 210 005.*

Citizens of Australia, New Zealand and South Africa should try the UK consulate.

## ENTERTAINMENT AND EVENTS

Latvia has a distinguished cultural tradition. The **National Opera/Riga Ballet** are currently performing in the **Kongress Zale** in Kronvalda Parks. The two main concert venues are the **Wagner Hall**, *R. Vagnera 4* and the **Concert Hall of the Philharmonic**, *Amatu iela 6*. Organ recitals are held every summer in the main churches. American **films** with Latvian subtitles are now showing at **Daile**, *Kr. Barona iela 31* and **Oskars**, *Skolas iela 2*. For details of what's on, see the listings magazine *Riga In Your Pocket*.

Riga's nightclub scene is constantly changing. One of the most popular places in town for discos and a whole range of art happenings is **Slepenais Eksperiments**, *Skunu 15* (open until 0500). **Underground**, *Slokas 1* (open until 0600) is a well-known conventional discotheque, while **Bimini**, *A. Čaka iela 67/9* has jazz nights, karaoke, techno and disco music.

### SHOPPING

Riga's main department store is the Soviet-style **Centrs**, *Audeju 16* (open Mon–Sat 0800–2000, Sun 1000–1630). For souvenirs, **Rukis**, *Gertrudes 32* (open Mon–Fri 1000–1700, Sat–Sun 1000–1600), sells a range of handicrafts and hand-made wooden toys.

### SIGHTSEEING

Riga's sights and monuments are concentrated in the highly picturesque **Vecriga** (Old Town), which is easily manageable on foot. This is a quite distinct area of cobbled streets, 17th-century burgher houses, with attractively painted façades and playful sculptures, and old warehouses. Also noteworthy sight is the **Latvian Parliament** building, *Jekaba iela 11*, in the style of a Florentine Renaissance palace.

### Churches
The towering green spire of **Sv. Petera baznica** (St Peter's Church), *Kungu iela*, now made of iron rather than wood, is a major landmark. Take the lift to the viewing platform at 72 metres for a magnificent panorama of the city. The charming courtyard of **Sv. Jana baznica** (St John's Church) *Skarnu iela*, incorporates part of the old city wall and was the site of Riga's first castle. Don't miss the grilled-over window in the south wall where two monks were bricked in for life in the 14th century. Riga's massive brick **Domu baznica**(Dom Cathedral), with walls 2 metres thick, dominates the enormous cobbled square of the same name. Begun in 1211, it contains an elegant pulpit and a powerful organ with more than 6700 pipes. Next door is the intriguing **Museum of History and Navigation** (open Wed–Sun 1100–1700). In Medieval times the 'sinners' bell' of the **Jekaba baznica**, *Jekaba iela*, tolled for criminals about to be executed. This attractive 13th-century Gothic building stood outside the city walls.

### The Castle
**Riga Pils** originally dates from the 14th century but has been rebuilt many times since. At various times in its chequered history it has been occupied by Swedish, Polish and Russian governors as well as by the Latvian president. The best views are from the **Vansu tilts** (Vanus bridge). The most impressive remnant of the old fortifications is the massive red brick **Pulvertornis** (Powder Tower), *Smilsu 20*, now a **War Museum** (open Tues–Sun 1000–1800). Between the old and the new town you can see part of the wholly separate 19th-century defences known as **Bastejkalns** (Bastion Hill).

### New Town
Modern Riga is largely 19th-century and was built under German as well as Russian influence. It's a spacious and sedate town with wide, elegant boulevards and parks and some striking Jugendstil architecture. The focal point is the **Freedom Monument** on *Brivibas bulvaris*. The statue, known as 'Milda' to the locals, holds a cluster of stars above her head, representing Latvia's three main regions – Kurzeme, Vidzeme and Latgale. Dating from 1935, it has come to stand as a symbol for all those Latvians who defied the post-war Soviet occupiers. It's worth taking trolley-bus no. 20 to the **Riga TV tower** for the excellent views across the city. From here you can see the attractive

woodland **Mezaparks**, home of Riga zoo.

## Museums

The Medieval **Juras Kirik** (St George's Church), *Skarnu iela 10,* is now the excellent **Museum of Applied Arts** (open Tues–Sun 1000–1700). Apart from the partially restored interior of the church there are exhibitions of tapestries, ceramics, jewellery and bookmaking. For a complete contrast, take bus no. 21 to the tongue-in-cheek **Motor Museum**, *Eisensteina 6* (open Tues–Sun 1000–1800), where you can see vehicles belonging to such notorious figures as Stalin, Brezhnev and the former East German leader, Erich Honecker, with their waxwork dummies at the wheel. The **Menczendorf House**, *Grecinieku 18* (open Wed–Sun 1000–1700), is an opportunity to see the former residence of a wealthy Riga merchant. There's a collection of contemporary furniture and 18th-century frescos and the English-speaking guide is a fund of knowledge on the subject.

## OUT OF TOWN

Just 20 km west of Riga is the beautiful seaside resort of **Jurmala**, where the Russian and German governing classes built their holiday homes in the 19th century. The name, meaning 'sea shore', actually applies to a string of small towns and resorts that hug the beaches, sand dunes and pine woods (all 30 km of them) along the Baltic shore. Following a five-year clean-up programme, the main beaches are now safe for swimming. There are shops, cafés and a new tourist information office on *Jomas iela* (Majori) which will book accomodation if you want to stay. Jurmala is reached by train (half hourly) to Majori or Dubulti, or by

boat along the Lielupe and Daugava rivers.

## SIDE TRACKS FROM RIGA

## LIEPAJA

**Tourist Office:** the travel agency at *Rigas 3* has brochures and maps for the Kurzeme region and will also help with accommodation.

**Railway and Bus Station:** *Station Square; tel (234) 512 84.* There are three trains daily to and from Riga.

The historic coastal town of Liepaja stands on an 18 km strip of land between Lake Liepaja and the Baltic Sea. It has only one hotel, the **Liva**, *Liela 11; tel: 25345,* but a good selection of shops, cafés and restaurants. The sights include some 17th-century warehouses and two historic churches, one of which boasts the largest mechanical organ in Europe. There are concerts in the **Summer Garden** and, in Aug, Latvia's annual rock festival, **Amber of Liepaja**. The area is typical of the northern Kurzeme, with tree-backed dunes and white sands.

## KULDIGA

The ancient Courland town of Kuldiga lies about 150 km west of Riga and can be reached by bus in 3½ hrs. It stands in a picturesque setting on the Venta River and has some interesting buildings, including a wooden 17th century **Town Hall**, and 18th-century granary and several churches, the most impressive of which is the Roman Catholic **Holy Trinity**, with its rich rococo interior. There are good views of the surrounding countryside from the castle hill just outside the town. 🔁

251

# RIGA-TALLINN

This route takes you through some of the more attractive parts of the Latvian and Estonian countryside. The landscape is generally flat and densely wooded, but look out for the occasional picturesque hamlet and even a goatherd or two!

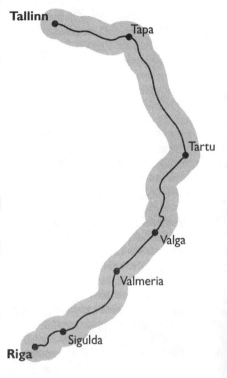

## TRAINS

**ETT Table:** 914

### FAST TRACK

Two through trains a day taking 6 to 8 hrs. Advance seat reservations required.

### ON TRACK

**Riga–Sigulda**
Frequent local service taking just over 1 hrs.

**Sigulda–Valmiera**
Seven trains a day. Journey time 1 hr 30 mins.

**Valmiera–Valga**
Just one train a day taking 1 hr.

**Valga–Tartu**
Seven trains a day with journey times of about 2 hrs.

**Tartu–Tallin**
Six trains each day taking 2 hrs.

FASTEST JOURNEY: 6 HRS

## SIGULDA

**Station:** *Stacijas iela.*
**Bus Station:** *Raina 3; tel: 972 106*
**Tourist Office:** *Lakstigalas 9; tel: 971 213*

## ACCOMMODATION AND FOOD

Probably the best place to stay is the **Hotel Siguldas Senleja,** *Turaidas iela 4; tel: 972 162,* nicely situated across the river from the town and with reasonable facilities including two bars, a restaurant and even a casino. The **Sigulda Hotel,** *Pils iela 6; tel: 872 263,* is handy for the station. For a stay in a summer cottage (also for bike and boat hire) contact the tourist office. There is little choice in the way of cafés and restaurants – most of what is available is within easy reach of the station. There are also refreshment points close to Turaida Castle

## SIGHTSEEING

If you're vigorous and healthy you can cover most of the sights on foot. Bus no. 12 runs a regular service to **Taraida** and **Krimalda** but it's a roundabout trip. A more enjoyable way of crossing the river is by cable car: the Sigulda stop is at the end of *Baumana iela.* Cars depart at 30-min intervals and you look down on the Gauja from a height of 40 metres. Sigulda commands a remarkably picturesque location at the foot of the Gauja valley gorge. The area is popular with tourists for its spectacular scenery and views, woodland trails, water and winter sports, ancient caves and ruined castles, and to top it all, the flora and fauna of the 920 sq km of the **Gauja National Park.** **Sigulda Castle** dates from the time in the 13th century, when the local Liv communities were terrorised by German crusading knights and Princes of the Church. From the ruins there are glimpses of the more imposing **Turaida Castle** on the opposite side of the valley. **Sigulda Church** also dates from the 13th century but the present building is 18th century. Beyond the ruined **Krimalda Castle and Manor House**

(19th century) is the splendidly restored **Turaida Castle** and **Church,** now a museum. The original fort was built in 1214 by order of the warrior Archbishop of Riga. You can learn more about the local history inside and there's a good look out from one of the towers. There are several caves in the area. The best known, **Gutmanis,** has graffiti dating back to the 17th century and descends to a depth of 14 metres.

## VALMIERA

**Station:** *Stacijas lauk; tel: 733 23.* 2 km from town centre
**Bus Station:** *Stacijas 1; tel: 247 28.*
**Tourist Office:** In the **Museum of Valmiera,** *Bruninieku 3; tel: 327 33..* Sells guidebooks and maps

The historic centre of the town (founded 14th century) is located between the meandering Gauja river and its tributary the Azkalna – take *Rigas* and *Bruninieku.* The most interesting architectural monument is **St Simanis Church,** one of the oldest stone buildings in Latvia.

## VALKA/VALGA

**Station:** *Jaama pst. 10; tel: 402 48.*
**Tourist Office:** *Kesk 11; tel: 458 27.*
The border divides the town (known as Valka in Latvia, Valga in Estonia). Take one of the through trains (twice daily) in order to avoid the isolated Lugazi station on the Latvian side of the frontier. Valga itself has little to offer the tourist but the surrounding area is attractive, scenic and ripe for discovery: for information about **Otepää Nature Reserve** contact *28 Kolga tee, EE2513 Otepää; tel: 558 76.*

## TARTU

**Station:** *tel: 309 67.* The ornate 19th-century weatherboard station is within easy walking distance of the town centre. There is a small currency exchange office, bar and restaurant, but no English spoken at the information counter. Tokens for left-luggage lockers must be bought from the stationmaster.

**Bus Station:** *Turu 2; tel: 761 19.*

**Tourist Office:** *Küütri 3; tel: 321 41,* open Mon–Fri 1000–1800 Ask for the very useful *Tartu this Week,* which has listings, maps and general information.

## ACCOMMODATION AND FOOD

There are about a dozen hotels in Tartu but most are very small. Fairly typical and reasonably priced is the **Park**, *Vallikraavi 23; tel: 336 63.* A more upmarket option is the modern **Taru Hotell**, *Rebase 9; tel: 737 00.* It's about 2 km from the centre of Tartu and has its own restaurant, bars and sauna; credit cards accepted. There are also several motels. For family accommodation contact **E-Tour**, *Kalevi 59; tel: 321 23.*

Most restaurants, cafés and bars are located in the streets off *Raekoja Plats.* There's a **Pizza-Bar** on *Tiigi 11* and a well-signposted bistro on *Rüütli.* The **Tarvas** on *Riia 2; tel: 322 53* claims to offer 'the best cuisine in Tartu'; or you might like to try the new **Central** restaurant, *Raekoja Plats 3; tel: 412 97.* It's open daily until 0200, there's a menu in English and German and an excellent choice of dishes, some bordering on the exotic – for example alligator in lemon sauce.

## SIGHTSEEING

**Buses** run from around 0600 weekdays, 0800 weekends to midnight. Tickets are obtainable from the driver and validated on the bus. There is a **taxi** rank near *Raekoja Plats; tel: 338 67*

Downtown Tartu has a genteel,

unruffled air and it's hard to believe this is Estonia's second city, with a population of 109,000. It's at its liveliest in term time when the students are in residence.

Although founded in the 11th century, little of medieval Tartu survives, with the notable exception of **St John's Church** on *Jaani*, which boasts a remarkable collection of terracotta statues. Most of the surviving architecture dates from the 18th-19th centuries and is neo-Classical in style. A distinguished example is the main building of the **University** (*Ülikooli*), though the handsome façade is in need of a lick of paint. Founded by Gustavus II Adolphus of Sweden in 1632 and closed for 100 years following the Great Northern War, the university now has some 8000 students, taught in more than 70 departments.

The historic centre of Tartu is **Raekoja Plats** (Market Square), where there are a number of fine 18th-century town houses. The salmon-coloured **Town Hall**, dating from 1778–84, has a restrained elegance. **Toomemägi** (Cathedral Hill) is Tartu's other main attraction. A fortified settlement in the 5th–6th centuries, the park contains several monuments to Estonian heroes and, more obviously, the extensive ruins of the massive red brick Gothic **Cathedral**. A little to the north on the site of the old bastion (known as the Hill of Kisses) is an ancient sacrificial stone.

Also worth a look is the 19th-century **Observatory**, now an astronomy museum and the two bridges spanning *Lossi* – the neo-Classical **Angel's Bridge** and the later (1913) **Devil's Bridge**. There are regular exhibitions (mainly modern art) at the **Art Museum** on *Vallikraavi* and the gallery on *Raekoja Plats 18.* For Tartu's history visit the **City Museum** on *Oru 2.*

# ST PETERSBURG

Russia's second city and former capital is the brainchild of one man, the westernising Tsar, Peter the Great. A place where almost every other building is a palace or architectural monument of some kind – there are more than 8000 listed for conservation – St Petersburg is still breathtakingly beautiful, despite the crumbling façades and peeling paintwork.

## TOURIST INFORMATION

There is at present no city information office in St Petersburg. The Intour or service desk in any large hotel will help with tours, restaurant bookings, theatre tickets, train and flight reservations, etc. The old Intourist offices, now the **St Petersburg Tourist Company**, *Isaakievskaya ploshchad 11; tel: 315 5129,* is only really useful for arranging tours. The main hotels are also the best source of up-to-date maps and English-language listings publications, provided free of charge. These include *St Petersburg Press* and *Neva Week*. Also very useful is the *Traveller's Yellow Pages and Handbook for Saint Petersburg*.

## ARRIVING AND DEPARTING

**Airport: Pulkovo,** *tel: 104 3444.* St Petersburg's international airport is located 17 kilometres south of the city centre. There are two terminals: Pulkovo 1, handling domestic flights including Moscow, and Pulkovo 2 for international arrivals and departures – there are daily flights to most European capitals and major US cities. The limited facilities include a small gift shop in arrivals; larger

duty-free shop and two bars serving light snacks in the departure lounge. The currency exchange office has limited opening hours and is generally unreliable. There is no efficient public transport link from Pulkovo to the city centre, so you'll either have to pre-book your transfer to the hotel or take a taxi. The following services offer English speaking drivers: **Matralen,** *Lyubotinsky proezd 5, tel: 298 1294;* **Pribaltiyskaya,** *Korablestroiteley ulitsa 14; tel: 356 1074.*

**Stations: Moskovsky Vokzal** (alternative name: Glavny), *Nevsky prospekt 85; tel: 168 0111* (metro: *Ploshchad Vosstaniya*) for trains to Moscow. Formerly known as the Nicholas Station, this terminal was the work of K. A. Thon who also designed the Great Kremlin Palace in Moscow. Many of the major revolutionary disturbances of 1917 took place in the square outside.

**Varshavsky Vokzal,** *Obvodnovo kanala naberezhnaya 118; tel: 168 0111* (metro: *Baltiyskaya*) for trains to Poland and the Baltic States. **Finlyandsky Vokzal,** *Lenina ploshchad 6; tel: 168 0111* (metro: *Ploshchad Lenina*) for trains to Helsinki. Lenin arrived here after travelling through Germany on the famous sealed train on 3 April 1917. In a large glass case on platform 5 you can see Locomotive 293, which carried him into hiding in Finland later in the year.

The facilities in all terminals are basic, with little more than a left luggage office and cheap snack bars. The only information in English is at the Intourist offices. Watch your bags at all times. All main line and international tickets must be paid for in hard currency. You can buy them either at the Intourist office or at a hotel or the Central Ticket Office (*Tsentralny Zheleznodorozhnye Kassy*), *Ekaterininsky (Griboedova) kanala naberezhnaya 24* (open Mon–Sat 0800–2000; Sun 0800–1600) at windows 100–104, 2nd floor.

**Ferries:** Sea Terminal, **Morskoy Vokzal**, *Morskoy Slavy ploshchad, Vasilevsky Ostrov; tel: 355 1616* trolleybus: 10 and 12.

### GETTING AROUND

While St Petersburg's majestic avenues are very fine to look at, they quickly become wearying to the tourist on foot. Fortunately, the public transport system is comprehensive and extremely cheap. All transport runs from 0530 to 0100. There is no official transport map, but most city maps include bus and tram routes as well as a metro plan. Lost property, *tel: 278 3690*.

### Tickets

Tickets for all forms of local transport (buses, trams, trolley-buses and the metro) are sold at metro stations and kiosks. Buy *yedinye bilyeti* and you'll be able to ride on any form of transport for a month. Tickets are either punched on board the vehicle or in the booking hall of the station. To travel on the metro you can also buy tokens (*talony*) which should be dropped into one of the turnstiles at the top of the escalator.

### Metro

A pale shadow of its Moscow counterpart, the St Petersburg underground is cheap and fairly reliable but far from comprehensive. All four lines are coloured coded. A basic knowledge of the Cyrillic alphabet is all but essential for negotiating the metro. Remember that each station has its own name, even two

stations on the same site but on different lines. Stations are indicated by a large red letter M. Indicator boards in the station give exit and transfer information. Check you're on the right line and heading in the right direction by studying the route map on the tunnel wall. If you're changing lines, look for a sign with the word *perekhod* and the name of the station you want. To get back to street level, follow the signs *vykhod*. Lost property, *tel: 222 2085*

### Other Transport

Look for the signs (T) for **trams**, (A) for **buses**, (m) for **trolley-buses**. Most vehicles, especially on the Nevsky Prospekt are extremely crowded and there is considerable amount or re-routing, often with no notice.

Not for nothing is St Petersburg known as the 'Venice of the North'. Apart from canal and river tours, there is a regular **hydrofoil** service (in summer) to Petrodvorets, departing from the Neva Embankment, outside the Hermitage, at half-hourly intervals. This involves a highly pleasurable trip along the Neva River and is still extremely cheap. However double-check the time of the last boat back to town!

### Taxis

There are plenty of taxis, but beware of the unofficial ones: the authorised cabs have a chequered pattern and the letter T on the side. It is best to order a cab in advance from the hotel (at least 1 hr in advance). Never take a taxi without agreeing a price in advance and never get into a cab where there is already another passenger. Official taxis: *tel: 312 0022*

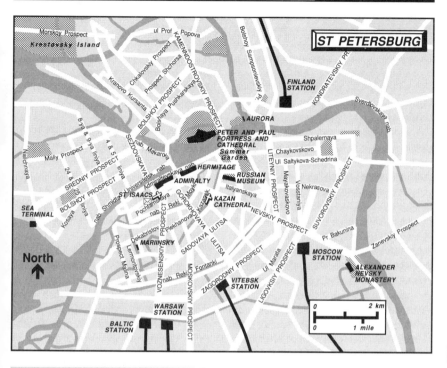

ST PETERSBURG

North ↑

## Accommodation

Most of the newer hotels are in the luxury class and, as in Moscow, there is a distinct shortage of good-value medium-price and budget accommodation.

Hotel chains in St Petersburg include Re. Several major hotels have been renovated and upgraded in recent years, including two famous pre-revolutionary establishments: the **Astoria**, *Bolshaya Morskaya ulitsa 39; tel: 210 5032* and the **Grand Hotel Europe**, *Mikhaylovskaya ulitsa 1/7; tel: 119 6000,* which recently made an appearance in the James Bond movie *Goldeneye.*

The **St Petersburg**, *Vyborgskaya naberezhnaya 5/2; tel: 542 9123,* metro: *Ploshchad Lenina,* has a nice location across the river from the Cruiser *Aurora.*

It's about 20 mins walk from the Winter Palace and the prices are more than reasonable for the facilities on offer.

The main drawback of the **Pribaltiyskaya Hotel**, *Korablestroiteley ulitsa 14; tel: 356 0158,* metro *Primorskaya* then bus, is its remoteness from the centre although it does offer fine views across the Gulf of Finland. The **Mir Hotel**, *Gastello ulitsa 17; tel: 108 5166,* metro *Moskovskaya,* is competitively priced and, while situated in the southern suburbs, is convenient for the metro.

Some of the old Soviet hotels are still a bargain if you're prepared to put up with minor inconveniences. The best located is the **Oktyabrskaya Hotel**, *Ligovsky prospekt 10; tel: 315 7501,* metro: *Ploshchad Vosstaniya,* just across the road from the Moscow station.

The **St Petersburg International**

Hostel, *3-ya Rozhdestvenskaya (Sovyet-skaya) ulitsa 28; tel: 277 0569*, metro *Ploshchad Vosstaniya*, is an American venture aimed at youngsters and backpackers and will help out in a general way with information, reservations etc. **Hostel 'Holiday'**, *Ulitsa Mikhailova 1; tel: 542 7364*, metro: *Ploshchad Lenina*, provides similar facilities and offers fine views across the Neva. It is now possible to stay with a Russian family in St Petersburg. However, to ensure that everything runs smoothly and that you're not disappointed, you should book through a recognised organisation such as the **Host Families Association**, *tel: 275 1992* which – most important – will also help arrange visas.

### Eating and Drinking

Eating out in St Petersburg is expensive. However, while private restaurants haven't proliferated to the same extent as Moscow, there is a reasonable amount of choice (though nothing specifically for vegetarians). A good starting point is the main shopping street, *Nevsky prospekt*, where you'll find eateries of all types, with the exception of the major western fast-food chains – surprisingly, perhaps, these haven't yet caught on here. If money is no object, you're probably best advised to head for the major hotels, most of which offer Russian and international cuisines. The Brasserie in the **Grand Hotel Europe** is fairly typical in its elegant surroundings and attentive service.

For an unusual setting, try the **Austeria**, *Petropavlovskaya krepost; tel: 210 5906*, where you'll be served classy Russian dishes in one of the bastions of the Peter-Paul Fortress. One of the best Georgian restaurants in St Petersburg is the **Tbilisi**, *Sytninskaya ulitsa 10; tel: 232 9391* – it's not very central but has a wel-

coming atmosphere, good food and fine Georgian wines. Known in the 18th century as **Wulf et Béranger**, the **Literaturnoe Café**, *Nevsky prospekt 18; tel: 312 6057*, is famous as the place where the poet Pushkin dined with his second before going off to be killed in a duel. The literary associations are traded on mercilessly. **Le Café**, *Nevsky prospekt 142*, is also expensive but has a homely atmosphere and American-style cooking. Two good lunch spots are the beautifully decorated **Dr Oetker**, *Nevsky prospekt 40*, and the **Beer Garden**, *Nevsky prospekt 86*.

Don't leave St Petersburg without visiting the city's famous pre-revolutionary delicatessen, still known as **Yeliseev's**, *Nevsky prospekt 52*. Even if you don't want to buy anything, the stained glass windows, marble counters and chandeliers are definitely worth a look. There are many western-run food stores, for example **Kalinka Stockmann Supermarket**, *Finlyandsky prospekt 1*, just behind the St Petersburg Hotel.

### Communications

**Central Post Office**, *Pochtamtskaya ulitsa 9; tel: 312 83 05* (open Mon–Sat 0900–2000, Sun 1000–1800). The most convenient poste restante (general delivery) is **St Petersburg 1904**, *Nevsky prospekt 64*.

**Telephones**: the local area code is 812. For local calls you'll need to buy *zhetony* (tokens) from a metro station. To make an international call, go to your hotel desk or the **St Petersburg International Telephone and Telegraph Office**, *Bolshaya Morskaya ulitsa 3–5* (open daily, except 1230–1300).

### Consulates
**South Africa:** *Naberezhnaya Reki Moyk*

**258**

11; *tel:* 553 1742, tram no. 12.
**UK:** *Proletarskoy Diktatury ploshchad 5; tel:* 119 6036, metro: *Chernyshevskaya.*
**USA:** *Furshtadtskaya ulitsa 15; tel:* 274 82 35, metro: *Chernyshevskaya.*

## ENTERTAINMENT AND EVENTS

Theoretically you can buy tickets to all major events and venues by simply turning up and asking; however this is not usually the way things work out in practice. Western visitors end up paying in hard currency by ordering through the service bureaux of hotels, though prices are not unreasonable. An alternative is the **Central Box Office No.1,** *Nevsky Prospekt 42; tel: 311 3183.*

St Petersburg's world renowned opera and ballet company still trades under two names: the **Mariinsky** or **Kirov,** *Teatralnaya ploshchad 1/2.* Nijinsky, Nureyev and Pavlova all danced at the Mariinsky, and Tchaikovsky's *Nutcracker* and *Sleeping Beauty* had their premieres here.An alternative is the **Maly Teatr,** *Ploshchad Iskusstv 1.* The main concert venues are the **Bolshoy Zal Filarmonii,** *Mikhailovskaya ulitsa 2,* the **Glinka Kapella,** *Reki Moyki naberezhnaya 20,* which continues the traditions of the Imperial Chapel Choir and the **Maly Zal,** *Nevsky prospekt 30,* the second venue of the St Petersburg Philharmonic. An all-purpose venue (rock concerts are often performed here) is the modern **Kontsertny Zal Oktyabrsky,** *Ligovsky prospekt 6.* Winter ice shows are performed at the **Yubileyni Sports Palace,** *Prospekt Dobrolyubova 18.* The **Circus,** *Ploshchad Belinskovo,* is closed in July and August.

Most films showing in the city have been dubbed into Russian. Check English-language listings magazines like *St Petersburg Press* for occasional private showings of films in English. Ice hockey matches are played throughout the year at the **Yubileyny Sports Palace,** *Prospekt Dobrolyubova 18.* The main soccer venue is the **Kirov Stadium,** on Krestovsky Island. For match details (the season is Mar–Oct) *tel: 235 5435.*

By far the most important festival in St Petersburg is the **Bely Nochy** (White Nights), 21 Jun–11 Jul, when the sun never sets and the city is bathed in a glowing twilight. Although there are special events in this season, the best places to be are the *Nevsky prospekt* or the river embankments, where parties are traditionally held and fireworks set off.

The **Russian Orthodox Christmas** (7 Jan) and **Easter** are marked by impressive church services. Russians go to town at **New Year** with parties and fireworks, and the restaurants are packed with inebriated revellers. Russia's newest public holiday, **Independence Day,** 12 Jun, is now marked with a wide range of special events.

## SHOPPING

St Petersburg's main shopping street is *Nevsky prospekt.* The beautiful shopping mall known as **Gostiny Dvor,** *Nevsky prospekt 35,* (founded in the 18th century) is still undergoing repairs – an alternative is **Passazh,** *Nevsky prospekt 48.* You can buy toiletries and other western necessaries at the 24-hour supermarket near Ploshchad Vosstaniya metro.

If you want typical Russian souvenirs, begin by looking in the vicinity of **Gostiny Dvor,** where bona fide street traders usually operate. For art books, try **Iskusstvo,** *Nevsky prospekt 52.*

## SIGHTSEEING

The **State Hermitage,** *Dvortsovaya naberezhnaya 34,* is not only one of the

**259**

world's largest and most magnificent picture galleries (on a par with the Louvre or the Vatican), but also the former residence of the Russian imperial family. The **Winter Palace** was designed by the Italian architect, Bartolomeo Rastrelli, in 1754-62. A tour of the royal apartments includes the sumptuous ballroom known as the **Nicholas Hall**, the **Malachite Hall** where Alexander Kerensky's Provisional Government surrendered to Lenin's Bolshevik forces in 1917, the **throne room of Peter the Great** and the **Gallery of 1812**, with its portraits of the heroes of the Napoleonic Wars. The Hermitage catalogue is akin to a roll-call of Old Masters. All the great names are here, from Raphael and El Greco to Leonardo, but the gallery is most famous for its collection of 19th- and 20th-century French paintings, some of which have only recently been brought out of storage. (Open Tues–Sun 1030–1800)

St Petersburg's elegant main avenue, *Nevsky prospekt*, extends 5 km eastward from Palace Square to the River Neva. The imposing frontages, elaborate bridges, stunning palaces and perfectly proportioned squares combine to make it a principal sight.

The avenue takes its name from the **Alexander Nevsky Monastery** at the far end of the avenue – the cemetery is the last resting place of a number of famous Russians, including the novelist Dostoevsky and the composer Tchaikovsky (open daily 0800–1400). Gracing the western end is the golden spire of the **Admiralty**, founded by Peter the Great.

Dating from 1703, the beautiful **Peter-Paul Fortress** was St Petersburg's first building. The present brick structure was conceived along Renaissance lines with massive perimeter walls interspersed with pentagonal bastion. The **Cathedral**

**of SS Peter and Paul** was designed by Domenico Trezzini in 1733 and is wholly western in character. Inside are the marble tombs of Russia's imperial rulers from Peter the Great onwards.

The **Trubetskoy Bastion** was a prison almost from the word go. During the 19th century most of the revolutionary opponents of the Tsarist regime were confined here, including Lenin's elder brother, Alexander Ulyanov, and Trotsky. The isolation cells are open to the public. Most of the other buildings are now interesting museums, including the **Commandant's House**, where political prisoners were interrogated (open Thurs–Tues 1100–1800, closed last Tues of the month).

Moored not far from the Peter-Paul Fortress is one of Russia's most famous warships, the **Cruiser Aurora**. On the night of 7 Nov 1917 a single blank round from the bow gun was the signal for the storming of the Winter Palace (*Petrogradskaya naberezhnaya 4,* open Tues–Thurs, Sat–Sun 1030–1600 group tours only).

## Other Sights

A complete contrast to the Winter Palace, the **Summer Palace and Gardens** (Letny Dvorets i Letny Sad) was Peter the Great's modest summer residence. A simple, two-storey brick building in the Dutch style, the rooms contain the original furnishings as well as an intriguing collection of Peter's personal possessions (open Wed–Mon 1100–1800). The **Kazan Cathedral**, *Kazanskaya ploshchad*, open Mon–Tues, Thurs–Sat 1100–1700, has a striking colonnade modelled on St Peter's in Rome. Once a museum of atheism, it has now been reconsecrated and contains a small exhibition on religion. One of the largest cathedrals in the world, **St Isaacs**,

260

is the work of French architect Auguste de Montferrand, and took 40 years to complete. No expense was spared on the interior, which was decorated with gold, bronze, precious stones, paintings and mosaics. You can climb the dome (91 metres) for panoramic views of the city (*Isaakievsky ploshchad*, open Thurs–Tues 1000–1700). The magnificent statue in the green *Senatskaya ploshchad* overlooking the river is Etienne Falconet's **Bronze Horseman**, immortalised in a poem of the same name by Pushkin; it was erected as a memorial to Peter the Great by Catherine the Great.

## Museums

Housed in one of the Grand Ducal palaces, the **Russian Museum** is a fascinating history of Russian painting from the 18th century onwards. The highlights are the canvases by artists of the Itinerant School, and the paintings by early 20th-century artists such as Mikhail Larionov and Natalya Goncharova, who also contributed stage designs and costumes for Diaghilev's *Ballets Russes*. (*Inzhenernaya ulitsa 4*, open Wed-Mon 1000–1800).

Russia's greatest poet, **Alexander Pushkin** lived in an apartment on the Moika Embankment from the autumn of 1836 until his death following a duel with Baron d'Anthès just a few months later. The rooms in the flat have been lovingly restored and contain many of Pushkin's personal possessions, including a blackamoor paperweight to remind him of his Abyssinian grandfather. (*Reki Moiki naberezhnaya 12*, open Wed–Mon 1030–1800).

No writer has closer associations with St Petersburg than the 19th century novelist, **Fyodor Dostoevsky**. Although he is most closely associated with the Haymarket, the setting for *Crime and Punishment*, it is his last home in the city that has been refurbished as a museum. Like all Russian literary museums, this wonderfully evokes the man and his times (*Kuznechny pereulok 5*, open Tues–Sun 1030–1730, closed last Wed of each month).

## OUT OF TOWN

Regular coach excursions to the environs of St Petersburg are organised by Intourist and other travel companies.

### Peterhof

The imperial palace at Peterhof (sometimes called Petrodvorets) was founded by Peter the Great in 1718 but not completed until the reign of his granddaughter, Catherine. A hydrofoil from St Petersburg (departing at half-hourly intervals from the pier on *Dvortsovaya naberezhnay* outside the Hermitage) will take you directly to the **Grand Cascade**, a magnificent sequence of gilded statues and fountains, only recently restored. The equally splendid baroque palace is mainly the work of architect Bartolomeo Rastrelli. Peter the Great actually lived in the smaller, less pretentious **Monplaisir Palace**, with its wonderful views across the Gulf of Finland.

### Tsarskoe Selo (Pushkin)

The main attraction here is Catherine the Great's summer residence, a stunning baroque confection designed by the architect of the Winter Palace, Rastrelli. The building was almost totally destroyed by the Nazis during World War II and is still being restored. Even so, twenty-two of the magnificent state rooms have been reopened to the public and the grounds can be explored. Trains leave from the Vitebsky Vokzal for Detskoe Selo station every 20 mins (journey time 30 mins).

# ST PETERSBURG–MOSCOW

Still one of the great Russian experiences, the rail journey between Moscow and St Petersburg beats air and road travel hands down for atmosphere, comfort and reliability. The fastest service is the high speed ER200 which does the journey in just five hours; most visitors however still fall for the romance (now somewhat tarnished) of the famed Red Arrow.

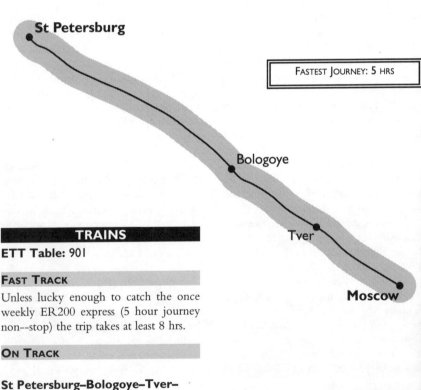

FASTEST JOURNEY: 5 HRS

St Petersburg

Bologoye

Tver

Moscow

## TRAINS

**ETT Table:** 901

### FAST TRACK

Unless lucky enough to catch the once weekly ER200 express (5 hour journey non--stop) the trip takes at least 8 hrs.

### ON TRACK

**St Petersburg–Bologoye–Tver–Moscow**

Thirteen trains a day make this journey. St Petersburg to Bologoye takes 4 hrs, Bologoye to Tver 2 hrs and Tver to Moscow 2–3 hrs.

## BOLOGOYE

**Station:** *tel: 220/4400*
Change here for Pskov, Tartu and Tallinn.

The twin locomotives known in Russian as *Krasnaya Strela* (Red Arrow) depart simultaneously from the **Oktyabrskaya** (formerly Leningrad) Station, Moscow and the **Glavny** (formerly Moscow) Station, St Petersburg at 2355 every night. The journey time for the 650 km trip is eight hours precisely. Most of the compartments are four-berth and for reasons of privacy and security it's worth booking the entire compartment. There's a primitive toilet and hand basin at the end of every carriage. Bring your own supplies of food and drink as the buffet facilities are limited. You can ask the guard for boiling water and tea from the samovar. The cost of bedding is inclusive in the price of the ticket but many attendants still seem to expect a tip. Security on the train is not all that it should be and there have been a number of much publicised incidents of theft, sometimes with violence. The best policy is to behave as unobtrusively as possible and make your own security arrangements. Take, where possible, strong suitcases with combination locks. Keep the door of your compartment locked at all times and even secure with a tie or scarf. If you're worried by other passengers, most conductors will listen very sympathetically to complaints. There's no point trying to buy a ticket at the station itself. Book in advance through the Intourist or information desk at any hotel – you'll have to pay in hard currency and you'll need to show your passport.

## TVER

**Station:** *tel: 332 846 /334 728*
**Tourist Office:** none
At the confluence of the Volga and Tvertsa Rivers, the modern industrial city of Tver is 130 km north of Moscow. Known in the Soviet era as Kallinin, it

## Early Russian Railways

Named originally after Tsar Nicholas I, the Moscow to St Petersburg railway was officially opened on 1 November 1851. On that day the journey took 22 hours because of an over-zealous official who thought to smooth the Tsar's progress by greasing the rails along 'his' stretch of the track. Nicholas himself insisted on personally inspecting the line at regular intervals. The project was completed in just eight years, partly thanks to American technical expertise. More than 50,000 serfs worked on the railway's construction, round the clock and in all weathers using only picks, shovels and wheelbarrows. Several thousand died in the process. There was some bemusement in the early days as to just what a train was capable of. There is the story of a merchant on his way to Moscow who boarded the train to St Petersburg by mistake. When he discovered his error, he was amazed: 'How marvellous! The same train that is taking you to St Petersburg, is taking me to Moscow'.

263

has a distinguished history and at one time rivalled the capital itself. Unfortunately much of the old town was destroyed during the Nazi occupation in World War II. However, the houses on the waterfront are worth a look as is the Belaya Troitsa (White Trinity) Church, commissioned by Ivan the Terrible in 1564. Catherine the Great's 18th-century palace is now the offices of the local government. There is a Motel run by Intourist, just off the St Petersburg Highway but, at the time of writing, only one or two adequate hotels in the town itself.

# SOFIA (SOFIJA)

Sofia is one of the oldest cities in Europe, but still one of its least known capitals. Archaeological or architectural traces of Thracians, Romans, Byzantines, Slavs and OttomanTurks can still be seen here. Since the fall of Communism in 1989, Sofia shows a more hospitable face to the world with its many new cafés, bars, restaurants and small private hotels. Its excellent museums, art gallerys and concerts, and the proximity of Mount Vitoša make a visit worthwhile.

## TOURIST INFORMATION

**Tourist Information: Balkantourist,** *1 Vitosha Blvd; tel: (02) 43 331* or *87 51 92*. (Mon–Sat 0800–2200 in summer) has English-language maps of Sofia which are also on sale at news-stands and in bookshops. Other agencies are: **InterBalkan**, which has offices at the airport, *tel: (02) 32 21 90*, and the station *tel: (02) 72 01 57*. **Rila**, *5 Gurko St; tel: (02) 87 07 77* can make international train reservations and sell tickets. Tickets are also sold by the **Travel Centre**, underneath the **National Palace of Culture**, *Ploshstad Bulgaria*. Expect to pay for printed information.

## ARRIVING AND DEPARTING

### Airport
**Sofia International,** *tel: (02) 88 44 33*, is 11 km from the centre. *Tel: (02) 72 06 72* for information on international flights or *72 24 14* for domestic flights.

### By Train
**Station: Central Railway Station,** *tel: (02) 31 111*, is located 1.5 km north of the city centre, on *Blvd. Knyaginya Maria Luisa*. For buses, taxis and tourist information, *tel: (02) 88 44 81*. Currency exchange and post office are all available.

## GETTING AROUND

Central Sofia is fairly compact and most areas of interest can be reached on foot. Maps tend to be clear and easy to follow, but remember that street names may have changed. There is a large network of trams, trolley-buses and buses; stops display the routes of each service using them. Buy tickets from kiosks or street vendors or from bus and tram drivers. A one-day pass is good value if you are planning more than three rides, but tickets are extremely cheap. Tram nos 1, 7 and 15 run from the station along *Blvd. Knyaginya Maria Luisa* and *Vitosha Blvd* through the town centre.

As in all east European countries, many, though not all taxi drivers will rip off passengers if given half a chance. Check that the meter is on, or agree a fare before getting in. Black and yellow taxis called **OK**, *tel: (02) 21 21* and the **Sofitaxis**, *tel: (02) 12 84*, provide efficient and properly metered rides.

## STAYING IN SOFIA

### Accommodation
**Balkantourist** books rooms in hotels and private apartments. More convenient however, are the agencies in the station, which offer reasonably priced and fairly

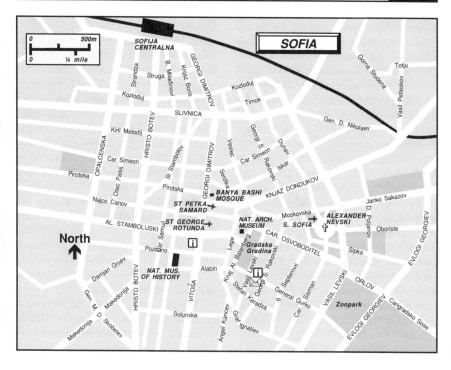

central private rooms. Ensure that whenever you book a room, the agency stamps your white statistical card (a remnant from the days of Communism). Private rooms are good value; if staying with friends you will have to arrange for the police to stamp your statistical card daily. Hotel chains with property in the city: *Sh, IH* and *Nv.* Balkantourist rents out private apartments at reasonable rates.

The outlying villages of **Simeonovo** and **Dragalevtsi** are noted for bed & breakfast establishments and small hotels, and both are only a few km from the city in the foothills of the Vitoša Mountain. For Simeonovo, take bus no. 67; for Dragalevtsi take bus no. 64.

### Eating and Drinking

Sofia's restaurant scene has been transformed in recent years. A constellation of new restaurants has opened in and around Sofia, many of which are favourable in terms of price.

Head for *Vitoša Blvd* and the surrounding side streets for a large collection of eateries. Despite the range of international restaurants, Bulgarian food is generally the best value, and good, moderately-priced places to try it are at the **Garden Club**, *ul Knyaz Boris 99*; at **Bey Genchu**, *Blvd. Dondukov*; or **Fram 1888**, near the National Palace of Culture. Pizza restaurants are very popular, and an excellent one is, **Venezia**, on *ul. Benovski 12*. In the foothills of the Vitosha Mountain are several traditional-style taverns serving Bulgarian specialities. One of the best aspects of Sofia's culinary scene is the abundance of street cafés and kiosks serving good cheap coffee and excellent cakes.

## Communications

The Central **Post Office** is at *ul. General Gurko 6*, opposite the Rila agency. International phone calls can be dialled directly, from the **Central Telephone Office** on *Stefan Karadza St*, diagonally behind the post office.

## Embassies

**UK:** *38 Levski Blvd; tel: (02) 88 53 61.*
**USA:** *Unit 1335, 1 Saborna St; tel: (02) 88 48 01.*

## Money

Bureaux de change have sprouted all over central Sofia, including some open 24 hrs on *Vitoša Blvd*. There are plenty of exchange facilities in the central station. It is often possible to get a better deal at bureaux than at banks, so check commission rates. Little of the black market remains.

## SHOPPING

*Vitoša Boulevard* and the adjoining streets are among the best places to shop, although small specialist private boutiques are springing up in various places. Good buys are arts and crafts, hand-knitted woollens, and modern jewellery made by young Bulgarian designers.

## ENTERTAINMENT

New street cafés and bars are gradually bringing the crowds to Sofia's streets. There are nightclubs, but most cater to the guests of the top hotels. Local clubs often consist of a few primitive poker machines, a pool table and a bar.

The best street life is on *Vitoša Blvd,* especially down at the south end towards *Patriarch Evtimi St*. Sofia's cinemas are very cheap and tend to show films with the original sound-track, merely adding subtitles.

## SIGHTSEEING

Sofia was a Thracian and Roman settlement before becoming the headquarters for the Turkish governor during the occupation of the Balkans. However, until it was declared capital of the unified Bulgaria, the city tended to be eclipsed by Plodiv in terms of cultural importance.

Today Sofia is a modern institutional city with a capital's quota of museums and churches, although none of them is compelling. The statue of Lenin has disappeared from the old Lenin Square.

Sofia was named after the 6th-century **St Sofia Basilica,** *Alexander Nevski Pl.* The dim interior is open daily to visitors. On one flank of the church the Eternal Flame flickers in memory of the Bulgarian war dead.

The best photo opportunity in Sofia is undoubtedly the **St Alexander Nevski Church,** a neo-Byzantine, gold-domed tribute to the Russians who died in the Russian-Turkish war of 1877–78. In the crypt, a fascinating collection of Bulgarian icons traces the development of Bulgarian icon-painting, from medieval times.

The 4th-century **St George Rotunda** provides an impressive block to the flow of *Dimitrov* and *Vitoša Blvds*. Within a few hundred yards are the 16th-century **Banya Bashi Mosque,** *Dimitrov Blvd,* and the 14th-century **St Petka Samardjiiska Church,** built below street level and now suffering the indignity of standing in a pedestrian underpass by the TSUM department store.

You can see relics from Bulgaria's eventful history in the **National Archaeological Museum,** 2 Saborna Blvd, and the **National Museum of History,** *2 Vitoša Blvd*. The 11th-century **Boyana Church,** at the foot of the Vitoša Mountain, is Sofia's contribution to the World Cultural Heritage List.

# SOFIA–ATHENS

From Sofia, the route quickly begins to climb into the rugged country of south-west Bulgaria, taking the relatively easy route through the Struma River valley (which becomes the Strymon after it enters Greek Macedonia). All along the route to the Greek border the great bulk of the Rila and Pirin Mountains beckon invitingly to the east.

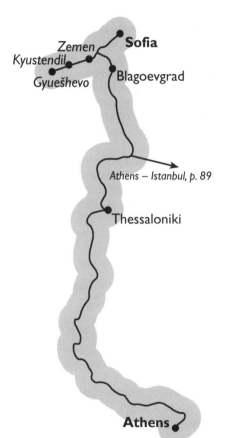

Athens – Istanbul, p. 89

FASTEST JOURNEY: 15 HRS

267

## TRAINS

ETT Tables: 975, 970.

### FAST TRACK

 One service a day changing trains at Thessaloniki and taking 15 hrs.

### ON TRACK

 **Sofia–Blagoevgrad**
Six trains a day taking just over 2 hrs.

**Blagoevgrad–Athens**
One service a day changing trains at Thessaloniki and taking 13 hrs.

 **SIDE TRACK FROM SOFIA**

Having traversed the western foothills of Mount Vitosa, the train passes through the grimy industrial town of **Pernik** then comes to **Radomir**, some 40 km from Sofia, after which the line splits, with the main route continuing south towards the Greek border. A side track, on which eight slow trains from Radomir leave every day, goes west through **Zemen**, which is noted for the 12th-century Zemen Monastery, 3km south-west of the village. From here the line swings south through an orchard-filled plain to **Kyustendil**, taking 1 hr 30 mins from Radomir, and then west again, three slow trains per day taking 1 hr 15 mins, through more rugged country to **Gyuševo** on the mountainous border with the Former Yugoslav Republic of Macedonia.

Modestly equipped hikers' chalets are the most promising accommodation in an area where hiking is the main leisure pursuit, but there are reasonable hotels in Kyustendil, including the **Pautalia**, *Ploschtad Velbâzhd 1; tel: (078) 245 61*, and the **Velbâzhd**, *Bld. Balgâriya 4; tel: (078) 202 46.*

### BLAGOEVGRAD

There is little of interest in Blagoevgrad, beyond some Turkish-era houses in the old centre. The town is more interesting as a base for hiking in the **Rila Mountains**, although this is better done from the small village of Bistritsa, about 7 km to the east, to which buses leave every hour or so. This leads also to an alternative route to the Rila Monastery (see Side Trip from Sofia in the Sofia–Istanbul chapter, pp. 275–280) around which there are numerous beauty spots and hikers' chalets

From Blagoevgrad, the line continues through **Sandanski**, noted for its nearby thermal springs and from where trails lead into the **Pirin Mountains**. Visit also **Melnik**, a small town in a stunning location of wind-sculpted sandstone cliffs. The Greek border is just beyond **Kulata**.

# SOFIA–BUCHAREST

This route takes an alternative track through Bulgaria to the country's Black Sea coast. It reaches the shore at a town which is one of the most animated in the country and is at the same time a real community in contrast to the artificial beach resorts built up under communism (although there is otherwise nothing wrong with the newer of these) as a means of soaking up tourists' foreign currency while they were soaking up the sun. In addition, the journey offers a detailed look at a part of Bulgaria that is off of the country's still rudimentary tourist trail, including much of natural beauty, local interest and the people's way of life.

FASTEST JOURNEY: **9** HRS

Silistra

Bucharest

269

Ruse

Sofia – Budapest, p. 274

Pleven

Varna

Gorna Orjahovitza

Veliko Tyrnovo

Mezdra

Sofia

## TRAINS

**ETT Tables:** 960, 962.

### FAST TRACK

 Two trains a day taking 9 hrs.

## ON TRACK

### Sofia–Mezdra–Pleven–Gorna Oryahovitsa

Ten trains a day make this journey calling at all stations. Sofia to Mezdra takes 1 hr 30 mins, Mezdra to Pleven 1 hr 15 mins, Pleven to Gorna Oryahovitsa 70 mins.

### Gorna Oryahovitsa–Ruse–Bucharest

The two through expresses take around 2 hrs between Gorna Oryahovitsa and Ruse and 2 hrs between Ruse and Bucharest

## MEZDRA

The route to Mezdra is via the Iskâr Gorge, the longest in Bulgaria, the train is the best way to see the impressive scenery and rock formations.

## PLEVEN

Pleven was considered to be an impregnable fortress town when it was attacked by Russian and Romanian troops and Bulgarian rebels during the liberation war against Turkey in 1877. Memorials and museum exhibits from the bloody struggle that finally forced the Ottomans' surrender are ubiquitous in the town, which is well placed as a base for exploring the central part of northern Bulgaria (by bus), north through the Danubian Plain to the Danube, and south to the Balkan Mountains.

### ACCOMMODATOPN

For accommodation, ask at the **Hotel Pleven**, *Ploschad Republiky 2; tel: (064) 200 62.*

## GORNA ORYAHOVITSA

This is another of those station towns on the Sofia–Varna route that are not so much interesting for themselves, but for where you can get to from them. Its main function is as a rail crossroads (it the largest railway station after Sofia) and many people use it as an overnight stop. Also, the prices are comparatively low.

In this case there are two possibilities: south to the town of Veliko Târnovo, and north to the Danube at Ruse.

 **SIDE TRACK FROM GORNA ORYAHOVITSA**

## VELIKO TÂRNOVO

The town has an assured place in the Bulgarian story, as it was the capital of Bulgaria from 1185–1393, before it fell to the Turks. The town is about 15 km from Gorna Oryahovitsa, with trains every hour or so in the morning and afternoon. The bus can be more convenient, however, and a frequent bus connects the railway station with the bus station, from where the no. 10 and no. 14 buses leave every 20 mins or so for the town.

**Station**: Both the railway and bus stations are inconveniently sited: the former being 2 km from the town centre (take bus no. 4 from outside the station), and the latter being more like 4 km (take bus no. 12 to the centre).

**Tourist Information**: The Tourist Information Office is located in the **Hotel Etur**, *ul. Ivailo 2; tel: (062) 24 195.* It can arrange accommodation at hotels, private homes and campsites in the town.

### ACCOMMODATION

For good budget accommodation try the **Hotel Etur**, *1 Ivailo St; tel: 2 68 61.* The town is very popular with Bulgarians, however, and accommodation is often fully booked at peak times.

### SIGHTSEEING

Veliko Târnovo is spectacularly sited on steep gorges overlooking the River Yantra. The heart of its historic district is the ruined **Tsarevets** (Tsar's Castle) on the Tsarevets Hill, which is romantically floodlit at night. This was both the royal and patriarchal centre of the town, protected by walls and stout fortifications. Visit the restored **Patriarchal Church of the Holy Assumption**.

Beside the river is the **Samovodska Charšiya** (Bazaar District), which has lost much of the bustle of a Turkish bazaar but is still a pretty quarter of workshops and cafés. The 19th-century **Sveti Nikolai** (St Nicholas) Church, the elegantly carved Ottoman **Sarafinova Kâšta** (Sarafina House), and the **Vâzrazhdane i Ureditelno Sâbranie** (National Revival and Constituent Assembly Museum) recalls the historic role of Veliko Târnovo where the first post-Turkish occupation Bulgarian parliament was held in 1879.

## RUSE

The River Danube port of Ruse has declined from its heyday as an important staging post on the overland and riverine route from western Europe to Istanbul before the direct rail link was built. It has also suffered visually from post-war industrial development. But enough remains of its National Revival and turn-of-the-century architecture to make it a pleasant place to visit. In addition, hydrofoil trips leave from the **Hydrofoil Station** on *Bld. Aleksandâr Stamboliiski* in summer.

From Ruse, it is not necessary to return to Gorna Oryahovitsa, as there are trains every 2 hrs direct to Varna.
**Station:** The station is several km south of the river, but trolleybus nos. 1, 11, 12 and 18 connect it with the city centre at Ploschad Tsar Svoboditel.
**Tourist Information:** Is available in the lobby of the **Hotel Riga**, *Bld. Aleksandâr Stamboliiski*; tel: (082) 22181. There are cheap rooms to be had in private houses

**SIDE TRACKS FROM RUSE**

## VARNA

The town is interesting and lively in its own right, as well as being a good base for exploring the coastline north towards Romania and south in the direction of Burgas. The town's tourist sector has grabbed private enterprise with both hands and lacks only a tourist boom to make the most of it. Although the shipbuilding and other declining industrial eyesores around the port area in the south detract somewhat from its slightly raffish air, Varna is well placed to benefit from the slowly increasing number of visitors, both Bulgarian and foreign.
**Station:** The train journey direct from Sofia takes about 8 hrs; if coming from Gorna Oryahovitsa it takes about 3 hrs. The railway station *tel: (052) 22 25 51,* stands on *Ploschad Slavejkov,* adjacent to the port and almost 1 km from the town centre around *Ploschad Varnenska Komuna*. To reach the centre, go north on *ul. Avram Gachev* until you arrive at the **Varna Accommodation Centre**.
**Tourist Information:** There are two main privately run Tourist Information offices in Varna, both of which are open from 0800–2000 in the summer season, with progressively earlier closing at less busy times, and have maps and brochures with some local information in English. One is just outside the station at the north end of *Ploschad Slavejkov*, at *ul. Avram Gachev 10; tel: 052 22 23 89.* The other one, which deals mostly with accommodation, is at *ul. Musala 3; tel: (052) 22 55 24.* Other private travel and accommodation agencies are

271

springing up and can be found in the area around the **Balkan Airlines office** on *ul. Shipka.*

### GETTING AROUND

Many of the non-beach attractions of Varna lie in an arc running east from *Ploschad Varnenska Komuna* then south towards the port. Central Varna, known as *Tsentâr,* is both easy and pleasant for getting around on foot and it is served by buses and trolleybuses for longer stretches. Many restaurants, along with nightlife and other entertainment possibilities are in the area around *Ploschad Nezavisimost,* on which stands the Opera House and Theatre. Privately owned bus networks now operate alongside the municipal one, so the system is in a state of flux. It is essential to get a transport map from the tourist office if you are planning to make trips to the beach and outlying resorts. Many street names have been changed and the process may not be fully completed yet.

### ACCOMMODATION

The tourist and accommodation offices listed under Tourist Information above can book all kinds of accommodation, from private rooms and campsites to the big hotels, but with many privately owned and operated hotels, guesthouses and pensions opening along the shore north and south of Varna, the tourist offices often don't have adequate information for booking. Few of these new properties are likely to be fully booked at present. If you prefer a seaview to a downtown option and you're not happy with what the tourist office or booking agency recommends, try

making a deal with a taxi driver to take you to one or two, giving an idea of your budget level if possible, or leave your bags at the railway station left-luggage office and walk: in general, out-of-town accommodation is cheaper than that in Varna itself. Purpose-built resorts along the coast have a central accommodation office, at which prices for non-reserved rooms will invariably be higher than for pre-booked package deals.

### SIGHTSEEING

Varna has a long and rich history, having been founded in the 6th century BC by Greek colonists and called Odessos. Its sheltered harbour has since then made it a valuable piece of real estate. When the Romans came on the scene 500 years later, the town really began to flourish, becoming the main port of the province of Moesia and one of the most important towns on the Black Sea coast. The Byzantines and later the Ottoman Turks continued this maritime tradition and built up Varna as a naval base.

In the town centre is a section of the **Roman Wall** and, on *ul. 27 Juli,* the **National Revival Museum** (open Tues–Sun 1000–1800), documents the struggle to throw off Ottoman rule. In the other direction is the excellent **Ethnographical Museum** on *ul. Panagyurište* (open Tues–Sun 1000–1700).

Further north, at *41 Osmi Primorski Polk* where it intersects *Bld. Slivnitsa,* the **Museum of History and Art** displays many historic treasures, most notably examples of exquisite Thracian gold jewellery, dating from 4000 BC. (many of these pieces were found in the Chalcolithic Necropolis on the edge of town). One cluster of attractions lies in the corner defined by the port and the sea, adjacent to *Bld. Primorski*. There are the ruins of the **Roman Thermae** (open Tues–Sun 1000–1700) dating from the 2nd century AD during the reign of Emperor Septimius Severus; their size is an indication of Varna's importance at that time. The nearby churches of **Sveti Atanas** from the 19th-century National Revival period, and **Sveta Bogoroditsa,** from the 17th century, contain fine icons and each has a beautifully embellished iconostasis. At *ul. 5 Noemvri 8* is the **Varna Museum** (open Tues–Sat 1000–1700), which has pictures and exhibits from the town's past, including its time as an Ottoman stronghold. On a lighter note, it documents Varna's claim to have invented the bathing beauty competition in the 1920s. On *Bld. Primorski* is another, but smaller **Roman Thermae.**

The flower-bedecked seafront gardens of the **Primorski Park** feature another collection of places worth visiting. Just outside its southern entrance stands the **Museum of Medical History** (open Mon–Fri 1000–1600), while just inside there is the **Bulgarian Navy Museum**, whose star attraction is the gunboat *Drâzhki,* which sank a Turkish cruiser in the war of 1912. Further in you will find an **Aquarium** (open Tues–Sun 0900–1700, Mon from 1400) beside the entrance to the **Municipal Beach,** and the **Copernicus Planetarium** (open daily 0800–1800), which has star-shows as well as standing exhibits on astronomy. In its eastern reaches there is the **National History Museum** (open Tues–Sun 1000–1700), the **Zoo** (open daily 0800–1700) and a **Dolphinarium** (open daily 1100–1500).

Most side trips from Varna will be made by bus to the nearby seaside resorts. Some of these are purpose-built beach resorts and others are based around an old fishing village. They include **Albena, Družba, Golden Sands** and **Balčik.** Although they can be very busy in July and Aug, there are always quiet and even deserted beaches to be found near the resorts.

One of the more interesting excursions is to **Château Euxinograd,** an estate some 10 km north of Varna that was the splendid summer residence built for Bulgarian Tsar Ferdinand I in 1891. In more recent times it was a hideaway for Bulgaria's Communist bosses and has now been opened to the public when it is not being used for official business. Bus nos 8 and 9 from Varna *Tsentâr* go there.

## SILISTRA

If you have not had enough of travelling on Bulgarian Railways by the time you arrive at Varna, there are a few side trips you can make by rail. One is Varna–Samuil, a town about halfway to the River Danube port of Ruse (which can also be reached as a side-trip from Varna instead of the route suggested above, from Gorna Oryahovitsa).

Don't stay at Samuil, but change there for **Silistra,** a sleepy town across the river from Romania, that was once an important Roman, Byzantine and Ottoman settlement (among its points of interest are a well-preserved Roman tomb).

# SOFIA–BUDAPEST

**Budapest**

This long journey provides a useful connection between Hungary and Bulgaria, allowing a transfer to the Bucharest–Budapest route (p. 129) at Craiova or Timĭoara if you wish to explore Romania..

FASTEST JOURNEY: 18 HRS 15 MINS

Timişoara

Bucharest-Budapest, p.129

Craiova

Vidin

Sofia

## TRAINS

**ETT Tables:** 97, 961, 954, 950.

### FAST TRACK

→ The through train runs via Yugoslavia and is best avoided at the moment.

### ON TRACK

**Sofia–Vidin**
Five trains a day make the 5 hr journey.

**Vidin–Craiova**
Vidin to Craiova involves a 15 min ferry crossing from Vidin to Calafat. Trains from Calafat to Craiova take 2 hrs.

**Craiova–Timişoara**
Eight trains a day. 5 hour journey.

**Timişoara–Budapest**
One direct service at inconvenient times. Other services are available by changing trains at Arad. Journey time at least 6 hrs.

## VIDIN

Vidin is noted for its medieval **Baba Vida Fortress** dominating both the town and the river. Hydrofoil tours operate on the Danube from here, but they have been suspended in recent years.

An alternative is to change to the branch line at the railway junction town of **Bojčinovci,** about half way to Vidin, for **Berkovica** in the Balkan Mountains. The local slow train takes more than 1 hr to get there. Berkovica is a pretty resort perched amidst the Balkan Mountains. There are hotels and holiday chalets in and around the town, and several nearby campsites.

# SOFIA–ISTANBUL

This route links the capital of Bulgaria, Sofia, a city that is slowly awakening from its long Communist slumber, with Istanbul, the vibrant European bridgehead of Islamic Turkey. It winds across Bulgaria and the European plain of Turkey, a historic and scenic yet too-little appreciated region. The route provides an insight into an area of Eastern Europe still seldom travelled by Westerners: trains are virtually devoid of backpackers.

| FASTEST JOURNEY: 12 HRS |
| --- |

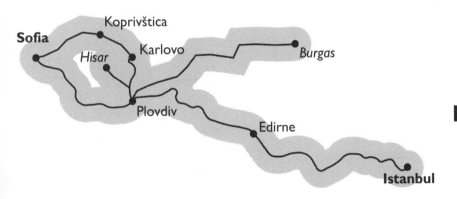

## TRAINS

**ETT tables:** 97b, 965, 960, 950.

### FAST TRACK

→ There is one direct train from Sofia to Istanbul, grandiosely called the 'Balkan Express' although it is a slow, fairly ramshackle, and often dirty affair. It comes from Budapest and Belgrade to Sofia and goes on to Istanbul. It takes about 12 hrs for the trip. On the train, sleeping cars are available but no refreshment service. Refreshments, including hot food, are available beside the Customs and Immigration office on the Turkish side of the border, and soft drinks, for a stiff overcharge, from sellers at Turkish stations en-route. It is best to stock up with drinks and snacks before leaving.

Note that on both the daylight and overnight service, the Bulgarian border police can be a major nuisance. On the Turkish side, the officers behave correctly and are even friendly, but on the Bulgarian side they look for excuses to increase their income. Any infringement of the rules, however minor, leads to an aggressive demand for payment of a 'fine'. German marks and US dollars are the only acceptable currencies; others have to be converted at exorbitant exchange rates.

Travellers should refuse to be intimidated by this shake-down, although they run the risk of being removed from the train as a result. The key thing is to have all one's visas and other papers perfectly in order, especially, when leaving Bulgaria, the *carte statistique,* with its stamps detailing one's stay in the country.

## ON TRACK

### Sofia–Plovdiv
There are ten express trains daily between Sofia and Plovdiv. The journey should take about 2 hrs 30 mins, but delays are common.

Some of the faster trains require reservations.

### Sofia–Koprivština
There are 4 trains each day taking just over 1hr 30 mins.

### Koprivština–Karlovo
Three express trains supplemented by 4 or 5 local services. The expresses take 40 mins, the locals 50 mins..

### Karlovo–Plovdiv
Nine trains a day taking 100 mins (1 fast express a day takes only 70 mins).

### Plovdiv–Edirne–Istanbul
The one through train a day takes 10 hrs. The stop at Edirne is during the night. The train carries sleeping compartments, but crosses the border early in the morning, so don't expect a good night's sleep. There is no refreshment service.

## KOPRIVŠTICA

**Station:** Although there is a station on the main line from Sofia to the Black Sea coast at Burgas called 'Koprivština', this is actually about 15km north of the town of that name. Buses meet the train at the station and ferry people to and from the town, taking about 30 minutes, plus waiting time.

**Tourist Information:** The **Balkantourist** office is on the corner of *Anton Ivanov St* and *Doganov St.* The **Museum Service Office** on *Apriltsi Mausoleum Square* (open Tues–Sun 0730–1200, 1330–1730), is the place to buy a combined ticket for visiting Koprivština's many museum houses, which are generally open during these same times.

## GETTING AROUND
There are a few buses and taxis but there is little point in using them as the best way to experience the town is to stroll around.

## ACCOMMODATION AND FOOD
The **Balkantourist** office can arrange accommodation in some of the village mansions, although these are usually already filled, especially at weekends, in summer and on public holidays. There are a few hotels in the town and others can be found in the surrounding countryside.

The excellent **Hotel Koprivština** in town can be very busy, but there are numerous other hotels, guest houses and private houses with rooms in the surrounding area, reachable by foot or taxi.

The wood-built **Dyado Liben** restaurant beside the River Topolnitsa is a magnificent hacienda-style place, with an upstairs restaurant and atmospheric courtyard bar.

### SIGHTSEEING

Koprivština is a small and delightful town surrounded by forest in an agricultural valley amid the pure air of the Sredna Gora Mountains. Most visitors to Bulgaria with limited time end up in Plovdiv for their excursion out of Sofia. In fact, Koprivština is in many ways a better choice. It is smaller, easier to get around on foot, and has none of the smoky industrial eyesores of its bigger counterpart. Furthermore, with its almost perfectly preserved 19th-century architecture and ambience, it is a glimpse of an older and seemingly more romantic Bulgaria.

Historically, Koprivština, and indeed the whole area, is noted for its gallant role in the April Rising of 1876 against Turkish rule, and the town's street names recall episodes and heroes from that bloody episode in Bulgarian history. But it is a peaceable place now, a kind of living museum.

Among the perfectly preserved houses in National Revival style to visit are the **House of Nincho Oslekov,** with its columns of Lebanese cypress supporting a fresco-painted facade, **the House of Georgi Benkovski,** and the **House of Todor Kableshkov,** the leader of the rising in Koprivština. In addition, there is the **Church of the Holy Virgin,** dating from 1817, and even the **village school** is worth a visit.

Because of its historical attachment and good looks, the town is often overrun by visitors, mostly Bulgarian, at peak times. The hilly forests around Koprivština makes for a good hike to escape the crowds and experience some of Bulgaria's unspoiled countryside.

Every five years, the **Koprivština Folklore Festival** takes place there (the next one is in 2000), with a veritable blizzard of groups in colourful costumes performing traditional Bulgarian folk dances and music. The air is alive with a cacophony of noise and charcoal smoke from kebab grills. At this time, the town and the fields around it are very crowded.

### KARLOVO

Karlovo is another of those Bulgarian towns noted for its 19th-century National Revival-style architecture, although in this case it is not so impressive as Plovdiv. However, it is a convenient base for touring the **Valley of the Roses,** which is well worth a visit for about six weeks from May onwards, because of the multicoloured masses of roses grown there (three-quarters of the world supply of attar of roses comes from the valley). If time is short, the sight can easily be appreciated from the train, on the line from Sofia to Karlovo. Out of the rose season, there is no special reason for visiting.

### PLOVDIV

**Station:** tel: *(032) 22 27 29,* about 1 km south-west of the centre on *Hristo Botev Blvd.* There are no exchange facilities at the station so travellers arriving from Turkey must walk into town in order to obtain Bulgarian currency. The city's two bus stations are within a hundred metres of the railway station in an easterly direction.

**Tourist Office: Puldin Tours** is at *34 Moskva Bld tel: (032) 55 28 07,* and is good at finding accommodation. **Hotel Trimontium,** *tel: (032) 23 491,* in the central square, is helpful for tourist information and sells reasonable city maps: open 0700–2200. The **Hotel Bulgaria,** *Evtimi St; tel: (032) 22 55 64,* also has maps. Other commercial accommodation agencies operate along *Georgi Dimitrov ul.*

277

### GETTING AROUND

It is 10–15 mins walk north-east along tree-lined *Ivan Yazov St,* diagonally across from the station, to Plovdiv's central square. Or take bus nos 1 or 7 from outside the railway station and stay on for three stops to the main Post Office and telephone building on *Tsentralen Square.* Here you will find the **Hotel Trimontium**. *Georgi Dimitrov ul* (a name that may well have been changed to another by this time), the pedestrianised main street, leads north towards the old town. Buses and trolley-buses run throughout Plovdiv, but much of the hilly old town is only accessible on foot.

### ACCOMMODATION AND FOOD

Hotel chains with properties in the city include *Nv* and *IH.* Plovdiv has six major hotels, including the **Trimontium** and **Bulgaria** already mentioned, but even the cheaper ones cost more than a private room. You may also find locals offering private accommodation at the station, and even in the street. There are several campsites with small bungalows, but all are a long way out from the centre.

There are many low-cost private snack bars in Plovdiv, selling hamburgers, Coca-Cola and such like, as well as bars beside some of the prominent tourist sites, such as the one overlooking the Roman Theatre in Trimontium. Many excellent, atmospheric (and, by Bulgarian standards, expensive) restaurants are to be found in converted National Revival-style houses in the Old Town.

### SIGHTSEEING

Situated on the River Maritsa in central Bulgaria, Plovdiv is the second largest city in the country. Plovdiv, Philippopolis to the Macedonians and Trimontium to the Romans, was described by Lucian in the

2nd century AD as 'the largest and most beautiful of all cities in Thrace'. Until the late 19th century it was more populous than Sofia and was the centre of Bulgarian cultural life. The unification of Bulgaria was announced here in 1885; but Sofia became capital of the unified state and Plovdiv's influence slowly declined.

Now Bulgaria's second city, Plovdiv is decidedly not a place of great beauty, ringed as it is by depressing industrial buildings and tower blocks. However, there is still much of interest in the central old town, where the coarsely cobbled streets, cluttered with houses from the Middle Ages and the National Revival Period, and dotted with Roman remains, possess a charm and character not found in Sofia.

Archaeological finds date Plovdiv to around 4000 BC, and the city was occupied by Thracians and Macedonians before the Romans took over in 72 BC. Remains of Trimontium, the 'city of the three hills', include the partially restored 2nd-century marble **Roman Theatre** *(Djoumaya Square),* one of Bulgaria's most notable archaeological sites. Nestling in the old town, the amphitheatre affords stark views over the modern Plovdiv suburbs to the mountains beyond. Gladiator tournaments took place in the Philippopolis Stadium, the few surviving seats of which are opposite a concrete cocktail bar terrace on *Piaţa Noemvri,* in the heart of the city. The remains of the Roman Forum, including marble floors, can be seen in the central square near Hotel Trimontium. The city's most important contribution to recent Bulgarian culture is the **Plovdiv National Revival Period house.** This refers not to a single house, but to many, scattered around the old city, which has

278

been designated an Archaeological-Historical Preserve. A cluster of fine examples of the style, mainly from the early 19th century, can be found towards the north end of the old town. The **Balabanov House** now hosts recitals and exhibits works by contemporary Bulgarian painters; the **Lamartine House** includes a museum room dedicated to the French writer and statesman.

The **Ethnographic Museum,** *Argit Koyumdjioglu House,* has exhibits on the local culture, while the **Archaeological Museum,** *1 Piaţa Saedineni,* contains relics from Plovdiv's earliest days right up to the National Revival.

### SIDE TRACKS FROM PLOVDIV

From Plovdiv you can visit the spa town of Hisar, some 50 km north of Plovdiv, on a spur line from the Plovdiv–Karlovo line. For a much longer side-track, four trains a day run east from Plovdiv to **Burgas** on the Black Sea, from where you can explore Bulgaria's tourist resorts. The journey takes about 4 hrs 30 mins.

Having long been a favourite destination for Eastern Europeans, the Black Sea coast is slowly establishing popularity with Western travellers.

## HISAR

**Tourist Office:** *Ul. Augusta 16.*
Hisar is noted for its mineral springs, which were already famous in ancient times. The Romans called the town Augusta and made it a place of baths, fountains and temples – Roman women were particularly attracted by the waters' supposed benefits during and after pregnancy. There are ruins of ancient buildings, including two basilicas, and a frescoed Roman tomb.

Many Bulgarians come to Hisar today for cures at the modern mineral baths in the town.

## BURGAS

**Station:** The station is on *Garov Ploshtad,* beside the bus station and the boat station, from which hydrofoils and ferries leave for other resorts up and down the coast. The **Railway Booking Office** is almost 1 km to the north, at *Ul Aleksandrovska 106; tel: (056) 4 70 23.*
**Tourist Office:** The **Balkantourist** office (open daily 0800–2000) is just outside the Railway Station, at *Ul. Aleksandrovska 2; tel: (056) 4 55 53.* The staff can book private rooms in the town and in the surrounding area, as well as in-town and resort hotels.

### GETTING AROUND

The centre of Burgas and the adjoining coastal strip along the Sea Gardens is small and can easily be done on foot. For trips to nearby resorts, leave from the **bus station** on *Garov Ploshtad.*

### ACCOMODATION AND FOOD

Balkantourist is the first place to try, although hawkers may already have approached you at the station with offers of private rooms at very cheap rates: get them to name their price and point out on a map where the property is located. There are some new private agencies on *Ul. Bogoridi.* Anyone who needs a bit of at least near-luxury should try to pre-book the **Hotel Bâlgariya,** *Ul. Aleksandrovska 21; tel (056) 45336.*

Some fancy cafés can be found on *Ul. Bogoridi,* between the Hotel Bâlgariya and the Sea Gardens, and also on the main thoroughfare, *Ul.*

*Aleksandrovska.* Hotel restaurants are at least reliable if rarely exciting, and the garden terrace of Burgaska Streshta, *Ul. Dimitrova,* is a pleasant place in the evening.

### SIGHTSEEING

Burgas itself is not one of the prettiest places on the coast, being more of a port and industrial town than a scenic seaside resort. But it does make a good place from which to explore the coast in the area, while being a bit better placed for getting back to the main Sofia–Istanbul line than is Varna further north.

It also lies on one of the main European bird-migrating routes, so a pair of binoculars might be a useful accessory. In town, the **Archaeological Museum** *(Ul. Bogoridi 21),* containing Greek, Roman and Byzantine remains, and the **Art Gallery** *(Vodenicharov 22)* are worth a visit. It is not safe to bathe in the sea at Burgas, due to severe environmental pollution in the bay. Resorts north and south of the town, such as Sozopol (the ancient Apollonia Pontica), are safe however. ⬛

### EDIRNE

It is possible to leave the Balkan Express at **Edirne,** about 40km along the railway line to Istanbul from the Bulgarian-Turkish border, and 230km from Istanbul itself. The onward journey by Turkish Railways Edirne–Istanbul service takes about 5hrs; and the bus takes about 4 hrs. **Station:** The railway station lies away from the centre, in the southern part of the city.

**Tourist Information:** The office on *Talapaşa Cad; 76/A; tel: (02 84) 2 25 52 60,* gives out maps and brochures and can help with accommodation.

### ACCOMMODATION

Perhaps the most memorable place to stay is **Rüstem Paşa Kervansaray Oteli;** *Iki Kapili Han Cad.; tel: (02 84) 2 12 61 91,* a centuries old converted caravansarai.

### SIGHTSEEING

The city stands in the Turkish part of the Thracian plain. Founded by the Roman emperor Hadrian in the second century AD as Hadrianopolis (Adrianople), the town was the site of a disastrous Roman military defeat in 378 against the Visigoths. Two-thirds of the Roman army, including the Emperor Valens, were killed and the Goths were able to establish themselves inside the empire. Later, under the Byzantines, Hadrianopolis was a fortified city defending the frontier with Bulgaria. Today, the town has many Islamic monuments, and is particularly rich in mosques. The colossal **Selimiye Camii** mosque is certainly Edirne's most impressive, and with its giant dome, and attached covered bazaar and gardens, forms a notable centre to the town. European Turkey's oldest mosque, the **Yildirim Camii** mosque, dates back to the 14th century.

On the island of Sarayiçi in the Tunca Nehri river, which flows through the city, are the ruins of the **Saray-i Cedid** (New Palace), built by Sultan Murad II in the 15th century. Today, the island is the scene of a colourful wrestling tournament every July, that dates back to the 14th century.

# TALLINN

Seen from far out at sea, the Estonian capital is a cluster of spires rising from a dark, mysterious mound. This is Toompea, the hill on which the city was founded back in the 11th century. Close to, Tallinn emerges as a perfectly preserved Hanseatic town of the 14th-15th centuries with traces of an even earlier Scandinavian presence. To do it justice you'll need to spend at least two or three days here.

## TOURIST INFORMATION

**Tourist Office**, *Raekoja Plats 18; tel: 666 959* Open 0900–1800 Mon–Fri, 1000–1500 Sat–Sun. The helpful English-speaking staff are happy to assist with accommodation, brochures tours and general information. You can also buy the listings magazine *Tallinn this Week* here and look out for the new *Tallinn In Your Pocket* (in preparation).

**Estravel**: *Liivalaia 33; tel: 315 565* (near the Hotel Olümpia) or *Suur-Karja 15; tel: 406 888* will also assist with accommodation and tours. **Estonian Holidays**, *Viru Väljak 4; tel: 630 1930* offer a walking tour of the old town as well as various other explorations of the city.

## ARRIVING AND DEPARTING

### Airport
**Tallinna Lennujaam**, *Lennujaama 2; tel: 211 092*. The terminal is 3 km south-east of the city centre. Tallinn airport operates international flights to and from Stockholm, Helsinki, Riga, Copenhagen, Frankfurt, Amsterdam, Moscow, St Petersburg and Vilnius. There is a 24-hr

service bureau, also ticket sales, information, payphones, car hire, café, shops, currency exchange and post office. You can take a taxi into town for about US$5; alternatively bus no. 22 leaves from in front of the terminal every 15–30 minutes.

### Station
**Baltijaam**, *Toompuiestee 35; tel: 446 756* The station, just outside the old town, is for international services to Riga, Warsaw, Moscow and St Petersburg. Facilities include a left luggage office downstairs, shops, a recently refurbished café and a separate suburban booking office to the side of the main terminal. Estonian railway timetables (*Reisirongide Soiduplaan*) are available in the booking hall.

### Buses and Ferries
From **Autobussijaan**, *Tartu maantee; tel: 422 549*, buses go to Riga, Vilnius, Klaipeda, St Petersburg, Kaliningrad, Warsaw and Berlin.

The four **ferry** terminals at Tallinn harbour are located about 1.5 km from the city centre. Terminal A is for Finland, B is for Sweden. The passenger terminals have ticket sales, currency exchange, bars, shops etc.

## GETTING AROUND
For maps of Tallinn ask at the Tourist Office.

### Public Transport
All the sights are within walking distance, but Tallinn is well-served with trams, trolley-buses, route taxis and taxis. Not

all services are reliable however and there is a lot of overcrowding. Public transport runs from 0600 to 2400. Tickets are sold at news stands and at stalls adjacent to the stops. Tickets should be validated on the vehicle.

Some useful routes are trams nos 1 and 2 for the port, nos 1 and 3 for Kadriorg, bus no. 65 from the port to the city centre. Bus no. 22 links up the bus and railway stations and the airport.

## Taxis

There are plenty of cabs about. Take the usual precautions – check there's a meter and that it is running, and agree on a price beforehand. As a rule of thumb, the better the car, the higher the price. There are taxi ranks on *Narva maantee* (near Hotel Viru), *Pärnu maantee*, junction with *G. Otsa* and the railway station. **Route taxis** run 1500–2400, departing from *Viru väljak* (near Hotel Viru). They travel on fixed routes and stop on request. Tickets are sold by the driver.

### STAYING IN TALLINN

## Accommodation

There's a wide range of accommodation, from the 4-star **Palace Hotel** to bed and breakfast. Probably the best value in its price range is the 3-star **Olümpia**, *Liivalaia 33; tel: 631 5315*. In its post-Soviet reincarnation, this hotel takes some beating – all rooms have satellite TV, hairdryers etc. and there's a wide choice of restaurants, cafés (one all night), bars, sauna, currency exchange and shop. For the time being at least the Olümpia is much superior to its main rival the **Viru** – and it's cheaper too. Among the smaller hotels, the **Mihkli** (*Endla 23; tel: 453 704*) and the **Central** (*Narva maantee 7; tel: 633 9800*) can be recommended. The

**Family Hotel Service Network**, *Mere puiestee 6; tel: 441 187*, advertises family stays and separate apartments at around US$10 a day; or you can try **Bed and Breakfast**, *Sadama 11; tel: 602 091* starting at about US$15 per day. The **Youth Hostel**, known as **The Barn**, is in an excellent old town location at *Viru 1; tel: 445 338*. For camping contact **Tourist Agency Silvest**, *Viljandi maantee 6; tel: 556 525* or **Kloostrimetsa Camping**, *Kloostrimetsa tee 56; tel: 238 686*

## Eating and Drinking

Visitors need look no further than charming *Raekoja Plats* and its cobbled surrounds. It's a lively scene in summer. The best cellar bars are in great demand, so if you see somewhere you'd like to eat out in, go in and book. Typical of what's on offer is **Eeslitall** (The Donkey's Stable), *Dukri 4/6; tel: 448 033*, reservations essential. If your taste is for homely Estonian cooking (Baltic herring and meatballs in sour cream for example), look no further than the sign of the fried egg at **Vanaema Juures**, *Ratatskevu 10/12; tel: 448 504*. There is a **McDonalds** at the gateway to the old town, *Viru 24*, which serves an early breakfast for overnight travellers. Another popular fast food outlet is **Peetri Pizza**, *Lai 4*. One of the friendliest bars in Tallinn is the Irish bar **Hell Hunt**, *Pikk 39* where, in the evenings, you can hear traditional Celtic sounds by courtesy of an Estonian band. For a quiet tête à tête, join the local clientele in **Tolli** bar, *Pikk 66*. There is a supermarket, **Kaubahall**, *Aia 7*, just 200 metres from the Hotel Viru.

## Communications

The **central post office** is at *Narva maantee 1; tel: 442 347*, open Mon–Fri

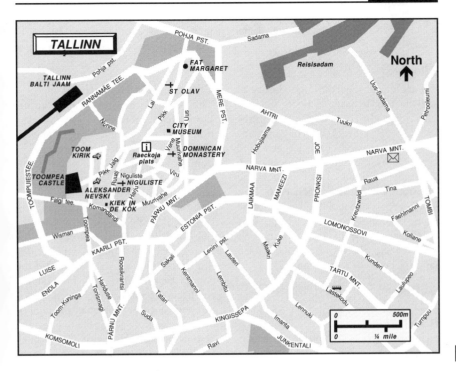

0800–2000 and Sat 0800–1700. There is also a post office in Toompea on *Lossi plats*. Stamps can be bought from hotels and the tourist office.

Public **telephones** are all operated by cards which are sold at post offices. To phone Tallinn from abroad dial your country's international code + 372 2.

## Money

There are currency exchange offices all over Tallinn. Most hotels, major restaurants and stores accept credit cards but have cash with you in case. Cash is available round the clock with Visa card in **Hotel Viru**. You can change travellers' cheques at **Tallinna Pank**, *Pärnu maantee 10*

## Consulates

**Canada:** *Toom-kooli 13*; *tel: 449 056*.
**UK:** *Kentmanni 20*; *tel: 631 3462*.

**USA:** *Kentmanni 20*; *tel: 631 2021*.
**Australia**, **New Zealand**, **Republic of Ireland**, **South Africa:** none. If necessary apply to the British Embassy.

## ENTERTAINMENT AND EVENTS

Nightlife is fairly thin on the ground in Tallinn. The hotels apart, most cafés and bars tend to empty out at 2300 or even earlier. An honourable exception is **Von Krahli Teatri Baar**, *Ratatskevu 10,* a popular student haunt where you can often hear some of the best local bands. If you like rock music, keep your ear to the ground for **Rock Summer**, held in July, the largest festival of its kind in Eastern Europe. If your taste is for classical music, **Estonia Teater**, *Estonia puiestee 4*, puts on opera and ballet performances to a high standard. There are nightclubs in the major hotels or you could try **Bel Air**,

*Vana-Viru 14*, or **Max Marine**, *Pärnu maantee 19*.

## SHOPPING

For traditional souvenirs a good place to start looking is *Saiakäik*, under the arch off *Raekoja plats*, or the little shop in the cellar of the Town Hall. For unpretentious but attractive Estonian glass and ceramics, try the souvenir shop at *Lai 4*. For something out of the ordinary the **Dominican Kloister Museum** sells fine pottery, candleholders, jars etc. made from Dolomite limestone. There is a small open air market under the city walls in *Müürivahe* where you can buy a small range of knitwear and clothing.

## SIGHTSEEING

### Raejoka Plats
Sightseeing, like everything else, begins at *Raekoja plats* (Town Hall Square). The grey stone **Town Hall** is remarkable for its slender Gothic tower. It's the oldest building of its kind in Europe – merchants began to trade from its arcades and cellars back in the 14th century. The interior is closed to the public with the exception of the tower, a steep climb but a must for its unsurpassed views across the old town and Tallinn harbour. Medieval Tallinn is wonderfully well preserved. Many of the houses, for example **Raeapteek** (the pharmacy) at *Raekoja plats 11* have been around for more than 350 years. The narrow streets off *Raekoja plats* with picturesque names like White Bread Passage (*Saiakäik*) preserve much of Tallinn's medieval history as a centre of commerce. The merchants' houses in this quarter, some of which date back from the 14th and 15th centuries, are superbly decorated with carved wooden doorways, paintings and stone reliefs. The

most famous example is the **house of the Brotherhood of Blackheads** at *Pikk 26*.

## Churches and Monasteries
The Gothic remains of the former **Dominican monastery**, *Vene 16*, date from the 13th century. Now a museum, it contains a fascinating collection of stone carvings and sculptures and visitors can explore the cloisters and what remains of the monks' living quarters (open daily 1000–1800). Tucked away to the side of *Saiakäik* is the beautiful 14th-century **Pühavaimu** (Church of the Holy Spirit), an unusual double-aisled structure – one aisle was reserved for the poor of the almshouses. The most important feature to survive the Reformation is a magnificent altar triptych by the Lübeck master, Bernt Notke, showing the descent of the Holy Spirit. The white-towered **Niguliste** (St Nicholas Church) on the street of the same name is a museum devoted to works of art from the Middle Ages. The exhibits include the church's own high altar (15th century) and a Dance Macabre fragment by Notke (open Wed 1400–1800; Thurs–Sun 1100–1800). At the far northern end of *Pikk* is Tallinn's most outstanding landmark, the **Oleviste** (St Olaf's Church). The dedicatee is King Olaf II of Norway and this was once the place of worship of Tallinn's large Scandinavian community.

## Musuems
A must for visitors is the quaintly named **Kiek in de kök** (Peep in the Kitchen) tower-museum. This massive bastion now houses a well-ordered display on Tallinn's military history – there are cannon, weapons, models, maps etc and when you get to the top you are rewarded with some fine views of the city

(open Tues–Fri 1030–1530; Sat–Sun 1100–1630). Another of Tallinn's mighty bastions, **Paks Margareeta** (Fat Margaret) *Pikk 70*, plays host to an entertaining exhibition on Tallinn's maritime history (open Wed–Sun 1000–1800). For visitors curious to see the inside of one of the merchant's houses, there's the **Linnamuuseum** (City Museum) with an exhibition on Tallinn in the 18th–19th centuries, open Apr–Nov, Wed–Mon 1030–1730 (1630 Dec–Mar). The **Town Hall prison** on *Raekoja Plats 4/6* is also open to the public (Apr–Sep, Thurs–Tues 1030–1930 (1630 Oct–Mar).

### Toompea

This ancient fortified settlement was once a town in its own right. Dominating the hill is the splendid **Toomkirik**. Tallinn's Cathedral Church was founded in 1233 but rebuilt after a fire in 1684. It's noted for its stone sarcophagi, which trumpet the virtues of Swedish military heroes and others. The most intrusive monument on Toompea is the garish 19th-century **Alexander Nevsky Cathedral**, a reminder that Tallinn, then known as Reval, was a part of the Russian Empire. The distinctive blue and black flag of Estonia flies proudly from one of the 14th-century turrets of Toompea fortress, now home to the parliament of Estonia.

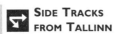

### SIDE TRACKS FROM TALLINN

#### PIRITA

Just a 15-min bus ride from Tallinn (nos 1, 8, 25, 34, 38 or 42) are the evocative ruins of the **Convent of St Birgitta**, completed on the eve of the Reformation only to be destroyed shortly thereafter. Armed with a map (available at the entrance) the visitor can trace the monastic life of the monks and nuns who once worshipped here: the cloisters, guest rooms, cellars as well as the great triangular facade of the main church can all be explored. Ask at the kiosk for a key to the tower for splendid views across Tallinn Bay.

#### HAAPSALU

**Information Office**, *Karja 2; tel: 450 37.*

The attractive town of Haapsalu has a number of sights worth visiting, including the castle ruins, a picturesque town hall (now a heritage museum), several churches and a bench on which the composer Tchaikovsky once sat! There are ferries to the two islands of Vormsi and Hiiumaa and a rewarding hinterland to explore, including a bird sanctuary in the **Matsalu Nature Reserve**. Three hours by train (infrequent) from Tallinn.

#### PÄRNU

**Station:** *Riia maantee, tel: 407 73*, is 5 km from the town centre (buses leave from outside). Three hours by local train from Tallinn.

**Tourist Office:** *Munga 2; tel: 455 33.*

Pärnu is the seaside resort with a small, picturesque old town and extensive sandy beaches beyond the **Rannapark**. Pärnu is well served with cafés, restaurants and shops. For snacks with drinks try the **Kroomi Cellar Bar**, *Haapsalu mnt 11* or **Vesuvio Pizza**, *Tallina mnt 89,* or, for more substantial fare, **Restaurant Rendez-Vous**, *Akadeemia 5; tel: 40 468,* which serves vegetarian as well as fish dishes.

# TALLINN–HELSINKI

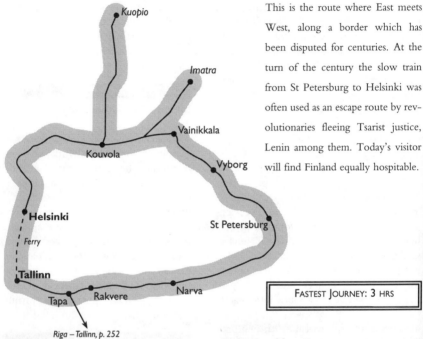

This is the route where East meets West, along a border which has been disputed for centuries. At the turn of the century the slow train from St Petersburg to Helsinki was often used as an escape route by revolutionaries fleeing Tsarist justice, Lenin among them. Today's visitor will find Finland equally hospitable.

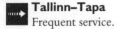

Riga – Tallinn, p. 252

| FASTEST JOURNEY: 3 HRS |
| --- |

## TRAINS

**ETT Tables:** 1255, 1295, 1297, 910, 902

### FAST TRACK

→ Ships, catamarans and hydrofoils cross the Gulf of Finland, taking between 3 and 4 hrs.

### ON TRACK

····▶ **Tallinn–Tapa**
Frequent service.

**Tapa–Rakvere**
4 trains a day taking 30 mins.

**Rakvere–Narva**
4 trains a day journey 2 hrs.

**Narva–St Petersburg**
Just one train a day links Narva to St Petersburg at unsociable hours.

**St Petersburg–Vyborg**
Two a day, reservations required, takes 1 hr 30 mins.

**Vyborg–Vainkkala–Kouvola**
Three trains a day taking 1 hr from Vyborg to Vainkkala and the same from Vainkkala to Kouvola.

**Kouvola–Helsinki**
Frequent trains taking 2 to 2½ hrs

## Ferries

There are several daily services Tallinn and Helsinki, operated by **Tallink**, tel: (Helsinki) 21 211, (Tallinn) 44 2440. The ferries complete the 80 km crossing in about 3½ hours. A faster alternative in summer only is the hydrofoil: **Tallink Express** runs a regular daily service which covers the distance in just 1½ hours. In Tallinn, ferries leaving for Finland use Terminal A in the main harbour; the Tallink Express terminal for hydrofoils is just to the rear at Linnahall. In Helsinki, Tallink services now depart from the Länsisatama (West Terminal). All the ships have a currency exchange office, duty-free shops, catering and bars. There are unsupervised luggage holds and lockers, not all of which will accommodate rucksacks or large cases. In summer many services are fully booked by Finnish passengers on cheap day shopping trips to Tallinn.

## RAKVERE

**Station**: *Jaama 8; tel: 42 008*
**Tourist Information**: *Turuplats 2; tel: 45 656*

This small town, one of the oldest in Estonia, was a wellspring of the Estonia Nationalist movement in the 19th century. The dominant sight is undoubtedly the **Order Castle** built by the Danes in the 13th century and now the setting for all kinds of summer events including rock concerts. There are some picturesque streets in the old town but little in the way of restaurants and bars.

## NARVA

**Station**: *Vaksali 23; tel: 24 065* The station is the frontier crossing into Russia.
**Tourist Information: Travel Agency**

**Viru Tuur** *Peetri Plats 3; tel: 22 012*
A bone of contention for centuries between Russia and Sweden, Narva is now part of Estonia, although the population is almost entirely Russian. Much of the old town was destroyed during World War II but you can still visit the impressive **Narva Castle** (and Town Museum), dating from the 13th century. If you're staying overnight the recently restored **Hotell Vanalinn**, *Koidula 6; tel: 22 486* is comfortable if expensive.

## VYBORG

**Station:** *Zheleznodorozhnaya ulitsa.* In the vicinity you'll find a customs post, souvenir shop, restaurant and the three-star **Druzhba Hotel** – there isn't much alternative accomodation in Vyborg.

This Russian port, situated on the north-eastern shore of the Gulf of Finland, is known as Viipuri to the Finns, who regard it as their own. It's easy to see why - most of the sights, the **Castle** for example, betray earlier Scandinavian influences and the historic churches are Lutheran rather than Russian Orthodox. There's even a ferry to the Finnish Lake District from here.

## KUOVOLA

**Station:** *tel: 742 711*
Kuovola's significance lies in its location as the gateway to the famous Finnish Lake District. There is a slow train from Kuovola to Helsinki which stops at Pasila, Riihimäki and Lahti. **Lahti** is best known as a ski resort - there's an international cross country ski race every February. You'll find other winter sports here too.

It's 1 hr by rail from here to **Imatra** with its spectacular waterfall; 3½ hrs to **Kuopio**, the cultural heart of Karelia and the point of embarkation for boat trips, steamers and general sightseeing.

# VENICE

The island city of Venice, with its chequered history and magnificent works of art and architecture has captured the imagination of travellers for centuries. Once a powerful maritime republic and a city of enormous prosperity, these days it defies all the odds in an effort to remain upright subject, as it is, to capricious tides, sinking mud and the tramp of nearly 10 million tourists' feet each year. Virtually unchanged over the centuries, the canals and alleys are still lined with curiously elaborate Gothic houses, Renaissance palaces and the baroque of the architect Longhena. Most extraordinary of all is its unique spider-web of canals which reach into every corner of the city. Venice is compact and many of its highlights can be absorbed in two or three days, but it will certainly reward a longer stay.

## TOURIST INFORMATION

The **Azienda Promozione Turistica** (**APT**), *Calle dell'Ascensione 71C, tel: (041) 522 6356 (off Piazza San Marco)* is open daily except Sun, 0830–1930 (Apr–Oct); 0830–1330 (Nov–Mar). APT also has offices at **Santa Lucia station**, *tel: (041) 719 078,* and at the *Lido, Gran Viale Santa Maria Elisabetta 6A, tel: (041) 526 5721.*

For youth information, contact the **Comune di Venezia Assessorato al Gioventù**, *San Marco 1529; tel: (041) 270 7650.* A **Carta Giovani** allows 14–29 year-olds cheap entry to museums, art gal-

leries, theatres, cinemas and cultural events, maps, cut-price shopping guide and reductions on public transport. It is free from the APT offices – take a photograph and your passport. A **Biglietto Cumulativo** is available to all to visit two out of five museums. The total cost of the card is L16,000.

## ARRIVING AND DEPARTING

### Airport
**Marco Polo International Airport** is 13 km north-east of Venice; flight information; *tel: (041) 661 262.* The ATVO bus no. 5 operates half-hourly (hourly in winter) between the airport and *Piazzale Romana*, where those travelling on into Venice must transfer to the city's waterborne public transport system (**ACTV**). The Co-operative San Marco ferry service operates from the airport (daylight hours, summer) via the Lido to the *Piazza San Marco* in the heart of Venice.

### Stations
To get to Venice proper, take a train terminating at **Santa Lucia** station; some trains will deposit you at **Mestre**, on the mainland. The two stations are 10 mins apart by rail, and all Santa Lucia trains call at Mestre. A frequent local service operates between Mestre and Santa Lucia. Santa Lucia has its own *vaporetto* (water-bus) stop, right outside the station, at the north-east end of the Grand Canal. Santa Lucia enquiries, *tel: (041) 715555.*

## GETTING AROUND

Europe's only roadless city is a joy to

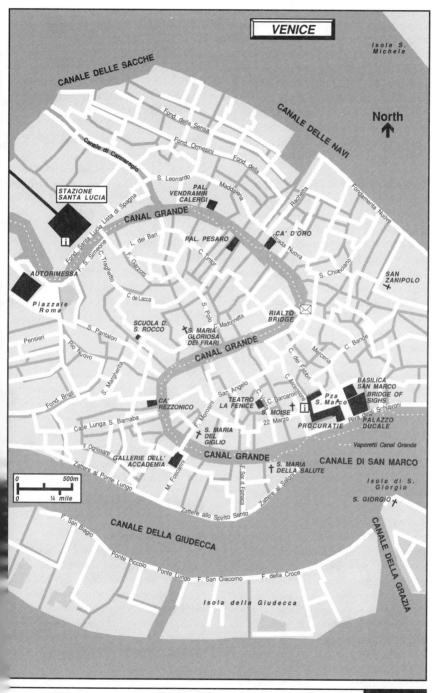

**VENICE**

*Isola S. Michele*

CANALE DELLE SACCHE

CANALE DELLE NAVI

North ↑

Fond. della Sensa

Fond. Ormesini

Fond. della

Canale di Cannaregio

S. Leonardo

Maddalena

**PAL. VENDRAMIN CALERGI**

Racheta

Fondamenta Nuova

**STAZIONE SANTA LUCIA**

**CANAL GRANDE**

Fond. Santa Lucia Lista di Spagna

F. S. Simeone

C. Traghetto

L. dei Bari

**PAL. PESARO**

**CA' D'OHO**

Strada Nuova

C. Tintor

**AUTORIMESSA**

F. Garzotti

C. de Lacca

S. Chiacano

**SAN ZANIPOLO** ✝

*Piazzale Roma*

**SCUOLA D. S. ROCCO**

✝ **S. MARIA GLORIOSA DEI FRARI**

S. Polo

C. Madonnetta

**RIALTO BRIDGE**

⊠

Pensieri

S. Pantalon

Rio Nuovo

S. Margherita

**CANAL GRANDE**

C. dei Fabbri

Merceria

C. Bande

**289**

Fond. Briati

San Angelo

C. Vaseri

C. Ascensione

C. Barcaroli

**TEATRO LA FENICE**

**S. MOISE**

22 Marzo

**Pza S. Marco**

**BASILICA SAN MARCO**

**BRIDGE OF SIGHS**

Riva degli Schiavoni

**CA' REZZONICO**

C. Morosini

**PROCURATIE**

**PALAZZO DUCALE**

Calle Lunga S. Barnaba

✝ **S. MARIA DEL GIGLIO**

F. Ognissani

**GALLERIE DELL' ACCADEMIA**

M. Foscarini

**CANAL GRANDE**

---- *Vaporetti Canal Grande*

Zattere al Ponte Lungo

✝ **S. MARIA DELLA SALUTE**

**CANALE DI SAN MARCO**

| 0 | 500m |
| 0 | ¼ mile |

F. Sor. d. Fornaca

Zattere al Saloni

*Isola di S. Giorgio*

**S. GIORGIO** ✝

F. San Biagio

Zattere allo Spirito Santo

CANALE DELLA GIUDECCA

Ponte Piccolo

Ponte Lungo

F. San Giacomo

F. della Croce

CANALE DELLA GRAZIA

*Isola della Giudecca*

explore, with its great public buildings and magnificent palaces overlooking the grand canal or unexpectedly tucked away on the maze of smaller canals called *rii* which separate the city's 100-plus islands. Prepare yourself for plenty of walking, and don't be surprised when you get lost. A good map, with *vaporetto* routes and street names, is available from the tourist office and at Venice's many news-stands.

## Tickets

A three-day *turisticche* (tourist ticket), cost L18000, enables you to use all *vaporetto* routes except the Line 2 express, and is ideal for those planning to explore some of Venice's outlying islands. Tickets are sold singly or in booklets of ten from kiosks at main stops, open 0600–2100, and must be validated in the machine provided at each pier before boarding. The line 2 express costs approximately 50% more than normal services. A **24-hour** pass is valid for unlimited travel on all lines – L9000. Anybody staying any longer should buy a **Carta Venezia** – valid for up to 3 years. It costs L8000 and is available from the ACTV central office, *Corte dell'Albero, tel: (041) 528 7886.*

## Vaporetto (water-bus)

Other cities have the bus, the train, the tram or the metro. Venice has the *vaporetto.* These water-buses, operated by the **ACTV** transport authority, run at 10–20 minute intervals in daytime and approximately hourly from midnight to 0600. The most useful lines are Line 1, which runs the length of the Grand Canal, stopping frequently, and Line 2, the express service connecting Santa Lucia station, the Rialto, *Piazza San Marco* and the Lido. *Vaporetto* piers bear the line number, but make sure you are heading the right way – it is easy to lose your bearings.

Other lines connect central Venice with its island suburbs in the lagoon. Line 5 is a round-the-islands service taking in Murano and handy if you are staying at the youth hostel on Isola del Giudecca, which has its own stop. **ACTV**, *Piazzale Roma, tel: (041) 520 7555.*

## Traghetto (gondola ferry)

The cheapest gondola ride in Venice is the *traghetto.* These two-gondolier boats cross the Grand Canal at many points along its length (signposted *Traghetto*) and cost less than a single water-bus ticket.

## Water Taxi

Water taxis are very expensive. You could take 40 trips on the Line 2 express for the cost of one taxi ride along the Grand Canal. The fare system is extremely complicated.

## Gondola

Gondola rides are costly, but if you decide to treat yourself to a once-in-a-lifetime experience you should go in the evening, when the canals and the buildings overlooking them are at their most magical. Official rates, which are set according to time, not distance, are available from the APT, but make sure you agree a price with your gondolier before setting out.

## STAYING IN VENICE

## Accommodation

Don't come to Venice looking for cheap and cheerful accommodation. Space is at a premium, and although the city has some of Europe's grandest luxury hotels (such as the legendary **Cipriani**) there are slim pickings for those on a tight budget, especially in summer, when booking ahead is strongly advisable. **AVA** (Venetian Hotel Association) has reservation desks at Santa

Lucia station, *tel: (041) 715 016 or (041) 715 288*, open daily Apr–Oct 0800–2200; Nov–Mar, 0800–2130, and at Marco Polo International Airport. Hotel chains with property in the city include: *Ch, BW, Ra, Ex, Pu.* The main HI **youth hostel** (Albergho per la Gioventù is on Isola del Giudecca *(vaporetto: line 5), tel: (041) 523 8211.* For further hostel information, contact the **Associazone Alberghi per la Gioventù**, *Palazzo della Civiltà del Lavoro, Quadrato della Concordia, 00144 Roma, tel: (06) 593 1702.* The nearest campsite is on the Lido, *Camping San Nicolò; tel: (041) 526 7415.*

## Eating and Drinking

Like all Italian cities, Venice takes pride in its distinctive regional cuisine. As you would expect of a race of lagoon-dwellers and mariners, Venetian cooking leans heavily toward sea-food.

In an expensive country for travellers, Venice is one of the more expensive cities, and the price of a meal or even a drink in one of the restaurants and cafés catering to tourists around the *Piazza San Marco* or *Rialto* will take your breath away. Drinks at a table cost up to three times as much as those taken at the bar. Wander off the beaten track and see where the Venetians are eating. There you'll find the best food and considerably better prices.

Good news for budget travellers is the array of eat-as-you-go snacks available; buy a slice of *pizza* from a snack-bar, absorb an *espresso* standing at the bar of a back-street café, and you will save enough money to eat well in the evening at a small trattoria – look for places catering to ordinary Venetians rather than tourists, though these are not always easy to find in a city so thoroughly devoted to tourism. Have a picnic lunch; buy the ingredients from a delicatessen, along with bottle of cold white wine which the vendor will be happy to open, and go and perch on the edge of a quiet canal.

## Communications

Main **post office: Poste Centrali,** *Rialto, Fontego dei Tedeschi, tel: (041) 522 0606.* To phone Venice from abroad: *tel: 39 (Italy) + 41 (Venice) + number;* to phone Venice from elsewhere in Italy: *tel: (041) + number.*

## Embassies and Consulates

UK: **Campo Santa Maria della Carità,** *1051, Dorsoduro, tel: (041) 522 7207.*

## Money

All central banks will change your money, as will bureaux de change in the city centre, at the station and at the airport. Ask for a supply of small-denomination bills – every shop and café in Italy is perennially short of change. **Thomas Cook** bureaux de change are located at *5126 Riva del Ferro (Rialto); tel: (041) 5287358* and *Piazza San Marco, 142; tel: (041) 5224751.*

## ENTERTAINMENT

The entertainment calendar is busier in summer than in winter, with events like the annual **Venice film festival** (late Aug to early Sept). Music – opera, classical and choral – is prominent. The free *Guest in Venice* guide, available from the APT and at most hotel front desks, will tell you what's on. The big event of the year is **Carnival,** ten days of masked balls, fancy dress parties and colourful street celebrations around Shrove Tuesday each year.

## Nightlife

Venice has numerous bars and clubs offering live music, dancing and late-night drinking. As everywhere in Italy, nightlife only begins to warm up at midnight. The best guide to nightlife venues and events is *Notturno Veneziana*, available at APT offices.

## Theatres, Cinemas and Concerts

Venice is not a great theatrical city and Italian drama is a closed book to non-natives. **Opera**, with its gorgeous costumes and magnificent arias is, on the other hand, accessible to everybody and the works of Verdi, Puccini and others are in performance virtually year-round. The main venue, the **Teatro La Fenice**, has been gutted by fire, but plans are being made to restore it.

Free concerts are often held in the city's churches, especially in tandem with other summer cultural events; enquire at APT offices for details of these. The *Palazzo del Cinema* on the Lido is the venue for the annual film festival and for frequent showings of international films all year round.

## SHOPPING

Bargain buys are thin on the ground, and many people touring the neighbouring islands of the lagoon, such as Murano, are disappointed to find prices are much the same as in the city centre. **Venetian glass** is the big shopping deal, but much of what is sold is over-priced; try major vendors such as **Cenedese** or **Salviati**, both on *Piazza San Marco*.

More affordable, and uniquely Venetian, are the painted papier-maché masks sold in many small stores. The best time to visit the **Rialto open-air market** is early morning; it's closed on Sun and quiet on Mon. Otherwise, shopping in this city, which is full of merchandise treasures, is much the same as you might find in Rome or Milan. You can always unearth a bit of old velvet from the antique shops, a gilded picture frame or a bit of coral jewellery.

## SIGHTSEEING

The beauty of sightseeing in Venice is that the city is a living museum with (as yet) no admission charge, although there is talk of introducing one. This causes problems: during the summer months its heart – **Piazza San Marco** and the surrounding neighbourhood – is densely-packed with tourists. There is, however, a steep entrance fee for almost all Venice's major sights. The biggest concentration of these is around the *Piazza San Marco*, making it the logical starting point for exploring the city. Almost all the rest – including the palaces of medieval Venice's great magnates – are strung out along the length of the S-shaped Grand Canal.

## Piazza San Marco

Close to the mouth of the Grand Canal and overlooking the Canale di San Marco, the *Piazza* is Venice at its most striking – and, in summer, at its most crowded. Here there are four highlights. The **Basilica di San Marco** (St Mark's), consecrated in 1094, has a sumptuous façade, curious Oriental-style domes, elaborate mosaics (the best of which date from the 13th century), and a museum containing sculpture and carvings from all over the medieval Venetian empire. The basilica was built to house the bones of St Mark the Evangelist – swiped from their resting place in Alexandria in the 9th century. There are ancient columns of rare, coloured marble, exquisite early pavements of inlaid marble, glass and porphyry and, best of all acres of ancient mosaic. See in particular the 13th-century originals in the atrium domes, the 11th-century image of the *Madonna and Saints* over the central door and the 14th-century scenes from the *Life of St John the Baptist* in the Baptistery.

One of the supreme prizes here are the legendary **Horses of St Mark** which adorn the external façade. Cast some time between the 3rd century BC and the 2nd century AD, and stolen from Byzantium by the Venetians in 1204, they are a powerful symbol of the Republic of Venice. The effects of pollution mean that the originals have had to be removed for safekeeping in the museum – those out in the *piazza* are recent copies.

Next to the basilica stands the **Palazzo Ducale** (the Doge's Palace) which was begun in 1309 then rebuilt in 1577. A sumptuous civic palace, built in an exotic, highly decorated Venetian Gothic style, it contains important Venetian works of art while providing an interesting view on the life and style of the Venetian rulers. The real business of state took place away from the grand rooms seen on a tour of the palace. On what is called the **Itinerari Segreti** (Secret Itinerary), you get to see into tiny, wood-panelled chambers, interesting, decorated meeting rooms, and the torture chamber. The **Bridge of Sighs** next to the palace leads to the **Palazzo delle Prigione**, the prison for petty offenders. Opposite the palace, the **Campanile di San Marco** (see p. 294) completes the quartet of the square's most important buildings.

### Canale Grande (Grand Canal): East Bank

Following the canal in its serpentine north-westward trend from *San Marco* you can stop off at the baroque church of **San Moise** and its neighbour **Santa Maria del Giglio**, and pass beneath the handsome **Ponte di Rialto**, built in 1592 at the geographic heart of the city, before stopping at the Gothic **Ca'd'Oro**, the most lavish of all the Venetian aristocratic palaces. Following a lengthy programme of restoration, it now houses the **Galleria Franchetti** in which is a magnificent collection of paintings (Mantegna, Guardi, for example), Renaissance bronzes and medallions. Last call is the Renaissance **Palazzo Vendramin Calergi** where Richard Wagner died in 1883.

### Canale Grande: West Bank

On the west bank of the canal, heading north-west from its junction with the Canale di San Marco, stands the **Galleria dell'Accademia**. The is the best place in the world in which to make a study of Venetian art. Here there are canvasses, altarpieces and frescos taken from churches and palaces around the city, among them important works by Bellini. But it is not devoted exclusively to the Venetian school, there are also works by artists of the Florentine Renaissance.

Nearby are two more splendid palaces. The **Ca'Rezzonico** (designed by Longhena in 1667), is the place where Browning died. Now it is the **Museo del Settecento Veneziano**, the Museum of Venice in the Eighteenth Century, and home to rococo furniture and a collection of 18th-century art. The **Ca'Foscari**, the second of the two important palaces, was built in 1437 for the Doge Francesco Foscari. Still on the Grand Canal, and not far from the Accademia, is the important **Peggy Guggenheim Museum** which contains a collection of 20th-century art, all of it put together by Peggy Guggenheim. From here it is only a short walk to the baroque church of **Santa Maria della Salute**, the masterpiece of the architect Longhena and built between 1631-81. Beyond, facing onto the Guidecca, is the church of **San Sebastiano** which contains astonishing illusionistic ceiling frescos by Veronese (c1555). A short walk west of the canal, between the *Rio della Frescada* and the *Campo di San Paolo*, is the **Scuola di San**

293

Rocco, once the headquarters of a charitable confraternity. Inside it houses a magnificent collection of canvases by Tintoretto. If you haven't time to see much in the city, then come here first. This is one of the finest cycles of painting in existence. Nearby is the Medieval church of the **Frari**, principal church of the Franciscan order – and burial place of the painter Titian and of Monteverdi. Built 1330 – 1469, this huge, brick-built, barn-like church is a repository of art: it contains works by Donatello, Bellini and Titian, amongst others. In fact Titian is buried here (see the tomb Antonio Canova designed for him) – as is Monteverdi.

## Other Sights

The **Fondazione Querini-Stampalia** (north-east of *Piazza San Marco*), housed in the 16th-century palace of the same name, is a good place in which to obtain an idea of the decor of an 18th-century Venetian residence. It is still decorated and furnished in contemporary patrician style and has a variety of paintings by Pietro Longhi, Bellini and Tiepolo. Not far away, the vast, brick-built Dominican church of **Santi Giovanni e Paolo** (begun 1246, rebuilt in 1333 and completed in 1430) is filled with the tombs of the Doges – there is a splendid array of Gothic and Renaissance sepulchral art. Outside is the equestrian statue of **Bartolomeo Colleoni**, the 15th-century condottieri who assisted the Venetians in establishing a realm beyond the watery confines of their city.

## View of Venice

The **Campanile di San Marco** on *Piazza di San Marco* is a 20th-century reconstruction of a thousand-year-old bell-tower which fell down in 1912. Take the lift to the top for a panoramic view of Venice and its lagoon. The view towards *Piazza di San Marco* from the island of San *Giorgio Maggiore* is also magnificent – particularly in the evening (if you go at dusk, make sure there is a way of getting back; San Giorgio Maggiore is an isolated island).

## The Islands

The **Lido** is the most glamorous of Venice's islands. Here you come to swim, lounge in the sun and, for those unwise enough to try them, eat in a vastly expensive restaurant. Made famous during the *Belle Époque* (and by Visconti – some of whose scenes from Thomas Mann's *Death in Venice* were filmed here). A free beach is at the island's north end. Organised sightseeing tours of the outlying island **Murano** and its neighbours **Burano** and **Torcello** are little more than showcase trips for the glass factories. You can visit these and other islands just as easily – and much more cheaply – on an ordinary *vaporetto*. Worth it for the view, but the big sights are all in Venice itself.

Facing Piazza di San Marco from the other side of the Grand Canal is the church of **San Giorgio Maggiore**, situated on the little island of San Giorgio Maggiore. Its delicate Renaissance façade is quite at odds with the Oriental jumble of St Mark's and the Palazzo Ducale which it faces. Beside it, the monastery buildings were partly designed by Palladio. A little way to the west, situated on one of the eight islands of the Giudecca, is Palladio's church of the **Redentore** (completed in 1592). It is one of the architect's most important works and was built to commemorate the ending of a horrific bout of plague that killed nearly 50,000 people. The event is still commemorated today in the *Festa del Redentore* (July).

# VENICE–VIENNA

This itinerary runs from Venice on the Adriatic to Austria's capital, Vienna. En route it passes through Trieste, crossroad between Eastern and Western Europe, and continues through Slovenia, part of the former Yugoslavia.

**Vienna**

**Budapest – Graz, p. 172**

| FASTEST JOURNEY: 8 HRS |
|---|

**Graz**

**Maribor**

**Ljubljana**   **Celje**

295

**Postojna**

**Venice**   **Trieste**

## TRAINS
**ETT Tables:** 88, 376, 930, 933, 830.

### FAST TRACK
Three through trains a day. Two day trains take 8 hr. Overnight train with sleeping cars and couchettes takes 10 hrs.

### ON TRACK

**Venice-Trieste**
Trains every hour, journey time 2 hrs.

**Trieste-Postojna**
Four trains a day cross the border from Italy to Slovenia. Journey takes 2 hrs.

**Postojna-Ljubljana**
Frequent service taking 1 hr.

**Ljubljana-Celje**
Almost hourly service taking 1 hr 30 mins.

**Celje-Maribor**
Frequent trains taking just over 1 hr.

**Maribor-Vienna**
Two through trains, another journey possible by changing at Spielfeld Strass. Takes at least 3 hrs 30 mins

## TRIESTE

Italy's easternmost city, once the chief port of the Austro-Hungarian Empire, is also the Istrian hinterland's window on the western world. Rebuilt in the 19th century, it is today a stately, solid place that relishes its role as a crossroads between east and west.

**Station: Stazione Centrale**, *Pza della Libertá 8, tel: (040) 418 207.*

**Tourist Office:** The central office is at *Via San Nicolo 20, tel: (040) 369 881*, and there is a second, smaller one in the station. The regional information office is at *Via Rossini 6, tel: (040) 363 952.*

## POSTOJNA

South west of Ljubljana is one of the world's largest caves, the karst cave outside the little town of Postojna. It is actually a system of caves, in all 27 km long and about 2 million years old and adorned with strange rock formations, stalachtites and stalachmites. A train takes you in and brings you back again and the tour reveals an awesome array of chambers with names like the Beautiful Caves, the Black Cave, the Winter Hall and the **Concert Hall** which can accommodate around 10,000 people for musical performances. There are caves nearby, which are well worth visiting: the Pivka and Black Caves, the Island Cave and Planina Cave are all within 5 km of Postojna.

## LJUBLJANA

See pp. 218–220.

## CELJE

The largest **castle** in Slovenia dominates Celje from the summit of a nearby hill. Built in the 13th century and much altered since, modern restorations have preserved the **Frederick Tower**. There is also a **Lower Castle** in Celje - the for-

mer residence of the Celje Counts who, before the advent of the Hapsburgs, were one of Central Europe's most powerful feudal dynasties. Much of the content of the **Celje Regional Museum**, housed in the 16th-century **Old County Palace**, is devoted to documenting their rule, as is the **Museum of Modern History**. The counts were buried in the Minorite **Church of Mary**, although their bones were removed this century. Other interesting churches include the **Abbey Church of St Daniel** (see the 15th-century Pieta in the Chapel of the Sorrowful Mother), and 15th-century **St Maximilian**. The **International Artisan Fair** is on in Sept.

## MARIBOR

Slovenia's second largest city has a distinctly Austrian heritage. It straddles the Drava River and has an attractive Old Town with a pretty river front. The chief sights are the 15th-century **Castle** which houses the **Maribor Regional Museum**, and the **Cathedral of St John the Baptist** which is adorned with virtually every architectural style from Romanesque to the present day. At the waterside are two interesting medieval landmarks - the 15th-century **Sodni Stolp** (the Judge's Tower) and the 16th-century **Vodni Stolp**, a water tower, which today houses Slovenia's oldest *vinoteka* where you can sample about 300 different Slovenian wines. Elsewhere in town there is an extraordinary 18th-century plague pillar - in the old medieval marketplace *Glavnis trg*, and there is a 15th-century synagogue alongside the Jewish Tower, the **Zidovski Stolp**.

Maribor has plenty of festivals including the June-July **International Baroque Music Festival** and a folkloric **Summer Festival**.

# VIENNA (WIEN)

Of Central Europe's three greatest cities – Vienna, Prague and Budapest – the Austrian capital is the most modern, the most truly cosmopolitan, and culturally the most lively. Vienna's chief attractions are a rich store of architecture, year-round events and hundreds of atmospheric places to eat and drink.

## TOURIST INFORMATION

The **Main Office** is *Kärntnerstr. 38; tel: (01) 513 88 92.* Open 0900–1900. There are also information and accommodation bureaux at **Westbahnhof**, 0615–2300; **Südbahnhof**, 0630–2200, (May–Oct) 0630–2100 (Nov–Apr); and **Schwechat Airport**, 0830–2300 (June–Sept); 0830–2200 (Oct–May). The Tourist Offices has a free map plus a mass of information leaflets. The youth information service, **Jugend Info**, has accommodation details: *Bellaria underground passage, Dr Karl-Renner-Ring* (U2/3 *Volkstheater*) Mon–Fri 1200–1900, Sat and school holidays, 1000–1900; *tel: (01) 526 4637.*

## ARRIVING AND DEPARTING

### Airport

**Schwechat International Airport** is 19 km east of Vienna; flight information, *tel: (01) 711 10-2231/2*; tourist information, *tel: (1) 711 10-0.* Bus transfers (ÖS70) run to the **City Air Terminal** (Hilton Hotel building), *tel: (01) 5800-35404*, 24 hours April–Oct, 0600–2430 Nov–March, and to Westbahnhof, via Südbahnhof, every hour 0640–2040. Taxi to the airport costs around ÖS450 which includes return trip.

### Stations

**Westbahnhof**, *Mariahilferstr./Europapl., tel: (1) 5800-310 60*, serves Austrian destinations west, Germany, Switzerland and Hungary. **Südbahnhof**, *Wiener Gürtel/Arsenalstr.; tel: (01) 5800-310 50*, serves the south, Italy, plus Czech Republic and Hungary. **Franz-Josefs-Bahnhof**, *Julius-Tandler-Pl.; tel: (01) 5800-310 20*, serves the north plus Berlin and Czech Republic. All three are 3–4 km outside *Ringstr.* and are connected to the centre by metro or tram. You can buy all Austrian rail tickets centrally at branches of the **Österreiches Verkhersbüro** travel agency at the same price as at stations. Two central branches are *Friedrichstr. 7; tel: (01) 588 00 0*, and *Opernring 3–5; tel: (01) 588 62 8.*

## GETTING AROUND

The old city (*Innenstadt*) was enclosed by bastions until 1857 and is now encircled by the famous *Ringstrasse*. Most sights are on or inside this. The tourist office offers a good free map with pictorial representation of the main sights. If you need a map with index the Falk one is useful.

**Public transport** is efficient, with U-Bahn, trams and buses all using the same tickets, on sale from all *Tabak/Trafik* (tobacconists and newsagents). Single tickets, sold in blocks of 5, and valid for one journey, are the most expensive option at ÖS17 each (ÖS20 on board). The 24-hr **Tageskarte Wien** is ÖS50 and the 72-hr **excursion ticket** ÖS130, an eight-day **Umwelt Streifnetzkarte** – a strip ticket punched each day used, ÖS265. A tourist option is the **Vienna Card** (ÖS180), available in hotels and Tourist Offices,

**297**

valid for 72 hrs transport plus reduced entry to tourist sights, discounts and more.

You must validate all tickets in the automatic puncher on the bus or tram or at the entrance to the U-Bahn. The fine for not doing so is ÖS520.

The marvellously clean and modern **U-Bahn** (underground railway) was built in the 1960s and has been continuously extended ever since. There are currently five lines, operating 0500–2400. Vienna's **trams** run on 33 radial routes plus in both directions round the *Ringstr.*, 0500–2400. **Buses** fill gaps not covered by trams during roughly the same hours, although there are some special all-night services on main routes (supplement payable), leaving *Schwedenpl.* on the canal edge of district 1.

A map of the transport network is included on the back of the free city map. **Information** is available at the offices in the underground stations of *Stephanspl., Karlspl.* and *Westbahnhof* 0630–1830 Mon–Fri, 0830–1600 Sat and Sun.

**Taxis** are not cheap, but extremely efficient and you may have to use them late at night, *tel: (01) 40 100, (01) 31 300, (01) 60 160, (01) 81 400, (01) 91 091.* Alternatively you can hail cabs with the *frei* sign lit or use one of the taxi ranks.

There are 500 km of **cycle** paths around Vienna and the Tourist Office lists bike-friendly accommodation. Train travellers get the best hire deals at the Westbahnhof 0400–2400, Wien Nord 0630–1930 and Südbahnhof 0600–2200. Hire is ÖS50 per day on production of the same day's ticket, otherwise ÖS90. For the cost of a half-price ticket, bikes are allowed on the U-Bahn except U6 0900–1500 and after 1830 Mon–Fri, after 0900 Sat and all day Sun. **Vienna Bike**, *Wasag. 28/2/5; tel: (01) 319 12 58*, offers daily tours by bike ÖS200 for two to three hours. Book two days ahead.

A 20-min tour by horse-drawn **Fiaker** is ÖS400, 40 mins ÖS800 and per hour ÖS1000 + 10% service tax. You will find fiakers next to Stephansdom, *Heldenpl.* in the Hofburg, and the Albertina.

## STAYING IN VIENNA

### Accommodation

There are lots of options but also lots of takers, so book well ahead May–Oct. The Tourist Board issues lists of hotels, *pensions* and summer *saisonhotels*. Don't expect much below ÖS500 per person a night. Major hotel groups represented in Vienna include *BW, GT, Hd, Hn, Ib, IC, Ma, Mc, Nv, RC, Rd, Rn, Rk, SA, Sc, Sf, Sn, Tp.*

At the top of the hotel options are **Hotel Bristol**, *Kärtner-Ring, 1; tel: (01) 515 16* (very expensive) and **Hotel Imperial**, *Kärtner-Ring, 16; tel: (01) 50 110 0.* **K&K Palais Hotel**, *Rudolfspl. 11; tel: (01) 533 13 53* (expensive), near the river, was once home to Emperor Franz Josef and his mistress. **Hotel Kummer**, *Mariahilferstr. 71A; tel: (01) 588 95* (expensive), is near Westbahnhof. **Pension Elite**, *Wipplingerstr. 32; tel: (01) 533 25 18 0* (moderate), is family-run and central. **Pension Sacher, Rotenturmstr. 1; tel: (01) 533 32 38** (moderate) right next to the cathedral, sees plenty of return business. **Hotel Goldene Spinne**, *Linke Bahng. 1A; tel: (01) 7124486* (budget) is close to the City Air Terminal.

There are nine hostels, but the most central are the **HI: Jugendherberge Wien**, *Myrtheng. 7/Neustiftg. 85; tel: (01) 523 63160;* and **Kolpingfamilie Wien-Meidling**, *Bendlg. 10; tel: (01) 8135487,* or there's the smaller **Hostel Zöhrer**, *Skodag. 26; tel: (01) 430730.* Just across the Danube Canal is **Aktive Camping**, *Neue Donau am Kleehaüfel; tel: (01) 2209310,* mid-May–mid-Sept.

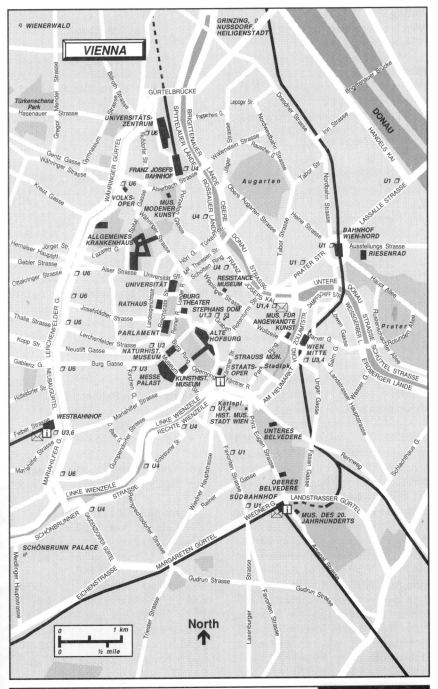

VIENNA

↖ WIENERWALD

GRINZING, NUSSDORF, HEILIGENSTADT

GÜRTELBRÜCKE

Türkenschanz Park
Hasenauer Strasse

Leipziger Str.

DONAU

HANDELS KAI

UNIVERSITÄTS-ZENTRUM
☐ U6

Papperheim G.
Dresdner Strasse
Nordwestbahn Strasse

Gentz Gasse
Währinger Strasse
Kreuz Gasse

FRANZ JOSEFS BAHNHOF
☐ U6
Alserbach Strasse

Augarten

U1 ☐

LASSALLE STRASSE

VOLKS-OPER
MUS. MODENER KUNST
☐ U4

Hernalser Haupstr.
Jörger Str.
Gebler Strasse

ALLGEMEINES KRANKENHAUS
Lazarett G.

BAHNHOF WIEN-NORD
U1 ☐
Ausstellungs Strasse
U1 ☐
RIESENRAD

Ottakringer Strasse
☐ U6

Alser Strasse
Universität Str.
UNIVERSITÄT
☐ U6

RESISTANCE MUSEUM

UNTERE

Thalia Strasse
☐ U6

RATHAUS
Josefstädter Strasse

BURG THEATER
STEPHANS DOM
U1,3 ☐
U1,4 ☐
MUS. FÜR ANGEWANDTE KUNST
Wollzeile

WIEN MITTE
☐ U3,4

Kopp Str.
Gablenz G.
☐ U6

Lerchenfelder Strasse
☐ U3
NATURHIST. MUSEUM
☐ U3
Burg Gasse

PARLAMENT
ALTE HOFBURG

STRAUSS MON.
Stadtpk.

Hüteldorfer Str.
NEUBAUGÜRTEL

MESSE PALAST
KUNSTHIST. MUSEUM
☐ i
STAATS-OPER
Kärntner R.

299

WESTBAHNHOF
Felber Strasse
☐ i
☐ U3,6

Karlspl.
☐ U1,4
HIST. MUS. STADT WIEN
LINKE WIENZEILE
RECHTE WIENZEILE
☐ U4

UNTERES BELVEDERE

Mariahilfer Strasse
☐ U6

☐ U4

☐ U1

OBERES BELVEDERE
SÜDBAHNHOF

LANDSTRASSER GÜRTEL

☐ U4

LINKE WIENZEILE
STRASSE

☐ U1
WIEDNER G.
☐ i
MUS. DES 20. JAHRHUNDERTS

SCHÖNBRUNN PALACE

MARGARETEN GÜRTEL

Gudrun Strasse

Gudrun Strasse

EICHENSTRASSE

**North**
↑

0 ____ 1 km
0 ____ ½ mile

## Eating and Drinking

Vienna not only gave the world the *Wiener Schnitzel* and *Sachertorte*, but is *the* place to eat food from the former Austro-Hungarian empire. Typically Viennese are the moderately priced *Beisl* or *Kellern*, atmospheric wine-bar/restaurants in cellars, and *Konditoreien* – coffee houses which serve hot food as well as their pastry specialities and, like Viennese cafés are an institution for people watching.

Some of the best cafés are **Café Central**, *corner Herreng. and Stauchg.* in Palais Ferstel, a recently restored 19th-century Gothic institution; **Café Hawelka,** *Dorotheerg. 6*, an intellectual hang-out; **Café Sperl,** *Gumpendorfstr. 11*, is a traditional coffeehouse dating to 1880; **Café Drechsler,** *Linke Wienzeile 22*, opening at 0400 is the place to round off a late night; **Café Landtmann,** *Dr-Karl-Lueger-Ring 14*, was Freud's favourite.

Best *Konditoreien* include **Oberlaaer,** *Neuer Markt 15*, and *Favoritenstr. 90*; **Gerstner,** *Kärntnerstr. 11-15,*. If you really want to splash out **Demel's Coffee House,** *Kohlmarkt 14,*, has achieved legendary status for both decor and baking.

*Konditorei* are not cheap at around ÖS60–120 for anything substantial. The university area (U2 or 4 near *Schottentor*) is better for cheap eats: **Fischerbrau,** *Billrothstr. 17*, offers homebrew and jazz; **D'Landsknecht,** *Porzellang. 13*, is a plain bistro; **Schweizerhaus,** *Strasse des 1 Mai,* a popular *biergarten.* Best value for money are student canteens, open to non-students. Try the **New University**, *Universitätsstr. 7*, 0800–1700; or **Academy of Fine Arts**, *Schillerpl. 3*, 0830–1700.

In the centre (meals around ÖS300–500) are **Bukarest,** *Braunerstr. 7,* offering Balkan food, **Gösser Bierklinik,** *Steindlg. 4,* offering beer and solid food, **Dubrovnik,** *Am Neumarkt, 5,* with a menu combining Croat, Balkan and Viennese; the **Glacisbeisl,** *Messepalast,* hidden in the trade fair centre off the *Ring*; **Alte Backstube**, *Langeg. 34*, offers Viennese and Hungarian food in an 18th-century bakery; **Figlmüller,** *Wollzelle 5,* is a *beisl* offering giant *Wiener Schnitzel.*

Eating out in style costs anything from ÖS700 upwards. Options include **Zu Den Drei Husaren,** *Weihburgg. 4*, nr *St Stephansdom*, with Viennese food and gypsy music; and **Huswirth,** *Otto-Bauerg. 20*, with wood panelled interiors and gardens. **Sachers,** *Philharmonikerstr. 4*, specialises in *Tafelspitz* and *rösti* potatoes – and for afters, naturally, *Sachertorte*. However, it is expensive (ÖS1000) and very touristy.

In delightful villages such as **Grinzing, Nussdorf, Sievering, Neustift am Walde,** and **Stammersdorf,** are the famous *Heurigen* taverns where young local wine is served with traditional food, (around ÖS250 depending on the establishment) mid-afternoon–midnight. Grinzing is the most touristy, Stammersdorf the cheapest. One of the best known is **Alter Klosterkeller im Passauerhof,** *Cobenzlg. 9, Grinzing*, has a menu dating to the last century and foundations to the 12th.

For the cheapest eating and fast food, try the counters in butchers' shops, *Würstelstände* (hot dog stalls), sandwich bars, and fast food stalls at the *Naschmarkt.*

## Communications and Money

The **Central Post Office** and poste restante is at *Fleischmarkt 19* (open 24 hrs). There are 24-hr post offices at the main stations. Some phones in the centre (e.g. *Wallnerstr.* and *Goldschmiedg.*) accept credit cards and have instructions in English.

To phone Vienna from abroad: *tel: 43 (Austria) + 1 (Vienna) + number*; to phone Vienna from elsewhere in Austria *tel: 01 + number*; however, older codes may apply.

Banks open Mon–Fri, 0800–1500 (–1730 Thurs in the centre); branch offices close for lunch, 1230–1330. There are exchange bureaux at Westbahnhof and Südbahnhof open extended hours. Credit cards and travellers' cheques are all widely accepted. Foreign currency can also be exchanged at the *Fleischmarkt 9* post office.

## Embassies and Consulates

**Australia**: *Mattiellistr. 2-4; tel: (01) 512 85 800.*
**Canada**: *Laurenzerberg 1; tel: (01) 531 38 30 00.*
**Republic of Ireland**: *Landstr./Hauptstr. 2; tel: (01) 715 4246.*
**New Zealand**: *Sprinsiedelg. 28; tel: (01) 318 85 05.*
**S. Africa**: *Sandg. 33; tel: (01) 32 64 93.*
**UK**: *Jauresg. 12: tel: (01) 713 15 75.*
**USA**: *Botzmanng. 16; tel: (01) 313 39.*

## ENTERTAINMENT

*Programm*, an indispensable monthly listing of all entertainment bar cinema, is free from Tourist Offices. Cinemas are listed in newspapers. Youth event details and discount tickets are available from *Jugend-Info* (see p. 297). Night life and trendies focus on the 'Bermuda Triangle', an area of lively bars, discos and pubs close to *Schwedenpl.*, but Vienna is better known as one of the world's great centres of classical music.

Specific events include the May, June **Vienna Festival** of plays, concerts, opera and exhibition, the **Vienna Summer of Music,** July and Aug, **dance festivals** in Feb and July/Aug, and **Modern Vienna,** Nov and Dec of little performed classic modern works.

The **Staatsoper,** considered one of the world's leading opera houses, stages productions Sept–June. The **Volksoper** offers operettas and musicals. To avoid high agency commissions apply for tickets for both the Staatsoper and Volksoper in writing to **Österreichischer Bundestheaterverband/Bestellbüro,** *Hanuschg. 3, A-1010 Vienna; fax: (01) 514 44 ext 2969* (direct dial) at least three weeks ahead. Credit card sales, *tel: (01) 513 1 513*, are only offered seven days in advance, and standing room tickets sold only before the performance.

Mozart operas are performed at the **Marionette Theatre** at the *Schönbrunn*. A cheaper substitute July and Aug is the free **Opera Film Festival** in the *Rathauspl.*

The **Vienna Boys' Choir** performs at the *Hofburg Chapel* Sun 0915, Sept–Jun, ÖS60–250, standing room free. Write to **Hofmusik Kapelle**, *Hofburg, A-1010 Vienna,* and collect and pay for tickets on the Sun 0830–0900. The choir also performs Fri 1530, May, June, Sept and Oct at the **Konzerthaus**, ÖS370/470. For tickets contact **Reisebüro Mondial**, *Faulmanng. 4, A-1040 Vienna; fax: (01) 587 12 68*, well ahead.

## SHOPPING

**Kärntnerstr.** is Vienna's busiest shopping street and together with **Graben** the place to promenade. But the smartest addresses are now smaller parallel streets like *Kohlmarkt*. *Mariahilferstr.* is home to the department stores. Ornamental objects are found at **Österreichische Werkstätten,** *Kärntnerst/ 26; tel: (01) 512 24 18.* A local speciality is **Augarten porcelain**, on sale at the factory in *Obere Augartenstr., tel: (01) 211 24*, or more conveniently at *Stock im Eisenpl. 3*, near the *Dom*. A good outlet for **Loden**, the heavy Austrian winter coats, is **Loden Plankel,** *Michaelerpl. 6.* The **Art and Antique market** *Am Hofpl.*, takes place Mar to Christmas. For original artwork and prints try **Kunstverlag Wolfrum**, *Augustinerstr. 10.*

There are tours of the city in a 1929 tram daily May–Oct from *Karlspl*. Wed, Sat and Sun 1330, and Sun 1000. The Tourist Office runs specialist walking tours (ÖS108), for example of Jewish Vienna. It's quite easy to see the basics yourself however, starting with the focal point of Vienna, the Romanesque and Gothic **Stephansdom** (St Stephen's Cathedral; U1: *Stephanspl*.) *tel: (01) 515 52 526*, with its jazzy green and gold roof. The loveliest parts are the Gothic **Albertine Choir** (1340) and the magnificent 14th-century 136.7 m South Tower (the '*Steffl*' – Steve – to locals), with 344 steps. Inside the cathedral, highlights include the pulpit (1510) and organ loft by Anton Pilgrim; a Gothic wing altar in the North Apse and the fabulous Renaissance tomb of Friedrich III in the South Apse.

The **Hofburg** is the great Habsburg residence (*Michaelerpl. 1; tel: (01) 587 55 54*) occupying a vast area of central Vienna with 18 wings, 54 stairways and 2600 rooms. The main sights are the **Burgkapelle**, home of the Vienna Boys' Choir; the **Schatzkammer** (Treasury), containing the crown of the Holy Roman Empire; the **Imperial Apartments**, preserved as the penultimate emperor, Franz Josef, had them; and the richly baroque **National Library**, containing one of the world's best collections of manuscripts.

Also housed in the Hofburg is the **Winter Riding School**, where the famous *Lippizaner* horses perform except July and Aug. Tickets for the main performance should be booked well ahead (ÖS220 plus around 25% commission for the agency – eg *Amex, Kärntnerstr. 21-3; fax: (01) 515 4070)*. If you can't get tickets queue at the door of the **Redoute**, *Josefspl.*, to see 'morning training' Tues–Sat 1000–1200.

## Galleries and Museums

Vienna's major museum is the **Kunsthistorisches Museum** (Museum of Art History), *Burgring 5; tel: (01) 54 77 0* (trams 1 and 2), based on the collection of the Habsburgs. The main museum contains classical and Egyptian antiquities, Palaeo-Christian art, decorative art and, above all, a picture gallery with a superb collection of Breughels as well as masterpieces by Rembrandt and Velazquez. Branches include the **Neue Burg** (part of the Hofburg) where musical instruments and armour are displayed; and the **Palace of Schönbrunn** (coaches and carriages). The superb 18th-century baroque **Belvedere Palace**, *Prinz-Eugenstr. 27; tel: (01) 79 80 700* (tram D), has two galleries and delightful gardens. The **Österreichische Galerie** (Austrian Gallery), *Oberes* (Upper) *Belvedere*, has important works by artists of the Biedermeier period (1814–1848), the Vienna Secession and Austrian Expressionism. The **Baroque Museum**, *Unteres* (Lower) *Belvedere*, at the *Rennweg* end of the park, contains works by leading baroque artists. **Gemäldegalerie Akademie der Bildenden Künste** (Academy of Fine Arts), *Schillerpl. 2; tel: (01) 58 816* (U 1/2/4 *Karlspl*.), includes generous numbers of Flemish works.

The **Museum für Angewandte Kunst** (Museum of Applied Art), *Stubenring 5; tel: (01) 711 36 0* (trams 1 and 2), is a recently up-dated cornucopia of Oriental, European and Austrian artefacts including pieces by Charles Rennie Mackintosh and early 20th-century Viennese design. The elegant café naturally draws designers and architects. Modern art enthusiasts will enjoy the **Museum des 20 Jahrhunderts** (Museum of the 20th Century), *Schweizer Garten; tel: (01) 78 25 50* (tram D) and the **Museum Moderner Kunst im Palas**

Liechstenstein, *Fürsteng. 1; tel: (01) 317 69 00* (tram D), with works by Austrian Expressionists and other leading European 20th-century artists such as Magritte. The **Albertina**, *Augustinerstr.; tel: (01) 534 83 (U1/2/4 Karlspl./Oper)*, has the world's greatest collection of drawings and prints. The delightful **Uhrenmuseum** (Clock Museum), *Schulhof 2; tel: (01) 533 22 65* (U-Bahn: *Schottentor*) features 900 clocks.

## Churches

In the Gothic **Augustinerkirche**, *Augustinerstr. 3* (U-Bahn: *Karlspl./Oper*, trams 1, 2), the hearts of the Habsburgs are kept in silver urns. The **Kapuzinerkirche**, *Neuer Markt* (U-Bahn: *Karlspl./Oper*), is above the Capuchin crypt where Habsburg bodies were laid to rest in impressive baroque tombs. Other examples of Viennese Gothic include the **Church of Maria am Gestade,** *Am Gestade* (trams 1 and 2), the **Minoritenkirche**, *Minoritenpl. 2A*, and the **Michaelerkirche**, *Michaelerpl.* (both U3 *Herreng.*). There are also two superb baroque churches: the 1708 **Peterskirche**, *Peterspl.* (U2/3 *Stephanspl.*), and the 1713 **Karlskirche**, *Karlspl.* (U1/2/4 *Karlspl./Oper*, trams 1 and 2).

## Other Sights

The fine baroque former **Rathaus** *Wipplingerstr. 8* (trams 1 and 2) now holds the **Museum of the Austrian Resistance Movement** (against Nazism). On the curious art nouveau **Anker Clock**, *Hoher Markt 10/11* (U1/4 *Schwedenpl.*), figures from Austrian history parade together at 1200. For an idea of the architectural splendours of the **Ringstrasse** era, take trams 1 or 2 around the *Ring*, passing the neo-Gothic **Rathaus** (City Hall), the **Burgtheater**, the **Parliament** and the **Opera**. In contrast is Joseph Olbrich's exhibition hall for

painters of the **Viennese Secession,** *Friedrichstr. 12; tel: (01) 587 5307*, with plain cream walls and gold dome.

The **Pasqualati House**, *Mölker Bastei 8* (trams 1/2) is one of innumerable lodgings used by Beethoven, who also has a museum at the **Heiligenstadt Testament Haus,** *Probusg. 6; tel: (01) 37 54 08* (buses 37A/38A) in *Heiligenstadt*. Mozart's lodging, the so-called **Figaro House,** *Domg. 5; tel: (01) 513 62 94* (U1/3 *Stephanspl.*) has memorial rooms. The **Schubert Museum** is at the composer's birthplace, *Nussdorfterstr.; 54 tel: (01) 345 99 24* (trams 37/38). **Haydns Wohnhaus**, *Haydng. 19, tel: (01) 596 1307*, is where the composer taught Beethoven. The Sigmund **Freud Museum,** *Bergg. 19; tel: (01) 319 15 96*, is set in the psychoanalyst's old consulting rooms. A leaflet from the tourist office highlights 20th-century buildings of interest. These range from the 1930s, with the 1 km of **Karl Marx public housing estate**, to the ecological and humanist playground of the **Hundertwasserhaus** (*Loweng./Kegelg.*) almost anarchic in combination of colours and shapes. Hundertwasser's **KunstHausWien,** *Untere Weissgerberstr. 13; tel: (01) 712 04 91* nearby, is an art museum in similar style.

## Further Out

**Schloss Schönbrunn,** *Schönbrunner Schlosstr. 13; tel: (01) 811 13 238* (U4 *Schönbrunn*, tram 58 from *Burgring*), is a grandiose rococo palace with a superb park with **Butterfly House** and the oldest **Zoo** in the world. The legendary **Prater** (U1 *Praterstern* trams O/5/21) is a vast park with a fun-fair and famous big wheel. Take care after dark. The **Wienerwald** (Vienna Woods) are a few thousand acres of wooded hills (tram 1 to *Schottentor* tram 38 to *Grinzing* and bus to *Kahlenberg*).

# VIENNA–BUDAPEST

This route runs between the twin capitals of the old Austro-Hungarian Empire. It branches around the Neusiedlersee to allow a visit to historic Sopron, or you can proceed directly via Győr; either choice affords the opportunity of branching off towards Esztergom and the beautiful region of the Danube Bend, north of Budapest.

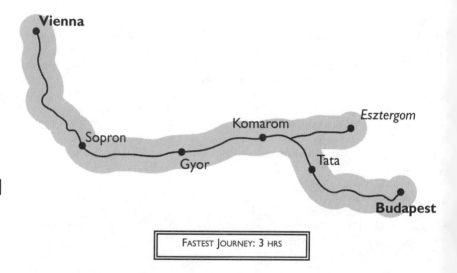

FASTEST JOURNEY: 3 HRS

## TRAINS

**ETT Tables:** 61, 830, 833, 890

### FAST TRACK

→ There are 7 trains a day. They take around 3 hrs.

### ON TRACK

**Vienna–Sopron**
Change trains at Wiener Neustadt. The overall journey takes around 3 hrs.

**Sopron–Budapest**
Eight trains a day taking between 2¾ and 3¼ hrs.

## SOPRON

**Station:** The main railway station is **GYSEV pályaudvar**, *Állomás utca,* just south of the old town. Train tickets issued by GYSEV, a private company, are not valid on the Hungarian state railway, MÉV.

**Tourist Office: Ibusz**, *41 Várkerület; tel: (99) 313 281* is open 0800–1600 weekdays, 0800–1230 Sat.

## ACCOMMODATION

The **Sziesta Hotel**, *37 Lövér; tel: (99) 314 260*, is a monolith up in the Lövér hills, surrounded by woodland. In town itself the **Palatinus**, *23 Új utca; tel: (99) 311 395*, is the most central but very small and not fully renovated. The **Pannonia**, *75 Várkerület; tel: (99) 312 180*, is now fully operational again after its refurbishment. Private rooms are usually as expensive as hotel rooms and very difficult to find, but you can ask at the tourist office. **Campsite: Löver camping**, *3 Pócsi-domb; tel: (99) 311 715*, with 1300 pitches and some bungalows, is up in the Lövér hills. **Özon Camping**, *3 Erdei malomköz; tel: (99) 331 144*, only has 150 places available

## SIGHTSEEING

Sopron is a mere 8 km away from the Austrian border. It is hardly surprising, therefore, that there is a strong Austrian influence in the city, and German is widely spoken. Nevertheless, the citizens voted in 1921 to remain part of Hungary, a decision commemorated in the title *urbs fidelissima* (most loyal city) in its charter. Sopron was a major point on the amber trade route between the Baltic and Italy during medieval times. Neither the Turks nor the Mongols could penetrate the town's defences, leaving it rich in antiquities, despite the damage that occurred during World War II.

For the energetic a walk up the spiral staircase in the 60-metre **Fire Tower**, *Fö tér*, will be rewarded with a splendid view. From here the heralds would trumpet out fire warnings and chime the hours. It is Sopron's landmark and is a

hotchpotch of architectural styles; the clock and dome were added in 1681–82. At the bottom of the tower stands **Loyalty Gate**, which depicts the charter given to the citizens of Sopron for their loyalty to Hungary.

The **Trinity Column** nearby was erected in 1695–1701 to commemorate a great plague. At *8 Fö tér*, next to the tower, is the **Storno House**, an old palace built in the Middle Ages. King Mátyás Corvinus lived in the house during the campaign against Vienna in 1483. Franz Lizst, too, lived there in 1872. There is a wide variety of exhibits such as porcelain and furnishings on the first floor. At *6 Fö tér* is the **Fabricius House**, where the history of the Amber Route is traced over 3000 years. The façade is baroque, but this hides the 14th- and 15th-century houses and Roman foundations. The **Lackner House**, containing a museum dedicated to archaeological finds, is next door at no. 7. On the other side of the square, at no 2 is the **Patikaház** (apothecary museum). **Kecske templom**, the 'Goat's Church', stands at the southern end. The uppermost parts were modelled on St Stephen's Cathedral in Vienna. In 1526 the Jewish population was evicted from Sopron; until then *Új utca* was known as *Zsidó utca*, Jews' street. This was divided from the rest of the town by a wall. The **Old Synagogue** at 20–22 and the **New Synagogue** at no. 11 were built in the 14th century in Gothic style. They are considered by many to be the finest buildings erected by the Jewish community in medieval Europe.

Sopron hosts a month-long festival of music in Jun–Jul, rock as well as classical, and at other times there is plenty of nightlife.

## GYŐR

**Station:** *Révai Miklós utca*, a short walk

**305**

from the town centre.

**Tourist Office: Ibusz,** *29–31 Szent István; tel:(96) 314 135,* is open 0800–1700.

Győr (in German, Raab, 'Raven'), is one of the most important industrial cities in Hungary; yet it has almost as many monuments, museums, galleries and buildings as Budapest and Sopron. It is easy to be put off by its industrial suburbs as you enter the place, but the old town centre is a gem.

The **Rába Hotel,** *34 Árpád utca; tel: (96) 315 533,* is a very imposing corner building, with prices to match its appearance. The **Klastrom,** *Bécsi kapu tér; tel: (96) 315 611,* is equally expensive and a little way out of the centre, but has good facilities. The **Aranypart,** *12 Aldozat utca; tel: (96) 326 033,* is small and very cheap. There are many good cafés and restaurants all over the town. The locals eat at **Sárkánlyul** (Dragon Hole), *29 Arany János utca.*

The beautiful **Carmelite Church** is in the baroque *Bécsi kapu tér* (Vienna Gate Square), where it takes pride of place. It is undergoing renovations at present. At no 5 is the **János Xánthus Museum,** a series of caves with minor Roman memorabilia. Napoleon's overnight stay in the town is recognised at **Napoleon Ház,** *4 Kiraly utca,* where there is an art gallery.

**Káptalandomb** (Chapter Hill), leading up to *Apor Vilmos püspök tere,* is the oldest part of town. The foundations of **Győr Cathedral** date back to the 11th century. There are some beautiful frescoes there. Inside the **Héderv**á**ry Chapel** is a gold bust of Herm of László, one of the first Hungarian Kings. In the same chapel is the statue of the **Weeping Icon of Mary,** brought to Hungary by an Irish bishop in the 17th century. **Vastuskós Ház** (Iron Log House), *94*

*Széchenyi tér,* is an unparalleled art gallery with canvasses by Chagal, Braque and Picasso as well as those of major Hungarian artists. Across the river at *5 Kossuth Lajos utca* is the very richly decorated 1869 **Synagogue.** It requires some persistence to gain access, but is worth the effort (try the old Jewish school next door, which is now the music academy).

## KOMÁROM

Change here for Esztergom and Visegrád if travelling from the Vienna direction

### SIDE TRACKS
### FROM KOMÁROM

## ESZTERGOM

**Tourist Office: Ibusz,** *1 Lörinc utca; tel:(33) 311 64,* is open 0800–1600. **Gran Tours,** *25 Széchenyi tér tel :(33) 313 756,* the visitors' centre operated by the city council, observes the same hours.

### ACCOMMODATION

Hotels are small and a little sparse. The **Esztergom,** *Nagy Duna sétány on Primate Island; tel:(33) 312 883,* is quite expensive, with a classy restaurant and roof terrace. For something different, try the seasonal **Korneuburg Ship Hotel,** moored on the Danube at *Sobieski sétány.* There are two **campsites, Gran Camping and Bungalow,** *3 Nagy Duna sétány; tel: (33) 311 327,* and **Gyopár Természetbarát,** *Vaskapu út; tel: (33) 311 401.*

### SIGHTSEEING

Esztergom is one of the oldest towns in Hungary, some 60 km away from Budapest at the end of the Danube

Bend, on the border with Slovakia. Like Budapest, it has a **Várhegy**, (Castle Hill) which was the site of the Roman settlement of Solva Mansio. In 997, Saint Stephen was crowned the first King of Hungary on the hill. Esztergom is the seat of the Primate of Hungary. The largest and most impressive **Cathedral** in the whole of Hungary was built on top of the hill in 1856, and dominates the town. For its inauguration, the *Esztergom Festival Mass* was composed by Franz Lizst. Inside there is the **Kincstár** or Cathedral Treasury, which houses the most superlative collection of ecclesiastica to be found in Hungary. The display of robes encrusted with precious stones, Byzantine treasures, crosses and chalices is overpowering.

Still on Castle Hill there are the remains of the **Királyi palota** (Royal Palace). Built in the 10th and 11th centuries, it is the oldest royal palace in the country, with a beautiful **Royal Chapel**.

The first public **baths** in Hungary opened in the 12th century between the Little Danube and the Fürdö. The outdoor thermal baths are open 0900–1800, May-Sept, the indoor ones all year round. The **Technical House**, *4 Imaház utca*, was once the Esztergom Synagogue. Built in 1888 in Moorish style, it has a monument in contrasting modernity to those who died in Auschwitz.

**Primás-Sziget** (Primate Island) is separated from the main town by the 'Little Danube', and makes a pleasant place for a picnic.

## VISEGRÁD

**Tourist Office:** There is no Ibusz or official Hungarian Service Tourist office in Visegrád, so information is limited. One of the travel agencies may be able to help.

### ACCOMMODATION

In the village of Visegrád itself, look out for signs saying *Szoba kiadó* (Rooms for rent) or even in German, *Zimmer frei*. **Hotel Silvanus**, *Feketehegy; tel: (26) 328 311,* is expensive, but the best hotel in the village, with cycle hire, ten pin bowling and a pretty terraced restaurant, and it is close to the citadel. **Elte**, *117 Fö utca; tel: (26) 328 165,* is in the very centre of town. The views from the sun deck are superb and most rooms have terraces. Visegrád is best seen in the summer months and most accommodation is open between May and Sept.

If you are camping you can choose from two **campsites**. **Jurta Camping**, *Mogyoró-hegy; tel: (26) 398 217,* has more amenities than the central **Visegrád Autós Camping**, *Fö utca; tel: (26) 398 102,* but is quite far out of the village and buses only run in the summer.

### SIGHTSEEING

This picturesque village is perhaps the diamond in the collection of jewels which is called the Danube BendThe name Visegrád was bestowed by the Slavs who settled in one of the Roman forts already in place, and means High Castle. King Béla IV built a second castle on the lower slopes to defend the residential one at the top. In 1316, King Charles of Anjou chose Visegrád as his summer residence, which meant the the status of the little town increased. The upper Palace was rebuilt by Italian Renaissance masters during the mid 15th century for King

307

Mátyás Corvinus. After the death of the King and the later Turkish sieges, Visegrád's importance declined. In 1702 Emperor Leopold of Austria demolished the remains. Houses were built on the slopes by the Austrians in the 18th century, using the rubble. In 1934 excavations discovered the complex and the rebuilding process began. **Salamontorony** (Solomon's Tower) has walls 8 metres thick. It is a relic of the lower castle and owes its name to a legend that King Solomon was kept a prisoner in the tower during the 11th century by Emperor Henry IV. The **Vizibástya** (Water bastion) was a watch tower and is now the setting for the **King Matthias Museum**, where there are royal relics to be seen. **Királyi plota** (Royal Palace), *Fö utca*, is a reconstruction and replica of the original, with a lion fountain, green canals and fishponds. The citadel itself has an interesting staircase and the views from the top of the hill are superb. ◪

### ⬌ Connection to Budapest

From Visegrád one can continue by train to **Budapest,** and indeed it is possible to visit both Esztergom and Visegrád by train as a day trip from the capital. If you are travelling from Budapest towards Vienna you can take in the Danube Bend towns in this way, joining the main route at Komárom.

## TATA

**Stations:** There are two rail stations, both within walking distance of the centre and both connected to the centtre by bus services.

**Tourist Office: Komturist,** *9 Ady Éndre út; tel: (34) 81805,* provides multilingual advice and a room booking service.

### ACCOMMODATION

The **Kristály,** *22 Ady Éndre út; tel: (34) 383 577,* is a charming hotel, 200 years old but refurbished recently. Close to Kristály Lake, its amenities are very good but it is extremely expensive. The **Laczházy Hotel,** *1a Épitök út; tel: (34) 341 071,* is very small, offers very little and is quite a way out, but is relatively inexpensive. **HI: Patak Motel,** *Fényesfasor; tel: (34) 382 853,* has 50 beds and a restaurant. There are two **campsites** in Tata: **Fényes-Fürdő,** *Fényes-fürdő; tel: (34) 381 591,* accommodates 600 and has bungalows. It is situated 2 km north of the city centre. The lakeside **Öreg-tó Camping,** *1 Fáklya út; tel: (34) 383 496,* also has bungalows available.

### SIGHTSEEING

Tata, the Town of Waters, is a resort town due to the many springs and **Öreg-tó,** the Old Lake. The lakes were formed by draining the marshes and they interconnect by means of canals. The oldest building in the town is the 1587 **Cifra-malom** (Cifra Mill), *3 Bartók Béla út.* The windows are made from the distinctive red marble seen in many splendid buildings in the area. A little distance away is the **Nepomucenus Mill** (1758), *2 Alkotmány utca;* unlike the Cifra Mill, this has been restored and now contains the **German Minority Museum**. **Öregvár Castle** houses the **Domokos Kuny Museum** with its archaeological finds. It stands on the banks of the Old Lake but only the five-storey tower remains intact. King Mátyás Corvinus extended the Palace to fortify it and Count Eszterházy, in 1727, bought the ruins in order to rebuild it. Eszterházy's house (1765) itself lies on the west bank of the lake at *3 Hősök tere.* Today it is a hospital.

# VIENNA–KOŠICE

This route offers the best introduction to Slovakia, one of the most underrated countries in Europe, combining cities and towns with splendid natural attractions. Arriving at Košice puts you on the Budapest–Kraków route (p.176), making this journey a prelude to a swing north to Poland and the Balti, or south to Hungary and the Balkans.

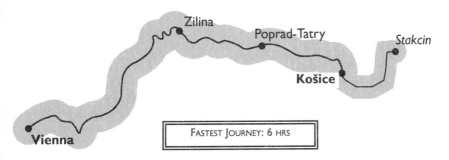

FASTEST JOURNEY: 6 HRS

## TRAINS

**ETT Tables: 888, 885**

### FAST TRACK

➡ No through trains operate, but there are four journeys possible each day by changing trains in Bratislava. The overall trip takes over 6 hours.

### ON TRACK

#### Vienna–Bratislava–Žilina

Four trains a day to Bratislava, taking 1 hr 15 mins; a train every 2 hrs throughout the day to Žilina, most with dining cars and supplements to pay.

#### Žilina–Poprad Tatry–Košice

At least ten trains a day, with no more than 2 hrs between trains, all calling at Poprad Tatry en route. Žilina to Poprad takes 2 hrs, Poprad to Košice 1 hr 20 mins.

## ŽILINA

**Station:** *tel: (089) 313 04.*At the end of *Národná ulica,* which leads southwest into the city centre. The bus station, *tel: (089) 209 50,* is east of the railway station, on *Hviezdoslavova ul.* The best way to the centre from here is to get to *Národná ulica* and walk from there.

**Tourist Office: Satur,** *Námestie L. Štúra 3; tel (089) 465 12 or 485 11* has information on Žilina and the region, but it is neither very detailed nor very extensive. Nevertheless, Satur is helpful with accommodation and will book rooms in hotels, guest houses and private accommodation. **Slovakotourist** at the Hotel Slovakia, *Námestie L. Štúra 2; tel (089) 478 60,* is good for both local information and arranging tours into the surrounding countryside.

### ACCOMMODATION

The two offices listed above can book a

**309**

wide range of possibilities. In Žilina itself, the **Hotel Slovakia**, *Námestie L. Štúra 2; tel (089) 465 72,* is the best option, but more expensive than others. For those on more restricted budgets, there may be student accommodation available at the **VŠDS** (Transport and Communications College), *Hlinská ul; tel: (089) 333 08,* but this is liable to be full in July and August; or try the **Hotel Metropol**, *Hviezdoslavova ul. 26; tel (089) 239 00.* Private accommodation can be found via Satur. Outside town the picture opens up, with many hotels, guest houses, chalets and campsites in and around the national park and nature reserve areas. **Tatratour**, *Mariánské nám. 21; tel: (089) 200 71,* as its name suggests, specialises in trips to the Tatra Mountains and can arrange accommodation in all such facilities. It is of course also possible to simply hike in and take your chance: there will always be something available.

## SIGHTSEEING

This small city on the River Váh is notable as a base for exploring the scenic hills and mountains round about. Within striking distance, either on an organised tour for a quick visit or, more satisfyingly, on a hiking trip of at least several days, are a national park, several nature reserves and pretty mountain resorts.

There are a few sights in Žilina. The old town is centred on *Mariánské nám.*, an elegant square surrounded by arcaded Renaissance houses. In the square stands the baroque **Kostol sv Pavla** (St Paul's Church, dating from 1743. Where the city wall once stood, on *Horný Val,* is the medieval **Kostol Najsvätejšie Trojice** (Holy Trinity Church).

In the high season, buses leave the bus station in Žilina *(Hviezdoslavova ulica)* every hour or so (more often at peak times) for the 75-minute journey to **Vrátná**, a village in a valley in the superb hiking country of the **Národný Park Malá Fatra** (Little Fatra National Park). From Vratná a cable-car reaches up 800m to **Chleb Mountain**, and from there a wide range of hiking trails begins. The Malá Fatra is less strenuous and, in winter and during bad weather, less risky than heading off into the High Tatra Mountains. Information on the national park is available from tourist offices in Žilina, and it is a good idea to buy a map, such as the highly detailed *Vratná-Martinské hole* map of the area.

The 14th-century **Strečno Castle** is dramatically sited atop a crag, guarding an important pass through the Little Fatra, outside Strečno, 10 km east of Žilina. It can be reached by bus from Žilina *(Hviezdoslavova ulica),* with departures every 2 hrs at peak times. The **Kysuce Nature Reserve** northwest of Žilina incorporates part of the Javorníky Mountains and the Beskydy Mountains and its forests and lakes have made it a popular tourist area with Slovakians.

Another possibility is to go by train or bus from Žilina (trains every 2 hrs; buses every hour), or from Martin further up the line, along the scenic Orava Valley to **Vodná Nádrž Orava** (Orava Lake).

## POPRAD

**Station:** *tel: (0969) 228 09.*1 km northwest of the town centre. You emerge on *Alžbetina ul.,* beside the Hotel Europa. The narrow-gauge train (the **Tatranská Električka Železnica,** or TEŽ) leaves from an upstairs platform at the railway station. If time is a problem, buses to the Tatras from the bus station adjacent to the railway station are quicker and more frequent, and the route is just as scenic. **Tourist Office:** The **Popradská**

**Informacná Agentúra** (Poprad Inform-ation Agency) is at *Námestie sv Egídia 2955; tel: (092) 636 36,* and can book accommodation. **Satur,** which does the same, but not only for the Poprad area, is nearby at *Námestie sv Egídia 95; tel: (092) 23651* or *23430.* **Tatratour,** *Námestie sv Egídia 9; tel: (092) 229 83,* specialises in the trips to the Tatra Mountains and can arrange accommodation there. If you are planning on hiking in the High Tatras, don't go without the hiking route map *Vysoké Tatry: Letná Turistická Mapa.*

## ACCOMMODATION

Bookings made by PIA or Satur are a good idea, because accommodation in the three main mountain resort villages gets filled easily. The **Hotel Satel,** *Mnohel'ova 826; tel: (092) 47 11 11,* is probably the best in Poprad, although the **Hotel Gerlach,** *Hviezdoslavova 2; tel: (092) 337 59,* is also good and the **Hotel Európa,** beside the railway and bus stations on *Alžbetina; tel (092) 327 44,* is a reasonable budget option. Beyond Poprad, there is a cluster of **campsites** around Tatranská Lomnica and others scattered in the foothills around the villages along the light railway line. Numerous mountain chalets can be found along the main hiking trails, and at the end of ski-lift, funicular and cable-car lines, ranging from very cheap to expensive by Slovak standards. If you are hiking and have not booked ahead from Poprad you shouldn't wait until evening to find a room. Some good low-priced options are: **Ubytovňa Športového Klubu,** Štrbské Pleso; *tel: (0969) 923 76.* **Penzión Sasanka,** Tatranská Lomnica; *tel: (0969) 25 35.* **Hotel Junior,** Horný Smokovec; *tel: (0969) 26 61.*

## SIGHTSEEING

Poprad itself is a fairly undistinguished town, although it retains some fine exam-ples of the wooden houses built by its for-mer German citizens. There is also the **Podtatranské Museum** (Mon–Sat 0900–1600), *Vajansková ul 72; tel: (092) 322 75.* One of the country's oldest museums, it houses exhibits about the ecology and geology of the High Tatras, as well as about human life there from Neanderthal Man onwards.

Poprad is important, however, because of its location beside the stunningly beau-tiful **High Tatra Mountains,** the high-est mountains of the Carpathian range, straddling the Slovak-Polish border. It is certainly the ideal base for exploring them. From here, a narrow-gauge railway wends its way into the mountains, stop-ping at the resort villages of **Starý Smokovec, Štrbské Pleso** and **Tatranská Lomnica.**

This area is the jewel of Slovakia, mar-vellously unspoiled, particularly the **Tatranský Národný Park** (High Tatras National Park), which was established by the merging of two previous parks in 1987. There are more than 300 km of hiking paths in the mountains. The mountains support a diverse flora and fauna, with many high-alpine varieties. It helps get a picture of the area to visit the **Múzeum Tatranského Národného Park** (Museum of the Tatra National Park), in Tatranská Lomnica; *tel: (0969) 967 951* (Mon–Fri 0830–1700).

The High Tatras are real mountains, and while their scenery can be appreci-ated from the light railway from Poprad, only a hiking trip, however short, can supply the genuine experience. Caution should be exercised, however; even in summer, showers of chilling rain are not uncommon. Good footwear, rainproof clothing and a supply of food and water are minimum requirements. The environmental protection rules – no fires, no litter, no picking of plants and flowers, etc – should of course be respected. If you are planning to do some serious off-trail hiking, it makes sense to call the **Horská Služba** (Mountain Patrol) in Starý Smokovec, tel: (0969) 2820 for advice on weather and other conditions.

South of Poprad lies the **Národný Park Slovenský Raj** (Slovakian Paradise National Park), more good hiking country, which is best accessed direct by bus from Poprad, or from there by train to Spišska Nová Ves. But if time allows only one trip, it is best to visit the High Tatras.

## KOŠICE

**Station:** East of the centre on *Staničné nám.*, a 5-min walk from the city wall that defines the old town, the centre being reached in a few more minutes along *Mlynská ul.* The bus station is adjacent.

**Tourist Office: Košice Informacná Agentúra** (Košice Information Agency) is at *Alžbetínska 16; tel: (095) 622 26 98.* **Satur** is at *Rooseveltova ul. 1; tel: (095) 622 38 47,* **Slovakotourist** at *Južná Trieda 5; tel: (095) 622 57 41.*

### ACCOMMODATION

Rooms in hotels, chalets, hostels and private houses, and places at campsites can be booked through Satur and Slovakotourist. The 3-star **Hotel Slovan**, *Hlavná ul. 1; tel: (095) 622 73 78,* is probably the best in town, for those who can afford it. Those on tighter budgets could try the **Domov Mládeže Hostel**, *Medická 2; tel: (095) 42 93 34.* Otherwise there are mid-priced hotels and offers of private accommodation at the tourist offices, with information from KIS and Satur (see above). An interesting option is the **Town Hall Penzión**,

*Bačíkova ul. 18; tel: (095) 622 86 01.*

### SIGHTSEEING

Košice is Slovakia's second biggest city, and a centre of heavy industry. Despite this it has some interesting architecture and other sites. Its many church steeples are its most distinctive markers. The main one is the **Dóm sv Alžbety** (St Elizabeth's Cathedral). The 19th-century **Jakabov Palác** (Jakab Palace) beside the **Municipal Park** was actually built with stones rejected from the cathedral, but it certainly doesn't look second-hand. The **Východoslovenské Muzeum** (Eastern Slovakia Museum) includes a stash of 920 Dutch and Hungarian gold coins dating from the 15th to the 17th centuries that were found by a group of (remarkably honest) workmen digging the foundations for a Košice Street in 1935. One scenic attraction that is outside Košice but easily reached by bus (every hour or so on weekdays; every 2 hrs at weekends) is the **Herl'any Gejzír** (Geyser), 30 km to the northeast. It erupts about 20 metres into the air, doing so every 36 hrs on average.

### ◤ SIDE TRACKS
### ◣ FROM KOŠICE

Trains and buses run southwest from Košice to **Moldava na Bodvou**, a good base for exploring the **Slovenský Kras** (Slovak Karst) a protected landscape of spectacular limestone caves and canyons. Going east from Košice by train leads to the pretty town of **Humenné** and the nearby **Vel'ká Domaša** (Lake Domaša), while continuing on the spur line to remote **Stakčín** puts one within striking distance of the rugged **Východné Karpaty** (Eastern Carpathian) mountains and nature reserve along the border with Ukraine. ◣

# VILNIUS

Vilnius is the most provincial of the Baltic capitals and the greenest – almost 50 per cent of the city is green space. Its strikingly baroque appearance originated in the 16th century with the arrival of the Jesuits who transformed Vilnius into a centre of learning and a bulwark against the encroachments of the Protestant Reformation. There's more to Vilnius than the obvious sights and tourist attractions: many of its charms are hidden away in the back streets, with their quaintly dilapidated houses (overrun by wild cats), old stables and grassy courtyards. Take Vilnius at a leisurely pace.

## TOURIST INFORMATION

There is no tourist office in Vilnius. **Lithuanian Tours**, *Seimyniskiu 18; tel: 353 931* will help with accommodation, excursions etc. Look out for the invaluable listings magazine, *Vilnius In Your Pocket*, on sale all over town. **Lithuanian Student and Youth Travel**, *tel: 650 145* offers bargain fares for students on planes, trains and buses.

## ARRIVING AND DEPARTING:

### Airport

**Aerouostas**, *Rodunes kelias 2; tel: 630 201/ 635 560*. Vilnius airport is situated  km south of the city. Flights depart to a number of major European destinations including Berlin, Frankfurt and London. The single terminal has two currency exchange offices (open 24 hrs) a café, restaurant and duty-free shop. Take a taxi only if you have to and don't pay more than about US$7. Bus no. 2 will take you to Vilnius's main street, *Gedimino Prospekt*. Flat rate tickets can be bought from kiosks at the airport.

### Station

**Gelezinkelio stotis**, *Gelezinkelio 16; tel: 630 086*. The advance booking office, for stations within the former USSR, is at *Sopeno 3; tel: 623 044*. All other tickets can be bought in the main booking hall. Little English is spoken, so buying tickets can be complicated and frustrating – make sure you have plenty of time to spare. This is especially important when leaving Vilnius for cross-border destinations: the border check for the St Petersburg–Warsaw–Berlin train is on platform 11/12, over the bridge.

Outside and to the left of the station is a currency exchange office, open from 0700. There is a baggage room open 24 hrs in the basement – the entrance is on the right facing the station. It's short walk to the centre of town and there are bus and trolley-bus stops in the forecourt.

### Buses

**Autobusu stotis**, *Sodu 22; tel: (information) 262 482; (international reservation) 635 277*. Buses leave for Kaliningrad, Klaipeda, Minsk, Riga and Warsaw as well as smaller towns within Lithuania.

## GETTING AROUND

### Public Transport

Most of Vilnius's sights are within walking distance of one another. There are

313

trolley-bus services operating in the centre of town and buses further afield.

All vehicles are unbearably crowded in summer and it's sometimes necessary to push vigorously to get off! Public transport operates from about 0530–0030 There is a local transport map in *Vilnius In Your Pocket*.

Flat fare tickets can be bought at kiosks or from the driver and should be punched on board.

## Taxis

Taxi drivers in Vilnius are predatory and inflate prices as a matter of course. Many of the vehicles are dilapidated and barely roadworthy and few are equipped with meters. Always agree on a price in advance or book through your hotel.

### STAYING IN VILNIUS

**314**

## Accommodation

Hotels, especially in the medium price range are still thin on the ground in Vilnius. Of the quality hotels, the most attractive is the 4-star newly renovated **Astorija Estate**, *Didzioji 35; tel: 224 0200.*

Many visitors prefer the smaller out-of-town hotels, among the most popular being the **Sarunas**, *Raitininku 4; tel: 353 888.* Owned by basketball star Sarunas Marciulionia, it caters specifically for western tourists. The rooms (all equipped with satellite TV) are comfortable and there's a small bar and restaurant.

**Litinterp** agency, *Bernardinu 7/2; tel: 223 850,* arranges bed and breakfast accommodation in private homes from about 60 Litas. There is a **Youth Hostel** information office 300 metres from the station at *Kauno 1a /407.* To stay at one of the three hostels you will need a Lithuanian Hostel Association card sold

on the spot for 20 Litas. The Filaretu, *Filaretu 17; tel: 696627* is a friendly hostel only a walk from the centre of town. There are no secure facilities for camping in the vicinity of Vilnius.

## Eating and Drinking

The most promising places to look for bars and restaurants are *Gedimino Prospektas, Pilies* and *Ausros Vartu.* **Stikliai Alude**, *Gaono 7; tel: 222 109* is a traditional hostelry with a distinctive middle-European flavour and lively folk band accompaniment. **Lokijs**, *Stikliu 8/10; tel: 629 046* serves exotic Lithuanian fare like elk sausages and wild boar, in a Gothic cellar – booking essential. **Medininki**, *Ausros vartu 8; tel: 614 019* is located in the chambers of a former monastery. The Russian-style menu is in Lithuanian only but both food and drink are good value.

A good place for afternoon coffee is the cool and sophisticated **Ladies' Happiness**, *Gedimino 31;* another boulevard café with a view is **Literatu Svetaine**, *Gedimino 1* – the salads are recommended. The fast food scene should improve with the arrival of **McDonalds** in 1996. There's no genuine pizzeria, although **Stikliai kavine**, *Stikliu 18* comes close. If all you want is a sandwich there's the kiosk **Submarinai** on the corner of *Gedimino* and *Cathedral Square* which rustles them up American-style.

There is a late-night **supermarket** next door to the Hotel Sarunas on *Raitiniku* and there's a branch of the Lithuanian **IKI** chain at *Jasinskio 16.* Also worth a look is the thriving **outdoor market** on *Bazilijonu* (closed Mon).

Vilnius doesn't offer much in the way of night bars. Youngsters flock to **Bix** *Etmonu 6,* founded by and named after Lithuania's premier rock band; or you can try the cellar bar underneath the

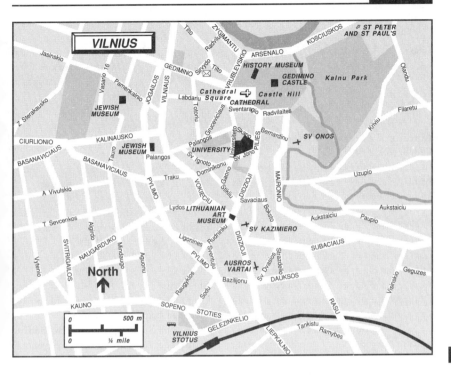

restaurant **Prie Parlamento**, *Gedimino 46*

## Communications

The **Central Post Office** is at *Gedimino 7; tel: 616759*. Open Mon–Fri 0800–2000; Sat–Sun 1100–1800. This is the best place to make a phone call. There is also a post office at *Vilniaus 33*. An increasing number of phones, especially in hotels, major buildings and offices take phone cards rather than cash. The local code for Vilnius is 22. To phone out abroad dial 8, then 10, then the country code.

## Money

Vinius is much a cash economy. Some hotels and the more upmarket restaurants will accept credit cards. Travellers' cheques may be exchanged in banks.

## Consulates

**Canada:** *Didzioji 8/5; tel: 220 898.*
**UK:** *Antakalnio 2; tel: 222 070.*
**USA:** *Akmenu 6; tel: 222 737.*
Citizens of **Australia, New Zealand, Republic of Ireland** and **South Africa** should contact the British Consulate in an emergency.

### ENTERTAINMENT AND EVENTS

Entertainment is a well-kept secret in Vilnius so you'll have to keep your ear to the ground. Outside the university, the only discos (with floor shows) are in the major hotels. There are several concert venues: *Ausros vartu 5* is the home of the **National Philharmonic**, *Vienuolio 1* is the opera and ballet theatre (closed July and August). Concerts and recitals are also held in the **Baroque Hall**, *Daukanto 1*, the **Academy of Music**, *Gedimino 42* and in the churches. There's a lively jazz scene – at **Leandra** on *Labdariu 8* every Sat night at 2000, at Langas, *Asmenos 8*, every Thurs and Fri (rock on Sat). A couple of cinemas show films in English with Lithuanian subtitles: **Lietuva**, *Pylimo 17a* and **Vilnius**, *Gedimino 5a*. Vilnius' **Summer Festival** takes place in July. It's largely folk-orientated, with dancing and musical ensembles, but there are also brass band concerts, recitals, jazz performances and other events.

## SHOPPING

Vilnius still has a long way to go on the road to market capitalism. The main, rather lacklustre shopping street is *Gedimino Prospektas*. There is a rather old-fashioned department store at no. 18 selling a wide range of goods. The best place to look for souvenirs is the area around *Pilies* in the old town. For religious memorabilia, look near the **Gates of Dawn** on *Ausros Vartu*. Amber necklaces and jewelry are typical local handicrafts; try, for example, **Amber**, *Ausros Vartu 9*.

## SIGHTSEEING

### Churches and monasteries

Vilnius is truly a treasure trove of Lithuanian baroque architecture. For sheer sensuality and delicate exuberance **Sv. Petro ir Povilo** (St Peter and Paul) on *Antakalnio* cannot be outdone. Commissioned by Lithuanian military commander Mykolos Kazimieras Pacas, in 1668, Italian sculptors were imported to decorate the walls, chapels and vaulted roof and the overall effect is stunning.

Vilnius' premier place of pilgrimage is the resplendent **Ausros Vartai** (Gates of Dawn) *Ausros vartu 12*. Originally a town gateway, the Carmelites from **Sv. Tereses** (St Teresa's) built a chapel above

in 1671 to display a sacred image of the Virgin. In Vilnius even the Orthodox Church of **Sv. Dvasios Cerkve** (The Holy Spirit), *Ausros vartu 10*, has a baroque exterior dating from the 17th century. Inside there's a hushed intimacy and a priest will point out the resting place of Saints Anthony, Ivan and Eustachius in the crypt.

The Jesuits founded Vilnius' oldest baroque church, **Sv. Kazimiero** (St Casimir), *Didzioji 34*, in 1604. In its time it has served variously as an Orthodox basilica, Protestant temple and, under the Soviets, Museum of Atheism. Roman Catholic services are now held here once more. The elaborate red brick facade of **Sv. Onos** (St Anne's), *Maironio 8*, late-Gothic in style (1520–72), is said to have enthused Napoleon Bonaparte.

Behind St Anne's is the **Bernadine Monastery**, currently undergoing extensive restoration. The brick-gabled **Sv. Mikalojaus** (St. Nicholas) *Sv. Mikalojaus 4*, is the oldest standing church in Lithuania (1320), even predating the country's conversion to Christianity.

Stridently out of step with the prevailing styles of Vilnius' church architecture is the **Arkikatedra Bazilika** (Cathedral). It's a neo-classical building, built over an ancient pagan site. The interior is unexceptional save for the baroque St Casimir's Chapel, which contains the mausoleum of the Lithuanian Grand Duke Alexander Jagiellon. The leaning **clock tower** outside the Cathedral is a remnant of the castle fortifications.

### Other Sights

**Vilnius University** occupies a prominent site between *Pilies* and *Universiteto*. The handsome bell tower of **Sv Jono** (St John's) graces the main courtyard, a perfectly harmonious example of the

Mannerist (pre-baroque) style of architecture. St John's predates the university by at least 200 years, although the existing pillar-clustered façade is 18th-century. The interior is only just recovering from its stint, in the Soviet era, as a museum of scientific thought. The university itself was founded by the Jesuits in 1579 and under Polish influence became one of the great centres of learning in the region.

The large tree-covered mound, known as **Gediminas Hill**, was where Vilnius was founded in the 14th century. Extensive excavations are now under way to recover what remains of the two castles. For the present all one can see is a single brick turret at the summit, capped by the national flag. Inside is a small museum devoted to the castles' history. Away to the east of Gediminas Hill is the **Hill of Three Crosses**, a 17th-century memorial to three monks said to have been martyred here. Since independence the site has become something of a national shrine.

### Museums and Galleries

The **Lithuanian State History Museum** is at *Arsenalo 1* (open Tues–Sun 1100–1800). More appealing to visitors perhaps is the neighbouring **Museum of Applied Art**, *Arsenalo 3*, which has some attractive examples of Lithuanian tapestry and ceramics (open Wed–Sun 1100–1900).

The **Lithuanian Art Museum** is housed in the neo-classical Town Hall building on *Rotuses aikste* (open Tues–Sun 1200–1800). Close to the Lietuva Hotel on *Ukmerges gatve*, the **National Gallery** is an all-purpose repository of Lithuanian culture home and abroad (open Wed–Sun 1100–1800). Before the Holocaust nearly half the population of Vilnius were Jews – a disturbing thought when all that survives is the impoverished contents of two museums, on *Pamenkalnio 12* and *Pylimo 4* (open Mon–Fri 0900–1700).

On the outskirts of town, at *Agrastu 17* is the pine forest where more than 100,000 victims of the Nazi genocide, mostly Jews, were murdered. (**Museum of Genocide**, open Wed-Mon 1100–1800).

In an unassuming building on *Auku 4* is another reminder of man's inhumanity to man. The **KGB museum** occupies the one-time headquarters of the notorious secret police. Former inmates and their relatives will show you the cells where Lithuanian dissidents were interrogated. (open Mon–Fri 1000–1300, 1400–1700; Sat–Sun 1100–1700; times liable to change)

### OUT OF TOWN

**Trakai Castle** is within easy reach of Vilnius and makes an enjoyable half-day excursion. The wholly, some say too perfectly, restored fortress dates originally from the late 14th century and became, under Grand Duke Vytautas and his successors, a vital centre of organised resistance to the depredations and incursions of the German crusading knights. The castle stands in a beautiful setting on a peninsula surrounded by three lakes. The various halls and chambers are open to the public as a rather eclectic **Museum of Lithuanian History** (open Tues–Sun 1000–1800).

Many of the wooden houses on the peninsula belonged to a community of Crimean Tartars who were first invited here by Vytautas in 1398 but who retain their language and customs including their own prayer house (1824) on *Karaimu 30*.

# VILNIUS–RIGA

This route takes travellers through Lithuania and across the border into Latvia, passing through largely unspoilt and increasingly flatter countryside and taking in the historic former capital, Kaunas – worth an overnight stay.

**Riga**

**Jelgava**

FASTEST JOURNEY: **7** HRS

**Siauliai**

**Radviliskis**

*Klaipeda*

## TRAINS

**ETT Table:** 919

### FAST TRACK

 Three trains a day taking just under 7 hrs.

**Kaunas**

### ON TRACK

 **Vilnius–Kaunas**
Five expresses taking 1 hr 30 mins.

**Vilnius**

**Kaunas–Radviliškis**
At least three trains a day, taking around 3 hrs.

**Radviliškis–Šiauliai**
A 30-min journey, 8 trains a day.

**Šiauliai–Jelgava**
4 a day, taking 2 hrs 30 mins.

**Jelgava–Riga**
8 trains a day, taking 1 hr.

## KAUNAS

**Station:** Stotis, *Ciurlionio 16; tel: 221 093 advanced booking tel: 292 408* The station hall promises much but delivers little in the way of facilities, not even a currency exchange. (The nearest office is just opposite on *Vytauto prospekt*.) The location, too, is inconvenient – a good 25 mins walk from the centre of town – look out for trolley-buses nos 3, 5, 7 and 14 **Tourist Office**: *Laisves aleja 88; tel: 200 621*. Ask for a copy of the indispensable

*Kaunas in Your Pocket*; also for help with accommodation.

## ACCOMMODATION AND FOOD

There are very few quality hotels in town. The situation is about to improve with the opening of the 5-star **Respublika** on *Karaliaus Mindaugo*. For the moment a popular choice is **'Perkuno Namai'**, *Perkuno aleja 61; tel: 209386*. This small, recently modernised hotel has a splendid position overlooking the old town.

There is more choice for budget travellers: the **Pienocentras Hotel**, *Kaunakiemio 1; tel: 202 763* is within striking distance of the railway station. For bed and breakfast contact **Litinterp**, *Kumeliu 15/4; tel: 228 718* (closed Sundays). The **Youth Hostel,** also handy for the train station, is at *Prancuzu 59; tel: 748 972*

Kaunas is more commercially minded than Vilnius. There are numerous pavement cafés and restaurants on the pedestrianised *Laisves aleja*, where smoking is forbidden in the street. The French restaurant and café, **Eliza**, on *Vilniaus 30* in the old town, is stylish and not overly expensive; for a view of the splendid St Michael's Church, try the **Café Zilinskas** in the art gallery of the same name. There are tables on the terrace in summer.

## SIGHTSEEING

Kaunas is well served by buses and trolley-buses, but they can be very crowded in summer. Tickets are sold on newsstands and should be punched on board. The most convenient place to pick up a bus is *Vytauto prospekt*.

There are state and private **taxis** – the latter are more comfortable and more expensive. State, *tel: 234 444, 235 555*; private, *tel: 239 880*

The central **post office** is at *Laisves aleja 102; tel: 226 220*. There are several public phone boxes on *Laisves aleja* – you can buy tokens at the post office.

The best place to look for **souvenirs** is *Laisves aleja,* alternatively *Vilniaus*. For films, cameras, etc., go to **Vezo** at *Laisves aleja 78*. There's a flower market on *Ciurlionio 23* and a servicable department store, **Merkurijus**, at *Laisves aleja 60*.

This important city, occupying both banks of the Nemunas River, was the capital of independent Lithuania during 1920–39 after Vilnius had been swallowed up by Poland. Today it's a large industrial centre but the charming old town has been surprisingly well preserved.

Most visitors however, will first encounter the magnificent, onion-domed **Church of St Michael the Archangel** at the east end of *Laisves aleja*. Despite its Byzantine appearance and the fact that it was built by Russian architects in the 1890s for the local garrison, this is now a Catholic place of worship.

The old town begins at the western end of *Laisves aleja* where *Vilniaus* leads to *Rotuses aikste* (Town Hall Square), an impressive ensemble of late-Gothic and Renaissance merchant houses. The **Town Hall** itself dates from 1542 and has served variously as an ammunition store, prison, palace, Orthodox church and currently, a registry office for weddings.

South of the square is the baroque **St Francis Xavier's Church** and former **Jesuit Monastery**. The substantial remains of **Kaunas Castle** extend along the river bank. The massive walls and fortified towers date from the 14th century. For a panoramic view of the city from **Zaliakalnis** (Green Hill), take the funicular railway from *Putvinskio*.

319

## RADVILIŠKIS

**Station:** *Laisves aleja 3; tel: 52 255*
This railway junction on the Šiauliai–
Jonava line is also a small but attractive
town surrounded by woods and parkland.

One stop down the line from (14 km)
is **Seduva** station *(tel: 56 495)* and the
**Daugyvene Cultural History and
Nature Reserve**. There are several outdoor museums in the vicinity, the most
important of which, at **Kleboniskiai
Village** *(tel: 44292)*, is devoted to 19th-
and early 20th-century rural life.

There's an important archaeological
site at **Raginenai**, where you'll find
ancient burial places, sacred stones and
mounds, including the celebrated **Hill of
Witches**. At **Burbiskio kaimas** there's
an attractive 17th-century **Manor
House** (currently being renovated) and a
landscaped park. Part of the house has
been converted into a hotel.

## ŠIAULIAI

**Station:** *Dubijos 44; tel: 430 652*
**Tourist Office: Paralele Tourism**,
*Vytauto 145; tel: 438 810* This bureau
will help with accommodation and local
tours.

There is a limited choice of accommodation – two hotels in the town itself, the
**Šiauliai**, *tel: 437 333* and the **Aronija**,
*tel: 423 672* are fairly central. There is a
café, popular with locals, called the
**Taskas** on *Ausros aleja and* restaurants in
the hotels.

Although there was a wooden castle in
Šiauliai as early as the 9th century, its official founding date is 1236, when a battle
was fought here between the Lithuanian
army and Teutonic knights. Šiauliai pros-
pered as a commercial centre in the late
19th century following the building of
the railway line to Riga.

There's not much to see today in the

town itself, with the notable exception of
the handsome white parish church of **SS
Peter and Paul**, which dates from 1634.

Most visitors will want to take the
short excursion (11 km) to the spectacular **Kryziu kalnas** (Hill of Crosses). Take
one of the regular bus services to Riga or
Mesluiciai and ask to be let off at *Kryziu
kalnas*. The first crosses are said to have
been planted on this site in the 14th century. The tradition was revived following
the rebellions of 1831 and 1863, when
large numbers of Lithuanians were exiled
to Siberia by the Russian occupiers.
More recently crosses were planted in
defiance of the Soviet authorities, who
periodically bull-dozed the site, only for
the crosses to stubbornly reappear. Today
the site is a place of Catholic pilgrimage.

 **SIDE TRACK
FROM ŠIAULIAI**

## KLAIPEDA

**Station:** *Priestoties 1; tel: 214 614.*
Advance reservations: *Taikos pr. 107;
tel: 296 356*
**Tourist Information:** *Tomo 2; tel:
213 977*

The classiest hotel is the **Klaipeda**,
*Naujoji Sodo gatve; tel: 219 960*, in a
convenient location, just off *Herkus
Manto* and with a good restaurant. It
gets heavily booked though in the
summer, so advanced reservations are
essential. There's a choice of seaside
hotels, for example the **Morena**,
*Audros 8a; tel: 298 456*, about 4 km
from the town centre, or you can stay
further afield in Palanga. For bed and
breakfast contact **Litinterp-Klaipeda**,
*Simkaus 21-8; tel: 216 962*. There's a
**Youth Hostel** at Palanga (300 metres
from the sea), *Neries 24; tel: 57 076.*

There is a rapid growth in the

number of cafés, bars and restaurants in Klaipeda. The best place to start is *H. Manto*. There is a good seafood restaurant, **Vaiva** *(H. Manto 11)* which serves meat dishes too. **Luja** at *H. Manto 20* delivers standard European cuisine in a modern setting. **Linas Baras**, *Naujoji sodo 3*, has a nice terrace in the summer and serves a hearty lunch. The best place for fast food is **Bambola**, on *S. Neries 10*, a Swedish-run establishment which serves extremely tasty pizzas.

Klaipeda is well-served with buses. Particularly useful for the tourist are nos 1 and 8, which travel the entire length of the main avenue, *Herkus Manto*, as far as *Taikos prospekt*. For beach-goers there are regular services to **Palanga** (every 45 mins until 2200) departing from the main bus station, *Butku Juze 9; tel: 214 863*. The nearest beaches are across the spit from **Smiltyne** and are reached by ferry. In summer, boats leave every half-hour 0700–2300, journey time 10 mins.

If you're looking for souvenirs, crafts and commercial art, head for the old town. The main shopping street is *H. Manto* – **Deimena**, at number 30, is an excellent foodstore, open 7 days a week.

A major port with a population of more than 200,000, Klaipeda is also a scenic holiday resort. Known for centuries as Memel – the Livonian Knights built Memelburg Castle in 1252 – Klaipeda was under German influence for much of its history and the town still attracts large numbers of German tourists.

Modern Klaipeda dates largely from the end of World War II, when much of the old town was destroyed by Soviet bombing. That being said, the restored streets south of the Dane River around *Turgaus aikste* (Market Square) are worth exploring. The stately **theatre** on *Teatro* dates from 1857. You'll find the site of **Memelburg Castle** just to the west side of *Pilies* – only the moat survives.

Most visitors come to Klaipeda for the sea and sand. The nearest beaches are across the Kursiai Lagoon at **Smiltyne**. There's an excellent **maritime museum and aquarium** here. The vicinity of **Nida** is wilder, with mile after mile of windswept dunes. If you're in Klaipeda for a while, you might think it worth making the 30 km trip to **Palanga,** a resort in its own right. ▲

## JELGAVA

**Station**: *Stacijas 1; tel: 42200*
**Tourist Office**: *Central Square 1; tel: 23461*

Jelgava's heyday was in the 18th and 19th centuries, when it was the capital of the Duchy (later Province) of Courland. Then known as Mitau, it was a fashionable winter resort for Russian high society. Today it's a large industrial town but despite this there are plenty of green spaces.

Unfortunately much of Jelgava's considerable architectural heritage was destroyed during World War II. The main tourist attraction is the **Palace of the Dukes of Courland** – you'll find it to the south-east of town by the Lielupe River. Comprising 300 rooms, it is one of the baroque masterpieces of Bartolomeo Rastrelli, architect of St Petersburg's Winter Palace (see p. 260). It's currently undergoing extensive restoration and may not be open to the public.

# VILNIUS–ST PETERSBURG

This journey connects Lithuania with Russia, crossing Latvia relatively briefly. Scenically, the best of the route is in the south. The most attractive stretch is through Latvia's Latgale region, with its clear blue lakes and gently undulating hills.

FASTEST JOURNEY: 15 HRS

## TRAINS

**ETT Table: 905**

### FAST TRACK

 Five through trains each day. They take 15 hrs.

### ON TRACK

 **Vilnius–Daugavpils–Rezekne–Pytalvo–Pskov**

Five trains a day with refreshments. Vilnius to Daugavpils takes 3 hrs, from there to Rezekne 1 hr 15 mins, Rezekne to Pytalovo 1 hr 15 mins, Pytalovo to Pskov 2 hrs.

**Pskov–St Petersburg**

Six trains a day make this 5 hr journey.

## DAUGAVPILS

**Station**: *Stacijas iela; tel: 34725*
**Bus Station:** *Lacplesa; tel: 22507*
**Tourist Offfice: Hotel Latvija**, *Gimnazijas 46; tel: 29003.*

Latvia's second city (population 127,000) occupies the northern bank of the broad river Daugava and is an important railway junction and industrial centre. Latvians are heavily outnumbered by Russians here and although the streets are no longer named after Lenin, Marx et al., Daugavpils is finding it difficult to shed its stolid Soviet imprint. Known variously in the past as Dünaberg to the Germans, Borisoglebsk to the Russians and Dvinsk to the Poles, the city was founded in 1275 when the German Livonian Knights built a castle. Nowadays there's little to see in the way of sights – perhaps the most interesting monument is the grassy remains of a massive 19th-century Russian fortress, until recently occupied by Soviet troops, and once serving as a Nazi concentration camp.

 **SIDE TRACK FROM DAUGAVPILS**

The line to Riga follows the northern bank of the Daugava River. The valley was a natural line of defence in the Middle Ages when knights built their castles on the slopes. The ruins of **Koknese Castle**, built by Bishop Albert of Riga in 1209, occupy a scenic position at the point where the River Perse flows into the Daugava. There's another 13th century castle at **Krustpils,** just across the river from **Jekabpils** where there's also an open air history museum. Some of these medieval fortifications were built on the site of ancient mounds, dating from as early as the 1st century BC. The mound at **Aizkraukle** (formerly Stucka) is overshadowed by the local hydro-electric power plant – the largest in the Baltic States. A little to the north of **Plavinas**, at **Mezezers**, there's a sports and recreation centre, *tel: 34858.* Facilities include accomodation in well-equipped cottages and hotel rooms, sports' hall and sauna. There's skiing in winter and fishing and excursions in summer.

## REZEKNE

**Stations: Rezekne 1**, *Brivibas iela; tel: 72115*; **Rezekne 2**, *Stacijas iela; tel: 72110* Rezekne stands at the junction of two railway lines: Rezekne 1 is on the route St Petersburg–Vilnius while Rezekne 2, at the other end of town, serves Riga–Moscow.

**Tourist Office: Latgale Tourism and Business Institute**, *Atbrivosanas aleja 90; tel: 24518.*

The centre of the beautiful Latgale region, Rezekne is a small, but charming town, refreshingly green and relatively unspoilt (the Soviet-style apartment blocks are kept well at bay). Known as Rositten in the Middle Ages, Rezekne was subsequently the object of a prolonged power struggle between Poland, Russia and Sweden. The town was part of independent Latvia from 1920 until World War II, when it was occupied by both Soviet and German forces. Its growth dates from the 19th century, when the two key railway lines were constructed.

### ACCOMMODATION AND FOOD

Rezekne has only one hotel worth talking about, the recently completed **Latgale** at *Atbrivosanas aleja 98; tel: 22067.* Medium priced and homely, there's a breakfast room and restaurant and the staff are friendly and helpful though mainly in Latvian! Ask to see the fine view of the town and surrounding countryside from the roof. Camping is possible at Luzda, one stop away from Rezekne by local train (about 25 km). **Camping Cirma**, *L. Ezerkrasta; tel: 23643*

There are a number of small cafés, as well as shops, along *Atbrivosanas aleja.* The best restaurant at present is the **Senatne**, located just across the square from the Hotel Latgale. The folksy interior is warm and relaxing, there's live music and dancing much appreciated by the locals who come here to eat traditional Latvian dishes (menu in Latvian only).

## SIGHTSEEING

The main artery, *Atbrivosanas aleja,* connects most of the sights. At the southern end, along *Latgales iela,* is the distinctive twin-tower Catholic **Church of the Sacred Heart of Jesus**, dating from the turn of the century. Across the river is a small park with a simple stone memorial commemorating 39 martyrs of the freedom movement, tortured by the Soviet secret police in June 1941. Off to the right on *Pils iela* are the ruins of the **Castle** (founded in the 9th century). The **Liberation Monument**, affectionately known as Mara, has a turbulent history: the bronze statue of a young woman defiantly holding a cross was erected in 1939 to commemorate the departure of the Bolsheviks 20 years earlier. In the decade 1940–50 the monument was twice torn down by the Soviets and the present structure, a replica, was unveiled in August 1992. On either side of the monument are two more churches, the pseudo-Romanesque **St Mary's** (Marian Catholic) and the classically proportioned Orthodox **Church of the Mother of God**, distinguished by its blue onion domes. There are some noteworthy civic buildings along *Atbrivosanas aleja,* notably the **Latgalian Culture and History Museum** at no. 102, which looks the same today as when it was first constructed at the beginning of the 19th century.

### ↱ SIDE TRACK
### FROM REZEKNE
South of Rezekne is an area of great natural beauty known traditionally as the **Land of Blue Lakes**. It's a comparatively hilly region too – the highest point, Lielais Liepukalns, reaches 289 metres. Of the lakes (there is a wide scattering of them throughout the region), the deepest is **Lake Dridzis** (65 metres); the largest, **Lake Razna** (area 55 sq km). This is a traditionally Catholic part of the country: in 1993 Pope John Paul II paid a visit to the shrine at **Aglona,** where there are religious festivities, including a candlelight procession, on the eve of the Feast of the Assumption (14 Aug). The basilica which dates from 1699 was once served by Dominican monks. There's a small hotel, **Hotel Arpa**, only 200 metres from the shrine but little else in the way of accommodation.

**Preili** is the local 'capital', though a modest one. It's an old town (founded in 1348) but there's not very much to see here. However, the travel agency on *Rainis blvd 19 room 12; tel: 22641* will help with excursions and tourist information. ⬛

**Station:** *tel: 23 737* The railway junction at Pskov earned its place in history when Tsar Nicholas II's military train was detained here shortly after the outbreak of the Russian Revolution in Feb 1917. Nicholas eventually abdicated the throne in the sumptuous surroundings of his private railway compartment.

**Tourist Information**: none

About 160 km south of St Petersburg, the ancient city of Pskov was one of the great cultural centres of medieval Russia. Still standing guard over the town is the well-preserved **Kremlin**, or fortress, from where the legendary military leader, Prince St Alexander Nevsky, led his army to victory against the Teutonic knights in 1242. Also of interest is the 12th-century **Mirozhsky Monastery,** the **Holy Trinity Cathedral** and **Pogankiny Palace**.

# WARSAW

Warsaw became Poland's capital in 1596, flourishing until the 17th-century Swedish invasion, and then expanding again in the late 18th century. After the partition of Poland in 1798, Warsaw was initially part of Prussia before Napoleon created the Grand Duchy of Warsaw, and subsequently came under Russian control. Poland regained independence in 1918, though Warsaw suffered terribly under the Nazis, which left the city almost completely destroyed. While Warsaw has its fair share of post-war concrete blocks, there are also areas of immense beauty and historic significance, which are a tribute to the extensive restoration undertaken, and Warsaw is now thriving under democracy.

## TOURIST INFORMATION

The **Informator Turystyczny (IT)**, *pl. Zamkowy 1/13, 00-262 Warsaw; tel: (02) 635 18 81*, opens Mon–Sat 0800–1800, Sun 1100–1700. While few brochures are free there is plenty to buy. **Orbis Travel (Thomas Cook** network member) on *ul. Marszałkowska 142; tel: (022) 276 766* also offers tourist services including hotel reservations, sightseeing/guides and Western Union money transfer. Larger hotels often have the free *Welcome to Warsaw* and *What, Where, When* magazines containing a city map, practical information and various listings. The *Warsaw Voice* (English-language newspaper) is also worth consulting.

## ARRIVING AND DEPARTING

### Airport

**Okęcie Airport,** *1A ul. Żwirki i Wigury; tel: (022) 46 17 31*, lies 10 km south of the city with two terminals (arrivals and departures) offering currency exchange, an Orbis travel office (where hotel reservations can be made throughout Poland), bank, post office, restaurant, fast food counter, Ruch kiosk, left luggage and washing facilities. Daily flights between London and various international destinations are operated by **LOT Polish Airlines**, with **British Airways** flying London–Warsaw. MZK's Airport Citybus (which is bright yellow), runs every 30 mins from 0630–2230 taking about 30 mins to reach the centre via Warszawa Centralna and major hotels with tickets at 3.5 złoty available from the driver. Bus no. 175 runs from 0500–2300 approximately every ten mins to the central railway station and Old Town.

### Stations

**Warszawa Centralna** (Central Railway Station), *al. Jerozolimskie 54; tel: (022) 20 50 10* for international information, *20 45 12* for national information and *20 03 61* to *9* for local details. Located about 20 mins walk from the Old Town or 10 mins by taxi, it offers currency exchange, left-luggage, café and washing facilities, but is also notorious for crime and best avoided at night. Other large stations are **Warszawa Wschodnia**; *tel: (022)18 34 97,* on the east bank of the Wisła (Vistula River), and the western suburban station, **Warszawa Zachodnia;** *tel: (022) 18 34*

**325**

97, which is 3 km west of Centralna, opposite the PKS bus station; *tel: (022) 23 63 94.*

## GETTING AROUND

The Vistula River divides Warsaw with most sights on the west bank, including the Old Town and main thoroughfares collectively known as *Trakt Królewski* (the Royal Way) starting on *Krakowskie Przedmieście*. Most tourist attractions are within walking distance, though public transport will probably be necessary at some stage. Street names are constantly changing (to remove Communist references) so don't be surprised if your map doesn't tally

### Tickets

Bus and tram tickets are sold at kiosks marked Bilety MZK and Ruch kiosks. Single journey, daily and weekly tickets are available which should be punched once. Spot checks are carried out.

### Public Transport

The 26 tram lines and 150 bus lines operate on a grid system. Buses, which are generally crowded, run from 0430–2300 on weekdays. Night buses run every 45 mins and cost three times the normal fare. Pick up taxis at ranks, outside larger hotels or by phoning *919*.

## STAYING IN WARSAW

### Accommodation

The tourist office can provide accommodation details, with a wide price range now available. The city's premier location is the **Hotel Bristol**, *Krakowskie Przedmieście 42/44; tel: (02) 625 25 25*, a beautifully restored art nouveau building, classified as a national monument, which is one of Europe's grandest hotels. There

are plenty of tourist class hotels run by **Orbis**, some pensions and budget hotels. Two **hostels** belonging to **HI** are at *ul. Smolna 30; tel: (022) 278 952* (central) and *ul. Karolkowa 53a; tel: (022) 328 829* (in Wola suburb, take tram nos 1, 13, 20 or 24 to *al. Solidarności*). There are six **campsites** (which tend to be located by busy thoroughfares and on the edge of town), with the best including *ul. Zwirki i Wigury 32; tel: (022) 25 43 91* and *ul. 7 Stycznia 32; tel: (022) 46 21 84.* Hotel chains include: *Fo, HI, Ma, Nv, Ic.*

### Eating and Drinking

Privatisation has revolutionised eating out with an international selection of restaurants thriving, while traditional Polish food has been joined by 'new wave' Polish, featuring lighter versions of classic dishes.

New wave pioneers include the **Malinowa** (within the Hotel Bristol) and **Fukier**, *Rynek Starego Miasta 27; tel: (022) 31 10 13.* For traditional Polish food in an Old Town burgher's house try **Bazyliszek**, *Rynek Starego Miasta 3/9; tel: (022) 31 18 41*, and **Swiętoszek**, *ul. Jezuicka 6/8; tel: (022) 31 56 34.* Snacks and fast food can easily be found along with plenty of alfresco cafés, particularly in the Old Town.

**Pijalnia Czekolady** (hot chocolate café) is an antique paradise on *ul. Szpitalna 8*, and mead bars, such as **Pszczółka** (Little Bee) on *ul. Pulawska 24*, are also Warsaw specialities. Delicatessens are usually open 0600–1900, and are particularly abundant in the Old Town and *Nowy Swiat*, with plenty of parks like **Ogród Saski** (Saxon Gardens) in which to enjoy picnics.

### Communications

The **Main Post Office**, *ul.*

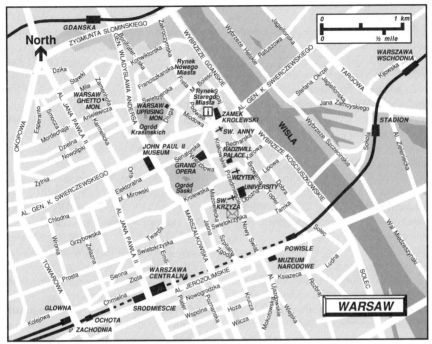

Świętokrzyska, 31/33, is open 0800–2000, for counter facilities and poste restante. Phones taking tokens are being phased out, though more reliable card-operated phones are still thin on the ground.

To phone Warsaw from abroad: *tel: 48* (Poland) + *22* (6 digit nos in Warsaw) or *2* (7 digit nos in Warsaw); to phone Warsaw from elsewhere in Poland: *tel: 022* (6 digit nos in Warsaw) or *02* (7 digit nos in Warsaw).

### Embassies

**Australia**: *ul. Estonska 3/5; tel: (02) 617 60 81.*
**Canada**: *ul. Matejki 1/5 (door on ul. Pieknej); tel: (022) 29 80 51.*
**New Zealand**: if necessary, contact the UK embassy.
**UK**: *Al. Róż 1; tel: (02) 628 10 01- 5.*
**USA**: *Al. Ujazdowskie 29/31; tel: (02) 628 30 41-9.*

### Money

When changing cash try to have undamaged notes without any writing on, as these may be refused. Some bureaux de change (generally termed kantor) will not cash travellers' cheques, in which case try **Orbis Travel** (Thomas Cook network member), *ul. Marszałkowska 142*, large hotels, or branches of **NBP,** one of which is *pl. Powstanców Warszawy*. Credit cards are accepted by many hotels, restaurants and larger shops. You can get cash advances on credit cards at Orbis Travel. Currency changes introduced in 1995 mean that 10,000 old złoty are worth 1 new złoty. Old złoty will remain in circulation and be phased out over the next couple of years. Prices are generally displayed in old and new złoty.

### ENTERTAINMENT

There is a good range of entertainment,

with plenty of bars, English and Irish pubs, and discos (including **Ground Zero** at *ul. Wspólna 62; tel: (02) 652 52 80*, and **Tango**, *ul. Smolna 15; tel: (02) 622 19 19*, live music, including rock and roll, jazz, and particularly classical music and opera. **Warsaw Opera House** is at *al. Solidarnosci 76; tel: (022) 25 75 10* and the **Narodowy Theatre** (National Theatre) is at *Pl. Marszałka Józefa Piłsudskiego; tel: (022) 26 40 50*. Chopin concerts are held every Sun at 1600, May–Oct by Chopin's monument in the **Łazienki Park**. The large number of cinemas increasingly show foreign (i.e. American) films subtitled rather than dubbed. The **Pałac Kultury i Nauki** (Palace of Culture and Science), a 'present' from Stalin, houses a casino, theatres, cinemas, nightclub and bookshop. **Festivals** include the International Poster Biennals (June–Sept), Bach International Organ Music Festival (July–Aug), Warsaw Autumn International Festival of Contemporary Music (Sept–Oct), Jazz Jamboree Festival (Oct), Warsaw Film Festival (Oct). The International Chopin Competition (Oct) is held every 5 years and is next due in the year 2000.

## SHOPPING

Local specialities include silver, leather, crystal and particularly amber, with **Cepelia** stores having the best selection of folk art. Some of the best shopping is in the Old Town, *Krakowskie Przedmieście* and *Nowy Swiat*, with leading hotels also having boutiques and shopping arcades. Street vendors are always busy in the Old Town, by the Palace of Culture and the **Russian Market, 10th Anniversary Stadium**, *Praga*. Try also the *Wola* antique market (on Sun) for clothes, furniture, and books. Take bus B, K or no. 159. Both markets are crowded by 1000.

## SIGHTSEEING

For various tours and excursions contact Orbis. Horse drawn carriages for city tours can be found in the Old Town Market Square.

### Rynek Starego Miasta

Very much a focal point, **Rynek Starego Miasta** (the Old Town Market Square) with its cafés, restaurants and boutiques, is lined with ornate burghers' houses which are exact post-war reconstructions, though you would never know it. The **Muzeum Historyczne Warszawy** (Warsaw Historical Museum) at *no. 28; tel: (02) 635 16 25*, is open Tues, Thur 1200–1900, Wed, Fri 1000–1530, Sat–Sun 1030–1700. Chronicling the city's turbulent history, a short film, *Warsaw After All*, includes footage shot by the Nazis documenting their systematic destruction of the city after the Warsaw Uprising. **The Muzeum Literatury im. Adama Mickiewicza** (The Literary and Adam Mickiewicz Museum) at *no. 28; tel: (022) 31 40 61*, is open Mon–Tues, Fri 1000–1500, Wed–Thur 1100–1800, Sun 1100–1700. The museum is a shrine to Polish literature and particularly Adam Mickiewicz, the romantic poet.

Behind the Old Town Market Square is the Gothic **Archikatedra sw. Jana**, the city's oldest church. The crypts contain the graves of Mazovian dukes and celebrated Poles such as the Nobel prize winning author Henryk Sienkiewicz. Continuing along *Swiętojanska* leads to pl. *Zamkowy*, dominated by **Zamek Królewski** (the Royal Castle); *tel: (02) 65 72 338*, open Tues–Sun 1000–1600. Essentially early baroque, it also includes Gothic and rococo elements. The castle became a royal residence when Warsaw became the capital in 1596, and also housed the Polish parliament. Looted and bombed in 1939, the Castle was completely destroyed five years later by the Nazis, with restoration only completed in the 1980s. Highly stylised interiors, such as the Royal Apartments, Marble Room and Ballroom, showcase a vast collection of furniture, tapestries, paintings and *objets d'art*. There is also a good souvenir shop. Standing before the Castle in *pl. Zamkowy* is Warsaw's oldest monument, the column of King Zygmunt III dating from 1644.

## North

The 16th-century **Barbakan** (Barbican), once part of the city walls, is now flanked by artists and street traders, and nearby is the 1855 statues of the **Warsaw Mermaid**, a symbol of the city. From here *ul. Freta* leads to *Rynek Nowego Miasta* (New Town Market Square) past **sw. Jacka** (St. Jack's Church) and the **Marie Skłodowskiej-Curie Museum** at *no. 16; tel: (022) 31 80 92*, open Tues–Sat 1000–1630, Sun 1000–1430 in the house where this distinguished scientist was born. The 18th-century **New Town Market Square**, less flamboyant than its Old Town counterpart, accommodates the **Church of the Blessed Sacrament**, founded in 1688 by Queen Maria in memory of her husband (King Jan III Sobieski) who defeated the Turks at Vienna. *Ul. Dluga* leads to *pl. Kraśinskich*, site of a Monument and Museum to the 63-day Warsaw Uprising, the **Raczyński Palace** (south-east) and **Kraśinski Palace**, fronting the Kraśinski Park.

## Museums

Pride of place goes to the **Muzeum Narodowe** (National Museum), *al. Jerozolimskie 3; tel: (02) 621 10 31*, open

Tues–Wed, Fri 1000–1700, Thur 1200–2000, Sat–Sun 1000–1700. This museum has an impressive collection of Polish and European paintings successfully hidden during the war. The **Muzeum Etnograficzne** (Ethnographic Museum), *ul. Kredytowa 1; tel: (022) 27 76 41*, open Tues, Thur, Fri 0900–1600, Wed 1100–1800, Sat–Sun 1000–1700, has a collection of Polish folk-art and worldwide tribal art. The new **Pope John Paul II Museum**, *pl. Bankowy 1; tel: (02) 620 27 25*, open Tues–Sun 1000–1700, has a huge collection of thematically arranged religious art, and European paintings ranging from Titian and Tintoretto to Breughel, Rembrandt and Rodin. The **Frederic Chopin Museum** within the **Ostrogski Palace** at *ul. Okólnik 1; tel: (022) 27 54 71* is open Mon, Wed, Fri 1000–1700, Thur 1200–1800, Sat–Sun 1000–1400, with a collection of memorabilia and a souvenir counter, while also being headquarters of the **International Chopin Society**. On *Krakowskie Przedmieście 5* within the **College of Fine Art**; *tel: (022) 26 62 51 ext 267*, is **Salonik Chopinów** (Chopin Family Salon) open Mon–Fri 1000–1400. This 18th-century room includes a piano on which Chopin played. **Muzeum Karykatury** (Caricature Museum), *ul Kozia 11; tel: (022) 27 88 95*, is open Tues–Sun 1100–1700. Warsaw's most romantic palace is within the **Łazienki Park**, *ul. Agrykola 1; tel: (02) 621 82 12*. **Pałac-na-Wyspie** (Palace-on-the-Isle), open Tues–Sun 0930–1600, was built in a neo-Classical style at the end of the 18th century, as the summer residence of Stanislaus Augustus Poniatowski, Poland's last king. Encircled by water it includes a marble rotunda, ballroom, Bacchus room with Delft tiles and various picture galleries. The

Łazienki Park also contains other palaces, a moated amphitheatre, Egyptian temple, orangery and the **Biały Dom** (White House) renowned for its Chinoiserie. The extravagantly baroque **Wilanów Palace,** *ul Wiertnicza 1; tel: (022) 42 07 95,* open Wed–Mon 0930–1430, is on the edge of town though easily reached by bus (nos. 122, 130, 180, 193 and 422). Wilanów was the residence of King Jan III Sobieski, and in addition to an extensive collection of furniture and works of art, the grounds include a baroque chapel, orangery, poster museum and Italianate gardens with water features.

### The Royal Way

The Royal Way starts at *Krakowskie Przedmieście* by the Stare Miasto (Old Town) and heads south for 10 km, under various names, all the way to **Wilanów**. The 15th-century **Kościół Sw. Anny** (St Anne's Church), *Krakowskie Przedmieście 68*, is the University church with interiors full of baroque and rococo extravagance, and a tower open for rooftop views. A small enclosed square is the site of the **Adam Mickiewicz Monument**. The adjacent **Radziwill Palace** (1643), now the Council of Ministers, where the Warsaw Pact was signed in May 1955. Opposite, in the **Ogród Saski** (Saxon Gardens) is the **Tomb of the Unknown Soldier** guarded around the clock. Dominating the adjacent *Pl. Teatralny* is the neo-classical **Grand Opera and Ballet Theatre** (1825–33), which faces the **Monument to the Heroes of Warsaw**. Back on *Krakowskie Przedmieście*, Chopin played the organ in the **Kościół Wizytek** (Church of the Nun's of the Visitation), while **Kościół Sw. Krzyża**, is a masterpiece of baroque and also the resting place of Chopin's heart. **Warsaw**

University, closed first by the Czar (1831–1915) and then the Nazis, is opposite the 17th-century **Kazimierz Palace.** A statue of astronomer Nicolaus Copernicus stands before the **Staszic Palace**, now the Academy of Sciences. Continuing along *Nowy Swiat* and across *al Jerolimski*, with its many shops and cafés, leads to *Pl. Zamkowy* beyond which is *al. Ujazdowskie,* where the **Łazienki Park** and palaces and the **Botanical Gardens** are located. The final stop on the Royal Way is **Wilanów Palace**.

### Jewish Warsaw

Before World War II, Warsaw had a large Jewish community, living mainly in the *Muranów* and *Mirów* districts. During the Nazi occupation, the population fell from 380,000 to just 300. There are two great monuments – to the **Heroes of the Warsaw Ghetto**, *ul. Zamenhofa*, and the white marble **monument to Concentration Camp Victims**, *Umschlarplatz*, at the site where Jews were herded onto trains bound for the nearby camps. The **Jewish Historical Institute**, *ul. Tłomackie 3/5; tel: (022) 27 92 21,* open Mon–Wed 0900–1500, Thur 1100–1900, and Sat–Sun by appointment, has a museum of the heroic Jewish resistance. **Nozyk**, *ul. Twarda*, is the only remaining synagogue.

### OUT OF TOWN

Within easy reach of Warsaw in Sochaczew is **Żelazowa Wola**; *tel: (0494) 223 00,* open Tues–Sun 0930–1730, the classical, manor house where Frederic Chopin was born in 1810. Set in its own landscaped park with lake, the interiors are true to the period and feature Chopin memorabilia, while the terrace is a venue for summer concerts. Orbis organises trips from Warsaw.

# WARSAW–GDAŃSK

FASTEST JOURNEY: 3 HRS 30 MINS

This route takes you through endless agricultural and pastoral landscapes in the northern flatlands, as well as some of Poland's most historic towns, with Gdańsk a major holiday destination on the Baltic coast. Gdańsk, Gdynia and Sopot are now referred to as the tri-city having merged geographically, though maintaining their individual characters, and extend over 30 km of coast line.

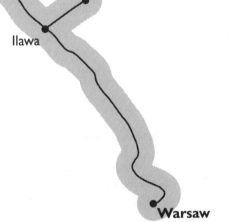

**331**

## TRAINS

**ETT Table:** 855.

### FAST TRACK

Direct service, total journey time is 3 hrs 30 mins.

### ON TRACK

**Warsaw–Iława–Gdańsk**
Frequent service throughout the day. Warsaw to Iława takes around 2 hrs, Iława to Gdańsk 1 hr 30 mins. Make seat reservation in advance.

## IŁAWA

**Tourist Information**: *ul. Jana III Sobieskiego 37a, 14-200 Iława; tel: (088) 48 58 00,* open Mon–Fri 0800–1500. There is plenty of town and regional information and advice on accommodation.
**Station**: *Iława, ul. Dworcowa 3; tel: (088)* 48 22 31, 48 32 00. Facilities include left-luggage, bar and kiosks. The centre is within walking distance.

### SIGHTSEEING

Various sightseeing and excursions can be booked through **Orbis**, *ul. Niepodległości 10; tel: (088) 18 33 30.*

Beautifully set on the side of a lake with its own beach, Iława is an established centre for 'water tourism,' being on the famous 81-km long Elbląg-Ostroda Canal route. It was built in the mid-19th century to join a series of lakes with man-made cuttings and slipways. There is little of historic interest to see, apart from the 14th-century **Gothic church** at *ul. Kościelnej* and remains of the 14th-century **city walls**.

## SIDE TRACK FROM IŁAWA

### OLSZTYN

**Tourist Information**: *ul. Marii Curie-Skłodowskiej 3, 10-109 Olsztyn; tel: (089) 27 27 38*, open Mon–Fri 0800–1800, Sat 1000–1400 (summer), Mon–Fri 0800–1600 (winter).
**Station: Olsztyn Główny**, *pl. Konstitucji 3 Maja; tel: (089) 33 66 87*, and *933* (train times). Facilities include left-luggage, restaurant, café, various kiosks (and currency exchange, opposite the main entrance, but still within the station complex).

### GETTING AROUND

Bus nos 1 and 4 depart from Olsztyn Główny to **Wysoka Brama** (Tall Gate) which is the entrance to the **Old Town**, although this is within walking distance.

### ACCOMMODATION AND FOOD

There are plenty of options at various prices. At the more comfortable on the edge of Lake Ukiel is the **Novotel**, *ul. Sielska 4a; tel: (089) 27 40 81*. **Dom Wycieczkowy** is a hostel at *ul. Staromiejska 1; tel: (089) 27 36 75*. **Campsites** include **Agro-Camping**, *ul. Młodziezowa 1; tel: (089) 23 66 66*,

and **Wanda-Mazury**, *ul. Sielska 12; tel: (089) 27 12 53*. There are plenty of restaurants, bars and cafés for all budgets around the Old Town Market Square. For traditional Polish food try **U Piotra**, *ul. Pana Tadeusza 6; tel: (089) 33 50 77*.

### SIGHTSEEING

Olsztyn's origins are 14th century, with the renowned Polish astrologer Nicolaus Copernicus living and studying in Olsztyn Castle in the early 16th century. Now a major tourist centre within the Mazurian lake district, Olsztyn is itself surrounded by six lakes. The key sights are concentrated in the Old Town, including the 14th-century **Wysoka Brama** (Tall Gateway), **Sw. Jakuba** (St. Jacob's) cathedral dates from 1445. The neo-Renaissance **Ratusz** (Town Hall) dates from 1912. Outside the Old Town, there is plenty of Secessionist (Polish art nouveau) and turn of the century eclectic architecture to see, with *ul. Warmińska* in particular having many fine examples. The 14th-century Gothic castle of the Cathedral Chapter is now the **Warmy i Mazury Muzeum Okręgowe** (Regional Museum), *ul. Zamkowa 2, tel: (089) 27 95 96*, open Tues–Sun 0900–1630 (June–Sept inclusive) otherwise Tues–Sun 1000–1530. Exhibits include regional history, local wildlife (stuffed), paintings, Medieval crafts and memorabilia from Nicolaus Copernicus's residence in the castle.

### GDAŃSK

**Tourist Information**: For information on Gdańsk, Gdynia and Sopot contact the main tourist office at *ul. Heweliusza 27, 80-861 Gdańsk; tel: (058) 31 43 55, 31 66*

37, open Mon–Fri 0800–1600. The office (a short walk from the station and Old Town) has local and national information (most of which must be bought), and can advise but not book accommodation. Another tourist information office, is at *ul. Długa 45; 80-827 Gdańsk; tel: (058) 31 93 27,* open Mon–Fri 0900–1800 (1900 in summer season) with local and national information accommodation details.

**Station: Gdańsk Główny,** *Podwale Grodzkie 1; tel: (058) 38 52 60, 31 11 12* (train information), *38 50 88, 38 59 68* (ticket office for travel in Poland), *38 54 15* (international timetable and tickets). The station is a magnificent red-brick neo-Gothic building dating from 1900. A basic tourist information point (no telephone), located by the ticket office, operates in the summer season throughout the week between 0930–1800, offering tourist information, advice on accommodation and help buying rail tickets (most ticket clerks don't speak English). Station facilities include left-luggage, fast food outlets, various shops and kiosks.

**Ferries:** PZB, the Polish Ferry Company operates from **Gdańsk Ferry Terminal,** *Gdańsk Nowy Port, ul. Przemysłowa 1; tel: (058) 43 18 87,* with services from Gdańsk to Oxelosund (Sweden) and Helsinki.

## GETTING AROUND

Most sights are within walking distance, with trams and trolley buses operating within each city. For travel between the three cities the railway is best, with sightseeing within walking distance of each Gdynia and Sopot station.

**Tickets:** Tram and bus tickets are available from Ruch kiosks, for single journeys, one-day or weekly travel. Tickets should be punched once on board (spot checks are carried out).

## ACCOMMODATION AND FOOD

Finding accommodation in the centre isn't difficult in expensive hotels (though rooms should be booked in advance for June-Sept), but much harder in less expensive hotels and pensions. Modern Orbis hotels include **Hevelius,** *ul. Heweliusza 22, tel: (058) 31 56 31,* which is a short stroll from the Old Town, with the modestly priced **Pensjonat Dom Aktora** located in an Old Town burgher's house at *ul. Straganiarska 55/56; tel: (058) 31 59 01.* **Youth hostels** are at *ul. Wałowa 21; tel: (058) 31 23 13 and ul. Kartuska 245B; tel: (058) 32 41 87.* An **Accommodation Bureau** is at *ul. Heweliusza 8; tel: (058) 31 26 34.* **Campsites** are located at *ul. Hallera 234, Gdańsk-Brzezno; tel: (058) 43 55 31,* and *ul. Jetlikowska 23, Gdańsk-Jelitkowo; tel: (058) 53 27 31.* A broad choice encompasses local specialities, ethnic and international fast food chains. For traditional Polish cuisine in a grand 16th-century setting the best choice is **Pod Łososiem,** *ul. Szeroka 54; tel: (058) 31 76 52.* The Old Town is full of inexpensive cafés, pizzerias and fast food outlets.

## Money

**Kantor** (currency exchange) are easily found and usually give a better rate than banks and hotels. Cash is preferred to travellers cheques, and try to have uncreased notes without anything written on them as these can be refused. Credit cards are increasingly accepted by hotels, restaurants and shops.

## ENTERTAINMENT

As a cultural centre there is plenty going on. **The Opera and Philharmonic Concert Hall** is at *al. Zwycięstwa 15; tel: (058) 41 05 63,* with leading theatres including **Teatr Wybrzeże,** *ul. Targ*

**333**

*Drzewny 1; tel: (058) 31 70 21,* and the **Puppet Theatre**, *al. Grunwaldzkia 16; tel:(058) 41 23 86.* Jazz is offered at **Cotton Club**, *ul. Złotników 25/29; tel: (058) 31 88 13* and **Piwnica u Filipa Club**, *ul Długa 45.*

**SHOPPING**

The Old Town, particularly *ul. Mariacka* and *Długi Targ*, are full of boutiques with traditional Polish specialites such as amber, leather goods and crystal.

**SIGHTSEEING**

Sightseeing and various excursions can be arranged through **Orbis**, *ul. Heweliusza 22; tel: (058) 31 22 32, 31 45 44*, while guides can be arranged through **PTTK**, *ul. Boguslawskiego 1; tel: (058) 31 60 96.* Boat services between Gdańsk and Westerplatte, Hel, Sopot and Gdynia, are operated by **Żegluga Ltd** departing from *Zielona Brama; tel: (058) 31 49 26.*

334

An important port and ferry terminal, scientific and cultural centre, Gdańsk is one of Poland's oldest settlements and already a thriving port in the early Middle Ages. Being granted exclusive rights to Poland's marine trade in the mid 15th century brought Gdańsk tremendous wealth, and the Medieval streets are full of Gothic and Renaissance architecture. After World War I Gdansk, then known as Danzig, had the status of a free city under the protection of the League of Nations. During World War II, which started in Gdańsk, much of the Old Town was destroyed, though extensive renovation has revived its former splendour.

Following the 'Royal Route' incorporates many of the key attractions, starting at the 16th-century **Brama Wyżynna** (Highland Gate), where visiting Polish King's were always greeted. Beyond this gate are Gothic and Renaissance buildings including the **Prison Tower, Torture Chamber** and **Dwór Bractwa Sw. Jerzego** (St. George's Brotherhood Court). Continuing along *ul. Długa* (Long Street) passing the **Ratusz Głównego Miasta** (Main Town Hall), which dates from the 14th century with the top floors part of the **City of Gdańsk Historical Museum**. *Długi Targ* (Long Market) features the 17th-century **Neptune's Fountain**, symbolising the union of Gdańsk with the sea, while the burgher's houses include boutiques and restaurants. The 16th-century **Zielona Brama** (Green Gate) marks the end of this route, and leads onto the **Motława river** and the pedestrianised waterfront with its historic granaries. An ideal way of returning to the Old Town is along *ul. Mariacka*, with burgher's houses featuring ornate terraces.

Beyond the Old Town, the **Cathedral** in **Oliwa** is renowned not only for being one of Poland's three largest churches, but also for its superb 13th-century Gothic architecture, the ornate organ, dating from 1763, and baroque altar. Bus nos. 6 and 12 make the journey from Gdańsk Główny to Oliwa in about 40 mins.

The **Westerplatte** peninsula is where World War II actually began, with this being the site of a Polish garrison and military transport depot. The German battleship Schleswig-Holstein began bombarding Westerplatte in Sept 1939, with the Poles resisting the German advance for over a week. A monument to the heroes of Westerplatte stands there. Boats for Westerplatte leave from Zielona Brama. The **Dominican Fair** is an antique and flea market, together with street entertainment. **Muzeum Narodowe** (National Museum) *ul. Toruńska 1; tel: (058) 31 70 61,* open Tues–Sun, 1000-1500, specialises in

Gothic art and Polish, Flemish and Dutch paintings. **Historical Museum of the City of Gdańsk**, *ul. Długa 47; tel: (058) 31 61 19*, open Tues–Sun, 1000-1700, has coins and medals and illustrates the city's reconstruction after World War II. **Central Maritime Museum**, *ul. Szeroka, 67/68; tel: (058) 31 86 11*, open Tues 1000–1600, Wed–Fri 0930–1600, Sun 1000–1600, has maritime paintings and artefacts recovered from shipwrecks. **Archaeological Museum**, *ul. Mariacka 25/26; tel: (058) 31 50 32*, open Tues–Sun 1000–1700.

### SIDE TRACKS
### FROM GDAŃSK

### SOPOT

Sopot was effectively established as a holiday resort and spa by Napoleon's former doctor. Many original buildings give the city great charm, with plenty of Secessionist villas.

**Tourist Information**: In addition to the tourist office in Gdańsk, **KMS**, *ul. Chopina 10, 81-752 Sopot; tel: (058) 51 12 77* gives tourist information, as does the **Accommodation Bureau**, *ul. Dworcowa 4; tel: (058) 51 26 17*.

**Station**: Sopot Główny, *ul. Dworcowa 7; tel: (058) 51 00 31/2/3, 51 54 11*. Facilities include left-luggage and a café. The Centre is within walking distance.

### GETTING AROUND

Sopot's main attractions are fairly close to each other. **Żegluga Ltd** runs boat services to Gdynia, Gdańsk, Westerplatte and Hel, departing from the *molo (pier) tel: (058) 75 04 37*. Yacht trips leave from the pier for a 1 hour journey between 0900-2000, *tel: 20 14 65*, or buy tickets on board.

### ACCOMMODATION AND FOOD

Sopot's options range from expensive hotels to budget and moderate boarding houses. At the top of the scale is the **Grand Hotel**, built in 1927 in the Secessionist style right on the edge of the beach, *ul. Powstańców Warszawy 12/14; tel: (058) 51 00 41*. **Camping** is at *ul. Bitwy pod Płowcami 69; tel: (058) 51 65 23*, and *ul. Zamkowa Góra 25/25, Sopot-Kamienny Potok; tel: (058) 51 80 11 ext.15*. There are plenty of inexpensive cafés and eateries, while more formal options with classic Polish cuisine include **Staropolska**, *ul. 3 Maja 7, tel: (058) 51 77 00*, and **Pod Strzechą**, *ul. Bohaterów Monte Cassino 17; tel: (058) 51 24 76*.

### SIGHTSEEING

Various sightseeing and excursions can be booked through **Orbis** at *ul. Bohaterów Monte Cassino 49; tel: (058) 51 41 42*, this street is also the main promenade and café/shopping area. The molo is the longest pier on the Baltic sea at 512 m. There are plenty of parks in Sopot, and forests also within walking distance.

### GDYNIA

Until the 1920s Gdynia was a fishing village and seaside resort, after which it was developed into an international port, designed to rival the port of Danzig (Gdańsk). The shipyards were also the birthplace of the Solidarity movement which led to the first post-War democratic elections in 1989, and was a catalyst for political change throughout the former Eastern Bloc.
**Station**: **Gdynia Główna**, *pl. Konstitucji 1; tel: (058) 21 67 01, 20 09 92*, has left luggage, cafés, delicatessen, kiosks, currency exchange, with a

**335**

tourist information point, *tel: (058) 23 02 08*, open Mon–Fri 0900–1600, Sat 0900–1300 providing city information and advice on accommodation.
**Tourist Office**: In addition to the offices in Gdańsk and Gdynia Główna, tourist information is also available from **Sports Tourist**, *ul. Starowiejska 35, 81-363 Gdynia; tel: (058) 21 99 21, 21 91 64*.
**Ferries**: **Lion Ferry** operates from the ferry terminal at *ul. Kwiatkowskiego 60; tel: (058) 21 36 21/2/3*, with services between Gdynia–Karlskrona, Sweden.

### GETTING AROUND

Gdynia is easily managed on foot, with the main points of interest at the seafront. Boat rides leave from **Żegluga Ltd's** passenger terminal at *Skwer Kościuszki; tel: (058) 20 26 42* with services to Gdańsk, Sopot, Westerplatte and Hel.

### ACCOMMODATION AND FOOD

Orbis hotels include **Gdynia**, *ul. Armii Krajowej 22; tel: (058) 20 66 61, 20 86 51*. The **Accommodation Bureau** is at *ul. Dworcowa 4, tel: (058) 51 26 17*. The **Youth Hostel** is at *ul. Morska 108C; tel: (058) 27 00 05*. The top-ranked **camping** site is at *ul. Swiętopełka 19/22; tel: (058) 29 29 00*.

Two of the best restaurants offering traditional Polish food are **Róża Wiatrów**, *ul. Zjednoczenia 2; tel: (058) 20 06 48*, and **Polonia**, *ul. Swiętojańska 92/94; tel: (058) 20 58 48*.

### ENTERTAINMENT

The **Danuta Baduszkowa Musical Theatre** is at *pl. Grunwaldzki 1; tel: (058) 20 95 21*. Festivals include the **Cepeliada Folk Festival** (Aug) and **Film Festival** (Sept).

### SIGHTSEEING

Sightseeing and various excursions can be booked through Orbis, *ul. Armii Krajowej 22* (within Hotel Gdynia); *tel: (058) 20 89 50*. **Kamienna Góra** (Stone Hill) by the town centre rises 52 m above sea level to give great views.

As Gdynia is such a young city, there is little of historic interest.

**Naval Museum**, *Bular Nadmorski; tel: (058) 26 35 65, 26 37 27* has maritime weapons from the 18th century to the present day. **Museum of Oceanography and Sea Aquarium of the Maritime Institute of Sea Fishing**, *al. Zjednoczenia 1; tel: (058) 21 70 21*, includes fish and various sea life. **Dar Pomorza**, *Skwer Kościuiszki (Nabrzeze Pomorskie); tel: (058) 20 23 71*, is a frigate museum with photographs and memorabilia. ⬛

---

## Hel

A sand bar 34 km long and between 200 m and 3 km wide, which separates Puck bay from the Baltic sea. It was formed by the action of the waves and sea winds which piled up sand dunes. Between Jastarnia and Hel the picturesque, sandy beaches support woods which are full of heather, with Hel inhabited by the Kaszubians, who are principally fishermen. Notable buildings include the lighthouse built in 1825, various early 19th-century timbered fisherman's houses, and the 15th-century St Peter and Paul's church, which is now a Fishing Museum with a good view from the spire. Ferries leave from **Zielona Brama** in Gdańsk and take about 1 hour, while trains leave from **Gdańsk Główny** and **Gdynia Główna**, the journey taking about 2 hours 30 mins.

# WARSAW–VILNIUS

Travelling from Warsaw to Białystok, close to the border with Belarus, passes through delightful countryside with rustic views, while the alternative journey via Suwalki, connects with the Vilnius–Riga route at Kaunas.

> FASTEST JOURNEY: 11 HRS

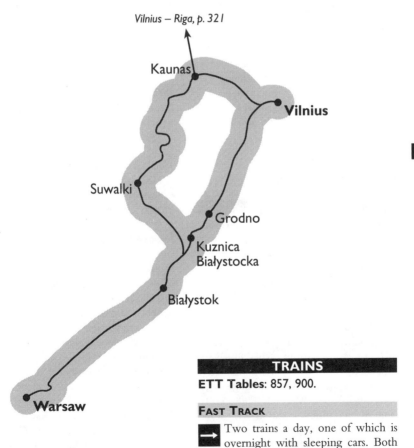

Vilnius – Riga, p. 321

Kaunas

Vilnius

**337**

Suwalki

Grodno

Kuznica
Białystocka

Białystok

Warsaw

## TRAINS

**ETT Tables:** 857, 900.

### FAST TRACK

Two trains a day, one of which is overnight with sleeping cars. Both travel through Belarus and a Belarus visa is required. The journey takes 11 hrs.

## ON TRACK

### ⟶ Warsaw–Białystok
Nine trains a day run between these cities taking just over 2 hr.

### Białystok–Kuznica Białystocka–Grodno
Five trains cross the border between Białystok and Grodno each day with the journey taking around 4 hr.

### Grodno–Vilnius
Two trains a day taking 4 hr.

### Białystok–Suwalki–Kaunas
The alternative route avoiding Belarus. Overall journey time 9 hrs, although the border checks can take much longer. Six trains run between Białystok and Suwalki and three between Suwalki and Kaunas. Change trains at Sestokai.

### Kaunus–Vilnius
Five expresses taking 1 hr 30 mins.

## BIAŁYSTOK

**Station**: Białystok, *ul. Kolejowa 26; tel: (085) 51 19 56,* and *910* (24-hour train information). This is a magnificent neo-classical building dating from the 1860s (though in need of restoration) with facilities including left-luggage and a restaurant.

**Tourist Information**: There is no 'it' tourist information office, though information is available from **Orbis**, *ul. Rynek Kościuszki 13, 15-091 Białystok, tel: (085) 42 16 27/8* (which is due to change to *44 13 20/33*), open Mon–Fri 0900–1700, (and in the summer season Sat 0900-1400). City information is limited, but there is also help with accommodation, a currency exchange counter, as well as various city sightseeing and excursions.

## GETTING AROUND
The centre is within walking distance of the station, with a bus service (tickets for single journeys, day or weekly travel are available from Ruch kiosks and should be punched once onboard).

Taxis are inexpensive with ranks at the station and *Rynek Kościuszki*.

## ACCOMMODATION
At the top end of the scale (though still modestly priced) is the centrally located **Hotel Cristal**, *ul. Lipowa 3/5, tel: (085) 250 61.* The **youth hostel** is at *ul. J Piłsudskiego 7B; tel: (085) 524 250.* The **campsite** is **OST Gromada Białystok**, *ul. Zwycięstwa 77; tel: (085) 511 641.*

## ENTERTAINMENT
**Teatr Dramatyczny im Al. Węgierki** is the main theatre at *ul. Elektryczna 12; tel: (085) 416 622.*

The Philharmonic Orchestra is at *ul. Podleśna 2, tel: (085) 32 73 43.* **Białostocki Teatr Lalek** is the puppet theatre at *ul. Kalinowskiego 1; tel: (085) 286 31.*

## SIGHTSEEING
Białystok dates from the 12th century, having originally been privately-owned by the Branicki family. With textiles and agriculture now the principal business, Białystok is renowned for its lack of pollution and natural beauty, with over a third of the Białystok voiovodship accounted for by forest, and is one of the region's termed 'the green lungs of Poland.'

From the station take *ul. Sw. Rocha* to the junction with *ul. Lipowa*, where the **Kościół p.w. Chrystusa Króla i św. Rocha** (Church of Christ the King and St. Rocha) stands, dating from 1927, with *ul. Lipowa* leading to *Rynek Kościuszki*, the main square, which includes the Renaissance **Farny** church.

Heading west to the adjoining *ul. Kilińskiego*, passing the turn-of-the-century neo-Gothic **pw. Wniebowzięcia NMP** (Cathedral of the Ascension of the Blessed Virgin Mary), leads to the main entrance of the **Branicki Palace** at *ul. Mickiewicza 1*. Built in the mid-17th century as one of the family's homes, its now a Medical Academy, but the porter will usually show you around between 0900–1700 if you ask.

The palace is also significant as the Ribbentrop-Molotov Pact was signed there, by the Nazis and the Soviets, which divided Poland between them before the outbreak of World War II. During the war it housed the Gestapo. The Palace's landscaped gardens include a maze and lakes, while a forest begins at the edge of the park.

Alternatively, heading east from *Rynek Kościuszki* along *ul. Lipowa* leads to the **Russian Orthodox church**, built in the 1840s, with a large collection of 19th-century icons and frescos of biblical scenes.

**Museums**

**Muzeum Okręgowe** (Regional Museum) within the **Ratusz** (City Hall), *Rynek Kościuszki, tel: (085) 42 14 73*, open Tues–Sun 1000–1700. Exhibits include Polish paintings from 1750–1930, folklore galleries, history of the Białystok region and archaeology of the earliest settlers 10,000 years ago.

Other branches of the Regional Museum include the **History Museum**, *ul. Warszawska 37; tel: (085) 41 65 91*, open Tues–Sun 1000–1700 with archaeology and ethnography. **Muzeum Wojskowe** (Army Museum), *ul. Kilińskiego 7; tel: (085) 41 64 49*, open

Tues–Sun 0930–1730, has military exhibits from 10th–19th century, as well as a small souvenir shop

**OUT OF TOWN**

The **Białowieza National Park**, comprising 58,000 hectares, is listed by UNESCO, with flora and fauna that includes bison roaming freely.

The **Narew Park** extends to 20,000 hectares and includes the town of **Tykocin** with its baroque buildings and ruined Medieval castle. For excursions contact Orbis.

**KUZNICA BIAŁYSTOCKA**

The border crossing from Poland to Belarus involves a 2hr 45mins stopover at this sprawling railway siding. The reason for the excruciating delay is that each individual bogey has to be converted from the standard European to the wider Russian guage. There are also the usual customs and passport checks - and the toilets are locked!

**339**

**GRODNO**

**Station: Zheleznodorozhniy vokzal**, *Ozheshko Ulitsa; tel: 687 1279*

**Tourist Information:** 'Grodnoturist', *Prospekt Ya. Kupaly 63; tel: 655 90* (The only source of information in Grodno is the **Hotel Tourist**)

This sprawling Belorussian town occupies both banks of the River Nieman. Visitors arriving here enter a time-warp where Soviet communism still reigns, right down to the street names. There are a dozen monuments commemorating Grodno's 'heroic' role in World War II when it was the scene of fierce fighting on the Russian western front. Surprisingly there's a small but highly attractive **old town** and some spectacular views of the meandering River Nieman and the forest beyond from the ramparts of the **'Zamok'**, the old fortress which is now the town's **History museum**.

If you want to stay the night there's only one tourist class hotel, **Gostinitsa 'Turist'**, *Prospekt Ya. Kupaly 63; tel: 655 90/ 690 19*. The rooms are clean and comfortable, there's an adequate restaurant and the staff are helpful but very little English is spoken and you'll need to take a taxi from the station.

## SUWAŁKI

**Tourist Information: Centrum Informacji Turystycznej 'Mewa,'** *ul. Kościuszki 55, 16-400 Suwałki; tel: (087) 66 69 69*, open Mon–Fri 0900–1700, has city and regional information, organising excursions, and advice on accommodation with a reservation service.
**Station: Suwałki**, *ul. Kolejowa; tel: (087) 66 22 35*, with facilities including left-luggage, cafe and kiosks.

### ACCOMMODATION AND FOOD

The choice of hotels includes **Wigry**, *ul. Zarzecze 26; tel: (087) 66 57 08*, which also has a good restaurant, **Hotel Hańcza**, *ul. Wojska Polskiego 2; tel (087) 66 66 44*, with a swimming pool and gym, in addition to a lakeside setting, and **Dom Nauczyciela**, *ul. Kościuszki 120; tel: (087) 62 900*. The **youth hostel** is at **SSM**, *ul. Wojska Polskiego 9; tel: (087) 66 58 78*. An **Accommodation Bureau** operates during the summer season only

at the travel agent **Wigry**, *ul. Kościuszki 84; tel: (087) 66 32 89*. Recommended restaurants are **Pod Temidą**, *ul. Kościuszki 82; tel: (087) 66 65 62*, together with the **Teinka cafe** at *ul. Kościuszki 76; tel: (087) 66 75 54*.

### SIGHTSEEING

Sightseeing and excursions can also be booked through **Orbis**, *ul. Noniewicza 48; tel: (087) 66 38 38*. Located close to the border with Lithuania and the Russian territory of Kaliningrad, Suwałki's architectural assets, like the 19th-century **Ratusz** (Town Hall) and various period buildings, are overshadowed by natural beauty, and its best known for the **Suwałki-Augustów Lake District**, created by an Ice Age that only retreated 10,000 years ago. **Muzeum Okręgowe** (Regional Museum), *ul. Kościuszki 81; tel: (087) 66 57 50*, is open Tues–Fri 0800–1600, Sat–Sun 1000–1700. **Muzeum Marii Konopnickiej**, *ul. Kościuszki 81; tel: (087) 66 41 33*, is dedicated to the eponymous Romantic author who was born in Suwałki. **Muzeum Historii i Tradycji Żołnierzy Suwalszczyzny** (Museum of the History and Traditions of Suwałki Soldiers), *ul. Wojska Polskiego 21; tel: (087) 66 22 22 extn. 551*, is open Tues–Sun 1000–1400.

## KAUNAS

See pp. 318–320.

# CONVERSION TABLES

## DISTANCES (approx. conversions)
1 kilometre (km) = 1000 metres (m)  1 metre = 100 centimetres (cm)

| Metric | Imperial/US | Metric | Imperial/US | Metric | Imperial/US |
|--------|-------------|--------|-------------|--------|-------------|
| 1 cm | 3/8ths in. | 10 m | 33 ft (11 yd) | 3 km | 2 miles |
| 50 cm | 20 in. | 20 m | 66 ft (22 yd) | 4 km | 2½ miles |
| 1 m | 3 ft 3 in. | 50 m | 164 ft (54 yd) | 5 km | 3 miles |
| 2 m | 6 ft 6 in. | 100 m | 330 ft (110 yd) | 10 km | 6 miles |
| 3 m | 10 ft | 200 m | 660 ft (220 yd) | 20 km | 12½ miles |
| 4 m | 13 ft | 250 m | 820 ft (275 yd) | 25 km | 15½ miles |
| 5 m | 16 ft 6 in. | 300 m | 984 ft (330 yd) | 30 km | 18½ miles |
| 6 m | 19 ft 6 in. | 500 m | 1640 ft (550 yd) | 40 km | 25 miles |
| 7 m | 23 ft | 750 m | ½ mile | 50 km | 31 miles |
| 8 m | 26 ft | 1 km | 5/8ths mile | 75 km | 46 miles |
| 9 m | 29 ft (10 yd) | 2 km | 1½ miles | 100 km | 62 miles |

## 24-HOUR CLOCK
(examples)

| | | |
|---|---|---|
| 0000 = Midnight | 1200 = Noon | 1800 = 6 p.m. |
| 0600 = 6 a.m. | 1300 = 1 p.m. | 2000 = 8 p.m. |
| 0715 = 7.15 a.m. | 1415 = 2.15 p.m. | 2110 = 9.10 p.m. |
| 0930 = 9.30 a.m. | 1645 = 4.45 p.m. | 2345 = 11.45 p.m. |

## TEMPERATURE
Conversion Formula: °C × 9 ÷ 5 + 32 = °F

| °C | °F | °C | °F | °C | °F | °C | °F |
|----|----|----|----|----|----|----|----|
| -20 | -4 | -5 | 23 | 10 | 50 | 25 | 77 |
| -15 | 5 | 0 | 32 | 15 | 59 | 30 | 86 |
| -10 | 14 | 5 | 41 | 20 | 68 | 35 | 95 |

## WEIGHT
1kg = 1000g  100 g = 3½ oz

| Kg | Pounds | Kg | Pounds | Kg | Pounds |
|----|--------|----|--------|----|--------|
| 1 | 2¼ | 5 | 11 | 25 | 55 |
| 2 | 4½ | 10 | 22 | 50 | 110 |
| 3 | 6½ | 15 | 33 | 75 | 165 |
| 4 | 9 | 20 | 45 | 100 | 220 |

## FLUID MEASURES
1 litre(l) = 0.88 Imperial quarts = 1.06 US quarts

| Litres | Imp.gal. | US gal. | Litres | Imp.gal. | US gal. |
|--------|----------|---------|--------|----------|---------|
| 5 | 1.1 | 1.3 | 30 | 6.6 | 7.8 |
| 10 | 2.2 | 2.6 | 35 | 7.7 | 9.1 |
| 15 | 3.3 | 3.9 | 40 | 8.8 | 10.4 |
| 20 | 4.4 | 5.2 | 45 | 9.9 | 11.7 |
| 25 | 5.5 | 6.5 | 50 | 11.0 | 13.0 |

## MEN'S CLOTHES

| UK | Europe | US |
|----|--------|----|
| 36 | 46 | 36 |
| 38 | 48 | 38 |
| 40 | 50 | 40 |
| 42 | 52 | 42 |
| 44 | 54 | 44 |
| 46 | 56 | 46 |

## MENS' SHOES

| UK | Europe | US |
|----|--------|----|
| 6 | 40 | 7 |
| 7 | 41 | 8 |
| 8 | 42 | 9 |
| 9 | 43 | 10 |
| 10 | 44 | 11 |
| 11 | 45 | 12 |

## LADIES' CLOTHES

| UK | France | Italy | Rest of Europe | US |
|----|--------|-------|----------------|----|
| 10 | 36 | 38 | 34 | 8 |
| 12 | 38 | 40 | 36 | 10 |
| 14 | 40 | 42 | 38 | 12 |
| 16 | 42 | 44 | 40 | 14 |
| 18 | 44 | 46 | 42 | 16 |
| 20 | 46 | 48 | 44 | 18 |

## MEN'S SHIRTS

| UK | Europe | US |
|----|--------|----|
| 14 | 36 | 14 |
| 15 | 38 | 15 |
| 15½ | 39 | 15½ |
| 16 | 41 | 16 |
| 16½ | 42 | 16½ |
| 17 | 43 | 17 |

## LADIES' SHOES

| UK | Europe | US |
|----|--------|----|
| 3 | 36 | 4½ |
| 4 | 37 | 5½ |
| 5 | 38 | 6½ |
| 6 | 39 | 7½ |
| 7 | 40 | 8½ |
| 8 | 41 | 9½ |

# HOTEL CODES
## AND CENTRAL BOOKING NUMBERS

The following abbreviations have been used throughout the book to show which chains are represented in a particular town. Most chains have a centralised worldwide-reservations system in every country where they have hotels (occasionally these do not cover hotels within the country itself). Most telephone calls are either completely free (usually incorporating *800*) or charged at the rate for a local call (e.g. 0345 in the UK). (Aus= Australia, Can=Canada, Ger=Germany, Ire=Ireland, NZ=New Zealand, SA =South Africa, UK=United Kingdom, USA=United States of America, WW=Worldwide.)

**Accor**
This is a group name that encompasses Ibis, Mercure, Novotel and Sofitel, with central reservation numbers (handled by Resinter worldwide) that cover them all
Aus *(1 800) 642 244*
Can *(800) 221 4542*
UK *(0171) 724 1000*
USA *(800) 221 4542*

BW **Best Western**
Aus *(1 800) 222 422*
Can *(800) 528 1234*
Ire *(1 800) 709 101*
NZ *(09) 520 5418*
SA *(011) 339 4865*
UK *(0800) 393130*
USA *(800) 528 1234*

Ch **Choice**
Aus *(008) 090 600*
Can *(800) 221 2222*
Ire *(1 800) 500 600*
NZ *(0800) 808 228*
UK *(0800) 444444*
USA:
*(800) 228 5150*
(Comfort)
*(800) 228 5151*
(Quality)

*(800) CLARION* (Clarion)
*(800) 228 3323*
(hearing impaired, TTY phone)

Do **Dorint**
WW: *(0800) 960024*

Ev **Exclusive**
See Forte (*FE*)

Ex **Excelsior**
UK *(0345) 40 40 40*

FE **Forte**
(Also covers Exclusive)
Aus *(008) 222 446*
Can *(800) 225 5843*
Ire *(01) 764 401*
NZ *(0800) 801 111*
SA *(011) 442 9201*
UK *(0345) 404040*
USA *(800) 225 5843*

Fm **Forum**
See Inter-Continental (*IC*)

Hd **Holiday Inn**
Aus *(800) 221 066*
Can *(800) 465 4329*
Ire *(1 800) 553 155*
NZ *(0800) 442 222*
SA *(011) 482 3500*
UK *(0800) 897121*

USA *(800) 465 4329*

HI **Hostelling International**
UK *(0171) 248 6547*

Hn **Hilton**
Aus *(1 800) 222 255*
Can *(800) 445 8667*
NZ *(0800) 448 002*
SA *(011) 880 3108*
UK *(0345) 581595*
USA *(800) 445 8667*

Hy **Hyatt**
Aus *(1 800) 131 234*
Can/USA *(800) 233 1234*
Ire *(1 800) 535 500*
NZ *(0800) 441 234*
SA *(011) 773 9888*
UK *(0345) 581 666*

Ib **Ibis**
See Accor

IC **Inter-Continental**
(Also covers Forum)
Aus *(008) 221 335*
Can/USA *(800) 327 0200*
NZ *(0800) 654 343*
SA *(011) 331 7422*
UK *(0345) 581444*

IH **Inter Hotel**
France: *(1) 42 06 46 46*
UK *(0171) 287 3231*
Ke **Kempinski**
Can *(800) 426 3135*
UK *(0800) 898588*
USA *(800) 426 3135*
(Also bookable
through Lufthansa)

Ma **Marriott**
Aus *(1 800) 251 259*
Can *(800) 228 9290*
NZ *(0800) 441 035*
UK *(0800) 221222*
USA *(800) 228 9290*

Mc **Mercure**
Can *(800) MERCURE*
UK *(0181) 741 3100*
USA *(800) MERCURE*
(Also see Accor)

Nv **Novotel**
Can *(800) NOVOTEL*
UK *(0181) 748 3433*
USA *(800) NOVOTEL*
(See also Accor)

Pe **Penta**
UK *(0990) 300200*

Pu **Pullman Hotels**
see Accor

Rd **Radisson**
See SAS

Re **Reso**
See Supranational

Rk **Romantik**
Ger*(06188) 95020*
Aus *(02) 968 1783* or
*(02) 957 0538*

Can *(416) 695 1449*
Ire *(01) 661 9466*
NZ *(09) 799 716*
UK *(0181) 392 1589*
or *(0171) 408 0111*
USA – bookable
through all AAA travel
agencies

Rm **Ramada**
Aus *(1 800) 222 431*
Can *(800) 854 7854*
Ire *(1 800) 252 627*
NZ *(0800) 441 111*
UK *(0800) 181737*
USA *(800) 854 7854*

Rz **Ritz Carlton**
Aus *(1 800) 252 888*
NZ *(800) 443 030*
UK *(0800) 234000*

SA **SAS**
(Also covers Radisson)
Aus *(1 800) 333 333*
Can *(800) 333 3333*
Ire *(1 800) 557 474*
NZ *(0800) 443 333*
UK *(0800) 191991*
USA *(800) 333 3333*

Sf **Sofitel**
Can *(800) SOFITEL*
UK *(0181) 741 9699*
USA *(800) SOFITEL*
(See also Accor)

Sh **Sheraton**
Aus *(008) 073 535*
Can *(800) 325 3535* or
*(800) 325 1717* (hear-
ing impaired)
Ire *(1 800) 535 353*
NZ *(0800) 443 535*
UK *(0800) 353535*

USA *(800) 325 3535*
or *(800) 325 1717*
(hearing impaired)

SL **Small Luxury**
Aus *(008) 251 958*
Can *(800) 525 4800*
NZ *(0800) 441 098*
SA *(011) 331 2911*
UK *(0800) 282124*
USA *(800) 525 4800*

Sn **Supranational**
(Also covers
Concorde, Reso,
Sokos and Welcome
Swiss)
Can *(800) 843 3311*
UK *(0500) 303030*
Ire *(01) 660 5000*
SA *(0800) 119 000*
USA *(800) 843 3311*
USA *(800) 336 3542*

Sw **Swissôtel**
Switz *(01) 812 54 51*
Can *(800) 637 9477*
UK *(0800) 614145*
USA *(800) 637 9477*
(Also bookable
through Swissair)

Tp **Top**
Ger *(0211) 57 80 75*
Aus *(008) 221 176*
Ire *(01) 872 3953*
NZ *(09) 303 4526*
SA *(011) 312 672*
UK *(0171) 402 8182*
or *(0181) 446 0126*
or *(0990) 300 200*
USA *(800) 223 6764* or
*(800) 44 UTELL*
(Also bookable
through Lufthansa)

**343**

# THROUGH ROUTES

Some travellers will want to start their journey in Western Europe and join the Eastern European routes in this book at the gateway cities of Berlin, Prague, Vienna or Venice. The following table shows a selection of possible through routes, as an aid to journey planning, with approximate summer frequencies. All these through routes may also be taken in the reverse direction to that shown but the number of trains per day may differ. Some of the trains require payment of supplements and many involve overnight travel. Not all services are daily. Always consult the international section in the latest issue of the *Thomas Cook European Timetable* (ETT), which gives up-to-date schedules for these and many other international long-distance trains. Services shown from London include travel through the Channel Tunnel.

| Through route | ETT table no. | Approx journey time | Trains daily | Notes |
|---|---|---|---|---|
| Amsterdam–Berlin | 22 | 7hrs | 4 | 1 overnight train |
| Amsterdam–Vienna | 28 | 13hrs | 3 | Change at Cologne on 2 services, 1 direct overnight service |
| Brussels–Berlin | 20 | 9hrs | 5 | Change at Cologne on 4 services |
| Brussels–Praha | 21 | 15hrs | 1 | Change at Cologne |
| Brussels–Venice | 43 | 15 hrs | 2 | Change at Milan |
| Brussels–Vienna | 21 | 13hrs | 2 | Change at Cologne 1 direct overnight service |
| Cologne–Praha | 57 | 12hrs | 2 | 1 overnight train |
| Cologne–Vienna | 66 | 10hrs | 6 | Direct, 2 overnight services |
| Copenhagen–Berlin | 50 | 9hrs | 3 | Change at Hamburg on 2 services |
| Hamburg–Praha | 60 | 10hrs | 3 | Change at Berlin on 2 services |
| London–Praha | 21 | 22hrs | 1 | Change at Brussels and Cologne |
| London–Venice | 43 | 20hrs | 1 | Change at Brussels and Milan |
| London–Vienna | 21 | 19hrs | 1 | Overnight service, change at Brussels |
| Paris–Berlin | 25 | 11hrs | 3 | Change at Brussels or Cologne, 1 direct overnight service |
| Paris–Praha | 30 | 15hrs | 2 | 1 overnight service |
| Paris–Venice | 44 | 13hrs | 3 | I direct overnight otherwise change in Milan |
| Paris–Vienna | 32 | 14hrs | 2 | Direct, 1 overnight service |
| Stockholm–Berlin | 50 | 18hrs | 2 | Change at Malmö |
| Warszawa–Moscow | 94a | 19hrs | 1 | Direct overnight service |
| Zurich–Berlin | 71 | 12hrs | 1 | Direct, overnight service |
| Zurich–Praha | 57 | 10hrs | 1 | Direct |
| Zurich–Venice | 84 | 8hrs | 2 | Direct, 1 overnight train |

**FORSYTH TRAVEL LIBRARY**

# BRITRAIL PASSES
Unlimited travel in England, Scotland & Wales
Prices are U.S. $ Effective until December 31, 1996

*AVAILABLE IN NORTH AMERICA ONLY*

**BRITRAIL CLASSIC PASS** – Unlimited travel every day

| Validity Period | Adult | | Senior (60 +) | Youth (16 - 25) |
| --- | --- | --- | --- | --- |
| | First | Standard | First | Standard |
| 8 Days | ❏ $325 | ❏ $235 | ❏ $275 | ❏ $189 |
| 15 Days | ❏ $525 | ❏ $365 | ❏ $445 | ❏ $289 |
| 21 Days | ❏ $665 | ❏ $465 | ❏ $565 | ❏ $369 |
| 1 Month | ❏ $765 | ❏ $545 | ❏ $650 | ❏ $435 |

**BRITRAIL FLEXIPASS** – Travel any days within 1 Month

| | | | | |
| --- | --- | --- | --- | --- |
| 4 Days / 1 Month | ❏ $289 | ❏ $199 | ❏ $245 | ❏ $160 |
| 8 Days / 1 Month | ❏ $399 | ❏ $280 | ❏ $339 | ❏ $225 |
| 15 Days / 1 Month | ❏ $615 | ❏ $425 | ❏ $490 | ❏ $340* |

*Youth pass valid for 2 months

*Phone Orders*
Call Toll Free
**1-800-367-7984**
*Charge to Visa, MasterCard or Discover*

### FREEDOM OF SCOTLAND TRAVEL PASS
| | | | |
| --- | --- | --- | --- |
| 8 Days ❏ $159 | | 22 Days ❏ $269 | |
| 15 Days ❏ $220 | | | |
| Any 8 Days in 15 Days ❏ $185 | | | |

### BRITRAIL SOUTHEAST PASS
| Duration | Adult | Standard |
| --- | --- | --- |
| 3 Days in 8 Days | ❏ $90 | ❏ $69 |
| 4 Days in 8 Days | ❏ $120 | ❏ $89 |
| 7 Days in 15 Days | ❏ $169 | ❏ $119 |

### BRITIRELAND PASS
Includes round-trip ticket on Stena Line Ferry between Britain and Ireland.
| Validity | First | Standard |
| --- | --- | --- |
| Any 5 Days in 1 Month | ❏ $405 | ❏ $299 |
| Any 10 Days in 1 Month | ❏ $599 | ❏ $429 |

### LONDON VISITOR TRAVELCARD (LVTC)
Unlimited Inner Zone on Underground and red buses.
| Duration | Adult | Child |
| --- | --- | --- |
| 3 Days | ❏ $25 | ❏ $11 |
| 4 Days | ❏ $32 | ❏ $13 |
| 7 Days | ❏ $49 | ❏ $21 |

### FREE! BRITRAIL KID'S PASS
Buy one Adult or Senior Pass and one Accompanying child (5-15) gets a pass of the same type & duration FREE! Additional children are half price of adult's regular pass price. You MUST request this pass when booking!

### GATWICK EXPRESS
Non-stop from Gatwick Airport to Victoria Station every 15 minutes. Takes only 30 minutes. Fastest way to London! Round-trip – buy two one-ways.
| | |
| --- | --- |
| First Class | ❏ $23 One-way |
| Standard | ❏ $17 One-way |

### EUROSTAR
Channel Tunnel Services

We are official agents for Channel Tunnel tickets and reservations. Passenger services from London operate non-stop to Paris and Brussels in 3 Hr. and 3:15 respectively. All seats require advance reservations and tickets. Various prices and advance purchase discounts available. Call for latest rates and reservations.

**SLEEPERS** – We can confirm overnight sleepers on Anglo-Scottish and West Country routes. Accommodation supplement is $50 per person First Class and $41 per person Second Class. **CHILDREN'S RATES** (5 - 15) are half fare for most passes. **SEAT RESERVATIONS, GROUP RATES, CROSS-CHANNEL SERVICES, IRISH SEA SERVICES** – call for rates.

**FORSYTH TRAVEL LIBRARY**

# ORDER FORM
## European Rail Passes
### Prices are U.S. $ Effective until December 31, 1996

AVAILABLE IN NORTH AMERICA ONLY

**EURAIL PASS (17 Countries) 1st Class**
| | |
|---|---|
| 15 Days | ❏ $522 |
| 21 Days | ❏ $678 |
| 1 Month | ❏ $838 |

| | |
|---|---|
| 2 Months | ❏ $1,148 |
| 3 Months | ❏ $1,468 |

**EURAIL FLEXIPASS – 1st Class**
| | |
|---|---|
| 10 Days in 2 Months | ❏ $616 |
| 15 Days in 2 Months | ❏ $812 |

**EURAIL SAVERPASS – 1st Class**
| | |
|---|---|
| 15 Days | ❏ $452 |
| 21 Days | ❏ $578 |
| 1 Month | ❏ $712 |

*Price is per person / 3 people must travel together at all times. (Two people may travel between Oct. 1st and March 31st) Children 4 - 11 half fare – Children under 4 free.*

**EURAIL YOUTHPASS\* – 2nd Class**
| | |
|---|---|
| 15 Days | ❏ $418 |
| 1 Month | ❏ $598 |
| 2 Months | ❏ $798 |

**EURAIL YOUTH FLEXIPASS\* – 2nd Class**
| | |
|---|---|
| 10 Days in 2 Months | ❏ $438 |
| 15 Days in 2 Months | ❏ $588 |

*\*Pass holder must be under age 26 on first day of use.*

**EURAIL & EURO DRIVE PASS**

There are excellent Rail/Drive programs that combine a Eurail or Euro Pass with either Avis or Hertz Rental cars in Europe. And, you can reserve your auto rentals before even leaving home! Call us for a complete brochure and prices.

**EUROPASS (5 Countries)**
France / Germany / Italy / Switz. / Spain
SPECIAL OFFER: The 2nd Adult traveler purchasing a EuroPass of any duration pays only half of the base pass price. Both travelers must travel together at all times.

**3 COUNTRIES EUROPASS – 1st Class**
| | |
|---|---|
| 5 Days in 2 Months | ❏ $316 |
| 6 Days in 2 Months | ❏ $358 |
| 7 Days in 2 Months | ❏ $400 |

**4 COUNTRIES EUROPASS – 1st Class**
| | |
|---|---|
| 8 Days in 2 Months | ❏ $442 |
| 9 Days in 2 Months | ❏ $484 |
| 10 Days in 2 Month | ❏ $526 |

**5 COUNTRIES EUROPASS – 1st Class**
| | |
|---|---|
| 11 Days in 2 Months | ❏ $568 |
| 12 Days in 2 Months | ❏ $610 |
| 13 Days in 2 Months | ❏ $652 |
| 14 Days in 2 Months | ❏ $694 |
| 15 Days in 2 Months | ❏ $736 |

*Note: You must specify the countries when ordering and countries must border each other.*

*EuroYouth Pass available for ages up to 26 in 2nd Class at substantial discounts. Call us for prices.*

**EUROPASS ASSOCIATE COUNTRIES**

These countries may be added to any EuroPass for a flat charge per country. They expand the geographic scope of the pass, not the duration.
| | |
|---|---|
| ❏ Austria $45 | ❏ Portugal $29 |
| ❏ Benelux $42 | ❏ Greece $90 |

*(Includes Brendisi-Patras ferry HML/ADN-RT)*

## For Travelers from North America
### CALL TOLL FREE  1-800-367-7984  – ASK FOR DEPT. OEE6
(Charge to Visa, Discover or MasterCard)
### FORSYTH TRAVEL LIBRARY, INC.
**9154 W. 57th, P.O. Box 2975 Dept. OEE6  •  Shawnee Mission, KS 66201-1375**

*Forsyth Travel Library, Inc., is the leading agent in North America for the European and British Railroads and distributor of the famous Thomas Cook European Timetable. We are international rail travel specialists. Members: ASTA, Better Business Bureau of Kansas City, MO and International Map Trades Association. Free catalogs upon request listing all rail passes, timetables, hostelling information and maps. All prices shown are US Dollars.*

FORSYTH
TRAVEL
LIBRARY

# ORDER FORM
### European Rail Passes
### Prices are U.S. $ Effective until December 31, 1996

AVAILABLE IN NORTH AMERICA ONLY

## AUSTRIA RAILPASS
Any 4 Days in 10 Days   ❏ $165 1st Class
  ❏ $111 2nd Class

## ITALIAN RAILPASS
*Please add a $15 admin. fee to the cost
of each Italian pass/non-refundable*

| | 1st Class | 2nd Class |
|---|---|---|
| 8 Days | ❏ $248 | ❏ $168 |
| 15 Days | ❏ $312 | ❏ $208 |
| 21 Days | ❏ $362 | ❏ $242 |
| 1 Month | ❏ $436 | ❏ $290 |

## ITALIAN FLEXI RAILCARD
| | | |
|---|---|---|
| Any 4 Days in 1 Month | ❏ $194 | ❏ $132 |
| Any 8 Days in 1 Month | ❏ $284 | ❏ $184 |
| Any 12 Days in 1 Month | ❏ $356 | ❏ $238 |

## ITALIAN KILOMETRIC TICKET
*3,000 Kilometers in 20 Trips.*
❏ $264 *1st Class*    ❏ $156 *2nd Class*

## HUNGARIAN FLEXIPASS
Any 5 Days in 15   ❏ $55 *1st Class*
Any 10 Days in 1 Month   ❏ $69 *1st Class*

## BULGARIAN FLEXIPASS
Any 3 Days in 1 Month   ❏ $70 *1st Class*

## EUROPEAN EAST PASS
Any 5 Days in 15   ❏ $195 *1st Class*
Any 10 Days in 1 Month ❏ $299 *1st Class*

## SWISS PASS
*Good on Swiss National Railroads,
most private railroads, lake steamers,
city transport, trams, etc.*

| | Adults | | Couples/each | |
|---|---|---|---|---|
| | 1st Cl. | 2nd Cl. | 1st Cl. | 2nd Cl. |
| 4 Days | ❏ $264 | ❏ $176 | ❏ $198 | ❏ $132 |
| 8 Days | ❏ $316 | ❏ $220 | ❏ $237 | ❏ $165 |
| 15 Days | ❏ $368 | ❏ $256 | ❏ $276 | ❏ $192 |
| 1 Month | ❏ $508 | ❏ $350 | ❏ $381 | ❏ $262⁵⁰ |

## SWISS FLEXIPASS
Any 3   ❏ $264   ❏ $176   ❏ $198   ❏ $132
Days in 15 Days
*(Couples Passes valid 5/1/96 - 10/31/96 only)*

## SWISS CARD
1 Month/1 Round Trip   ❏ $142   ❏ $116

## GERMAN RAILPASS – Adult
| Validity | 1st Cl./Twin* | 2nd Cl./Twin* |
|---|---|---|
| 5 Days in 1 Mo. | ❏ $260/$390 | ❏ $178/$267 |
| 10 Days in 1 Mo. | ❏ $410/$615 | ❏ $286/$429 |
| 15 Days in 1 Mo. | ❏ $530/$795 | ❏ $386/$579 |

*Twin: Total price valid for 2 people traveling
together. Youth rates available.*

## PRAGUE EXCURSION PASS
*From any Czech Republic border crossing to
Prague and return First Class – within 7 days.*
❏ $49 Adult   ❏ $39 Youth   ❏ $25 Child

## CZECH FLEXIPASS
Any 5 Days in 15    ❏ $69 *1st Class*

## ROMANIAN PASS
Any 3 Days in 15    ❏ $60 *1st Class*

347

SHIPPING There is a $9.50 handling and priority shipping charge for all US, APO/FPO orders using 2nd Day/AIR UPS. Rush service with overnight delivery is available for $25. We can not ship overseas. RAIL/DRIVE Programs are available for many countries. Call for rates and free brochures.

RAIL PASSES NOT SHOWN FOR: Spain, Benelux, France, Hungary, Portugal, Greece, Scandinavia, Finland and Norway. Call for rates and plans.

# INDEX

348

# READER SURVEY

If you enjoyed using this book, or even if you didn't, please help us improve future editions by taking part in our reader survey. Every returned form will be acknowledged, and to show our appreciation we will give you £1 off your next purchase of a Thomas Cook guidebook. Just take a few minutes to complete and return this form to us.

When did you buy this book?

_____

Where did you buy it? (Please give town/city and if possible name of retailer)

_____

When did you/do you intend to travel in Eastern Europe?

_____

For how long (approx.)? _____

How many people in your party? _____

Which cities and other locations did you/do you intend mainly to visit?

_____

_____

_____

_____

Did you/will you:
- ☐ Make all your travel arrangements independently?
- ☐ Travel on an Inter-Rail pass? ☐ Travel on a Eurail Pass?
- ☐ Use other passes or tickets, please give brief details: _____

Did you/do you intend to use this book:
- ☐ For planning your trip?
- ☐ During the trip itself?
- ☐ Both?

Did you/do you intend also to purchase any of the following travel publications for your trip?

Thomas Cook European Timetable

Thomas Cook New Rail Map of Europe

Thomas Cook European Travellers Phrase Book

Other guidebooks or maps, please specify

_____

Have you used any other Thomas Cook guidebooks in the past? If so, which?

_____

Please rate the following features of On the Rails around Eastern Europe for their value to you (Circle VU for 'very useful', U for 'useful', NU for 'little or no use'):

| | | | |
|---|---|---|---|
| The 'Travel Essentials' section on pages 15–26 | VU | U | NU |
| The 'Travelling by Train' section on pages 27–35 | VU | U | NU |
| The 'Country by Country' section on pages 36–77 | VU | U | NU |
| The recommended routes throughout the book | VU | U | NU |
| Information on towns and cities | VU | U | NU |
| The maps of towns and cities | VU | U | NU |
| The colour rail maps | VU | U | NU |

Please use this space to tell us about any features that in your opinion could be changed, improved, or added in future editions of the book, or any other comments you would like to make concerning the book:

_____

_____

_____

_____

_____

_____

_____

_____

**352**

_____

_____

Your age category: ☐ 21-30 ☐ 31-40 ☐ 41–50 ☐ over 50

Your name: Mr/Mrs/Miss/Ms
(First name or initials) _____
(Last name) _____

Your full address: (Please include postal or zip code)

_____

_____

_____

Your daytime telephone number: _____

**Please detach this page and send it to: The Project Editor, On the Rails around Eastern Europe, Thomas Cook Publishing, PO Box 227, Peterborough PE3 8BQ, United Kingdom.**

We will be pleased to send you details of how to claim your discount upon receipt of this questionnaire.

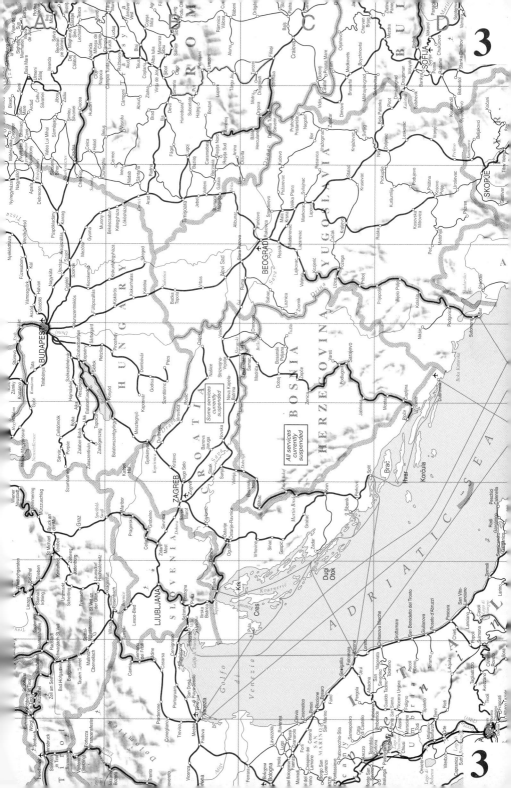